Bumpty-
Bumpty-
Bump!

The Stephen King Daily Reader

Michael Roch

Here there be spoilers . . .

CONTENTS

INTRODUCTION

Bumpty presents dates from and about Stephen King's fiction. Other than as provided in one of his novels, his private life is not covered.

In most cases, release dates are given for the first widely available edition, although a few special editions may be shown. Dates of re-releases and alternate forms (e.g., paperback, audio) are not tracked.

The criteria for entry onto the Best Seller Lists have evolved. You'll notice some of King's early works have entered the List before their accepted release dates. That doesn't happen anymore.

By the nature of this book, there are spoilers everywhere. I let you know whether the butler did it and a little of how he did it. This is just a starting point. While I tell you some of what happens, get the books you don't have and let Stephen King show you everything.

January
Happenings

January 1

1 January 1962

<u>George Amberson's second timeline</u>: 2703 Mercedes Street was vacant. George installed a surveillance lamp in the combination living room-kitchen. [*11/22/63*]

1 January 1974

Barton Dawes tripped on a mescaline pill he had taken before he went to Wally Hamner's New Year's Eve party. Phil Drake drove him home. [*Roadwork*]

Joyland owner Bradley Easterbrook died in his condo on John Ringling Boulevard in Sarasota, FL. [*Joyland*]

1 January 1975

Norm Lawson and Charlie Norton found Carol Dunbarger's body near Strimmer's Brook. [*The Dead Zone*]

1 January 1979, Monday, early a.m.

Arnie Cunningham drove Dennis Guilder home after seeing in the New Year. Dennis saw Roland LeBay's corpse driving. In the rearview mirror, he saw the corpses of Rita LeBay, Veronica LeBay, Buddy Repperton, and Richie Trelawney. The town and his development looked as they had in 1959. [*Christine*]

1 January 1983, 12:01 a.m.

Billy Halleck quit smoking but started gaining weight faster. [*Thinner*]

1 January 1984

Pet Sematary stayed at number 2 on *The New York Times* Fiction Best Seller List, its ninth week on the List.

1 January 1995

Insomnia rose to number 4 on *The New York Times* Fiction Best Seller List, its eleventh week on the List.

1 January 1999

Stephen King had a nightmare about Baby Mordred and 6/19/99 O Discordia. [*The Dark Tower VI: Song of Susannah*]

1 January 2007, afternoon

Edgar Freemantle woke up from a nap where he had dreamed of the perfect orange shell to paint in a Mexican sunset. He walked far down the beach and found a suitable shell. Without realizing it, he had walked farther than he had before. He saw a man—Wireman—wave from a beach chair. Edgar waved back as he turned to go home. This began his Great Beach

Walks. Each day, he walked longer and farther than the day before. [*Duma Key*]

1 January 2012

11/22/63 stayed at number 1 on *The New York Times* Fiction Best Seller List, its sixth week on the List.

1 January ≥2018

Scott Carey asked Mike Badalamente to take Bill D. Cat while Scott visited his [fictional] Aunt Harriet in California a few weeks later. [*Elevation*]

January 2

2 January 1972

Rita Billings's mother was in a car accident. ["The Boogeyman"]

2 January 1977

Charlene MacKenzie and Herb Smith married at the Southwest Bend Congregational Church. Hector Markstone (her dad) and the Hazletts—Denny, Sarah, and Walter—attended. Johnny Smith was the best man. They honeymooned in Miami Beach and planned to live on a twenty-acre farm in Biddeford, ME. [*The Dead Zone*]

2 January 1979

The Rocky Mountain *News* mentioned Ralph Dugan's marriage to Annie Wilkes. A year and a half later, he divorced her because of mental cruelty. [*Misery*]

2 January 1983

Different Seasons rose to number 8 on *The New York Times* Fiction Best Seller List, its twenty-second week on the List.

2 January 1994

Lois Chasse and Ralph Roberts married. Harold Chasse gave his mother away. Many Harris Avenue Old Crocks were there. [*Insomnia*]

Nightmares & Dreamscapes dropped to number 4 on *The New York Times* Fiction Best Seller List, its twelfth week on the List.

2 January 1999

Stephen and Owen King spent the night at Hyatt Harborside in Boston. [*The Dark Tower VI: Song of Susannah*]

2 January 2000

Hearts in Atlantis rose to number 6 on *The New York Times* Fiction Best Seller List, its fourteenth week on the List.

2 January 2009

The Stand: Captain Trips #4 of 5 (Marvel Comics, $3.99) published

Stephen King started *11/22/63* in Sarasota, FL.

2 January 2011

Full Dark, No Stars rose to number 6 on *The New York Times* Fiction Best Seller List, its sixth week on the List.

January 3

3 January 1979, 10:00 a.m.

Elton Curry helped the limping Johnny Smith on the Amtrak train in Phoenix. The train left at 10:30. [*The Dead Zone*]

3 January 1982

Cujo stayed at number 4 on *The New York Times* Fiction Best Seller List, its twenty-first week on the List.

3 January 1988

After two weeks off, *Misery* re-entered *The New York Times* Fiction Best Seller List at number 14, its twenty-ninth week on the List.

The Tommyknockers stayed at number 1 on *The New York Times* Fiction Best Seller List, its sixth week on the List.

3 January 1993

Gerald's Game stayed at number 9 on *The New York Times* Fiction Best Seller List, its twenty-fifth week on the List.

Dolores Claiborne stayed at number 1 on *The New York Times* Fiction Best Seller List, its fifth week on the List.

3 January 1999

Stephen and Owen King left for Florida. Steve and Tabby considered buying a home there. [*The Dark Tower VI: Song of Susannah*]

Bag of Bones stayed at number 2 on *The New York Times* Fiction Best Seller List, its thirteenth week on the List.

3 January 2010

Under the Dome rose to number 3 on *The New York Times* Fiction Best Seller List, its sixth week on the List.

3 January 2016

The Bazaar of Bad Dreams stayed at number 4 on *The New York Times* Hardcover Fiction Best Seller List, its seventh week on the List.

January 4

4 January 1946

William Robert Shearman was born. He grew up in Harwich, CT. ["Blind Willie" (*Hearts in Atlantis*)]

4 January 1976

A front-page Portland *Press-Herald* article reported an overnight accident, where Mr. Gordon Phillips's car struck a Central Maine Power utility pole. Blood was found at the scene. A search of the area didn't find Mr. Phillips or his family. [*'Salem's Lot*]

4 January 1981

Carlos Detweiller sent a query letter for *True Tales of Demon Infestations* to Zenith House, Publishers. The manuscript included the following sections: "The World of the Aether," "The World of the Living Dead," "The World of Spells," and "The World of Voodoo." [*The Plant* Book One: *Zenith Rising*]

Firestarter rose to number 3 on *The New York Times* Fiction Best Seller List, its twentieth week on the List.

4 January 1982

Afterword to *Different Seasons*

4 January 1987

IT stayed at number 1 on *The New York Times* Fiction Best Seller List, *IT*'s seventeenth week on the List.

4 January 1991

Peter Goldsmith-Redman was born—six pounds, nine ounces—by caesarean section. He looked like Jess Rider, his biological father. [*The Stand: The Complete & Uncut Edition*]

4 January 2004

The Dark Tower V: Wolves of the Calla (as *The Dark Tower*: Volumes 1–5) stayed at number 5 on *The New York Times* Fiction Best Seller List, its seventh week on the List.

4 January 2009

Just After Sunset stayed at number 6 on *The New York Times* Fiction Best Seller List, its sixth week on the List.

4 January 2015

Revival rose to number 2 *The New York Times* Hardcover Fiction Best Seller List, its sixth week on the List.

January 5

5 January 1946

Gatlin, NE, resident Yemen Hollis was born Edward Hollis. ["Children of the Corn"]

5 January 1965, dusk

Yemen Hollis was sacrificed to He Who Walks Behind the Rows. ["Children of the Corn"]

5 January 1974

The Dankmans were scheduled to move. Route 784 was going to go through their street, Crestallen Street West. [*Roadwork*]

5 January 1979

A postcard from Richard McCandless gave George LeBay's address. Dennis Guilder got LeBay's phone number from Paradise Falls, OH, information.

night: Christine and the dead Roland LeBay chased Pennsylvania State Police Detective Rudy Junkins at more than 120 MPH. They battered and ran his car off the road near Blairsville, killing him, their seventh victim. [*Christine*]

5 January 1986

Skeleton Crew rose to number 6 on *The New York Times* Fiction Best Seller List, its twenty-ninth week on the List.

5 January 1992

Needful Things stayed at number 2 on *The New York Times* Fiction Best Seller List, its twelfth week on the List.

5 January 1997

Desperation rose to number 5 on *The New York Times* Fiction Best Seller List, its thirteenth week on the List.

Richard Bachman's *The Regulators* rose to number 12 on *The New York Times* Fiction Best Seller List, its thirteenth week on the List.

5 January 2003

From a Buick 8 rose to number 9 on *The New York Times* Fiction Best Seller List, its tenth week on the List.

5 January 2014

Joyland dropped to number 13 on *The New York Times* Paperback Trade Fiction Best Seller List, its twenty-second and last week on the List.

Doctor Sleep stayed at number 5 on *The New York Times* Hardcover Fiction Best Seller List, its thirteenth week on the List.

January 6

6 January 1974

Marjorie Duvall, Beadie's last victim, was born. ["A Good Marriage"]

6 January 1979, Saturday

Johnny Smith arrived at New York's Grand Central Station. Taxi driver George Clements drove him to the Port Authority Terminal, where Johnny got a Greyhound bus to Portsmouth, NH. That evening, he checked in to the Portsmouth Holiday Inn. [*The Dead Zone*]

"DARNELL INVESTIGATOR MURDERED NEAR BLAIRSVILLE" appeared in the Libertyville *Keystone*. The caption under a picture of his wrecked car read, "DEATH CAR." Library research confirmed Rudy Junkins had investigated the murders of Christine's victims. That night, Dennis Guilder called George LeBay, who told him the darker side of Roland LeBay's past. This confirmed Guilder's suspicions that the dead Roland LeBay and Christine were killing. He decided to destroy Christine. [*Christine*]

6 January 1980

The Dead Zone stayed at number 9 on *The New York Times* Fiction Best Seller List, its eighteenth week on the List.

6 January 1985

The Talisman stayed at number 1 on *The New York Times* Fiction Best Seller List, its eleventh week on the List.

6 January 1991

Two-day-old Peter Goldsmith-Redman had Captain Trips. [*The Stand: The Complete & Uncut Edition*]

The Stand: The Complete & Uncut Edition stayed at number 11 on *The New York Times* Fiction Best Seller List, its thirty-second week on the List.

Four Past Midnight stayed at number 2 on *The New York Times* Fiction Best Seller List, its seventeenth week on the List.

6 January 2002

Black House rose to number 7 on *The New York Times* Fiction Best Seller List, its fourteenth week on the List.

6 January 2019

Elevation rose to number 7 on *The New York Times* Hardcover Fiction Best Seller List, its eighth week on the List.

January 7

7 January 1974, 10:15 a.m.

Philip T. Fenner gave Barton Dawes relocation form 6983–73–73. The city felt Dawes was planning a public display on the 20th, the day the Crestallen Street West demolition for the Route 784 extension was to begin. Fenner offered an extra $5,000 and to keep Olivia Brenner's living with him private if he completed the form. He agreed. (They knew Olivia had spent a night with him because they had bugged his house.) [*Roadwork*]

7 January 1984

Maura Dunbarton killed her husband, two children, and Slugger, their dog. Sentenced to life, she became inmate #4028200–1 at Dooling Correctional Facility for Women. [*Sleeping Beauties*]

7 January 1990

The Dark Half rose to number 1 on *The New York Times* Fiction Best Seller List, its tenth week on the List.

7 January 1991

Tom Cullen, Kojak, and Stu Redman spent the night in Golden, CO, twenty miles from the Free Zone. [*The Stand: The Complete & Uncut Edition*]

7 January 1996

After fourteen weeks off, *Rose Madder* entered *The New York Times* Fiction Best Seller List at number 14, its fourteenth and last week on the List.

7 January 2001

On Writing stayed at number 11 on *The New York Times* Non-Fiction Best Seller List, its twelfth week on the List.

7 January 2007

Lisey's Story rose to number 8 on *The New York Times* Fiction Best Seller List, its ninth week on the List.

7 January 2018

Sleeping Beauties rose to number 9 on *The New York Times* Hardcover Fiction Best Seller List, its thirteenth week on the List.

January 8

8 January 1948

"AIR FORCE CAPTAIN KILLED CHASING UFO; Mantell's Final Transmission: 'Metallic, Tremendous in Size;' Air Force Mum" appeared in the Kentucky *Courier Journal*. [*Dreamcatcher*]

8 January 1974

Barton Dawes visited Sal Magliore, who sent two men in a Ray's TV Sales and Service van to clean bugs from Barton's house. They found listening devices in his bedroom, dining room, and two phones. Dawes asked Magliore for explosives. [*Roadwork*]

8 January 1979, Monday

Libertyville High School's first day of classes after the Christmas break [*Christine*]

8 January 1984

Pet Sematary stayed at number 2 on *The New York Times* Fiction Best Seller List, its tenth week on the List.

8 January 1991, ~1:00 p.m.

Tom Cullen, Kojak, and Stu Redman walked when their snowmobile ran out of gas. Excited about almost being home, they had forgotten to fill its tank. [*The Stand: The Complete & Uncut Edition*]

8 January 1995

Insomnia stayed at number 4 on *The New York Times* Fiction Best Seller List, its twelfth week on the List.

8 January 2012

11/22/63 stayed at number 1 on *The New York Times* Fiction Best Seller List, its seventh week on the List.

January 9

9 January 1974

Barton Dawes filled out the relocation form for his house and received a cashier's check for $68,500. He deposited half in the checking account and took the rest in cash. [*Roadwork*]

9 January 1983

Different Seasons stayed at number 8 on *The New York Times* Fiction Best Seller List, its twenty-third week on the List.

9 January 1991

Peter Goldsmith-Redman began recovering from Captain Trips because of his inherited half-immunity. Fran Goldsmith, his mother, was immune; Jess Rider, his father, wasn't.

Lucy Swann was four months pregnant.

~8:20 p.m.: Billy Gehringer, a Free Zone sentry, spotted Tom Cullen, Kojak, and Stu Redman in the center of town. Stu quit smoking. [*The Stand: The Complete & Uncut Edition*]

9 January 1994

Nightmares & Dreamscapes rose to number 3 on *The New York Times* Fiction Best Seller List, its thirteenth week on the List.

9 January 2000

Hearts in Atlantis stayed at number 6 on *The New York Times* Fiction Best Seller List, its fifteenth week on the List.

9 January 2002

[Ridley Pearson's] *The Diary of Ellen Rimbauer: My Life at Rose Red*, edited by Joyce Reardon, Ph.D. (Hyperion, $22.95) published with a first printing of 200,000 copies

9 January 2011

Full Dark, No Stars rose to number 5 on *The New York Times* Fiction Best Seller List, its seventh week on the List.

9 January 2013

The Dark Tower: The Gunslinger—Sheemie's Tale #1 of 2 (Marvel Comics, $3.99) published

January 10

~10 January 1965

Paul Landon had the bad-gunky so bad, cutting him wouldn't let it out; he was dangerous. For three weeks, his father and brother had kept him chained in the basement. They tried drugging him so Scott Landon could take him to Boo'ya Moon to cure him. The first two tries didn't work, perhaps because Paul wasn't awake. Scott suggested drugging him enough to subdue him, but not knock him out—big mistake. Paul opened his mouth wide enough to encompass Scott's head. Before Paul could kill Scott, their father grabbed Paul's hair, pulled his head back, and shot him under the chin with a .30-06 deer rifle. With the bad-gunky gone, Scott had no trouble taking him to Boo'ya Moon to bury him. [*Lisey's Story*]

10 January 1978

Jerry, Janey, and Francie Lumley were going to visit Janey's sister in Cumberland, ME. In a blizzard, their car went off the road near Jerusalem's Lot, about six miles south of Tookey's Bar. While Jerry walked to the bar for help, vampires bit his wife and daughter. He returned with Booth and Tookey to find his car empty. Janey bit him. Tookey threw a Bible at Francie when she was about to bite Booth, whom she had under her spell. ["One For the Road"]

10 January 1982

Cujo stayed at number 4 on *The New York Times* Fiction Best Seller List, its twenty-second week on the List.

10 January 1988

Misery rose to number 13 on *The New York Times* Fiction Best Seller List, its thirtieth and last week on the List.

The Tommyknockers stayed at number 1 on *The New York Times* Fiction Best Seller List, its seventh week on the List.

10 January 1993

Gerald's Game rose to number 7 on *The New York Times* Fiction Best Seller List, its twenty-sixth week on the List.

Dolores Claiborne stayed at number 1 on *The New York Times* Fiction Best Seller List, its sixth week on the List.

10 January 1999

Bag of Bones stayed at number 2 on *The New York Times* Fiction Best Seller List, its fourteenth week on the List.

10 January 2010

Under the Dome stayed at number 3 on *The New York Times* Fiction Best Seller List, its seventh week on the List.

10 January 2016

The Bazaar of Bad Dreams dropped to number 6 on *The New York Times* Hardcover Fiction Best Seller List, its eighth week on the List.

January 11

11 January 1974

Sal Magliore agreed to sell explosives to Barton Dawes for $9,000. [*Roadwork*]

11 January 1979

At his trial for raping and assaulting Miss Cora Ann Hooper, Morris Bellamy pleaded guilty, blamed the Jack Daniels, and threw himself at the mercy of the court. The judge sentenced him to life in Waynesville State Prison. [*Finders Keepers*]

11 January 1981

Firestarter stayed at number 3 on *The New York Times* Fiction Best Seller List, its twenty-first week on the List.

11 January 1987

IT stayed at number 1 on *The New York Times* Fiction Best Seller List, *IT*'s eighteenth week on the List.

11 January 1991

Stu Redman's leg was rebroken and set properly. His cast came off three months later. [*The Stand: The Complete & Uncut Edition*]

11 January 2004

The Dark Tower V: Wolves of the Calla (as *The Dark Tower*: Volumes 1–5) stayed at number 5 on *The New York Times* Fiction Best Seller List, its eighth week on the List.

11 January 2009

Just After Sunset stayed at number 6 on *The New York Times* Fiction Best Seller List, its seventh week on the List.

11 January 2012

The Dark Tower: The Gunslinger—The Way Station #2 of 5 (Marvel Comics, $3.99) published
The Stand: Night Has Come #6 of 6 (Marvel Comics, $3.99) published

11 January 2015

Revival dropped to number 4 *The New York Times* Hardcover Fiction Best Seller List, its seventh week on the List.

11 January 2017

The Dark Tower: The Drawing of the Three—The Sailor #4 of 5 (Marvel Comics, $3.99) published

January 12

12 January 1974

Alan and Ray, two of Sal Magliore's men, met Barton Dawes at the Revel Lanes Bowladrome. As they bowled, they told Dawes about the explosives he would get. Later, they made the explosives-$9,000 exchange behind the Town Line Tavern. [*Roadwork*]

12 January 1975

Johnny Smith spoke in his coma. [*The Dead Zone*]

12 January 1986

Skeleton Crew stayed at number 6 on *The New York Times* Fiction Best Seller List, its thirtieth week on the List.

12 January 1992

Needful Things stayed at number 2 on *The New York Times* Fiction Best Seller List, its thirteenth week on the List.

12 January 1997

Desperation rose to number 3 on *The New York Times* Fiction Best Seller List, its fourteenth week on the List.

Richard Bachman's *The Regulators* rose to number 9 on *The New York Times* Fiction Best Seller List, its fourteenth and last week on the List.

12 January 2003

From a Buick 8 dropped to number 10 on *The New York Times* Fiction Best Seller List, its eleventh and last week on the List.

12 January 2011

The Dark Tower: The Gunslinger—The Little Sisters of Eluria #2 of 5 (Marvel Comics, $3.99) published

12 January 2014

Doctor Sleep rose to number 3 on *The New York Times* Hardcover Fiction Best Seller List, its fourteenth week on the List.

January 13

13 January 1974

Barton Dawes gave Phil Drake $5,000 for the Drop Down Mamma Coffeehouse. [*Roadwork*]

13 January 1980

The Dead Zone rose to number 7 on *The New York Times* Fiction Best Seller List, its nineteenth week on the List.

13 January 1985

The Talisman stayed at number 1 on *The New York Times* Fiction Best Seller List, its twelfth week on the List.

13 January 1991

The Stand: The Complete & Uncut Edition rose to number 10 on *The New York Times* Fiction Best Seller List, its thirty-third week on the List.

Four Past Midnight stayed at number 2 on *The New York Times* Fiction Best Seller List, its eighteenth week on the List.

13 January 2002

Black House dropped to number 11 on *The New York Times* Fiction Best Seller List, its fifteenth and last week on the List.

13 January 2010

The Talisman: The Road of Trials #3 of 6 (Del Rey Comics, $3.99) published

13 January 2019

Elevation stayed at number 7 on *The New York Times* Hardcover Fiction Best Seller List, its ninth week on the List.

January 14

14 January 1921

Cora Leonard Newall gave birth to a girl without arms but with fingers growing from an eye socket. The girl died six hours later. Her tombstone in Gates Falls, ME, read, "GOD GRANT SHE LIE STILL." ["It Grows on You"]

14 January 1976

Red ended his story about Andy Dufresne with Andy's escape. ["Rita Hayworth and Shawshank Redemption"]

14 January 1982

The Boulder *Camera* reported that Annie Wilkes became Head Maternity Ward Nurse at Boulder Hospital. [*Misery*]

Mother Abagail received a letter from President Reagan, congratulating her for reaching her 100th year. Four Republicans were older. [*The Stand: The Complete & Uncut Edition*]

14 January 1990

The Dark Half stayed at number 1 on *The New York Times* Fiction Best Seller List, its eleventh week on the List.

14 January 2001

On Writing rose to number 10 on *The New York Times* Non-Fiction Best Seller List, its thirteenth week on the List.

14 January 2006

Sword in the Darkness, Chapter 71, Part 1, appeared in *The Weekend Australian*.

14 January 2007

Lisey's Story dropped to number 14 on *The New York Times* Fiction Best Seller List, its tenth and last week on the List.

14 January 2018

Sleeping Beauties dropped to number 12 on *The New York Times* Hardcover Fiction Best Seller List, its fourteenth and last week on the List.

January 15

15 January 1909

Ellen and John Rimbauer moved into their new home. They hosted a Grand Opening party, which became an Annual Inaugural Ball. More than 250 guests, including a famous baseball player, the mayor of Seattle, Tanner Longford, Jeanine Sabino, Marjorie Savoy, Bradley Webster, and a senator, attended. Dinner, with beef from Chicago and Kansas City, chocolate from Switzerland, fresh fish, pork from Nebraska, and tea from England, was served in six rooms. Grand Ballroom dancing followed. They had Cuban cigars, French champagne, and wine from abroad.

Adam Rimbauer was conceived. [*The Diary of Ellen Rimbauer: My Life at Rose Red*]

15 January 1910, Second Annual Inaugural Ball

Ellen Rimbauer wore the same white gown she had worn the year before. The Rimbauers had about 400 guests. [*The Diary of Ellen Rimbauer: My Life at Rose Red*]

15 January 1916, Annual Inaugural Ball

Charlie Chaplin and Elizabeth Paige, a famous opera singer, attended. [*The Diary of Ellen Rimbauer: My Life at Rose Red*]

15 January 1946, Annual Inaugural Ball

Deanna Petrie, a great film actress, disappeared at Rose Red. [*The Diary of Ellen Rimbauer: My Life at Rose Red*]

15 January 1974

Barton Dawes gave Sal Magliore $15,000 to invest with the dividends going to Olivia Brenner. Another $3,000 was for Magliore to find Brenner and set up her trust fund. [*Roadwork*]

15 January 1981

Apex Corporation's chief comptroller Harlow Enders implied to Roger Wade that Zenith House had a year to improve their sales or Zenith House may be sold. [*The Plant* Book One: *Zenith Rising*]

15 January 1984

Pet Sematary rose to number 1 on *The New York Times* Fiction Best Seller List, its eleventh week on the List.

15 January 1995

Insomnia stayed at number 4 on *The New York Times* Fiction Best Seller List, its thirteenth week on the List.

15 January 2012

11/22/63 dropped to number 2 on *The New York Times* Fiction Best Seller List, its eighth week on the List.

January 16

16 January 1882

John and Rebecca Freemantle's last child, Abagail, was born in Hemingford Home, NE. For more than a hundred years, she lived there all except the last six weeks of her life. She far outlived her husbands—Nate Brooks, Henry Hardesty, and David Trotts. She was best known as Mother Abagail. [*The Stand: The Complete & Uncut Edition*]

16 January 1909

John Rimbauer left a rose on Ellen Rimbauer's pillow. When she told Sukeena its color was rose red, she knew the name of the new grand house would be Rose Red. Sukeena guaranteed Ellen would be pregnant from the previous night's lovemaking. She also warned Ellen to stay out of the Billiard Room because she had seen Indian spirits there. [*The Diary of Ellen Rimbauer: My Life at Rose Red*]

16 January 1974

Barton Dawes sent the checkbook, representing half the money from the house, to his wife. [*Roadwork*]

16 January 1981

Zenith House editor John Kenton asked Carlos Detweiller for a synopsis and the first three chapters of *True Tales of Demon Infestations*. [*The Plant* Book One: *Zenith Rising*]

16 January 1983

Different Seasons dropped to number 9 on *The New York Times* Fiction Best Seller List, its twenty-fourth week on the List.

16 January 1994

Nightmares & Dreamscapes stayed at number 3 on *The New York Times* Fiction Best Seller List, its fourteenth week on the List.

16 January 2000

Hearts in Atlantis dropped to number 16 on *The New York Times* Fiction Best Seller List, its sixteenth and last week on the List.

16 January 2004

Eleanor Druse's [Richard Dooling's] *The Journals of Eleanor Druse: My Investigation of the Kingdom Hospital Incident* (Kingswell, $22.95) published

16 January 2011

Full Dark, No Stars dropped to number 12 on *The New York Times* Fiction Best Seller List, its eighth and last week on the List.

January 17

17 January 1974

Mary Dawes received $34,250 from Barton Dawes—her half of the proceeds from their house. She called to talk about divorce. [*Roadwork*]

17 January 1982

Cujo stayed at number 4 on *The New York Times* Fiction Best Seller List, its twenty-third week on the List.

17 January 1988

The Tommyknockers stayed at number 1 on *The New York Times* Fiction Best Seller List, its eighth week on the List and eighth week at number 1.

17 January 1993

Gerald's Game dropped to number 14 on *The New York Times* Fiction Best Seller List, its twenty-seventh week on the List.

Dolores Claiborne stayed at number 1 on *The New York Times* Fiction Best Seller List, its seventh week on the List.

17 January 1999

Bag of Bones dropped to number 9 on *The New York Times* Fiction Best Seller List, its fifteenth week on the List.

17 January 2010

Under the Dome dropped to number 10 on *The New York Times* Fiction Best Seller List, its eighth week on the List.

17 January 2016

The Bazaar of Bad Dreams rose to number 5 on *The New York Times* Hardcover Fiction Best Seller List, its ninth week on the List.

January 18

18 January 1974

Barton Dawes hadn't secured the Waterford relocation site. Steve Ordner told him The Blue Ribbon Laundry's corporate owners decided not to continue the industrial laundry service. They kept the Laundromats but changed their names to Handi-Wash. [*Roadwork*]

18 January 1979, Thursday

Leigh Cabot and Dennis Guilder ate Kentucky Fried Chicken. In the parking lot, they discussed ways of destroying Christine, whose murder toll stood at seven. Arnie Cunningham/Roland LeBay threatened them, and then LeBay's corpse sped away. Dennis and Leigh thought LeBay and Christine would go after them next. [*Christine*]

18 January 1981

Firestarter rose to number 2 on *The New York Times* Fiction Best Seller List, its twenty-second week on the List.

18 January 1993

A Grayson, KY, high school senior shot and killed his English teacher and the school custodian; he held the class hostage for twenty minutes. The C his English teacher gave him for his essay on *Rage* set him off.

18 January 1987

IT dropped to number 2 on *The New York Times* Fiction Best Seller List, *IT*'s nineteenth week on the List.

18 January 2004

The Dark Tower V: Wolves of the Calla (as *The Dark Tower*: Volumes 1–5) dropped to number 7 on *The New York Times* Fiction Best Seller List, its ninth and last week on the List.

18 January 2009

Just After Sunset dropped to number 12 on *The New York Times* Fiction Best Seller List, its eighth and last week on the List.

18 January 2015

Revival dropped to number 6 *The New York Times* Hardcover Fiction Best Seller List, its eighth week on the List.

January 19

19 January 1977

George Staub was born. [*Riding the Bullet*]

19 January 1979

Christine and the dead Roland LeBay enticed Michael Cunningham, their eighth victim, inside Christine, where they killed him with her exhaust. The newspapers reported he slipped on the ice and the car rolled on top of him.

In the school's parking lot before school, Dennis Guilder persuaded LeBay, in Arnie Cunningham, to meet him later that night at Darnell's Garage with Christine. At the Garage, Leigh Cabot and Dennis used Petunia, Johnny Pomberton's large GM septic-system tanker truck, to batter Christine into a pile of scrap.

Arnie Cunningham and his mother, Regina, drove toward Penn State to talk with the dean of the College of Arts and Sciences. As Christine battled Petunia, LeBay struggled with Arnie and his mother. Traveling about 45 MPH in light snow, they crossed the Pennsylvania Turnpike's median and ran head-on into a truck. The car exploded. The truck driver suffered a broken arm and said there were three people in the car. Police found only two bodies.

Aftermath: Dennis had overstrained his leg while trying to open the stuck door to Darnell's Garage. Dr. Arroway treated him in the hospital. Rick Mercer supervised a two-man crew put Christine in Will Darnell's crusher; she came out a 2' x 2' x 2' cube. She bit a crewman; he needed stitches. About three years later, she and LeBay killed Sander Galton at a Los Angeles drive-in movie theater. [*Christine*]

19 January 1986

Skeleton Crew dropped to number 12 on *The New York Times* Fiction Best Seller List, its thirty-first week on the List.

19 January 1990

A final five hours finished *The Waste Lands*. A voice in Stephen King's head told him to stop; he ended with a cliffhanger. The 800 pages-plus manuscript needed few edits. [*The Dark Tower VI: Song of Susannah*]

19 January 1992

Needful Things dropped to number 3 on *The New York Times* Fiction Best Seller List, its fourteenth week on the List.

19 January 1997

Desperation dropped to number 16 on *The New York Times* Fiction Best Seller List, its fifteenth and last week on the List.

19 January 1999

Dick Hallorann died of a heart attack. He was eighty-one. [*Doctor Sleep*]

19 January 2014

Doctor Sleep dropped to number 6 on *The New York Times* Hardcover Fiction Best Seller List,

Michael Roch

its fifteenth week on the List.

January 20

20 January 1973

A Route 784 extension was going to go through Crestallen Street West. Hank Albert, the Arlins, the Dankmans, the Darbys, the Daweses, the Hobarts, the Langs, the Quinns, the Stauffers, and the Upslingers were told they had one year to move. Albert moved to Waterford. When they filed a relocation form, the Dawses would receive a check for $63,500, based on their tax assessment. The Hobarts moved the following November. The Langs moved to Minnesota after a job transfer. By December 6, the Upslingers had moved to Iowa. [*Roadwork*]

There were no *New York Times* articles for this date in Ur 4,121,989. 19 November 1962 was the last archive date in that Ur. ["Ur"]

20 January 1974

The deadline for Barton Dawes to evacuate his house arrived. Early in the morning, he spread explosives throughout his house and garage. Later, he started a shootout with sixteen police officers; one was shot in the arm, Dawes in the right leg. Dave Albert, WHLM, Channel 9, News interviewer, worked his way to Barton Dawes's house; Dawes let him in. Later, Dawes threw out his guns, but detonated the explosives, killing himself. WHLM won a Pulitzer Prize for their "Dawes' Last Stand" coverage and their "Roadwork" documentary. [*Roadwork*]

20 January 1979, Saturday

Greg Stillson held a feedback meeting in Coorter's Notch, NH. [*The Dead Zone*]

20 January 1980

The Dead Zone dropped to number 9 on *The New York Times* Fiction Best Seller List, its twentieth week on the List.

20 January 1985

The Talisman dropped to number 2 on *The New York Times* Fiction Best Seller List, its thirteenth week on the List.

20 January 1991

The Stand: The Complete & Uncut Edition dropped to number 11 on *The New York Times* Fiction Best Seller List, its thirty-fourth week on the List.

Four Past Midnight dropped to number 4 on *The New York Times* Fiction Best Seller List, its nineteenth week on the List.

20 January 2016

The Dark Tower: The Drawing of the Three—Lady of Shadows #5 of 5 (Marvel Comics, $3.99) published

20 January 2019

Elevation dropped to number 14 on *The New York Times* Hardcover Fiction Best Seller List, its tenth and last week on the List.

January 21

21 January 1979, Sunday

Rick Mercer talked with Dennis Guilder in the hospital. Because Rick was a close friend of Rudy Junkins, Dennis told him the whole Christine/Arnie Cunningham/Roland LeBay story for two hours, off-the-record. [*Christine*]

The Stand entered *The New York Times* Fiction Best Seller List at number 15. It was on the List for two weeks.

21 January 1981

In response to John Kenton's request, Carlos Detweiller sent a letter saying he'd send the entire *True Tales of Demon Infestations* manuscript soon. He wrote that, without his body leaving home, he had joined covens in Flagstaff, AZ, Fall River, MA, and Omaha, NE. [*The Plant* Book One: *Zenith Rising*]

21 January 1990

The Dark Half dropped to number 4 on *The New York Times* Fiction Best Seller List, its twelfth week on the List.

21 January 2001

On Writing dropped to number 11 on *The New York Times* Non-Fiction Best Seller List, its fourteenth week on the List.

21 January 2006

Sword in the Darkness, Chapter 71, Part 2, appeared in *The Weekend Australian*.

21 January 2009

In Ur 1,000,000, *The New York Times* reported that Hillary Clinton succeeded Albert Arnold Gore as 44th President of the United States. ["Ur"]

January 22

22 January 1981

Carlos Detweiller sent human-sacrifice photographs and the *True Tales of Demon Infestations* manuscript to John Kenton. [*The Plant* Book One: *Zenith Rising*]

22 January 1984

Pet Sematary stayed at number 1 on *The New York Times* Fiction Best Seller List, its twelfth week on the List.

22 January 1995

Insomnia dropped to number 9 on *The New York Times* Fiction Best Seller List, its fourteenth week on the List.

22 January 2008

Duma Key (Scribner, $28) published with a first printing of 1,000,000 to 1,500,000 copies

22 January 2012

11/22/63 dropped to number 4 on *The New York Times* Fiction Best Seller List, its ninth week on the List.

January 23

23 January

Paradise Lines, Inc., cruise ship *Callas* sank in a storm. Ex-surgeon Richard Pine escaped in a lifeboat. Pine was on his way home from Saigon with $40,000 worth of heroin. It had a United States street value of $350,000, enough to bribe back his revoked medical license. ["Survivor Type"]

23 January [1974]

Blaze prepared to kidnap Joseph Gerard IV, the baby of a wealthy couple. At the Baby Shoppe of Hager's Mammoth Department Store, he told the saleslady he wanted it all for his six-month-old nephew. Working on commission, Nancy Moldow loaded him up with almost $340 of baby stuff. She sold him everything from clothes and furniture to food and place settings. [*Blaze*]

23 January 1981

John Kenton received Carlos Detweiller's letter. The manuscript would be on its way soon. [*The Plant* Book One: *Zenith Rising*]

23 January 1983

Different Seasons dropped to number 11 on *The New York Times* Fiction Best Seller List, its twenty-fifth week on the List.

23 January 1984

The Spring Semester started at the University of Maine at Orono. Louis Creed ran University Medical Services. [*Pet Sematary*]

23 January 1994

Nightmares & Dreamscapes dropped to number 9 on *The New York Times* Fiction Best Seller List, its fifteenth week on the List.

January 24

24 January

Richard Pine washed up on a small island after his lifeboat was damaged on a reef. The boat sank. He kept two knives, a fork, a spoon, his heroin, some matches, a logbook, a pencil, four gallons of water, a sewing kit, and a first aid kit. ["Survivor Type"]

24 January [1974], night

On Portland, ME's Jolly Jim's Giant Groceries parking lot, Blaze swapped his Ford's license plates with those from a Volkswagen. After dinner, he spray-painted the green car Skylark Blue. [*Blaze*]

24 January 1979, Wednesday

Arnie Cunningham, Michael Cunningham, and Regina Cunningham were buried in a family plot in Libertyville Heights Cemetery. Pennsylvania State Police Inspector Rick Mercer went to the funeral. [*Christine*]

24 January 1982

Cujo dropped to number 8 on *The New York Times* Fiction Best Seller List, its twenty-fourth week on the List.

24 January 1988

The Tommyknockers dropped to number 2 on *The New York Times* Fiction Best Seller List, its ninth week on the List.

24 January 1993

Gerald's Game rose to number 13 on *The New York Times* Fiction Best Seller List, its twenty-eighth and last week on the List.

Dolores Claiborne dropped to number 3 on *The New York Times* Fiction Best Seller List, its eighth week on the List.

24 January 1999

Bag of Bones dropped to number 11 on *The New York Times* Fiction Best Seller List, its sixteenth week on the List.

24 January 2006

Cell (Scribner, $26.95) published with a first printing of 1,100,000 copies

24 January 2007

Edgar Freemantle and Pam Freemantle exchanged emails. He told her about his paintings and attached a couple of .jpgs. He thought her "hands-off" gardening gloves would be great for a sunset painting, so he asked to borrow them. [*Duma Key*]

24 January 2010

Under the Dome stayed at number 10 on *The New York Times* Fiction Best Seller List, its ninth and last week on the List.

24 January 2016

The Bazaar of Bad Dreams dropped to number 8 on *The New York Times* Hardcover Fiction Best Seller List, its tenth week on the List.

January 25

25 January [1974], night

Blaze robbed Tim & Janet's Quik-Pik for the second time that month. Although Blaze wore a stocking over his face this time, clerk Harry Nason recognized him from the first time. [*Blaze*]

25 January 1978

"OVERLOOK COMBINE CALLS IT QUITS" appeared in *Resort* Magazine. Albert Shockley, on The Overlook Hotel's Board of Directors, said they wouldn't rebuild the hotel. ["After the Play"]

25 January 1980: Russell Bowie's Funeral

Russell Bowie and Stewie McClelland had ridden Stewie's snowmobile on the frozen Reach. The ice broke; they fell in. Russell died, and Stewie lost a foot to frostbite. ["Do the Dead Sing?" / "The Reach"]

25 January 1981

John Kenton wrote Ruth Tanaka, his fiancée. He feared Carlos Detweiller might have been another crazy like General Hecksler. [*The Plant* Book One: *Zenith Rising*]

Firestarter dropped to number 4 on *The New York Times* Fiction Best Seller List, its twenty-third week on the List.

25 January 1987

IT stayed at number 2 on *The New York Times* Fiction Best Seller List, *IT*'s twentieth week on the List.

25 January 2003

Introductions to *The Dark Tower: The Gunslinger, Revised and Expanded Edition*, and the Viking re-issues of *The Dark Tower II: The Drawing of the Three*, *The Dark Tower III: The Waste Lands*, and *The Dark Tower IV: Wizard and Glass*

25 January 2015

Revival dropped to number 10 *The New York Times* Hardcover Fiction Best Seller List, its ninth week on the List.

January 26

26 January

Richard Pine started a diary. ["Survivor Type"]

26 January [1974]

morning: Blaze went to Apex Hardware in Apex Center. He bought a Craftwork Lightwork Supreme aluminum extension ladder for $30 on clearance.

11:00 p.m.: He woke up and fell back asleep, missing a chance to kidnap Joseph Gerard IV. [*Blaze*]

26 January 1986

Skeleton Crew dropped to number 15 on *The New York Times* Fiction Best Seller List, its thirty-second and last week on the List.

26 January 1992

Needful Things stayed at number 3 on *The New York Times* Fiction Best Seller List, its fifteenth week on the List.

26 January 2014

Doctor Sleep dropped to number 13 on *The New York Times* Hardcover Fiction Best Seller List, its sixteenth week on the List.

January 27

27 January [1974], night

Blaze missed another opportunity to kidnap Joseph Gerard IV. [*Blaze*]

27 January 1980

The Dead Zone stayed at number 9 on *The New York Times* Fiction Best Seller List, its twenty-first week on the List.

27 January 1985

The Talisman stayed at number 2 on *The New York Times* Fiction Best Seller List, its fourteenth week on the List.

27 January 1991

Four Past Midnight dropped to number 6 on *The New York Times* Fiction Best Seller List, its twentieth week on the List.

27 January 2002

The Diary of Ellen Rimbauer: My Life at Rose Red entered *The New York Times* Fiction Best Seller List at number 15. It was on the List for eleven weeks.

27 January 2007

Edgar Freemantle's Great Beach Walk took him two hundred yards from Wireman.

UPS delivered Pam Freemantle's gardening gloves. *Friends with Benefits* exploded from Edgar's brushes. The painting showed Pam, wearing only panties, with two naked men. Max Stanton was the man on the way out of Pam's life. Tom Riley, Edgar's best friend of thirty-five years, was the man on his way in. [*Duma Key*]

January 28

28 January

Richard Pine killed and ate a seagull, raw. ["Survivor Type"]

28 January 1962

Annie Wilkes poisoned Peter Gunn, a cat that belonged to her and USC nursing-student roommate Andrea Saint James. She put him at the top of the stairs for Andrea to trip over. Andrea was dead on arrival at Mercy Hospital in Los Angeles. Peter Gunn was assumed to have eaten rat poison from the basement. [*Misery*]

28 January [1974], night

Blaze bought three comic books at the beer store in Apex Center. After dinner, he fell asleep while reading. [*Blaze*]

28 January 1977

The Shining (Doubleday, $8.95) published with a first printing of 25,000 to 26,000 copies

28 January 1981, Wednesday

John Kenton received Carlos Detweiller's manuscript and photographs. He dismissed most of the pictures, but four of a "Black Mass" seemed to show a human sacrifice. He called the Central Falls Police Department and told Chief of Police Barton Iverson. Before the police received the photos, Iverson sent Riley to confirm Carlos Detweiller still worked at the House of Flowers. After seeing the photos, they brought Detweiller in. Riley recognized the dead man in the pictures as Norville Keen, a living, breathing human being he had seen at the House of Flowers that morning. They released Detweiller. [*The Plant* Book One: *Zenith Rising*]

28 January 1990

The Dark Half rose to number 3 on *The New York Times* Fiction Best Seller List, its thirteenth week on the List.

28 January 1991

Stephen King finished *Needful Things*.

28 January 2001

On Writing stayed at number 11 on *The New York Times* Non-Fiction Best Seller List, its fifteenth week on the List.

28 January 2007, afternoon

Edgar Freemantle reached Wireman.

After a nap, Edgar Freemantle listened to a message from Jack Cantori. Jack's mother had set up an appointment with Dario Nannuzzi to look at Edgar's artwork. He should bring up to ten finished pieces to the Scoto Gallery on Friday, 4:00–5:00 p.m.

Edgar Freemantle had a vision of Tom Riley, missing an eye. He thought this suggested Tom would commit suicide. Edgar called Tom but got a recording saying he was on his annual cruise. [*Duma Key*]

28 January 2009

The Dark Tower: Treachery #5 of 6 (Marvel Comics, $3.99) published

The Stand: Captain Trips #5 of 5 (Marvel Comics, $3.99) published

January 29

29 January 1962

"USC STUDENT DIES IN FREAK FALL" appeared in the *Los Angeles Call*. [*Misery*]

29 January 1966

Steve King's "The 43rd Dream" appeared in Vol. 3 No. 4 of the Lisbon High School newsletter *The Drum*, "Lisbon's Best Selling Newspaper."

29 January [1974]

12:00 a.m.: Blaze woke up to go the bathroom. He was having second thoughts about the kidnapping. The George Rockley in his mind persuaded him to go.

1:15 a.m.: He left.

2:00 a.m.: He arrived at the Oakwood condominium tower. At the far end of the parking lot, he scratched his leg climbing over the Cyclone chain-link fence. He cut through four acres of deserted parkland across from the Gerard estate. The Gerards' hedge had an electrified wire, so he jumped over it. He cut his scratched leg, leaving blood on the hedge and snow. He climbed into an unlocked second-floor window over the kitchen and went into the hall. The fourth door he opened was the baby's room. He took Joseph Gerard IV downstairs to the kitchen. The nineteenth step creaked enough to wake Norma Gerard. He broke the lower kitchen windowpane to get out. Norma Gerard went to see what she thought the cat might have knocked over and found Blaze in the kitchen. He coldcocked her before she could scream. Back home, a jar of Gerber Peas stopped Joe from crying.

afternoon: He bought a copy of *Child and Baby Care* and the *Evening Express* at Walgreens. The cover of the *Express* had police artist John Black's rendition of him. With letters cut from magazines and comic books, he made a $1 million ransom note. [*Blaze*]

29 January 1982

Annie Wilkes killed a baby in Boulder Hospital's Maternity Ward. [*Misery*]

29 January 1984

~8:00 a.m.: Norma Crandall died of a stroke. [*Pet Sematary*]

Pet Sematary dropped to number 2 on *The New York Times* Fiction Best Seller List, its thirteenth week on the List.

29 January 1995

Insomnia dropped to number 10 on *The New York Times* Fiction Best Seller List, its fifteenth week on the List.

29 January 2001

"All That You Love Will Be Carried Away" (collected in *Everything's Eventual*) appeared in the January 29th issue of *The New Yorker*.

29 January 2007, Wednesday afternoon

Wireman introduced Edgar Freemantle to Miss Elizabeth Eastlake. After tea and *Oprah*, Edgar read her a Frank O'Hara poem from *Good Poems*, edited by Garrison Keillor.

At home, Edgar called Pam Freemantle and asked her to confront Tom Riley. She denied any connection with Riley but relented after she was sure Edgar knew. He pushed her into letting Tom know she'd tell everyone his upcoming accidental death would be suicide. [*Duma Key*]

29 January 2012

11/22/63 dropped to number 6 on *The New York Times* Fiction Best Seller List, its tenth week on the List.

January 30

30 January [1974]

3:00 p.m.: Outside the Giant Kleen Kloze U-Wash-It, Blaze mailed the ransom note and talked with Georgia Kingsbury's son. He stole Jerry Green's 1970 Mustang from the parking lot.

4:30 p.m.: Nancy Moldow called FBI Agent Sterling. She told him she had seen Blaze's driver's license when he opened his wallet to pay for baby products. Blaze became the prime suspect. [*Blaze*]

30 January 1981

John Kenton wrote Ruth Tanaka, telling her about Carlos Detweiller's "Black Mass" photographs. [*The Plant* Book One: *Zenith Rising*]

30 January 1983

Different Seasons stayed at number 11 on *The New York Times* Fiction Best Seller List, its twenty-sixth week on the List.

30 January 1994

Nightmares & Dreamscapes dropped to number 10 on *The New York Times* Fiction Best Seller List, its sixteenth week on the List.

30 January 2007

Thursday, 2:00 p.m.: Edgar Freemantle showed Wireman sixteen drawings and paintings. One was *Hello*, the pencil sketch of a tanker he drew his first night on Duma Key. They gave Wireman an emotional bang. [*Duma Key*]

Stephen King's Full Disclosure Introduction to Richard Bachman's *Blaze*

January 31

31 January

Donald Knowles gave Edie Rowsmith an engagement ring. They played around, but he wanted to wait until they married to go all the way. His last words to her: "Will you remember to take the milk out of the icebox before you go up?" [*Sword in the Darkness*]

31 January

Richard Pine killed and ate another seagull. ["Survivor Type"]

31 January [1974]

5:30 a.m.: Blaze and Joseph Gerard IV left Blaze's Apex, ME, home, two hours before police roadblocks. They went to Hetton House, the county home where Blaze had lived as a child. It had been boarded up for fifteen years.

5:00 p.m.: In the dark and snow, Blaze walked to Cumberland Center, three miles to the north. The Exxon on Route 289 had a pay phone. He gave his real name to the operator when he made a collect call to the Gerards to arrange a ransom. The FBI traced the call. [*Blaze*]

31 January 1982

Cujo rose to number 7 on *The New York Times* Fiction Best Seller List, its twenty-fifth week on the List.

31 January 1988

The Tommyknockers stayed at number 2 on *The New York Times* Fiction Best Seller List, its tenth week on the List.

31 January 1993

Dolores Claiborne stayed at number 3 on *The New York Times* Fiction Best Seller List, its ninth week on the List.

31 January 1999

Bag of Bones dropped to number 16 on *The New York Times* Fiction Best Seller List, its seventeenth week on the List.

31 January 2005

Afterword to *The Colorado Kid*

31 January 2007

Friday, 4:00–5:00 p.m.: Jack Cantori took Edgar Freemantle and Wireman to the Scoto Gallery. Edgar showed eight pieces, including *Roses Grow from Shells* and *Sunset with Seagull*. Mr. Dario Nannuzzi thought Edgar's work was quite good for a beginner. He classified Edgar as an American primitive, like Grandma Moses and Jackson Pollock. Mr. Costenza, a patron of the gallery, offered to buy *Sunset with Seagull*, but it wasn't for sale yet. Although they didn't meet, Edgar and Mary Ire became aware of each other—he a new artist, and she an art critic.

Edgar, Jack, and Wireman had dinner at Zoria's on Main Street in Sarasota, FL. While waiting for Jack to get the rented van after dinner, Wireman had a small seizure. He said he was just falling asleep. On Casey Key Road, Edgar saw Wireman have a petit mal seizure that lasted about twenty seconds. [*Duma Key*]

Marvel Spotlight #14: The Dark Tower—Stephen King's Magnum Opus (Marvel Comics, $2.99) published

~31 January 2011

Holt Ramsey told Darcy Anderson he had wanted to ask her husband a few questions. Since he couldn't, he thought he'd ask her. He told her about his suspicions that her husband was serial killer Beadie. Witnesses had seen Bob Anderson's vehicles near the murder victims' homes. He asked her straight out whether her husband was Beadie. Fearing he was recording her, she answered with a gesture. Before leaving, Holt told her she had done the right thing. ["A Good Marriage"]

31 January 2016

The Bazaar of Bad Dreams dropped to number 12 on *The New York Times* Hardcover Fiction Best Seller List, its eleventh and last week on the List.

January

January 1880

Skinner Sweet and his gang killed a three-year-old and others while robbing a Bakersville, Colorado, bank. They got away with a mining company's payroll of almost $20,000 and stashed it in the abandoned mine where they had been hanging out. [*American Vampire*]

January 1918

Dick Hallorann was born. He inherited the shining from his maternal grandmother. [*The Shining*][*Doctor Sleep*]

January 1946

Kermit William Hodges was born. [*End of Watch*]

January 1951

Patrick Hockstetter worried that his parents might replace him with his baby brother. Suffocating Avery Hockstetter with a pillow awakened an enjoyment in killing. For the rest of his life, he killed bugs then small animals. [*IT*]

January 1953

Johnny Smith ice-skated backward into a hockey game on Runaround Pond in Durham, ME. He fell and hit his head, knocking himself out. When Chuck Spier woke him up, Johnny foresaw him in an explosion (February 1953). For the next seventeen years, Johnny had occasional hunches about things that would happen. [*The Dead Zone*]

January 1959

Roland LeBay ran a Western Auto hose from Christine's exhaust into her passenger compartment to kill his wife. Veronica's death was recorded as a suicide, which ended months of depression. Six months earlier, their daughter, Rita, died inside Christine. These two deaths gave Christine a supernatural power where she became self-repairing. [*Christine*]

January 1960

Thaddeus Beaumont entered his story, "Outside Marty's House," into *American Teen* magazine's writing contest. He heard from them five months later. [*The Dark Half*]

January 1964

Dolores St. George reverted to her maiden name, Dolores Claiborne. The previous summer, she killed her husband and made it look like an accident. [*Dolores Claiborne*]

January 1971

"The Blue Air Compressor" and "In the Key-Chords of Dawn" appeared in the Spring issue (Vol. 1, No. 1) of *Onan*, the University of Maine at Orono's literary magazine.

January 1973, 6:45 p.m.

Vinnie Corey, David Garcia, and Bob Lawson pushed Kathy Slavin off her apartment building's roof to make room for Garcia in Jim Norman's class. ["Sometimes They Come Back"]

January 1975

On the first day after the Christmas break, Castle Rock Middle School history teacher Miss Chiles hosted Curiosity Day. Each student could ask a history-related question. She'd put any question she couldn't answer up for class discussion. Gwendy Peterson's question stimulated the most conversation: if pushing a magic button caused someone to disappear or something to be blown up, who should die or what should be blown up? Most students suggested foreign countries they perceived as a threat. [*Gwendy's Button Box*]

January 1977

Sam Landry started *Scarlet Town*, his first Clyde Umney novel. He wrote four more in the next ten years. ["Umney's Last Case"]

January 1980

New Tales of the Cthulhu Mythos, edited by Ramsey Campbell (Arkham House, $14.95), with "Crouch End" (collected in *Nightmares & Dreamscapes*), published

January 1981

Alva Thornton gave Brett Camber a puppy. Charity Camber paid $9 for rabies and distemper shots. A couple of months later, they called him Willie. [*Cujo*]

January 1983

"The Word Processor" (collected as "Word Processor of the Gods" in *Skeleton Crew*) appeared in the January issue (Volume 40, Number 1) of *Playboy*.

January 1984

full moon: GS&WM flagman Arnie Westrum waited out a blizzard in a tool and signal shack, nine miles from Tarker's Mills, ME. The Beast broke into the shack and killed him. [*Cycle of the Werewolf*]

Danny Torrance found Horace Derwent in his closet. Danny locked him away in his mind. [*Doctor Sleep*]

January 1985

Researching copyrights at the Library of Congress, Steve Brown found that Stephen King owned the copyright to *Rage*, Richard Bachman's first book.

"Dolan's Cadillac," part 1 of 5 (collected in *Nightmares & Dreamscapes*), appeared in the January 1985 issue (Vol. 1, No. 1) of *Castle Rock: The Stephen King Newsletter*.

January 1992

Shock Rock: The New Sound of Horror, edited by Jeff Gelb (Pocket Books, $4.99), with "You Know They Got a Hell of a Band" (collected in *Nightmares & Dreamscapes*), published

The Dark Tower III: The Waste Lands (Plume, $17.95) published

January 1998

Robert Bloch's Psychos, edited by Robert Block (Pocket Books, $6.99), with "Autopsy Room Four" (collected in *Everything's Eventual*), published

The Best of the Best: 18 New Stories by America's Leading Authors, edited by Elaine Koster and Joseph Pittman (Signet, $22.95), with "L. T.'s Theory of Pets" (collected in *Everything's Eventual*), published

January 2007

Azzie visited Charlie Hayes in The Helen Rivington House's Alan Shepard Suite. Nurse Claudette Albertson paged Doctor Sleep to help Charlie pass on. [*Doctor Sleep*]

January 2012

"Final Dispatch," an alternate final chapter to *11/22/63*, available on www.stephenking.com

January 2015

Johnny Shining Path Parker had the item Alden McCausland wanted; it cost $2,000. Two or three days later, Alden went to pick it up; it was in a nailed crate. Johnny showed him a video of the Close Encounters of the Fourth Kind (CE4). Alden and his mother opened it the next day. It was much bigger than the one in the video. They stowed the CE4, the only firework Alden bought that year, in the garage. ["Drunken Fireworks"]

January 2016

Sunday: Janice Ellerton killed Martine Stover with an oxycodone overdose in Martine's feeding tube then suffocated herself in the bathtub.

Monday:

morning: Detective Pete Huntley consulted with Holly Gibney and retired detective Bill Hodges on the Stover-Ellerton murder-suicide. Holly found a Zappit Commander between the arm and cushion of Mrs. Ellerton's chair.

Brady Hartsfield extended his middle finger at Nurse Ruth Scapelli. Two of her uniform buttons popped. He smiled. That afternoon, Nurse Scapelli reached into Brady's shirt, grabbed a nipple, and pinched and twisted it. His non-reaction angered her more. She threatened to do his testicles if he ever gave her the finger again. He did and smiled. She didn't know Dr. Babineau had a nanny-cam with a fisheye lens in Brady's room. At 8:00 p.m., the doctor confronted Ruth Scapelli about assaulting and criminally threatening a mentally-deficient patient. He gave her a Zappit and said it would all be forgotten if she tapped pink fish in the Fishin' Hole demo until their numbers summed to a 9-digit number. Dr. Babineau left; Brady Hartsfield entered through her Zappit and persuaded her to kill herself. She slashed her arms with a butcher knife.

Tuesday:

Dr. Wendell Stamos told Bill Hodges his pancreatic cancer had spread to the liver. Bill needed chemo and radiation.

Listening to a voice—Brady Hartsfield—from her Zappit, Barbara Robinson cut school. Brady tried to talk her into suicide as she walked along Martin Luther King Avenue in Lowtown. When Barbara stepped on the curb, with a black truck approaching, Dereece Neville grabbed her and clowned around with her, taking her Zappit. She kicked Neville in the shins, snatched her Zappit, and ran into the street—in front of a panel truck. Dereece tried to push her out of the way. With a broken leg, she was sent to Kiner Memorial. She told Bill Hodges that Dereece may have saved her life.

Holly Gibney found that the company that owned the Zappits, Sunrise Solutions, had gone bankrupt.

~8:00 p.m.: Brady Hartsfield, inside Al Brooks as Z-Boy, killed Mrs. Cora Babineau. He transferred from Al Brooks into Dr. Babineau. At Freddi Linklatter's apartment, he had Freddi start a repeater to search for Zappits. After five minutes, it had found one.

Wednesday:

~2:00 a.m.: In Kiner Memorial's Room 217, Brady Hartsfield returned to his body to take enough Vicodin and Ambien to kill it then went back into Dr. Babineau. He headed for Dr. Babineau's hunting camp.

>10:00 a.m.: The repeater had found and updated forty-five Zappits. At an I-47 rest area, Brady persuaded Ellen Murphy to jump out her second-floor bedroom window. The snow may have saved her life, but she broke her collarbone and three ribs.

Bill Hodges talked with Todd Schneider, the Sunrise Solutions bankruptcy trustee. Myron Zakim had bought $80,000 worth of Zappit Commanders. They were sent to Gamez Unlimited, 442 Maritime Drive, c/o Ms. Frederica Linklatter, Brady's co-worker back in his Cyber Patrol days.

>11:04 a.m.: From Heads and Skins, the hunting camp Dr. Babineau co-owned with other doctors, Brady had Jamie Winters shoot himself.

Bill Hodges, Holly Gibney, and Jerome Robinson went to Freddi Linklatter's. Jerome cut the repeater's cables. Freddi told them Brady Hartsfield had perfected personality projection; sometimes, Z-Boy and Dr. Z were Brady.

Brady's laptop reported 248 Zappits found, but the repeater was offline. zeetheend.com showed more than 9,000 visitors.

It didn't take much shaming about her weight and overeating for Brady Hartsfield to convince Jane Ellsbury she'd be better off dead. She took her father's thirty back pain pills, OxyContin, five at a time.

Bill got in touch with Nurse Becky Helmington and found Dr. Babineau co-owned Head and Skins, a hunting camp near Thurston's Garage north of the city. Holly and Bill rented a Ford Expedition from the Hertz at the airport. Mr. Thurston directed them to the camp. Brady caught them by surprise as they crawled in the snow toward the house. He knocked Holly out with a gun butt. A second swing broke Bill's right wrist. Inside, he had Hodges play the Fishin' Hole demo. As it relaxed Bill, and as Brady started to enter Bill's mind, a text alert on Bill's phone broke the mood. They fought. Holly woke up and shot Brady in the shoulder; he ran outside.

Brady had Dr. Babineau's FN SCAR 17S, which fired 650 rounds a minute. He set it to FULL AUTO and opened fire on the house, sweeping back and forth across the great room. Something with bright lights approached. He fired at the Tucker Sno-Cat. Driver Jerome Robinson jumped out; the Sno-Cat ran over Brady. In agony and unable to move, he pleaded with Bill Hodges to kill him. Instead, Hodges left one bullet in a Victory .38 and put the gun in Brady's hand. When Brady couldn't move it, Holly Gibney placed his hand beside his head, with the gun's muzzle against his temple. His finger wasn't on the trigger, so he pulled it telekinetically.

On the way back, Bill read the text. His daughter, Allie, wished him a happy seventieth birthday. He passed out. [*End of Watch*]

January ≥2018

Scott Carey lied when he told Doctor Bob he was still losing up to two pounds a day, Zero Day was still early March, and his current weight was 106. His true weight was around seventy pounds with Zero Day later in January.

three days later: After losing so much weight but keeping his muscle mass, walking was a series of leaps, almost like walking on the moon with its lower gravity. Scott Carey jumped down the front steps to get the mail but slipped on the crust-covered snow, slid down his front yard, and smacked into the mailbox post. He couldn't stand without slipping and falling again. With the mailbox flag, he broke through the crust to make holes for a knee then a foot. Many such holes helped him back to the steps.

Monday:

At his home, Scott Carey hosted the Dr. Ellis Party's last meal. He came clean and told them he had stopped weighing himself when his rate was three pounds a day. It had been difficult moving around with little weight but with the strength of a full-grown man.

He weighted himself: 30.2 pounds.

Doctor Bob had Bill D. Cat in a pet carrier to take him to Mike Badalamente.

following Sunday:

morning: 2.1 pounds

evening: Scott called Deirdre McComb. She strapped him in a wheelchair that kept him from floating away. She wheeled him to his front lawn; Missy Donaldson and Myra and Bob Ellis stood at the street. Deirdre released his harness. He floated above the house. When he was high enough to see Main Street and the town square, he lit a SkyLight firework. After the last sparks died out, he left Earth's gravitational field. [*Elevation*]

February
Happenings

February 1

1 February

Cass Knowles killed her son, Donald, with a hatchet and held his genitals in her apron. Years earlier, she had had an extramarital affair with a Bangor & Aroostook Railroad conductor. She thought their son, Donald, was the Devil's bastard. When Donald proposed to Edie Rowsmith, Cass couldn't allow them to marry and spawn more Devil's children. [*Sword in the Darkness*]

1 February

While waving at an overhead plane, Richard Pine broke his right ankle in a pile of rocks. ["Survivor Type"]

1 February 1952

In his article, "Millionaire Exec to Sell Colorado Investments," Rodney Conklin wrote about Horace Derwent selling The Overlook Hotel to Charles Grondin and other investors from California. [*The Shining*]

1 February [1974]

dawn: FBI Agent Bruce Granger gave Agent Albert Sterling the latest intelligence. Blaze had lived at Hetton House in Cumberland, ME, not far from the source of the traced ransom call.

5:45 a.m.: Several FBI Agents and about twenty state police troopers headed to Cumberland.

6:15 a.m.: Blaze woke up. Because he had given his real name to the operator, he realized they'd know he had lived at Hetton House and would check there. He took Joe to a cave beyond Hetton House's Victory Garden.

7:15 a.m.: Blaze went back to Hetton House to get the rest of the baby food and supplies.

7:30 a.m.: On his way back to the cave, Blaze killed State Trooper Corliss, who had gotten too close. Agent Granger broke his leg in a deadfall.

7:45 a.m.: Agent Granger saw Blaze enter the cave.

8:10 a.m.: Agent Granger fired a shot into the cave. A granite chip cut Joe's face. Furious, Blaze ran from the cave, toward the shot's source, and leaped at Granger. The agent got off two shots before Blaze choked him to death; one shot grazed Blaze's forearm. Blaze got Joe and ran across a logging road to the Royal River. Cumberland County Sheriff's Deputies fired several shots. One hit his right calf; a second hit the back of a knee. Another shot went into his right buttock and shattered his hip. Agent Sterling shot him in the lower back, cutting his spinal cord. Blaze fell, paralyzed below the waist. Sterling, standing over him, killed him with a second shot.

Joseph Gerard IV reunited with his parents. Blaze was buried in South Cumberland, within ten miles of Hetton House. [*Blaze*]

1 February 1981

Firestarter stayed at number 4 on *The New York Times* Fiction Best Seller List, its twenty-fourth week on the List.

1 February 1984

Brookings-Smith Mortuary handled Norma Creed's funeral. Reverend Laughlin led the services at North Ludlow Methodist Church and the Mount Hope Chapel at the cemetery. Pallbearers included Louis Creed, two of Jud Crandall's second or third cousins, and Norma's brother. Because of the frozen ground, she and her steel-gray American Eternal casket weren't buried until spring. [*Pet Sematary*]

1 February 1987

IT dropped to number 3 on *The New York Times* Fiction Best Seller List, *IT*'s twenty-first week on the List.

The Eyes of the Dragon entered *The New York Times* Fiction Best Seller List at number 1. It was on the List for twenty-six weeks.

1 February 1999

Storm of the Century (Gallery Books, $18) published

Postscript to *The Girl Who Loved Tom Gordon*

1 February 2015

Revival dropped to number 14 *The New York Times* Hardcover Fiction Best Seller List, its tenth and last week on the List.

February 2

2 February

With dark rocks on the island's light sand, Richard Pine spelled, "HELP." He had lost about twenty-five pounds since washing up on the island. ["Survivor Type"]

2 February 1979, Friday

Johnny Smith moved to the Jackson House in Jackson, NH. He cased the town hall, where Greg Stillson had a feedback meeting scheduled for the next day. Stuart Clawson failed the written test while trying to renew his driver's license. [*The Dead Zone*]

2 February 1981

Roger Wade learned that Apex Corporation was seeking buyers for Zenith House. In a memo, he urged John Kenton to find something publishable. [*The Plant* Book One: *Zenith Rising*]

2 February 1987

The Eyes of the Dragon (Viking, $18.95) published with a first printing of 400,000 to 500,000 copies

2 February 1992

Needful Things dropped to number 5 on *The New York Times* Fiction Best Seller List, its sixteenth week on the List.

2 February 1996

A Moses Lake, WA, middle school student killed two students, wounded another, and killed his fifth-period algebra teacher. He uttered a line to a quote from *Rage*. The gym teacher went into the classroom and offered himself as a hostage. The coach disarmed the gunman.

2 February 2011

The Stand: No Man's Land #1 of 5 (Marvel Comics, $3.99) published

2 February 2014

Doctor Sleep dropped to number 15 on *The New York Times* Hardcover Fiction Best Seller List, its seventeenth week on the List.

February 3

3 February 1979, Saturday, 10:10 a.m.

Matt Robeson and his mother attended Greg Stillson's feedback meeting at the Jackson, NH, town hall. When Stillson arrived, Johnny Smith, who had been waiting in the gallery above the hall since 4:00 a.m., fired three shots at Stillson and missed. Stillson's security team, led by Sonny Elliman and including Moochie, killed Johnny. Stuart Clawson took a picture of Stillson using Matt Robeson as a shield from Johnny's gunfire. The picture ended Stillson's political career. Later, Johnny was buried at The Birches. [*The Dead Zone*]

3 February 1980

The Dead Zone dropped to number 12 on *The New York Times* Fiction Best Seller List, its twenty-second week on the List.

3 February 1985

The Talisman dropped to number 3 on *The New York Times* Fiction Best Seller List, its fifteenth week on the List.

3 February 1991

After a week off, *The Stand: The Complete & Uncut Edition* re-entered *The New York Times* Fiction Best Seller List at number 15, its thirty-fifth and last week on the List.

Four Past Midnight dropped to number 12 on *The New York Times* Fiction Best Seller List, its twenty-first week on the List.

3 February 2002

The Diary of Ellen Rimbauer: My Life at Rose Red rose to number 10 on *The New York Times* Fiction Best Seller List, its second week on the List.

February 4

4 February, 9:45 a.m.

Ex-surgeon Richard Pine's broken right ankle worsened. He decided to amputate his foot. He started by snorting heroin. Three hours later, he began the operation, finishing at 1:50 p.m. At 5:00 p.m., he washed and ate the foot. ["Survivor Type"]

4 February 1981

Carlos Detweiller wrote a letter to Mr. John "Judas Priest" Kenton. It said he wasn't going after Kenton but could "fix" him. [*The Plant* Book One: *Zenith Rising*]

4 February 1990

The Dark Half dropped to number 9 on *The New York Times* Fiction Best Seller List, its fourteenth week on the List.

4 February 2001

On Writing stayed at number 11 on *The New York Times* Non-Fiction Best Seller List, its sixteenth and last week on the List.

February 5

5 February

Richard Pine's diary discussed how snorting heroin was instrumental in dealing with the pain during the amputation the day before. ["Survivor Type"]

5 February 1984

Pet Sematary rose to number 1 on *The New York Times* Fiction Best Seller List, its fourteenth week on the List.

5 February 1995

Insomnia dropped to number 14 on *The New York Times* Fiction Best Seller List, its sixteenth and last week on the List.

5 February 2012

11/22/63 stayed at number 6 on *The New York Times* Fiction Best Seller List, its eleventh week on the List.

February 6

6 February 1958

<u>George Amberson's first timeline</u>: Harry Dunning died at Khe Sanh in the Vietnam War's Tet Offensive. [*11/22/63*]

6 February 1983

Different Seasons rose to number 10 on *The New York Times* Fiction Best Seller List, its twenty-seventh week on the List.

6 February 1994

Nightmares & Dreamscapes dropped to number 11 on *The New York Times* Fiction Best Seller List, its seventeenth week on the List.

6 February 1998

Stephen King finished *Bag of Bones*.

6 February 2003

Forward to *The Dark Tower: The Gunslinger, Revised and Expanded Edition*

February 7

7 February 1981

John Kenton wrote Ruth Tanaka to tell her Carlos Detweiller had left town. [*The Plant* Book One: *Zenith Rising*]

7 February 1982

Cujo stayed at number 7 on *The New York Times* Fiction Best Seller List, its twenty-sixth week on the List.

7 February 1988

The Tommyknockers stayed at number 2 on *The New York Times* Fiction Best Seller List, its eleventh week on the List.

7 February 1993

Dolores Claiborne dropped to number 6 on *The New York Times* Fiction Best Seller List, its tenth week on the List.

7 February 1996

Audrey Wyler noticed that, while Seth Garin liked his Cassie Styles action figure, Tak got off on it sexually. [*The Regulators*]

7 February 2007

The Dark Tower: Gunslinger Born #1 of 7 (Marvel Comics, $3.99) published

February 8

8 February

Richard Pine amputated and ate his left foot. ["Survivor Type"]

8 February 1981

Firestarter dropped to number 5 on *The New York Times* Fiction Best Seller List, its twenty-fifth week on the List.

8 February 1987

IT dropped to number 4 on *The New York Times* Fiction Best Seller List, *IT*'s twenty-second week on the List.

The Eyes of the Dragon dropped to number 2 on *The New York Times* Fiction Best Seller List, its second week on the List.

8 February 1998

The X-Files, Season 5, Episode 10 ("Chinga"), screenplay by Stephen King and Chris Carter, aired.

8 February 2017

The Dark Tower: The Drawing of the Three—The Sailor #5 of 5 (Marvel Comics, $3.99) published

February 9

9 February

In his sophomore college year, a Hollis warder (a ward of the state, living with the Hollises) received a letter from the dean. The school canceled his scholarship because of failing grades. ["Nona"]

9 February 1985

"CARL SAGAN: 'NO, WE ARE NOT ALONE;' Prominent Scientist Reaffirms Belief in ETs Says, 'Odds of Intelligent Life Are Enormous'" appeared in the Portland, ME, *Press-Herald*. [*Dreamcatcher*]

Richard Bachman died of cancer of the pseudonym. The *Bangor Daily News* reported evidence that Stephen King wrote as Richard Bachman. Years earlier, Stephen King's publishers feared he would oversaturate the market. They wanted to limit his published output. Richard Bachman was their compromise.

9 February 1992

Needful Things dropped to number 7 on *The New York Times* Fiction Best Seller List, its seventeenth week on the List.

9 February 2011

The Dark Tower: The Gunslinger—The Little Sisters of Eluria #3 of 5 (Marvel Comics, $3.99) published

9 February 2014

Doctor Sleep rose to number 14 on *The New York Times* Hardcover Fiction Best Seller List, its eighteenth week on the List.

February 10

10 February 1974

Joseph Gerard Jr. gave a public announcement that his baby son, Joseph Gerard III, was OK and the family was going on vacation. Blaze had kidnapped the baby. [unpublished *Blaze*]

10 February 1980

The Dead Zone stayed at number 12 on *The New York Times* Fiction Best Seller List, its twenty-third week on the List.

10 February 1985

The Talisman stayed at number 3 on *The New York Times* Fiction Best Seller List, its sixteenth week on the List.

10 February 1991

Four Past Midnight dropped to number 13 on *The New York Times* Fiction Best Seller List, its twenty-second and last week on the List.

10 February 2002

The Diary of Ellen Rimbauer: My Life at Rose Red rose to number 6 on *The New York Times* Fiction Best Seller List, its third week on the List.

10 February 2008

Duma Key entered *The New York Times* Fiction Best Seller List at number 1. It was on the List for nine weeks.

10 February 2010

The Dark Tower: Battle of Jericho Hill #3 of 5 (Marvel Comics, $3.99) published

February 11

11 February 1979

After two weeks off, *The Stand* entered *The New York Times* Fiction Best Seller List at number 13, its second and last week on the List.

11 February 1990

The Dark Half dropped to number 10 on *The New York Times* Fiction Best Seller List, its fifteenth week on the List.

11 February 2007

afternoon: Edgar Freemantle returned Pam Freemantle's call. She told him how upset Tom Riley had gotten when she said she worried he was planning suicide. Pam didn't believe Edgar had known about the suicide plans from a painting he had done.

Wireman went on a repair job at a Duma Key rental homes. Edgar Freemantle stayed with Miss Elizabeth Eastlake. While she napped, Edgar's missing right arm itched. To relieve it, he sketched a china figurine of a woman. It became Pam Freemantle and showed what she was doing. Just after a shower, she was sitting in a new rocking chair, reading a book, and eating a Grandma's oatmeal cookie. A cat slept under a new flat-screen TV. He called Pam to show he wasn't crazy because he had known about Tom Riley's suicide plans. He told her what she was doing when he called. Although it scared her, she no longer thought he was crazy. [*Duma Key*]

February 12

12 February

From the wreckage of his lifeboat, Richard Pine ate seaweed and kelp and kept the wood for fire. ["Survivor Type"]

12 February 1984

Pet Sematary stayed at number 1 on *The New York Times* Fiction Best Seller List, its fifteenth week on the List.

12 February 1985

Foreword to *Silver Bullet*, including *Cycle of the Werewolf* and the *Silver Bullet* screenplay

12 February 2006

Cell entered *The New York Times* Fiction Best Seller List at number 1. It was on the List for eight weeks.

12 February 2009

"Ur" (Kindle, $2.99) published (collected in *The Bazaar of Bad Dreams*)

12 February 2012

11/22/63 rose to number 5 on *The New York Times* Fiction Best Seller List, its twelfth week on the List.

February 13

13 February

Richard Pine ate a crab. ["Survivor Type"]

13 February 1983

Different Seasons dropped to number 11 on *The New York Times* Fiction Best Seller List, its twenty-eighth week on the List.

13 February 2007, night

Edgar Freemantle dreamed of a young Ilse Freemantle in a rowboat approaching a derelict ship at sunset. She had false red hair and wore an "I WIN YOU WIN" tic-tac-toe shirt. He awoke and painted the scene, calling the picture *Girl and Ship No. 1*. [*Duma Key*]

13 February 2013

The Dark Tower: The Gunslinger—Sheemie's Tale #2 of 2 (Marvel Comics, $3.99) published

13 February 2015

News at Noon reported Keith Frias and Krista Countryman's double suicide. They had overdosed in his bedroom. As both were City Center Massacre victims, Brady Hartsfield figured his score went from eight to ten and wanted more. [*End of Watch*]

February 14

14 February

After losing his college scholarship five days earlier, a Hollis warder quit school and hitch-hiked west. At Joe's Good Eats on 202 in Augusta, ME, he met Nona. Norman Blanchette gave them a ride to the Gardiner exit, eight miles away. The Hollis warder stabbed Blanchette in the throat with Nona's nail file. He strangled a witness, threw the two bodies down a hill, and stole the witness's pickup truck. On 136 between Harlow and Castle Rock, they skidded on an icy bridge. Essegian, a police officer, lost traction and slid into them. While Nona talked with the officer, the Hollis warder killed him with a socket wrench and threw him over the bridge. The pickup truck wouldn't start, so they took the police car. They made love on a disused logging road off Route 7. ["Nona"]

14 February

Richard Pine rebuilt his "HELP" sign. A storm had knocked it out of place a few days earlier. During the next week, he amputated each leg at the knee for food. ["Survivor Type"]

14 February 1976

Mrs. Gertrude Hersey reported her aunt, Mrs. Fiona Coggins, missing from her home on Smith Road in West Cumberland, ME. ['Salem's Lot]

14 February 1982

Cujo dropped to number 11 on *The New York Times* Fiction Best Seller List, its twenty-seventh week on the List.

14 February 1984, full moon

The Beast, also known as The Full Moon Killer and The Werewolf, went in Stella Randolph's window and killed her. [*Cycle of the Werewolf*]

14 February 1988

The Tommyknockers stayed at number 2 on *The New York Times* Fiction Best Seller List, its twelfth week on the List.

14 February 1993

Dolores Claiborne dropped to number 9 on *The New York Times* Fiction Best Seller List, its eleventh week on the List.

14 February 1999

After a week off, *Bag of Bones* re-entered *The New York Times* Fiction Best Seller List at number 14, its eighteenth week on the List.

14 February 2007, 3:16 p.m.

Candy Brown kidnapped twelve-year-old Tina Garibaldi from the loading docks behind Bealls Department Store at the Crossroads Mall in Sarasota, FL. Security cameras caught much of it. A scene where he held her wrist, and she looked up at him innocently, trusting him, was repeatedly shown on TV. Before returning home, he tortured and killed her. Her body was found in a ditch behind the Wilk Park Little League field. [*Duma Key*]

February 15

15 February

A Hollis warder and Nona dug themselves out from a logging road a snow plow had blocked. Two power company men, who had been servicing a fallen electrical line on Stackpole Road, stopped them. The warder killed one with a shotgun from the police car they had stolen; the other ran away. Nona took the warder to a mausoleum in a graveyard. She showed him his old college girlfriend, dead, with rats using her body for a nest. Nona turned into a rat when he embraced her. ["Nona"]

15 February 1981

Firestarter stayed at number 5 on *The New York Times* Fiction Best Seller List, its twenty-sixth week on the List.

15 February 1987

IT dropped to number 5 on *The New York Times* Fiction Best Seller List, *IT*'s twenty-third week on the List.

The Eyes of the Dragon stayed at number 2 on *The New York Times* Fiction Best Seller List, its third week on the List.

15 February 2007, morning

Candy Brown returned to work at the Sarasota E-Z Jet Wash. A coworker told police the guy on the news looked a lot like Brown. [*Duma Key*]

15 February 2012

The Dark Tower: The Gunslinger—The Way Station #3 of 5 (Marvel Comics, $3.99) published

Road Rage #1, with part 1 of "Throttle," by Joe Hill and Stephen King (IDW Publishing, $3.99) published

February 16

16 February 1992

Needful Things dropped to number 14 on *The New York Times* Fiction Best Seller List, its eighteenth week on the List.

16 February 2007

Edgar Freemantle painted *Girl and Ship No. 2* and *Girl and Ship No. 3*. In No. 2, Ilse Freemantle wore a polka-dotted blue dress. No. 3 showed her with blond hair and wearing the sailor-blouse she had worn when she had broken her arm as a child. [*Duma Key*]

16 February 2014

Doctor Sleep rose to number 13 on *The New York Times* Hardcover Fiction Best Seller List, its nineteenth week on the List.

February 17

17 February 1917

April Rimbauer disappeared from Rose Red's Kitchen. Sukeena had been with her. One minute April was there, the next she was gone. Fifty police officers searched the house and grounds without luck. Within a couple of days, her death was reported as an accident: she had fallen through the ice on Lasky Pond. After Sukeena was questioned, a police officer approached her in the Solarium. She had the plants devour him, leaving only his belt.

Ellen Rimbauer thought Rose Red told her April was in a tower that wasn't built yet. [*The Diary of Ellen Rimbauer: My Life at Rose Red*]

17 February 1978

Night Shift (Doubleday, $8.95) published with a first printing of 12,000 copies

17 February 1980

The Dead Zone stayed at number 12 on *The New York Times* Fiction Best Seller List, its twenty-fourth week on the List.

17 February 1985

The Talisman stayed at number 3 on *The New York Times* Fiction Best Seller List, its seventeenth week on the List.

17 February 2002

The Diary of Ellen Rimbauer: My Life at Rose Red rose to number 1 on *The New York Times* Fiction Best Seller List, its fourth week on the List.

17 February 2008

Duma Key dropped to number 2 on *The New York Times* Fiction Best Seller List, its second week on the List.

17 February 2010

The Talisman: The Road of Trials #4 of 6 (Del Rey Comics, $3.99) published

The Stand: Soul Survivors #4 of 5 (Marvel Comics, $3.99) published

February 18

18 February 1917, early a.m.

Sukeena was arrested for the disappearances of April Rimbauer and a police officer. For three days, she was locked in City Hall's basement without food, sleep, or a toilet. She was beaten and perhaps raped to force a confession she never gave. She lost three front teeth and suffered broken ribs, a broken left wrist, and much bruising and bleeding. Her nose had to be bandaged. [*The Diary of Ellen Rimbauer: My Life at Rose Red*]

18 February 1990

The Dark Half dropped to number 13 on *The New York Times* Fiction Best Seller List, its sixteenth week on the List.

18 February 2007

Police interviewed Candy Brown's good-hearted but mentally challenged wife. [*Duma Key*]

February 19

19 February 1923, teatime

Sukeena, dressed provocatively, teased—almost seduced—John Rimbauer and hinted she wanted him. He followed her to the Tower, where she said she had a quilt. Ellen Rimbauer closed the door from inside the Tower; there was no quilt. She and Sukeena helped April Rimbauer force him through the stained-glass window. He plunged fifty feet to his death on the flagstone terrace. [*The Diary of Ellen Rimbauer: My Life at Rose Red*]

19 February 1928

Several days earlier, Sukeena disappeared from the Health Room (formerly known as the Solarium). Ellen Rimbauer planned to fire the staff and live alone to coerce Rose Red into letting her visit Sukeena. [*The Diary of Ellen Rimbauer: My Life at Rose Red*]

19 February 1953

John Rothstein wrote a thank-you letter to Flannery O'Connor. She had sent him an inscribed novel, *Wise Blood*. Later, the letter was published in *Dispatches from Olympus: Letters from 20 Great American Writers in Their Own Hand*. [*Finders Keepers*]

19 February 1981

As Roberta Solrac, Carlos Detweiller sent a letter to John Kenton. Roberta was a big Anthony LaScorbia fan. To thank John, LaScorbia's editor, she said she was sending him a plant via UPS.

James Saltworthy submitted *The Last Survivor* to Zenith House, his twenty-fourth publisher. [*The Plant* Book One: *Zenith Rising*]

19 February 1984

Pet Sematary stayed at number 1 on *The New York Times* Fiction Best Seller List, its sixteenth week on the List.

19 February 2006

Cell stayed at number 1 on *The New York Times* Fiction Best Seller List, its second week on the List.

19 February 2012

11/22/63 dropped to number 6 on *The New York Times* Fiction Best Seller List, its thirteenth week on the List.

February 20

20 February 1915

Douglas Posey drove to Rose Red and parked off to the side. He sneaked through the new construction and made his way to the Parlor. Adam Rimbauer and April Rimbauer found him atop a ladder. He threw his cowboy hat to Adam and a red rose to April then jumped, hanging himself. April screamed and stopped speaking. [*The Diary of Ellen Rimbauer: My Life at Rose Red*]

20 February 1983

Different Seasons dropped to number 15 on *The New York Times* Fiction Best Seller List, its twenty-ninth week on the List.

February 21

21 February 1917, early a.m.

Ellen Rimbauer heard sounds of sawing wood above her chambers. She found a secret passage that led past views of the guest quarters, a bathroom, and her bed. (She then knew John Rimbauer was aware of Sukeena's sharing her bed.) The passage led to the attic, where she found a warm saw and a newly framed door, by itself, in the middle of the room.

Before, she had stopped all sexual relations with John. She negotiated with him. In exchange for Sukeena's return, she'd open her chambers to him whenever he wanted. He arranged for Sukeena's release and had her treated in a hospital. [*The Diary of Ellen Rimbauer: My Life at Rose Red*]

21 February 1982

Cujo dropped to number 13 on *The New York Times* Fiction Best Seller List, its twenty-eighth week on the List.

21 February 1984

Doubleday had received more than 3,000 letters asking about Stephen King's *The Dark Tower*. Sam Vaughn, the Doubleday editor of King's *Pet Sematary*, called to tell him.

Stephen King joked about writing a story about a psychotic rare-book dealer. [*The Dark Tower VI: Song of Susannah*]

21 February 1988

The Tommyknockers stayed at number 2 on *The New York Times* Fiction Best Seller List, its thirteenth week on the List.

21 February 1993

Dolores Claiborne dropped to number 13 on *The New York Times* Fiction Best Seller List, its twelfth week on the List.

21 February 1999

Storm of the Century entered *The New York Times* Paperback Fiction Best Seller List at number 15. It was on the List for four weeks.

21 February 2007

With a warrant, police searched Candy Brown's home. They found a child's blood-spattered underwear. [*Duma Key*]

21 February 2012

The Dark Tower 4.5: The Wind Through the Keyhole (Donald M. Grant, $75 5,000-copy limited Artist Edition) published

February 22

22 February 1917

John Rimbauer brought Sukeena home. He hired a nurse, Carol, to care for her. [*The Diary of Ellen Rimbauer: My Life at Rose Red*]

22 February 1981

Firestarter stayed at number 5 on *The New York Times* Fiction Best Seller List, its twenty-seventh week on the List.

22 February 1987

IT stayed at number 5 on *The New York Times* Fiction Best Seller List, *IT*'s twenty-fourth week on the List.

The Eyes of the Dragon stayed at number 2 on *The New York Times* Fiction Best Seller List, its fourth week on the List.

22 February 2007

Candy Brown was arrested. [*Duma Key*]

February 23

23 February

Richard Pine ate a dead, rotten fish. During the next week, he amputated and ate his thighs, earlobes, and a hand. ["Survivor Type"]

23 February 1981

Zenith House's market position was to be evaluated in January 1982. Harlow Enders told Roger Wade the evaluation had moved up to September 1981.

Suspicious of a plant from Carlos Detweiller, John Kenton sent a memo to Riddley Walker of the mail room. Riddley should get rid of any package from Roberta Solrac. [*The Plant* Book One: *Zenith Rising*]

23 February 1992

Needful Things rose to number 12 on *The New York Times* Fiction Best Seller List, its nineteenth week on the List.

23 February 2007

A newspaper quoted Candy Brown as saying, "I got high and did a terrible thing." Royal Bonnier, Brown's court-appointed lawyer, held a press conference. He stated that, because of Candy Brown's problems, he would plead not guilty by reason of insanity.

Wireman lost the sight in his left eye and asked Edgar Freemantle to come over. At Dr. Hadlock's suggestion, Edgar took him to Sarasota Memorial Hospital.

6:00 p.m.: They left the hospital. On the way home, Wireman had Edgar pull over at the Crossroads Mall. Outside Bealls Department Store, he told Edgar a bullet in his brain caused his seizures and lost sight. Eight months after losing his wife and daughter in separate tragic accidents, he had shot himself.

Edgar Freemantle left a message for Dario Nannuzzi. He asked whether Nannuzzi would want to show his work. [*Duma Key*]

23 February 2014

Doctor Sleep dropped to number 14 on *The New York Times* Hardcover Fiction Best Seller List, its twentieth week on the List.

February 24

24 February 1980

The Dead Zone stayed at number 12 on *The New York Times* Fiction Best Seller List, its twenty-fifth week on the List.

24 February 1985

The Talisman dropped to number 4 on *The New York Times* Fiction Best Seller List, its eighteenth week on the List.

24 February 1999

Afterword (Longboat Key, FL) to *'Salem's Lot: Illustrated Edition*, including deleted scenes, "Jerusalem's Lot," and "One For the Road"

24 February 2002

The Diary of Ellen Rimbauer: My Life at Rose Red dropped to number 4 on *The New York Times* Fiction Best Seller List, its fifth week on the List.

24 February 2007

early a.m.: Edgar Freemantle painted a picture of Candy Brown without his nose and mouth. Brown suffocated in his sleep.

Wireman invited Edgar to breakfast to celebrate Candy Brown's death. Edgar took one of Wireman's X-rays.

Dario Nannuzzi left Edgar a message saying he'd be happy to show his work.

With a Sharpie, Edgar drew on cardboard inserts from new shirts. In twenty minutes, he had a picture of Wireman's brain, without the bullet. After lunch, Wireman called and told him his long-term headache was gone. When he asked whether Edgar had done anything, Edgar told him and invited him to come for a full portrait. He would try to restore the sight in Wireman's left eye. Later, he started the portrait and took several digital pictures to work from. [*Duma Key*]

24 February 2008

Duma Key dropped to number 3 on *The New York Times* Fiction Best Seller List, its third week on the List.

24 February 2010

The Dark Tower: Battle of Jericho Hill #4 of 5 (Marvel Comics, $3.99) published

February 25

25 February 1987, Wednesday

Best-selling author Paul Sheldon finished his *Fast Cars* manuscript. It was his first novel since killing off his popular Misery character in *Misery's Child*, published in 1986. He completed it in the same Boulderado Hotel room he had used for manuscript completion since 1974. He celebrated with champagne. Driving drunk on Route 9, he crashed about five miles from Sidewinder, CO. Annie Wilkes saw his overturned car and found him, unconscious. She took him home and splinted his shattered legs with pieces of aluminum crutches. She kept him in a first-floor room. Annie, Paul's self-proclaimed Number One Fan, was upset when she learned Misery had died. For four months, she kept Paul prisoner while he brought Misery back in *Misery's Return*. Not liking *Fast Cars*, she made him burn his only copy of the manuscript. [*Misery*]

25 February 1990

The Dark Half stayed at number 13 on *The New York Times* Fiction Best Seller List, its seventeenth week on the List.

25 February 2007

The Scoto Gallery's Dario Nannuzzi and Jimmy Yoshida stopped by to see Edgar Freemantle's work. Edgar showed them forty-one paintings, five from the *Girl and Ship* series. They left a sample contract for his agent, Wireman, to look over. [*Duma Key*]

25 February 2008

Introduction to *Just After Sunset*, in Sarasota, FL

25 February 2009

The Dark Tower: Treachery #6 of 6 (Marvel Comics, $3.99) published

25 February 2014

Astrid Soderberg wrote Charlie Jacobs to ask for help with her lung cancer. [*Revival*]

February 26

26 February 1915

Sukeena warned Ellen Rimbauer that Rose Red wasn't just possessed by spirits, she was alive. The house fed on those who disappeared within her. As Rose Red grew, more people would disappear to feed her. [*The Diary of Ellen Rimbauer: My Life at Rose Red*]

26 February 1923

Adam Rimbauer returned home for John Rimbauer's funeral. Hundreds of people attended. That night, Adam's mother, Ellen Rimbauer, took him to Rose Red's Tower to talk with April Rimbauer's presence. [*The Diary of Ellen Rimbauer: My Life at Rose Red*]

26 February 1981

Zenith House editor John Kenton had an editorial meeting at work. [*The Plant* Book One: *Zenith Rising*]

26 February 1984

Pet Sematary stayed at number 1 on *The New York Times* Fiction Best Seller List, its seventeenth week on the List.

26 February 2006

Cell stayed at number 1 on *The New York Times* Fiction Best Seller List, its third week on the List.

26 February 2007

Edgar Freemantle had coffee with Wireman and Elizabeth Eastlake at the end of their boardwalk. He left the Scoto contract with Wireman, offering him 15%. Wireman agreed to no more than 10% of sales. [*Duma Key*]

26 February 2012

11/22/63 rose to number 5 on *The New York Times* Fiction Best Seller List, its fourteenth week on the List.

February 27

27 February 1976, morning

Frank Vickery found his father-in-law, John Farrington, dead from massive hemorrhage or internal bleeding. [*'Salem's Lot*]

27 February 1977

Forward to *Night Shift*

27 February 1981

Bill Gelb owed Riddley Walker $75.40 from playing dice.

Zenith House received a plant from Roberta Solrac. Riddley saw that it looked like harmless ivy and put it on a shelf in his janitor/mail room. The card identified the Tibetan *kadath* ivy as Zenith. To those outside its circle, Zenith appeared as Common Ivy. To those within its circle—Bill Gelb, Sandra Jackson, John Kenton, Herb Porter, Roger Wade, and Riddley—Zenith grew, creating a virtual jungle on the fifth floor of Zenith House. They experienced telepathy where they could read one another's thoughts. Later, they could read the thoughts of others in the building. Zenith inspired the circle; they developed ideas for best seller books to save their failing publishing company. [*The Plant* Book One: *Zenith Rising*]

27 February 1983

Different Seasons rose to number 12 on *The New York Times* Fiction Best Seller List, its thirtieth week on the List.

27 February 1994

After two weeks off, *Nightmares & Dreamscapes* re-entered *The New York Times* Fiction Best Seller List. At number 15, this was its eighteenth and last week on the List.

27 February 2007

Candy Brown's cause of death was reported as congestive heart failure.

10:00 a.m.: Wireman called Edgar Freemantle with changes to the Scoto Gallery contract. The contract called for a 50/50 split of proceeds. Wireman suggested 60/40 after $250,000 of sales, then 70/30 after $500,000. He also wanted to reduce the 180-day termination clause to ninety days to not be locked in with Scoto for so long. [*Duma Key*]

February 28

28 February 1982

Cujo dropped to number 15 on *The New York Times* Fiction Best Seller List, its twenty-ninth week on the List.

28 February 1988

The Tommyknockers dropped to number 4 on *The New York Times* Fiction Best Seller List, its fourteenth week on the List.

28 February 1993

Dolores Claiborne rose to number 11 on *The New York Times* Fiction Best Seller List, its thirteenth week on the List.

28 February 1999

After a week off, *Bag of Bones* re-entered *The New York Times* Fiction Best Seller List at number 16, its nineteenth week on the List.

Storm of the Century rose to number 10 on *The New York Times* Paperback Fiction Best Seller List, its second week on the List.

28 February 2012

Reverend George Winston died of kidney failure. Mrs. Granger, his housekeeper, suspected suicide. Too many of his prescription pills were missing. ["Morality"]

February 29

29 February 2012

Chad and Nora Callahan moved from Brooklyn, New York, to a house about twenty miles from Montpelier, VT. Reverend George Winston had given Nora $200,000 to hit a small child in the mouth, drawing blood. She and Chad used the money to buy the new house. ["Morality"]

February

February 1953

Chuck Spier lost an eye while jump-starting his 1948 DeSoto; the battery exploded. He was in Lewiston General Hospital for more than a week. Johnny Smith foresaw the accident a month earlier. [*The Dead Zone*]

February 1961

Arnie Cunningham was born. He grew up on Laurel Street in Libertyville, PA. [*Christine*]

February 1964

Odetta Holmes spent three days in an Oxford Town, MS, jail after her arrest in a Civil Rights protest. When Andrew Feeny, her chauffeur, brought her home, she got a headache and became Detta Walker. House detective Jimmy Halvorsen pursued Detta for shoplifting at Macy's in New York. Roland entered her mind and brought her to his world. Odetta and Detta became aware of each other briefly. They were The Lady of Shadows. [*The Dark Tower II: The Drawing of the Three*]

February 1965

The Fergusons took Andy Morton and Con Morton skiing at Goat Mountain Resort. Norm Ferguson and Con raced. Norm hit a mogul and stretched his arm. His ski pole hit Con in the neck. Three days after returning home, Con lost his voice. [*Revival*]

February 1972

The boogeyman came out of Andy Billings's closet, broke his neck, and killed him. The death looked as if Andy had tried to climb out of his crib and had fallen. ["The Boogeyman"]

"Suffer the Little Children" (collected in *Nightmares & Dreamscapes*) appeared in the February issue (Vol. 22, No. 4) of *Cavalier*.

February 1973

Chip Osway, afraid of Davie Garcia and Bob Lawson, quite school and ran about from home. Vinnie Corey transferred from Milford High (Milford Cemetery) to Harold Davis High School. He joined Jim Norman's class.

They killed Sally Norman. Jim Norman summoned the Dark Father to get rid of them. ["Sometimes They Come Back"]

Devin Jones, a University of New Hampshire junior, worked in the Commons cafeteria on a work-study program. Someone had left a copy of *Carolina Living* on a lunch tray. In the classified section, he found an ad for a job at the Joyland amusement park. He called the number; they sent an application. [*Joyland*]

Morris Bellamy and his mother argued after she made disparaging remarks about John Rothstein's Jimmy Gold trilogy. Morris, 17, hung out near a liquor store at a strip mall three blocks away. The third guy he approached agreed to get a quart of whiskey for $5. He took it to a stream in the undeveloped land behind his house and got drunk. After a joyride in a stolen car, he urinated on the dashboard. Rent-a-cops responded to an alarm he tripped in a Sugar Heights house he had broken into. They fought; one broke his nose and knocked him out with a nightstick. He spent nine months in Riverview Youth Detention. In weekly counseling sessions with Larsen, he blamed his mother for his incarceration and, secondarily, the wino who bought the whiskey. [*Finders Keepers*]

February 1975

Stephen King started *The Stand*.

February 1976

Johnny Smith moved to Kittery, ME. [*The Dead Zone*]

February 1977

Mrs. Laura Morton, Jamie's mother, died of ovarian cancer. She was fifty-one. [*Revival*]

February 1978

Ellie Creed was born in Chicago, IL. [*Pet Sematary*]

"The Night of the Tiger" appeared in the February issue (#321; Volume 54, Number 2) of *The Magazine of Fantasy & Science Fiction*.

February 1979

Stephen King started *Pet Sematary*.

February 1981

"The Oracle and the Mountain" (collected in *The Dark Tower I: The Gunslinger*) appeared in the February issue (#357; Volume 60, Number 2) of *The Magazine of Fantasy & Science Fiction*.

February 1983

Dr. Karl Hofferitz was the Manderses' doctor. He told Shirley McKenzie about Roberta McCauley's (Charlie McGee) staying with the Manderses. [*Firestarter*]

February 1985

"Dolan's Cadillac," part 2 of 5 (collected in *Nightmares & Dreamscapes*), appeared in the February 1985 issue (Vol. 1, No. 2) of *Castle Rock: The Stephen King Newsletter*.

February 1989

Old and near the end of his life, Andre Linoge wanted to make a child his protégé. He went to Little Tall Island, ME, during their snowstorm of the century. To show he meant business, he killed several Islanders. He promised to go away if they gave him what he wanted. If they didn't, he'd kill all the children and cause a mass suicide where everyone would walk into the ocean. He left Little Tall with Ralphie Anderson, the Town Constable's son. [*Storm of the Century*]

February 1992

Stephen King finished *Dolores Claiborne*.

February 1993

Raymond Andrew Joubert had been robbing crypts and mausoleums in small towns in

Maine and New Hampshire for about nine years. He stole jewelry, pulled teeth with gold fillings, and mutilated bodies. While staking out Homeland Cemetery in February, Sheriff Norris Ridgewick and Deputy John LaPointe caught Joubert. Police found body parts and around fifty jars of eyes, fingers, lips, testicles, and toes in Joubert's home.

Jessie Burlingame recognized Joubert from the newspaper as Death, whom she had seen when she was handcuffed to the bed in October. [*Gerald's Game*]

February 2002

Jonesy had a Teflon-and-steel hip replacement after having his mending hip dislocated at Quabbin Reservoir's Shaft 12. [*Dreamcatcher*]

February 2008

Gracie Goodhugh Dickerson became depressed after her baby was stillborn during a snow-storm. It had a congenital heart defect.

Carl Goodhugh's father could no longer afford a companion to care for him. ["Fair Extension"]

February 2010

Wednesday: Pete Saubers's parents had been arguing because of the strain of living on her reduced salary. Tina Saubers called the arguments arkie-barkies. Honor Roll students could go home early if they didn't have any academic classes after lunch. To escape an arkie-barkie, Pete went through the undeveloped land behind his house. Down by the creek, some of the embankment had fallen away, exposing tree roots. Under the tree, he found a trunk, stuck. He went home, got a spade from the garage, went back, and covered the trunk.

Friday: Faking illness, Pete stayed home from school. After the family had left, he freed the trunk from beneath the tree. It weighed nearly sixty pounds. Inside, he found about a hundred leather notebooks and dozens of bank envelopes, each with $400 worth of twenties and fifties. He repacked the notebooks in the trunk, put the trunk back in the hole, and took the money home. Anonymously, Peter started sending $500 a month to his parents. As the money rolled in, the arkie-barkies became occasional. It may have saved the marriage. [*Finders Keepers*]

February 2016

Detective Pete Huntley retired. [*End of Watch*]

February ≥2017

Same-sex couple Missy Donaldson and Deirdre McComb opened Holy Frijole, a Mexican-vegetarian restaurant, in Castle Rock, ME. [*Elevation*]

March
Happenings

March 1

1 March 1923

After returning home for his father's funeral, Adam Rimbauer was back in school. [*The Diary of Ellen Rimbauer: My Life at Rose Red*]

1 March 1976

With a hammer, Todd Bowden killed a wino who slept near Cienaga Way. The bad dreams from killing the first wino the previous June stopped. ["Apt Pupil"]

1 March 1981

RainBo Soft Drinks had a 6.5% share of the soft drink market. [*The Plant* Book One: *Zenith Rising*]

Firestarter dropped to number 7 on *The New York Times* Fiction Best Seller List, its twenty-eighth week on the List.

1 March 1985

Mike Hanlon saw a balloon with his face on it tied to the Derry Public Library door. The balloon burst. [*IT*]

1 March 1987

IT stayed at number 5 on *The New York Times* Fiction Best Seller List, *IT*'s twenty-fifth week on the List.

The Eyes of the Dragon stayed at number 2 on *The New York Times* Fiction Best Seller List, its fifth week on the List.

1 March 1992

Needful Things rose to number 9 on *The New York Times* Fiction Best Seller List, its twentieth and last week on the List.

1 March 2007

Edgar Freemantle had been painting Wireman's portrait from the digital photos he had taken. He didn't need them anymore. [*Duma Key*]

March 2

2 March 1963

<u>George Amberson's second timeline</u>: The Oswalds moved to 214 West Neely Street in Dallas, TX. They had the upstairs apartment of the two-unit building. George Amberson lived below. [*11/22/63*]

2 March 1969

A Manchester, NH, *Union-Leader* clipping reported seventy-nine-year-old Ernest Gonyar's death at Saint Joseph's Hospital. Nobody knew Annie Wilkes had killed him. [*Misery*]

2 March 1980

The Dead Zone stayed at number 12 on *The New York Times* Fiction Best Seller List, its twenty-sixth week on the List.

2 March 1985, Saturday, ~11:00 a.m.

Crack dealer Richie Bender robbed a Payless Shoe Store, shooting the clerk in the head twice. Detectives Harley Bissington and Norman Daniels investigated. The clerk at the bottle-redemption center next-door told them Richie Bender did it and where Bender lived. They found Wendy Yarrow, in her underwear and high on crack, in the Railroad Motel's Unit 12. They forced their way in, injuring her severely. Bissington raped her then flushed the condom down the toilet. He cut Daniels's forehead with a nail file to give credence to a beating. They had the wrong room; Bender lived next-door. Because of the nail file cuts, they got off with reprimands. Later, Yarrow hired a lawyer. Daniels killed her before she could go to court. [*Rose Madder*]

2 March 2000

Bradley Trevor was born. He grew up on a farm in Canton County, IA. [*Doctor Sleep*]

2 March 2007

Wireman brought Edgar Freemantle a revised Scoto Gallery contract to sign.

Edgar called the portrait *Wireman Looks West*.

Dario Nannuzzi wanted Edgar to give a lecture and present photos of his work. The lecture was important to start the buzz about his work before the show. Sixty to seventy art patrons would attend. [*Duma Key*]

2 March 2008

Duma Key stayed at number 3 on *The New York Times* Fiction Best Seller List, its fourth week on the List.

2 March 2011

The Stand: No Man's Land #2 of 5 (Marvel Comics, $3.99) published

2 March 2014

Doctor Sleep rose to number 13 on *The New York Times* Hardcover Fiction Best Seller List, its twenty-first and last week on the List.

March 3

3 March 1976

Placerville High School chemistry-physics teacher John Carlson made fun of Charlie Decker for doing a problem on the board incorrectly. Charlie started hitting the board with a pipe wrench. Charlie hit Carlson in the head when Carlson tried to grab him. At Central Maine General Hospital, Carlson was operated on for almost four hours. The charges were dropped, but Charlie was suspended. That night, Carl Decker, Charlie's dad, hit Charlie with a belt buckle and cut his cheek for attacking Mr. Carlson. The fight stopped when Carl picked up a rake and Charlie a hatchet. [*Rage*]

3 March 1978

Boston FBI agent Edgar Lancte investigated politicians and illegal real estate deals. He had been monitoring Greg Stillson since 1976 or earlier. His car exploded, killing him when he turned on its ignition. [*The Dead Zone*]

3 March 1981

General Hecksler escaped from Oak Cove Asylum in Cutlersville, NY. He stabbed Nurse Alicia Penbroke and orderlies Norman Abelson and John Piet in the throat with a pair of barber's shears. New York State Police spokesperson: Lieutenant Arthur P. Ford. [*The Plant Book One: Zenith Rising*]

Richard Bachman's *Roadwork* (Signet, $2.25) published

3 March 1985

The Talisman stayed at number 4 on *The New York Times* Fiction Best Seller List, its nineteenth week on the List.

Richard Bachman's *Thinner* entered *The New York Times* Fiction Best Seller List at number 8. It was on the List for twenty-five weeks.

3 March 2002

The Diary of Ellen Rimbauer: My Life at Rose Red stayed at number 4 on *The New York Times* Fiction Best Seller List, its sixth week on the List.

3 March 2010

Stephen King's N. #1 of 4 (Marvel Comics, $3.99) published

March 4

4 March 1978

"FBI AGENT MURDERED IN OKLAHOMA," an article about Edgar Lancte's death, appeared in *The New York Times*. [*The Dead Zone*]

4 March 1981

"INSANE GENERAL ESCAPES OAK COVE ASYLUM, KILLS THREE!!" appeared on page 1 of *The New York Post*.

Bill Gelb did fairly well at dice with Riddley Walker. [*The Plant* Book One: *Zenith Rising*]

4 March 1984

Pet Sematary stayed at number 1 on *The New York Times* Fiction Best Seller List, its eighteenth week on the List.

4 March 1990

The Dark Half dropped to number 14 on *The New York Times* Fiction Best Seller List, its eighteenth week on the List.

4 March 2007

Edgar Freemantle finished *Wireman Looks West*, which showed a Wireman of about twenty-five. Later, Wireman called; the sight was back in his left eye. [*Duma Key*]

4 March 2012

11/22/63 dropped to number 6 on *The New York Times* Fiction Best Seller List, its fifteenth week on the List.

4 March 2014

Charlie Jacobs wrote to Jamie Morton. Charlie's work was in its final stage, and he would need Jamie later that summer. He enclosed Astrid Soderberg's letter of February 25th to coerce Jamie to help. [*Revival*]

March 5

5 March 1981

Bill Gelb lost more to Riddley Walker; his bill grew to $81.50. [*The Plant* Book One: *Zenith Rising*]

5 March 1991

Author's Note to *The Dark Tower III: The Waste Lands*

5 March 2006

Cell dropped to number 2 on *The New York Times* Fiction Best Seller List, its fourth week on the List.

5 March 2007

Edgar Freemantle gave the portrait to Wireman, who was speechless upon seeing it. Wireman set it aside to go with the other NFS (Not For Sale) paintings at the Scoto Gallery exhibition. [*Duma Key*]

5 March 2008

The Dark Tower: The Long Road Home #1 of 5 (Marvel Comics, $3.99) published

March 6

6 March 1981

John Kenton called Ruth Tanaka; he got her answering machine. [*The Plant* Book One: *Zenith Rising*]

6 March 1983

Different Seasons dropped to number 13 on *The New York Times* Fiction Best Seller List, its thirty-first week on the List.

6 March 1988

The Tommyknockers rose to number 3 on *The New York Times* Fiction Best Seller List, its fifteenth week on the List.

6 March 1992

Coretta Vele wrote Stephen King to ask whether he could tell her how *The Dark Tower* story ended. She would probably be gone by 7/4/1992 and wouldn't be able to read the rest as it came out. [*The Dark Tower VI: Song of Susannah*]

March 7

7 March 1981

John Kenton got Ruth Tanaka's answering machine again. [*The Plant* Book One: *Zenith Rising*]

7 March 1982

Cujo rose to number 13 on *The New York Times* Fiction Best Seller List, its thirtieth week on the List.

7 March 1993

Dolores Claiborne dropped to number 14 on *The New York Times* Fiction Best Seller List, its fourteenth and last week on the List.

7 March 1999

Bag of Bones stayed at number 16 on *The New York Times* Fiction Best Seller List, its twentieth and last week on the List.

Storm of the Century rose to number 7 on *The New York Times* Paperback Fiction Best Seller List, its third week on the List.

7 March 2007

The Dark Tower: Gunslinger Born #2 of 7 (Marvel Comics, $3.99) published

March 8

8 March 1918

George Meader had been cornering and groping Sukeena. She arranged to meet him in Rose Red's Health Room at midnight. [*The Diary of Ellen Rimbauer: My Life at Rose Red*]

8 March 1957

"STRANGE RINGED CRAFT CRASHES IN MATO GROSSO! 2 WOMEN MENACED NEAR PONTO PORAN! 'We heard Squealing Sounds from Within,' They Declare" appeared in the Brazilian *Nacional*. [*Dreamcatcher*]

8 March 1963, Friday afternoon

George Amberson's second timeline: George Amberson bought a Colt .38 Police Special revolver from a pawn shop on Greenville Ave. (He had bought the same kind in Derry.) He agreed to pay $12 if the dealer threw in a box of bullets. [*11/22/63*]

8 March 1981

Again John Kenton got Ruth Tanaka's answering machine. He wrote her. [*The Plant* Book One: *Zenith Rising*]

Firestarter stayed at number 7 on *The New York Times* Fiction Best Seller List, its twenty-ninth week on the List.

8 March 1987

IT rose to number 4 on *The New York Times* Fiction Best Seller List, *IT*'s twenty-sixth week on the List.

The Eyes of the Dragon stayed at number 2 on *The New York Times* Fiction Best Seller List, its sixth week on the List.

8 March 2008

"Sunset Notes" to *Just After Sunset*

March 9

9 March 1918

12:00 a.m.: Drunk, George Meader arrived at Rose Red's Health Room. Sukeena danced provocatively then summoned a bee to sting him. Vines covered and scratched his body. His cause of death was listed as an allergic reaction to a bee sting.

Ellen Rimbauer ordered the construction of a Tower at Rose Red. [*The Diary of Ellen Rimbauer: My Life at Rose Red*]

9 March 1980

The Dead Zone rose to number 11 on *The New York Times* Fiction Best Seller List, its twenty-seventh week on the List.

9 March 1981

The Boulder, CO, *Camera* reported that Annie Wilkes became a Boulder Hospital nurse. [*Misery*]

In a letter to Herb Porter, General Hecksler wrote he hadn't forgotten Herb and was going after him. Herb Porter was an editor at Zenith House. He had rejected Hecksler's *Twenty Psychic Garden Flowers* submission three years earlier. [*The Plant* Book One: *Zenith Rising*]

9 March 2008

Duma Key dropped to number 5 on *The New York Times* Fiction Best Seller List, its fifth week on the List.

9 March 2015

"A Death" (collected in *The Bazaar of Bad Dreams*) appeared in the March 9th issue of *The New Yorker*.

March 10

10 March 1915

A letter from the Cheshire Academy in Portland, OR, to John Rimbauer was postmarked on this date. [*The Diary of Ellen Rimbauer: My Life at Rose Red*]

10 March 1963, Sunday

<u>George Amberson's second timeline</u>: George saw a white-over-red Plymouth Fury from Arkansas drive past Sadie Dunhill's. [*11/22/63*]

10 March 1981

John Kenton still hadn't gotten in touch with Ruth Tanaka. Worried, he sent her a Mailgram. She responded with a Dear John letter. It said she still loved him, hoped they could still be friends, yadda-yadda-yadda. [*The Plant* Book One: *Zenith Rising*]

10 March 1982

Andy McGee wrote six letters describing his trouble with the Shop and Lot Six. Three were to *The New York Times*, the Chicago *Tribune*, and the Toledo *Blade*. The others were to his US Congressmen from Ohio. Shop agent Charles Payson saw him mail these letters in Bradford, NH.

1:15 p.m.: Postman Robert Everett emptied the mailbox outside the Bradford general store. Five miles from Teller, NH, Shop agents Orville Jamieson and George Sedaka took Andy McGee's letters from him. [*Firestarter*]

10 March 1985

The Talisman dropped to number 6 on *The New York Times* Fiction Best Seller List, its twentieth week on the List.

Richard Bachman's *Thinner* dropped to number 10 on *The New York Times* Fiction Best Seller List, its second week on the List.

10 March 2002

The Diary of Ellen Rimbauer: My Life at Rose Red rose to number 3 on *The New York Times* Fiction Best Seller List, its seventh week on the List.

March 11

11 March 1975, 9:00 p.m.

Andy Dufresne was locked in his Shawshank State Prison cell, as was routine. Within an hour and a half, he carried out an escape he had planned for almost thirty years. He was never caught. ["Rita Hayworth and Shawshank Redemption"]

11 March 1981

John Kenton received Ruth Tanaka's Dear John letter. [*The Plant* Book One: *Zenith Rising*]

11 March 1984

Pet Sematary dropped to number 2 on *The New York Times* Fiction Best Seller List, its nineteenth week on the List.

11 March 2009

The Stand: American Nightmares #1 of 5 (Marvel Comics, $3.99) published

11 March 2012

11/22/63 dropped to number 10 on *The New York Times* Fiction Best Seller List, its sixteenth week on the List.

March 12

12 March 1957

"MATO GROSSO HORROR! Reports of Grey Men with Huge Black Eyes; Scientists Scoff! Reports Persist!" VILLAGES IN TERROR!" appeared in the Brazilian *Nacional*. [*Dreamcatcher*]

12 March 1975

Shawshank State Prison Captain of the Guards Rich Gonyar discovered Andy Dufresne's cell empty. Warden Norton ripped a poster off Andy's cell wall. Behind it, a hole led to a sewer pipe, which emptied fourteen Cellblock 5 toilets into a stream. Andy had been creating the hole for about twenty-five years. He had covered his progress with current pinup posters. He started with Rita Hayworth in 1949 and ended with Linda Ronstadt in 1975. Marilyn Monroe, Jayne Mansfield, and Raquel Welch appeared between them. ["Rita Hayworth and Shawshank Redemption"]

12 March 1981

morning: John Kenton resigned. Roger Wade asked him to wait until after drinks that night.

evening: John and Roger drank at Four Fathers. Roger asked John to stay until June, preferably the end of the year, to help wrap things up if Apex decided to terminate the company. They agreed to hold the resignation until the end of the month. [*The Plant* Book One: *Zenith Rising*]

12 March 2006

Cell stayed at number 2 on *The New York Times* Fiction Best Seller List, its fifth week on the List.

March 13

13 March 1909, afternoon teatime

Connie Fauxmanteur and Melissa Ray visited Ellen Rimbauer at Rose Red. Mrs. Fauxmanteur spun the globe in the corner of the Parlor. As she spoke foreign words, the globe continued to spin on its own. Trancelike, she left the room. Ellen and Melissa followed, but couldn't find her. After searches that included the police, she was never found. She had had relations with John Rimbauer. Sukeena believed the globe was one of many portals to Rose Red's soul. [*The Diary of Ellen Rimbauer: My Life at Rose Red*]

13 March 1915

A letter from the Cheshire Academy in Portland, OR, to John Rimbauer was delivered. They had accepted Adam Rimbauer for the first grade. [*The Diary of Ellen Rimbauer: My Life at Rose Red*]

13 March 1981

Hungover, John Kenton didn't go to work. [*The Plant* Book One: *Zenith Rising*]

13 March 1983

Different Seasons stayed at number 13 on *The New York Times* Fiction Best Seller List, its thirty-second and last week on the List.

13 March 1988

The Tommyknockers stayed at number 3 on *The New York Times* Fiction Best Seller List, its sixteenth week on the List.

March 14

14 March 1909

The police continued looking for Mrs. Fauxmanteur. Tina Coleman suggested Ellen Rimbauer consult a medium. [*The Diary of Ellen Rimbauer: My Life at Rose Red*]

14 March 1982

Cujo stayed at number 13 on *The New York Times* Fiction Best Seller List, its thirty-first week on the List.

14 March 1997

"HUGE UFO SIGHTED NEAR PRESCOTT; DOZENS DESCRIBE 'BOOMERANG-SHAPED' OBJECT; Switchboard at Luke AFB Deluged with Reports" appeared in the Phoenix *Sun*. [*Dreamcatcher*]

14 March 1999

Storm of the Century dropped to number 10 on *The New York Times* Paperback Fiction Best Seller List, its fourth and last week on the List.

14 March 2000

Riding the Bullet e-book (Scribner/Philtrum Press, $2.50) published (collected in *Everything's Eventual*)

14 March 2009

Stephen King finished *Under the Dome*.

14 March 2014

The e-book *Bad Little Kid* (collected in *The Bazaar of Bad Dreams*) was published in only French (*Sale Gosse*) and German (*Böser Kleiner Junge*). These editions were Stephen King's thank you to his French and German fans for their warm welcome during his 2013 European visit.

March 15

15 March 1981

Firestarter dropped to number 8 on *The New York Times* Fiction Best Seller List, its thirtieth week on the List.

15 March 1987

IT dropped to number 7 on *The New York Times* Fiction Best Seller List, *IT*'s twenty-seventh week on the List.

The Eyes of the Dragon stayed at number 2 on *The New York Times* Fiction Best Seller List, its seventh week on the List.

15 March 2001, Thursday, 11:00 a.m.

David Defuniak, 19, had an appointment with Jonesy. David had aced the European History midterm in a class where he didn't excel. Jonesy knew David must have cheated, so he offered a take-home essay. Three thousand words on the short-term results of the Norman Conquest would make up for the missed exam. David, a student at John Jay College in Boston, MA, had the flu the day of the midterm. He thought nobody would know someone else took the exam for him because a grad student proctored the test that day.

Jonesy started to take a Boston *Phoenix* and his briefcase with an egg salad sandwich to have lunch on a bench across the Charles River. Big Mistake. At the intersection of Mass Avenue and Prospect Street, near Harvard Square in Cambridge, across the river from John Jay College, he thought he saw Duddits across the street and crossed without looking. A retired BU history professor in the early stages of Alzheimer's hit Jonesy. He woke up in Mass General with a shattered hip, two broken ribs, and a cracked skull. [*Dreamcatcher*]

15 March 2004

Kellie Gervais's body was found in the woods behind a landfill. A few days earlier, Bob Anderson had gone on a business trip to Brattleboro, NH, to see George Fitzwilliam, a Benson, Bacon & Anderson client. Beadie killed Gervais, his eighth victim, who lived in nearby Keene, NH. ["A Good Marriage"]

~15 March 2007

A lecture at Selby Library's Geldbart Auditorium was part of the pre-show promotion of Edgar Freemantle's art exhibition. Around two hundred people, including some friends and family from Minnesota, attended. After Dario Nannuzzi's ten-minute introduction, a standing ovation welcomed Edgar on stage. He showed twenty-two slides. Nine were photos of pencil sketches, and thirteen were pictures of paintings. A reception at the Scoto Gallery followed the lecture. [*Duma Key*]

15 March ≥2018: Zero Day

With his weight loss close to two pounds a day, Scott Carey moved the day he'd run out of pounds to March 15th. [*Elevation*]

March 16

16 March 1909, 1:30 p.m.

Tina Coleman's carriage took Ellen Rimbauer and Sukeena to Tina's house. Ellen, Sukeena, Tina, and Tina Coleman's maid, Gwen, went to see Madame Lu, who told them Mrs. Faux-manteur's spirit was conscious, but her body wasn't alive as we know it. Also, there was a presence at Rose Red. [*The Diary of Ellen Rimbauer: My Life at Rose Red*]

16 March 1968, first day of strawberry spring

11:10 p.m.: John Dancey found Gale Cerman's body. Springheel Jack had slit her throat in the New Sharon Teachers' College Animal Sciences parking lot. ["Strawberry Spring"]

16 March 1980

The Dead Zone dropped to number 13 on *The New York Times* Fiction Best Seller List, its twenty-eighth week on the List.

16 March 1989

Stephen King finished *The Dark Half*.

16 March 2008

Duma Key dropped to number 9 on *The New York Times* Fiction Best Seller List, its sixth week on the List.

16 March 2011

The Dark Tower: The Gunslinger—The Little Sisters of Eluria #4 of 5 (Marvel Comics, $3.99) published

March 17

17 March 1968

The police arrested Carl Amalara as a Springheel Jack suspect. They thought he may have killed Gale Cerman, his girlfriend. ["Strawberry Spring"]

17 March 1985

The Talisman dropped to number 11 on *The New York Times* Fiction Best Seller List, its twenty-first and last week on the List.

Richard Bachman's *Thinner* rose to number 4 on *The New York Times* Fiction Best Seller List, its third week on the List.

17 March 2001, Saturday, St. Patrick's Day

Henry Devlin and Jonesy had planned to visit Duddits in Derry, ME. They didn't because Jonesy had been in a serious accident two days earlier. [*Dreamcatcher*]

17 March 2002

The Diary of Ellen Rimbauer: My Life at Rose Red dropped to number 4 on *The New York Times* Fiction Best Seller List, its eighth week on the List.

~17 March 2007, afternoon

Art critic Mary Ire interviewed Edgar Freemantle. After the interview's publication, Dario Nannuzzi and Jimmy Yoshida scheduled more, including one with Channel 6. [*Duma Key*]

17 March 2010

American Vampire #1 (Vertigo Comics, $3.99), with Stephen King's "Bad Blood," published

March 18

18 March 1968

Springheel Jack beheaded Ann Bray. ["Strawberry Spring"]

18 March 1981, 7:00–9:30 p.m.

the first of five evenings Ruth Tanaka would be at home to take John Kenton's call if he chose to do so [*The Plant* Book One: *Zenith Rising*]

18 March 1984

Pet Sematary stayed at number 2 on *The New York Times* Fiction Best Seller List, its twentieth week on the List.

18 March 1990

After a week off, *The Dark Half* re-entered *The New York Times* Fiction Best Seller List at number 15, its nineteenth and last week on the List.

18 March 1991

Sam and Linda Landry's son, Daniel, died. The stress from the loss gave Sam a permanent case of shingles. Linda became depressed. ["Umney's Last Case"]

18 March 1992

Linda Landry committed suicide by overdose. Sam became depressed and considered pills. Instead, he worked on his book. ["Umney's Last Case"]

18 March 2012

11/22/63 stayed at number 10 on *The New York Times* Fiction Best Seller List, its seventeenth week on the List.

March 19

19 March 1846

Stefan Toren was Calvin Tower's great-great-great-grandfather. He kept his will in an envelope labeled with "Dead Letter" and his name. It identified Roland Deschain as the only person who could acquire the Turtle Bay vacant lot (Lot #298, Block #19). [*The Dark Tower V: Wolves of the Calla*]

19 March 1968

The police released Carl Amalara. They had arrested him as a Springheel Jack suspect two days earlier. Springheel Jack killed Ann Bray while Carl was in jail. ["Strawberry Spring"]

19 March 1969

A Manchester, NH, *Union-Leader* obituary mentioned eighty-four-year-old Hester "Queenie" Beaulifant's death in Saint Joseph's Hospital. Nobody knew Annie Wilkes had killed her. [*Misery*]

19 March 1970

A Harrisburg, PA, *Herald* article reported a new Riverview Hospital staff, which included Annie Wilkes. [*Misery*]

19 March 2002

Everything's Eventual: 14 Dark Tales (Scribner, $28) published with a first printing of 1,250,000 copies

19 March 2006

Cell dropped to number 4 on *The New York Times* Fiction Best Seller List, its sixth week on the List.

19 March 2013

Ghost Brothers of Darkland County (Concord Music Group, $49.99) was published. Stephen King wrote the musical's *libretto*.

March 20

20 March 1900

Emlyn McCarron was born at Harriet White Memorial Hospital. The hospital had been named after his father's first wife. ["The Breathing Method"]

20 March 1968

Donald Morris had the flu. On his way to eat, he fainted in the New Sharon's Teachers' College parking lot. A campus security officer thought he was dead. ["Strawberry Spring"]

20 March 1969

Hester "Queenie" Beaulifant had Foster's Funeral Home viewings at 2:00 p.m. and 6:00 p.m. Annie Wilkes had killed her. [*Misery*]

20 March 1988

The Tommyknockers dropped to number 5 on *The New York Times* Fiction Best Seller List, its seventeenth week on the List.

20 March 1997

"'PHOENIX LIGHTS' REMAIN UNEXPLAINED; Photos Not Doctored, Expert Says; Air Force Investigators Mum" appeared in the Phoenix *Sun*. [*Dreamcatcher*]

20 March 2001

Dreamcatcher (Scribner, $28) published with a first printing of 1,250,000 copies

20 March 2002

Stephen King finished *From a Buick 8*.

March 21

21 March 1968

Springheel Jack killed Adelle Parkins. On her windshield, he wrote, "HA! HA!" in her blood. ["Strawberry Spring"]

21 March 1969, 4:00 p.m.

Hester "Queenie" Beaulifant, whom Annie Wilkes had killed, was buried in Mary Cyr Cemetery. [*Misery*]

21 March 1981

Carlos Detweiller wrote to Mr. John "Poop-Shit" Kenton. He reminded John that he hadn't forgotten him. [*The Plant* Book One: *Zenith Rising*]

21 March 1982

Cujo rose to number 13 on *The New York Times* Fiction Best Seller List, its thirty-second week on the List.

21 March 2004

The Journals of Eleanor Druse: My Investigation of the Kingdom Hospital Incident entered *The New York Times* Fiction Best Seller List. At number 13, this was its only week on the List.

21 March 2012

Road Rage #2, with part 2 of "Throttle," by Joe Hill and Stephen King (IDW Publishing, $3.99), published

March 22

22 March 1968

Most of Adelle Parkins was found behind the wheel of her 1964 Dodge, with some of her in the backseat, some in the trunk.

The police arrested Hanson Gray, a sociology graduate student. ["Strawberry Spring"]

22 March 1981

John Kenton received Carlos Detweiller's letter. Detweiller hadn't forgotten him. [*The Plant* Book One: *Zenith Rising*]

Firestarter stayed at number 8 on *The New York Times* Fiction Best Seller List, its thirty-first week on the List.

22 March 1987

IT stayed at number 7 on *The New York Times* Fiction Best Seller List, *IT*'s twenty-eighth week on the List.

The Eyes of the Dragon dropped to number 3 on *The New York Times* Fiction Best Seller List, its eighth week on the List.

22 March 2017

In a water rights dispute, the Bright Ones entered a forty-four-day standoff with the ATF and the FBI. [*Sleeping Beauties*]

March 23

23 March 1962

Margaret Brigham married Ralph White. [*Carrie*]

23 March 1968, last day of strawberry spring

Springheel Jack killed Marsha Curran with a knife. ["Strawberry Spring"]

23 March 1980

The Dead Zone dropped to number 14 on *The New York Times* Fiction Best Seller List, its twenty-ninth week on the List.

23 March 1992

Stephen King wanted to answer Coretta Vele's 3/6/1992 letter to tell her he didn't yet know what would happen in the rest of *The Dark Tower* story. [*The Dark Tower VI: Song of Susannah*]

23 March 2008

Duma Key dropped to number 13 on *The New York Times* Fiction Best Seller List, its seventh week on the List.

March 24

24 March 1957

Carlos Detweiller was born. [*The Plant* Book One: *Zenith Rising*]

24 March 1968

The police released Springheel Jack suspect Hanson Gray. Springheel Jack killed Marsha Curran while Gray was in jail. ["Strawberry Spring"]

24 March 1974

Charlene McGee was born with inherited paranormal abilities. Pyrokinetic, Charlie could start fires with her mind. She was also telekinetic, telepathic, and had precognition. As the Z factor, the strength of her abilities exceeded the sum of her parents'. At one week of age, she smoldered her pillow and burned her cheek. [*Firestarter*]

24 March 1982

Rainbird agreed to bring the McGees to Captain Hollister. In return, Rainbird could have Charlie McGee when the Shop finished with her. [*Firestarter*]

Annie Wilkes had killed several babies in Boulder Hospital's Maternity Ward. The Boulder *Camera* reported an investigation's conclusions: the babies might have died from tainted formula. [*Misery*]

24 March 1984

Rachel Creed and Ellie Creed went shopping. Louis Creed took Gage Creed next-door to Mrs. Vinton's field to fly a Vulture kite. This was the last day Louis was happy. [*Pet Sematary*]

24 March 1985

Richard Bachman's *Thinner* rose to number 3 on *The New York Times* Fiction Best Seller List, its fourth week on the List.

24 March 1989

The Dark Tower II: The Drawing of the Three (Plume, $12.95) published

24 March 2002

The Diary of Ellen Rimbauer: My Life at Rose Red dropped to number 6 on *The New York Times* Fiction Best Seller List, its ninth week on the List.

24 March 2010

The Stand: Soul Survivors #5 of 5 (Marvel Comics, $3.99) published

March 25

25 March 1963

Lee Harvey Oswald picked up a 6.5-millimeter Mannlicher-Carcano rifle with a 4X scope at the Post Office. Klein's Sporting Goods, in Chicago, had sent it Registered, Insured. [*11/22/63*]

25 March 1981

Aunt Olympia told Riddley Walker his mother died of a heart attack. Riddley left for Blackwater, AL. [*The Plant* Book One: *Zenith Rising*]

25 March 1984

Pet Sematary dropped to number 4 on *The New York Times* Fiction Best Seller List, its twenty-first week on the List.

25 March 1987

Someone drove up Annie Wilkes's driveway. She handcuffed Paul Sheldon, tied the cuffs to the bed, and stuffed a rag in his mouth. The visitors told her that her property taxes were due; if she didn't pay, a lien would be put on her house. When she told Paul, he gave her $400 from his wallet and suggested she pay that day. She did. [*Misery*]

25 March 2012

11/22/63 dropped to number 12 on *The New York Times* Fiction Best Seller List, its eighteenth week on the List.

25 March 2015

The Dark Tower: The Drawing of the Three—House of Cards #1 of 5 (Marvel Comics, $3.99) published

March 26

26 March 1981: Operation Hotfoot

General Hecksler burned Mr. and Mrs. Hubert D. Leekstodder in their Shady Rest Mortuary crematorium. He raked out their ashes then put in a bum. He pulled his two gold teeth and burned them and his lighter from General MacArthur with the bum to make the ashes appear to be his. On a corpse's earlobe in the composing room, he left a note. It identified the Leekstodders as foremen of the antichrist. [*The Plant* Book One: *Zenith Rising*]

26 March 2006

Cell dropped to number 5 on *The New York Times* Fiction Best Seller List, its seventh week on the List.

March 27

27 March 1901

When Bradley Colson preached in Ilium, ME, the previous August, he said the town was a haven and shouldn't be named after an Italian. On March 27th, Ilium voted to change its name to Haven. Methodist Reverend Donald Hartley voted against the change. Fred Perry, a deacon at Reverend Hartley's church, voted for it. [*The Tommyknockers*]

27 March 1977

The Shining entered *The New York Times* Fiction Best Seller List at number 8. Stephen King's first Best Seller hardcover was on the List for one week.

27 March 1981, Friday

"MAD GENERAL DIES IN MORTUARY HORROR!" appeared on page 1 of *The New York Post*. Long Island Police spokesperson: Lieutenant Rodney Marksland.

Apex Corporation chief comptroller Harlow Enders met with Teddy Graustark, Vice President in charge of Print Media. In the magazine market, Apex will keep *Third World Mercenary* and *Your Pregnancy* but will drop *Horny Babes*, *Hot Tools*, and *Raw Cycle*. By the end of June, Zenith House must have three books that will hit *The New York Times* Bestseller List by the end of the year. If they don't, Zenith House will close at the end of October. These orders were direct from Sherwyn Redbone, Number One Apex Big Chief & Big Honcho. [*The Plant Book One: Zenith Rising*]

27 March 1982

Since the 24th, Don Jules worked with Rainbird to capture Andy McGee and Charlie McGee. Outside Granther McGee's cottage, he shot Andy in the back of the neck with a Thorazine-drugged .22 dart. Rainbird shot Charlie in the throat with an Orasin-drugged dart. The Shop's ID code for Andy: 14112, for Charlie: 14111. [*Firestarter*]

27 March 1988

The Tommyknockers dropped to number 6 on *The New York Times* Fiction Best Seller List, its eighteenth week on the List.

March 28

28 March 1927

"STORM PROVES TREASURE-HUNTING BOON TO AMATEUR DIVER" appeared in the Venice *Gondolier*. Alice, an out-of-season Florida hurricane, had uncovered a debris field of miscellaneous rickrack left by a damaged ship years before. Perse was a china doll buried in the debris field. Speaking through Elizabeth Eastlake's doll, Noveen, she had told Elizabeth to draw the storm. Among the "treasure" John Eastlake brought to shore was the china doll Perse. He gave it to Elizabeth. [*Duma Key*]

28 March 1981, Saturday

Tina Barfield sent a letter to John Kenton's home address, which few people knew. She warned that he and others at Zenith House were in danger from Carlos Detweiller. She asked him to visit on Tuesday, and she mentioned his dead brother. [*The Plant* Book One: *Zenith Rising*]

28 March 1996

The Green Mile, Part One: The Two Dead Girls (Signet, $2.99) published with a first printing of 2,000,000 copies

28 March 2012

The Dark Tower: The Gunslinger—The Way Station #4 of 5 (Marvel Comics, $3.99) published

March 29

29 March 1901

Faith Clarendon gave birth to traveling revival preacher Bradley Colson's eight-pound baby boy. Cora Simard delivered the blue-eyed, black-haired baby. Paul Clarendon knew the boy wasn't his. He cut the baby's throat, his wife's throat, and then his own. [*The Tommyknockers*]

29 March 1981

1990 hours: For Operation Bookworm, General Hecksler planned to get Designated Jew—Herb Porter—the following weekend. [*The Plant* Book One: *Zenith Rising*]

Firestarter dropped to number 11 on *The New York Times* Fiction Best Seller List, its thirty-second week on the List.

29 March 1987

IT dropped to number 8 on *The New York Times* Fiction Best Seller List, *IT*'s twenty-ninth week on the List.

The Eyes of the Dragon stayed at number 3 on *The New York Times* Fiction Best Seller List, its ninth week on the List.

29 March 1990, Thursday

Curry & Trembio's All-Star Circus and Travelling Carnival acrobat, The Amazing Joe, performed while drunk and sprained his neck. He was taken to a Cedar Rapids hospital and couldn't speak at Friday's Rotary Club meeting. Craig Jones told Sam Peebles that Sam would have to. ["The Library Policeman"]

March 30

30 March 1980

The Dead Zone rose to number 13 on *The New York Times* Fiction Best Seller List, its thirtieth week on the List.

30 March 1981

In a memo to Roger Wade, Harlow Enders told about the decisions made on March 27th. Roger sent memos to the Zenith House editors, asking for ideas by noon. He approved Sandra Jackson's idea of a joke book. They'd call it *World's Sickest Jokes* and write it themselves. Herb Porter suggested having Olive Barker write a biography of Iron-Guts Hecksler. [*The Plant* Book One: *Zenith Rising*]

30 March 1990, Friday

Naomi Higgins suggested Sam Peebles go to the library for jokes to open his speech and poetry to close it. Librarian Ardelia Lortz picked two books—*The Speaker's Companion*, edited by Kent Adelmen, and *Best Loved Poems of the American People*, selected by Hazel Felleman. That night, his speech, "Small-Town Businesses: The Lifeblood of America," earned him a standing ovation and six drinks. ["The Library Policeman"]

30 March 2008

Duma Key dropped to number 14 on *The New York Times* Fiction Best Seller List, its eighth week on the List.

30 March 2011

The Stand: No Man's Land #3 of 5 (Marvel Comics, $3.99) published

March 31

31 March 1899

Author John Rothstein was born. He was best known for his Jimmy Gold trilogy. [*Finders Keepers*]

31 March 1963, Sunday

Marina Oswald snapped a picture of Lee Harvey Oswald holding his new rifle. [*11/22/63*]

31 March 1981, Tuesday

John Kenton and Roger Wade visited Tina Barfield at the House of Flowers in Central Falls, RI. She explained that Carlos Detweiller had a power and had killed several people, including his mother and Don Barfield, Tina's husband. After he died, Detweiller would still live on as a tulpa, so they shouldn't relax when they hear of his death. Zenith the Common Ivy will get much more powerful and will need blood, which it will take from the evil or the insane. When they have gotten what they needed from Zenith, they should kill it. They should be careful because it was psychic and would know when they went to do it. [*The Plant* Book One: *Zenith Rising*]

31 March 1985

Richard Bachman's *Thinner* stayed at number 3 on *The New York Times* Fiction Best Seller List, its fifth week on the List.

31 March 2002

The Diary of Ellen Rimbauer: My Life at Rose Red dropped to number 10 on *The New York Times* Fiction Best Seller List, its tenth week on the List.

31 March 2010

The Talisman: The Road of Trials #5 of 6 (Del Rey Comics, $3.99) published

31 March 2016

the Spring 2016 issue (Volume 9, #2) of *VQR*, with "Cookie Jar," published

31 March ≥2018: Zero Day

As the rate of his weight loss increased beyond a pound a day, Scott Carey figured March 31st would be the day he'd lose his last pound. [*Elevation*]

March

March 1922

During the winter, Arlette James inherited a hundred acres of Hemingford Home, NE, land. She wanted to sell, but her husband, Wilfred, wanted to add them to their farm. By March, Wilfred had decided he hated his wife, and she should die. ["1922"]

March 1939

René Michaud worked for the Bangor & Aroostook Railroad. One night in a storm, he was killed between two train cars. [*Pet Sematary*]

March 1946

The cookie jar in the attic was still full. Rhett Alderson took it to his room and dumped it on his bed. He kept dumping as the jar refilled; cookies spilled onto the floor. When the jar finally emptied, he looked inside. In place of the jar's bottom, he saw Lalanka, what he had thought was his mother's delusional fantasyland. As if looking through a bombsight without crosshairs, he watched Gobbits attack a peddler. He spent the next three nights filling four galvanized steel trash cans with cookies. On the third night, he loaded them in a pickup truck. He meant to dump them in the river, but memories of starving Holocaust victims stopped him. He couldn't just throw away good food, so he left the cans for the homeless of a nearby Hooverville camp. A week or so later, he put the cookie jar in the attic. The jar was full. ["Cookie Jar"]

March 1958

After school, Henry Bowers, Victor Criss, and Belch Huggins chased Richie Tozier from Derry Elementary School to Freese's Department Store. Richie lost them in the toy department. [*IT*]

March 1971

"I Am the Doorway" (collected in *Night Shift*) appeared in the March issue (Vol. 21, No. 5) of *Cavalier*.

March 1973

During spring break, Devin Jones went to Heaven's Bay, NC. His fifteen-minute interview with Fred Dean resulted in a summer job as a Happy Helper at the Joyland amusement park. Dean gave him a Visitor's day-pass and told him to walk around and ride the Carolina Spin, one of the few operational rides. He talked with Lane Hardy, the Spin's operator, and Rosalind Gold—Madame Fortuna. She told him two children were in his future. One was a little girl who wore a red hat and carried a doll, the other a little boy. One of the two had the sight. Later, he secured a second-floor room at Mrs. Shoplaw's Beachside Accommodations for the summer. Over soup and melted-cheese sandwiches, she told him about Linda Gray, the ghost at Joyland. Pictures taken at Joyland couldn't identify her killer but showed his hand had a bird tattoo. [*Joyland*]

"The Boogeyman" (collected in *Night Shift*) appeared in the March issue (Vol. 23, No. 5) of *Cavalier*.

March 1974

Mike Ross died. His wishes were to be cremated. [*Joyland*]

Kurt Barlow and Richard Straker applied for visas to the United States. ['*Salem's Lot*]

"Sometimes They Come Back" (collected in *Night Shift*) appeared in the March issue (Vol. 24, No. 5) of *Cavalier*.

March 1976

A Type Three vampire infected Lupe Delgado with AIDS. [*The Dark Tower V: Wolves of the Calla*]

March 1977

"Children of the Corn" (collected in *Night Shift*) appeared in the March issue (Volume 8, Number 7) of *Penthouse*.

March 1979

Gwendy Peterson was ready to push a button for the Three Mile Island meltdown. When the crisis was resolved, she felt off the hook. [*Gwendy's Button Box*]

March 1980

Ninety-five-year-old Stella Flanders saw her dead husband, Bill, beckoning her to cross the Reach. She did so and died on the other side. While crossing, she saw many dead friends and neighbors. Her body was found with Bill's hat on her head. An autopsy showed advanced cancer. ["Do the Dead Sing?" / "The Reach"]

March 1981

Mrs. Massey visited Danny Torrance in Florida. Feeding on his shining, she became more physical than a ghost. Dick Hallorann told him how to deal with her. When she visited a week later, he put her away in a lockbox in his mind. [*Doctor Sleep*]

Stephen King finished *Cujo*.

March 1983

Roberta McCauley (Charlie McGee) had been staying with the Manderses. Shirley McKenzie told Hortense Barclay. Ten days later, Hortense Barclay told Christine Traegger, who told her husband and friends. [*Firestarter*]

Lars Arncaster let Taduz Lemke's Gypsies camp on his farm for a few days. Billy Halleck and his wife were on their way home from the Shop 'N Save when Susanna Lemke walked in front of their car from between two parked cars. Billy hit and killed her. His wife was giving him a hand-job and pulled up her skirt, the only time she had done so in the car. Traveling at 35 MPH with the Gypsy woman 150 feet away, he had time to stop, but his attention was on his wife, not the road. [*Thinner*]

March 1984, full moon

The Beast killed an unknown drifter. [*Cycle of the Werewolf*]

March 1985

Through *Castle Rock: The Stephen King Newsletter*, King confirmed he was Richard Bachman.

"Dolan's Cadillac," part 3 of 5 (collected in *Nightmares & Dreamscapes*), appeared in the March 1985 issue (Vol. 1, No. 3) of *Castle Rock: The Stephen King Newsletter*.

March 1990

Traveling at 70+ MPH on the way to Hemphill's Market, Annie Pangborn hit a tree on Route 117. Usually, she wore her seat belt but didn't that day. She and her son, Todd, were killed. Her autopsy revealed a small brain tumor. [*Needful Things*]

March 1992

Gerald and Jessie Burlingame began bondage practices with scarves and handcuffs. Bondage was Gerald's game. She had lost interest but continued because he enjoyed it so much. They did this at their Portland home. At their summer home, they did their standard Tarzan on top of Jane. [*Gerald's Game*]

March 1993

In Room 317 of Derry Home Hospital's Intensive Care Unit, Carolyn Roberts died of a brain tumor. She had been suffering severe headaches for a year. [*Insomnia*]

March 1998

Larry McFarland gave his daughter, Trisha, a Red Sox cap signed by Tom Gordon. [*The Girl Who Loved Tom Gordon*]

March 2007

"Graduation Afternoon" (collected in *Just After Sunset*) appeared in the Spring issue (Number 10) of *Postscripts* (PS Publishing, £12/$25).

March 2010

"Tommy" (collected in *The Bazaar of Bad Dreams*) appeared in the March issue (Volume 57, Number 2) of *Playboy*.

March 2014

Jenny Knowlton took Astrid Soderberg to see Charlie Jacobs. The next morning, Charlie healed Astrid of her lung cancer. [*Revival*]

Pete Saubers wanted to sell some Rothstein notebooks so his sister could go to Chapel Ridge, the private school her friends from the old neighborhood attended. He found three local book dealers who bought and sold first editions. He told Mr. Ricker, his English teacher, he had a signed, first edition copy of John Rothstein's *The Runner* and asked his opinion of the dealers. Teddy Grissom Jr. was honest, but wouldn't pay a fair price. Buddy Franklin specialized in old atlases and maps so he wouldn't be interested. If Pete could get Franklin to value the book, he could take that to Grissom for a better price. He advised Peter to stay away from Andrew Halliday, who was shady. [*Finders Keepers*]

April
Happenings

April 1

1 April 1909

Laura Hirtson disappeared at Rose Red. She was last seen going from the Solarium toward the Carriage House. Someone, probably Daniel, had raped her in the hay wagon. Ellen Rimbauer suspected John Rimbauer had had relations with Laura. Because she often prayed that any woman who had relations with her husband be cursed, she thought either her prayers had been answered or Sukeena had taken care of her. [*The Diary of Ellen Rimbauer: My Life at Rose Red*]

1 April 1911

April Rimbauer was born with a withered right arm, a deformity caused by the sexually transmitted disease her mother had contracted from her father in April 1908. After a rough childbirth, Ellen couldn't have any more children. [*The Diary of Ellen Rimbauer: My Life at Rose Red*]

1 April 1943

Annie Wilkes was born in Bakersfield, CA. [*Misery*]

1 April 1981, Wednesday

James Whitney's article, "COMMUTER CRASH KILLS 7 IN R.I.," appeared on page B–1 of *The New York Times*. Ocean State Airways Flight 14, a shuttle from Central Falls, RI's Barker Field to New York City's LaGuardia Airport, crashed two minutes after takeoff. Pilot John Chesterton, co-pilot Avery Goldstein, and seven passengers, including Tina Barfield, Dallas Mayr, and Robert Weiner, died. Carlos Detweiller had cast a spell that brought the plane down to kill Tina.

Tina Barfield had told John Kenton the one he was looking for was in the purple box. John found James Saltworthy's *The Last Survivor*. He knew it was going to be one of the three books to save Zenith House. [*The Plant* Book One: *Zenith Rising*]

1 April 1983

Paul Sheldon gave *Misery's Hobby*, a joke pamphlet, to friends. [*Misery*]

1 April 1984

Pet Sematary stayed at number 4 on *The New York Times* Fiction Best Seller List, its twenty-second week on the List.

1 April 2008

Dr. John Bonsaint woke up from an Ackerman's Field dream showing seven stones. He went to the Field. With the summer solstice approaching, there were seven stones. He looked through his camera to bring back the eighth. ["N."]

1 April 2012

11/22/63 dropped to number 14 on *The New York Times* Fiction Best Seller List, its nineteenth week on the List.

1 April 2015

The Dark Tower: The Drawing of the Three—House of Cards #2 of 5 (Marvel Comics, $3.99) published

April 2

2 April 1919

George Gregson played poker with Darrel Baker, Henry Brower, Jason Davidson, Andrew French, and Jack Wilden. With a straight flush, Brower beat Gregson's flush and won about $1,000. Davidson shook Brower's hand to congratulate him. In terror, Brower ran from the club and left his money. After Gregson caught him, Brower shook a dog's paw. Gregson went to get Henry's money. When he returned, Brower was gone, and the dog was dead. ["The Man Who Would Not Shake Hands"]

2 April 1981, ~9:45 a.m.

The Zenith House editors shared telepathy, courtesy of Zenith. Herb Porter learned that Sandra Jackson had been having sex with Riddley Walker. He approached her about it. She said Riddley was big and used it well. She knew she aroused something in Herb, causing him to want to sniff her chair. Excited by this, she offered to do him. He declined because of a longtime impotence problem. She suggested he go to Zenith, breathe deep, and then join her in the sixth-floor ladies' room. He did so and took care of her. [*The Plant* Book One: *Zenith Rising*]

2 April 2006

Cell dropped to number 7 on *The New York Times* Fiction Best Seller List, its eighth and last week on the List.

2 April 2008

The Dark Tower: The Long Road Home #2 of 5 (Marvel Comics, $3.99) published

April 3

3 April 1919

Henry Brower moved out of his East Village tenement. Jason Davidson, who shook Brower's hand the day before, died of coronary thrombosis. ["The Man Who Would Not Shake Hands"]

3 April 1962

Margaret White was admitted to Westover Doctors Hospital for a miscarriage after falling. [*Carrie*]

3 April 1981, Friday

In a memo to Roger Wade, Bill Gelb documented his idea for a book. Combine alien abduction with stock investing, where aliens abduct a stockbroker then reward him with stock tips. Common, general investment advice would be sprinkled throughout. Bill thought Dawson Postlewaite would be a good author. In a return memo, Roger told him to go for it. Bill knew *Alien Investing* would sell three million copies.

With no flights until Sunday, Riddley Walker boarded the Silver Meteor, Amtrak's Train 36 from Birmingham, AL, to New York. [*The Plant* Book One: *Zenith Rising*]

3 April 1988

The Tommyknockers rose to number 5 on *The New York Times* Fiction Best Seller List, its nineteenth week on the List.

3 April 1999

Stephen King started *From a Buick 8*. Over the next three years, he wrote the story in Bangor, ME, Boston, MA, Naples, FL, Lovell, ME, and Osprey, FL.

3 April 2013

The Dark Tower: The Gunslinger—Evil Ground #1 of 2 (Marvel Comics, $3.99) published

April 4

~4 April 1930

Wilfred James had lost his farm, moved to Omaha, and worked at the Bilt-Rite Clothing Factory. The rats, which nobody else could see, found him. He left that job for a librarian position at the Omaha Public Library. When he pulled volume Ra-St of the Britannica Encyclopedia for an elderly patron and saw a rat behind it, he left and never went back. He checked in to the Magnolia Hotel in Omaha, NE. ["1922"]

4 April 1981, Saturday

9:16 a.m.: George Patella, Executive Vice President of RainBo Soft Drinks, let General Hecksler in 490 Park Avenue South in New York City. Patella was going to work to document a marketing concept—soda bottles dancing to "Somewhere Over the Rainbow."

10:37 a.m.: Frank DeFelice worked at Tallyrand Office Supply on the seventh floor at 490 Park Avenue South. He needed to pick up some paperwork to prepare for a pre-inventory meeting the following Monday morning. A Checker Cab dropped him off in front of the building. He held the door for Carlos Detweiller.

10:38 a.m.: The door to Zenith House was unlocked from General Hecksler's entry. Carlos went in.

11:15 a.m.: Hungry, Carlos Detweiller looked for food. When he opened Sandra Jackson's office door, General Hecksler hooked an arm around his throat. They fought.

11:28 a.m.: Detweiller activated Sandra Jackson's Rainy Night Friend, an illegal weapon to combat muggers. Through Zenith, Bill Gelb, Sandra, John Kenton, Herb Porter, Roger Wade, and Riddley Walker heard the piercing siren in their heads. Each went to the office.

11:29 a.m.: Detweiller pushed the Rainy Night Friend's red button and sprayed Hi-Pro gas in General Hecksler's face. Thinking he incapacitated Hecksler, Detweiller tried for the door. Hecksler killed him with a stab to the heart.

11:33 a.m.: General Hecksler couldn't see. Zenith guided him out, deep into Zenith's growth, wrapping itself around him, killing him, getting the blood of insanity.

At the office, Bill, Sandra, John, Herb, Roger, and Riddley found that Zenith had eaten General Hecksler. They felt Zenith had had enough, so they got rid of Carlos Detweiller's body themselves.

4:45 p.m.: Bill Gelb and Riddley Walker loaded an old panel truck Bill had rented from a neighbor. They put Detweiller's body in one of several Port-a-Potties scheduled to be crushed at the Peterborough Disposal Co. Landfill the following Monday morning. [*The Plant* Book One: *Zenith Rising*]

4 April 1982

After a week off, *Cujo* re-entered *The New York Times* Fiction Best Seller List at number 13, its thirty-third week on the List.

April 5

5 April 1974

Carrie (Doubleday, $5.95) published with a first printing of 3,000 to 30,000 copies

5 April 1981

Firestarter dropped to number 13 on *The New York Times* Fiction Best Seller List, its thirty-third week on the List.

5 April 1987

IT dropped to number 11 on *The New York Times* Fiction Best Seller List, *IT*'s thirtieth week on the List.

The Eyes of the Dragon stayed at number 3 on *The New York Times* Fiction Best Seller List, its tenth week on the List.

5 April 1990, Thursday

Housekeeper Mary Vassar gave Sam Peebles's old newspapers to Dave Duncan. Sam's library books were in the papers. ["The Library Policeman"]

5 April 1992

Barney, Jagger, Keenan, and Sarge robbed a Portland-Bangor Federated armored truck near Carmel. They killed three guards and netted $480,000. ["The Fifth Quarter"]

April 6

6 April 1963, Saturday, 2:00 a.m.

<u>George Amberson's second timeline</u>: While spending the weekend with Sadie Dunhill at the Candlewood Bungalows, George woke up. Outside, he saw a white-over-red Plymouth Fury from Oklahoma. Sadie woke up and had a cigarette. George told her his real first name. He said if the next week went well, he wanted to marry her. She agreed, so long as he wasn't already married. [*11/22/63*]

6 April 1980

The Dead Zone stayed at number 13 on *The New York Times* Fiction Best Seller List, its thirty-first week on the List.

6 April 1981, Monday morning

Carlos Detweiller's body was in a Port-a-Potty scheduled to be crushed at the Peterborough Disposal Co. Landfill. Off Route 27 in Paramus, NJ, the landfill was rumored to be Mafia-owned and Jimmy Hoffa's resting place. [*The Plant* Book One: *Zenith Rising*]

6 April 1990

Sam Peebles's library books were due. He didn't think about them.

Sam Peebles gave Naomi Higgins a $20 bonus for suggesting he use a joke and poem in his speech. ["The Library Policeman"]

6 April 1999

The Girl Who Loved Tom Gordon (Scribner, $16.95) published with a first printing of 1,250,000 copies

"The New Lieutenant's Rap," a Philtrum Press chapbook, was distributed at Stephen King's twenty-fifth publishing anniversary party. The story was revised and incorporated into "Why We're in Vietnam," in *Hearts in Atlantis*.

6 April 2008

Again there were seven stones. It took longer for Dr. John Bonsaint to bring back the eighth. He misspelled words in his diary. ["N."]

Duma Key dropped to number 15 on *The New York Times* Fiction Best Seller List, its ninth and last week on the List.

6 April 2013

Stephen King started *Revival*.

April 7

7 April 1985

Richard Bachman's *Thinner* stayed at number 3 on *The New York Times* Fiction Best Seller List, its sixth week on the List.

7 April 1990, Saturday, 4:45 p.m.

Ardelia Lortz told Sam Peebles his library books were overdue and extended the deadline to Monday. Sam asked Dave Duncan about the newspapers and library books. Dave didn't remember any books and told Sam he took the papers to the recycling center. Sam tried to pay for the books. The library hadn't heard of Ardelia Lortz, the librarian who lent him the books. ["The Library Policeman"]

7 April 2002

The Diary of Ellen Rimbauer: My Life at Rose Red dropped to number 14 on *The New York Times* Fiction Best Seller List, its eleventh and last week on the List.

Everything's Eventual entered *The New York Times* Fiction Best Seller List at number 1. It was on the List for eleven weeks.

7 April 2004

Stephen King finished the *Dark Tower* series.

7 April 2007

The Dark Tower: Gunslinger Born #3 of 7 (Marvel Comics, $3.99) published

7 April 2010

Stephen King's N. #2 of 4 (Marvel Comics, $3.99) published

April 8

8 April 1974

Squad D member Josh Bortman, in the hospital with hemorrhoid trouble, took a picture of the rest of Squad D. In Ky Doc, Squads A, C, and D crossed the Ky River in separate places. The Viet Cong blew up the bridge that Squad D crossed. Jack Bradley, Billy Clewson, Rider Dotson, Charlie Gibson, Bobby Kale, Jack Kimberly, Andy Moulton, Staff Sgt. I Jimmy Oliphant, and Asley St. Thomas died. Bortman sent copies of the Squad D photograph to their families. ["Squad D"]

8 April 1984

Pet Sematary stayed at number 4 on *The New York Times* Fiction Best Seller List, its twenty-third week on the List.

8 April 1985

Josh Bortman hanged himself in the garage. Since returning from Vietnam, he had been depressed. It was worse in April. When he died, his image appeared in the Squad D pictures he had taken eleven years earlier. ["Squad D"]

8 April 1990

Sam Peebles left Dave Duncan a note asking about Ardelia Lortz. Dave told Sam he couldn't talk about her. ["The Library Policeman"]

8 April 2001

Dreamcatcher entered *The New York Times* Fiction Best Seller List at number 1. It was on the List for fifteen weeks.

8 April 2009

The Dark Tower: Guide to Gilead #1 (Marvel Comics, $3.99) published

8 April 2012

11/22/63 dropped to number 15 on *The New York Times* Fiction Best Seller List, its twentieth week on the List.

April 9

9 April 1930

At the Magnolia Hotel, Wilfred James hung a "Do Not Disturb" sign on the door. ["1922"]

9 April 1971

Vietnam veteran Robert S. Deisenhoff escaped from Quigly Veterans Hospital in Ohio. He took the name Robert Drogan. ["The Old Dude's Ticker"]

9 April 1985

Dale Clewson was the father of a Squad D member killed in Vietnam. He noticed that Josh Bortman started appearing in a picture Bortman had taken of Squad D. Clewson called Bortman's family. They told him Josh had committed suicide the day before. Peter Moulton, the father of another killed Squad D member, also called Bortman's family. He learned the same news. ["Squad D"]

Cycle of the Werewolf (Signet, $8.95) published

9 April 1990

After The Library Policeman threatened Sam Peebles, Sam and Naomi Higgins went to Pell's Book Shop in Des Moines. He bought *Best Loved Poems of the American People* and *The Speaker's Companion* for $22.57.

Naomi and Sam met Dave Duncan behind the library. The Library Policeman pulled Dave inside. Naomi and Sam followed, finding themselves in a 1960 library. The Library Policeman threw Dave onto a fire extinguisher. Sam threw his books and $5 at the Library Policeman. His fine was paid. The Library Policeman turned into a creature that resembled Ardelia Lortz then into a creature with a large proboscis. Sam fought the Ardelia-thing, putting a ball of licorice in its proboscis. The creature expanded and exploded. The library returned to its 1990 appearance. Before dying, Dave warned that Ardelia Lortz waits. ["The Library Policeman"]

9 April 1997

"FOOD POISONING OUTBREAK UNEXPLAINED; REPORTS OF 'RED GRASS' DISCOUNTED AS HOAX" appeared in the Paulden, AZ, *Weekly*. [*Dreamcatcher*]

9 April 2009, Thursday

Janice Cray went to wait in line for the next day's First Annual City Job Fair. She couldn't afford a babysitter to stay all night, so she took her daughter, Patti, along. [*Mr. Mercedes*]

Tom Saubers and Todd Paine went to City Center to wait for the job fair. On Marlborough Street, they saw a hundred or more people were already in line. [*Finders Keepers*]

Mr. Harvey Galen pigged out on Mexican food at Tijuana Rose. [*End of Watch*]

April 10

10 April 1963

The article, "Las Vegas Group Buys Famed Colorado Hotel," reported that High Country Investments bought The Overlook Hotel. [*The Shining*]

George and Jeanne de Mohrenschildt celebrated Jeanne's birthday at the Carousel Club.

George Amberson's second timeline: ~3:00 p.m.: Sadie Dunhill returned home after meeting with her library aides after school. She didn't see the white-over-red Fury parked down the street. She went through the open front door and followed a trail of her slashed undergarments to the bedroom. Nasty words were written in her lipstick on the walls. Johnny Clayton grabbed her and said he'd kill her if she tried to fight.

This was the day to be sure Lee Harvey Oswald was an assassin and the day to kill him. Al Templeton thought if Oswald had acted alone when he tried to kill ex-General Edwin Walker, then it was a near certainty Oswald was an assassin and he—and he alone—had killed President Kennedy. If Oswald hadn't acted alone, then George de Mohrenschildt was his most-likely accomplice. Before George Amberson left to confirm this, Johnny Clayton called and gave him until 7:30 p.m. to get to Sadie Dunhill's. He heard Sadie scream when Clayton slashed her face.

Lee Harvey Oswald got his rifle. He had hidden it behind an ivy-colored fence board in an alley near Major General Walker's home.

On his way, George called Deke Simmons to meet at the house behind Sadie's. He had Deke create a diversion at the front of the house while George let himself in the back. Clayton dropped his Smith & Wesson .38 revolver when Deke threw a chop suey casserole at him. George entered the front room, slapped Clayton around, and punched him in the nose, breaking it and knocking him out. Clayton slashed his own throat when he came to.

9:00 p.m.: From General Walker's backyard, Lee Harvey Oswald's shot narrowly missed. He returned the gun behind the fence then mingled with people leaving the Oak Lawn Church of Latter-day Saints. He took a bus home.

Sadie was in fair condition at Parkland Memorial Hospital. With a severed facial nerve, the damage was more than cosmetic. The face below her left eye would always droop, and she'd have difficulty eating on the left side of her mouth. [*11/22/63*]

10 April 1968

Lily Cavanaugh received an Academy Award nomination for Best Supporting Actress for her performance in *Blaze*. To celebrate, she and her husband, Phil Sawyer, spent three weeks at the Alhambra Inn & Gardens, where they conceived Jack Sawyer. They watched Ruth Gordon win the Oscar. [*The Talisman*]

10 April 1983

Christine entered *The New York Times* Fiction Best Seller List at number 3. It was on the List for thirty-two weeks.

10 April 1988

The Tommyknockers dropped to number 8 on *The New York Times* Fiction Best Seller List, its twentieth week on the List.

10 April 2009, Friday: City Center Massacre

Mr. Harvey Galen called 911 because of chest pains. EMTs Rob Martin and Jason Rapsis responded. Galen had indigestion and felt much better after a few burps and a fart, so he declined to go to the hospital.

~5:00 a.m.: A line of people waited outside City Center for the First Annual City Job Fair. Many had been waiting all night. Brady Hartsfield, in Mrs. Trelawney's gray Mercedes-Benz sedan, approached, accelerated, and plowed into the applicants. He killed eight, maimed three, and severely injured twelve. Seventeen were treated and released.

<6:00 a.m.: Rob Martin and Jason Rapsis were the first EMTs on the scene. On their way, a gray Mercedes, traveling in the opposite direction, almost hit them. They made eight runs to Ralph M. Kiner Memorial Hospital. Martine Stover was their first.

Hartsfield parked the car behind a lakeshore warehouse. He wiped the car's inside with bleach to destroy any DNA.

The car had ridden over Tom Saubers. Krista Countryman had broken arms and ribs; spinal injuries responded to therapy. Keith Frias lost an arm and had four broken ribs and other internal injuries. Later, Krista and Keith met at Recovery is You therapy. Martine Stover was paralyzed; her mother, Janice Ellerton, cared for her. Todd Paine was in a coma. [*Mr. Mercedes*][*Finders Keepers*][*End of Watch*]

April 11

11 April 1922

Since winter, Arlette and Wilfred James had been arguing about the hundred acres she had inherited from her father. She wanted to sell them to the Farrington Company, and he wanted to add them to their eighty-acre farm. Wanting all the money at once, she declined his offer to buy it from her, paying her over eight to ten years. Instead, she told him they could sell both properties, split the money, and go their separate ways. She would take Henry James with her, of course. Wilfred started alienating his son against her. He told him his mother wanted to move them away from farm life to city life. Henry wouldn't be able to see Shannon Cotterie anymore. The only way out was to kill Arlette. Later that month, Henry sought comfort with Shannon, getting her pregnant. ["1922"]

11 April 1930, Friday

From his hotel room, Wilfred James wrote a confession detailing how he had killed his wife, Arlette. He hurried because of rats in the room. Many rats he had seen over the years had pieces of bloodstained burlap from the sack that was over Arlette's head like a snood. As he neared the end, a rat bit his ankle. He heard three corpses—Arlette, Henry James, and Shannon Cotterie—in the hall. The doorknob turned.

late afternoon: He had a gun but never used it. A chambermaid heard his cries of pain as he bit himself to death. He bit his arms, legs, ankles, and toes. He chewed his paper confession then his wrists. ["1922"]

11 April 1963, Thursday

George Amberson's second timeline: "RIFLEMAN TAKES SHOT AT WALKER," by Eddie Hughes, appeared on page 1 of the Dallas *Morning News*. The article covered the attempted shooting of Major General Edwin A. Walker. [*11/22/63*]

11 April 1983

Heidi and Billy Halleck left for a Mohonk vacation. [*Thinner*]

11 April 1988

In his lecture at the North Conway Public Library, Henry K. Verdon said walk-ins were a myth. [*The Dark Tower VI: Song of Susannah*]

11 April 1990

Funeral services for Dave Duncan were held at St. Martin's, with a wake at Angle Street.

As a small creature on Naomi Higgins's neck, Ardelia Lortz had partial control of her. Several appendages pierced Naomi's brainstem. Sam Peebles wrapped it in red licorice then put the licorice on a train track. A train ran over the Lortz-infested licorice. ["The Library Policeman"]

11 April 2009, Saturday

The City News released the names of those killed, maimed, and seriously injured in the City Center Massacre. [*Mr. Mercedes*]

EMTs Rob Martin and Jason Rapsis took a stroke victim to Ralph M. Kiner Memorial Hospital. Martine Stover was in the ICU. [*End of Watch*]

April 12

12 April 1963, Friday

<u>George Amberson's second timeline</u>: "MENTAL PATIENT SLASHES EX-WIFE, COMMITS SUICIDE," by Mack Dugas, appeared on page 7 of the Dallas *Morning News*. The AROUND TOWN column reported that the de Mohrenschildts celebrated Jeanne de Mohrenschildt's birthday at the Carousel Club on Wednesday night. The accompanying picture showed both partying. [*11/22/63*]

12 April 1981

Firestarter rose to number 10 on *The New York Times* Fiction Best Seller List, its thirty-fourth week on the List.

12 April 1987

IT rose to number 10 on *The New York Times* Fiction Best Seller List, *IT*'s thirty-first week on the List.

The Eyes of the Dragon dropped to number 5 on *The New York Times* Fiction Best Seller List, its eleventh week on the List.

12 April 1988

Logan Merrill's article, "LOCAL SOCIOLOGIST DISMISSES 'WALK-IN' TALES," appeared in the North Conway, NH, *Mountain Ear*. It discussed Henry K. Verdon's lecture at the North Conway Public Library. [*The Dark Tower VI: Song of Susannah*]

12 April 1989

Robbie Henderson was born in Giles County, TN. ["Ur"]

12 April 2017

Authors' Note to *Sleeping Beauties*

April 13

13 April 1920

Lenny Stillmach was born in Sheboygan, WI. He and Sally Druse became lovers. They made love once, but it was for the ages. He served in the Navy for twenty years, fighting in World War II and the Korean Conflict. On his deathbed in Kingdom Hospital, he helped Sally Druse communicate with Mary. [*The Journals of Eleanor Druse*]

13 April 1930, Sunday

A Magnolia Hotel guest complained about a bad smell coming from Wilfred James's room. The Hotel's Chief of Security entered and found Wilfred's badly bitten body and unloaded pistol. Wilfred's body was taken to Omaha County Morgue. Dr. Tattersall said he would be buried in public ground if no next of kin claimed the body. ["1922"]

13 April 1963, Saturday

George Amberson's second timeline: Bobbi Jill Allnut and Mike Coslaw had set up an appointment with Dr. Ellerton at Parkland Memorial Hospital. They, George Amberson, Ellen Dockerty, and Deke Simmons discussed Sadie Dunhill's prospects. The damage was beyond Dr. Ellerton's (and 1963 medicine's) ability to correct. He was sure they would've been able to fix her injuries, had they happened twenty to thirty years later. [*11/22/63*]

13 April 2011

The Dark Tower: The Gunslinger—The Little Sisters of Eluria #5 of 5 (Marvel Comics, $3.99) published

April 14

14 April 1865

Two levels below the DALLAS (NOVEMBER 1963)/FEDIC door was a door to Ford's Theater, allowing one to witness Lincoln's assassination. Ford's Theater presented *Our American Cousin* that night. [*The Dark Tower VII: The Dark Tower*]

14 April 1930

"Librarian Commits Suicide in Local Hotel, Bizarre Scene Greets Security Man," an article in the Omaha *World-Herald*, reported Wilfred James's strange death. ["1922"]

14 April 1965, Passover

Dory and Irwin Goldman visited the Cabrons. They left eight-year-old Rachel alone with her sister, Zelda, who had spinal meningitis. Trying to stop Zelda from choking, Rachel strained her back lifting her. Zelda choked to death. That night, Rachel awoke from a nightmare and a sore back. She thought Zelda gave her spinal meningitis after she died. The bad dreams lasted eight years. Uncomfortable with death, Rachel hadn't gone to a funeral until her son died. [*Pet Sematary*]

14 April 1983

Billy Halleck weighed 232 pounds. At his most-recent physical before his curse, he weighed 249 pounds. [*Thinner*]

14 April 1985

Richard Bachman's *Thinner* stayed at number 3 on *The New York Times* Fiction Best Seller List, its seventh week on the List.

14 April 1996

The Green Mile, Part One: The Two Dead Girls entered *The New York Times* Paperback Fiction Best Seller List at number 1. It was on the List for twenty-five weeks.

14 April 2001

Stephen King and Peter Straub finished writing *Black House*.

14 April 2002

Everything's Eventual stayed at number 1 on *The New York Times* Fiction Best Seller List, its second week on the List.

14 April 2018

A Dayton Landscaping & Pools panel truck was stolen. Later that month, Heath Holmes (the outsider) used it to abduct Amber and Jolene Howard. [*The Outsider*]

April 15

15 April

Mom sent a Morris Toy Company miniature army unit package to John Renshaw after he killed her son. The Organization had contracted Renshaw to kill Hans Morris. ["Battle-ground"]

15 April

Two hundred Walkers had already been chosen—100 Prime Walkers and 100 backups. April 15th was the first of two dates Prime Walkers could back out. [*The Long Walk*]

15 April 1984

Pet Sematary rose to number 3 on *The New York Times* Fiction Best Seller List, its twenty-fourth week on the List.

Introduction to *Skeleton Crew*

15 April 1987

Paul Sheldon had 267 pages of *Misery's Return*, an average of twelve a day. While Annie Wilkes was away, he used a bobby pin he had found a month earlier to open the bedroom door. The exterior doors had locks he couldn't pick; the ground was too muddy for his wheelchair, anyway. He got food from the pantry. In the parlor, he learned about her murderous past from her scrapbook. [*Misery*]

15 April 1991

According to the Census Bureau (previously the Census Committee), the Free Zone population was about 11,000. [*The Stand: The Complete & Uncut Edition*]

15 April 1997

limited edition of *Six Stories* (The Philtrum Press, $80) published with a first printing of 1,100 copies

15 April 2001

Dreamcatcher stayed at number 1 on *The New York Times* Fiction Best Seller List, its second week on the List.

15 April 2007

"The View From Duma," an art exhibition featuring Edgar Freemantle's work, was held at the Scoto Gallery in Sarasota, FL. All For-Sale work—thirty-two paintings and fourteen sketches—sold for $506,000, the largest sale of any single-artist exhibition at the Scoto. Elizabeth Eastlake went in a wheelchair. During her tour of Edgar's work, the *Girl and Ship* series of paintings upset her. They took her into the office, where she had a seizure after warning Edgar that "she" (Perse) was awake again.

11:19 p.m.: Elizabeth Eastlake died during or after surgery at Sarasota Memorial Hospital. [*Duma Key*]

15 April 2009

The Dark Tower: Sorcerer #1 (Marvel Comics, $3.99) published

The Stand: American Nightmare #2 of 5 (Marvel Comics, $3.99) published

15 April 2012

11/22/63 rose to number 13 on *The New York Times* Fiction Best Seller List, its twenty-first and last week on the List.

April 16

16 April 1983

227 pounds: Heidi and Billy Halleck drove home from their Mohonk vacation. [*Thinner*]

16 April 1996

Stephen King wrote "The Importance of Being Bachman," a second Introduction to re-releases of the Bachman books, in Lovell, ME.

16 April 2007

"WELL-KNOWN ART PATRON STRICKEN AT FREEMANTLE SHOW," a two-paragraph story about Elizabeth Eastlake's seizure, appeared in the Tampa *Trib*.

Elizabeth Eastlake left an estate worth about $160 million to Jerome Wireman.

6:00–8:00 p.m.: Elizabeth Eastlake viewing at Abbot-Wexler Funeral Parlor

The artwork Edgar Freemantle made entirely himself was safe. The Perse-influenced work, however, was dangerous, especially the *Girl and Ship* series. He called Tom Riley, who had bought Edgar's *Hello* sketch. Riley's answering machine greeting indicated Riley was on his way to kill Pam Freemantle. Edgar called Pam and was relieved when she answered. She said Tom Riley had killed himself by driving his car at 70+ MPH into a retaining wall. Later, she told him Dr. Xander Kamen had died of a heart attack at Starbucks. [*Duma Key*]

April 17

17 April 1907

Ellen Rimbauer expected John Rimbauer to propose within a month. [*The Diary of Ellen Rimbauer: My Life at Rose Red*]

17 April 1908

Ellen Rimbauer had been having premonitions of the grand house being built. She told John Rimbauer there would be no second Breakfast Room window because the pantry had to go there. That evening, John received a telegram saying that.

Ellen had her suspicions, so she lied and told John she had visions of him with young native women. His reaction increased her suspicions. [*The Diary of Ellen Rimbauer: My Life at Rose Red*]

17 April 1983

Christine stayed at number 3 on *The New York Times* Fiction Best Seller List, its second week on the List.

17 April 1987, 4:00 a.m.

After being away for a couple of days, Annie Wilkes had trouble opening Paul Sheldon's door. She opened the lock and found a piece of bobby pin. She saw that boxes in the bathroom had been moved, black marks on the doorjambs, a butcher knife under his mattress, and many broken hairs. (She had three hairs on her scrapbook and hairs throughout the house and shed. Sheldon had broken the scrapbook hairs, but most of the others had already broken. She thought he had broken them.) She injected him and told him she knew he had been out of his room. To make it harder for him to get around, she cut off his left foot with an ax and cauterized the stump with a propane torch. [*Misery*]

17 April 1988

The Tommyknockers dropped to number 11 on *The New York Times* Fiction Best Seller List, its twenty-first week on the List.

17 April 2007

Pete Jacobs left his house and went into fog that took him to unknown places in the past and future. Once, it took him to a future city where a skyscraper's cornerstone showed 17 April 2007. ["The Other Side of the Fog"]

2:04 a.m.: Edgar Freemantle remembered that Ilse Freemantle had *The End of the Game*, a dangerous drawing. He called her and persuaded her to burn it in the oven. When she had done so, he felt she was safe.

Mary Ire was influenced by the *Girl and Ship* painting she had bought at Edgar Freemantle's exhibition. She conned her way into Ilse Freemantle's apartment and drowned her in the bathtub. Afterward, she sat on Ilse's couch and shot herself in the mouth.

>7:15 a.m.: A message from Pam Freemantle told Edgar that Ilse was dead.

12:00–2:00 p.m.: Elizabeth Eastlake viewing at Abbot-Wexler Funeral Parlor

12:45 p.m.: Edgar Freemantle, Jack Cantori, and Wireman drove to the long-abandoned, original Heron's Roost estate at the south end of Duma Key. Much of the house was gone, lost in a long-ago storm.

 5:15 p.m.: From Elizabeth Eastlake's childhood drawings, Edgar Freemantle suspected that Perse was in the cistern behind the tennis court. With a ladder from the barn, Edgar descended into the cistern. The water had leaked out long ago. A crack in the ceramic Table Whiskey keg had allowed most of the water to leak out of it, too. Without much fresh water around her, Perse had awakened. In the cistern, Edgar had both arms. He picked up the Table Whiskey keg and smashed it on his knee twice to break it open. He put Perse in his shirt pocket to open the flashlight, take out the batteries, and pour Evian water in.

 ~7:15 p.m., sundown: Perse came to life and started to chew into Edgar's chest. He put her in the flashlight tube, but, with his right arm gone again, he couldn't screw the cap on. He called Jack Cantori to give him a hand. With Perse safely in the water-filled flashlight, they went home. [*Duma Key*]

April 18

18 April 1963, Thursday

<u>George Amberson's second timeline</u>: Deke Simmons drove Sadie Dunhill home from the hospital. [*11/22/63*]

18 April 1982

After two weeks off, *Cujo* re-entered *The New York Times* Fiction Best Seller List at number 15, its thirty-fourth and last week on the List.

18 April 1994

Norman Daniels gave Rose Daniels a bloody nose for spilling iced tea on his hand. [*Rose Madder*]

18 April 2007, 10:00 a.m.

Elizabeth Eastlake's funeral was held at Unitarian Universalist Church in Osprey. Her cremation followed at Abbot-Wexler Funeral Parlor. [*Duma Key*]

April 19

19 April 1896

Jason Davidson was born. ["The Man Who Would Not Shake Hands"]

19 April 1908

Charles Hammer, Hipshoo, and about thirty natives took the Rimbauers, two British couples, and a couple from Cleveland, OH, through the bush in Kenya, Africa. Marishpa and Sukeena tended to Ellen Rimbauer's needs. [*The Diary of Ellen Rimbauer: My Life at Rose Red*]

19 April 1927

Big boy, a large frog with teef, chased Laura Eastlake and Tessie Eastlake to the water at the south end of Duma Key. They thought the undertow would carry them to a ship, their only escape. Instead, hands from the water pulled them under, first Laura, then Tessie. They drowned in the Gulf of Mexico. As undead, they served Perse. (Once, at Nan Melda's suggestion, Elizabeth Eastlake had tried to get rid of Perse by drawing her, then erasing her. Instead of making Perse go away, it angered her and may have hurt her. She had Elizabeth's sisters drowned to punish Elizabeth.) [*Duma Key*]

19 April 1981

Firestarter dropped to number 15 on *The New York Times* Fiction Best Seller List, its thirty-fifth and last week on the List.

19 April 1987

IT dropped to number 15 on *The New York Times* Fiction Best Seller List, *IT*'s thirty-second week on the List.

The Eyes of the Dragon stayed at number 5 on *The New York Times* Fiction Best Seller List, its twelfth week on the List.

19 April 1994

Rose Daniels woke up with a drop of blood on her sheet. After fourteen years of beatings from her husband, she wondered whether he might kill her or what the next twenty years would be like. She left, leaving everything except her maiden name, Rose McClendon. When Norman Daniels found his wife had left him, he decided to kill her. He picked up a woman that resembled Rose and took her to the far side of the lake. He strangled her while doing her then dumped the body behind a grain-storage tower. [*Rose Madder*]

19 April 2011

the May 2011 issue (Vol. 307, No. 4) of *The Atlantic*, with "Herman Wouk is Still Alive" (collected in *The Bazaar of Bad Dreams*), published

19 April 2018, Thursday

Mary and Johnny Hollister hired a guy to distribute Tommy and Tuppence Pub and Café leaflets over a nine-block area. Merlin Cassidy ditched the dirty white van, with the key in the ignition, in a free city parking lot in Dayton, OH. The guy put Pub leaflets under wipers in the lot. [*The Outsider*]

April 20

20 April

John Renshaw received the Morris Toy Company miniature army unit from Mom. The little army attacked him. He threw a Molotov cocktail in the footlocker they came in. It detonated their nuclear bomb, killing him. ["Battleground"]

20 April 1973

Stephen King returned the contracts for *Carrie*—both initialed—to editor Bill Thompson. Hardcover advance: $2,500.

20 April 1980

The Dead Zone re-entered *The New York Times* Fiction Best Seller List at number 14, its thirty-second and last week on the List.

20 April 1981

Danse Macabre (Everest House, $13.95) published with a first printing of 60,000 copies

20 April 1983, Wednesday

221 pounds: Billy Halleck talked with Dr. Houston about his weight-loss. [*Thinner*]

20 April 1994

Rose McClendon's bus arrived at a large, lakeside city in the Midwest. She asked Peter Slowik where a woman who had left her husband after fourteen years of hell and imprisonment could go. He referred her to Daughters and Sisters. Anna Stevenson took care of her. [*Rose Madder*]

20 April 1995

Kyra Elizabeth Devore was born. [*Bag of Bones*]

20 April 2010

Blockade Billy (Cemetery Dance, $25) published with a first printing of 10,000 copies (collected in *The Bazaar of Bad Dreams*)

20 April 2016

The Dark Tower: The Drawing of the Three—Bitter Medicine #1 of 5 (Marvel Comics, $3.99) published

20 April 2018, Friday

Fredo's Place on Northwoods Boulevard in Dayton, OH, had too much Italian-restaurant competition. Mary and Johnny Hollister re-opened their restaurant as The Tommy and Tuppence Pub and Café, specializing in British food. [*The Outsider*]

April 21

21 April 1983, Thursday

Dr. Houston gave Billy Halleck a physical examination. [*Thinner*]

21 April 1985

Richard Bachman's *Thinner* dropped to number 4 on *The New York Times* Fiction Best Seller List, its eighth week on the List.

21 April 1996

The Green Mile, Part One: The Two Dead Girls stayed at number 1 on *The New York Times* Paperback Fiction Best Seller List, its second week on the List.

21 April 2002

Everything's Eventual dropped to number 2 on *The New York Times* Fiction Best Seller List, its third week on the List.

21 April 2010

The Dark Tower: Battle of Jericho Hill #5 of 5 (Marvel Comics, $3.99) published

American Vampire #2 (Vertigo Comics, $3.99), with Stephen King's "Deep Water," published

21 April 2018, Saturday

Heath Holmes started a weeklong vacation. He visited his mother in Regis, OH, thirty miles from Dayton. Mrs. Holmes corroborated his alibi and many people saw him in Regis that week.

~12:00 p.m.: The Maitlands flew Southwest Airlines and arrived in Dayton. They stayed at the Fairview Hotel. Terry visited his father at the Heisman Memory Unit three times during their trip. Marcy and the girls went to a Disney matinee, swam in the hotel pool, and visited the Art Institute. As a family, they took in two or three movies, the air force museum, and Boonshoft, a science museum. They ate at the hotel restaurant, once at IHOP, and twice at Cracker Barrel. [*The Outsider*]

April 22

22 April 1923

George T. Amberson was born. Later, he was buried in the graveyard at St. Cyril's. Al Templeton created an identity in this name. Jake Epping used it to travel to the past to save President Kennedy. [*11/22/63*]

22 April 1934

Melvin Purvis and the Gees shot into the front of a lodge in Little Bohemia, WI. Johnnie Dillinger, Jack Hamilton, and Homer Van Meter slipped out the back and got away via the lakeshore. They stole a carpenter's Ford coupe and headed toward St. Paul, MN. Hamilton's rag as a sweatband around his head attracted the attention of Wisconsin police. Jack was hit in the back when the police chased them and tried to shoot their tires. After losing the coppers, they flagged down Deelie Francis, Roy Francis, and Buster Francis. They took the family's car and dropped them off in a small town twenty miles away. They went to Chicago, where they rented a room for five nights at Murphy's, an Irish saloon on the South Side.

In the shootout with the Gees, Dillinger Gang member Lester Nelson shot several Gees. He killed one before escaping. ["The Death of Jack Hamilton"]

22 April 1984

Pet Sematary dropped to number 8 on *The New York Times* Fiction Best Seller List, its twenty-fifth week on the List.

22 April 2001

Dreamcatcher stayed at number 1 on *The New York Times* Fiction Best Seller List, its third week on the List.

April 23

23 April 1977

When Andy Dufresne was convicted of murder in 1948, he created a second identity. He invested $14,000 in the name of Peter Stevens. A safe-deposit box in Portland's Casco Bank held stock certificates, tax-free municipal bonds, and bearer bonds. (By 1967, the $14,000 had grown to $370,000.) The key was under a rock near a stone wall in a Buxton, ME, hayfield. Andy had told Red about it. Out on parole, Red found the rock off The Old Smith Road. Under it were twenty $50 bills and a letter from Andy inviting him to Mexico. ["Rita Hayworth and Shawshank Redemption"]

23 April 1980, Wednesday

James Cogan had something to do in Maine.

6:45 a.m. Mountain Daylight Time: He went to work at Mountain Overlook Advertising as usual.

10:20 a.m. MDT: He finished talking with George the Artist. Outside, a car waited to take him to the airport.

10:55 a.m. MDT/12:55 p.m. Eastern Daylight Time: At Stapleton airport, he got on a private jet bound for Maine.

4:05 p.m. EDT: He landed at Bangor International Airport. A local driver, ready and waiting, took him to Tinnock, ME.

5:30 p.m.: He ate fish and chips at Jan's Wharfside.

6:00 p.m.: He took the last ferry to Moose-Lookit Island. [*The Colorado Kid*]

23 April 1983, Saturday

217 pounds: Dr. Houston said Billy Halleck was OK and could stand to lose another thirty pounds. [*Thinner*]

23 April 1985

IT killed Adam Terrault on Adam's way home after band practice. [*IT*]

23 April 1990

Institute for Advanced Theater Training (Harvard University), with "An Evening at God's," published

23 April 2018, Monday

10:00 a.m.: Amber and Jolene Howard left their Trotwood, OH, school early.

<12:00 p.m.: Surveillance video showed them carry sodas and candy bars to the counter. The clerk didn't wait on them because they belonged in school. The video also showed Heath Holmes (the outsider) looking in the window.

12:19 p.m.: Video at a gas station showed Heath Holmes (the outsider) hand sodas through the driver's side window to Amber Howard. He drove the stolen Dayton Landscaping & Pools panel truck.

The outsider brutalized, molested, and killed the girls.

>6:00 p.m.: A waitress and a short-order cook saw him at a Waffle House. He explained the

blood on this face, hands, and shirt as coming from a nosebleed. He cleaned himself up then ordered takeout. Doubting blood on the back of his shirt and pants was from a nosebleed, the waitress called the police. [*The Outsider*]

April 24

24 April 1963

<u>George Amberson's second timeline</u>: George Amberson parked across from the Greyhound Bus Terminal on South Polk Street. Pretending to read *The Spy Who Loved Me*, he watched the Oswald family see Lee Harvey off for New Orleans. [*11/22/63*]

24 April 1980, Thursday

12:00 a.m.–2:00 a.m.: On Moose-Lookit Island's Hammock Beach, James Cogan ate six to seven bites of steak. He died before swallowing the eighth.

6:15 a.m.: Jogging schoolkids Nancy Arnault and Johnny Gravlin found his body. With no identification, he became known as John Doe.

His autopsy determined he had choked to death. He wasn't identified until October 1981. [*The Colorado Kid*]

24 April 1983, Sunday

Billy Halleck weighed 215 pounds. [*Thinner*]

Christine rose to number 2 on *The New York Times* Fiction Best Seller List, its third week on the List.

24 April 1985

Adam Terrault's body was found near West Broadway in Derry, ME. IT had killed him the day before. [*IT*]

24 April 1988

The Tommyknockers dropped to number 14 on *The New York Times* Fiction Best Seller List, its twenty-second week on the List.

24 April 2012

The Dark Tower 4.5: The Wind Through the Keyhole (Scribner, $27) published

April 25

25 April 1996

The Green Mile, Part Two: The Mouse on the Mile (Signet, $2.99) published with a first printing of 2,000,000 copies

25 April 1999

The Girl Who Loved Tom Gordon entered *The New York Times* Fiction Best Seller List at number 2. It was on the List for eighteen weeks.

25 April 2012

The Dark Tower: The Gunslinger—The Way Station #5 of 5 (Marvel Comics, $3.99) published

25 April 2018, Wednesday

A mail carrier found Amber and Jolene Howard dead and mutilated in a ravine in Trotwood Community Park, not far from their home. The panel truck was found in the Regis municipal parking lot, less than a half mile from Heath Holmes's mother's house. It had blood in the back and fingerprints from Holmes and the girls. [*The Outsider*]

April 26

26 April 1949

Bobby Garfield was born. His father died when he was three. Bobby and his mother moved to an apartment at 149 Broad Street, in Harwich, CT. ["Low Men in Yellow Coats"]

26 April 1960, Tuesday morning

Sheemie Ruiz opened a hole to Bridgeport, CT. Ted Brautigan left Devar-Toi and landed next to the Merritt Parkway in April 1960. In a Town Taxi, Ted arrived at his new home, a rented room on the third floor at 149 Broad Street in Harwich, CT. A Breaker, he evaded the low men in yellow coats. They caught people like him to break the Beams for the Crimson King. ["Low Men in Yellow Coats"] [*The Dark Tower VII: The Dark Tower*]

26 April 1987

IT rose to number 13 on *The New York Times* Fiction Best Seller List, *IT*'s thirty-third week on the List.

The Eyes of the Dragon rose to number 3 on *The New York Times* Fiction Best Seller List, its thirteenth week on the List.

26 April 1988

A San Gabriel, CA, high school senior took about sixty students hostage. Another student tackled and disarmed him thirty minutes later. A friend of the gunman said he was inspired by *Rage*.

26 April 1997

"Before the Play," a prologue to *The Shining*, appeared in Issue 2300 (Vol. 45, No. 17) of *TV Guide*.

26 April 2018, Thursday

Nurse Candy Wilson saw orderly Heath Holmes (the outsider) at the Heisman Memory Unit. Mrs. Kelly asked why he was in on his vacation. He answered he needed to get something from his locker and thought he'd look in on a couple of patients. Mrs. Kelly thought that odd because orderlies don't have lockers and they call patients, "residents."

Cam Melinsky saw Holmes slip and fall coming out of B–5, Peter Maitland's suite. The orderly grabbed Terry Maitland's arm; Terry helped him up. Halfway down the hall, Terry saw his wrist was bleeding. He figured the orderly's fingernail must have cut him. [*The Outsider*]

April 27

27 April 1934

Mickey McClure, of Murphy's Irish saloon, recommended Joe Moran to treat Jack Hamilton. After talking with Moran, Johnnie Dillinger didn't want him treating Jack, so Moran suggested Volney Davis. Dillinger, Hamilton, and Homer Van Meter went to the Barker Gang's hideout in Aurora, IL. Davis, Dock Barker, and Rabbits were staying there after the Barker Gang's failed Bremer kidnapping. (Ma Barker was in Florida.) ["The Death of Jack Hamilton"]

27 April 2018, Friday

The Maitlands flew home from Dayton, OH. [*The Outsider*]

April 28

28 April 1934

Without anesthetic, Volney Davis's girlfriend, Rabbits, dug the bullet out of Jack Hamilton's lung. ["The Death of Jack Hamilton"]

28 April 1963, Sunday night

<u>unaltered timeline</u>: John Clayton slashed Sadie Dunhill with a knife in her home. Deke Simmons and Miss Ellen Dockerty brought a tuna casserole and bread pudding for dinner. Miss Dockerty threw the casserole at Clayton then Deke disarmed him of his pistol. Clayton slashed his own throat. Deke and Miss Dockerty couldn't stop the bleeding. [*11/22/63*]

28 April 1983, Thursday

195 pounds: While representing a client before Judge Hilmer Boynton, Billy Halleck held up his pants through his jacket pockets. [*Thinner*]

28 April 1985

Richard Bachman's *Thinner* rose to number 1 on *The New York Times* Fiction Best Seller List, its ninth week on the List.

28 April 1996

Stephen King finished *The Green Mile*.

The Green Mile, Part One: The Two Dead Girls stayed at number 1 on *The New York Times* Paperback Fiction Best Seller List, its third week on the List.

28 April 2002

Everything's Eventual stayed at number 2 on *The New York Times* Fiction Best Seller List, its fourth week on the List.

28 April 2018, Saturday

Police questioned Heath Holmes as a person of interest. [*The Outsider*]

April 29

29 April 1983

Christine (Viking, $16.95) published with a first printing of 250,000 to 270,000 copies

29 April 1984

Pet Sematary dropped to number 9 on *The New York Times* Fiction Best Seller List, its twenty-sixth week on the List.

29 April 2001

Dreamcatcher dropped to number 2 on *The New York Times* Fiction Best Seller List, its fourth week on the List.

April 30

30 April 1934, midafternoon

Johnnie Dillinger walked on his hands for Jack Hamilton. His .38 fell out and went off. The bullet grazed Johnnie's upper lip and right cheek then hit a fly Homer Van Meter had roped for Jack. Jack died shortly after. Johnnie and Homer buried him in a gravel pit outside Aurora. They burned off Jack's fingerprints and face with lye, but there were enough other body marks to identify him. ["The Death of Jack Hamilton"]

30 April 1961

Gatlin, NE, child Ruth Clawson was born Sandra Clawson. ["Children of the Corn"]

Lee Harvey Oswald married Marina Prusakova. [11/22/63]

30 April 1963

<u>unaltered timeline</u>: "MENTAL PATIENT SLASHES EX-WIFE, COMMITS SUICIDE," by Ernie Calvert, appeared in the Dallas *Morning News*. [*11/22/63*]

30 April 1970

Stephen King finished the unpublished *Babylon Here / Sword in the Darkness*.

30 April 1975

Todd Bowden had been neglecting his schoolwork while blackmailing Arthur Denker, whom he discovered was Kurt Dussander, a Nazi war criminal. He didn't blackmail for money. He wanted firsthand Holocaust stories, especially the "gooshy" concentration camp parts. On this night, he thought about killing Denker. With Dussander dead, nobody would know Todd had been harboring a war criminal. ["Apt Pupil"]

30 April 1983

Roberta McCauley (Charlie McGee) left the Manderses' just before the Shop came to get her. [*Firestarter*]

30 April 2018, Monday

With overwhelming evidence—witnesses, surveillance video, fingerprints, Jolene Howard's blond hair, the girls' bloody underwear, and DNA—police arrested Heath Holmes. [*The Outsider*]

April 31

31 April

Two hundred Walkers—100 Prime Walkers and 100 backups—had already been chosen. April 31st was the second of two dates Prime Walkers could back out. [*The Long Walk*]

April

April 1908

John Rimbauer was sick for about three weeks with a sexually transmitted disease he picked up while being unfaithful to his wife. A couple of weeks into it, Ellen Rimbauer became sick. [*The Diary of Ellen Rimbauer: My Life at Rose Red*]

April 1911

Grondin had used substandard material when paving the road from Estes Park to The Overlook Hotel. Sixty miles needed repaving. ["Before the Play"]

April 1927

John Eastlake saw the undead Emery Paulson try to drown Adriana Eastlake Paulson in the water off Shade Beach at the south end of Duma Key. He fired his spear-pistol at Paulson; the harpoon struck Adriana in the throat. Nan Melda tussled with the undead Laura Eastlake and Tessie Eastlake. Thinking Nan Melda was harming his daughters, John shot her in the chest. Realizing what he had done, he screamed long and hard enough to cause a cerebral hemorrhage. He bled from his nose and an eye.

Elizabeth Eastlake put Perse in a ceramic Table Whiskey keg filled with pool water. She dropped the barrel in the cistern behind the tennis court.

John Eastlake dropped the bodies of Nan Melda and his daughter Adriana in the cistern. [*Duma Key*]

April 1945

Rhett Alderson helped liberate the concentration camp at Buchenwald. Two weeks later, the Allies liberated Dachau. Rhett volunteered for most of his life after the war. ["Cookie Jar"]

April 1957

The New Jersey Titans lost both catchers in Spring Training. They called up Billy Blakely from the Davenport Cornhuskers, part of their farm system. Although Billy hit well, he became known for stopping players from scoring at the plate. The Newark *Evening News* nicknamed him Blockade Billy after he stopped Baltimore's Gus Triandos. Newark fans started displaying orange road-construction signs reading, "ROAD CLOSED BY ORDER OF BLOCKADE BILLY." [*Blockade Billy*]

April 1958

Henry Bowers, Victor Criss, and Belch Huggins broke Richie Tozier's glasses frames. [*IT*]

April 1965

Claire Morton and Jamie Morton took Con Morton to the parsonage. Reverend Charlie Jacobs cured Con's lost voice with his Electrical Nerve Stimulator invention. [*Revival*]

April 1972

John Swithen's "The Fifth Quarter" (collected in *Nightmares & Dreamscapes*) appeared in the April issue (Vol. 22, No. 6) of *Cavalier*.

April 1974

Dev Jones and Annie Ross went to Heaven's Bay. They put some of Mike Ross's ashes in a pocket attached to Mike's kite—Mike flew. Annie spread the rest on the beach. [*Joyland*]

April 1976

Donald Callahan saw a Type Three vampire feed on Lupe Delgado. With a meat cleaver from Home's kitchen, he killed it, his first of many Type Three vampire kills. [*The Dark Tower V: Wolves of the Calla*]

April 1977

Sarah and Walter Hazlett's daughter, Janis, was born. She grew up at 12 Pond Street in Bangor, ME. [*The Dead Zone*]

Jack Torrance beat up George Hatfield for cutting his tires. The Stovington Preparatory Academy's Board of Directors fired him. Drinking buddy Al Shockley was on The Overlook Hotel's Board of Directors. He gave Jack the opportunity to be the hotel's caretaker during the next winter. [*The Shining*]

April 1980

Rose McClendon married Norman Daniels. On their wedding night, he pulled her hair and bit her shoulder for slamming a door. [*Rose Madder*]

afternoon: Harry Streeter and Gwendy Peterson flew a kite on the high school's baseball field. Harry's attention was on the kite, so he didn't see Mr. Farris's hat appear at the treeline. It moved—against the wind—toward them, circled Gwendy, and then went behind the bleachers. [*Gwendy's Button Box*]

"The Way Station" (collected in *The Dark Tower I: The Gunslinger*) appeared in the April issue (#347; Volume 58, Number 4) of *The Magazine of Fantasy & Science Fiction*.

April 1982

Dr. Pynchot tested Andy McGee's mental-domination ability at the Shop. McGee tried, without success, to push Dick Albright. Andy thought he might have lost his power. For the next four months, they kept him drugged on Thorazine; he became addicted. [*Firestarter*]

April 1983

In Billy Halleck's hearing for vehicular manslaughter, Judge Cary Rossington dismissed the case. Sheriff Duncan Hopley hadn't investigated Susanna Lemke's death, so no evidence was presented. Billy, the Sheriff, and the judge were friends who looked out for their own. Outside the courthouse, Taduz Lemke cursed Halleck to lose weight continuously. Later, Lemke cursed Hopley with severe acne and Rossington with reptile-like scales. [*Thinner*]

April 1984, full moon

Brady Kincaid lost track of time flying his kite near the War Memorial. The Beast decapitated and disemboweled him. [*Cycle of the Werewolf*]

April 1985

The movie about Prom Night sickened Sue Snell. [*Carrie*]

"Dolan's Cadillac," part 4 of 5 (collected in *Nightmares & Dreamscapes*), appeared in the April 1985 issue (Vol. 1, No. 4) of *Castle Rock: The Stephen King Newsletter*.

April 1993

Ralph Roberts had insomnia. He started waking at 6:00 a.m., after about six and a half hours' sleep. Short of smoking marijuana, he tried just about everybody's remedies without success. By early October, his waking time was around 2:00 a.m., with two and a half hours' sleep. [*Insomnia*]

April 2001

Shortly after arriving in Frazier, NH, Dan Torrance struck up a conversation with Billy Freeman. Billy recommended Dan for a spring-cleaning job. Casey Kingsley, Dan's new boss, helped him stop drinking. [*Doctor Sleep*]

April 2004

For ten days, Scott Landon had a cold with a cough. He gave a reading from The Secret Pearl for the Pratt College English Department in Bowling Green, KY. Several times, he went to Boo'ya Moon to heal himself in the pool, but the long boy blocked the path. He collapsed at the reception after the reading. Emergency surgery removed fluid from both lungs and air trapped in his brain. He lived long enough for Lisey Landon to fly and see him. [*Lisey's Story*]

The Great Mysterio performed at Abra Stone's backyard birthday party. For his final trick, he hung six spoons from his face, including one from his nose. Abra, wanting to be like Minstrosio, dangled all the kitchen spoons from the kitchen ceiling. [*Doctor Sleep*]

April 2007

N.'s OCD got worse. ["N."]

April 2009

Detectives Bill Hodges and Pete Huntley had The Mercedes Killer case. They didn't like Mrs. Trelawney, so it was easy for them to blame her for the killings. Sure she left her key in the car, they questioned her repeatedly. She insisted she had only one key. Ross Mercedes head mechanic Howard McGrory said they delivered all their cars with two. [*Mr. Mercedes*]

April 2010

Police found blood in the Davises' summer cabin. Sheila Davis had been missing since she had served divorce papers to Donnie Davis. [*Mr. Mercedes*]

April 2011

Pete Simmons napped in the closed Burger King of the shutdown rest area at Mile 81 of I-95. A muddy, nondescript station wagon drove through the cones blocking the entrance ramp and stopped. To attract Good Samaritans, the driver's door opened, but nobody got out. Anybody who came in contact with the car stuck to it as it sucked them in. It ate insurance agent Doug Clayton, horse-lady Julie Vernon, Johnny Lussier and his wife Carla, and Trooper Jimmy Golden. Rachel Lussier's screaming at the 911 operator that her parents were dead woke Pete Simmons. He made the station wagon-shaped alien go away by burning it with a magnifying glass. ["Mile 81"]

April 2014

Alden McCausland met with Howard Gamache at the Harvest Hotel in Oldtown. They went to Howard's house, where he had fireworks under a tarp in the garage. Alden bought $500 worth of cakes, which fired off many rockets at a time. At home, Alden and his mother celebrated with Dirty Hubcaps. ["Drunken Fireworks"]

April 2016

Fred Carling, an orderly at The Helen Rivington House, went out for a cheeseburger. A drunk driver hit and mortally wounded him. With the local ambulances at a four-car pileup in nearby Castle Rock, the police took him to The Helen Rivington House. Carling asked for Dan Torrance. He knew he was going but worried about his mutt, Brownie. Dan told him he'd give Brownie to his niece (Abra Stone) then helped Fred pass on. [*Doctor Sleep*]

April 2018

Merlin Cassidy, 12, ran away from home to escape his abusive stepfather. He left Spuytenkill, NY, in Carl Jellison's dirty white 2007 Ford Econoline van. (His Uncle Dave had taught him to drive.) [*The Outsider*]

May
Happenings

May 1

1 May: The Long Walk Begins

The Long Walk is an annual event held in a future America (or, perhaps, a United States in an alternate reality) with fifty-one states, the Potomac River on dimes, thirty-one days in April, and no millionaires. The Walk starts at the USA/Canada border and progresses south. The Major assigns numbers to the Walkers, who are arranged in alphabetical order. They form a 10-by-10 array in any order they want. Once they start, they cannot stop—not at night, not to go to the bathroom, never. Soldiers on half trucks monitor their speed. If a Walker drops below 4 MPH, he receives a Warning, after which he has thirty seconds to pick up the pace or get another Warning. Instead of a fourth Warning, a Walker is shot. A Warning is dropped for each hour the Walker walks without another Warning. The Walk continues until just one Walker remains. The winner gets a lot of cash and The Prize—whatever he wants for the rest of his life.

9:00 a.m.: Long Walkers Art Baker (#3), Ray Garraty (#47), Pete McVries (#61), and Hank Olson (#70) started the Long Walk together. By 11:10 p.m., they had traveled sixty miles.

11:05 a.m.: Curley (#7) had a charley horse in his right leg, received three Warnings, and was the first Walker shot. About three miles before Limestone, ME, he had walked almost nine miles.

~4:30 p.m.: An hour and a half after cutting his knee on railroad tracks and needing stitches, Zuck (#100) was the fourth Walker shot.

~5:45 p.m.: With stomach cramps and diarrhea, Travin was the fifth Walker shot.

~7:45 p.m.: Fenter (#12) was the sixth Walker shot. He had traveled about forty miles to south of Caribou, ME.

>8:40 p.m.: Larson (#60) slowed on a steep hill. He sat to rest and got up too late. He was the seventh Walker shot.

~9:00 p.m.: Toland fainted while walking up a steep hill and was the ninth Walker shot.

~11:00 p.m.: Gary Barkovitch (#5) yelled at Rank (#84). Rank tried to hit him and got a Warning. Barkovitch continued to taunt him and received a Warning. Rank received two more Warnings and was shot. [*The Long Walk*]

1 May 1983

Christine stayed at number 2 on *The New York Times* Fiction Best Seller List, its fourth week on the List.

1 May 1988

The Tommyknockers stayed at number 14 on *The New York Times* Fiction Best Seller List, its twenty-third and last week on the List.

1 May 2011

Stephen King started *Doctor Sleep*.

1 May 2017, Monday evening

In the Coughlin High School parking lot after a Tri-Counties Curriculum Committee meeting, Dorothy Harper remarked that Lila Norcross must be proud of her niece, Sheila Norcross, a star on the basketball court. Lila thought that was odd because Clint didn't have a brother. [*Sleeping Beauties*]

May 2

2 May

3:30 a.m.: Davidson (#8) was the twenty-fifth Walker shot. He had Walked seventy-five miles.

5:25 a.m.: After about eighty-two miles, Yannick (#98) was the twenty-eighth Walker shot.

~6:45 a.m.: Gribble (#48) ran to two girls dressed in tight shorts and middy blouses. He embraced one; she wrapped herself around him, and they kissed. He got three Warnings and, fifteen seconds before he would have been shot, he broke the embrace and continued walking. A bit later, he slowed from a cramp and was the thirtieth Walker shot. By walking at least a hundred miles, he had made the Century Club.

~7:00 a.m.: A little over an hour after receiving three Warnings for stopping to massage a cramped foot, Harkness (#49) was the thirty-first Walker shot. He made the Century Club but wouldn't write the Long Walk book he had planned.

7:45 a.m.: Art Baker received two Warnings when he slowed to defecate. He had traveled ninety-four miles.

7:45–8:00 a.m.: Percy (#81), the thirty-second Walker shot, made the Century Club.

~8:30–9:00 a.m.: Wayne (#94) was among the thirty-fifth to thirty-sixth Walkers shot. He had walked about ninety-nine miles, just missing the Century Club.

9:10 a.m.: Ray Garraty and Pete McVries joined the Century Club.

9:10–9:30 a.m.: Frank Morgan (#64) was the thirty-seventh Walker shot. With about a hundred miles, he just made the Century Club.

~10:25 a.m.: Walker #38 ran and tried to climb a half truck. He was knocked off; the half-track ran over his legs. He was the thirty-ninth Walker eliminated; he made the Century Club.

~12:00 p.m.: Suffering from sunstroke, Tressler (#92) was the forty-first Walker shot. His ~110 miles put him in the Century Club.

12:55 p.m.: Aaronson's (#1) feet cramped, and he couldn't keep up the pace. He was the forty-third Walker shot. With 115 miles, he made the Century Club.

~1:15 p.m.: Gary Barkovitch limped after 116 miles.

>2:30 p.m.: After walking more than 121 miles, Jensen ran off the road and was the forty-eighth Walker shot. He made the Century Club.

Roger Fenum (#13) was the fiftieth Walker shot. He made the Century Club.

~8:45 p.m.: Hank Olson tried to climb a Long Walk half truck and disarmed a soldier. Other soldiers gut-shot him; his intestines fell out. Some hair turned gray before he died; he was the fifty-third Walker eliminated.

~8:55 p.m.: Art Baker, Ray Garraty, and Pete McVries were still walking together. They had traveled 147 miles, just thirteen miles from Oldtown, ME. [*The Long Walk*]

2 May 1945

Nazi war criminal Kurt Dussander lived as Arthur Denker. As part of Denker's fictitious past, his German regiment surrendered to the Allies. Hackermeyer gave him a chocolate bar. ["Apt Pupil"]

2 May 1999

The Girl Who Loved Tom Gordon rose to number 1 on *The New York Times* Fiction Best Seller List, its second week on the List.

2 May 2007

The Dark Tower: Gunslinger Born #4 of 7 (Marvel Comics, $3.99) published

2 May 2008

Dr. John Bonsaint saw CTHUN, the thing with the helmet head, at Ackerman's Field. He brought back the eighth stone. ["N."]

2 May 2017, Tuesday morning

Lila Norcross found "COUGHLIN PHENOM LEADS TIGERS TO TOURNEY FINALS" in an internet search. It mentioned Shannon Parks was Sheila Norcross's mother. Pretending to investigate identity theft, Sheriff Lila Norcross illegally asked the Coughlin High School principal for the girl's school records. They showed Clint Norcross as Sheila's father. [*Sleeping Beauties*]

May 3

3 May

~1:00 a.m.: Johnny watched Ray Garraty defecate. Betty scooped it up as a Long Walk souvenir.

~10:10 a.m.: Joe and Mike had led the Long Walkers through more than half the Walk. Mike got cramps in his abdomen. Scramm (#85), favored to win, had pneumonia. Mike and Scramm sat in the path of the soldiers' vehicle. With ~200 miles, they made the Century Club when they were among the fifty-eighth to sixtieth Walkers shot.

2:38 p.m.: With ~219 miles to make the Century Club, Joe was the sixty-first Walker shot.

~6:00 p.m.: Gallant was the sixty-third Long Walker shot. He made the Century Club.

evening: Long Walkers Art Baker, Ray Garraty, and Pete McVries were near Augusta, ME, after walking ~250 miles.

Walkers #62 and #63 were each named Milligan. One had traveled more than 250 miles, making the Century Club, before being shot.

>10:00 p.m.: Harold Quince (#82) was shot, then Gary Barkovitch clawed his throat, fell, and was shot. With more than 250 miles, the sixty-seventh and sixty-eighth Walkers shot easily made the Century Club. [*The Long Walk*]

3 May 1987

IT dropped to number 15 on *The New York Times* Fiction Best Seller List, *IT*'s thirty-fourth week on the List.

The Eyes of the Dragon dropped to number 5 on *The New York Times* Fiction Best Seller List, its fourteenth week on the List.

3 May 1988

A letter from Amelia Jenks to Sandra Jenks described telekinetic activity with two-year-old Annie Jenks. [*Carrie*]

3 May 2017, Wednesday evening

Warden Janice Coates had Mexican for dinner.

Fearing Clint had had a daughter with another woman, Lila Norcross went to the girls' basketball game to get a look at her. In case Clint called, she texted him that she was working a nasty accident scene on Mountain Rest Road; cat litter was everywhere. Seeing Sheila Norcross do the Cool Shake with a teammate removed any doubt she may have had. Clint and Jared did the Shake all the time. Clint had taught the Little League boys and must have taught his daughter. [*Sleeping Beauties*]

3 May ≥2018: Zero Day

When Scott Carey discovered he was losing about a pound a day, he thought he had enough weight to last until May 3rd. [*Elevation*]

May 4

4 May

<6:40 a.m.: Near Brickyard Hill, Charlie Field was the seventy-fifth Walker shot. He had walked more than 250 miles to make the Century Club.

9:00 a.m.: Ray Garraty received three Warnings when he stopped in front of Wolman's Free Trade Center on US 1 to hold his mother's and girlfriend Jan's hands. Pete McVries received three Warnings in stopping to prevent Ray from being shot.

Klingerman (#58) was among the seventy-seventh to seventy-ninth Walkers shot. Continuing to walk after appendicitis that morning, he made the Century Club.

~2:45 p.m.: Long Walkers Art Baker, Ray Garraty, and Pete McVries were forty-four miles from New Hampshire.

~3:00 p.m.: Tubbins (#93), insane, was the eightieth Walker shot. He made the Century Club.

~6:00 p.m.: Collie Parker climbed into a half truck and disarmed and killed a soldier. Another soldier killed him, the eighty-first or eighty-second Walker shot. He made the Century Club.

11:40 p.m.: Marty Wyman (#97) lay down and was the eighty-third Walker shot. He made the Century Club. [*The Long Walk*]

4 May 1982

Richard Bachman's *The Running Man* (Signet, $2.50) published

4 May 2008

Dr. John Bonsaint's manuscript on N. ended with his plans to jump from the Bale Road Bridge, thirty feet to the shallow, rock-lined Bale Stream. The doctor's suicide was ruled an accidental fall. Sedatives had made him disoriented enough to fall over a railing. ["N."]

4 May 2017, Thursday: Aurora Day One

dawn: Supernatural Evie Black (her real name unpronounceable by humans) emerged from the Mother Tree, which had appeared near Truman Mayweather's trailer in Dooling, WV. She killed Mayweather and Jacob Pyle; she didn't bother Tiffany Jones and let Dr. Garth Flickinger escape through the bathroom window. As she left, she lit a circular and tossed it in Trume's meth lab.

Sheriff Lila Norcross arrested Evie Black. So the sheriff would take her to the prison so she couldn't hurt herself, Evie bashed her face against the wire mesh between the front and back seats.

7:37–7:57 a.m.: The first woman was infected with a sleeping sickness. Later that morning, NewsAmerica anchor George Alderson reported the sickness, which affected only women. Australians called it the Australian Fainting Flu; in Asia, it was the Asian Fainting Sickness. It spread to Hawaii, California, Colorado, and on to North and South Carolina. It took on the name the Female Sleeping Flu before settling on the Aurora Flu, or just Aurora. Women fell asleep and didn't wake up; a cotton-like substance grew around them. Disturbing their cocoons caused the women to attack—often kill—those who woke them. (While their bodies slept, the Dooling women found themselves in a vacant Dooling, abandoned and neglected for years. They called this world beyond the Tree "Our Place." Time advanced faster than in the old world; hours in the old world were days in the new. They created a society and learned they could exist without men. Some married women reverted to their maiden names. Although they cast off their names from men—their husbands—they took on names from other men—their fathers. When a sleeping woman died in the old world, she popped out of existence from Our Place. When a woman died in Our Place, her body became a soul-less zombie in the old world.)

~9:00 a.m.: Dr. Norcross checked in with Captain Vanessa Lampley. He asked how the smash-up on Mountain Rest Road had affected her commute the previous night. She said it must have cleared before she went to work. She mentioned a PetSmart truck had spilled cat litter and dog food the previous fall. Clint realized Lila had lied to him.

During the inmates' lunch break, Officer Don Peters told Jeanette Sorley to go with him to clean the visitors' room. He took Ree Dempster, too, after Officer Tig Murphy reminded him that no male officer could be alone with a female inmate. Peters had Jeanette give him a sexual favor between the vending machines. Ree saw the assault and pleaded with Officer Vanessa Lampley to see the warden.

In a public statement, Kinsman Brightleaf, leader of the Bright Ones, said the feds had poisoned their water to infect their women with the sleeping sickness. On air, he cut Kins-woman Brightleaf's cocoon and bent to kiss her. She bit off part of his nose. The Bright Ones' standoff with federal agents ended.

12:30 p.m.: Home for lunch, Anton Dubcek found his mother, Magda Dubcek, sleeping. Un-aware of the dangers of disturbing a cocoon, he cut the membrane and pulled it from her face. She growled, looked around the room, and hit Anton on the head twice with his plastic shake jar. She jumped on his back when he fell. With plastic shards, she stabbed him in the neck and ear, killing him. She went back to sleep and grew a new cocoon.

~2:05 p.m.: Ms. Leanne Barrows and her two-year-old son Gary had been napping for about three hours. Gary woke up and tore her cocoon. She dropped Gary at next-door neighbor Al-fred Freeman's feet and went back to bed.

Shackled to a bench in the Coughlin County Courthouse, the Griner brothers—Lowell and Maynard—waited for their hearing. Judge Wainer had fallen asleep. The bailiff woke her; she killed him and went back to sleep as the Griner brothers watched through reinforced glass. They busted the bench and went into the conference room. Without disturbing the judge, they took the dead bailiff's keys, gun, and Taser. They unlocked their cuffs and shackles and fled in the bailiff's GMC pickup. In a campground parking lot, they killed a man at and took his Silverado to a hunting cabin.

In an interview with NewsAmerica's George Alderson, Dr. Erasmus DiPoto suggested mass hysteria caused the sleeping sickness. On air, Stephanie Koch became hysterical, yelled at Dr. DiPoto, clobbered him with her headset, and slashed his face.

NewsAmerica correspondent Michaela Morgan left for Dooling, WV.

Warden Coates fired Don Peters for forcing a sexual favor from inmate Jeanette Sorley. While Peters waited in her office after she had sent for him, he found her Xanax and spiked her coffee. She passed out.

~5:00 p.m.: Deputy Roger Elway opened Jessica Elway's cocoon. She woke up, chased him outside, and killed him with two bricks. She bit a neighbor who tried to stop her from bash-ing Roger after he was dead. A crowd formed. Sheriff Norcross arrived and commanded her to drop the bricks; she dropped one but ran after Curt McLeod. The Sheriff killed her.

Ree Dempster fell asleep in her cell. Since Ree had just fallen asleep, Claudia Stephenson thought she could safely awaken her. Ree bit off Claudia's earlobe and tried to bite her throat. Officer Lampley shot her in the forehead.

Curt McLeod tried to rape the sleeping Zolnik in her home. She woke up, ripped off his genitals, and went back to sleep. He bled out.

9:00–11:00 p.m.: Clint asked why Lila had lied to him the night before. She told him she had watched Sheila Norcross play basketball and implied it was he, not she, who had lied. Deputy Terry Coombs interrupted to tell Sheriff Norcross they had forgotten baby Platinum Elway. The officers went to get her. [*Sleeping Beauties*]

May 5

5 May

12:20 a.m.: Abraham (#2) began coughing.

1:15 a.m.: Bobby Sledge tried to run into the crowd and was the eighty-fourth or eighty-fifth Walker shot. He made the Century Club.

1:40 a.m.: Art Baker fell, hit his head, and received three Warnings.

~dawn: Abraham was the ninetieth or ninety-first Walker shot. He made the Century Club.

9:00–9:40 a.m.: Bruce Pastor was the ninety-second or ninety-third Walker shot. He made the Century Club.

George Fielder was the ninety-fourth Walker shot, making the Century Club.

10:45 a.m.: Bill Hough was the ninety-fifth Long Walker shot. He made the Century Club.

11:30 a.m.: Walkers #62 and #63 were each named Milligan. One was shot two days earlier. The other was the ninety-sixth Walker shot. Each made the Century Club.

>11:30 a.m.: Forty-nine miles from Boston, Art Baker and Pete McVries couldn't go on and stopped. They were the ninety-seventh and ninety-eighth Walkers shot.

8:00 p.m.: Stebbins (#88) dropped dead; as a formality, his body was shot. Ray Garraty had won the Long Walk but didn't know it; he kept seeing another Walker ahead of him. [*The Long Walk*]

5 May 1976

Chuck Chatsworth had Jackson's Syndrome, a reading phobia where people have trouble reading and retaining what they have read. Part of the problem was his father's success. Although his father didn't pressure him, he felt he had to succeed, too. His dad, Roger Chatsworth, hired Johnny Smith to tutor him. (Johnny had answered his *Maine Times* ad.) [*The Dead Zone*]

5 May 1983

188 pounds: Billy Halleck set up an appointment for a three-day series of tests at the Henry Glassman Clinic in New Jersey. [*Thinner*]

5 May 1985

Richard Bachman's *Thinner* stayed at number 1 on *The New York Times* Fiction Best Seller List, its tenth week on the List.

5 May 1996

The Green Mile, Part One: The Two Dead Girls stayed at number 1 on *The New York Times* Paperback Fiction Best Seller List, its fourth week on the List.

5 May 2002

Everything's Eventual dropped to number 3 on *The New York Times* Fiction Best Seller List, its fifth week on the List.

5 May 2010

Stephen King's N. #3 of 4 (Marvel Comics, $3.99) published

5 May 2017, Friday: Aurora Day Two

Frank Geary had Dr. Flickinger examine his sleeping daughter. Without disturbing Nana, Dr. Flickinger removed a small piece of her cocoon and found the fiber inconsistent with human chemistry. He burned it; a blaze bloomed larger than expected, moved in a circle, and then burned out into an eclipse of moths. Realizing Aurora and the cocoons were other-worldly, there was nothing to do but go to the Squeaky Wheel. Frank learned a woman at the prison could sleep without growing a cocoon and wake up. The woman could lead to a cure; Frank wanted Dr. Flickinger to examine her.

~1:00 a.m.: Michaela Morgan arrived at the prison to check on her mother, Warden Janice Coates. Officer Quigley told her the warden was asleep. Michaela went to the Squeaky Wheel, where she hooked up with Garth Flickinger. His drugs helped her stay awake.

2:11 a.m.: Zolnik's door was open. Deputy Terry Coombs found the remains of Curt McLeod.

The Norcrosses discussed Sheila Norcross. Lila said Sheila resembled Jared so much she could be Jared's twin. Jared found a picture online; she didn't look like him at all. Sheila's doing the Cool Shake with a teammate proved Clint was a cheater and a liar. Clint called the operator for Shannon Parks's phone number. While Lila talked with Shannon, Clint explained to Jared that Shannon had invented the Cool Shake and had taught Clint. Naturally, she had taught her daughter, too.

Mrs. Ransom had fallen asleep in a lawn chair. Lila moved her inside then fell asleep in Unit One in Mrs. Ransom's driveway. Terry Coombs became acting Sheriff.

afternoon: Judge Oscar Silver swore in Eric Blass, Frank Geary, and Don Peters as volunteer deputies.

Evie Black used the prison's rats to make Assistant Warden Lawrence Hicks give her his cell phone. She called prison psychiatrist Clint Norcross and told him Dooling men would kill her when she refused to end Aurora. When she died, the rest of the women would fall asleep, and the men would eventually die. She could end it but wouldn't for a few days. (The women needed time to adjust and fall in love with Our Place so they would never want to come back). Dr. Norcross would have to persuade other men to help protect her until then.

Fake news reported that the cocoons spread the sickness. To stop Aurora's proliferation, Blowtorch Brigades popped up to hunt and burn sleeping women. [*Sleeping Beauties*]

May 6

6 May 1969

Quincey Tremont had told Andy McGee about Dr. Wanless's psychology experiment, which paid $200. Quincey's girlfriend had arranged for Andy to be one of twelve subjects in the forty-eight-hour Lot Six experiment. In Harrison State College's Jason Gearneigh Hall, Room 100, the subjects filled out a questionnaire and received on introduction. Andy McGee met Vicky Tomlinson. [*Firestarter*]

6 May 1979, Friday: The Shower Incident

Margaret White believed sex and reproduction happened only to sinners, so she didn't feel the need to explain menstruation to her daughter. In the shower after playing volleyball in Period 1 gym class, Carrie White had her first period. She thought she was bleeding to death. Tina Blake, Fern, Ruth Gogan, Chris Hargensen, Helen Shyres, Sue Snell, Rachel Spies, Donna Thibodeau, Mary Lila Grace Thibodeau, and Jessica Upshaw teased her mercilessly when she freaked out. She stopped screaming after Rita Desjardin, her gym teacher, slapped her and explained menstruation, during which Carrie popped a light bulb telekinetically. Principal Pete Morton sent Carrie home for the rest of the day. While in his office, she pushed his ashtray on the floor telekinetically. On her way home, Tommy Erbter harassed her outside Mrs. Yorraty's house. Without touching him, she caused him to fall off his bike. At home, her mother, thinking Carrie must have sinned with boys, kicked her a few times and sent her to the closet to pray for seven hours. [*Carrie*]

6 May 1983

Billy Halleck weighed 186 pounds. [*Thinner*]

6 May 1984

Pet Sematary rose to number 6 on *The New York Times* Fiction Best Seller List, its twenty-seventh week on the List.

6 May 1985

IT drowned two-and-a-half-year-old Frederick Cowan in a toilet. He was found with a cracked skull and a broken back. [*IT*]

6 May 2001

Dreamcatcher dropped to number 4 on *The New York Times* Fiction Best Seller List, its fifth week on the List.

6 May 2017, Saturday

Retired deputy Jack Albertson was reinstated. [*Sleeping Beauties*]

May 7

7 May 1983

Billy Halleck weighed 183 pounds. [*Thinner*]

7 May 2008

The Dark Tower: The Long Road Home #3 of 5 (Marvel Comics, $3.99) published

7 May 2017, Sunday

Acting Sheriff Terry Coombs and Frank Geary caught Roger Dunphy with loot stolen from sleeping Crestview Nursing Home patients. Terry offered to let him go if he returned the goods. [*Sleeping Beauties*]

May 8

8 May 1983

Billy Halleck weighed 181 pounds. [*Thinner*]

Christine stayed at number 2 on *The New York Times* Fiction Best Seller List, its fifth week on the List.

8 May 1985

Two days after Frederick Cowan's death, his mother was sent to the Bangor Mental Health Institute. She was not expected to recover quickly. [*IT*]

8 May 2008

the Spring 2008 issue (Issue 27) of *McSweeney's Quarterly Concern* (McSweeney's, $24), with "A Very Tight Place" (collected in *Just After Sunset*), published

8 May 2017, Monday: Aurora Day Five

morning: Acting Sheriff Terry Coombs had Judge Oscar Silver issue an order to transfer Evie Black into his custody. Terry and Frank Geary took it to the prison. Dr. Norcross said they needed a county judge to order the transfer. Evie had fallen asleep, so it didn't matter. Clint sent a photo of Wanda Denker in her cocoon, with Evie's ID, to Terry's phone.

Lowell Griner wanted to tie up loose ends—the evidence and witness against them. At gunpoint, they took Fritz Meshaum's Russian bazooka.

Garth Flickinger took Michaela Morgan to Truman Mayweather's trailer to get Trume's superb Purple lightning crystal meth. He found it taped to a ceiling panel. Michaela wanted to interview Eve Black, so they went to the prison.

Eric Blass took Don Peters to where Old Essie Wilcox, a homeless woman, was sleeping. Peters gave Blass his lighter and Blass set her cocoon afire. The cocoon flashed; Essie sat up. The fireball rose and extinguished into an eclipse of moths that flew toward the high school. They enjoyed the show and didn't care that they had just killed a woman.

Judge Oscar Silver drove toward Coughlin to meet Harry Rhinegold, a retired FBI agent. The judge wanted to enlist him as an advisor and negotiator when Frank Geary's posse went after Evie Black. Evie didn't want outside help, so she caused a fatal accident. The judge veered through the guardrails on Dorr's Hollow Bridge and toppled into Dorr's Hollow Stream.

After talking with Dr. Norcross at the prison, Dr. Flickinger and Mickey Morgan picked up Barry Holden and his sleeping family. At the Sheriff's office, Barry told Linny Mars that Terry Coombs had ordered them to take weapons to the prison. They loaded Barry's RV. Don Peters and Eric Blass pulled up while they were inside. Willy Burke told them he heard shots at the hardware store. Willy joined Barry's group. They picked up Jared Norcross on their way to the prison.

afternoon: Frank Geary organized an assault team of nineteen men—seven deputies, three reinstated retired deputies, three civilian deputies (including himself), and six civilians—to raid the prison and take Eve Black. Terry Coombs added Johnny Lee Kronsky for his explosives expertise.

Clint Norcross had four other men on his defense team: Willy Burke and Officers Tig Murphy, Rand Quigley, and Billy Wettermore.

Deputies Reed Barrows and Vern Rangle stopped Barry Holden's RV on the road leading to the prison. As Reed Barrows took a call from Terry Coombs, Barry Holden led Vern Rangle away from the RV. Willy Burke drove away. Vern, trying to shoot the RV's tire, fired into the side of the RV. The bullet hit and woke Gerda Holden. Garth Flickinger tackled her as she went after Michaela Morgan. They bumped the back door open and fell onto the road. Garth hit his head and died. Barry wrestled Vern and broke his nose so he couldn't shoot again. Vern killed Barry by cracking his skull with his gun butt. Gerda bit onto Vern Rangle's throat. Reed Barrows shot and killed her and pried her off Rangle. The others made it to the prison.

In a 180, Evie Black told Dr. Norcross his defending her from the outside mob—his not turning her over, his not letting her die—would prevent the women from starting their much better life. She berated him for fighting a war—typical male behavior—she had told him to fight.

When Dr. Norcross refused his last chance to turn over Eve Black, Terry Coombs gave up and left.

Fritz Meshaum burned his wife in her cocoon.

evening: Van Lampley's husband, who had been trying to stay awake with her, fell asleep watching a cooking show. Van didn't want to burden Tommy with caring for her cocooned body, so she rode away on a Suzuki ATV to shoot herself. From a ridge past the woods, she saw two men leave a hunting cabin. Sleep-deprived, she didn't recognize them. She went to the cabin and saw a picture of Big Lowell Griner; the two men were the Griner brothers. Why, she wondered, were two men, who were supposed to be in jail, going into town when they should be fleeing? She followed and watched then gun up at Fritz Meshaum's.

The Griner brothers broke into the back of Drew T. Barry Indemnity, across Main Street from the Sheriff's office. Two bazooka shots through the front window destroyed much of the Sheriff's office, including the sleeping Linny Mars and the evidence against them. They camped east of the prison, in a field perfect to fire the bazooka.

Van Lampley's ATV had run out of gas. She filled it at the Shell station then went to see whether Fritz Meshaum knew where the Griners were going next. He didn't but said they had taken his bazooka; he had a GPS tracker on it. Meshaum shot her in the hip with a pistol from under the table. When he leaned over her, she grabbed his wrist with her wrestling arm and twisted. Two shots missed before bones broke and he dropped the gun. She beat him to death.

>8:00 p.m.: Clint Norcross and Tig Murphy lit the tires that had been doused with gasoline earlier that day. Smoke blew over the assault team's camp. Bert Miller and another took fire extinguishers to put out the fire between the prison fences. Billy Wettermore shot Miller in the left thigh. The assault team dropped to eighteen. [*Sleeping Beauties*]

May 9

9 May 1977, 8:25 a.m.

At the intersection of Forty-Third Street and Fifth Avenue in New York City, Jake Chambers was both killed and saved from death.

<u>In the timeline where he died</u>: Walter influenced Jack Mort, dressed as a priest, to push him in front of a blue 1976 Cadillac Sedan de Ville, driven by a fat man wearing a blue hat. The car ran over and killed Jake; he transferred to a way station in Roland's world. Jake hid from Walter. He traveled with Roland, but, to catch Walter, Roland had to let Jake fall to his second death in a chasm under the mountains.

<u>In the timeline where he lived</u>: At the corner of Fifth Avenue and Forty-Second Street while walking to school, Jake became part of a *ka-tet*, a group of people ruled by *ka*—fate. Members of *ka-tets* experience *khef*, where they have ESP-like transmission and reception of one another's thoughts. They also share dreams. (Eddie Dean, Susannah Dean, Oy, and Roland were the *ka-tet*'s other members.) At the pushing place, he knew he was about to be pushed but wasn't. Roland, inside Jack Mort's mind, took control and prevented Mort from pushing Jake in front of the car. (Knowing this dual timeline would make Roland crazy, Walter let Jake live). Jake began remembering he died in this world and lived—then died—in Roland's world. He remembered these things but knew they never happened. Voices in his head battled between these events happening and not happening. He thought he was going crazy. Soon, he developed a fascination with doors, sure that Roland's world was behind each one. It was just his world, though, when he opened them. [*The Dark Tower III: The Waste Lands*]

9 May 1979, Monday after school

Rita Desjardin gave a week's detention to the girls who harassed Carrie during The Shower Incident. [*Carrie*]

9 May 1983

Billy Halleck weighed 180 pounds. [*Thinner*]

9 May 1999

The Girl Who Loved Tom Gordon dropped to number 2 on *The New York Times* Fiction Best Seller List, its third week on the List.

9 May 2012

Stephen King's introduction to "Throttle" in the hardcover edition of *Road Rage*

Joe Hill's introduction to "Throttle" and Richard Matheson's "Duel" in the hardcover edition of *Road Rage*

9 May 2017, Tuesday: The Great Awakening

4:30 a.m.: Frank Geary's prison assault started with three Caterpillar bulldozers to bust through the fences. Four men walked behind each dozer. The first Caterpillar hit the front doors.

Acting Sheriff Terry Coombs had been drinking through the Aurora Crisis. He killed himself with Unit Four's exhaust in his garage.

The Griner brothers enjoyed watching the bulldozers then fired two bazooka shells at the prison. The first hit C Wing and killed fourteen sleeping women, including Kitty McDavid, the witness against them. The second bounced off the parking lot and hit the bulldozer by the front doors.

Vanessa Lampley tracked the Griners with Fritz Meshaum's phone. She killed them then slept.

The assault team lost half its troops. One left, three were injured, and six were killed, including two by their team. The defense team lost three. In a standoff outside Evie Black's cell, Evie tried to trick the assault team into killing her, lying that her death would make the women wake up. Clint explained she was manipulating them; the only chance to get the women back was to let Evie return to where she came from. Willy Burke had heart trouble; when Evie revived him, all agreed to let her go.

8:10 a.m.: A six-vehicle motorcade drove to Truman Mayweather's trailer. The fox led Evie Black and the others to the Tree. The Dooling women represented all women. If every Dooling woman chose to come back, all sleeping women the world over would awaken. If any Dooling woman chose to stay, the rest of the world's women would join them, leaving the men to die off. Drew T. Barry wanted some insurance, so he pointed his gun at Michaela Morgan and urged her to go with Evie to persuade her mother, who could then persuade any holdouts.

In Our Place, Evie explained the women's choices. Michaela told them what had happened in Dooling: several men had died before Dr. Norcross talked some sense into the vigilantes. The Dooling women had a dim view of men. They liked the new life but missed much of the old. They wanted to return for their sons, not so much their husbands. Every woman voted to return. Elaine Nutting, who had tried to burn The Tree to prevent the women from ever returning, agreed because Nana Geary wanted to go back. It disappointed Evie that the women wanted to return to a world with men.

After returning, the Dooling women were more open in their dislike—hatred, in some cases—of the entire male gender. Even Nana Geary, who had once understood her mother shared the responsibility for her father's anger, started casting boys in a negative light. The only woman who grew from the experience was Angel Fitzroy, who had killed five men and brutally attacked two others in her previous life. [*Sleeping Beauties*]

May 10

10 May 1969, Saturday, 9:00 a.m.

Dr. Wanless's Lot Six trial began. Andy McGee and Vicky Tomlinson talked telepathically and fell in love. The test gave Andy a mental domination ability (where he could "push" people) and mild precognition; he was the X factor. Vicky, the Y factor, got a mild telekinetic ability. (Five years later, their daughter, Charlie, was born the Z factor.) Shop agents Norville Bates and John Mayo began working together at this experiment. Ralph Baxter, another Shop agent, posed as a graduate student subject. [*Firestarter*]

10 May 1981

Annie Wilkes killed a Boulder Hospital patient. [*Misery*]

10 May 1983

Billy Halleck weighed 179 pounds. [*Thinner*]

10 May 1987

The Eyes of the Dragon dropped to number 6 on *The New York Times* Fiction Best Seller List, its fifteenth week on the List.

May 11

11 May 1907, 10:15 a.m.

John Rimbauer picked up Ellen Rimbauer in his Olds motorcar and took her to the construction site of what would become the grandest mansion in the state. While the Rimbauers were there, Harry Corbin made a delivery to the Rose Red construction site that the foreman, Mr. Williamson, refused to accept. After an argument, Corbin shot Mr. Williamson twice with a shotgun, killing him. Later, he was arrested drinking beer at the Merchant Café. Instead of being hanged, he received a twenty-five-year sentence because he was considered insane after explaining that an Indian climbed from the excavation, gave him a shotgun, and told him to shoot Mr. Williamson. (Rose Red was built on an Indian burial ground.) It was rumored that he clawed out his eyes and bled to death in prison.

On the way back home, Ellen accepted John's marriage proposal. [*The Diary of Ellen Rimbauer: My Life at Rose Red*]

11 May 1983

Billy Halleck weighed 176 pounds. [*Thinner*]

11 May 2011

The Stand: No Man's Land #4 of 5 (Marvel Comics, $3.99) published

11 May 2016

The Dark Tower: The Drawing of the Three—Bitter Medicine #2 of 5 (Marvel Comics, $3.99) published

11 May 2017, Thursday

Michaela Morgan took her mother, Janice Coates, to an oncologist. She had cervical cancer. [*Sleeping Beauties*]

May 12

12 May

Employees arrived at The Overlook Hotel for the new season. [*The Shining*]

12 May 1939

Paul Emory Wilkes, Annie's older brother, was born in Bakersfield Receiving Hospital. [*Misery*]

12 May 1965

"STATE POLICEMAN FIRES AT UFO; Claims Saucer Was 40 Feet Above Highway 9; Tinker AFB Radar Confirms Sightings" appeared in the *Oklahoman*. [*Dreamcatcher*]

12 May 1979, Thursday after school

Chris Hargensen skipped her detention. She received three days' suspension and was barred from the Ewen High Spring Ball. [*Carrie*]

12 May 1985

Richard Bachman's *Thinner* stayed at number 1 on *The New York Times* Fiction Best Seller List, its eleventh week on the List.

12 May 1996

The Green Mile, Part One: The Two Dead Girls dropped to number 2 on *The New York Times* Paperback Fiction Best Seller List, its fifth week on the List.

The Green Mile, Part Two: The Mouse on the Mile entered *The New York Times* Paperback Fiction Best Seller List at number 7. It was on the List for seventeen weeks.

12 May 2002

Everything's Eventual dropped to number 6 on *The New York Times* Fiction Best Seller List, its sixth week on the List.

May 13

13 May 1973, Mother's Day

A Doubleday agent told Stephen King that New American Library had purchased the paperback rights to Carrie. Doubleday and King each got $200,000, eighty times his hardcover advance.

13 May 1975

Stephen King sent the first draft of *The Shine* to Doubleday editor Bill Thompson. The book was published as *The Shining*. In the first draft, Wendy Torrance's name was Jenny.

13 May 1979, Friday

Lawyer John Hargensen, Chris's father, threatened Principal Henry Grayle with a lawsuit if Grayle didn't allow Chris to the Spring Ball. He dropped it after Grayle promised to countersue on Carrie White's behalf because of Chris Hargensen's involvement in the Shower Incident (6 May 1979). [*Carrie*]

13 May 1983

Duncan Hopley's acne from Taduz Lemke's curse got so bad that he shot himself. [*Thinner*]

13 May 1984

Pet Sematary dropped to number 8 on *The New York Times* Fiction Best Seller List, its twenty-eighth week on the List.

13 May 1990

The Stand: The Complete & Uncut Edition entered *The New York Times* Fiction Best Seller List at number 1. It was on the List for thirty-five weeks.

13 May 2001

Dreamcatcher stayed at number 4 on *The New York Times* Fiction Best Seller List, its sixth week on the List.

13 May 2009

The Dark Tower: Fall of Gilead #1 of 6 (Marvel Comics, $3.99) published

13 May 2012

The Dark Tower 4.5: The Wind Through the Keyhole entered *The New York Times* Fiction Best Seller List at number 1. It was on the List for eight weeks.

13 May 2015

The Dark Tower: The Drawing of the Three—House of Cards #3 of 5 (Marvel Comics, $3.99) published

13 May 2017, Saturday

Janice Coates started chemotherapy. [*Sleeping Beauties*]

May 14

14 May 1958

Charles N. Brown had borrowed Stephen W. Meader's *Bulldozer* from the Derry Public Library. It was due on the 14th. [*IT*]

14 May 1973

Mrs. Shoplaw served champagne, as was her tradition of starting the summer with the seasonal-hire renters. She had four renters—Miss Tina Ackerley (the local librarian) and Joyland summer hires Erin Cook, Devin Jones, and Tom Kennedy. [*Joyland*]

14 May 1981

Annie Wilkes killed a Boulder Hospital patient. [*Misery*]

14 May 1983

172 pounds: Billy Halleck returned home after three days of tests at the Henry Glassman Clinic. Dr. Yount thought his problem was psychological anorexia. When Billy got home, he found his wife had sent his daughter away. He tried smoking again but didn't like it. [*Thinner*]

14 May 1984, Saturday

Gage Creed found a new game: run away from his parents. The Micmac burying ground influenced people who had been there. To increase its hold over Louis Creed, it caused Gage to run in front of an Orinco truck on Route 15. Louis ran after Gage, dove, and touched the back of his jumper but couldn't catch him. The truck hit the boy and dragged him about a hundred yards, knocking him out of his cap, jumper, and sneakers; his jumper was turned inside out, and his hat was full of blood. The Ellsworth, ME, truck driver had not been drinking or using drugs but was overcome by the Micmac burying ground and floored it. Later, he was released on $1,000 bail, his wife and kids left him, and he failed an attempt to kill himself by hanging. [*Pet Sematary*]

May 15

15 May

Opening day at the Joyland amusement park [*Joyland*]

The Overlook Hotel's annual season started. [*The Shining*]

15 May 1908

Ellen Rimbauer had been unconscious or delirious from the sexually transmitted disease John Rimbauer had given her. Sukeena took care of her with bitter teas and other remedies. With Sukeena's help, Ellen vowed to emotionally and financially ruin John for his infidelity. Sukeena would continue the trip and return home with them. [*The Diary of Ellen Rimbauer: My Life at Rose Red*]

15 May 1972

George Amberson's second timeline: With a .38 handgun (probably a Victory), Arthur Bremer assassinated President George Wallace at a Laurel, MD, shopping mall. Wallace was campaigning for re-election. [*11/22/63*]

15 May 1973, 7:00 a.m.

Erin Cook, Dev Jones, and Tom Kennedy started their summer jobs at Joyland. Teams consisted of a Hollywood Girl, five Happy Helpers, and a Joyland veteran as the leader. Erin, Dev, and Tom were assigned to Team Beagle. Each team member learned different rides and stands then taught the others. Dev Jones worked with Lane Hardy on the Carolina Spin, an Aussie (counterclockwise) Ferris wheel. Dressing as Howie the Happy Helper was called wearing the fur. Dev was so good at entertaining the kids that park owner Bradley Easterbrook made sure he wore the fur often. [*Joyland*]

15 May 1983

Billy Halleck weighed 170 pounds. [*Thinner*]

Christine stayed at number 2 on *The New York Times* Fiction Best Seller List, its sixth week on the List.

15 May 2000

"MYSTERY LIGHTS ONCE AGAIN REPORTED IN JEFFERSON TRACT; Kineo Town Manager: 'I Don't Know What They Are, but They Keep Coming Back,'" appeared in the Derry, ME, *Daily News*. [*Dreamcatcher*]

May 16

16 May 1979, Monday

Carrie White practiced her telekinesis. She pushed a brush off her bureau but couldn't hold it in the air. [*Carrie*]

16 May 1983

Billy Halleck weighed 167 pounds. [*Thinner*]

16 May 1999

The Girl Who Loved Tom Gordon stayed at number 2 on *The New York Times* Fiction Best Seller List, its fourth week on the List.

16 May 2017

Gwendy's Button Box (Cemetery Dance, $25), by Stephen King and Richard Chizmar, published with a first printing of 60,000 copies

May 17

17 May 1966

A *Bakersfield Journal* clipping mentioned that Annie Wilkes graduated with honors from USC nursing school. [*Misery*]

17 May 1975

3:15 p.m.: Johnny Smith came out of his coma. He had psychic experiences when he touched people. He could see events in their lives, see what was happening or has happened to family members, and see what they were thinking. When he saw an event, he didn't just see it, he lived it. When he got a reading from touching someone, they felt something, and the look in his eyes changed. This tired him; he suffered headaches. Some psychic experiences had holes. Because part of his brain had died—his dead zone—he couldn't see some things and couldn't remember others, particularly place names. Part of his parietal lobe had become more active.

3:55 p.m.: Marie Michaud, an Eastern Maine Medical Center nurse, touched Johnny. Immediately, he knew her name and that she had three children.

Dr. Jim Brown examined him but didn't tell him how long he'd been asleep. He grabbed Dr. Brown's hand and discovered he had been in a coma for fifty-five months. [*The Dead Zone*]

17 May 1979, Tuesday

To atone for her part in The Shower Incident, Sue Snell asked her boyfriend, Tommy Ross, to take Carrie White to the Ewen High Spring Ball.

Again, Carrie moved a brush off her bureau. She held it then lowered it for a smooth landing. Her respiration slowed, her heart rate and blood pressure rose, and her body temperature fell. She lifted the end of her bed three inches but dropped it. [*Carrie*]

17 May 1981

Danse Macabre entered *The New York Times* Non-Fiction Best Seller List at number 13. It was on the List for five weeks.

17 May 1984, Tuesday

Gage Creed had two closed-coffin viewings at Brookings-Smith Mortuary's East Room, 10:00–11:30 a.m. and 2:00–3:30 p.m. Rachel Creed and Ellie Creed couldn't be at the morning viewing; Jud Crandall and Steve Masterton stayed with them. Between viewings, Jud and Steve had lunch with Rachel, Ellie, and Louis Creed at Benjamin's in Bangor, ME. During the second viewing, Louis Creed and Irwin Goldman had a fistfight; they knocked over Gage's coffin. Jud stayed with Ellie, who didn't go to the afternoon viewing. [*Pet Sematary*]

17 May 1987

The Eyes of the Dragon dropped to number 7 on *The New York Times* Fiction Best Seller List, its sixteenth week on the List.

17 May 2018

"Laurie" online at www.stephenking.com

May 18

18 May 1961, 7:45 p.m.

<u>George Amberson's second timeline</u>: George Amberson was the director of Denholm County Consolidated High School's junior-senior play. After being nervous with stage fright all day, Mike Coslaw rang George's bell. George reminded him that, at football games, he had performed in front of larger, more-hostile crowds. [*11/22/63*]

18 May 1984, Wednesday

2:00 p.m.: Gage Creed was buried in Pleasantview Cemetery near Bangor International Airport. His coffin was the American Casket Company's $600, rosewood, Eternal Rest model.

3:00—6:00 p.m.: A wake was held at the Creed house. Joan Charlton came with quiche, Jud Crandall with Mr. Rat (rat cheese), Missy Dandridge with key lime pie, the Dannikers with baked ham, the Goldmans with cold cuts and cheeses, Surrendra Hardu with apples, and Steve Masterton and his wife with a hamburger-and-noodle casserole.

9:45 p.m.: Louis Creed suggested that Rachel Creed and Ellie Creed visit Rachel's parents in Chicago. He would follow in three or four days, enough time to bring Gage back to life and rekill him if it didn't work out. [*Pet Sematary*]

May 19

19 May 1961

George Amberson's second timeline: The kids got a standing ovation at opening night for *Of Mice and Men*, Denholm County Consolidated High School's junior-senior play, directed by George Amberson. [*11/22/63*]

19 May 1979, Thursday

After Period 5 Study Hall, Tommy Ross asked Carrie White to the Ewen High Spring Ball. [*Carrie*]

19 May 1980

Castle Rock High School finals week started. [*Gwendy's Button Box*]

19 May 1981

After arriving in New York City from Sacramento, CA, Donald Callahan visited Rowen Magruder in Room 577 of Riverside Hospital. The Hitler Brothers had been hired to kill Callahan and brutally attacked Magruder to find out where he was; Magruder didn't know. Callahan walked toward Home, to see it one last time before leaving town. Near the vacant lot at Second Avenue and Forty-Sixth Street, the Hitler Brothers grabbed him and escorted him to the deserted Turtle Bay Washateria on Forty-Seventh Street. They duct-taped his hands behind his back. One kicked him in the right side of the face, breaking his jaw in four places, and then started to carve a swastika on his forehead. He was interrupted after carving just a cross. Two men came forward with a gun and a bright light. They had the Hitler Brothers take off their shoes and pants and leave the premises. Callahan didn't know the two men were Aaron Deepneau and Calvin Tower. Not long after they left, an ambulance arrived and took him to Riverside Hospital. He got Room 577; Rowan Magruder had died. The Hitler Brothers were found dead by the end of the month, killed for failing to get Callahan. [*The Dark Tower V: Wolves of the Calla*]

19 May 1984, Thursday

Rachel Creed and Ellie Creed to visit Rachel's parents in Chicago. Before going, Ellie dreamed that Gage Creed's coffin was empty and there was dirt in his crib. On the plane, she dreamed that Gage was alive and had Louis Creed's scalpel. Also, she dreamed that Paxcow (Victor Pascow) had taken her to the Pet Sematary and told her that her father was going to do something he shouldn't.

Louis bought $58.60 worth of grave digging tools (a pick, rope, two shovels, an 8' x 8' tarp, and work gloves) in Brewer, ME. Under the name Dee Dee Ramone, he checked in to the Howard Johnson's Motor Lodge on Odlin Road in Bangor, ME.

Uneasy about Ellie's dreams, Rachel headed home. Delta Airlines Reservations clerk Kim booked flights from Chicago to Bangor. Rachel flew from Chicago to New York, New York to Boston, and Boston to Portland. She missed her Portland-to-Bangor plane because of a late shuttle bus. [*Pet Sematary*]

19 May 1985

Richard Bachman's *Thinner* stayed at number 1 on *The New York Times* Fiction Best Seller

List, its twelfth week on the List.

19 May 1987

Stephen King finished *The Tommyknockers*.

19 May 1996

The Green Mile, Part One: The Two Dead Girls stayed at number 2 on *The New York Times* Paperback Fiction Best Seller List, its sixth week on the List.

The Green Mile, Part Two: The Mouse on the Mile rose to number 1 on *The New York Times* Paperback Fiction Best Seller List, its second week on the List.

19 May 2002

Everything's Eventual dropped to number 8 on *The New York Times* Fiction Best Seller List, its seventh week on the List.

19 May 2010

American Vampire #3 (Vertigo Comics, $3.99), with Stephen King's "Blood Vengeance," published

The Dark Tower: The Gunslinger—The Journey Begins #1 of 5 (Marvel Comics, $3.99) published

May 20

20 May 1963, 11:00 a.m.

<u>George Amberson's second timeline</u>: George Amberson parked on Greenville Avenue, four blocks from Faith Financial. He intended to bet $500 on Chateaugay to Place at the Kentucky Derby. (He didn't want to be greedy by betting for the Win.) As he approached Faith Financial, he saw the bookie in the doorway, looking at a Lincoln with Florida plates across the street. George had a hunch the Lincoln was associated with Eduardo Gutierrez, so he left. [*11/22/63*]

20 May 1976

Johnny Smith started tutoring Chuck Chatsworth. They read Max Brand's *Fire Brain*. [*The Dead Zone*]

On page 17, the Portland *Press-Herald* reported the Maine State Wildlife Service suspected a pack of wild dogs had been roaming the Jerusalem's Lot-Cumberland-Falmouth area. For about a month, dead sheep had been found with mangled throats and bellies. [*'Salem's Lot*]

20 May 1978, Saturday: Coin & Stamp Show at the Castle Rock VFW

Gwendy Peterson sold two mint condition 1891 Morgan silver dollars for $800 each, cash, to Jon Leonard. Frankie Stone and Jimmy Sines were checking for unlocked cars when they saw Gwendy leaving the VFW. Frankie felt her leg and made inappropriate sexual remarks. She took her opportunity to escape when Lenny asked if the boys were bothering her. Their confidence at outnumbering Lenny two-to-one waned when he flicked his knife, engraved with *Semper Fi*. The boys ran off. [*Gwendy's Button Box*]

20 May 1984

Friday: After missing her Portland-to-Bangor flight because of a late airport shuttle bus, Rachel Creed rented a car. The Wendigo, the power of the Micmac burying ground beyond the Pet Sematary, caused her to drowse. She stopped for coffee. When she was ready to go, her car wouldn't start; a trucker fixed a disconnected battery cable.

Jud Crandall had been waiting by his front window to stop Louis Creed from doing the unspeakable. The Wendigo caused him to sleep while Louis exhumed Gage Creed and reburied him in the Micmac burying ground. Gage returned home for Louis's scalpel. Jud awoke to noises in his house; the demon within Gage killed him with the scalpel. Rachel arrived and, expecting a hug from Gage, got killed by the demon. In Chicago, Ellie Creed dreamed that Oz the Gweat and Tewwible killed her mother.

>9:00 a.m.: Louis Creed rekilled Winston Churchill, his daughter Ellie's cat, with a 75 mg injection of morphine then rekilled Gage. After removing Rachel's body, he burned Crandall's house then buried Rachel in the Micmac burying ground. She came back. [*Pet Sematary*]

Pet Sematary dropped to number 12 on *The New York Times* Fiction Best Seller List, its twenty-ninth week on the List.

20 May 1990

The Stand: The Complete & Uncut Edition stayed at number 1 on *The New York Times* Fiction Best Seller List, its second week on the List.

20 May 2001

Dreamcatcher stayed at number 4 on *The New York Times* Fiction Best Seller List, its seventh week on the List.

20 May 2012

The Dark Tower 4.5: The Wind Through the Keyhole dropped to number 2 on *The New York Times* Fiction Best Seller List, its second week on the List.

May 21

21 May 1911

Delora White, a maid with whom John Rimbauer may have had relations, disappeared in Rose Red. [*The Diary of Ellen Rimbauer: My Life at Rose Red*]

21 May 1979, Saturday night

Carrie's telekinesis had strengthened. She raised her bureau to the ceiling and guided it back down. She also lifted her bed, with herself on it. Earlier that week, she had pushed a parked car. [*Carrie*]

May 22

22 May 1975

Johnny Smith told Dr. Weizak the doctor's mother was still alive; she hadn't died in 1939 during the Nazis' Warsaw occupation. After marrying Helmut Borentz and living in Switzerland, she lived in Carmel, CA, as Johanna Borentz. Helmut died in 1963 or later.

Over the next few months, Johnny compared Ridgeway, NH mayor Greg Stillson to Hitler. He decided to kill him. [*The Dead Zone*]

22 May 1983

Christine stayed at number 2 on *The New York Times* Fiction Best Seller List, its seventh week on the List.

22 May 1985

John Feury's body was found under the porch at 29 Neibolt Street. IT had killed him and removed his legs. [*IT*]

22 May 2018

The Outsider (Simon & Schuster, $30) published

May 23

23 May 1979

Chris Hargensen slept with Billy Nolan to persuade him to help her seek revenge against Carrie White, whom she blamed for being prohibited from the Spring Ball. She had brought it on herself for harassing Carrie during The Shower Incident, then skipping the detention. [*Carrie*]

Olive Kepnes jumped off the Suicide Stairs. [*Gwendy's Button Box*]

23 May 1981

Annie Wilkes killed a Boulder Hospital patient. [*Misery*]

23 May 1985

Andrew Rademacher arrested Harold Earl for the murder of John Feury. Blood was found on his clothes, but it was deer blood. He had been drinking paint thinner, so they sent him to the Bangor Mental Health Institute. [*IT*]

23 May 1988

An article about Thad and Liz Beaumont appeared in *People* magazine's BIO section. The piece made public that George Stark was Thad's pseudonym. Thad killed Stark and began writing under his own name again. They staged a fake burial at Homeland Cemetery, near Danforth Keeton's plots. Mike Donaldson wrote the article, and Phyllis Myers, whose idea it was to have a George Stark tombstone, was the photographer. [*The Dark Half*]

23 May 1999

The Girl Who Loved Tom Gordon dropped to number 4 on *The New York Times* Fiction Best Seller List, its fifth week on the List.

23 May 2014, Friday

Peter Saubers introduced himself as James Hawkins to Drew Halliday at Andrew Halliday Rare Editions. He showed photocopies of handwritten pages from unknown John Rothstein notebooks. Hawkins had a copy of *Dispatches from Olympus: Letters from 20 Great American Writers in Their Own Hand* for handwriting comparison. The book included a letter Rothstein had written to Flannery O'Connor. Halliday lowballed him and said a private collector might pay $50,000 and offered a 50–50 split. Hawkins insisted on 70–30; Halliday countered with 60–40. Halliday knew he'd get around $250,000, so he was willing to give the kid 60% of $50,000. He told Hawkins to return in a week.

Dispatches from Olympus had a purple sticker on the spine, meaning a Garner Street Library book that didn't circulate. The MEET OUR STAFF page of the library's website showed Mr. Peter Saubers, the boy who called himself James Hawkins. Halliday knew there were more than six notebooks. The entire collection could fetch $50 million. With Bellamy in prison, it would be Halliday's. [*Finders Keepers*]

May 24

24 May 1979, Thursday

At school, Gwendy Peterson heard that Olive Kepnes had committed suicide. Gwendy blamed herself; had she not let their friendship fade, Olive might not have jumped. Before midnight, Gwendy parked in the Castle Rock View Recreational parking lot and headed toward the Suicide Stairs. Deciding she could make it so that nobody else jumped off, she went home. [*Gwendy's Button Box*]

24 May 1981

Danse Macabre rose to number 12 on *The New York Times* Non-Fiction Best Seller List, its second week on the List.

24 May 1987

After two weeks off, *IT* re-entered *The New York Times* Fiction Best Seller List at number 15, *IT*'s thirty-fifth and last week on the List.

The Eyes of the Dragon rose to number 6 on *The New York Times* Fiction Best Seller List, its seventeenth week on the List.

24 May 2010, Monday

Bill Hodges received a four-page letter from The Mercedes Killer, whom Hodges called Mr. Mercedes. The letter praised his career, reminded him that he didn't catch The Mercedes Killer, and mentioned that retired cops often commit suicide. If Hodges wanted to get in touch, Mr. Mercedes had set up an account for him on Under Debbie's Blue Umbrella. Before going to bed, Hodges looked up Under Debbie's Blue Umbrella and found that it was a social site for people who wanted to converse and exchange interesting ideas in anonymity. [*Mr. Mercedes*]

24 May 2011

trade paperback version of *Full Dark, No Stars* (Gallery Books, $16) published; includes "Under the Weather," a new short story not included in the first (hardcover) edition ("Under the Weather" was collected in *The Bazaar of Bad Dreams*)

May 25

25 May 1975

Bangor *Daily News* reporter David Bright interviewed Johnny Smith. They talked about the accident, coming out of his coma after four-and-a-half years, and the recovery challenges facing him. When Bright asked about Johnny's sixth sense, Johnny said he wasn't psychic. [*The Dead Zone*]

25 May 1979

1:00–6:00 a.m.: The northeastern corner of the Castle View Recreational Park, including the Suicide Stairs, collapsed. [*Gwendy's Button Box*]

For plausible deniability, Tina Blake went for a Coke while Chris Hargensen studied the Prom Committee's Spring Ball floor plan and seating chart.

Billy Nolan and others slaughtered Irwin Henty's two sows for their blood. [*Carrie*]

25 May 1981

A van took Donald Callahan and three or four others from Riverside Hospital to a welfare rehabilitation facility in Queens. [*The Dark Tower V: Wolves of the Calla*]

25 May 1994, Wednesday

Rose McClendon wanted to pawn her wedding ring at Liberty City Loan & Pawn. Bill Steiner told her the stone was cubic zirconia; she declined his $50 offer for the $10 stone in a $200 setting. A picture selling for $75 or best offer caught her attention. The painting was behind glass, which was odd for an original oil. It showed a woman whom she called Rose Madder (because of the writing on the back) on top of a hill, facing away from the viewer. Bill traded it for her ring.

Outside, Rob Lefferts asked her to read from David Goodis's *Dark Passage*. He offered her a job reading books for an audio cassette series. [*Rose Madder*]

25 May 1997

Stephen King started *Bag of Bones*.

25 May 2010, Tuesday

Bill Hodges tore down the letter from Mr. Mercedes. It was authentic, from the killer. Bill profiled Mr. Mercedes as educated and younger than fifty. He used digits for numbers, instead of spelling them out, and used 'perk' for 'perp.' Later, Bill looked up articles on The Mercedes Killer. On the Monday after the attack, *The City News* published the photo of the smiley face found on the steering wheel. The letter from Mr. Mercedes and its envelope each had the same smiley face (with sunglasses and showing teeth). [*Mr. Mercedes*]

Blockade Billy (Scribner, $14.99) published with a first printing of 500,000 copies (collected in *The Bazaar of Bad Dreams*)

25 May 2015, Memorial Day

Alden McCausland and his mother took the Close Encounters of the Fourth Kind to their cabin at the lake. ["Drunken Fireworks"]

May 26

26 May 1979, Saturday

The Castle Rock *Call* reported the collapse of the northeastern corner of the Castle View Recreational Park. Sheriff George Bannerman said they needed more investigation to find out if the destruction was natural or man-made. [*Gwendy's Button Box*]

26 May 1985

Richard Bachman's *Thinner* dropped to number 7 on *The New York Times* Fiction Best Seller List, its thirteenth week on the List.

26 May 1994, Thursday

Anna Stevenson from Daughters and Sisters had found Rose McClendon a room at 897 Trenton Street for $320 a month. Rose moved in. [*Rose Madder*]

26 May 1996

The Green Mile, Part One: The Two Dead Girls dropped to number 3 on *The New York Times* Paperback Fiction Best Seller List, its seventh week on the List.

The Green Mile, Part Two: The Mouse on the Mile stayed at number 1 on *The New York Times* Paperback Fiction Best Seller List, its third week on the List.

26 May 2002

Everything's Eventual stayed at number 8 on *The New York Times* Fiction Best Seller List, its eighth week on the List.

26 May 2010, Wednesday

A game warden found bones in an old gravel pit less than two miles from Donnie Davis's summer cabin. Later, the body was identified as Sheila Davis.

Bill Hodges drove around then parked opposite the late Mrs. Trelawney's house at 729 Lilac Drive. Later, private security officer Radney Peeples asked why he was sitting there so long. Hodges, a retired police detective, struck up a rapport with Peeples and learned about Mrs. Trelawney's sister. That evening, he called Directory Assistance for Janelle Patterson's phone number. He called her and set up an appointment for the next day. [*Mr. Mercedes*]

May 27

27 May 1975

David Bright's article, "JOHN SMITH, MODERN RIP VAN WINKLE, FACES LONG ROAD BACK," appeared on Page One of the Bangor *Daily News*. [*The Dead Zone*]

27 May 1979

Investigators from Portland were expected in Castle Rock to help investigate the collapse of part of the Castle View Recreational Park. [*Gwendy's Button Box*]

Prom Night: Tommy Ross took Carrie White to the Ewen High 1979 Spring Ball. Carrie began to feel she fit in with others. Third on the Spring Ball King and Queen ballot, Carrie and Tommy voted for themselves. For the first time in Spring Ball history, there was a tie; two couples each had sixty-three votes. Carrie and Tommy beat Jessica MacLean and Frank Greer in a tiebreaker. At the King and Queen crowning, Chris Hargensen dumped pig blood on them. A bucket hit Tommy in the head and killed him. Carrie's telekinesis became violent; she was the Angel's Fiery Sword. An electrical fire and an oil-tank explosion burned the school. Destruction followed Carrie home. Teddy's Amoco and Tony's Citgo exploded. A gas main explosion wiped out West End. Fire consumed Chamberlain Center and the north side of Carlin Street. Carrie's house, the Carlin Street Congregational Church, the Chamberlain *Clarion* office, the billiard parlor, the Blue Ribbon Laundry, Duffy's Bar and Grille, the Kelly Fruit Company, Woolworths, and much of the business district burned. 440–458 people died, including 67 of 119 high school seniors expecting to graduate. Just twelve people who went to the Spring Ball lived. [*Carrie*]

27 May 1980, Tuesday: Castle Rock High School Graduation

After the ceremony, Gwendy Peterson and Harry Streeter went to Gwendy's to change for a party at Brigette Desjardin's. Gwendy's parents had gone to a neighbor's for dinner, so she thought it odd that the front door was slightly open. They didn't notice it had been jimmied. In her bedroom, Gwendy and Harry made love for half an hour. When Gwendy opened the closet to dress, Frankie Stone pulled her in. Harry, thirty pounds heavier, wrestled Stone to the floor. Frankie kneed him in the crotch, jabbed his fingers in Harry's eyes, and bludgeoned him to death with Gwendy's button box. To keep Frankie from pushing a button, Gwendy opened her bra. At knifepoint, he told her to get on the bed; he wanted to cut off her panties. She struck out with her leg. The knife pierced her foot; her kick knocked Stone into the closet. She grabbed her button box, hit the red button, and told Frankie to rot in hell; he decayed in front of her. She couldn't explain that so she hit the red button while imagining him gone; his remains disappeared. Later, she told the police he ran away. [*Gwendy's Button Box*]

27 May 1984

Pet Sematary stayed at number 12 on *The New York Times* Fiction Best Seller List, its thirtieth week on the List.

27 May 1985

Fifth-grader Jerry Bellwood's body was found in pieces near Kansas Street in Derry, ME. On a nearby wall, "Come Home" was written three times in his blood—a message to the Losers. [*IT*]

27 May 1988

Tom Carroll retired from the University of Maine English Department. [*The Dark Half*]

27 May 1990

The Stand: The Complete & Uncut Edition dropped to number 2 on *The New York Times* Fiction Best Seller List, its third week on the List.

27 May 2001

Dreamcatcher dropped to number 5 on *The New York Times* Fiction Best Seller List, its eighth week on the List.

27 May 2010, Thursday

10:00 a.m.: Bill Hodges hoped to persuade Janelle Patterson to help him. She was eager to have him involved; the police didn't seem to care about who drove her sister to suicide. She showed him a two-page letter her sister had received. Similar to the note Hodges had received, it had a smiley-face with sunglasses, and the font was American Typewriter. Again, the writer used 'perk' for 'perp,' and all compound words had hyphens. Mrs. Patterson told him Mrs. Trelawney suffered from anxiety and was obsessive-compulsive. Bill began to doubt Mrs. Trelawney had left her key in her car.

~4:00 p.m.: At home, Bill and his handyman, Jerome Robinson, went to Under Debbie's Blue Umbrella. He asked Jerome to research the site to see whether it was real or set up just for him. While walking to the shopping center for ice cream cones, Bill made up a story about a car that wasn't broken into but was moved without the owner's knowledge. Jerome knew it was about The Mercedes Killer. He told Hodges his mother had never known her spare car key was with the car's documentation in the glove compartment. Even if Mrs. Trelawney's key had been in the glove compartment, Bill thought, how did the thief take it from the locked car?

That evening, Jerome got back to Hodges. Under Debbie's Blue Umbrella was an Extreme Privacy site, where everything was encrypted. If someone had set up a username for Bill, then that someone had paid the first $30 monthly fee. [*Mr. Mercedes*]

27 May 2012

The Dark Tower 4.5: The Wind Through the Keyhole dropped to number 8 on *The New York Times* Fiction Best Seller List, its third week on the List.

May 28

28 May 1957

Dorsey Corcoran's stepfather, Richard P. Macklin, fractured Dorsey's skull with a hammer. At Derry Home Hospital, Macklin said the boy fell from a step ladder in the garage. Three days later, never regaining consciousness, Dorsey died. [*IT*]

28 May 1975

Raymond Ruopp, the surgeon who started the technology of lengthening human ligaments with plastic ones, operated on Johnny Smith. [*The Dead Zone*]

28 May 1979

When Carrie White returned home after Prom Night, Margaret White tried to kill her, stabbing her in the shoulder. Carrie stopped her mother's heart then left home. Outside The Cavalier, Billy Nolan and Chris Hargensen tried to run her down. She caused his car to crash into the tavern, killing Billy and Chris. Sue Snell found Carrie, weak from her stab wound. They exchanged thoughts without talking. Carrie said Sue and the others tricked her. Again. Sue invited Carrie to look inside her, to see that Sue hadn't done this to her. They were linked when Carrie died. Ambulance #16 took her to Westover Mercy Hospital, where Harold Kuebler, M.D., pronounced her DOA. FM did her autopsy, which showed abnormal brain tissue, and RM wrote the hospital's death record. [*Carrie*]

Many Castle Rock High School teachers and students attended Olive Kepnes's funeral. After the graveside service, Mr. Kepnes told Gwendy Peterson everything would be OK. [*Gwendy's Button Box*]

28 May 1980, Wednesday morning

Gwendy Peterson and Harry Streeter had planned to leave for a weeklong camping trip at Casco Bay. [*Gwendy's Button Box*]

28 May 1985

Mike Hanlon felt the nine IT-type murders between July 1984 and May 1985 were enough to call the other Losers. A picture from Georgie Denbrough's photo album was found near Dennis Torrio's body. Mike called Richie Tozier, Stan Uris, Ben Hanscom, and Eddie Kaspbrak. Ben, Eddie, and Richie left for Maine. Stan committed suicide; in blood on the bathroom wall, he wrote, "IT." In 1958, he was the only one who knew IT was pregnant. [*IT*]

28 May 2001, Monday, Memorial Day

Jonesy watched fireworks. [*Dreamcatcher*]

28 May 2003

Wordslinger's Note to *The Dark Tower VI: Song of Susannah*

28 May 2008

Sheila Bonsaint LeClair wrote to Charlie Keen. She was sure her brother's death was suicide and asked Charlie to read the late Johnny Bonsaint's manuscript about N. Its folder was marked, "BURN THIS." ["N."]

28 May 2009

The Stand: American Nightmares #3 of 5 (Marvel Comics, $3.99) published

28 May 2010, Friday

Bill Hodges left a message for Mr. Mercedes on Under Debbie's Blue Umbrella. Withheld evidence showed that merckill (username for Mr. Mercedes) was not the killer.

Brady Hartsfield was furious that Hodges didn't believe he was The Mercedes Killer. He wanted to hurt Hodges indirectly, perhaps by poisoning Odell, Jerome Robinson's dog. In response, Brady reminded Hodges about the bleach used to clean the Mercedes and the hairnet left in the car. The media hadn't reported those.

Donnie Davis turned himself in for killing his wife. He also confessed to the Turnpike Joe killings. Turnpike Joe was the name given to a serial killer who had raped and murdered five women, from 1994 to 2008, at rest stops from the Midwest to Pennsylvania.

Bill Hodges and Janelle Patterson visited Mrs. Elizabeth Wharton, Janelle and Mrs. Trelawney's mother. She said that Livvy (Mrs. Trelawney) had a pen pal, Frankie, who made her stop taking her pills. Frankie said he had taken the same meds, and they caused him to kill those people. Livvy killed herself because of the ghosts. Baby Patricia cried in the night, and the baby's mother accused Livvy and screamed, "Why did you let him murder my baby!"

Hodges left another message for Mr. Mercedes. Again, merckill couldn't be the killer; otherwise, he would have mentioned the valet key. Hodges told him to watch the news. The guy who confessed to killing his wife would also admit to the City Center Massacre.

Enraged at Bill Hodges's message, Brady Hartsfield responded that there was no key in the ignition and no valet key, only the spare in the glove compartment. He left it as an exercise for Bill to figure out how he had gotten into the car. [*Mr. Mercedes*]

May 29

29 May 1963

<u>unaltered timeline</u>: Sadie Dunhill had been discharged from the hospital. "JODIE LIBRAR-IAN LEAVES HOSPITAL," appeared on page 20 of the Dallas *Morning News*. [*11/22/63*]

29 May 1976

A front-page article in the Portland *Press-Herald* reported that Daniel Holloway, his wife, and their two children had disappeared a month after moving to Taggart Stream Road in Jerusalem's Lot. His grandfather had become concerned when the Holloways stopped answering his calls. [*'Salem's Lot*]

29 May 1983

Christine stayed at number 2 on *The New York Times* Fiction Best Seller List, its eighth week on the List.

29 May 1985

Mike Hanlon called Bill Denbrough and Beverly Rogan. Bill hadn't stuttered for twenty-one years. He started again after Mike called him in England. Immediately, he went back to Derry, ME, checking in to Room 311 of the Derry Town House. As Beverly prepared to leave for Derry, Tom Rogan beat her with a belt and his fists. She surprised him by throwing makeup and toiletries at him and overturning a vanity cabinet on him. She left before he got his second wind. Late that night, she checked in to the Derry Town House, Room 518.

Henry Bowers heard the voices of Victor Criss and Belch Huggins coming from the moon. IT told him the Losers were coming back, and, because he was the only one left alive, he must kill them. [*IT*]

29 May 1994, Sunday

Norman Daniels had more than thirty off-days, which he decided to use to find his wife. [*Rose Madder*]

29 May 2000

Stephen King finished *Dreamcatcher* in Lovell, ME.

29 May 2002

Author's Note to *From a Buick 8*

29 May 2010, Saturday

Bill Hodges left a message for Mr. Mercedes on Under Debbie's Blue Umbrella. He lied that it wasn't the spare key because Mrs. Trelawney had both keys. The valet key under the bumper was missing, however.

Brady had a rough plan. He'd kill Odell with Gopher-Go, let Bill Hodges stew a bit before killing him, and then go out in a terrorist act at the 'Round Here concert at the MAC.

Jerome Robinson explained to Bill Hodges that modern car keys are part of Passive Keyless Entry (PKE) systems. Instead of putting the key into the lock, the operator pushed a button to lock the car, and another to unlock it. For about $100, a person could build a device to capture the code when somebody used their key.

Mrs. Elizabeth Wharton, Mrs. Olivia Trelawney's mother, died. Family—Charlotte Gibney, Holly Gibney, and Henry Sirois—arrived. Janey Patterson reserved rooms for them at the Holiday Inn.

That evening, Brady mixed two cups of Gopher-Go into a pound of ground beef. He put it in a mini fridge in the garage. [*Mr. Mercedes*]

29 May 2012

the June/July issue (Vol. 157, No. 6 & 7) of *Esquire*, with part 1 (of 2) of "In the Tall Grass," a Stephen King-Joe Hill short-story collaboration, published

May 30

30 May 1938

The *Bakersfield Journal* listed Crysilda Berryman's marriage to Carl Wilkes. She became Crysilda Wilkes, mother of Annie. [*Misery*]

30 May 1985, The Reunion

2:04 a.m.: IT killed John Koontz and freed Henry Bowers from Juniper Hill. Bowers hid near Route 9 during the day then got a ride. When he got close to Derry, ME, he killed the old man who gave him a ride. IT told him where to get his old clothes and switchblade.

Tom Rogan followed Beverly Rogan to Maine. In Bangor, he used the name Mr. Barr to buy a car.

Bill Denbrough bought Silver, his childhood bicycle, for $20 at Secondhand Rose, Secondhand Clothes at the bottom of Up-Mile Hill on Kansas Street. At Mike Hanlon's, he got it running again, complete with Bicycle playing cards and clothespins.

Audra Denbrough followed Bill from Fleet, England, to Derry.

The Losers met in a private room at Jade of the Orient, a restaurant on Mall Road in Derry. Mike Hanlon brought them up to date on why he thought IT was active again. They decided to try again to kill IT. Before leaving, they opened their fortune cookies and found messages from IT. That night at the library, they refreshed their memories about the events of summer 1958. Their hands bled from the 1958 Coke bottle cuts. They re-formed their circle, felt a power, and remembered everything about IT and Derry. [*IT*]

30 May 1994, Monday

Rose McClendon started her new job earning $120 a day reading for "Women in Disguise," an Audio Concepts unabridged audio series. Richard Racine's *The Manta Ray* was her first book. Trying not to vomit after many beatings from her husband had given her excellent breath control.

Dusk: After compelling Peter Slowik into telling him he referred Rose to Daughters and Sisters, Norman Daniels bit Slowik more than eighty times. [*Rose Madder*]

30 May 1996

The Green Mile, Part Three: Coffey's Hands (Signet, $2.99) published with a first printing of 2,000,000 copies

30 May 1999

The Girl Who Loved Tom Gordon stayed at number 4 on *The New York Times* Fiction Best Seller List, its sixth week on the List.

30 May 2007

At on Old-Time Tent Revival show in St. Louis, MO, Evangelist C. Danny Jacobs healed Robert Rivard of his Muscular Dystrophy. [*Revival*]

30 May 2010, Sunday

Bill Hodges, Janey Patterson, Charlotte Gibney, Holly Gibney, and Henry Sirois had breakfast at the Holiday Inn's buffet. Henry and the Gibneys stayed at Mrs. Trelawney's place for the rest of the time they were in town for Elizabeth Wharton's funeral.

afternoon: Brady Hartsfield sold Mr. Tastey products at the Little League games at McGinnis Park. When he returned home, he saw his mother had fixed herself a hamburger with mayonnaise. Half his strychnine-laced meat was in the kitchen refrigerator. His mother had found it in the garage. Having gotten drunk first, she hadn't noticed it tasted wrong. Brady found her dying on the couch. He couldn't call 911, so he went downstairs to wait for her to die. [*Mr. Mercedes*]

30 May 2014, Friday

Peter Saubers went to Drew Halliday's bookshop without the notebooks. He wanted Drew's number from consulting potential buyers. $30,000 wasn't enough, so he'd only agree to a 70–30 split. Halliday said he knew who he was and knew much about his family. He threatened to turn Pete and his family in to the police. Pete could save himself and his family by turning over all the notebooks. Pete countered. The police would believe his parents had nothing to do with it. Not much would happen to Pete, either; he was a minor and wasn't even born when the notebooks were stolen. Pete knew Halliday had taken out a third mortgage on his bookshop. If Halliday turned him in, Halliday would lose a large payday. It was just a matter of time before the bank took the shop. Pete left to think; he said he'd return the following Friday. [*Finders Keepers*]

May 31

31 May 1977

Jake Chambers attended The Piper School, a prestigious, private, middle school in New York City. Bonita Avery gave him an A+ on *My Understanding of the Truth*, his English Comp Final Essay, which contributed 25% to the semester's grade. Piper School students didn't ask to go to the bathroom; they asked to step out. He stepped out, left the school, and wandered around the city, missing his French final. Near the corner of Fifty-Fourth Street and Lexington Avenue, he realized the voices in his head had stopped. *ka* led him to a Second Avenue bookstore. Calvin Tower sold *Charlie the Choo-Choo* by Beryl Evans and *Riddle-De-Dum! Brain Twisters for Everyone* to him for $7 plus tax. The Evans book was an old fourth-printing copy; the riddle book was free for Jake, the boy whom Tower said was going to "light out for the territories." During the transaction, Tower mentioned the Donald M. Grant editions of books. *ka* led Jake to the corner of Second Avenue and Forty-Sixth Street. He expected Tom and Gerry's Artistic Deli would be the door to Roland's world. Instead, he found a boarded, vacant lot where the deli used to be. Inside, he found a key, a single growing rose, a Turtle Bay Luxury Condominiums sign, and graffiti highlighting a Turtle and a Beam. The rose opened and showed him light from many suns. He touched it. Six hours later, he woke up and found a brick with blood on it. He took the key and went home. That night, he dreamed of a young Eddie Dean, who told him to go to Co-Op City at 3:00 p.m. the next day. Eddie would lead him to a portal to Roland's world. [*The Dark Tower III: The Waste Lands*][*The Dark Tower V: Wolves of the Calla*]

Todash Number One: After eating muffin-balls near Calla Bryn Sturgis, Jake Chambers went todash—a passing between worlds—and found himself back in New York City with Oy. In Mid-World, only a dull gray glow remained where his body had been. He turned the corner from Fifty-Fourth Street onto Second Avenue and greeted Eddie Dean. They felt something wasn't right; although they were in bright sunlight, it just seemed dark in a way. When going todash, they were mostly in New York but not entirely. New Yorkers couldn't see them but, sometimes, could sense them. Jake and Oy saw the Jake of 1977 walk past them on his way to The Manhattan Restaurant of the Mind. They followed him and saw him buy *Charlie the Choo-Choo*, by Claudia y Inez Bachman (nineteen letters), yet they remembered Beryl Evans had written the book. They thought Calvin Tower's TODAY'S SPECIALS sign differed from when Jake went there on 31 May 1977 the first time. They followed Jake out of the store then went back in when Enrico Balazar, Jack Andolini, and George Biondi showed up. Because they weren't there physically, they could walk through the locked door to the backroom. They learned that Calvin Tower owned the vacant lot with the rose. [*The Dark Tower V: Wolves of the Calla*]

~31 May 1977

"TWO MEN FOUND SHOT TO DEATH IN CONEY ISLAND. COPS SAY 'IT LOOKS LIKE A MOB JOB,'" appeared in the New York *Post*. The Hitler Brothers had been killed, with their hands and faces burned with acid (for failing to kill Donald Callahan). [*The Dark Tower V: Wolves of the Calla*]

31 May 1985

~2:15 a.m.: Henry Bowers and Mike Hanlon fought at the Derry Public Library. Bowers stabbed Mike in the thigh and right hand. Mike bloodied Henry's nose and cut him in the forearm and across the chest. Mike's letter opener broke in Bowers's stomach when he lunged at Mike. IT, as a dead, decaying Belch Huggins, drove Bowers to the Derry Town House in a 1958 red and white Plymouth Fury. In a fight with Eddie Kaspbrak, Henry broke Eddie's arm, and Eddie stabbed him in the stomach with a broken Perrier bottle. Bowers died.

Eddie and the remaining Losers (Bill Denbrough, Ben Hanscom, Beverly Marsh, and Richie Tozier) went to kill IT. Beyond the small, three-foot-high door, the Ritual of Chüd began again. Bill missed IT's tongue; his consciousness was hurled toward the deadlights, where the real IT was. Richie grabbed IT's tongue and was thrown after Bill; he grabbed Bill's hand. He used his voices on IT, hurting IT until IT brought them back. Eddie squirted his aspirator on IT; he died after IT bit off his right arm. Bill, Ben, and Richie ran after the dying, bleeding IT. They found some of IT's miscarriaged eggs. Ben stayed to crush the eggs and the rat-sized baby ITs. Knowing IT's young were dying, IT stopped to fight. With power from the Final Other, Bill forced his body into IT's body, found IT's heart and crushed it. While IT was hurt and dying, Derry suffered severe storms, with hurricane-like weather, and an earthquake. Some of downtown Derry fell into a hole. During the next two weeks, the hole got bigger, and more of Derry fell in. Sixty-seven people died, 320 were injured.

Audra Denbrough had gone to Derry Town House to find Bill. Tom Rogan had taken her to IT; he died when he saw IT in IT's pure form. The Losers found Audra, catatonic, wrapped in silk in IT's web. Bill sent her to the hospital. [*IT*]

Beaver Clarendon was attending a junior college in downstate Maine. Henry Devlin was at Harvard. Jonesy was in finals week. Pete Moore was bumming around the West Coast. [*Dreamcatcher*]

31 May 1987

The Eyes of the Dragon stayed at number 6 on *The New York Times* Fiction Best Seller List, its eighteenth week on the List.

31 May 1988, Tuesday, 8:00 p.m.

Thad and Liz Beaumont threw a retirement party for Tom Carroll. [*The Dark Half*]

31 May 1994, Tuesday

For $50 at Elaine's Dreams, Rose McClendon changed her hair color and style to match Rose Madder's blond, plaited hair. [*Rose Madder*]

31 May 2008

Sheila Bonsaint LeClair wrote a second letter to Charlie Keen, telling him to burn Johnny Bonsaint's manuscript instead of reading it. For closure with Johnny's death, she had gone to Ackerman's Field. In the letter, she counted things. ["N."]

31 May 2010, Monday

Brady Hartsfield saw Mrs. Elizabeth Wharton's obituary in the paper.

Janelle Patterson gave Bill Hodges a brown fedora because he was her private detective. [*Mr. Mercedes*]

May

May 1905

Amsel Bickford, Andy DeLesseps, Davey Hartwell, and Claude Heroux tried to organize a union for Maine's lumbermen, but the loggers strongly opposed unions. They checked in to the Brentwood Arms Hotel in Derry, ME. Richard Bowie, William Mueller, and Hamilton Tracker took part in violence that resulted in the disappearance of DeLesseps and the deaths of Bickford and Hartwell. Bickford's body was found in the Kenduskeag River with his head axed off. Hartwell's body, minus his legs, was also found in the river. [*IT*]

May 1923

The Overlook Hotel opened under the new management of Texas cattle and oil men Cecil Brandywine and Clyde Brandywine. ["Before the Play"]

May 1931

Sheriff Catlett and three deputies beat up Wild Bill Wharton for trying to molest a nine-year-old girl. [*The Green Mile*]

May 1938

In 1994, writer Sam Landry thought he'd be happier in 1930s Los Angeles. Typing on his computer, he physically entered *Umney's Last Case* in May 1938 to replace Private Detective Clyde Umney. He walked into Umney's office, bought the business for $5,000, and then wrote Umney out of town. Umney woke up as Samuel D. Landry in 1994. He didn't like his new world. He learned how to use Landry's laptop word processor so he could write himself back to 1930s Los Angeles and kill Landry. ["Umney's Last Case"]

May 1957

Joe DiPunno, manager of the New Jersey Titans, learned that Billy Blakely, their new star catcher wasn't Billy Blakely, but Gene Katsanis, a hired hand on the Blakely farm. Katsanis had killed the Blakelys and played with the Titans as Billy.

Home plate umpire Hi Wenders made a bad call in the top of the sixth inning against the White Sox, a call that may have lost the game. Spurred on by pitcher Danny Doo's recent bad-mouthing of Wenders and the crowd's chanting, "KILL THE UMP, KILL THE UMP," Katsanis slit Wenders's throat after the game. Proud of himself for preventing more bad calls from Wenders, he didn't flee. In Essex County Jail, awaiting extradition to Iowa, he swallowed a bar of soap and choked to death. Every Titans game he played was canceled out. The Titans made them up in doubleheaders the rest of the season. [*Blockade Billy*]

May 1958

At Kitchener Ironworks, Mike Hanlon saw IT as Rodan, a bird-monster he had seen in a movie the night before. He ran away, and the bird followed, pecking his head. Rodan grabbed and lifted him until he shook free and hid in a fallen smokestack. He hit the bird in the eye with a piece of broken tile when the bird tried to squeeze in after him. He stayed until the bird left. [*IT*]

May 1963

The Man Who Loved Flowers killed his sixth victim on Seventy-Third Street near Third Avenue in New York. He bought flowers for his victims then bludgeoned them with a hammer when he found out they weren't Norma. ["The Man Who Loved Flowers"]

May 1969

Andy McGee graduated from Harrison State College, third of the English majors, fortieth in his class of 506. [*Firestarter*]

May 1973

Ben Mears hit a wet spot while riding his motorcycle with Miranda Mears in New York. Miranda was killed when they slid into a yellow moving van; Ben wasn't hurt. Because of a Breathalyzer test, tabloids incorrectly reported he was drunk. He never rode again. ['*Salem's Lot*]

May 1975

"The Lawnmower Man" (collected in *Night Shift*) appeared in the May issue (Vol. 25, No. 7) of *Cavalier*.

May 1976

Charlie Decker shot and killed Mrs. Underwood and Mr. Vance. He and the Algebra II students talked freely about personal things they normally wouldn't share. Maine State Police sharpshooter Daniel Malvern shot him through the window. The bullet hit Titus, The Helpful Padlock, in his breast pocket over his heart. The shot knocked him down and knocked the wind out of him. He let Irma Bates go to the bathroom; she came back. The class gave Ted Jones much oral and some physical abuse. After Charlie let the class leave, Frank Philbrick came in and shot him three times when Charlie pretended to grab something from behind a plant. [*Rage*]

"Weeds" appeared in the May issue (Vol. 26, No. 7) of *Cavalier*.

May 1978

Roland LeBay put Christine with a For Sale sign on his front lawn. [*Christine*]

May 1980

An amber-eyed, growling monster in Tad Trenton's closet identified itself as Frank Dodd. [*Cujo*]

May 1984

Saturday, full moon: The Beast disemboweled and killed Clyde Corliss in Grace Baptist Church. [*Cycle of the Werewolf*]

"Mrs. Todd's Shortcut" (collected in *Skeleton Crew*) appeared in the May issue (Volume 163, Number 1) of *Redbook*.

May 1985

Norman Daniels punched Rose Daniels in the stomach three times for reading Paul Sheldon's *Misery's Journey*. Caroline Daniels, with whom Rose was four months pregnant, died in a miscarriage. [*Rose Madder*]

"Dolan's Cadillac," part 5 of 5 (collected in *Nightmares & Dreamscapes*), appeared in the May 1985 issue (Vol. 1, No. 5) of *Castle Rock: The Stephen King Newsletter*.

May 1987

In Nassau, William Wilson taped two pounds of cocaine under Eddie Dean's arms. Organized crime figure Enrico Balazar had sent Eddie Dean to smuggle the cocaine into the US. Eddie was to give it to his brother, Henry Dean, who was to give it to Balazar. In seat 3A on Delta Flight 901 to New York, Roland entered his mind. Flight attendant Jane Dorning, suspicious that Eddie was a terrorist or a smuggler, voiced her concerns to Captain McDonald, who alerted Federal Customs agents. On landing, Roland had Eddie go through the door to Roland's world, drop the cocaine, and come back. Federal Customs agents picked him up at Kennedy International Airport but let him go two hours later when they couldn't find any drugs.

Balazar, concerned that Eddie left Nassau with the cocaine but arrived in New York without it, sent some men to talk with Henry Dean and sent Jack Andolini and Col Vincent to get Eddie. Balazar's men gave Henry a heroin overdose, unintentionally killing him. Back at Balazar's office, Jack Andolini and Claudio Andolini (Jack's brother) took Eddie/Roland into the bathroom to search him, including a cavity search. Eddie/Roland pulled Jack Andolini into Roland's world. After losing a fight, Andolini ran toward the ocean. The lobstrosities killed him. Eddie and Roland returned to Balazar's office, separately.

In a shootout, Eddie shot Balazar in the shoulder with Roland's gun; Balazar shot Eddie in the left arm. Tricks Postino killed Dario by mistake with The Wonderful Rambo Machine, his M-16. Eddie killed George Biondi and Postino. Biondi fell on Rudy Vechhio and broke three of Vechhio's ribs. Roland shot and killed Balazar and several of his men, including Claudio Andolini, 'Cimi Dretto, and Jimmy Haspio. After the shootout, Kevin Blake gave Henry Dean's head to Eddie. Roland shot and killed him in the doorway of Balazar's office. Eddie and Roland went to Roland's world. [*The Dark Tower II: The Drawing of the Three*]

The Dark Tower II: The Drawing of the Three (Donald M. Grant, $35) published with a first printing of 30,000 copies

May 1990

Daniel Landry knocked himself unconscious when he fell off a park swing. The hospital gave him a pint of AIDS-infected blood. ["Umney's Last Case"]

The Stand: The Complete & Uncut Edition (Doubleday, $24.95) published with a first printing of 400,000 to 900,000 copies

May 1992

Gerald's Game (Viking, $23.50) published with a first printing of 1,500,000 copies

May 2005

Transgressions: Ten Brand-New Novellas, edited by Ed McBain (Forge Books, $27.95), with "The Things They Left Behind" (collected in *Just After Sunset*), published

May 2007

N. had nightmares about CTHUN, a monster with a helmet head he had seen at Ackerman's Field. The dream reminded him he'd been neglecting his duties. In his house, he arranged things in crop circles to keep the force that attacks thin places at bay.

5:00 a.m.: N. woke after another nightmare and drove to Ackerman's Field. He touched all eight stones; the darkness in the center was gone. ["N."]

May 2008

Evangelist C. Danny Jacobs healed Mabel Jergens of her spinal cord injury at a revival show in Albuquerque, NM. [*Revival*]

May 2014

Every five years, Miss Cora Ann Hooper appeared at Morris Bellamy's parole hearings. Because Miss Hooper still suffered, Bellamy was denied parole. In an off-year hearing in 2014, the Parole Board granted his parole. Miss Hooper had cancer and no longer objected.

Morris moved into a room on the ninth floor of an old apartment building. A job had been arranged; he started working as a part-time file clerk and computer operator at the Midwest Culture and Arts Center (MAC). Ellis McFarland was his Parole Officer.

Bellamy went to the stream in the undeveloped land behind his old house. He dug enough to see the trunk was still there. [*Finders Keepers*]

May 2015

Brady Hartsfield wanted to use Zappits to persuade kids who had gone to the 'Round Here concert to kill themselves. He had Dr. Babineau set up a Gamez Unlimited bank account and fund it with $150,000. The money bought $80,000 worth of Zappits and a new apartment and expensive computer equipment for Freddi Linklatter. The Zappits would be sent to her new apartment, and she'd used the computer equipment to install rootkits on them. When activated, a repeater would search for active Zappits and download a program to them. The program modified the Fishin' Hole demo screen to provide pink number-fish, blue flashes with subliminal messages directing users to zeetheend.com, and a self-destruct mechanism that waited for the user to start it. Dr. Z brought her a thumb drive for her to set up zeetheend.com, a suicide website.

Krista Countryman and Keith Frias had planned to marry, but they had committed suicide three months earlier. [*End of Watch*]

June
Happenings

June 1

1 June 1910, Wednesday

After two years of high-expense construction, Bob T. Watson's Overlook Hotel had its Grand Opening. A chef scalded his arm, a woman fainted at the ribbon-cutting ceremony, Mrs. Arkinbauer slipped in a bathroom and broke her wrist, and a Congressman (whom Bob T. Watson had bribed to build the hotel) choked on a piece of meat and died. ["Before the Play"]

1–2 June 1979

Prom Night's dead were buried in three ceremonies over two days. [*Carrie*]

1 June 1982

"HEAD MATERNITY NURSE QUESTIONED IN INFANT DEATHS," Michael Leith's article in the Denver *Post*, reported that Annie Wilkes was questioned about baby deaths in Boulder Hospital then released. [*Misery*]

1 June 1985

Bryant Gumble of ABC's *Today* show interviewed Andrew Keene about his seeing the Derry Standpipe collapse the previous morning (while IT was dying). [*IT*]

1 June 1977

Skipping school, Jake Chambers bought a sausage and a soda at Broadway and Forty-Second. A cop stopped him. He pulled out the key he found in the vacant lot and said his name was Tom Denby (Denby's Discount Drug was across the street). The cop let him go. He took the subway to the Castle Avenue and Brooklyn Avenue station in Brooklyn's Co-Op City. Brooklyn Avenue led him to Markey Avenue, where Eddie Dean and Henry Dean, as children, passed him. He followed them to the Markey Avenue playground, where they played basketball outside their apartment. Henry then took Eddie to The Mansion, a haunted house on Rhinehold Street in Dutch Hill. Jake followed and waited for them to leave before he went in. In the kitchen doorway, two large, bloated spiders dropped on his head; one bit his neck. He found a door labeled THE BOY, but The Mansion began collapsing into itself, forming a large face with long arms. This doorkeeper reached for him. He opened the door but dirt blocked his way until the adult Eddie Dean opened the door from the other side—from Roland's world. The doorkeeper grabbed him and dragged him. Roland jumped in and saved him with a Demon that occupied the area on Roland's side. The Demon lodged in the doorkeeper's throat, causing it to drop Jake. The voices and Jake's insanity were gone, but his neck became infected from the spider bite. [*The Dark Tower III: The Waste Lands*]

1 June 1988, Wednesday, ~12:45 a.m.

Dolly Arsenault saw Homer Gamache pick up a strange hitchhiker in a suit and tie. George Stark beat Homer to death with Homer's artificial arm. Stark took Gamache's truck and abandoned it in Connecticut. On his way home from fishing Strimmer's Brook, Frank Gavineaux found Gamache's body. He told his mother, who called the sheriff. [*The Dark Half*]

1 June 1993

Insomniac Ralph Roberts's wake-up time was 4:30–4:45 a.m., with about five to five and a quarter hours' sleep. [*Insomnia*]

1 June 1994, Wednesday

In the Hot Pot, Norman Daniels saw Rose McClendon, his wife, from behind but didn't recognize her new slim, blond look. [*Rose Madder*]

1 June 1999

1:19 p.m.: Susannah Dean and Mia appeared at the corner of Second Avenue and Forty-Sixth Street. Susannah's body grew legs as Mia became dominant. After Mia took Trudy Damascus's bag of shoes, they went to a small park across Second Avenue. The chap had been ready for birth since leaving Calla Bryn Sturgis; Mia held off the labor awhile then Susannah did. Susannah, sitting on a park bench, found an old, ivory turtle in a Velcro pocket in Black Thirteen's bowling bag.

Susannah used the turtle to hypnotize Mr. Mathiessen van Wyck, a Swedish businessman. She commanded him to rent a room at the New York Park-Plaza Hyatt on the corner of First Avenue and Forty-Sixth Street. After giving him enough time to do so, Susannah/Mia went to the hotel, Room 1919. They stashed Black Thirteen and their Oriza plates then palavered while they waited for the phone to ring. Richard P. Sayer told Mia to go to the Dixie Pig at Lexington Avenue and Sixty-First Street.

Mia took full control and led them to The Dixie Pig, where Richard P. Sayre and about seventy-five low men, low women, and vampires were waiting. They were escorted to the Arc 16 Experimental Station in Fedic. Mia's life force was separated out of Susannah, into Mia's body, lying in a bed. Susannah was in the next bed. Steel hoods, connected by a steel hose, were placed on Mia and Susannah to finish transferring the baby from Susannah to Mia. Mordred was born.

evening: Without Black Thirteen (Mia and Susannah had taken it) Roland, Eddie Dean, Jake Chambers, Pere Callahan, and Oy enlisted the Manni to help open the Unfound Door so they could follow Susannah and Mia. The Pere, Jake, and Oy found themselves in New York City on June 1st. They went to the Park-Plaza Hotel, where Stephen King had left them an envelope with a key to Room 1919. They retrieved Black Thirteen from the closet and nineteen Oriza plates from the safe. Later, Oy found a little turtle, which Susannah had dropped for them, outside The Dixie Pig restaurant on the corner of Lexington Avenue and Fifty-Ninth Street. They drew their weapons and went in. [*The Dark Tower VI: Song of Susannah*]

Pere Callahan kept the low men, low women, and Type Three Vampires busy while Jake Chambers and Oy made their way to the kitchen. With 'Riza plates, Jake killed cat-thing and the menacing-looking Chef Warthog. Three more plates killed three low men. Jochabim, who had been washing dishes, told Jake to "mind the mind trap."

Susannah Dean had been through the kitchen. Oy tracked her into a pantry, through a door in the corner, down a long flight of more than 120 stairs, across a lobby, and into a corridor. In the lobby, a sign said tickets were still available for 9/11/2001. To Jake, the corridor appeared as the jungle with a triceratops from *The Lost Continent*, a movie he had seen on TV. When Jake realized it was the mind trap and it didn't affect Oy, he and Oy exchanged places. Oy, in Jake's body, carried him. When they got through the trap, they switched back.

Flaherty, Lamla, and fifteen low men and vampires followed. At the end of the corridor was New York/Fedic door #9. He called to Susannah, who told him the password: *chassit.* The door opened and Susannah pulled Jake and Oy in. The door closed; Flaherty and the others couldn't open it.

With the touch, Jake told Roland Deschain where they were. [*The Dark Tower VII: The Dark Tower*]

1 June 2007

N. had his first session with psychiatrist Dr. John Bonsaint. For the previous ten months, N. had insomnia and three clusters of obsessive-compulsive disorder (OCD) symptoms. First, he counted things, needing an even number. Second, he touched things, such as his stove burners, light switches, and his car roof. Then, he placed things in the proper orientation to keep the order of the world intact. ["N."]

1 June 2008

"WOMAN JUMPS FROM BRIDGE, MIMICS BROTHER'S SUICIDE," an article by Julia Shumway, appeared in The Chester's Mill *Democrat.* County Coroner Richard Chapman ruled Sheila Bonsaint LeClair's fall from the Bale Road Bridge a suicide. ["N."]

1 June 2010, Tuesday

Bill Hodges asked Marlo Everett, of the police Records Department, to research car break-ins from summer 2007 through spring 2009. Later, she said there were twelve, with the last reported in March 2009.

10:00 a.m.–1:00 p.m.: viewing for Mrs. Elizabeth Wharton in the Eternal Rest parlor at Soames Funeral Home

Brady Hartsfield used Thing Two, a device he built to capture cars' PKE codes, to get the code to Bill Hodges's car. [*Mr. Mercedes*]

1 June 2011

The Dark Tower: The Gunslinger—The Battle of Tull #1 of 5 (Marvel Comics, $3.99) published

June 2

2 June 1965

"'ALIEN GROWTH' A HOAX, FARM BUREAU REP DECLARES; 'Red Weeds' Said to Be Work of Spray-Gun, Teenagers" appeared in the *Oklahoman*. [*Dreamcatcher*]

2 June 1977

Todash Number Two: After eating muffin-balls near Calla Bryn Sturgis, Jake Chambers, Eddie and Susannah Dean, Roland Deschain, and Oy went todash (with the help of Black Thirteen, which was in the Calla). They met near the corner of Second Avenue and Fifty-Fourth Street in New York City. As in Todash Number One, they again sensed a darkness that Roland realized was because they were in Black Thirteen. Jake led them down Second Avenue, toward the vacant lot. "19th Nervous Breakdown," by The Rolling Stones, was playing in Tower of Power Records near Fifty-First Street. As they crossed Forty-Eighth Street and got closer to the rose, they had pleasant memories and feelings that everything was all right. At the vacant lot, most of the posters were the same as when Jake was there the first time. The sign about Turtle Bay Condominiums that Jake had moved out of the weeds the first time was still where he left it, but he thought the phone number was different. As they approached the rose, they saw people from their pasts. The rose's nineteen petals opened. It was one of two hubs of existence—the Tower, which the rose was, was the other. The rose, sick, was holding things together until the Tower's Beams were restored. Susannah had stayed outside with Oy. She screamed at the sight of vags—dead people who hadn't yet realized or accepted their deaths. When Susannah screamed, Jake picked up something from next to the rose—where the key was before. Back at camp, they saw that it was a pink bowling bag, stamped, "NOTHING BUT STRIKES AT MID-WORLD LANES." After Jake had bowled a 282, Timmy had given him a bag stamped, "NOTHING BUT STRIKES AT MID-TOWN LANES." [*The Dark Tower V: Wolves of the Calla*]

1–2 June 1979

Prom Night's dead were buried in three ceremonies over two days. [*Carrie*]

2 June 1983

Taduz Lemke's Gypsies passed through Falmouth, ME. [*Thinner*]

2 June 1985

Richard Bachman's *Thinner* stayed at number 7 on *The New York Times* Fiction Best Seller List, its fourteenth week on the List.

2 June 1988

Connecticut State Police Trooper Warren Hamilton found Homer Gamache's pickup truck abandoned on an I–95 McDonald's parking lot near Westport, CT. A lot of blood was in the cab. This was the third time he drew his gun in the line of duty. [*The Dark Half*]

2 June 1994, Thursday

Rose McClendon entered another world through her Rose Madder picture. She rescued Rose Madder's baby from Erinyes, the bull that hung out in and around the maze beyond the Temple of the Bull. [*Rose Madder*]

2 June 1996

The Green Mile, Part One: The Two Dead Girls dropped to number 4 on *The New York Times* Paperback Fiction Best Seller List, its eighth week on the List.

The Green Mile, Part Two: The Mouse on the Mile stayed at number 1 on *The New York Times* Paperback Fiction Best Seller List, its fourth week on the List.

2 June 2002

Everything's Eventual dropped to number 9 on *The New York Times* Fiction Best Seller List, its ninth week on the List.

2 June 2010, Wednesday

After Elizabeth Wharton's memorial service, Bill Hodges rode with Holly Gibney, Charlotte Gibney, and Henry Sirois. Janey Patterson wore Bill's fedora and drove his car. Brady Hartsfield detonated a bomb he had planted behind the driver's seat of Bill's car. Janey was killed.

Later, at Mrs. Trelawney's, Jerome Robinson introduced himself to Holly Gibney as working with Bill Hodges. Together, they searched Mrs. Trelawney's computer and found an audio file. It was the ghost sounds Mrs. Trelawney had heard at night. Holly found Looking Glass hidden in her email contacts folder. It allowed someone to access the computer remotely. They supposed her IT guy, her geek freak, must have installed it. They couldn't find any documentation—business card, invoice, or contact—on the IT guy. [*Mr. Mercedes*]

Stephen King's N. #4 of 4 (Marvel Comics, $3.99) published

2 June 2015

Finders Keepers, book 2 of the Bill Hodges trilogy (Scribner, $30), published

June 3

3 June

Pete McVries and Priscilla lost their virginities at the Shady Nook motel. Each worked in the Plymouth Sleepwear pajama factory in Newark, NJ. [*The Long Walk*]

3 June 1977

the school year's last day at The Piper School [*The Dark Tower III: The Waste Lands*]

3 June 1979

Ewen High had a service in memory of those who died on Prom Night. [*Carrie*]

3 June 1984

Pet Sematary rose to number 11 on *The New York Times* Fiction Best Seller List, its thirty-first week on the List.

~3 June 1988

George Stark killed Frederick Clawson, the man who had discovered that Stark was Thaddeus Beaumont's pseudonym and had tried to blackmail Beaumont. Thad, with Stark's hand, wrote, "THE SPARROWS ARE FLYING AGAIN," in blood, on the wall. [*The Dark Half*]

3 June 1990

The Stand: The Complete & Uncut Edition rose to number 1 on *The New York Times* Fiction Best Seller List, its fourth week on the List.

3 June 2001

Dreamcatcher rose to number 3 on *The New York Times* Fiction Best Seller List, its ninth week on the List.

3 June 2010, Thursday

While peeing in the early morning, Bill Hodges realized Mrs. Trelawney didn't have an IT guy. She used an IT services company. He had Jerome pretend to be a paralegal and call Vigilant Guard Service to see whether any of their employees could help identify Mrs. Trelawney's IT guy. Mr. Peoples called back. He didn't know who the particular guy was, but Cyber Patrol was in the neighborhood often. Bill and Jerome found Cyber Patrol on the Discount Electronix website. It showed the names and photos of their three employees.

Holly Gibney found Discount Electronix emails in Mrs. Trelawney's junk mail folder. She saw 30% off coupons for her next Cyber Patrol call. Hoping Bill Hodges and Jerome Robinson would make the Cyber Patrol connection, she drove to Birch Hill Mall to wait for them. They did. While Bill was inside, Holly asked Jerome to go to Whitey's Happy Frogurt Shoppe. She wanted ice cream, but yogurt would do. Jerome recognized one of the Cyber Patrol guys he had seen on the website as the ice cream man.

Mrs. Robinson took her daughter and her daughter's friends (Hilda Carver, Betsy DeWitt, and Dinah Scott) to the 'Round Here concert.

Brady Hartsfield went to the concert, masquerading as a person with disabilities going for his son, who was killed in the same accident that had disabled Brady. He waited in the handicapped area for the right time to detonate the bomb he had hidden in his wheelchair.

At the Hartsfields' house, Holly hacked into Brady's computer and found an email thanking him for buying a ticket to that night's 'Round Here concert. Identifying themselves as police at the MAC Center, Bill, Holly, and Jerome gained access to the auditorium through the back gate. As Holly was the only one whom Brady wouldn't recognize, she went to the handicapped area. With Bill's Happy Slapper, she walloped Brady on the side of the head twice. She disabled the bomb's remote detonator by removing its batteries. [*Mr. Mercedes*]

With irreparable brain damage, Hartsfield was in a coma for fifteen months. He spent the rest of his life in Room 217 of the Lakes Region Traumatic Brain Injury Clinic at Kiner Memorial. Dr. Felix Babineau, head of the Neurology Department, used Brady as a guinea pig, giving him experimental drug 649558 (Cerebellin). Human trials were years away, but Dr. Babineau took advantage of using a murderous degenerate who was unlikely to come out of his persistent vegetative state. He ran nine trials over fourteen months. [*End of Watch*]

The Stand: Hardcases #1 of 5 (Marvel Comics, $3.99) published

3 June 2012

The Dark Tower 4.5: The Wind Through the Keyhole dropped to number 9 on *The New York Times* Fiction Best Seller List, its fourth week on the List.

3 June 2014

Mr. Mercedes, book 1 of the Bill Hodges trilogy (Scribner, $30) published

June 4

4 June 1960, Saturday

For a dollar a week, Ted Brautigan hired Bobby Garfield to watch for low men in yellow coats or signs of their presence.

Mr. Coughlin drew Sully-John's name for a week at Camp Winiwinaia, a YMCA camp on Lake George. ["Low Men in Yellow Coats"]

4 June 1976

Widow Mrs. Elaine Tremont was admitted into Cumberland Receiving Hospital for a heart attack after seeing a grinning face looked in her bedroom window on Back Stage Road in Cumberland, ME. [*'Salem's Lot*]

4 June 1979

So many Chamberlain, ME, residents had moved after Prom Night that Chamberlain Mills and Weaving had to drop to one shift. [*Carrie*]

4 June 1985

Bill Denbrough visited Mike Hanlon in the hospital, where Mike offered Bill his house for a week. Richie Tozier flew back to California. [*IT*]

4 June 1988, Saturday

morning: Sheriff Pangborn and two state police troopers visited Thad Beaumont at his Ludlow, ME, home. They wanted to take him to the Orono State Police Barracks and question him about Homer Gamache's murder. With his fingerprints on Gamache's truck, he was a suspect. He refused to go, so they talked with him at home. Tom Carroll's retirement party was his alibi. While the police were there, he heard sparrows, the first time since his operation in 1960.

7:00 p.m.: Sheriff Pangborn returned with a six-pack of beer. Thad was also a suspect in Frederick Clawson's murder; his fingerprints were found at the scene. The Sheriff didn't think Thad was a killer. They speculated that the fingerprints were planted. [*The Dark Half*]

4 June 1994, Saturday

Norman Daniels staked out the restrooms at the Daughters and Sisters Swing Into Summer Picnic to wait for Rose. He tore off Cynthia Smith's blouse, bit her shoulder, and broke her nose. Gert Kinshaw threw him into a wheelchair, belly flopped on top of him, and peed on him. He fled. Later, he found Rose's address. Officers Lee Babcock and Alvin Demers, Rosie McClendon's police protection, watched her building from their Caprice. When they helped a man appearing to be having a heart attack, Daniels broke Babcock's neck and sat him in the cruiser's passenger seat. Daniels stabbed Demers in the throat with a letter opener and tossed him in the trunk to die. Rose and Bill Steiner arrived and fought him off. He followed them to her room and through a doorway into another world. Rose Madder clawed out his tongue and bit him, slowly, painfully, to death. [*Rose Madder*]

4 June 2008

The Dark Tower: The Long Road Home #4 of 5 (Marvel Comics, $3.99) published

4 June 2013

Joyland (Hard Case Crime, $12.95) published with a first printing of more than a million copies

4 June 2017

Gwendy's Button Box entered *The New York Times* Hardcover Fiction Best Seller List at number 7. It was on the List for three weeks.

June 5

5 June 1979

Prom Night's death toll reached 409, with another forty-nine missing. [*Carrie*]

5 June 1983

Christine stayed at number 2 on *The New York Times* Fiction Best Seller List, its ninth week on the List.

5 June 1985

Audra Denbrough, still catatonic, was scheduled to be transferred from Derry Home Hospital to the Bangor Mental Health Institute. She and Bill Denbrough moved into Mike Hanlon's place for a week while Mike was in the hospital. Mike began forgetting about IT and the Losers. Beverly Rogan went back to Hemingford Home, NE, with Ben Hanscom. [*IT*]

5 June 1994, Sunday

After waking, Rose McClendon and Bill Steiner made love. They married five months later. [*Rose Madder*]

5 June 2008

Charlie Keen emailed Chrissy, asking her to cancel the following week's appointments. He was going to Maine, where his childhood friends—Johnny Bonsaint and Sheila Bonsaint LeClair—both committed suicide. He thought it would make a good OCD story. ["N."]

5 June 2013

The Dark Tower: The Gunslinger—Evil Ground #2 of 2 (Marvel Comics, $3.99) published

5 June 2014, Thursday

10:45 a.m.: James Mallon, an Oliver Madden alias, had paid for an airplane with a bad check. Dwight Cramm had paid Bill Hodges $20,000 to get his plane back. Hodges arrived at the loading zone of the airport's Fixed-Based Operator (FBO) area beyond the main terminal. He ate a veggie burger and a salad with lo-cal French dressing.

James Mallon intended to buy licenses for casinos on Grand Belle Coeur and P'tit Grand Coeur.

11:37 a.m.: Mallon's plane landed. Madden went into the Zane Aviation office to have his plane hangared. Hodges chatted him up when he came out. As Madden opened a Lincoln Navigator's driver-side door, Hodges hit him across the left temple with the Happy Slapper, a sock filled with ball bearings. Hodges helped him into the driver's seat and handcuffed him to the steering wheel. After telling Madden he knew about several cons, including details of scamming Cramm out of his private jet, he gave Madden an offer he couldn't refuse. A ticket to Los Angeles waited for him at the Delta terminal. Take the flight, leave the plane, and stay a free man. Or, Hodges turns him in to the authorities. He took the flight. After Madden left, Hodges called Pete Huntley and told him where he could find one of the FBI's Ten Most Wanted.

After lunch, Drew Halliday played a message from Pete Saubers. Pete had forgotten about the school's weekend retreat for class officers, so he rescheduled their Friday appointment to Monday.

If the police got involved, Pete didn't want them finding the notebooks. He packed them into a couple of boxes he labeled KITCHEN SUPPLIES. The basement of the shutdown Birch Street Rec was filled with junk, including boxes labeled KITCHEN, the perfect place to hide his boxes. (His father was the real estate agent trying to sell the property.)

3:30 p.m.: Back at the office, Bill Hodges talked with Barbara Robinson and Tina Saubers. Tina was worried that her brother had stolen a lot of money and was in trouble because it was gone. Barb knew Bill and had suggested Tina talk with him. [*Finders Keepers*]

5 June 2017

Geneva peace talks, to ease tensions in India and Pakistan, failed. ["Summer Thunder"]

"After the Play," an epilogue to *The Shining*, appeared in *The Shining: The Deluxe Special Edition* (Cemetery Dance; 3,000-copy Gift Edition, $95; 750-copy Artist Edition, $275; 52-copy Lettered Artist Edition, $1250).

June 6

6 June 1944

Rhett Alderson stormed the beaches at Normandy. ["Cookie Jar"]

6 June 1985

The police-courthouse building had received some structural damage after IT died. An old, heavy tramp-chair broke through the attic floor and fell on Derry Police Chief Andrew Rademacher as he worked late at his fifth-floor desk. Officer Bruce Andeen found his body.

Richie Tozier's Derry memories faded. He thought Stan Uris's name was something like Underwood. [*IT*]

6 June 1988, Monday

morning: At Dr. Hume's recommendation, Thad Beaumont had a CAT-scan and cranial X-rays. He had been hearing sparrows again. He went into a trance during the sparrow episodes, after which he didn't remember what had happened. George Stark took over during these episodes. Real sparrows landed near him. Sparrows are psychopomps; they guide dead souls to and from the land of the living.

When Miriam Cowley got home, George Stark pulled her inside, so roughly that she broke a cheekbone and two teeth. He called Thad and cut her left cheek. Thad and Stark were linked; Thad, through Stark, wrote something on the wall in Miriam's blood. Stark didn't know. Stark cut Cowley's throat. She and her ex-husband, Rick Cowley, were Thad's literary agents and had publicized the death of the Stark pseudonym.

Thad called Sheriff Pangborn and told him he felt Rick Cowley might be in danger. They discussed a psycho pretending to be George Stark and killing people responsible for killing Stark. [*The Dark Half*]

6 June 1990

Fran Goldsmith found out she was pregnant, the result of losing her virginity with Jess Rider at Ogunquit's beach one weekend in April. They were twelve feet above the high tide line, thirty-six feet east of the seawall. The pill didn't work. [*The Stand: The Complete & Uncut Edition*]

6 June 1998, Saturday

Quilla McFarland took her children, Pete and Trisha, for a six-mile hike on the Appalachian Trail. At a fork, one trail led to their destination of North Conway, the other to Kezar Notch. Nine-year-old Trisha wanted a break from the fighting, so she took the Kezar Notch path then went off the trail to pee. To make up for lost time, she cut through the woods to get to the other path. She didn't find it, so she followed a stream. On her Walkman that night, she listened to Castle Rock radio station WCAS as Tom Gordon pitched his eighteenth save of the season. [*The Girl Who Loved Tom Gordon*]

6 June 1999

The Girl Who Loved Tom Gordon dropped to number 6 on *The New York Times* Fiction Best Seller List, its seventh week on the List.

6 June 2007

The Dark Tower: Gunslinger Born #5 of 7 (Marvel Comics, $3.99) published

6 June 2014, Friday

Morris Bellamy visited Charlie Robeson, a friend from Waynesville State Prison, to collect a favor. (In prison, Morris had written letters to the Innocence Project to help free Charlie on DNA evidence.) Morris needed a car to get the Rothstein notebooks. Roberson showed him a small panel truck and promised to leave the keys under the right front tire.

After work, Morris got the truck and killed time until dark. He drove to the Birch Street Rec. Through the basement window, he saw a bunch of boxes—a good place to keep the notebooks. He found the path and followed it to the stream. It took an hour to chop through the roots around the trunk. It slid out easily; it was too light. He opened it. No notebooks. No money. [*Finders Keepers*]

6 June 2017

Stemming from tensions in India and Pakistan, a nuclear holocaust hit. Peter Robinson's wife, Diana, and daughter, Ellen, were killed in Boston while checking out Emerson College. Peter moved to their summer home on Vermont's Lake Pocomtuck to live out his last days. Most residents of the area had fled to Canada on rumors it was free of radiation. Howard Timlin stayed in his cottage on Woodland Acres, two miles from Robinson's home. ["Summer Thunder"]

June 7

7 June 1975

Sarah Hazlett visited Johnny Smith at Eastern Maine Medical Center. When she kissed him goodbye, he told her where to find the wedding ring she lost on her honeymoon. [*The Dead Zone*]

7 June 1981

After a week off, *Danse Macabre* re-entered *The New York Times* Non-Fiction Best Seller List at number 14, its third week on the List.

7 June 1982

At Strawford Park, Josie Rinkenhauer found her way behind a Derry, Bangor, and Aroostook Railroad fence near The Barrens. She slipped on the leaves and slid to the bottom of a sloping drainpipe; she couldn't climb out. Later, a lost-child poster mentioned she was last seen on the Park's softball field. [*Dreamcatcher*]

7 June 1985

Bill Denbrough's Derry memories waned. He thought Eddie Kaspbrak's name was something like Kerkorian. [*IT*]

7 June 1987

The Eyes of the Dragon dropped to number 7 on *The New York Times* Fiction Best Seller List, its nineteenth week on the List.

Misery entered *The New York Times* Fiction Best Seller List at number 1. It was on the List for thirty weeks.

7 June 1988, Tuesday

George Stark killed Michael Donaldson, Phyllis Myers, Rick Cowley, and Darla Gates. Donaldson had written the *People* magazine article that killed Thad Beaumont's Stark pseudonym; Myers was the photographer. Cowley was Beaumont's literary agent who had handled publicizing that Stark was a pseudonym. Gates, a secretary in Darwin Press's accounting department, had helped Frederick Clawson discover that Stark was Beaumont.

Dave and Wes installed bugs, trace equipment, and recording equipment on Thad's Ludlow phones. Later, George Stark called and said he killed the last one at noon. Sheriff Pangborn told Thad about the murders of Miriam Cowley, Mike Donaldson, and Phyllis Myers in New York. Thad told him he thought it was his pseudonym, George Stark, who came to life. The Sheriff didn't believe him. [*The Dark Half*]

7 June 1998, Sunday

Instead of leading Trisha McFarland out of the woods, the stream petered out into a Maine bog. Imagining Tom Gordon was with her, she waded across the knee-deep, stagnant water. On the way, she saw a deer's head and a tree that something with large claws had knocked down. That evening, she found a brook, larger than the first. She followed it, hoping to find her way out. She listened to the Yankees beat the Red Sox 8-6. Something watched her while she slept. [*The Girl Who Loved Tom Gordon*]

7 June 2007

N. had his second session with psychiatrist Dr. John Bonsaint. He told Dr. Bonsaint about the cause of his insomnia and OCD symptoms—his first trip to Ackerman's Field, in August 2006. ["N."]

7 June 2014, Saturday

Morris Bellamy figured only Andy Halliday knew about the notebooks and money, so he went to Andrew Halliday Rare Editions. With a hatchet, he escorted Andy into the back office and chopped Halliday's buttock. Andy told Bellamy he didn't have the books, but Peter Saubers, who lived in Bellamy's old house, had been trying to sell them. He expected the kid to come to the shop Monday after school. Four hatchet whacks killed Halliday. Bellamy took Andy's keys and the money from his wallet. [*Finders Keepers*]

7 June 2016

End of Watch, book 3 of the Bill Hodges trilogy (Scribner, $30), published

7 June 2018

Heath Holmes hanged himself in Montgomery County Jail. He was buried in Peaceful Rest Cemetery. [*The Outsider*]

June 8

8 June 1960, Wednesday

On Colony Street, Bobby Garfield saw a piece of red cloth on someone's television antenna. He wasn't sure it was a sign of low men; he expected kite tails on telephone lines. ["Low Men in Yellow Coats"]

8 June 1962

Lee Harvey and Marina Oswald left Russia on the SS *Maasdam*, bound for the United States.

George Amberson's second timeline: On the last day of school, Bobbi Jill Allnut and Mike Coslaw gave George Amberson a thank-you gift—a boxed, Waterman fountain pen, with his initials engraved on the clip. Amberson had put on a benefit jamboree to fund facial reconstruction surgery for Bobbi Jill. Dr. Ellerton had performed the surgery in Dallas. [*11/22/63*]

8 June 1982

After graduation rehearsal, Beaver, Henry Devlin, Jonesy, and Pete Moore got Duddits to help them find Josie Rinkenhauer. From Strawford Park, they followed Duddits, who could see the line, through a break in a Derry, Bangor, and Aroostook Railroad fence near The Barrens. Pete found her at the bottom of a sloping concrete drainpipe. Holding one another in a human chain, Pete went in first, held by Beaver, then Henry, then Jonesy. She climbed up enough for Pete to grab her wrist and save her. [*Dreamcatcher*]

8 June 1985

The names of the Losers were fading from Mike Hanlon's address book. [*IT*]

8 June 1987

Misery (Viking, $18.95) published with a first printing of 900,000 to 1,000,000 copies

8 June 1998, Monday

With Tom Gordon beside her, Trisha McFarland continued following the brook. In the afternoon, she crossed into New Hampshire, thirty miles from the search teams. She found a checkerberry patch and some deer eating beechnuts. She ate her full of checkerberries, then picked more and gathered a few nuts for later. The Red Sox had the night off, so she fell asleep watching a meteor shower. [*The Girl Who Loved Tom Gordon*]

8 June 2004

The Dark Tower VI: Song of Susannah (Donald M. Grant, $30) published with a first printing of 650,000 copies

8 June 2011

The Stand: No Man's Land #5 of 5 (Marvel Comics, $3.99) published

8 June 2014, Sunday

Bill Hodges visited Brady Hartsfield at the John M. Kiner Memorial Hospital's Traumatic Brain Injury Clinic. Semi catatonic, Hartsfield didn't seem to know Hodges was there. While Bill talked to him, a framed picture of Brady and his mother on the table fell over. Bill set the picture back up as he left. Brady looked up and smiled; the picture fell again. [*Finders Keepers*]

8 June 2016
The Dark Tower: The Drawing of the Three—Bitter Medicine #3 of 5 (Marvel Comics, $3.99) published

June 9

9 June 1922

John Rimbauer had become violent. The headwaiter quit after John threatened him with a carving knife for the beef being too rare.

John had cut Rose Red's construction budget in half. As construction slowed, April Rimbauer's appearances became less frequent. Ellen Rimbauer decided John must be removed from the picture. [*The Diary of Ellen Rimbauer: My Life at Rose Red*]

9 June 1979

date of Ewen High School Principal Henry Grayle's resignation letter to Peter Philpott, Superintendent of Schools [*Carrie*]

9 June 1981

Annie Wilkes killed a Boulder Hospital patient. [*Misery*]

9 June 1982, 12:00 p.m.

Beaver Clarendon, Henry Devlin, and Jonesy graduated from Derry High School. Pete Moore graduated from his junior year. [*Dreamcatcher*]

9 June 1985

Richard Bachman's *Thinner* stayed at number 7 on *The New York Times* Fiction Best Seller List, its fifteenth week on the List.

9 June 1996

The Green Mile, Part One: The Two Dead Girls dropped to number 5 on *The New York Times* Paperback Fiction Best Seller List, its ninth week on the List.

The Green Mile, Part Two: The Mouse on the Mile dropped to number 2 on *The New York Times* Paperback Fiction Best Seller List, its fifth week on the List.

The Green Mile, Part Three: Coffey's Hands entered *The New York Times* Paperback Fiction Best Seller List at number 1. It was on the List for fifteen weeks.

9 June 1998, Tuesday

The brook led Trisha McFarland to another marsh, one less nasty than the first. She didn't want to cross it, so she turned north. Had she crossed it, she would have stumbled on civilization soon after. [*The Girl Who Loved Tom Gordon*]

9 June 2002

Everything's Eventual dropped to number 14 on *The New York Times* Fiction Best Seller List, its tenth week on the List.

9 June 2014, Monday

2:15 p.m.: Morris Bellamy went to Andrew Halliday Rare Editions to wait for Peter Saubers. Holly Gibney, Bill Hodges, and Jerome Robinson left the office to talk with Peter. Bill went to the school's front entrance. In case Peter left by another exit, Holly watched from Garner

Street and Jerome from Westfield Street.

3:00 p.m.: Pete left through the school's main entrance. Bill stopped him and told him he was a friend of the Robinson family. Tina Saubers was worried about Pete. Barbara Robinson had suggested Tina talk with Bill because he used to be a detective. They talked in Bill's air-conditioned Prius. Pete didn't break. He said he hadn't sent the money, and there was no trouble. He excused himself because he had to get his father's prescription filled. Bill had Jerome watch City Drug to see where Pete went after the drugstore.

3:40 p.m.: Bill Hodges realized Peter had made up a story for the pharmacist to let Peter out the back. On a Holly-hunch, Bill, Holly, and Jerome talked with Mr. Ricker to see if Peter had ever approached him with a problem. Mr. Ricker remembered Pete had a signed, first edition copy of John Rothstein's *The Runner*. He got it from his uncle, who had won it in a poker game. Mr. Ricker thought Peter had made up that part; it was too movie-like. Pete wanted to sell the book so his sister could go to a private school. He asked Mr. Ricker about a few booksellers. Mr. Ricker advised him to stay away from Andrew Halliday—too shady.

Peter went in Andrew Halliday Rare Editions. Bellamy told him Andy was expecting him in the office, to knock and go in. Bellamy put a gun to Pete's head and told him to turn on the lights; they needed to talk about the notebooks Peter had stolen. They argued. Pete threw two liquor decanters at Bellamy. The next closest object was the hatchet Bellamy had used on Halliday. Pete threw it. Bellamy blocked it with his forearm but dropped the gun. Pete ran out.

Holly, Bill, and Jerome headed for Lacemaker Lane. Holly was sure Peter had gone to Halliday but not to sell a book. On her iPad, she pulled up a Manchester *Union-Leader* article. Three men had killed John Rothstein, broken into his safe, and stolen money and notebooks with material Rothstein had written after he retired. They figured the robbers had hidden the loot, and Peter had found it. Peter sent the money to his parents then tried to sell the notebooks. He had gone to Halliday because a reputable bookseller wouldn't deal with them.

Andrew Halliday Rare Editions was closed, but the door was unlocked. They found Halliday's body. As Bill reached for his phone to call the police, Pete called from Government Square, needing his help. Bill told him to stay there; they would pick him up, take him home, and listen to his story.

Bellamy parked at the Birch Street Rec and walked through the undeveloped land to the Sauberses' house. Inside, he shot Linda Saubers in the head and grabbed Tina Saubers. With Tina's phone, he told Pete he was taking her some place safe and Pete should call back when he had the notebooks. Bellamy took Tina to the Birch Street Rec's basement.

Eager to get home, Pete took the bus to North Side. He called Bill and told him he was on his way home and the guy who had killed Rothstein and Halliday used to live in Pete's house. Pete found his mother. A bullet had grazed the right side of her head, exposing her skull. He called 911, took a couple of items from his father's desk, and left. Through the Birch Street Rec's basement window, he heard a man's voice. Pete went in the front. He took off his shoes so his walking wouldn't be heard downstairs.

Bill, Holly, and Jerome arrived at the Sauberses'. Bill went in the open front door. Mrs. Saubers spoke in broken sentences, but Bill learned Peter had taken the key to the Birch Street Rec and there was a path behind the house. Holly stayed with Mrs. Saubers, while Bill and Jerome took the path.

Pete hid in the pantry. He called Tina's phone: the notebooks were in the Saturday Movie Palace on the Rec's second floor. Bellamy went up; Peter went down. On the second floor,

Peter and the notebooks weren't there. Back in the basement, Bellamy found Peter holding a lit lighter over a pile of Moleskine notebooks soaked in lighter fluid. They bantered, Morris threatening to hurt Tina, Pete threatening to destroy two more Jimmy Gold novels.

Bill found the Rec's front door open and went in. Pete's shoes were in the kitchen. He threw them onto the basement floor. Startled, Pete dropped the lighter; the Moleskines caught fire. Hodges and Bellamy fought; Hodges broke Bellamy's wrist to make him drop the gun. Bellamy ran to the burning notebooks. The flames had spread, burning the stairs. Jerome Robinson helped Tina, Bill, and Hodges through the window. Bellamy stayed with the notebooks and burned. [*Finders Keepers*]

June 10

10 June 1958, Tuesday

Henry Bowers promised Ben Hanscom he would get Ben for refusing the let Henry copy his math test answers. [*IT*]

10 June 1960, Friday, last day of school

Bobby Garfield saw a yellow crescent moon and star next to a purple hopscotch grid on a sidewalk—a sign that low men were about. He didn't want to tell Ted Brautigan until he saw more signs. ["Low Men in Yellow Coats"]

10 June 1982

The Dark Tower: The Gunslinger (Donald M. Grant, $20) published with a first printing of 10,000 copies

10 June 1984

Pet Sematary dropped to number 15 on *The New York Times* Fiction Best Seller List, its thirty-second and last week on the List.

10 June 1985

Bill Denbrough forgot why Audra Denbrough was catatonic, but he wanted to try to cure her with the last of the fading Derry magic. He took her for a ride on Silver, his old bicycle, during which her catatonia and his stuttering went away.

Foxy Foxworth, retired Aladdin Theater manager and concessions clerk, spent two weeks in the hospital after the bleachers collapsed at a Bassey Park horse race. He punctured a testicle and broke a leg in the accident. [*IT*]

10 June 1986

Stephen King was living on Turtleback Lane in Lovell, ME, when he wanted to write more of *The Dark Tower*. [*The Dark Tower VI: Song of Susannah*]

10 June 1988, Friday

Thad Beaumont shopped at Dave's Market. George Stark called him there and told him he wanted Thad to write another Stark novel. If he didn't start in a week, Stark would kill his children, wife, and him. Thad had an idea for a Stark novel called *Steel Machine*.

When Thad heard sparrows, he was linked with Stark. So far, the episodes happened when they happened. That night, however, he made it happen. He heard sparrows and Stark wrote, with Thad's hand, about Miriam Cowley's death and that he wanted to write to continue to live. [*The Dark Half*]

last day of school for third-grade teacher Robinson ["Dolan's Cadillac"]

10 June 1990

The Stand: The Complete & Uncut Edition stayed at number 1 on *The New York Times* Fiction Best Seller List, its fifth week on the List.

10 June 1993

Stephen King started *Rose Madder*.

10 June 1995, Saturday

While Hugh Hobart and his father distributed religious brochures, Hugh saw a MotoKops Dream Floater Power Wagon in the Wylers' yard. Later, he stole it. Upset at not having his Dream Floater, Tak made Audrey and Herb Wyler's lives miserable for three days. [*The Regulators*]

10 June 2001

Dreamcatcher dropped to number 4 on *The New York Times* Fiction Best Seller List, its tenth week on the List.

10 June ≥2008, Saturday

Ramona Norville hosted a Books & Brown Baggers meeting at her home in Brewster, MA. ["Big Driver"]

10 June 2012

The Dark Tower 4.5: The Wind Through the Keyhole dropped to number 10 on *The New York Times* Fiction Best Seller List, its fifth week on the List.

10 June 2015

The Dark Tower: The Drawing of the Three—House of Cards #4 of 5 (Marvel Comics, $3.99) published

10 June 2018

The Outsider entered *The New York Times* Hardcover Fiction Best Seller List at number 1. It was on the List for twenty weeks.

June 11

11 June 1960, Saturday

Mrs. Anita Gerber and Rionda Hewson took Angie Avery, Bobby Garfield, Carol Gerber, Ian Gerber, Tina Lebel, Yvonne Loving, and Sully-John to Savin Rock, an amusement park at the beach. Bobby and Carol kissed at the top of the Ferris wheel, the kiss by which all others in Bobby's life would fall short. Herb McQuown, the Monte Man at Savin Rock, showed them how easy it was to win at three-card monte then won $1.25 from Rionda and Sully-John. Bobby, who could see into McQuown's mind (a side effect from having touched Ted Brautigan that morning), played twice, winning back $1.20. ["Low Men in Yellow Coats"]

11 June 1970

"Slade," Chapter 1, appeared in *The Maine Campus*.

11 June 1979

Rita Desjardin, Carrie White's gym teacher, resigned from teaching. [*Carrie*]

11 June 1995, 6:00 a.m.

While Seth Garin/Tak slept, a life-size projection of their missing Dream Floater Power Wagon appeared outside. When Tak awoke, he vandalized the kitchen telekinetically. [*The Regulators*]

11 June 2013

"Afterlife" (collected in *The Bazaar of Bad Dreams*) appeared in the Summer 2013 issue (Volume 14, Number 4; Issue #56) of *Tin House*.

11 June 2017

Gwendy's Button Box dropped to number 14 on *The New York Times* Hardcover Fiction Best Seller List, its second week on the List.

June 12

12 June 1960, Sunday

Police arrested John T. Anderson for stealing shopping carts. They found more than fifty in his backyard, with some from Stansbury, CT's IGA market and more than twenty from Harwich, CT's A&P and Total Grocery. ["Low Men in Yellow Coats"]

12 June 1983

Christine dropped to number 3 on *The New York Times* Fiction Best Seller List, its tenth week on the List.

12 June 1995

Tak made Herb Wyler punch himself in the eye, blackening it. [*The Regulators*]

12 June 1999

Stephen King decided to take a ten-day vacation then work on a how-to-write book. [*The Dark Tower VI: Song of Susannah*]

Stephen King had less than 200 hours to live. Walter had arranged his death so the final three *Dark Tower* books wouldn't be written, clearing the way for the Tower to fall. [*The Dark Tower VII: The Dark Tower*]

12 June 2007

Richard Bachman's *Blaze* (Scribner, $25) published

June 13

13 June 1962

The SS *Maasdam*, with Lee Harvey and Marina Oswald on board, docked in Hoboken, NJ. [*11/22/63*]

13 June 1986

Stephen King woke up with the image of Roland Deschain telling him to resume *The Dark Tower* with the lobstrosities. [*The Dark Tower VI: Song of Susannah*]

13 June 1990, 2:37:16 a.m.

An accident occurred on the Army's Project Blue viral warfare project. Captain Trips got out and killed many Project Blue personnel. Private, Tech Second Class, Frank D. Bruce died with his face in a bowl of Campbell's Chunky sirloin soup in the cafeteria. Nobel Prize recipient Dr. Emmanual Ezwick died in the viral biology lab.

When Charles D. Campion saw a viral detection device go active, he ran and escaped his post about thirty seconds before it was sealed. The California Army base closed twenty-three seconds after he and his family left. Resisting the virus for about fifty hours, he spread Captain Trips unknowingly. By dawn, they reached Nevada.

Of $7,000 Columbia royalties for "Baby, Can You Dig Your Man?," Larry Underwood had $800 left. He had spent the rest on his car, beach house, and a weeklong party. He still owed $9,200 to Dewey the Deck for marijuana and cocaine, $1,400 in party damage to the beach house, $600 for party liquor, $400 for party food, and more for his car. Wayne Stukey talked him into leaving town until he could pay his debts with his next royalty check. Wayne also persuaded Dewey the Deck to wait awhile for the money Larry owed him. [*The Stand: The Complete & Uncut Edition*]

13 June 1995, Tuesday

Herb Wyler bought *The Regulators* video for Seth Garin/Tak, who watched it often. [*The Regulators*]

13 June 1998, Saturday

Trisha McFarland had been lost for a week. Halfway across a meadow, she found a post with a ringbolt. Tom Gordon helped her figure out it was a gatepost. She saw a hinge and determined how the gate had been positioned to show the road or path it was on. Tom helped her find another post. For seven hours, she found the remains of more posts that Elias McCorkle had used to mark a trail ninety-five years earlier. They led to another gate, on a rutted old woods road. She spent the night in the woods, near an old truck cab, just off the road. She woke to a thunderstorm and the feeling of being watched. She sought shelter in the truck cab. [*The Girl Who Loved Tom Gordon*]

13 June 1999

The Girl Who Loved Tom Gordon stayed at number 6 on *The New York Times* Fiction Best Seller List, its eighth week on the List.

13 June 2008, Friday, 7:00 p.m.

Evangelist C. Danny Jacobs held a revival show at Norris County Fairgrounds, twenty miles east of Denver, CO. The Gospel Robins, featuring Devina Robinson, and soul singer Al Stamper performed. [*Revival*]

13 June 2010

Blockade Billy entered *The New York Times* Fiction Best Seller List at number 9. It was on the List for two weeks.

June 14

14 June 1960, Tuesday

Liz Garfield arranged for Ted Brautigan to stay with Bobby Garfield while she was on a business trip the following week. Even after seeing a lost-pet poster for Phil, Bobby didn't want to tell Ted about the signs of low men he had seen because he didn't want to jeopardize Camp Broad Street, where Ted was going to watch him. ["Low Men in Yellow Coats"]

14 June 1962, Thursday

Delta Flight 194 took Lee Harvey and Marina Oswald from Newark, NJ, to Dallas, TX, with a stop in Atlanta. They lived with Lee's brother, Robert Oswald, for a while then moved in with Lee's mother.

George Amberson's second timeline: George Amberson drove to Love Field, an airport northwest of Dallas, 40+ miles from where he lived in Fort Worth, TX. He paid seventy-five cents to park then sat in a restaurant booth and waited to see the Oswalds arrive in Texas.

To satisfy the six-week residence requirement to get a divorce in Reno, NV, Sadie Dunhill took a Frontier Airlines flight from Love Field. In Reno, she lived in a rooming house and worked as a cocktail waitress. [*11/22/63*]

14 June 1981

Danse Macabre rose to number 7 on *The New York Times* Non-Fiction Best Seller List, its fourth week on the List.

14 June 1987

The Eyes of the Dragon dropped to number 9 on *The New York Times* Fiction Best Seller List, its twentieth week on the List.

Misery stayed at number 1 on *The New York Times* Fiction Best Seller List, its second week on the List.

14 June 1988

Norton Briggs, who hit his wife of twenty years often, knocked her out with a frying pan. Thinking he killed her, he shot himself with a handgun. She regained consciousness, saw her dead husband, and attempted suicide by sticking her head in the oven. Paramedics saved her. [*The Dark Half*]

14 June 1990

Charles D. Campion's wife and daughter woke up with Captain Trips in Salt Lake City, UT. Sally and Baby LaVon died within two days.

Larry Underwood left California and headed for New York. [*The Stand: The Complete & Uncut Edition*]

14 June 1991

Lucy Swann and Larry Underwood's baby was due. [*The Stand: The Complete & Uncut Edition*]

14 June 1998, Sunday

Trisha McFarland woke up and saw a circle dug around the truck cab in which she had slept.

She walked the road most of the day; something kept pace in the woods to her right. [*The Girl Who Loved Tom Gordon*]

14 June 2007

N. had his third session with psychiatrist Dr. John Bonsaint. He told Dr. Bonsaint about his second trip to Ackerman's Field, in early September 2006. ["N."]

14 June 2008, Saturday, 2:00 p.m. and 7:00 p.m.

Evangelist C. Danny Jacobs held revival shows at Norris County Fairgrounds, twenty miles east of Denver, CO. The Gospel Robins, featuring Devina Robinson, and soul singer Al Stamper performed. [*Revival*]

June 15

15 June 1908

Ellen Rimbauer and Sukeena stopped at a teahouse in Cairo, Egypt. Ellen showed her coin purse—with bills visible—when she paid. A commotion was staged at the front of the teahouse. Ellen and Sukeena left through the back, where two men waited with knives. Sukeena spoke strange words, causing the men to collapse and writhe in pain. [*The Diary of Ellen Rimbauer: My Life at Rose Red*]

15 June 1962

George Amberson's second timeline: George Amberson bought a pair of Bausch & Lomb binoculars. From his window at 2706 Mercedes Street in Fort Worth, TX, he could see in 2703's window. Lee Harvey Oswald and family would be moving into 2703. [*11/22/63*]

15 June 1981

Annie Wilkes killed a Boulder Hospital patient. [*Misery*]

15 June 1986

Stephen King continued writing *The Dark Tower*, picking up with Roland Deschain on the Western Sea beach. From a series of doors, Roland drew characters from our world; Eddie Dean was the first. [*The Dark Tower VI: Song of Susannah*]

15 June 1990, overnight

Charles D. Campion woke up with Captain Trips. [*The Stand: The Complete & Uncut Edition*]

15 June 1998, Tuesday

With pneumonia in her lungs, Trisha McFarland woke up coughing blood. The old woods road ended in a better east-west dirt road. She turned west so the morning sun wouldn't be in her eyes. About forty-five minutes later, she heard tires on a road and branches breaking near her. She seemed relieved when she saw what had been following her was only a 400-pound, seven-foot, North American black bear. Without showing fear, she faced it, keeping still, like Tom Gordon getting ready to pitch for a save. The bear came and sniffed her face. She kept still—she didn't even blink—holding her Walkman the way Tom Gordon held a baseball. It stood on its hind legs and swatted at her, missing on purpose. She looked into its eyes and started her pitch. Caught off-guard, expecting her to run instead of stepping forward, it stepped back. Travis Herrick, hunting out-of-season deer to eat, shot the bear in the ear. Trisha followed through with her pitch, hitting it between the eyes for a called third strike. The bear ran off; Herrick carried Trisha to safety. [*The Girl Who Loved Tom Gordon*]

15 June 2005

Introduction (Center Lovell, ME) to '*Salem's Lot: Illustrated Edition*, including deleted scenes, "Jerusalem's Lot," and "One For the Road"

15 June 2007

the July issue (Vol. 148, No. 1) of *Esquire*, with "The Gingerbread Girl" (collected in *Just After Sunset*), published

15 June 2008, Sunday, 2:00 p.m. and 7:00 p.m.

Evangelist C. Danny Jacobs held revival shows at Norris County Fairgrounds, twenty miles east of Denver, CO. The Gospel Robins, featuring Devina Robinson, and soul singer Al Stamper performed. [*Revival*]

June 16

16 June 1965

Eve Tobin was the first person in Gatlin, NE, born a worshiper of He Who Walks Behind the Rows. ["Children of the Corn"]

16 June 1980, <2:00 p.m.

Cujo chased Br'er Rabbit into a hole that opened into a cave on Seven Oaks Farm. A rabid brown insectivorous bat bit him. He never had a rabies shot. The rabbit died in the cave. [*Cujo*]

16 June 1981

Annie Wilkes killed a Boulder Hospital patient. [*Misery*]

16 June 1985

Richard Bachman's *Thinner* stayed at number 7 on *The New York Times* Fiction Best Seller List, its sixteenth week on the List.

16 June 1990

Charles D. Campion almost lost consciousness on US 93. Driving erratically, he knocked off three gas pumps at Hapscomb's Texaco in Arnette, TX. He infected Norm Bruett, Hank Carmichael, Bill Hapscomb, Victor Palfrey, and Tommy Wannamaker with Captain Trips; he exposed Billy Verecker, Monty Sullivan, and Carlos Ortega of Arnette Volunteer Ambulance, and Stu Redman. Stu didn't get sick. [*The Stand: The Complete & Uncut Edition*]

16 June 1996

The Green Mile, Part One: The Two Dead Girls dropped to number 8 on *The New York Times* Paperback Fiction Best Seller List, its tenth week on the List.

The Green Mile, Part Two: The Mouse on the Mile stayed at number 2 on *The New York Times* Paperback Fiction Best Seller List, its sixth week on the List.

The Green Mile, Part Three: Coffey's Hands stayed at number 1 on *The New York Times* Paperback Fiction Best Seller List, its second week on the List.

16 June 2002

Everything's Eventual stayed at number 14 on *The New York Times* Fiction Best Seller List, its eleventh and last week on the List.

16 June 2010

The Dark Tower: The Gunslinger—The Journey Begins #2 of 5 (Marvel Comics, $3.99) published

June 17

17 June

Elise and John Graham arrived in Willow, ME, to spend the summer at the Hempstead Place. Henry Eden and Laura Stanton warned them about Rainy Season, suggesting they leave town and return the next day. The Grahams didn't believe the tale of literally raining toads every seven years. That night, it rained large toads with big, sharp teeth. The toads broke into their windows and trapped them in the basement. When they finished barricading the four cellar windows, the coal-chute broke open. Many toads fell in and killed them. By noon the following day, the toads had melted in the sun and seeped into the earth. Willow prospered for another seven years. ["Rainy Season"]

17 June 1922, Saturday

Henry James agreed to help Wilfred, his father, kill Arlette, his mother. A few days later, Arlette drank too much wine. After Wilfred put her to bed, Henry slipped a burlap sack over her head. Wilfred slit her five times with a butcher knife and wrapped her in a counterpane and quilt. They dumped her in the old well behind the barn. Their story was she ran off to St. Louis or Chicago.

About a week later, for an excuse to fill the well, they led Elphis, an old, cranky cow that produced little milk, to the old well cap. She broke through and fell in. Wilfred finished her with his .22 varmint gun. ["1922"]

17 June 1958

Joseph Brennan had borrowed Stephen W. Meader's *Bulldozer* from the Derry Public Library. It was due on the 17th. [*IT*]

17 June 1990

Lila Bruett woke up with Captain Trips, which she caught from Norm Bruett, her husband; they infected their son Luke. Lila infected Cheryl Hodges while babysitting for Sally Hodges. That afternoon, the Bruetts, Hank Carmichael, the Hodgeses, Tony Leominster, Parker Nason, Chris Ortega, Vic Palfrey, Stu Redman, Monty Sullivan, Tommy Wannamaker, and other Arnette, TX, residents were sent to the Atlanta Plague Center. Joe Bob Brentwood caught Captain Trips from Bill Hapscomb, his cousin.

Fran Goldsmith told Jess Rider she was pregnant. He offered to marry her or pay for her abortion.

Coroner Finnegan and Dr. James examined the dead Campions. They called in three pathologists from Houston and the Atlanta Plague Center. [*The Stand: The Complete & Uncut Edition*]

The Stand: The Complete & Uncut Edition dropped to number 4 on *The New York Times* Fiction Best Seller List, its sixth week on the List.

17 June 1999

Rand Holston and Mark Carliner talked with Stephen King about doing *Rose Red* or *Kingdom Hospital* after *Storm of the Century*. [*The Dark Tower VI: Song of Susannah*]

17 June 2001

Dreamcatcher dropped to number 6 on *The New York Times* Fiction Best Seller List, its eleventh week on the List.

17 June 2009

The Dark Tower: Fall of Gilead #2 of 6 (Marvel Comics, $3.99) published

17 June 2012

The Dark Tower 4.5: The Wind Through the Keyhole dropped to number 11 on *The New York Times* Fiction Best Seller List, its sixth week on the List.

17 June 2018

The Outsider stayed at number 1 on *The New York Times* Hardcover Fiction Best Seller List, its second week on the List.

June 18

18 June 1970
"Slade," Chapter 2, appeared in *The Maine Campus*.

18 June 1988
Thad Beaumont missed his deadline to start writing another George Stark novel. Stark killed Tom Chatterton and Jack Eddings, Liz Beaumont's police protection. He kidnapped Liz and the kids and took them to their Castle Rock home.

At his office, Thad heard sparrows and went into a trance; Stark typed—on Thad's typewriter—that he killed the state troopers at the house and kidnapped Thad's family. He wanted Thad to meet him at the Castle Rock home and start a new story. Thad lost Steve Harrison and Manchester, his police protection, and went to Castle Rock. Harrison and Manchester returned to the Ludlow home and found two dead cops. They told Sheriff Pangborn that Thad killed the officers and might be heading to Castle Rock. After more research, the Sheriff believed there was a George Stark; he went to Castle Rock alone.

When Thad got to Lake Lane in Castle Rock, he saw millions of sparrows. Thad and Stark wrote in the study; they fought. The sparrows broke through the study's door and walls. Thad ordered them to take Stark back to hell. They picked him up and carried him away. Thad and Sheriff Pangborn burned the house and Stark's car. [*The Dark Half*]

18 June 1990
Texas State Patrolman Joe Bob Brentwood infected Harry Trent with Captain Trips while giving him a speeding ticket. Later, Joe Bob was taken to the Atlanta Plague Center. [*The Stand: The Complete & Uncut Edition*]

18 June 1999, Thursday
"'WALK-IN' PHENOMENON IN WESTERN MAINE CONTINUES TO RESIST EXPLANATION" headlined the Portland *Press-Herald*.

Naomi and Owen arrived to celebrate Father's Day with Stephen King. [*The Dark Tower VI: Song of Susannah*]

9:19 p.m.: Ted Brautigan, Dinky Earnshaw, Dani Rostov, and Fred Worthington helped Sheemie Ruiz open a hole in the Keystone World to see when it was. A Times Square news ticker showed June 18, 1999, 9:19 p.m. The digits in the time summed to nineteen, confirming it was the Keystone World.

Bryan Smith spent the night at the Million Dollar Campground, outside Lovell, ME, on the Stoneham side. [*The Dark Tower VII: The Dark Tower*]

18 June 2013
Hard Listening: The Greatest Rock Band Ever (of Authors) Tells All (Coliloquy, $9.99–$16.99 e-book), with "The Rock and Roll Dead Zone," published

18 June 2017
Gwendy's Button Box rose to number 13 on *The New York Times* Hardcover Fiction Best Seller List, its third and last week on the List.

June 19

19 June 1834

A 5′ x 2-1/2′ x 3′ crate with a six-legged, green-gold-eyed monster was sent to Horlicks University via Julia Carpenter. The creature was still alive when the crate was found in the basement of Amberson Hall 140 years later. ["The Crate" / "The Crate" from *Creepshow*]

19 June 1921

Grand Opening of Rose Red's new Tower [*The Diary of Ellen Rimbauer: My Life at Rose Red*]

19 June 1958, last day of school: The Losers' Club formed

Henry Bowers, Victor Criss, and Belch Huggins saw Ben Hanscom go into the Derry Public Library. When Ben came out, Criss and Huggins held him while Bowers carved an "H" on his chest. He broke free and fell down a hill. Bowers fell after him; Ben kicked him in the balls and hid in a hole in the Barrens for two hours. While looking for Ben, they destroyed Bill Denbrough and Eddie Kaspbrak's dam in the Barrens. Eddie suffered a nosebleed and an asthma attack after he was punched. Bill stayed with him until they met Ben, who stayed with Eddie while Bill took Silver to get an aspirator from Norbert Keene. Bill, Ben, and Eddie became the first Losers.

IT, as the Creature from the Black Lagoon, beheaded ten-year-old Eddie Corcoran in Bassey Park, near Derry's Canal.

From a picture in Georgie Denbrough's photo album, Georgie winked at Bill Denbrough. The picture bled. [*IT*]

19 June 1964

Civil rights activists James (Jimmy) Cheney, 21, Andrew (Andy) Goodman, 21, and Michael Schwerner, 24, disappeared near Philadelphia, MS. [*The Dark Tower VI: Song of Susannah*]

19 June 1970

Stephen King started the *Dark Tower* series.

19 June 1980

Donald Grant wanted to publish Stephen King's Dark Tower stories as *The Dark Tower: The Gunslinger* in a 10,000-copy limited edition, with another 500 signed and numbered. King said OK. [*The Dark Tower VI: Song of Susannah*]

19 June 1983

Christine stayed at number 3 on *The New York Times* Fiction Best Seller List, its eleventh week on the List.

19 June 1986

In a letter to Kathi Goodlowe, newlywed Pat Allen told about Lake Mohonk's having been haunted for four years by what people thought were a mother and son [Audrey Wyler and Seth Garin]. She found a Cassie Styles action figure in the gazebo of the Mother and Son Meadow. Nobody knew who it was because the MotoKops hadn't been created yet. [*The Regulators*]

19 June 1987

Stephen King received an author's copy of *The Drawing of the Three* from Donald Grant. He wanted NAL to do both *Dark Tower* books as trade paperbacks. He got drunk to celebrate. [*The Dark Tower VI: Song of Susannah*]

19 June 1988

Stephen King joined Alcoholics Anonymous. [*The Dark Tower VI: Song of Susannah*]

19 June 1989

Stephen King hit his one-year AA anniversary. He did not get drunk to celebrate. He wanted to get back into *The Dark Tower*, but it wasn't working out. He found it harder to write while sober. [*The Dark Tower VI: Song of Susannah*]

19 June 1990

3:45 a.m.: Larry Underwood arrived in New York City and parked outside his mother's house. Alice Underwood called in sick when she saw her son outside. She spent the morning with him then went to work late. Larry slept for eighteen hours.

The National Guard took over the WBZ-TV station in Boston.

Fran Goldsmith told her parents she was pregnant. Carla Goldsmith called her a bitch and forbade her from living in the house with the baby. Peter Goldsmith, Fran's dad, slapped Carla and said Fran could stay. Fran moved to the Harborside Hotel.

Vacationing Edward M. Norris and his family caught Captain Trips from Harry Trent outside Babe's Kwik-Eat in eastern Texas. Trent also infected Babe and some of Babe's help. [*The Stand: The Complete & Uncut Edition*]

19 June 1995

morning: William Hobart found the windows of his 4WD broken and all four tires flattened. Tak had attacked. [*The Regulators*]

Stephen King was ready to start the next *Dark Tower* volume. [*The Dark Tower VI: Song of Susannah*]

19 June 1999, Saturday

tentative title for Stephen King's how-to-write book: *On Writing*

12:00 p.m.: Joe and his family arrived to celebrate Father's Day with Stephen King.

In one timeline:

afternoon: Bryan Smith took his eyes off the road while driving the Slab City Hill part of Route 7 in Lovell, ME. Bullet, one of Smith's Rottweilers, was interested in ground beef in a cooler behind the seat. Smith struck Stephen King.

6:02 p.m.: Stephen King was pronounced dead of extensive head injuries at Northern Cumberland Memorial Hospital in Bridgton. [*The Dark Tower VI: Song of Susannah*]

While in another timeline:

>3:55 p.m.: Jake Chambers, Roland Deschain, and Oy pulled up behind Stephen King as he walked along Route 7. Roland got out and fell to his knees when his hip gave out. Jake jumped out and grabbed King by the waist. Bryan Smith's out-of-control van ran over Jake

and hit King, who was injured severely but lived. When King's hip broke, the pain in Roland's was gone. He buried Jake 200 paces into the woods. [*The Dark Tower VII: The Dark Tower*]

George Amberson's second timeline: Vermont's Yankee nuclear reactor exploded, spreading radiation over New England and Quebec, Canada. [*11/22/63*]

19 June 2011

Bree Donlin married George Hughes in a Long Island church. As a wedding present, Hugh Yates chartered a Gulfstream jet to take them to Hawai'i for their honeymoon. [*Revival*]

~19 June 2012

George Hughes and Bree Donlin's first child was born. [*Revival*]

June 20

20 June

Frank Kalowski had a nervous breakdown. Earlier, his wife, Rita, died of a brain tumor and his daughter, Miriam, committed suicide. [unpublished *Babylon Here / Sword in the Darkness*]

20 June 1921, 12:00 a.m.

Ellen Rimbauer and Sukeena went into Rose Red's new Tower to talk with April Rimbauer's presence. Ellen was sure she heard April's voice and saw her face as part of the stained-glass window. [*The Diary of Ellen Rimbauer: My Life at Rose Red*]

20 June 1958

Eddie Corcoran's mother, Monica Macklin, reported him missing after he didn't come home from school the day before.

The previous day's dam had been washed and kicked away. Under Ben Hanscom's instruction, Bill Denbrough, Eddie Kaspbrak, and Ben built a dam six feet long, two feet wide, and three feet deep. Richie Tozier and Stanley Uris became Losers when they stopped to help. During Mr. Nell's investigation of Derry drains backing up, he found their dam and made them take it apart.

Bill and Richie looked at Georgie Denbrough's photo album. The picture that had bled was gone. They saw a picture of themselves in 1930 Derry, ME. The still became a moving picture with sound. In the Canal, they saw IT as Georgie dressed as a clown. Bill reached into the picture. Richie pulled him out—Bill's fingers were cut. [*IT*]

20 June 1983

For most of June, Billy Halleck had been trying to find the Gypsies so he could persuade Taduz Lemke to lift the curse. On the 20th, he found out the Gypsies had been in Falmouth eighteen days earlier. [*Thinner*]

20 June 1990, Friday

2:00–4:00 p.m.: Ed Norris took his sick family to Dr. Sweeney's office in Polliston, KS. Sarah Bradford and Dr. Sweeney caught Captain Trips. Sarah infected her family, Angela Dupray, and her bridge club. The Norrises died within two weeks.

~6:00 p.m.: Poke Freeman and Lloyd Henreid had arranged with Gorgeous George to rob him and give him 25% of the take. They robbed him, but they killed him, too, getting drugs, guns, a Mustang, and $26.60.

Ray Booth, Mike Childress, Vince Hogan, and Billy Warner beat and robbed Nick Andros after seeing Nick at Zack's Place in Shoyo, AK. Nick broke one of their noses. The fight stopped when Doc Soames pulled up.

10:00 p.m.: Sarah Bradford and Angela Dupray celebrated their bridge club success at a cocktail bar, infecting more people. [*The Stand: The Complete & Uncut Edition*]

20 June 1999

Sunday: Ray Routhier's article, "STEPHEN KING DIES NEAR LOVELL HOME," with two subtitles, "POPULAR MAINE WRITER KILLED WHILE TAKING AFTERNOON WALK," and

"INSIDER CLAIMS MAN DRIVING LETHAL VAN 'TOOK EYES OFF THE ROAD' AS HE AP-PROACHED KING ON ROUTE 7," appeared in the Portland Sunday *Telegram*. [*The Dark Tower VI: Song of Susannah*]

The Girl Who Loved Tom Gordon dropped to number 8 on *The New York Times* Fiction Best Seller List, its ninth week on the List.

20 June 2010

Blockade Billy dropped to number 13 on *The New York Times* Fiction Best Seller List, its second and last week on the List.

20 June 2012

The Dark Tower: The Gunslinger—Man in Black #1 of 5 (Marvel Comics, $3.99) published

June 21

21 June 1957

Gatlin, NE, child Rachel Stigman was born Donna Stigman. ["Children of the Corn"]

21 June 1958, Saturday

Henry Bowers, Victor Criss, Belch Huggins, and two others went to the Aladdin Theater. After the movie, they trapped Ben Hanscom, Beverly Marsh, and Richie Tozier in an alley next to the theater. Ben knocked Bowers down with a trashcan. Ben and the others fought until they could run away. Beverly became a Loser. [*IT*]

21 June 1960, Tuesday, 7:00 a.m.

Don Biderman picked up Liz Garfield and, with Bill Cushman and Curtis Dean, drove to Providence, RI, for a three-day *Real Estate in the Sixties* seminar at the Warwick Hotel. ["Low Men in Yellow Coats"]

21 June 1975

A second ligament operation was scheduled for Johnny Smith for the 21st. [*The Dead Zone*]

21 June 1976, dusk

Rachel Stigman was sacrificed to He Who Walks Behind the Rows. ["Children of the Corn"]

21 June 1981

Danse Macabre dropped to number 11 on *The New York Times* Non-Fiction Best Seller List, its fifth and last week on the List.

21 June 1983

Billy Halleck learned the Gypsies had been in Boothbay Harbor thirteen days earlier. [*Thinner*]

21 June 1985

Skeleton Crew (Putnam, $18.95) published with a first printing of 500,000 copies

21 June 1987

~4:00 p.m.: National Guard helicopters had spotted Paul Sheldon's car. Colorado State Police Trooper Duane Kushner talked with Annie Wilkes. When Paul threw an ashtray through the bedroom window and yelled, she stabbed the trooper in the back with the cross from her cow's grave. He tried to crawl away; she ran over his arm and head with a riding lawn mower. She hid the trooper and his car in the barn. She put Paul on a mattress on a dark, damp, dirty floor in the basement, leaving him a Pepsi, food, and a hypodermic needle with scopolamine, a morphine-based painkiller. Thinking she left something lethal in the hypo, he injected himself. After dark, she took the cop's car and body away. [*Misery*]

The Eyes of the Dragon dropped to number 11 on *The New York Times* Fiction Best Seller List, its twenty-first week on the List.

Misery stayed at number 1 on *The New York Times* Fiction Best Seller List, its third week on the List.

21 June 1988

While marking trees to cut for firewood, Bobbi Anderson tripped over a metallic object protruding from the ground. For an instant, she felt a vibration. That night, she dreamed of green light and of her teeth falling out. [*The Tommyknockers*]

21 June 1990

Lila Bruett, Luke Bruett, and Bill Hapscomb were alive at the Atlanta Plague Center, but their conditions were classified. Norm Bruett and Bobby Bruett were dead. Hank Carmichael died that day.

Sheriff Baker jailed Mike Childress, Vince Hogan, and Billy Warner for beating and robbing Nick Andros. Ray Booth left town to avoid capture. Too sick to work that night, Sheriff Baker deputized Nick, whom he had already hired for small jobs around the office, to feed and watch the prisoners.

9:30 p.m.: Joe Bob Brentwood died from Captain Trips. [*The Stand: The Complete & Uncut Edition*]

21 June 2007

The summer solstice was the most dangerous day. Keeping the eight stones intact required more effort. (The winter solstice in December was the least dangerous.) N. canceled his appointment with Dr. Bonsaint and spent the day at Ackerman's Field, touching and counting the stones. ["N."]

21 June 2015

Finders Keepers entered *The New York Times* Hardcover Fiction Best Seller List at number 1. It was on the List for ten weeks.

June 22

22 June 1960, Wednesday

Ted Brautigan took Bobby Garfield to The Corner Pocket in Bridgeport, CT, to bet $500 on that night's Albini-Haywood fight. Ted had learned Haywood was going to take a dive in the eighth round. With 4-to-1 odds, he'd win $2,000.

night: In a scheduled twelve-round fight at Madison Square Garden, Tommy "Hurricane" Haywood, 23, knocked Eddie Albini, 36, around for five rounds. Eddie did OK in rounds six and seven; he knocked Hurricane out with a right hook in the eighth.

Liz Garfield didn't want to take part in Don Biderman, Bill Cushman, and Curtis Dean's S&M games. She had known the trip involved sex but went because she needed her job. She didn't like their bizarre antics and tried to run. They chased and fought her. She fought back but suffered two black eyes, a broken nose, a split lip, a removed fingernail, and many bruises. ["Low Men in Yellow Coats"]

22 June 1964

Odetta Holmes had been staying at the Blue Moon Motor Hotel for a civil rights activist event in Oxford, MS. At a meeting at John Bambry's First Afro-American Methodist Church of Oxford, it was announced that, because of the disappearance of Cheney, Goodman, and Schwerner three days earlier, anybody could go home. Nineteen, including Odetta, stayed. [*The Dark Tower VI: Song of Susannah*]

22 June 1988

Robinson flew to California to watch Jimmy Dolan's house for signs of preparations for Dolan's arrival. Dolan, a Las Vegas crime boss, had a home at 1121 Aster Drive in Hollywood Hills. Seven years earlier, Dolan had Robinson's wife, Elizabeth, killed. From *Nevada's Road Signs*, Robinson learned that miles 440–472 of US Route 71, westbound, would be repaved 1–22 July. He planned his revenge for the three-day national holiday, when Dolan would travel home to Los Angeles and nobody would be working on the road. ["Dolan's Cadillac"]

22 June 1990

Doc Soames had Captain Trips.

Alice Underwood called in sick for work, this time with Captain Trips. Larry Underwood took her to Mercy Hospital.

Randall Flagg participated in blowing up a power station in Laramie, WY. [*The Stand: The Complete & Uncut Edition*]

22 June 1998

"That Feeling, You Can Only Say What It Is In French" (collected in *Everything's Eventual*) appeared in the June 22nd issue of *The New Yorker*.

22 June 2014

Mr. Mercedes entered *The New York Times* Hardcover Fiction Best Seller List at number 1. It was on the List for ten weeks.

June 23

23 June 1960, Ugly Thursday

afternoon: Richie O'Meara and Willie Shearman held Carol Gerber while Harry Doolin hit her with a baseball bat. They ran away when she screamed after her shoulder popped. Bobby Garfield found her and took her to Ted Brautigan. Ted saw her wounds weren't serious and replaced her dislocated shoulder. Bobby had dropped his Alvin Dark baseball glove while helping Carol; Shearman went back and took it. Liz Garfield returned home early, saw a beaten Carol on Ted's lap and, having been sexually assaulted herself, assumed Ted had molested her—with Bobby's help. She threatened to tell the police she saw his hand in her clothes if he didn't leave. While walking Carol home, she learned where Ted would be that night. She called the low men at a number on one of many posters inquiring about Brautigan, an apparent lost pet. Later that night, she received $300.

9:45 p.m.: Outside The Corner Pocket, low men surrounded Ted Brautigan and brought Bobby Garfield to him. They said they'd kill Bobby and Carol Gerber if he escaped again, so Ted agreed to go with them and work willingly as a Breaker. Bobby went into the Corner Pocket and got Ted's winnings from Len Files by saying if Len gave him what he wanted, he and the low men would go away. He gave the money to his mother, who used it to become a partner of and invest in a friend's real estate business in Massachusetts. ["Low Men in Yellow Coats"] [*The Dark Tower VII: The Dark Tower*]

23 June 1975, dusk

Todd Bowden stabbed a wino thirty-seven times with a butcher knife at an abandoned train yard. He had bad dreams for almost a year. ["Apt Pupil"]

23 June 1977, Thursday

Lightning struck during the Durham High School graduation party held at Bruce Carrick's Cathy's Roadhouse in Somersworth, NH. A fire killed eighty-one people and burned thirty more. About forty escaped. Because of Johnny Smith's fears of fire at Cathy's, half the class had gone to Chuck Chatsworth's party instead. Johnny left New England to escape the publicity. In gratitude for saving his son's life, Roger Chatsworth paid Johnny's outstanding medical bills. [*The Dead Zone*]

3:14 p.m.: Eddie Dean used Black Thirteen and the Doorway Cave to go to New York City to see what day it was. He found The Manhattan Restaurant of the Mind closed and Enrico Balazar's car parked nearby. Inside, he saw chess pieces strewn on the marble, an overturned coffee cup, and Calvin Tower's broken glasses on the floor. In the office, Jack Andolini and George Biondi tried to persuade Tower to sell the vacant lot to The Sombra Corporation. Eddie surprised them by going in and talking to them as if he knew them (he did but years later). After hitting Biondi in the head three times and Andolini across the nose with his gun, Eddie sent them off with a message for Balazar. Tower was going to sell the vacant lot to the Tet Corporation instead of Sombra, and Tower was under the protection of people far more powerful than Balazar. Sure Balazar would retaliate, Eddie suggested Tower get out of New York until July 15th. After Tower figured out where he was going, he should have Aaron Deepneau write the ZIP code on the end of the vacant lot's fence on the Forty-Sixth Street side. Eddie also wanted Tower to agree to sell the vacant lot to the Tet Corporation (Eddie and his *ka-tet*). Tower agreed to do so if Eddie mentioned the name in Stefan Toren's (Tower's great-great-great-grandfather's) will. Eddie said it was either Roland Deschain or

Steven Deschain (it was Roland). Although he couldn't see it, Tower knew Eddie had a door to another place. He had Eddie help him pass his bookcase of valuable books through it. [*The Dark Tower V: Wolves of the Calla*]

23 June 1980

Over lunch at Portland's The Yellow Submarine, admen Roger Breakstone and Vic Trenton planned a ten-day trip to keep the Sharp account after the Red Razberry Zingers fiasco. They would go to Boston, New York, and Cleveland to meet with Image-Eye Studios, Summers Marketing and Research, and the Sharp Company. Later, they called this their Magical Mystery Tour. [*Cujo*]

23 June 1985

Richard Bachman's *Thinner* stayed at number 7 on *The New York Times* Fiction Best Seller List, its seventeenth week on the List.

Skeleton Crew entered *The New York Times* Fiction Best Seller List at number 1. It was on the List for thirty-two weeks.

23 June 1987

Annie Wilkes moved Paul Sheldon from the basement to his room. He took a can of lighter fluid from the basement. Investigating Colorado State Police Trooper Duane Kushner's disappearance, Troopers McKnight and Wicks visited Annie. She talked with them, and they left. Paul had a plan to get even, so he didn't yell. [*Misery*]

23 June 1988

Prime Evil: New Stories by the Masters of Modern Horror, edited by Douglas E. Winter (Dutton Books, $18.95), with "The Night Flier" (collected in *Nightmares & Dreamscapes*), published

23 June 1990

morning: Two of the stolen pickup's tires blew in New Mexico. A Lincoln Continental owner with his wife and daughter stopped to help. Poke Freeman and Lloyd Henreid killed the family and stole their car. Poke shot the man between the eyes with his Pokerizer.

Sheriff Baker and Vince Hogan died from Captain Trips in Shoyo, AK.

Sick with Captain Trips, Carla Goldsmith was taken to Sanford Hospital. She died within four days.

Poke and Henreid killed Mrs. Storm in a Burrack, AZ, café/store/gas station. Bill Markson, a store patron, shot Poke, removing the left side of his face. Pop, the proprietor, finished him with a shotgun. Henreid killed Markson. The Arizona State Police caught him outside and sent him to Apache County Jail in Phoenix, AZ. [*The Stand: The Complete & Uncut Edition*]

23 June 1996

The Green Mile, Part One: The Two Dead Girls dropped to number 10 on *The New York Times* Paperback Fiction Best Seller List, its eleventh week on the List.

The Green Mile, Part Two: The Mouse on the Mile stayed at number 2 on *The New York Times* Paperback Fiction Best Seller List, its seventh week on the List.

The Green Mile, Part Three: Coffey's Hands stayed at number 1 on *The New York Times* Paperback Fiction Best Seller List, its third week on the List.

23 June 2003

The Dark Tower: The Gunslinger: Revised and Expanded Edition (Viking, $25) published with a first printing of 60,000 copies

23 June 2010

American Vampire #4 (Vertigo Comics, $3.99), with Stephen King's "One Drop of Blood," published

23 June 2013

Joyland entered *The New York Times* Paperback Trade Fiction Best Seller List at number 2. It was on the List for twenty-two weeks.

June 24

24 June 1977, 12:00 p.m.

Direct from Calla Bryn Sturgis's Doorway Cave, Donald Callahan arrived outside Chew Chew Mama's in New York City. He found The Manhattan Restaurant of the Mind sealed with yellow *POLICE INVESTIGATION* tape; the bookstore had been torched in the night. As he approached Forty-Sixth Street on his way to the vacant lot, he could hear the rose. On the fence on the Forty-Sixth Street side, he saw Calvin Tower's ZIP code. At the New York Public Library, he found it was the ZIP code of East Stoneham, ME, about forty miles north of Portland. [*The Dark Tower V: Wolves of the Calla*]

24 June 1983

Billy Halleck found out the Gypsies had been in Bangor eleven days earlier. [*Thinner*]

24 June 1986

John Corcoran, a reporter for *The Topeka Capital-Journal* from the Topeka, KS, in a world like ours, reported about a superflu raging throughout the country. Dr. Morris Hackford estimated twenty to thirty million people in the United States had died. Dr. April Montoya estimated that, for every person killed, another six to twelve were sick. [*The Dark Tower IV: Wizard and Glass*]

24 June 1988, evening

Jim Gardener, on tour with the New England Poetry Caravan, gave a reading in Fall River. The Caravan had contracted him after Billy Claughtsworth died. [*The Tommyknockers*]

24 June 1990

So nobody could trace the Captain Trips epidemic to the United States, Billy Starkey ordered Len Creighton to tell Jack Cleveland to have his spies throughout the world release the Captain Trips virus from their vials.

On US 51 in Idaho, Randall Flagg walked south toward Nevada.

~12:00 p.m.: Nick Andros let Mike Childress, sick with Captain Trips, out of jail after Billy Warner died.

Alice Underwood died at Mercy Hospital. [*The Stand: The Complete & Uncut Edition*]

The Stand: The Complete & Uncut Edition stayed at number 4 on *The New York Times* Fiction Best Seller List, its seventh week on the List.

24 June 1995, Saturday, 5:45 a.m.

Tak broke every window in the Hobarts' house. [*The Regulators*]

24 June 2001

Dreamcatcher dropped to number 7 on *The New York Times* Fiction Best Seller List, its twelfth week on the List.

24 June 2012

The Dark Tower 4.5: The Wind Through the Keyhole dropped to number 14 on *The New York Times* Fiction Best Seller List, its seventh week on the List.

24 June 2018

The Outsider dropped to number 2 on *The New York Times* Hardcover Fiction Best Seller List, its third week on the List.

June 25

25 June 1947

"FIRE CONTROL OFFICER SPOTS 'FLYING SAUCERS' Kenneth Arnold Reports 9 Disc-Shaped Objects 'Shiny, Silvery, Moved Incredibly Fast'" appeared in the *East Oregonian*. [*Dreamcatcher*]

25 June 1970

"Slade," Chapter 3, appeared in *The Maine Campus*.

25 June 1975

Todd Bowden and his parents left for a Hawaiian vacation. ["Apt Pupil"]

25 June 1983

Billy Halleck was close to finding the Gypsies. [*Thinner*]

25 June 1988

Jim Gardener, on tour with the New England Poetry Caravan, gave a reading at B. U. in Boston. [*The Tommyknockers*]

25 June 1990

early a.m.: Randall Flagg walked near the Idaho-Nevada border.

Sheriff Baker's wife, Jane, died from Captain Trips.

Wes Swann caught the superflu.

Curtis Beauchamp and Freddy Delancey manned an armed barricade to keep people out of Ogunquit, ME.

Guard Shockley paid Mathers a pack of cigarettes to knee Lloyd Henreid in the crotch. [*The Stand: The Complete & Uncut Edition*]

June 26

26 June 1977

Black Thirteen helped Donald Callahan go through the door in Calla Bryn Sturgis's Doorway Cave. In New York City, he went to the New York Public Library's men's room to get *Yankee Highways*, a book he had stashed there two days before. On page 119 was a picture of the East Stoneham Methodist Meeting Hall, Built 1819 (digits add up to nineteen). He returned to the Cave. [*The Dark Tower V: Wolves of the Calla*]

26 June 1983

118 pounds: Billy Halleck found the Gypsies in Tecknor, ME. He checked in to Unit 37, Frenchman's Bay Motel, in Bar Harbor, ME. Taduz Lemke refused to lift the curse. With a slingshot, Gina Lemke shot a hole in Billy's left hand. [*Thinner*]

Christine stayed at number 3 on *The New York Times* Fiction Best Seller List, its twelfth week on the List.

26 June 1987

Newscaster Glenna Roberts and a KTKA news team visited Annie Wilkes. They left when Annie fired a gun in the air. [*Misery*]

26 June 1988

Bobbi Anderson began digging up the metal object she found in her property a few days earlier. She dug a trench about fifteen feet long and around four feet deep. From the object's curvature, she suspected a flying saucer with an estimated diameter of ninety-five yards. She felt it vibrate.

Ron Cummings, not knowing about Jim Gardener's drinking problems, invited him to get drunk. They were thrown out of the Stone Country Bar and Grill after Gard started a fight over nuclear power plants. [*The Tommyknockers*]

26 June 1990

The Bruetts' house exploded; the gas had been left on when they were taken to the Atlanta Plague Center.

Marcy Swann caught Captain Trips.

Andy Devins, Lloyd Henreid's court-appointed lawyer, visited Henreid in jail.

9:01 a.m.: WBZ-TV employees George Dickerson, Bob Palmer, Charles Yorkin, and six to seven others reclaimed the station from the National Guard and broadcast the truth about Captain Trips.

10:45 a.m.: Sergeant T. L. Peters led an eighteen-man patrol from Carthage, MO, to get Ray Flowers off the air. Twenty men were ordered to go; two were shot for refusing.

11:45 a.m.: Sergeant Peters shot and killed Ray Flowers for talking about Captain Trips on Ray's radio show. Three of Peters's men shot and killed him for killing Flowers.

7:16–7:22 p.m.: Colonel Albert Philips commanded Units 12, 13, 16, 17, and 20 to kill the many Kent State University students they were containing on campus.

7:28–7:30 p.m.: Sergeant First Class Roland Gibbs changed his name to Brother Zeno after he and other soldiers took over a San Francisco Army base. Major Alfred Nunn had them killed.

8:30 p.m.: Peter Goldsmith died from Captain Trips at home.

9:16–10:45 p.m.: Radical black Army men executed Master Tech Sergeant Roger Petersen and sixty-one others on WCSH–TV, Portland, ME.

11:15 p.m.: Boulder, CO, residents felt the US Meteorological Air Testing Center on Broadway was a front for biological research. Desmond Ramage blew it up and died in the explosion. [*The Stand: The Complete & Uncut Edition*]

26 June 2016

End of Watch entered *The New York Times* Hardcover Fiction Best Seller List at number 1. It was on the List for nine weeks.

June 27

27 June 1958, Friday

Thinking IT had killed Georgie Denbrough and other Derry children, Bill Denbrough and Richie Tozier went to 29 Neibolt Street to kill IT. Bill took a slingshot and his father's pistol. They entered through a cellar window under the porch. IT as a werewolf came downstairs. Richie climbed up a coal pile and out another window. Bill shot at IT three times, hitting IT at least once, before following Richie. IT grabbed Bill's leg; Richie pulled him free. Bill turned and shot IT in the head, and Richie threw sneezing powder in IT's face. While IT sneezed, they ran for Silver. IT ran after them awhile but couldn't catch them.

IT talked to Beverly Marsh from her bathroom sink's drain. IT used the voices of Matthew Clements, Veronica Grogan, and Betty Ripsom—all IT murder victims—before spewing blood from the drain. Her father couldn't see the blood, so he beat her for screaming without reason. [*IT*]

27 June 1977

With Black Thirteen's help, Donald Callahan stepped through the door in Calla Bryn Sturgis's Doorway Cave to the East Stoneham Methodist Church. On his way to the General Store, he saw that Mobil gasoline was forty-nine cents a gallon. At the General Store, he bought a Portland *Press-Herald* for ten cents and some salami by the slice. He got directions to the Post Office, where he left a letter for Aaron Deepneau or Calvin Tower, General Delivery. The note told how they could let him know where they were. As Roland Deschain had instructed, he signed the note, *Callahan, of the Eld.* Leaving the Post Office, he noticed Eddie Dean wasn't in the Cave. He went back and saw a Sherlock Holmes book propping Black Thirteen's box open, which kept the door ajar. Outside the Cave, Eddie was about to fall over a 700-foot drop. Callahan pulled him back to safety. [*The Dark Tower V: Wolves of the Calla*]

27 June 1983, Monday

116 pounds: Richard Ginelli sent Fander, who used to be a doctor, to treat Billy Halleck's hand. Ginelli, who had done a lot of business with Greely, Penschley, and Kinder, called Kirk Penschley to stop Barton Detective Services, Inc., from tracking Billy. He told Penschley to send phony reports to Dr. Houston and Heidi Halleck. [*Thinner*]

27 June 1987

Local Sidewinder, CO, police talked with Annie Wilkes about the missing state trooper. [*Misery*]

27 June 1988

Bobbi Anderson noticed improvements in her aging dog. Peter's cataract, although smaller, glowed green. She took him to Dr. Etheridge. When Peter came out of the Augusta Veterinary Clinic, Eric bit Mrs. Perkins, his owner. She required stitches.

Arberg introduced the New England Poetry Caravan poets, including Jim Gardener, at Northwestern University. After the readings, he gave a party. Anti-nuke Gardener argued with Ted. When Arberg tried to throw Gard out, Gard elbowed him in the chest. Arberg had a heart attack; he died on the way to the hospital. Gard left after Patricia McCardle called the police. [*The Tommyknockers*]

27 June 1990

Wes Swann, sick with Captain Trips, slipped into a coma.

~11:45 a.m.: Rita Blakemoor joined Larry Underwood in New York's Central Park.

Fran Goldsmith buried her father in his garden.

~10:00 p.m.: Stu Redman killed Dr. Elder at the Stovington Plague Center. Dr. Elder, an Army Project Blue operative, had orders to kill him. Stu escaped the Center and headed for the ocean. [*The Stand: The Complete & Uncut Edition*]

27 June 1996

The Green Mile, Part Four: The Bad Death of Eduard Delacroix (Signet, $2.99) published with a first printing of 2,000,000 copies

27 June 1999

The Girl Who Loved Tom Gordon dropped to number 10 on *The New York Times* Fiction Best Seller List, its tenth week on the List.

27 June 2004

The Dark Tower VI: Song of Susannah entered *The New York Times* Fiction Best Seller List at number 1. It was on the List for ten weeks.

June 28

28 June 1958

Ben Hanscom, Eddie Kaspbrak, and Stan Uris helped Beverly Marsh clean up the blood from her bathroom. [*IT*]

28 June 1968, Friday, 2:00 a.m.

Warwick, foreman of a Gates Falls, ME, textile mill, recruited Hall to clean the basement during the mill's weeklong break for the Fourth of July. They'd work the graveyard shift when it wouldn't be as hot. ["Graveyard Shift"]

28 June 1983, Tuesday

Richard Ginelli helped Billy Halleck with Taduz Lemke and the Gypsies. He poisoned their seven fighting pit bulls and fired a Kalashnikov AK-47 automatic assault rifle over their heads and under their cars. [*Thinner*]

28 June 1987

Sidewinder, CO, teenagers harassed Annie Wilkes. [*Misery*]

The Eyes of the Dragon dropped to number 12 on *The New York Times* Fiction Best Seller List, its twenty-second week on the List.

Misery stayed at number 1 on *The New York Times* Fiction Best Seller List, its fourth week on the List.

28 June 1988, Wednesday

At the spaceship dig site, Bobbi Anderson found five dead birds, without flies. Over the next few days, she was busy and lost track of the time. Her water ran on LP gas from Dead River Gas in Derry, ME; she modified it to run on twelve D flashlight batteries. She added another gear to her Tomcat mini tractor—UP. She updated her typewriter to accept input from her thoughts; it had a five-to-ten-mile range. Mostly while she slept, she wrote *The Buffalo Soldiers*, which took place in an early 1850s Kansas range war. She dedicated this 400-page novel, her twelfth Western, to Jim Gardener. She adapted other things to use batteries, but she didn't understand the modifications she learned from the ship's Tommyknocker influence. She put Peter in the shed and used him as a power source. [*The Tommyknockers*]

28 June 1990

That day's lunch was the last meal served to the Phoenix municipal jail prisoners. The Pokeno Killer, who had killed his wife and brother-in-law while playing a penny Pokeno game, hanged himself in his cell. Trask, awaiting his trial for assault and armed robbery, in the cell next to Lloyd Henreid, died from Captain Trips. Henreid and a rat shared his leg over the next few days. [*The Stand: The Complete & Uncut Edition*]

28 June 1995, late morning

Courtesy of Tak, Irene Hobart suffered a worse-than-normal nosebleed. An ambulance took her to the hospital. Within two hours, she was home. [*The Regulators*]

28 June 2007

At his fourth session with Dr. John Bonsaint, N. told the doctor about the effect of the summer and winter solstices on Ackerman's Field. N. also said he no longer needed his services. Dr. Bonsaint made an appointment for July 5th in case N. changed his mind. ["N."]

28 June 2015

Finders Keepers dropped to number 2 *The New York Times* Hardcover Fiction Best Seller List, its second week on the List.

June 29

29 June 1967

Darlene Stamnacher, of Maxton, NC, disappeared. [*Joyland*]

29 June 1969

Harding gang members Bull Run, Hash, Jig, Marty, Webs McCullough, Peter, and Spooner started a riot to coincide with black activist Marcus Slade's arrival in town. [unpublished *Babylon Here / Sword in the Darkness*]

29 June 1983, Wednesday evening

still 116 pounds: Billy Halleck's weight-loss was causing heart trouble. Richard Ginelli told Gina Lemke he would kill her and two small Gypsy boys if Taduz Lemke didn't lift his curse. They arranged a meeting between Taduz Lemke and Halleck. [*Thinner*]

29 June 1987

Paul Sheldon finished *Misery's Return*. He asked for a cigarette. Annie Wilkes agreed but just one match. Paul soaked a pile of blank paper—the top piece was *Misery's Return*'s cover sheet—with lighter fluid. When Annie came in, he lit it. When she tried to put out the fire, he dropped the fifty-pound typewriter on her back. He jumped on her and stuffed burning paper in her mouth. She threw him off, got up, fell over the typewriter, and hit her head on the mantelpiece. Paul got out and shut the door. Colorado State Police Troopers McKnight and Wicks returned with a search warrant. They found Paul alive. Annie was in the barn, dead, holding a chainsaw. [*Misery*]

29 June 1988, Wednesday

Los Angeles Security Services and Big Joe's Cleaning Service began preparing Jimmy Dolan's house. To confirm Dolan was going to Los Angeles for the weekend, Robinson pretended to be Bill, and called Big Joe's about a party at Dolan's on Saturday night. Big Joe's said Dolan wasn't due until Sunday. ["Dolan's Cadillac"]

While cleaning a closet, Rebecca Paulson found her husband's pistol. She shot herself in the head when she fell from the ladder she was using. That evening, she had a Band-Aid on her head but had forgotten what had happened. ["The Revelations of 'Becka Paulson"]

29 June 1990

7:00 a.m.–1:00 p.m.: Lloyd Henreid bloodied his hands freeing a cot leg, which he used to make noise, but there was no one to hear. He killed a rat in Trask's cell with it. That evening, he retrieved the rat and saved it to eat later. His trial was scheduled for this day; Arizona sought the death penalty.

Arthur Stimson stepped on a rusty nail after swimming. Within three days, he died while amputating his gangrenous foot.

~9:10 p.m.: Ray Booth returned to Shoyo and attacked Nick Andros. Ray jammed his thumb in Nick's eye, and Nick's gun went off, the bullet grazing his right thigh. Nick shot and killed Booth. He didn't lose his eye, but it bled and his vision was impaired. He almost died from the infected leg wound, however.

~11:00 p.m.: Marcy Swann, Lucy's daughter, died from Captain Trips. Lucy buried her. [*The*

Stand: The Complete & Uncut Edition]

29 June 2014

Mr. Mercedes dropped to number 2 on *The New York Times* Hardcover Fiction Best Seller List, its second week on the List.

June 30

30 June

Johnny Rockwell's inspection sticker expired at midnight. Bob Driscoll gave Rocky a sticker for his car that couldn't pass inspection. They drank beer with Leo Edwards. ["Big Wheels: A Tale of the Laundry Game (Milkman #2)"]

30 June 1980, Monday

With a fifty-cent lottery ticket she bought at the Agway Market, Charity Camber won $5,000 with green #76 and red #434. She'd get around $4,200 after taxes.

Donna Trenton had been having an affair with Steve Kemp. When she called it off, he wrote an anonymous note to Vic Trenton, telling him of the affair.

That evening, Vin Marchant became the oldest Castle Rock resident when Aunt Evvie Chalmers died of a heart attack at her kitchen table. [*Cujo*]

30 June 1981

deadline for Zenith House to have three books that will hit *The New York Times* Bestseller List by the end of the year [*The Plant* Book One: *Zenith Rising*]

30 June 1983, Thursday, ~7:00 p.m.

Richard Ginelli dropped off Billy Halleck at Fairmont Park in Bangor and watched from a distance. Gina Lemke killed Ginelli and severed his hand. She disposed of the body but left the hand in the car for Halleck. Taduz Lemke gave Halleck a pie and explained that *purpurfargade ansiktet* was alive in Billy, eating him. To get rid of it, he had to put a knife in his wounded hand, bleed into the pie, and get somebody else to eat it within a couple of weeks. He called home and found that his daughter was staying with her Aunt Rhoda. His weight increased to 122 pounds. [*Thinner*]

30 June 1985

Richard Bachman's *Thinner* dropped to number 9 on *The New York Times* Fiction Best Seller List, its eighteenth week on the List.

Skeleton Crew stayed at number 1 on *The New York Times* Fiction Best Seller List, its second week on the List.

30 June 1990

Al and Virge served in the Army during the Captain Trips epidemic; the rest of their unit was dead.

At her insistence, Rita Blakemoor and Larry Underwood buried the monster-shouter, whom they found murdered in New York's Central Park.

Mark Braddock met Perion McCarthy in Albany, NY.

The Trashcan Man set fire to Cheery Petroleum Company, Inc.'s #1 unleaded gasoline storage tank. It and other tanks blew. He broke his right wrist running away. [*The Stand: The Complete & Uncut Edition*]

30 June 1995

"Luckey Quarter" (collected in *Everything's Eventual*) appeared in *USA Weekend*.

30 June 1996

The Green Mile, Part One: The Two Dead Girls rose to number 9 on *The New York Times* Paperback Fiction Best Seller List, its twelfth week on the List.

The Green Mile, Part Two: The Mouse on the Mile dropped to number 6 on *The New York Times* Paperback Fiction Best Seller List, its eighth week on the List.

The Green Mile, Part Three: Coffey's Hands stayed at number 1 on *The New York Times* Paperback Fiction Best Seller List, its fourth week on the List.

30 June 2003

"Harvey's Dream" (collected in *Just After Sunset*) appeared in the June 30th issue of *The New Yorker*.

30 June 2013

Joyland rose to number 1 on *The New York Times* Paperback Trade Fiction Best Seller List, its second week on the List.

30 June 2015

"Drunken Fireworks" (Simon & Schuster Audio, $9.99) published (collected in *The Bazaar of Bad Dreams*)

June

June 1915

Bob T. Watson and his son became The Overlook Hotel's caretakers after Watson sold the hotel to James Parris for $180,000. ["Before the Play"]

June 1925

Two-year-old Elizabeth Eastlake fell from her carriage and struck the right side of her head on a stone. The contrecoup injury damaged the left side of her brain. She temporarily lost her language ability but kept her sight. In the Port Charlotte *Weekly Echo*, M. Rickert reported her newfound art talent and called her a child prodigy. Her ability attracted the attention of Perse, who used Elizabeth and her artwork for evil. [*Duma Key*]

June 1932

Wild Bill Wharton raped and murdered Cora and Kathe Detterick. John Coffey found them and tried to heal them, but it was too late. Deputy Rob McGee's posse found Coffey holding the dead girls. They mistook his saying he couldn't help it as a confession. Wild Bill killed a pregnant woman and two more people in a holdup, a crime for which he was to be executed. [*The Green Mile*]

June 1951

Greg Stillson graduated at the top of his high school class. [*The Dead Zone*]

June 1960

Thaddeus Beaumont's January entry of a story in *American Teen* magazine's writing contest could have won Second Prize in the Fiction category. He was too young for the teenagers' contest, but he got an Honorable Mention. They sent him a Certificate of Merit by insured, registered mail. Six years later, they bought a story, his first professional sale. [*The Dark Half*]

June 1963

A week after school finished, Tanya Caron and Selena St. George went to Lake Winthrop for the summer. Reverend Huff needed two girls who swam well to be counselors at the Methodist Church Camp. [*Dolores Claiborne*]

June 1964

Steve King's *The Star Invaders* (Triad, Inc., and Gaslight Books, 20 cents) self-published

June 1966

Three gunmen killed Vito Gienelli and his bodyguards in The Overlook Hotel's Presidential Suite. The article "Gangland-Style Shooting at Colorado Hotel" detailed the event. [*The Shining*]

June 1970

Dr. Younger diagnosed an inoperable brain tumor on Charlie Dawes's nineteenth day in Doctors Hospital. [*Roadwork*]

June 1973

"Trucks" (collected in *Night Shift*) appeared in the June issue (Vol. 23, No. 8) of *Cavalier*.

June 1974

During a thunderstorm, Jamie Morton took Astrid Soderberg to Skytop, near Goat Mountain Resort. They watched lightning strike a twenty-foot iron rod, driven into the rock. The rod glowed a blue so bright they had to close their eyes. When they opened them, the rod was red then faded to black. Six balls of St. Elmo's fire followed another lightning bolt. To the east, they could see Brunswick, Freeport, and Jerusalem's Lot. In an old cabin, Astrid had Jamie make love to her. Each lost their virginity. [*Revival*]

In the sixth-grade, Frankie Stone called the overweight Gwendy Peterson, "Goodyear," after the Blimp. Other kids picked up on the nickname. After school ended for the year, she climbed the 305 Suicide Stairs to go to the playground on Castle View. She vowed to do this every day during the summer so she wouldn't be Goodyear when she started the seventh grade at Castle Rock Middle School. [*Gwendy's Button Box*]

June 1975

Gwendy Peterson's glasses hurt her eyes. She found she could see better without them. At optician Dr. Emerson's, she read the entire chart without her glasses. She attributed her improved eyesight to the tiny chocolate treats. [*Gwendy's Button Box*]

Stephen King finished *'Salem's Lot*.

June 1976

Lupe Delgado died. After Lupe's funeral, Donald Callahan fell off the wagon and left Home. [*The Dark Tower V: Wolves of the Calla*]

Johnny Smith recommended a year of prep school before college for Chuck Chatsworth. Roger Chatsworth agreed and paid him a $500 bonus for Chuck's improvement. [*The Dead Zone*]

Bookstore clerk Andy Halliday told Morris Bellamy that booksellers believed John Rothstein had continued writing after he stopped publishing. He suggested Bellamy get the unpublished work. Andy could sell it to a private collector after a five-year cooling-off period. [*Finders Keepers*]

June 1977

Summer 1976 was the first time Gwendy Peterson wore a bathing suit in public. Best friend Olive Kepnes called it her granny suit. The following June, Gwendy's mother took her to the mall for flip-flops and two bikinis. [*Gwendy's Button Box*]

"The Cat From Hell" (collected in *Just After Sunset*) appeared in the June issue (Vol. 27, No. 8) of *Cavalier*.

June 1980

Two days after Brock came home from school sick, his younger sister, Marcy, had a virus. After Red Razberry Zingers for breakfast, she vomited what looked like blood. A large batch of Zingers with a bad red dye had gone out. The dye stayed red as it passed through the body, making it appear as if Marcy had vomited blood. This started the Red Razberry Zinger fiasco for Roger Breakstone and Vic Trenton. [*Cujo*]

June 1981

"The Jaunt" (collected in *Skeleton Crew*) appeared in the June issue (Volume 1, Number 3) of *The Twilight Zone Magazine*.

June 1982

Terrors, edited by Charles L. Grant (Berkley, $2.95), with "Survivor Type" (collected in *Skeleton Crew*), published

June 1983

Billy Halleck told his wife about the Gypsy curse. Heidi Halleck and Dr. Houston did the paperwork to have him committed into a mental hospital. [*Thinner*]

The Creeds bought Bill Cleveland's house in Ludlow, ME. Bill's wife, Joan, had died in 1981; Bill had moved to an old folks' apartment in Orrington, ME. [*Pet Sematary*]

June 1984

full moon: Reverend Lowe went into the Chat 'n Chew café, transformed into The Beast, and killed proprietor Alfie Knopfler. [*Cycle of the Werewolf*]

Gwendy Peterson graduated *summa cum laude* from Brown University. After she packed to go home to Castle Rock, she saw a hat sitting on her desk. Mr. Farris called her into the kitchen. He congratulated her on her proprietorship of the button box, in never using it for ill intent. He set her mind at ease about what the box had and had not done. It had averted many disasters but hadn't prevented everything. Some things for which she blamed the box would have happened anyway: Jim Jones was crazy, and Olive Kepnes had issues, mainly her stepfather molesting her. He admitted Harry Streeter may have lived had she never had the box. Before Mr. Farris left with the box, he told a little of her future. The Iowa Writer's Workshop would accept her application. As a writer, she would use different button boxes —a typewriter then a computer. Finally, she would die, with little pain, among friends. When Mr. Farris was gone, Gwendy found an 1891 Morgan silver dollar in place of his hat on her desk. [*Gwendy's Button Box*]

"The Ballad of the Flexible Bullet" (collected in *Skeleton Crew*) appeared in the June issue (#397; Volume 66, Number 6) of *The Magazine of Fantasy & Science Fiction*.

June 1987

Masques II, edited by J. N. Williamson (Maclay & Assoc, $19.95), with "Popsy" (collected in *Nightmares & Dreamscapes*), published

June 1988

Night Visions 5, edited by Douglas E. Winter (Dark Harvest, $22), with "Dedication" (collected in *Nightmares & Dreamscapes*), "The Reploids," and "Sneakers" (collected in *Nightmares & Dreamscapes*), published with a first printing of 7,500 copies

June 1989

Book of the Dead, edited by John Skipp and Craig Spector (Bantam, $5.99), with "Home Delivery" (collected in *Nightmares & Dreamscapes*), published

June 1990

Nadine Cross found Joe on the Rockway's lawn. He had been bitten in the ankle; she nursed him back to health in three days. [*The Stand: The Complete & Uncut Edition*]

June 1995

Rose Madder (Viking, $25.95) published with a first printing of 1,750,000 copies

June 2002

Tom Goodhugh's wife, Norma, died of cancer. Dave Streeter's promotion at the bank earned him a six-figure salary. The Columbia School of Journalism admitted Dave's daughter, May, to their graduate school. ["Fair Extension"]

June 2003

2:47 a.m.: Harvey Stevens dreamed that Frank Friedman's Volvo was dented, perhaps from hitting someone while driving drunk. Harvey's daughter Trisha called and told him the police called her because they didn't have his number. One of his other daughters, Jenna or Stephanie, had been killed. Harvey screamed himself awake before he learned which one.

After Harvey told his wife about the dream later that morning, the phone rang. ["Harvey's Dream"]

June 2006

Calling himself Zack McCool, James Dooley harassed Lisey Landon on behalf of Professor Woodbody to coerce her to donate her late husband's, popular writer Scott Landon, professional memorabilia to the University of Pittsburgh. At one point, Dooley mutilated Lisey with an Oxo can opener. Sure that Dooley would kill her when they next met, she healed herself in Boo'ya Moon's pool then enticed Dooley to return. She took him to Boo'ya Moon, where she smashed his face with the same spade she had used on Gerd Allen Cole in August 1988. She had planned to kill him with that spade, but he wandered off the path into the woods. It was after sunset, and the commotion woke the long boy, a living mass of swirling bad-gunky, which consumed Dooley. [*Lisey's Story*]

June 2007

Edgar Freemantle and Jerome Wireman took a boat to the middle of Lake Phalen in Minnesota. Wireman had Perse in a sealed, custom-made silver cylinder. He dropped it into a 380-foot fissure beneath the freshwater lake. [*Duma Key*]

June 2008

Bree Donlin took computer classes at CU. Jamie Morton asked her to research C. Danny Jacobs. She found many websites that debunked his cures. The cancerous tumors he removed were just pig livers or goat guts. Jamie suspected the tumor removals were for show, like the electrical demonstrations before selling Lightning Portraits. [*Revival*]

June 2009

The Big Book of NECON, edited by Bob Booth (Cemetery Dance Publications, $50), with "The Old Dude's Ticker," published

June 2011

Al Templeton went through the time portal in the back of his diner to 1958 to prevent the JFK assassination. Four years in, he had to return because of lung cancer; he wouldn't live long enough to finish. While there, he wrote a notebook on Lee Harvey Oswald. He told Jake Epping about the portal and his mission. Jake went into the past to save Carolyn Poulin from being shot by Andy Cullum, to stop Frank Dunning from killing his family, and to save President Kennedy. [*11/22/63*]

June 2012

Nurse Sadie MacDonald had another mini-seizure at the window. Brady Hartsfield went in. He could control her body but worried he'd be caught, so he read her thoughts. He also dropped thoughts in her mind—she led her father on; she enjoyed it; she was responsible for his death; she didn't deserve to live. After this, he found he could enter her easily, without mini-seizures from the flashes of sunlight. He continued dropping thoughts. [*End of Watch*]

June 2013

Alden McCausland needed bigger, better fireworks, so Pop Anderson got him some M-120s and twelve Chinese Peonies bottle rockets for $30. Pop threw in a few firecrackers and Twizzlers. ["Drunken Fireworks"]

June 2014

For ten years, Charlie Jacobs tracked people with any of eight specific, rare illnesses that were incurable with secret electricity. The list grew to hundreds of names. As Charlie learned more, and as the people died, hundreds dropped to dozens. By June 2014, he had three names. He eliminated two, leaving Mary Fay, whom he called Patient Omega. [*Revival*]

June 2015

In 1986, Ollie Franklin and friends went to Highpockets. A young man with silver glitter on his cheeks, long blond hair, and wearing a sleeveless blue T-shirt and white shorts walked in and joined a group of young men. Noah Freemont called him Mister Yummy.

Over two weeks in June 2015, Ollie saw a representation of Mister Yummy. Each time he saw him, Mister Yummy was closer. He first saw him at the end of the Lakeview Assisted Living Center's drive. Every couple of days, he saw him again—on the porch steps, on a bench at the administration office, and then in the common room. After recreating four missing puzzle pieces, he said he was tired and excused himself. A nurse found him dead on his bed that evening. ["Mister Yummy"]

June 2017

Peter Robinson found a small, gray dog scratching at his door. He took him in, gave him food and water, and named him Gandalf the Gray. ["Summer Thunder"]

July
Happenings

July 1

1 July

Carolyn Broadmoor was buried next to Amanda Drogan. Seventy-year-old Broadmoor had lived with the Drogans for two years before Sam stole her breath. ["The Cat From Hell"]

1 July, early a.m.

After drinking beer for several hours, Leo Edwards and Johnny Rockwell left Bob Driscoll's gas station. Spike Milligan caused them to crash into a 1959 Mercury, the car owned by a murder victim in The Devon Woods. (The murder victim and his girlfriend had been parking. Their bodies were found strewn throughout the car.) Leo and Rocky died in the crash. Milligan headed for Driscoll's house. ["Big Wheels: A Tale of the Laundry Game (Milkman #2)"]

1 July 1967

Darlene Stamnacher's body was found in a lean-to near Elrod. The Funhouse Killer had cut her throat. [*Joyland*]

1 July 1968, Monday, 11:00 p.m.

Thirty-six men, including Hall and Harry Wisconsky, assembled to clean the basement level of a Gates Falls, ME, textile mill. Warwick supervised. ["Graveyard Shift"]

1 July 1983, Friday

Richard Ginelli's body was found in the basement of a Bangor apartment on Union Street near Fairmont Park. He was believed to have been the victim of a Mafia hit. [*Thinner*]

1 July 1988, Friday

Robinson loaded his van and put stolen license plates on it. He began preparing Jimmy Dolan's trap on a detoured section of US Route 71. ["Dolan's Cadillac"]

Bobbi Anderson stopped her Central Maine Power service. She didn't need it because she knew how to power everything with batteries. [*The Tommyknockers*]

1 July 1990

Garvey joined Al and Virge.

Glen Bateman and Kojak met Stu Redman on US 302 in New Hampshire.

In Gary, IN, one of The Trashcan Man's fire-setting devices malfunctioned, scorching his left arm. More than 108 oil tanks blew; all of Gary burned.

~4:20 p.m.: Rita Blakemoor and Larry Underwood left New York through the Lincoln Tunnel to New Jersey. They had split after an argument and entered the tunnel separately. She caught up to him. [*The Stand: The Complete & Uncut Edition*]

The Stand: The Complete & Uncut Edition stayed at number 4 on *The New York Times* Fiction Best Seller List, its eighth week on the List.

1 July 1991

In a Winnebago, Fran Goldsmith, Peter Goldsmith-Redman, and Stu Redman left the Free Zone. They expected to be in Maine by the end of the month. On the way, they stopped at Mother Abagail's old house in Hemingford Home, NE. [*The Stand: The Complete & Uncut Edition*]

1 July 1995

Tak caused William Hobart to fall down the stairs and break a hip and leg. An ambulance took him to County General Hospital. [*The Regulators*]

1 July 1999

In a joint effort between North Central Positronics and the Sombra Corporation, the New York Plaza-Park Hotel became the Regal U. N. Plaza Hotel. [*The Dark Tower VI: Song of Susannah*]

1 July 2001

Dreamcatcher rose to number 6 on *The New York Times* Fiction Best Seller List, its thirteenth week on the List.

1 July 2007

Richard Bachman's *Blaze* entered *The New York Times* Fiction Best Seller List at number 2. It was on the List for five weeks.

1 July 2009

On a Cyber Patrol call to Mrs. Trelawney, Brady Hartsfield installed a program that allowed remote access to her computer. He also put on SPOOKS, an audio file. [*Mr. Mercedes*]

1 July 2012

The Dark Tower 4.5: The Wind Through the Keyhole dropped to number 16 on *The New York Times* Fiction Best Seller List, its eighth and last week on the List.

1 July 2014

Charlie Jacobs called Jamie Morton and told him to be ready. He was getting close to his final experiment. [*Revival*]

1 July 2018

The Outsider stayed at number 2 on *The New York Times* Hardcover Fiction Best Seller List, its fourth week on the List.

July 2

2 July 1958

Gard Jagermeyer, a friend of Henry Bowers, pushed Richie Tozier down, breaking Richie's glasses. [*IT*]

2 July 1968, Tuesday, 2:00–4:00 a.m.

A large rat bit and hung on to Ray Upson's hand while he cleaned the basement of a Gates Falls, ME, textile mill. Charlie Brochu knocked it off. ["Graveyard Shift"]

2 July 1970

"Slade," Chapter 4, appeared in *The Maine Campus*.

2 July 1982

"THREE MORE INFANT DEATHS IN BOULDER HOSPITAL," a Rocky Mountain *News* article, reported that more babies died. Annie Wilkes was responsible. [*Misery*]

2 July 1983

127 pounds: Billy Halleck called Rhoda Simonson and found out Linda Halleck would stay there until he got home. [*Thinner*]

2 July 1988, Saturday

Starting in the early morning, Robinson cut forty-two squares in the asphalt and moved them to a ditch with a $315,000 Case-Jordan bucket loader. After sleeping for a few hours, he started digging a 42' x 5' x 5' hole, big enough for Jimmy Dolan's Cadillac. ["Dolan's Cadillac"]

2 July 1990

Rita Blakemoor and Larry Underwood left Passaic, NJ, and reached Quarryville, NY.

Fran Goldsmith and Harold Lauder left Ogunquit, ME, for the Stovington Plague Center.

Stu Redman continued without Glen Bateman and Kojak.

While drunk, Clewiston, FL, resident Mrs. Eileen Drummond smoked in bed. She died in the fire.

Irma Fayette fired her father's old .45 pistol at a drunkard she thought wanted to rape her. She died when the gun exploded.

Trapped in a walk-in freezer in the basement of her apartment building, Judy Horton starved.

~9:45 a.m.: Ten-year-old Sam Tauber fell in an old well behind Hattie Reynolds's house in Murfreesboro, GA, and broke his legs. His siblings and parents had died from Captain Trips.

11:15 a.m.: George McDougall died of a heart attack while running. His family had already perished from Captain Trips. [*The Stand: The Complete & Uncut Edition*]

2 July 1995

Rose Madder entered *The New York Times* Fiction Best Seller List at number 3. It was on the List for fourteen weeks.

2 July 2008

The Dark Tower: The Long Road Home #5 of 5 (Marvel Comics, $3.99) published

The Dark Tower: The End-World Almanac (Marvel Comics, $3.99) published

The Stand Sketchbook (Marvel Comics, Free) published

July 3

3 July

In seeking revenge for Drogan Pharmaceuticals' killing 15,000 cats during four years of Tri-Dormal-G testing for FDA approval, Sam had killed Drogan's sister, Amanda Drogan, and her companion, Carolyn Broadmoor. Drogan had Dick Gage take Sam to the vet to be put to sleep. On the way, Sam killed Gage. ["The Cat From Hell"]

3 July 1958, ~1:00 p.m.

Henry Bowers, Victor Criss, Peter Gordon, Belch Huggins, and Moose Sadler were going to the dump to light some firecrackers, M–80s, and cherry bombs when they saw Mike Hanlon. They chased him from the train yards to a gravel pit near the Barrens. Hanlon threw chunks of coal at them, hitting Bowers a couple of times. One guy threw an M–80 at Hanlon. The Losers heard this and ran to help by throwing rocks at Bowers and the others. Everybody took a beating, but the Losers made the others leave. Mike Hanlon became a Loser. [*IT*]

3 July 1968, Wednesday, ~1:00 a.m.

A foot-long rat bit Carmichael on the chest while he cleaned the basement of a Gates Falls, ME, textile mill. ["Graveyard Shift"]

3 July 1979

Richard Bachman's *The Long Walk* (Signet, $1.95) published

3 July 1980, Thursday

Lewis Belasco sold a Jörgen chainfall to Charity Camber for $1,241.71 including tax. Ronnie DuBay and Joe Magruder delivered it that afternoon. [*Cujo*]

3 July 1983

131 pounds: Billy Halleck arrived home. After a late dinner, he gave the pie to Heidi Halleck and went to bed. Linda Halleck, who had been staying with her Aunt Rhoda, came home early. She and her mother each had a piece of cursed Gypsy pie meant for her mother. [*Thinner*]

Christine stayed at number 3 on *The New York Times* Fiction Best Seller List, its thirteenth week on the List.

3 July 1988, Sunday

Robinson stopped digging the hole at forty feet long. He covered it with canvas, which had a yellow line that matched Route 71's yellow line, then removed a flashing arrow and road cones that blocked the detoured highway section. When he saw Jimmy Dolan coming, he removed the detour signs, replacing them after Dolan's car fell into the hole. While burying Dolan, he declined Dolan's $1 million and $5 million offers for freedom. ["Dolan's Cadillac"]

3 July 1990

Nick Andros left Shoyo, AK, and headed for Nebraska. Ronnie joined Al, Garvey, and Virge.

Rita Blakemoor and Larry Underwood reached Bennington, VT, and stayed at Twelve-Mile Point. Rita died that night after a drug overdose. [*The Stand: The Complete & Uncut Edition*]

3 July 1995

Tak identified himself to Audrey Wyler. Until then, she had thought Tak had been another Seth Garin personality, whom she called the Stalky Little Boy for the way he walked without bending his knees. [*The Regulators*]

3 July 2016

End of Watch stayed at number 1 on *The New York Times* Hardcover Fiction Best Seller List, its second week on the List.

July 4

4 July, twilight

Jordy Verrill saw a meteorite fall on his property. It broke in two and oozed hot, oatmeal-like stuff when he poured water on it to cool it. The meteorshit burned the fingers of his right hand when he touched it. He would need Big Thinking to deal with the meteorite. The college wouldn't buy a broken one. ["The Lonesome Death of Jordy Verrill" / "Weeds"]

4 July 1864

Hugh Crane didn't become the Thirteenth Earl of Montville because his father, the Twelfth Earl of Montville, disinherited him for fighting against the British in the American Revolutionary War. In 1813, Crane bought what is now Haven, ME, from the Commonwealth of Massachusetts for its timber. Derry was twenty miles away to float his timber to sea. In 1816, his land earned municipal status and became known as Montville Plantation. Later, he incorporated the 22,000 acres of Montville Plantation, the 193rd town incorporated in the Massachusetts Province of Maine. In 1831, Montville Plantation became Coodersville, due, perhaps, to businessmen George and Hiram Cooder. During the Civil War, Ellis Montgomery died fighting with the 20th Maine at Gettysburg. On 4 July 1864, Coodersville was renamed to Montgomery. In 1878, the townspeople changed the name to Ilium, to fit in with other classically named towns. Later, Ilium became Haven, ME. [*The Tommyknockers*]

4 July 1894

The Arcadia Beach Carousel began operation. [*The Talisman*]

4 July 1908, morning

In Crete, Greece, Ellen and John Rimbauer had sex for the first time since April. He apologized for his infidelity, and they did it again. Ellen and Sukeena knew Ellen was pregnant. [*The Diary of Ellen Rimbauer: My Life at Rose Red*]

4 July 1912

The drunkard Stanny Bouchard was found dead in a road, killed by his poisoned liver. In the early 1800s, Stanny's grandfather, a fur trapper, traded with the Micmac Indians. They told him about their soured burial ground. He told Stanny's father, who told Stanny, who in turn told Jud Crandall. Many years later, Jud told Louis Creed. [*Pet Sematary*]

4 July 1958

While marching in the Neibolt Street Church School band for the annual Fourth of July parade, Mike Hanlon saw Pennywise the Clown give balloons to children. He recognized Pennywise from several of his father's old pictures. [*IT*]

4 July 1968, Thursday

3:30 a.m.: While cleaning the basement of a Gate Falls, ME, textile mill, the cleanup crew found a trapdoor to a subcellar.

4:00 a.m.: Hall, Warwick, and Harry Wisconsky went to see whether the many rats they had seen were breeding down there. When they passed under the mill's outer wall, they found crow-sized bats and large rats. Wisconsky went back; Hall forced Warwick to continue.

Farther on, they found blind, three-foot long rats without rear legs. With a high-powered water hose, Hall pushed Warwick over a ledge, where the *magna mater* ate him. On Hall's way back, large, mutated rats and bats killed him.

5:00 a.m.: After only Wisconsky returned, Charlie Brochu, Brogan, Dangerfield, Cy Ippeston, Nedeau, and Stevenson went to see what was keeping Hall and Warwick. ["Graveyard Shift"]

4 July [1973]

George Rackley discovered the Gerards had a baby. He had been waiting for one final score, one large enough to set him up for life. He planned the kidnapping with Blaze but was killed before they could do it. The following January, Blaze tried it by himself. [*Blaze*]

4 July 1973, Wednesday, 3:45 p.m.

Devin Jones, wearing the fur as Howie the Happy Hound, saved Hallie Stansfield, who was choking on a two-inch bite of Pup-A-Licious hot dog. One of Hollywood Girl Erin Cook's photographs accompanied articles in several newspapers, including the Heaven's Bay *Weekly* and the Wilmington *Star-News*. Hallie, wearing a red Howie dogtop hat and holding a Raggedy Ann doll, was one of the two children Rosalind Gold had told Dev was in his future. [*Joyland*]

4 July 1983, morning

132 pounds: Billy Halleck found his daughter at home. When he saw two plates and forks in the sink, he realized his daughter had a piece of the cursed pie. So he ate some. [*Thinner*]

4 July 1984

Uncle Al brought assorted fireworks when he visited the Coslaws for the holiday. Late that night, Marty Coslaw went to light them. The Beast stopped by. Marty lit a pack of firecrackers and threw them in The Beast's face. The Beast lost its left eye. [*Cycle of the Werewolf*]

4 July 1988, Monday

morning: Robinson replaced the asphalt he had taken off Route 71. ["Dolan's Cadillac"]

Bobbi Anderson had lost thirty pounds since finding the spaceship about two weeks earlier.

Hilly Brown began building battery-powered gadgets for better magic tricks.

Jim Gardener woke up and met Jack on the beach near the Arcadia Funworld Amusement Park and the Alhambra in Arcadia Beach, NH. He hitchhiked to Haven, ME, walking the last three miles to Bobbi Anderson's place. That night, green light from the sleeping Bobbi's eyes shone on him; his sore throat and fever were cured. [*The Tommyknockers*]

4 July 1990

Randall Flagg freed Lloyd Henreid from the Phoenix municipal jail. Lloyd became Flagg's right-hand man.

Fran Goldsmith and Harold Lauder traveled on Honda motorcycles. She carried a small deer rifle. Stu Redman joined them on US 302 in Fabyan, NH. Within four hours, he fell in love with Fran. They met Glen Bateman in Woodsville, NH.

Larry Underwood continued from Bennington, VT, on a Harley-Davidson motorcycle. He spent the night in Brattleboro, VT. [*The Stand: The Complete & Uncut Edition*]

4 July 1992

On Carmen's Folly, Cappy MacFarland buried the money Barney, Jagger, Keenan, and Sarge robbed in April. Only Cappy knew where it was. He drew a map marking its location and cut it into four pieces, one for each man. Because the serial numbers were recorded, they planned to get together in five years. They would either split the money or wait another five years. ["The Fifth Quarter"]

Stephen King fan Coretta Vele expected to pass away before this date. It saddened her that she wouldn't be able to read the rest of *The Dark Tower* series as it came out. [*The Dark Tower VI: Song of Susannah*]

4 July 1998, Saturday, ~11:00 a.m.

After arguing with her mother about when they would go to the beach, Kyra Devore sneaked out and went by herself. Mike Noonan found her walking the centerline of Route 68. Fearing she might get hit, he led her off the road. Mattie Devore, Kyra's mother, discovered her missing and found her with Mike. [*Bag of Bones*]

4 July 1999

The Girl Who Loved Tom Gordon rose to number 8 on *The New York Times* Fiction Best Seller List, its eleventh week on the List.

4 July 2001

Jonesy ate watermelon. [*Dreamcatcher*]

4 July 2004

The Dark Tower VI: Song of Susannah dropped to number 2 on *The New York Times* Fiction Best Seller List, its second week on the List.

4 July 2007

The Dark Tower: Gunslinger Born #6 of 7 (Marvel Comics, $3.99) published

4 July 2012: the Fourth of July Arms Race

Alden McCausland had bought fireworks from Pop Anderson at Anderson's Cheery Flea Mart. He and his mother sat on their summer cabin's dock to drink Bucket Lucks and wave a couple of sparklers. Across Abenake Lake, the Massimos waved bigger, colorful, longer-lasting sparklers then played waah-waah-waah on a trumpet.

The McCauslands lit a few firecrackers. The Massimos lit packs of firecrackers then played waah-waah-waah.

Alden and his mother lit a couple of cherry bombs. The Massimos lit M-80s; waah-waah-waah.

Whatever the McCauslands did, the Massimos' responded with a grander display. The trumpet was maddening. ["Drunken Fireworks"]

4 July 2013

Alden McCausland and his mother sat on their summer cabin's dock and drank Orange Driver. Alden started the Arms Race with packs of firecrackers. The Massimos did the same, waved a few sparklers, and lit M-80s. The McCauslands lit M-120s.

When it looked as if the Massimos had nothing more, Alden and his mother lit Twizzlers on Styrofoam and floated them on the lake. The Massimos ignited an explosive almost as big as a softball. It was the night's loudest and brightest firework. They followed with a long waa-aaaah on a trumpet.

Alden set up twelve beer and soda cans with the Chinese Peonies. The Massimos set off bigger rockets and played waah-waah-waah on the trumpet. ["Drunken Fireworks"]

4 July 2014

Word of the annual Arms Races had spread. More than 600 people showed up at the lake. Alden McCausland started with a Pyro Monkey. The Massimos lit a bigger, longer-lasting one then played waah-waah-waah on a trumpet.

Alden set off a Declaration of Independence. The Massimos topped it then played waah-waah-waah.

Alden lit the extra-special Ghost of Fury. Everybody applauded, even the Massimos. Paul Massimo had a better one, followed by a large trumpet blast. ["Drunken Fireworks"]

4 July 2015: the Great Fourth of July Arms Race

More than a thousand people went to watch. Paul Massimo hired a professional fireworks crew. They put on a twenty-minute show, ending with a Double Excalibur and a Wolfpack. For an encore, they put an Excellent Junk in the sky and the American flag on the beach.

Alden McCausland and his mother drank Moonquakes. Alden lit the Close Encounters of the Fourth Kind's thick fuse. The seven-foot-square box lifted off. At fifty feet, it exploded and unfolded into a paper flying saucer, shooting fireballs in all directions. The fireballs exploded and shot off more fireballs. Parachutes opened to hold the saucer in the sky. The wind blew it over the lake toward Massimo's Twelve Pines summer home. The saucer and parachutes caught fire then crashed into two pines on either side of Massimo's porch. A burning branch fell on the porch roof, setting it ablaze. The saucer broke in two. One piece landed safely on the lawn; the other on Massimo's roof. The house burned. The Massimos scattered, leaving the trumpet on the dock.

Officer Ardelle Benoit arrested Alden. While Alden's mother, Hallie, dealt with that, a couple of Massimo's boys sneaked into the cabin, put some fireworks next to the McCauslands' woodstove, and fired it up. After the boys were long gone, the fireworks caught, went off, and burned the cabin. ["Drunken Fireworks"]

July 5

5 July

Jordy Verrill felt sick when he woke up. A green mossy weed grew from his fingers. Throughout the day, the weed grew from whatever body parts and items at home he had touched. Much of the weed grew near the meteorite he found the day before; he could hear it grow. By midnight, the weeds had grown over him and his farm; he was a large, fuzzy, green blob. The weeds helped him kill himself with his .410 Remington. ["The Lonesome Death of Jordy Verrill" / "Weeds"]

5 July 1962, 5:00 p.m.

George Amberson's second timeline: George Amberson had dinner with Ellie Dockerty and Deke Simmons at Al's Diner. After dinner, he and Deke went to the high school football field. Talking with Coach Borman, George learned about Duffer's omnidirectional microphone. [*11/22/63*]

5 July 1973, Thursday

Joyland owner Bradley Easterbrook was grateful for the extra, free publicity Devin Jones's heroics of the previous day gave the park. With Joyland's small profit margins, he couldn't afford to give Dev a bonus, so he offered to owe Dev a favor. [*Joyland*]

5 July 1984

Reverend Lowe woke up without his left eye, painless. He then knew he was The Beast. He began wearing an eye patch. [*Cycle of the Werewolf*]

5 July 1987

The Eyes of the Dragon dropped to number 15 on *The New York Times* Fiction Best Seller List, its twenty-third week on the List.

Misery stayed at number 1 on *The New York Times* Fiction Best Seller List, its fifth week on the List.

5 July 1988

Bobbi Anderson could clearly read the minds of others, but she could barely read Jim Gardener because of his steel plate. She told Gard that Peter died of old age a week earlier. With a shotgun, she persuaded him to help her at the dig, which was 200 feet long by twenty-five to forty feet wide. After telling him much of what had happened in the past week, she took him to the ship and had him touch it. His steel plate picked up a radio station and his nose bled. She believed the ship affected the townspeople. [*The Tommyknockers*]

5 July 1990

Tom Cullen joined Nick Andros in May, OK.

Fran Goldsmith began a diary. [*The Stand: The Complete & Uncut Edition*]

5 July 2007

After reading N.'s obituary, Dr. John Bonsaint called N.'s home phone and spoke with C., N.'s daughter. She invited him to the funeral. N. had sealed the garage door cracks with an even number of towels and had killed himself with the car's fumes. He left a short note, "Am so tired." ["N."]

5 July 2013

Pop Anderson told Alden McCausland there were more-impressive fireworks, but he wouldn't risk his vendor's license or anybody's life to get them for drunks to light off. Pop referred Alden to Howard Gamache of Indian Island, ME. ["Drunken Fireworks"]

5 July 2015

Alden McCausland gave a statement to Police Chief Andrew Clutterbuck and arresting Officer Ardelle Benoit. His story started with his father's buying the cabin, told of two financial windfalls for the McCauslands, and concluded with the annual Fourth of July Arms Races.

Paul Massimo treated Hallie McCausland to brunch at Lucky's Diner. He told her he wasn't pressing any charges; both families were at fault. He suggested they let bygones be bygones. Massimo expressed sorrow that Alden had left his fireworks so close to the stove. ["Drunken Fireworks"]

Finders Keepers dropped to number 3 *The New York Times* Hardcover Fiction Best Seller List, its third week on the List.

July 6

6 July

The weeds that consumed Jordy Verrill reached the highway on their way to town. ["The Lonesome Death of Jordy Verrill" / "Weeds"]

6 July 1958

The Losers started an underground clubhouse at the Barrens. Bill Denbrough, Ben Hanscom, and Richie Tozier decided the Losers would go to 29 Neibolt Street to kill IT with a silver bullet. [*IT*]

6 July 1988

Jim Gardener began helping Bobbi Anderson dig out the spaceship. [*The Tommyknockers*]

Rebecca Paulson built a zigzag attachment for her sewing machine. ["The Revelations of 'Becka Paulson"]

6 July 1990

On bicycles, Nick Andros and Tom Cullen left May, OK. When a tornado hit that afternoon, Tom took Nick to a storm cellar under a barn near Rosston, OK.

Glen Bateman joined Fran Goldsmith, Harold Lauder, and Stu Redman in Woodsville, NH. [*The Stand: The Complete & Uncut Edition*]

6 July 1998

While his family went to Oxford to see *Armageddon*, Stephen King wrote some of his Vietnam story, starring Sully John, Bobby Garfield, and Ted Brautigan. [*The Dark Tower VI: Song of Susannah*]

6 July 2003, Sunday

Mrs. Wanda Junkins used a stepladder to dust high places. She fell, cracked her skull, and suffered a small brain-bleed. From across the street, two-year-old Abra Stone alerted Chetta Reynolds and Lucy Stone, who found Mrs. Judkins in the dining room. Had they not found her so soon, she would not have recovered. [*Doctor Sleep*]

6 July 2011

The Dark Tower: The Gunslinger—The Battle of Tull #2 of 5 (Marvel Comics, $3.99) published

6 July 2014

Mr. Mercedes dropped to number 4 on *The New York Times* Hardcover Fiction Best Seller List, its third week on the List.

July 7

7 July 1962

George Amberson's second timeline: George Amberson went to Satellite Electronics to see whether Silent Mike McEachern could get him an omnidirectional microphone. He could. [*11/22/63*]

7 July 1967

Kevin Anthony Kenton, John Kenton's brother, died of a brain tumor. [*The Plant* Book One: *Zenith Rising*]

7 July 1973, Saturday

Dev Jones wore the fur for a public ceremony at the intersection of Joyland Avenue and Hound Dog Way. Hallie Stansfield's parents thanked him for saving their daughter. After the ceremony, he met with the parents in the Joyland Customer Service Center. The girl's father offered $500. Dev declined because the man was trying to get a contracting firm started, and they had a second child on the way. [*Joyland*]

7 July 1980, Monday

Roger Breakstone and Vic Trenton started their trip to keep the Sharp account. Yancy Harrington agreed to star in a Sharp Cereal Professor apology commercial.

Brett Camber and Charity Camber went to Stratford, CT, to visit her sister.

Joe Camber and Gary Pervier planned to go to Boston for the week while Charity and Brett were away. That morning, Cujo killed Gary, his first victim. Around noon, Joe found Gary's body, and then Cujo killed him in Gary's kitchen.

Donna Trenton and Tad Trenton took their car to Camber's for repairs; it stalled and wouldn't start. Cujo trapped them in the car. Tad recognized Cujo as the monster from his closet, the one that identified itself as Frank Dodd. [*Cujo*]

7 July 1985

Richard Bachman's *Thinner* stayed at number 9 on *The New York Times* Fiction Best Seller List, its nineteenth week on the List.

Skeleton Crew stayed at number 1 on *The New York Times* Fiction Best Seller List, its third week on the List.

7 July 1988, Thursday

Rebecca Paulson began reading the thoughts of others, thoughts she believed came from a picture of Jesus on her TV. She discovered her husband's affair with Nancy Voss, whom she called The Hussy. [*The Tommyknockers*]

7 July 1990, evening

Nick Andros and Tom Cullen entered Kansas.

Glen Bateman left Kojak in Woodsville, NH, when he, Fran Goldsmith, Harold Lauder, and Stu Redman went to the Stovington Plague Center. Harold wanted to be sure the Center was deserted. [*The Stand: The Complete & Uncut Edition*]

7 July 1996

The Green Mile, Part One: The Two Dead Girls dropped to number 11 on *The New York Times* Paperback Fiction Best Seller List, its thirteenth week on the List.

The Green Mile, Part Two: The Mouse on the Mile dropped to number 7 on *The New York Times* Paperback Fiction Best Seller List, its ninth week on the List.

The Green Mile, Part Three: Coffey's Hands dropped to number 2 on *The New York Times* Paperback Fiction Best Seller List, its fifth week on the List.

The Green Mile, Part Four: The Bad Death of Eduard Delacroix entered *The New York Times* Paperback Fiction Best Seller List at number 7. It was on the List for thirteen weeks.

7 July 1998, Tuesday, 6:00 p.m.

Mike Noonan had dinner with Kyra Devore and Mattie Devore. Mike told Mattie that John Storrow was available to help in her custody battle for Kyra with half-billionaire Max Devore. He brought a set of Magnabets—refrigerator magnets of the alphabet—for Kyra. During the next two weeks, the Devores found words, mostly names, spelled with the magnets. Kyra called the spirits responsible for this "fridgeafator people." [*Bag of Bones*]

7 July 2007

Dr. John Bonsaint went to N.'s funeral, first the church services then at the cemetery. ["N."]

7 July 2013

Joyland stayed at number 1 on *The New York Times* Paperback Trade Fiction Best Seller List, its third week on the List.

July 8

8 July 1947

"AIR FORCE CAPTURES 'FLYING SAUCER' ON RANCH IN ROSWELL REGION; Intelligence Officers Recover Crashed Disc" appeared in the Roswell, NM, Daily Record. [*Dreamcatcher*]

8 July 1980, Tuesday

Vic Trenton and Roger Breakstone had a wrap-up business lunch with Rob Martin of Image-Eye Studios in Boston. Martin agreed to the apology commercial.

~3:30 p.m.: Steve Kemp ransacked several rooms in the Trentons' house.

Tad Trenton retreated to a duck pond in his mind.

~8:15 p.m.: Donna Trenton tried to reach the house. Cujo chased her back to her car and bit her stomach and leg. Repeatedly, she slammed the car door on his head and body; he nearly lost an ear. [*Cujo*]

8 July 1988, Friday

Justin Hurd, Bobbi Anderson's nearest neighbor, had gone crazy from the Tommyknocker spaceship on Bobbi's farm long before she unearthed it. Thinking it was May 1951, forty-two-year-old Hurd plowed his fields of growing crops.

After learning that her husband had been cheating on her, Rebecca Paulson rigged the TV to electrocute Joe when he turned it on. She ran to him when he did so; both died, and their house burned. [*The Tommyknockers*]

8 July 1990

Glen Bateman, Fran Goldsmith, Harold Lauder, and Stu Redman reached Stovington, VT. Fran was falling in love with Stu. Harold made a sign saying they were going to Nebraska.

The Trashcan Man reached Iowa after crossing the Mississippi.

Nick Andros and Tom Cullen spent the night near Dearhead, KS. [*The Stand: The Complete & Uncut Edition*]

The Stand: The Complete & Uncut Edition rose to number 3 on *The New York Times* Fiction Best Seller List, its ninth week on the List.

8 July 1994

Stoneham, ME, resident Charles McCausland died in a hit-and-run while walking Route 7, the same road Stephen King walked. [*The Dark Tower VI: Song of Susannah*]

8 July 1995, ~9:00 a.m.

A Mayflower van arrived at the Hobarts' house. They moved after too much Tak terror. [*The Regulators*]

8 July 2001

Dreamcatcher dropped to number 15 on *The New York Times* Fiction Best Seller List, its fourteenth week on the List.

8 July 2007

Richard Bachman's *Blaze* dropped to number 3 on *The New York Times* Fiction Best Seller List, its second week on the List.

8 July 2009

The Stand: American Nightmares #4 of 5 (Marvel Comics, $3.99) published

8 July 2010

The Stand: Hardcases #2 of 5 (Marvel Comics, $3.99) published

8 July 2014

the August issue (Vol. 162, No. 1) of *Esquire*, with "That Bus Is Another World" (collected in *The Bazaar of Bad Dreams*), published

8 July 2018

The Outsider dropped to number 3 on *The New York Times* Hardcover Fiction Best Seller List, its fifth week on the List.

July 9

9 July 1947

"AIR FORCE DECLARES SAUCER WEATHER BALLOON" appeared in the Roswell, NM, *Daily Record*. [*Dreamcatcher*]

9 July 1970

"Slade," Chapter 5, appeared in *The Maine Campus*.

9 July 1972

Sarah Bracknell and Walter Hazlett married at the First Methodist Church of Bangor. They honeymooned in Montreal. [*The Dead Zone*]

9 July 1977

Jack Andolini and a team of hit men ambushed Roland Deschain and Eddie Dean outside the East Stoneham General Store in Maine. Roland killed seven, and Eddie killed six, including George Biondi and Tricks Postino. Eddie suffered gunshots to the left arm and right calf. John Cullum led them a quarter mile through the woods to his motorboat, docked on Keywadin Pond. Cullum took them to Calvin Tower to sign the bill of sale for the vacant lot at the corner of Second Avenue and Forty-Sixth Street. [*The Dark Tower VI: Song of Susannah*]

~3:30 p.m.: County Sheriff Eldon Royster arrested Jack Andolini and three others trying to get around a police roadblock in Auburn, ME. [*The Dark Tower VII: The Dark Tower*]

9 July 1980, Wednesday

12:34 a.m.: Billy radioed Officer Roscoe Fisher to have him check the Trentons' house after Vic Trenton expressed concern that no one answered the phone. Fisher found the house trashed with nobody home. Later, Sheriff Bannerman called Trenton in Boston and told him his house had been vandalized and his family was missing. Vic left Boston.

Police picked up Steve Kemp in Massachusetts and sent him to the Maine State Police barracks in Scarborough, MA. He remained silent after they found drugs in his van. Later, he admitted to vandalizing the Trentons' home but said no one was home.

7:20 a.m.: As a formality, Sheriff Bannerman went to Camber's Garage to see whether Donna Trenton's car was there. He saw Frank Dodd in Cujo, who gutted and killed him, Cujo's third victim.

12:20 p.m.: Vic needed to do something, so he drove to Camber's Garage. He saw Joe Camber's car at Gary Pervier's. When he found the two men dead in Gary's house, he rushed to Camber's.

>12:30 p.m.: Donna Trenton beat Cujo with a taped baseball bat Brett Camber had left near the driveway. After two blows, he had broken ribs and hindquarter bones. He tried to get away. She hit him across the back, splitting the bat where it was taped. He lunged for her throat and landed on the pointy, broken handle; it pierced his right eye and brain. She continued beating him after he died until Vic stopped her.

12:50 p.m.: Vic found Tad Trenton dead of advanced dehydration. He broke into the Cambers' house and to call the police and an ambulance.

3:45 p.m.: Detective Andy Masen called Charity Camber in Stratford, CT, to tell her about Joe Camber's death.

The Portland *Evening Express* reported the incident in "RABID DOG KILLS 4 IN BIZARRE THREE-DAY REIGN OF TERROR, Lone Survivor at Northern Cumberland Hospital in Guarded Condition." [*Cujo*]

9 July 1990, morning

Glen Bateman, Fran Goldsmith, Harold Lauder, and Stu Redman left Stovington, VT, and headed for Nebraska. [*The Stand: The Complete & Uncut Edition*]

9 July 1992

Claire Bowie gave N101BL clearance to land at Cumberland County Airport in Maine. The Night Flier ripped his throat open and sucked most of his blood. Ninety dollars cash was found on his body. ["The Night Flier"]

9 July 1994

After reading about Charles McCausland in the Lewiston *Sun*, Tabby King was upset that Stephen King wanted to take his daily walk. McCausland was killed on the same road Steve walked. [*The Dark Tower VI: Song of Susannah*]

9 July 1995

Rose Madder rose to number 2 on *The New York Times* Fiction Best Seller List, its second week on the List.

9 July 2018, Monday

Monday was the first day of the three-day Tri-State Teachers of English mid-summer conference, held at the Sheraton in Cap City, OK, that year. [*The Outsider*]

July 10

10 July 1910

John Rimbauer caught Douglas Posey in a compromising position with a male accountant in Posey's Omicron Oil office.

evening: Douglas and Phillis Posey attended a dinner at the Rimbauers' to celebrate Washington's being the first state to allow women to vote. That night, Ellen Rimbauer became pregnant. [*The Diary of Ellen Rimbauer: My Life at Rose Red*]

10 July 1980, Thursday

"FATHER TELLS OF WIFE'S DOOMED STRUGGLE TO SAVE SON" appeared in the morning Portland *Press-Herald*.

Brett Camber and Charity Camber left Stratford, CT, to go home.

"MRS. TRENTON RESPONDING TO RABIES TREATMENT, DOCTOR SAYS" and sidebar "DOG HAD NO SHOTS: LOCAL VET" appeared in the evening *Press-Herald*. [*Cujo*]

10 July 1983

Christine dropped to number 4 on *The New York Times* Fiction Best Seller List, its fourteenth week on the List.

10 July 1988

Postal worker Nancy Voss built a battery-powered Tommyknocker mail sorter. [*The Tommyknockers*]

10 July 1990, >4:00 p.m.

Nick Andros and Tom Cullen met Julie Lawry in Pratt, KS. She invited Nick to bed and got angry when he wouldn't sleep with her a second time. Later, she disabled their bicycles and shot at them. Nick and Tom spent the night in a barn three miles north of Pratt. [*The Stand: The Complete & Uncut Edition*]

10 July 1998, 10:00 a.m.

Judge Rancourt had appointed Elmer Durgin as Kyra Devore's guardian *ad litem*, where he was to recommend to the custody court where he felt Kyra's best interests lay. He held a deposition with Mike Noonan about the events of July 4th. Rancourt and Durgin were on Max Devore's payroll. [*Bag of Bones*]

10 July 2003, Thursday

Eight-year-old Amy St. Pierre was the Fisherman's first victim; he ate her liver and tongue. Later, he wrote a letter to Armand St. Pierre. The letter was like those Albert Fish had written to his victims' families. [*Black House*]

10 July 2012

the August issue (Vol. 158, No. 1) of *Esquire*, with part 2 (of 2) of "In the Tall Grass," a Stephen King-Joe Hill short-story collaboration, published

10 July 2016

End of Watch stayed at number 1 on *The New York Times* Hardcover Fiction Best Seller List, its third week on the List.

10 July 2018, Tuesday

10:00 a.m.: The Flint City High School English Department—Debbie Grant, Terry Maitland, Billy Quade, and Ev Roundhill—went to the Tri-State Teachers of English conference to see Harlan Coben, the keynote speaker. They left the school in Ev's BMW and arrived in time for the banquet lunch. After lunch, Terry and Billy went to Second Edition, a used bookstore.

3:00 p.m.: Josephine McDermott's ten-minute-plus introduction preceded Harlan Coben's forty-minute speech. The Flint City English Department sat at a table near the front. Cap City Channel 81's video, HARLAN COBEN SPEAKS TO TRI-STATE ENGLISH TEACHERS, showed Terry Maitland stand to ask a question. In Flint City, Mrs. Arlene Stanhope saw Frankie Peterson walk his bike with a broken chain across the parking lot as she left Gerald's Fine Groceries. Terry Maitland (the outsider) got out of a dirty white van with an orange license plate and talked with Frankie. They put the bike in the back, and Terry drove Frankie to Mulberry Avenue.

~4:30 p.m.: The Question & Answer session ended. Terry, Billy, and Ev went to the newsstand. Terry took the heavy *A Pictorial History of Flint County, Douree County, and Canning Township* from the top shelf, saw it was $79.99, and put it back. He left a thumbprint on the cover and four fingerprints on the back.

Debbie and the men got in the long autograph line.

>5:30 p.m.: They reached the autograph table.

They and five English teachers from Broken Arrow dined at the Firepit.

Terry Maitland (the outsider) killed Frankie Peterson in Flint City's Figgis Park. The outsider bit open his throat, ate bits of flesh, sodomized him with a twenty-two-inch-long, three-inch-wide branch, and ejaculated on the back of his legs. Frankie died of exsanguination.

6:15 p.m.: Riley Franklin ate with Carlton Scowcroft at Shorty's Pub. Riley had mac and cheese.

6:15–6:25 p.m.: June Morris saw Terry Maitland (the outsider), bloody, walk from woods at Figgis Park. He told her a branch had hit his nose. He got in a dirty white van and drove down Barnum Street. Jon Ritz, walking his beagle, Dave, in the park, had seen the dirty white van and heard an engine start. Dave pulled him off the gravel path and through the trees to a clearing. Frankie Peterson's body lay behind a bloody, granite bench. Jon vomited.

7:00 p.m.: Riley and Carlton ordered dessert then smoked out back. A dirty white van with New York license plates parked next to a Subaru and Terry Maitland (the outsider) got out. He wore a white shirt with blood on the front and blood-spattered pants. He told Carlton and Riley he had a nosebleed. Scowcroft gave him directions to a nearby walk-in clinic. Maitland left the keys in the cup holder in case someone needed to move the van and drove off in the Subaru.

The outsider left the Subaru and bloody clothes on a boat landing at the end of Iron Bridge.

8:00 p.m.: In Cap City, the English Department attended the evening panel discussion. Debbie and Ev went to their rooms early.

8:40 p.m.: Cab dispatcher Clint Ellenquist took a call from Gentlemen, Please in Flint City. He referred the caller to the cabstand outside the club. Security official Claude Bolton saw Terry Maitland (the outsider) hang up the payphone. He knew Terry and shook his hand;

Terry's fingernail cut him. Terry wore a yellow shirt, jeans with a horse's head belt buckle, and fancy sneakers. Willow Rainwater drove him from the club to the Amtrak station in Dubrow. He tipped her $20 for getting him there in time for the train to Dallas–Fort Worth. He wore a nice button-up shirt and clean, faded blue jeans with a horse's head belt buckle.

9:30 p.m.: In Cap City, Terry Maitland and Billy Quade had a beer at the bar then went up to 644, the double room they shared. In Flint City, Detective Ralph Anderson interviewed Mr. Jonathan Ritz for the record.

9:33–9:39 p.m.: Terry Maitland (the outsider) entered the Amtrak station from the north and exited to Montrose Avenue—he didn't board the train.

The outsider shed his clothes and Terry skin in the Elfmans' barn in Canning Township. [*The Outsider*]

July 11

11 July 1965

Adam Greenlaw was the second Gatlin, NE, resident—the first boy—born a worshiper of He Who Walks Behind the Rows. ["Children of the Corn"]

11 July 1989

Stephen King found a copy of Richard Adams's *Shardik*, a story about a mythological bear, on his bookshelf. [*The Dark Tower VI: Song of Susannah*]

11 July 1990, ~11:00 a.m.

Nick Andros and Tom Cullen reached Iuka, KS, and got new bikes.

Mark Braddock and Perion McCarthy joined Glen Bateman, Fran Goldsmith, Harold Lauder, and Stu Redman in Albany, NY. [*The Stand: The Complete & Uncut Edition*]

11 July 1999

The Girl Who Loved Tom Gordon stayed at number 8 on *The New York Times* Fiction Best Seller List, its twelfth week on the List.

11 July 2004

The Dark Tower VI: Song of Susannah dropped to number 4 on *The New York Times* Fiction Best Seller List, its third week on the List.

11 July 2018, Wednesday

morning: Terry Maitland worked out in the Cap City Sheraton Hotel's fitness room. He and Billy Quade checked out; Billy paid with his MasterCard.

Dr. Felicity Ackerman, Flint County Chief Medical Examiner, performed Frankie Peterson's autopsy. Dr. Alvin Barkland assisted. [*The Outsider*]

July 12

12 July 1963, Friday

George Amberson's second timeline: This was the first night of the second *Jodie Jamboree*'s two-night show. Proceeds went to Sadie Dunhill's medical bills. Bobbi Jill Allnut and Mike Coslaw danced an energetic Lindy to Glenn Miller's "In the Mood." [*11/22/63*]

12 July 1980

"STATE HEALTH AGENCY BLAMES RABID FOX OR RACOON FOR DOG'S CASTLE ROCK RAMPAGE" was on page 4 of the Portland *Press-Herald*. [*Cujo*]

12 July 1987

The Eyes of the Dragon stayed at number 15 on *The New York Times* Fiction Best Seller List, its twenty-fourth week on the List.

Misery stayed at number 1 on *The New York Times* Fiction Best Seller List, its sixth week on the List.

12 July 1990

Ralph Brentner joined Nick Andros and Tom Cullen on US 281 near Iuka, KS. They traveled in his pickup truck. Dick Ellis and Gina McCone joined the group within ten days.

Stu Redman's group spent the night near Guilderland, NY. [*The Stand: The Complete & Uncut Edition*]

12 July 1996, Friday

Steve Ames had been running the soundboard at Deke Abelson's Club Smile, a blues nightclub. Deke had moved to San Francisco to run a new club; Steve could have a job there, if he wanted, and his first task would be to truck Abelson's stuff to California. On Friday, Steve left New York with a Ryder truck full of Abelson's belongings. [*The Regulators*]

12 July 2011

Rose the Hat felt the ping of a steamhead in Iowa. She, Barry the Chink, and Grampa Flick found Bradley Trevor by triangulation. They took him behind an abandoned ethanol-processing plant. Pain purified steam, so Rose tortured him with a knife for a long time. She licked his blood from her hands. Bradley had a few red spots, indicating measles. The True Knot thought nothing of it because they didn't catch rube diseases.

During the torture, Rose detected a looker [Abra Stone]. Rose didn't know who it was but was sure it was probably a girl, a huge steamhead that was growing stronger. [*Doctor Sleep*]

12 July 2015

Finders Keepers dropped to number 4 *The New York Times* Hardcover Fiction Best Seller List, its fourth week on the List.

12 July 2017

"Thin Scenery" appeared in the Summer 2017 issue (Issue #133; Volume 43, Number 2) of *Ploughshares*.

12 July 2018, Thursday

1:00 p.m.: Detective Ralph Anderson interviewed Mrs. Arlene Stanhope for the record.

5:45 p.m.: Detective Anderson interviewed June Morris for the record. Mrs. Francine Morris, her mother, sat in.

9:30 p.m.: Ralph interviewed Mr. Carlton Scowcroft for the record. [*The Outsider*]

July 13

13 July 1963, Saturday

George Amberson's second timeline: After breakfast, George Amberson asked Sadie Dunhill whether she'd go somewhere they could fix her face, even if it meant never returning to Jodie, TX. When she asked whether he had come from the future, he said he had, forty-eight years. In answer to her next question, he told her someone was going to kill President Kennedy in four months. She fainted; he caught her.

She believed him but needed to be sure, so she asked him to tell her something that would happen. He told her Tom Case would defeat Dick Tiger in a fifth-round knockout. She wanted to wait until after the fight before discussing going back with him. [*11/22/63*]

13 July 1990

Nadine Cross and Joe followed Larry Underwood, whom they had first seen in Epsom, NH. [*The Stand: The Complete & Uncut Edition*]

13 July 2011

dawn: The True Knot buried Bradley Trevor's body behind the abandoned plant.

Danny Torrance saw flies around a person's face when they were ill. The more flies, the worse it was. He saw three or four around Billy Freeman. [*Doctor Sleep*]

13 July 2014

Mr. Mercedes stayed at number 4 on *The New York Times* Hardcover Fiction Best Seller List, its fourth week on the List.

13 July 2016

The Dark Tower: The Drawing of the Three—Bitter Medicine #4 of 5 (Marvel Comics, $3.99) published

13 July 2018, Friday

sunrise: George Czerny went to the Iron Bridge on Old Forge Road (Route 72) to go fishing. Off the road at the end of the bridge, he saw a knocked-down fence and a green Subaru Outback on the boat landing. There were bloody clothes on the passenger seat and bloody sneakers on the floor. He called 911.

7:45 a.m.: Detective Ralph Anderson interviewed Mr. Riley Franklin for the record.

8:15 a.m.: Officer Ronald Wilberforce interviewed Mr. George Czerny for the record.

Donelli Brothers handled Frankie Peterson's memorial service, funeral, and graveside service.

11:40 a.m.: Detective Ralph Anderson interviewed Ms. Willow Rainwater for the record.

2:30 p.m.: Lieutenant Yune Sablo reviewed security footage with Michael Camp, Security Director at Vogel Transportation Center, the bus-train depot in Dubrow. It showed Terry Maitland (the outsider) enter from the north side, pay cash for a paperback book at a newsstand, and exit to Montrose Avenue, without getting on the train. His horse's head belt buckle and yellow shirt were visible.

4:30 p.m.: Detective Anderson interviewed Mr. Claude Bolton for the record. [*The Outsider*]

July 14

14 July 1963, Sunday, 9:00 a.m.

George Amberson's second timeline: George Amberson met with Freddy Quinlan to see about placing a $500 bet on Tommy Case. Freddy suggested Akiva Roth at Faith Financial in Dallas or Frank Frati at a Fort Worth pawn shop. He said Roth had Mob ties but would give better odds.

George placed the bet with Frati, who offered 4–1 for a knockout in the first five rounds. [*11/22/63*]

14 July 1985

Richard Bachman's *Thinner* rose to number 8 on *The New York Times* Fiction Best Seller List, its twentieth week on the List.

Skeleton Crew stayed at number 1 on *The New York Times* Fiction Best Seller List, its fourth week on the List.

14 July 1990

Stu Redman's group reached Batavia, NY.

The Trashcan Man crossed the Missouri River into Nebraska.

Larry Underwood spent the night in North Berwick, ME. [*The Stand: The Complete & Uncut Edition*]

14 July 1996

The Green Mile, Part One: The Two Dead Girls dropped to number 12 on *The New York Times* Paperback Fiction Best Seller List, its fourteenth week on the List.

The Green Mile, Part Two: The Mouse on the Mile dropped to number 10 on *The New York Times* Paperback Fiction Best Seller List, its tenth week on the List.

The Green Mile, Part Three: Coffey's Hands dropped to number 4 on *The New York Times* Paperback Fiction Best Seller List, its sixth week on the List.

The Green Mile, Part Four: The Bad Death of Eduard Delacroix rose to number 1 on *The New York Times* Paperback Fiction Best Seller List, its second week on the List.

14 July 1998, Tuesday evening

Mattie Devore and custody lawyer John Storrow went to the softball game at Warrington's Lodge to get a glimpse of Max Devore. It was the first time Max missed a Tuesday-night game since returning to TR–90 in 1997. [*Bag of Bones*]

14 July 2003, Monday

Johnny Irkenham was the Fisherman's second victim. Later, the Fisherman wrote to Helen Irkenham. Within three days of Johnny's death, Spencer Hovdahl found his dismembered body in the henhouse of John Ellison's abandoned farm. Some body parts, hanging from the rafters, had bite marks. [*Black House*]

14 July 2011

morning: Dan Torrance took Billy Freeman to Greg Fellerton's office in Lewiston, ME. The doctor diagnosed a Ping-Pong ball-sized abdominal aortic aneurysm.

evening: Azzie visited Mr. Ben Cameron after dinner. Nurse Loretta Ames paged Doctor Sleep. [*Doctor Sleep*]

14 July 2013

Joyland stayed at number 1 on *The New York Times* Paperback Trade Fiction Best Seller List, its fourth week on the List.

14 July 2018, Saturday

evening: With overwhelming evidence—blood, fingerprints, and a chain of witnesses—Detective Ralph Anderson had Officers Troy Ramage and Tom Yates arrest Terry Maitland in front of 1,588 at the Flint City Golden Dragons City League tournament semi-final game at Estelle Barga Field. The Dragons lost to the Bears by one run.

In a police station conference room, Terry, with Howie Gold, his lawyer, presented his alibi to Ralph and Flint County District Attorney Bill Samuels: he and the Flint City High School English Department were at the Tri-State Teachers of English mid-summer conference in Cap City, seventy miles to the north.

Howie had his investigator, Alec Pelley, go to the Cap City Sheraton. Alec reviewed their security footage and learned Channel 81 had covered the conference.

The Petersons hosted a wake for Frankie. Fifty to sixty people gave their condolences. During the cleanup, Arlene Peterson had a heart attack in the kitchen. [*The Outsider*]

July 15

15 July 1958

Nine-year-old Jimmy Cullum's body was found in the Barrens. It had washed into the Kenduskeag River from the Derry drain system. IT, as a large bird, had pecked away his face. [*IT*]

15 July 1976

Calvin Tower and the Sombra Corporation entered an agreement. For one year, Tower would not lease or encumber the Lot #298 (digits add up to nineteen) property (the vacant lot at the corner of Second Avenue and Forty-Sixth Street). Sombra paid Tower $100,000 and had first right of purchase of the property. Tower and Sombra representative Richard Patrick Sayre (nineteen letters) signed the agreement. [*The Dark Tower V: Wolves of the Calla*]

15 July 1977

The agreement between Calvin Tower and the Sombra Corporation expired. Sombra wanted to buy the vacant lot. [*The Dark Tower V: Wolves of the Calla*]

15 July 1988

Haven, ME, Tommyknocker Wendy Fannin had lost three teeth by this date. Beach Jernigan had also lost some teeth. Ruth McCausland's office and home phones weren't working. [*The Tommyknockers*]

15 July 1990

Nadine Cross and Joe joined Larry Underwood in Wells, ME, after Joe tried to attack Larry with a knife. They spent the night on the Wells public beach. [*The Stand: The Complete & Uncut Edition*]

The Stand: The Complete & Uncut Edition dropped to number 6 on *The New York Times* Fiction Best Seller List, its tenth week on the List.

15 July 1996, Monday afternoon

Tak launched four MotoKops attacks on Poplar Street in Wentworth, OH. In the first attack, with Snake Hunter's Tracker Arrow, they killed Cary Ripton, delivery boy for the *Shopper*, a local freebie newspaper, and Hannibal, the Reeds' German Shepherd.

Four Power Wagons were in the second attack, where David Carver and Mary Jackson were killed. The survivors congregated in Tom Billingsley's house and the Carvers' house next-door. Groups from each house tried to take the path behind the houses to get help. Steve Ames and Collie Entragian went first. A cat-freak attacked. They ran back into the other group. Not knowing what was running toward them, Jim Reed shot and killed Collie. When Jim saw what he had done, Tak pushed him over the edge; he shot himself in the head. Later, when Cammie Reed learned that an entity inside Seth Garin was responsible for the carnage, she intended to kill Seth.

After the third MotoKops attack, in which Pie Carver was killed, the remaining survivors grouped in the Carvers' house. Characters from *The Regulators*, a 1958 Western, and other old Western TV shows joined the MotoKops in all six Power Wagons. They opened fire on every house except the Carvers' then lined up outside the Carvers' house.

Tak had possessed the autistic Seth for two years. Telepathically, Seth had Audrey Wyler put Ex-Lax in his chocolate milk; Tak left Seth's body when Seth went to the bathroom. On his telepathic signal, he had Audrey go to her safe place in 1982 Mohonk Lake; he followed. They left their bodies behind. He had also signaled Cammie Reed to shoot. Two shots killed Seth's and Audrey's empty bodies. Tak, as little dancing red lights, tried to enter Cammie through the eyes, bursting them. Her head couldn't contain him and exploded. Seth and Audrey continued out-of-body experiences in 1982 Mohonk Lake, causing many guests to swear there were mother and son ghosts in a Mohonk meadow. The attacking MotoKops on Poplar Street disappeared; police and emergency equipment arrived. [*The Regulators*]

15 July 2001

Dreamcatcher stayed at number 15 on *The New York Times* Fiction Best Seller List, its fifteenth and last week on the List.

15 July 2007

Richard Bachman's *Blaze* dropped to number 7 on *The New York Times* Fiction Best Seller List, its third week on the List.

15 July 2011

Billy Freeman recovered after surgery. [*Doctor Sleep*]

15 July 2015

The Dark Tower: The Drawing of the Three—House of Cards #5 of 5 (Marvel Comics, $3.99) published

15 July 2018, Sunday

Cap City Channel 81's website had a video showing Terry Maitland at the conference in Cap City. Alec Pelley texted a link to Bill Samuels. Later, at the police station, Samuels played it for Detective Ralph Anderson.

~9:10 a.m.: Mrs. Arlene Peterson died in Mercy Hospital.

The state police took cheek swabs from Terry Maitland to Cap City for DNA testing.

Jeannie Anderson supported Ralph's decision to arrest Terry. If Terry had a doppelgänger, perhaps it was the imposter at the conference. At her suggestion, he went to the Cap City Sheraton to look for forensic evidence. Security footage showed Terry at the hotel the day of the murder. At the gift shop, Lorette Levelle remembered Terry. He had asked about the book on the top shelf, *A Pictorial History of Flint County, Douree County, and Canning Township*, took it down and put it back after seeing its high price. He remarked that his family had lived in Canning Township. Ralph bought the book.

Ralph found a thumbprint on the front cover and four fingerprints on the back, all matching Terry's.

>5:00 p.m.: Alec Pelley returned to the Cap City Sheraton. Ms. Levelle told him Ralph Anderson had purchased the book Terry Maitland had handled.

Merlin Cassidy pulled his stolen Buick with Oklahoma plates onto a Walmart Supercenter parking lot in El Paso, TX, to sleep. A cop woke him because he looked too young to drive. The officer took him to Harrison Avenue for processing and to wait for social services. [*The Outsider*]

The Outsider stayed at number 3 on *The New York Times* Hardcover Fiction Best Seller List, its sixth week on the List.

July 16

16 July 1932

Old Toot-Toot played Arlen Bitterbuck in the rehearsals of Bitterbuck's execution. [*The Green Mile*]

16 July 1986

Stephen King's *The Drawing of the Three* manuscript was 300 pages. Although the story just flowed from him, he felt as if something didn't want him to write it. [*The Dark Tower VI: Song of Susannah*]

16 July 1988, Saturday

Ruth McCausland lost a tooth overnight. That day, she began thinking tongue twisters so the Tommyknockers couldn't read her thoughts of going to the state police on Tuesday. [*The Tommyknockers*]

16 July 1990, ~11:00 a.m.

Continuing south on US 1, Nadine Cross, Joe, and Larry Underwood reached Ogunquit, ME, and, after reading Harold Lauder's sign, decided to go to the Stovington Plague Center. They returned to Wells to spend the night. [*The Stand: The Complete & Uncut Edition*]

16 July 1995

Tak wanted to use Herb Wyler's body to have sex with Audrey Wyler. Herb refused, so, in the garage, Tak made him put a gun in his mouth and shoot himself. Tak, a mental vampire, had been sucking him dry. Herb was too tired to go on, so he escaped Tak when he died. [*The Regulators*]

Rose Madder stayed at number 2 on *The New York Times* Fiction Best Seller List, its third week on the List.

16 July 2018, Monday: Terry Maitland's arraignment . . .

. . . didn't happen. Because of the outrage at a child's brutal murder and Terry's public arrest, an unruly crowd had formed outside the courthouse. Detective Ralph Anderson saw a burned man with a yellow bandanna on his head. Distraught at the loss of his brother and mother, Ollie Peterson shot Terry. Someone bumped Detective Anderson as he took his first shot. It hit a CBS TV camera; shards went into the cameraman's eye. Ralph's second shot took out Ollie Peterson. Before dying, Terry said he did not kill Frankie Peterson.

That morning, Dr. Bogan called and told Ralph the DNA from the semen sample matched Terry's. [*The Outsider*]

July 17

17 July 1932

Cherokee Indian Arlen Bitterbuck, nicknamed The Chief, was executed on Cold Mountain State Penitentiary's Old Sparky. [*The Green Mile*]

17 July 1958, The Smoke-Hole

The Losers had completed their underground clubhouse. Boards with grass sod glued on them covered the top. A person who didn't know about it could stand on the clubhouse without realizing there was anything unusual. The Losers had an Indian Smoke-Hole Ceremony, hoping for visions. Stan Uris, Ben Hanscom, Eddie Kaspbrak, and Beverly Marsh each left the clubhouse when the smoke became too much. Bill Denbrough left after the clubhouse looked much bigger than it was. Mike Hanlon and Richie Tozier shared a vision of the Barrens millions of years ago. They saw IT arrive on Earth. Bill and Ben pulled them out when they heard screaming. Mike and Richie vomited. [*IT*]

17 July 1983

Christine stayed at number 4 on *The New York Times* Fiction Best Seller List, its fifteenth week on the List.

17 July 1984, Tuesday

John Garton saw Adrian Mellon in an I Love Derry hat, which he had won at the Canal Days Festival in Bassey Park. Not liking a Derry cap on a gay man, Garton wanted to hurt him. Officer Frank Machen talked him out of it. [*IT*]

17 July 1988

In Hilly Brown's Second Gala Magic Show, Hilly unwittingly sent his brother, Davey, to Altair-4 and couldn't bring him back. Ev Hillman took Hilly to a doctor in Derry, ME, because he wasn't well and to get him out of Haven. Ev rented a room on Lower Main Street while his grandson was in Derry Home Hospital. [*The Tommyknockers*]

17 July 1990

Al, Garvey, Ronnie, and Virge kidnapped Rachel Carmody and Susan Stern near Columbus, OH. They had taken to kidnapping women, whom they kept drugged and raped often.

Nadine Cross, Joe, and Larry Underwood left Wells, ME, on Honda motorcycles. They lunched in Epsom, NH, had dinner in Concord, NH, and spent the night near Warner, NH.

The Trashcan Man entered Colorado. [*The Stand: The Complete & Uncut Edition*]

17 July 1998, Friday, almost midnight

With a plastic bag, Max Devore suffocated himself in the bathtub. [*Bag of Bones*]

17 July 2003, Thursday afternoon

The Fisherman took ten-year-old Irma Freneau, his third victim, from the sidewalk outside a Chase Street video store. At Ed Gilbertson's abandoned Ed's Eats & Dawgs shack, he beat her to keep her quiet, removed her clothing below the waist, and killed her. He cut off and took her right leg to eat later but left the foot. [*Black House*]

17 July 2007, midday

To write his case study on N., Dr. John Bonsaint visited Ackerman's Field. He found the dirt road with the chain across it, parked at Serenity Ridge Cemetery, and walked to the Field. In a Baggie in a bush was a white envelope addressed to him from N. The envelope had a note, "Sorry, Doc," and the key to the chain. On his way out, he turned and saw only seven stones. In the center, a darkness moved. Knowing there needed to be eight stones to be safe, he looked through the Baggie to bring out the eighth. When he got home, he threw away the key. ["N."]

17 July 2012

Stephen King finished *Doctor Sleep.*

17 July 2016

End of Watch dropped to number 4 on *The New York Times* Hardcover Fiction Best Seller List, its fourth week on the List.

July 18

18 July 1957

Carl Wilkes, Annie's father, tripped over a pile of clothes and fell down the stairs. He died from multiple skull fractures and a broken neck. Dr. Frank Canley was the attending physician at Hernandez General Hospital. [*Misery*]

18 July 1963, Thursday

Vera Donovan fired Karen Jolander for dropping a cracked plate. After Dolores St. George talked with her, Vera had Dolores call Karen back. Vera had hired Karen to clean for a weekend eclipse party. [*Dolores Claiborne*]

18 July 1967

Richard Macklin served in Shawshank State Prison for killing Dorsey Corcoran, his stepson. Three years after being released on parole, IT visited him as the dead Eddie Corcoran, Dorsey's brother. Macklin hanged himself. [*IT*]

~18 July 1979, ~10:40 a.m.

An otherworldly Buick Roadmaster had been abandoned at the Jenny station at the intersection of Pennsylvania State Road 32 and Humboldt Road in Statler County, PA. Trooper Ennis Rafferty had the Buick towed to Troop D's Shed B. It stayed there for at least the next twenty-seven years. From time to time, the Buick put on spectacular light shows, which Troop D called lightquakes. They interfered with the DSS satellite TV dish, the dispatcher's radio, and the microwave oven. During or after a lightquake, creatures from another world entered our world through the Buick's trunk. Our atmosphere and/or environment were fatal to them. Twice, a person was sucked from our world—Trooper Rafferty and arrestee Brian Lippy. The temperature in Shed B dropped far below the outside temperature before, during, and after a lightquake. [*From a Buick 8*]

18 July 1988, Monday

After two days of organizing and leading the search for David Brown, Ruth McCausland collapsed from exhaustion. Ad McKeen took her home. [*The Tommyknockers*]

18 July 1990

Lucy Swann joined Larry Underwood's group in Enfield, NH. They spent the night in Queche, VT.

Trash joined The Kid on Highway 34 in Colorado. They spent the night in Golden, CO. The Kid put a gun up Trash's butt and told Trash to masturbate him. [*The Stand: The Complete & Uncut Edition*]

18 July 1998, Saturday

2:00 a.m.: Max Devore's personal assistant, Rogette Whitmore, held a press conference after Max's death to reassure Wall Street that Visions, his software company, would continue to be run successfully. [*Bag of Bones*]

Introduction to Storm of the Century

18 July 1999

The Girl Who Loved Tom Gordon dropped to number 10 on *The New York Times* Fiction Best Seller List, its thirteenth week on the List.

18 July 2003, Friday, <9:12 a.m.

In the mirror of a Maxton Elder Care men's room, Charles Burnside saw Tyler Marshall outside the facility. He summoned Gorg, a speaking crow, to hold Tyler's attention then went into a stall. As all toilets and urinals flushed, Burny disappeared from the men's room. Outside, he thrust an arm through the hedge, grabbed Tyler, and hit him over the head with Butch Yerxa's pet rock. Tyler Marshall was the Fisherman's fourth victim.

Page 5 of the *La Riviere Herald* had a blurb about Milly Kuby's third-place standing in a state-wide spelling bee. She had misspelled 'opopanax' as 'opopanix.' [*Black House*]

18 July 2004

The Dark Tower VI: Song of Susannah dropped to number 7 on *The New York Times* Fiction Best Seller List, its fourth week on the List.

18 July 2007

Dr. John Bonsaint retrieved the key from the trash and put it in a desk drawer. ["N."]

18 July 2012

The Dark Tower: The Gunslinger—Man in Black #2 of 5 (Marvel Comics, $3.99) published

18 July 2018, Wednesday

Bill Samuels told Ralph Anderson that Merl Cassidy had stolen the dirty white van in New York and left it in Ohio. [*The Outsider*]

July 19

19 July 1880

Ella Langum, James Book's fiancée, died. Skinner Sweet had sent her poisoned wine that appeared to be a gift from Book. [*American Vampire*]

19 July 1933

The Castle Rock *Call* article, "VETERAN GUIDE, CARETAKER, CANNOT SAVE DAUGHTER," reported Carla Dean's death. The wind shifted, driving wildfires about two hundred men had been fighting to an area of TR–90 considered safe. Hilda Dean put her children in the car. While Hilda stowed things in the trunk, Carla left the car without her mother's knowledge. When Carla was discovered missing, Fred Dean went back, found her, and took her to the lake to escape the surrounding fires. She slipped away from him and drowned. That was how it was reported. Actually, Hilda left Carla behind intentionally, and Fred drowned her. [*Bag of Bones*]

19 July 1949

Wesley Smith was born. ["Ur"]

19 July 1957

"BAKERSFIELD ACCOUNTANT DIES IN FREAK FALL" appeared in the *Bakersfield Journal* the day after Annie Wilkes's father died. [*Misery*]

19 July 1963, Friday

So far, eighteen guests had arrived for Vera Donovan's eclipse-watching party that weekend. [*Dolores Claiborne*]

19 July 1964

In Oxford, MS, for a civil rights activist event, Odetta Holmes and others would go behind the Blue Moon Motor Hotel, where they were staying, to sing along with Delbert Anderson's guitar. This night, Odetta sang along with "Man of Constant Sorrow," by Ralph Stanley. Afterward, she and Darryl, another activist, made love and slept under the moon. [*The Dark Tower VI: Song of Susannah*]

19 July 1977

Stephen King thought about selling the chapters of *The Dark Tower* as individual stories to *Fantasy and Science Fiction*. [*The Dark Tower VI: Song of Susannah*]

19 July 1981, 4:45 a.m.

The tenants of the Tennis Club Apartments in River City were stuck in their building when the external doors wouldn't open. The front and back foyers had locked internal doors, which worked. Tim Hill discovered that neither the external doors, which had no locks, nor the fire door would open. The daylight didn't look right. If you looked at something too long, you'd see it there, then gone, then there again. Everything had a wavy look that made some tenants feel seasick. [*The Cannibals*]

19 July 1982

The Denver *Post* and the Rocky Mountain *News* reported Annie Wilkes's arrest in connection with infant deaths at Boulder Hospital. [*Misery*]

19 July 1984

"The Revelations of 'Becka Paulson" (revised and incorporated into *The Tommyknockers*) appeared in the July 19/August 2 double issue of *Rolling Stone*.

19 July 1987

The Eyes of the Dragon stayed at number 15 on *The New York Times* Fiction Best Seller List, its twenty-fifth week on the List.

Misery stayed at number 1 on *The New York Times* Fiction Best Seller List, its seventh week on the List.

19 July 1988, Tuesday

Ruth McCausland put off going to the state police to rejoin the search for David Brown. At home, her collectible dolls weren't in their proper places. On their little blackboard, they wrote her a note that said David Brown was on Altair-4. As part of her Tommyknocker becoming, which she tried to resist, her dolls spoke to her; she could hear the Haven Tommyknockers' thoughts. [*The Tommyknockers*]

19 July 1990

Stu Redman's group reached Girard, OH.

~10:30 a.m.: Stalled traffic stopped Trash and The Kid on I–70, about twelve miles east of the closed Eisenhower Tunnel.

7:15 p.m.: Larry Underwood's group arrived in Stovington, VT, and, after reading another of Harold Lauder's signs, decided to go to Nebraska.

~8:00 p.m.: Randall Flagg sent a pack of more than twenty-four wolves to help Trash. The Kid killed three and took shelter in an Austin. Later, hungry and thirsty, he came out. The wolves attacked; he strangled the one that gave him his death wounds. Some wolves led Trash west, through the Eisenhower Tunnel. Trash served Flagg and said, "My life for you." [*The Stand: The Complete & Uncut Edition*]

19 July 1992

Gerald's Game entered *The New York Times* Fiction Best Seller List at number 1. It was on the List for twenty-eight weeks.

19 July 1995

Stephen King was more than two hundred pages into the next *Dark Tower* manuscript. [*The Dark Tower VI: Song of Susannah*]

19 July 1998, Sunday, ~12:00 a.m.

Mike Noonan went to bed and found himself walking The Street, which led him to the October 1900 Fryeburg Fair. From home, Kyra Devore went up many stairs and saw Mike at the Fair. Sara Tidwell, performing with the Red-Top Boys, scared her, so they headed out. Seven dead men, including Harry Auster, Fred Dean, and Jared Devore came out of Freak Alley, blocked their exit, and demanded Mike hand over Kyra. Mike picked her up and ran into the Ghost House. Kyra returned home through a door with a red tricycle on it. [*Bag of Bones*]

19 July 2003, Saturday morning

8:10–8:12 a.m.: In a two-minute 911 call from the pay phone outside 7-Eleven, the Fisherman said he left a body at Ed's Eats & Dawgs. After taking the call, Officer Hrabowski told his wife, Paula, swearing her to secrecy. She told Myrtle Harrington and one other friend; rumors of five to six victims' bodies spread throughout town. Many French Landing residents went to satisfy their morbid curiosity. Officers Pam Stevens and Danny Tcheda stopped them from entering by the main access road; later, some of the Thunder Five helped. Others got in by way of a disused road behind Goltz's French County Farm Equipment dealership. Among those who entered were Toots Billinger, Wendell Green, Teddy Runkleman, Freddy Saknessum, Doodles Sanger, and the Thunder Five. Green had paid Billinger, Runkleman, Saknessum, and Sanger $20 each to create a diversion on his signal. While the police and the Thunder Five were busy chasing them, Green went inside and took photos of the dead girl. Beezer St. Pierre exposed his film, ruining the pictures. Green offered 10% of the proceeds to Jack Sawyer if Jack let him back in to take more photos; Jack punched him in the stomach. After seeing a crowd at the crime scene, Wisconsin State Police detectives Jeff Black and Perry Brown relieved French Landing Chief of Police Dale Gilbertson and took over the Fisherman investigation.

~6:30 p.m.: Charles Burnside planted Polaroid pictures of the Fisherman's child victims in George Potter's closet. Andy Railsback saw him in the hall as Burny went to leave Maxton Elder Care through the men's room. Railsback found the pictures and had Morty Fine, the Nelson Hotel's night clerk, call the police. (Burnside framed Potter because Potter beat him out of a lucrative federal housing deal in Chicago more than thirty years earlier.)

7:03 p.m.: Chief Gilbertson and Officers Bobby Dulac and Tom Lund arrested George Potter at Lucky's Tavern, next-door to the Nelson Hotel. Tansy Freneau led a mob of about 250 to lynch Potter. Jack Sawyer, with lilies from the Territories, convinced Tansy that Potter wasn't the Fisherman. When Wendell Green tried to re-incite the crowd, Arnold Hrabowski knocked him out with a flashlight. [*Black House*]

19 July 2015

Finders Keepers dropped to number 5 *The New York Times* Hardcover Fiction Best Seller List, its fifth week on the List.

19 July 2018, Thursday

>12:00 a.m.: Gracie Maitland screamed at a man outside her second-story bedroom window. Her sister, Sarah, screamed when G told her about the man. After Marcy Maitland comforted them, they dismissed it as a nightmare. The man had short, black hair that stood up, a lumpy, Play-Doh face, and straws for eyes.

~3:00 a.m.: Fred Peterson took a footstool and a rope to a tree in the backyard and hanged himself. A footstool's height wasn't enough drop to break his neck. As he strangled, survival instinct took over. His flailing broke the branch with a loud snap; he fell. As he lost consciousness, he saw a man with straws for eyes.

Mrs. June Gibson, suffering a recent bout of sciatica, sat in her living room, fiddling with her iPhone. She looked out when she heard a gunshot. Mr. Peterson lay under a tree. She loosened the rope around his neck. Mr. Jagger walked over as she resuscitated Fred; she had him call 911. She kept Fred alive until the EMTs arrived. In a coma with minimal brain function, he existed on life support in Mercy Hospital's ICU Room 304.

morning: Donelli Brothers handled the double funeral for Arlene Peterson and Ollie Peterson.

afternoon: Terry Maitland was buried in Memorial Park Cemetery.

3:30 p.m.: Ralph Anderson had found a piece of a takeout menu under the van's front seat during his investigation. He thought it might give more information about the dirty white van's history. In the police evidence room, he found the scrap. It was from The Tommy and Tuppence Pub and Café on Northwoods Boulevard in Dayton, OH. [*The Outsider*]

July 20

20 July

Bud Brown, Mrs. Carmody, Mrs. Clapham, Ambrose Cornell, Billy Drayton, David Drayton, Amanda Dumfries, Buddy Eagleton, Jim Grondin, Michael Hatlen, Myron LaFleur, Mr. McVey, Dan Miller, Norm, Brent Norton, Hilda Reppler, Sally, Arnie Simms, Tom Smalley, Hattie Turman, Hank Vannerman, Walter, and Ollie Weeks were trapped at Federal Food Supermarket in Bridgton when the mist with creatures hit. Mrs. Carmody preached that they needed a human sacrifice to save themselves. At first, the others dismissed her as crazy. A mild panic started after a large bug-like creature got in the store and killed Smalley. Mrs. Clapham suffered a broken leg from being trampled. Norm was killed when he went outside to clear a clogged exhaust. Brent Norton and his Flat-Earth Society died when they tried to get help. ["The Mist"]

20 July 1958

Eddie Kaspbrak went to the Center Street Drug Store on an errand for his mother. Norbert Keene gave him a free ice cream soda and told him his asthma was psychosomatic. Henry Bowers, Victor Criss, Patrick Hockstetter, and Moose Sadler beat up Eddie outside the Costello Avenue Market. Mr. Gedreau came out to help, but Bowers forced him back inside. Eddie ran; they caught him when he ran into Richard Cowan. Bowers broke Eddie's arm. Mr. Nell chased Bowers and the others away. Pennywise the Clown drove the ambulance that took Eddie to the hospital. [*IT*]

20 July 1963, Saturday, Eclipse Day

Vera Donovan and her thirty to forty guests watched the eclipse from the *Island Princess*, which she had chartered. [*Dolores Claiborne*]

The Mahout family went to New Hampshire for the eclipse. Tom Mahout couldn't go and stayed with ten-year-old Jessie Mahout. She sat on Tom's lap as they watched the eclipse from their summer home on Dark Score Lake. Her constant wiggling to get comfortable caused an erection in her father. He fondled her and ejaculated on her buttocks. She went inside to change her underwear. This incident triggered multiple personalities to develop within Jessie. In 1975, she married Gerald Burlingame. [*Gerald's Game, Dolores Claiborne*]

Two years earlier, Dolores St. George stopped Joe St. George from beating her by threatening him with an ax. During their marriage, she put up with his habitual drinking and gambling, but his molesting their daughter and stealing the kids' bank account money was too much. During the eclipse while the kids were away and the neighbors were off watching it, she killed Joe. She compelled him to chase her in the backyard, where she jumped over an old, abandoned well. He didn't jump and fell in. Later, when she checked on him, he had climbed mostly out. She bashed his face with a rock. He fell back in, dead. [*Dolores Claiborne*]

20 July 1964

Most of the activists attending a civil rights event in Oxford, MS, were in jail. Bathroom breaks weren't allowed; eventually, Odetta Holmes had to go in her slacks. [*The Dark Tower VI: Song of Susannah*]

20 July 1980, Sunday

"TRAGIC BATTLE IN MAINE AS MOM BATTLES KILLER SAINT BERNARD" appeared in a national tabloid. [*Cujo*]

20 July 1988, Wednesday

Ruth McCausland brought in the State Police to handle the search for David Brown. [*The Tommyknockers*]

20 July 1990

early a.m.: The Trashcan Man emerged from the west end of the Eisenhower Tunnel.

~12:00 noon: Trash broke into a Vail, CO, apartment, where he spent the night. [*The Stand: The Complete & Uncut Edition*]

20 July 2003, Sunday

The Thunder Five found Black House. A large dog-like creature not of this Earth bit Mouse Baumann's leg, infecting him with something alive. The others shot the creature, hitting it several times, more than enough to kill an Earthly creature but only enough to run this one off. The rest of the Five took Mouse to Beezer St. Pierre's house, where he waited for Jack Sawyer. They covered the windows with blankets because light melted his skin. His body decayed from the inside; the melted parts ate through the couch. When Jack arrived, among the things Mouse told him was a word Jack would need to help save Tyler Marshall: *D'Yamba*. He died at almost 8:00 p.m. By 3:00 a.m., there was little of him left; Beezer and the others washed his remains down the bathtub.

1:40 p.m.: Jack visited Judy Marshall and flipped to the Territories to where Sophie, Judy's Twinner, was. Sophie and Parkus explained that Tyler Marshall had abilities to become among the best Breakers for the Crimson King, who kidnapped Breakers and used them to break the Beams that hold the Dark Tower—and the worlds as their inhabitants knew them—in place. Although Jack's once touching the Talisman wouldn't help him defeat the Crimson King, it could be enough for him to rescue Ty Marshall.

7:14 p.m.: With Henry Leyden's hedge clippers in hand, Charles Burnside (with Mr. Munshun inside him) stood outside Henry's studio as Henry listened to tapes from the Fisherman. He went in and mortally wounded Henry with the clippers; Leyden stabbed Burny. Back in the Maxton Elder Care men's room, Burnside bandaged his abdomen and right arm. He killed Georgette Potter on his way to Chipper Maxton's office then killed Maxton in the office. Mr. Munshun was still with him; they went to Black House. [*Black House*]

20 July 2014

Mr. Mercedes stayed at number 4 on *The New York Times* Hardcover Fiction Best Seller List, its fifth week on the List.

20 July 2018, Friday

Dougie Elfman's father sent him in an old Dodge pickup truck for milk cans and horse-tack from one of their disused barns. He loaded four galvanized cans into the truck's bed, but there wasn't any tack. He found new blue jeans, Jockey underpants, expensive sneakers, and a horse's head belt buckle, all encrusted with what looked like semen.

4:00 p.m.: Dougie pulled off Route 79 and called his father. He said someone had been staying in the barn. Because of the belt buckle like Terry Maitland's on the news, he told his father to call the police.

Canning Township's old graveyard, with many of Terry Maitland's ancestors, was less than half a mile away.

5:45 p.m.: Lieutenant Yune Sablo and the Mobile Crime Lab investigated at the barn.

Ralph Anderson was on administrative leave following the Ollie Peterson shooting, and Betsy Riggins was having a baby, so Jack Hoskins was called back from vacation three days early. After two vodka-tonics at Gentlemen, Please, he went to Canning Township. The outsider stroked the back of his neck. Jack spun around; no one was there.

8:00 p.m.: Ralph Anderson talked with Marcy Maitland about their trip to Dayton, OH, in April. From the kitchen doorway, Sarah Maitland heard some of the conversation. When Ralph asked whether anything unusual had happened, Sarah said her father had been cut. Marcy added they thought an orderly's fingernail had cut Terry. [*The Outsider*]

July 21

21 July, ~9:30 a.m.

David Drayton, Buddy Eagleton, Jim Grondin, Mike Hatlen, Dan Miller, Hilda Reppler, and Ollie Weeks left the Federal Foods Supermarket. They went to the Bridgton Pharmacy next-door to get drugs for Mrs. Clapham's broken leg. Dog-sized spiders with twelve to fourteen legs shot silk at them and killed four. David, Hilda, and Ollie returned to the supermarket. ["The Mist"]

21 July 1958

The Losers practiced shooting at ten cans, twenty feet away, with a slingshot. They chose Beverly Marsh, with the most hits—nine of ten—to shoot IT. That evening, they visited Eddie Kaspbrak in the hospital and told him their plan to kill IT: they would make two silver slugs from Ben Hanscom's silver dollar, and Beverly would shoot IT at 29 Neibolt Street using Bill Denbrough's slingshot. They signed Eddie's cast. [*IT*]

21 July 1961, Friday

George Amberson's second timeline: Mimi Corcoran and Deke Simmons married in a small, private ceremony at Deke's house. Her sister and his parents attended. [*11/22/63*]

21 July 1963, Sunday

Vera Donovan had given Dolores Claiborne the day off. Dolores called Gail Lavesque, in charge of Vera's housekeeping while Dolores was away, and asked whether Joe St. George had stopped by; he hadn't come home the night before. Later, she called some of Joe's friends to see whether they had seen him. [*Dolores Claiborne*]

21 July 1984, Saturday

After leaving the Canal Days Festival in Bassey Park, Steven Dubay, John Garton, and Chris Unwin waited for Adrian Mellon outside the Falcon, a gay bar. When Mellon and Dan Hagarty came out, they beat Hagarty and threw Mellon over a bridge, into the water. IT killed Mellon. [*IT*]

21 July 1985

Richard Bachman's *Thinner* dropped to number 9 on *The New York Times* Fiction Best Seller List, its twenty-first week on the List.

Skeleton Crew stayed at number 1 on *The New York Times* Fiction Best Seller List, its fifth week on the List.

21 July 1996

The Green Mile, Part One: The Two Dead Girls dropped to number 13 on *The New York Times* Paperback Fiction Best Seller List, its fifteenth week on the List.

The Green Mile, Part Two: The Mouse on the Mile dropped to number 12 on *The New York Times* Paperback Fiction Best Seller List, its eleventh week on the List.

The Green Mile, Part Three: Coffey's Hands dropped to number 6 on *The New York Times* Paperback Fiction Best Seller List, its seventh week on the List.

The Green Mile, Part Four: The Bad Death of Eduard Delacroix stayed at number 1 on *The New*

York Times Paperback Fiction Best Seller List, its third week on the List.

21 July 1998, Tuesday

In celebration of Max Devore's death, Rommie Bissonette, George Kennedy, Mike Noonan, and John Storrow went to a cookout at Mattie Devore's. Dickie Osgood drove by while George Footman opened fire with a Glock 9-millimeter automatic weapon. Kyra Devore, napping, was unharmed. Rommie, George, and John were wounded; Mattie was killed. Max Devore had arranged the shooting before he died, wiring $2 million to a Grand Caymans bank account for Footman.

After putting Kyra to bed at Sara Laughs, Mike went to dig up and destroy Sara Tidwell's remains so her hold over the town and the killings would stop. Jo Noonan's ghost held off Sara and an Outsider long enough for Mike to do this. [*Bag of Bones*]

21 July 2003, Monday

Because help for Tyler Marshall was coming, Charles Burnside took Ty from his Black House cell to his special place off Conger Road in Sheol. He handcuffed Ty's left wrist in a shackle on the back wall. When Burny adjusted his position to get the cuff for the right wrist, Ty grabbed and squeezed his balls, puncturing one. Thinking this wasn't enough, Ty thrust his hand into Burny's stabbed abdomen, pulled out some intestines, and yanked them back and forth. The shock was too much for Burny's eighty-five-year-old body; it died.

Outside, Black House looked like a black-painted, three-story house. Inside, it was infinite; a person would easily lose her way and wander forever. Jack said, "*d'yamba.*" The Queen of the Bees, the queen of many bees swarming outside, entered and led them through Black House, past Tyler's cell, to another world outside.

Lord Malshun caught Tyler as he left Burny's shack, picked him up, and carried him toward Station House Road, where they'd board a monorail train to Din-tah. Jack Sawyer, Dale Gilbertson, Doc, Beezer, and a swarm of bees stopped them on Conger Road. The Sawyer Gang was victorious, partly because Jack had touched the Talisman years before, and defeated Malshun. Before going home, Jack had Tyler destroy the Big Combination, machinery powered by many children kidnapped from their home worlds. The Crimson King felt it when Tyler broke the Big Combination. [*Black House*]

21 July 2010

The Dark Tower: The Gunslinger—The Journey Begins #3 of 5 (Marvel Comics, $3.99) published

21 July 2013

Azzie visited Eleanor Ouellette. [*Doctor Sleep*]

Joyland stayed at number 1 on *The New York Times* Paperback Trade Fiction Best Seller List, its fifth week on the List.

21 July 2018, Saturday

10:00 a.m.: Ralph Anderson met State Police Lieutenant Yune Sablo at O'Malley's Irish Spoon near the train station in Dubrow. Yune had investigated the clothes at the Elfman barn and found three weird things:

weird #1: Terry Maitland's fingerprints were on the horse's head belt buckle, but the Forensics Unit tech said they were like the prints of a seventy-to-eighty-year-old. A second set of prints was blurred but similar to the unknown set from the van. Ralph and Yune thought they were from the same unsub. They considered Terry might have had an accomplice who drove the van to Oklahoma.

weird #2: An unknown substance on the clothes looked like dried semen but there was far too much. The same substance on hay had turned the hay black.

weird #3: The set of clothes—501 jeans, Jockey underpants, white athletic socks, expensive sneakers, and a horse's head belt buckle—matched the clothes Claude Bolton had described, but the yellow shirt was missing.

Later, Ralph wondered whether the burned man outside the courthouse had the yellow shirt wrapped around his head instead of a long bandanna. The man was beside another in a cowboy hat. He and Jeannie Anderson reviewed videos from the four major stations and Channel 81. They saw the man in the cowboy hat but not the man with the burned, scarred, lumpy face. Jeannie suggested a creature like a vampire that casts no mirror reflections and couldn't be captured on camera. [*The Outsider*]

July 22

22 July

Mrs. Carmody had picked up about fifteen devout followers, including Marty LaFleur and Mr. McVey. They wanted Billy Drayton to be a human sacrifice to protect them from the creatures in the mist. Her group disbanded after Ollie Weeks shot and killed her. Ambrose Cornell, Billy Drayton, David Drayton, Amanda Dumfries, Hilda Reppler, Mrs. Turman, and Ollie Weeks left the store, heading for Drayton's Scout. Cornell ran back to the supermarket after Mrs. Turman and Ollie Weeks were killed. The others arrived at a Howard Johnson's in southern Maine. They saw no end to the mist. ["The Mist"]

22 July 1934

Outside Chicago's Biograph Theater, the Gees ambushed Johnnie Dillinger as he ran down an alley. It was rumored that somebody else was shot that day and that Dillinger got away and lived the rest of his life in Mexico. ["The Death of Jack Hamilton"]

22 July 1943

Timmy Baterman was buried with military honors in Pleasantview Cemetery. The seventeen-year-old was killed when he charged a machine gun nest near Rome the week before. He was posthumously awarded the Silver Star. About three days after his burial, his father, Bill Baterman, exhumed his body and reburied him in the Micmac burial ground beyond the Pet Sematary. Touched by the Wendigo, Timmy came back zombie-like, psychic, and stinky. His coming back not himself caused his dad to go crazy. About a week after Timmy's return, Bill Baterman shot and killed him, set fire to the house, and then shot himself. [*Pet Sematary*]

22 July 1958

After eating Rena Davenport's baked beans, Henry Bowers, Victor Criss, Belch Huggins, and Patrick Hockstetter lit one another's farts at the dump. After the others left, Hockstetter opened a refrigerator he used to suffocate animals. Flying leeches, courtesy of IT, attacked. He ran and passed out from blood loss. IT as a man dragged him to Derry's sewer system, where he died.

Beverly Marsh had been at the dump to practice with a slingshot. She saw everything up to where Hockstetter ran away. She opened the refrigerator; a flying leech landed on her arm, scarring it for life. After she told the Losers about Hockstetter, all except Eddie Kaspbrak went to look in the refrigerator. When they opened it from the far end of a clothesline, they saw a blood-written message from Pennywise on the inside of the door. The message warned the Losers to stop or else he would kill them. [*IT*]

22 July 1961, Saturday

George Amberson's second timeline: George Amberson met Miss Sadie Dunhill at Mimi and Deke Simmons's wedding reception. As the accident-prone Sadie approached during the introduction, she tripped over a folding chair. George caught her. [*11/22/63*]

22 July 1963, Monday

Dolores St. George told Vera Donovan she wouldn't be in; Joe St. George had been missing for two nights. She developed her story: They argued about booze and money. Joe choked her.

She crossed Russian Meadow on her way to East Head to watch the eclipse. Satisfied with her story, she reported Joe's disappearance to Garrett Thibodeau, Little Tall Island's town constable. [*Dolores Claiborne*]

22 July 1988, Friday

Ev Hillman told David Bright of the Bangor *Daily News* about Haven, ME. Bright thought he was crazy.

Ruth McCausland tried to leave Haven but couldn't get through an invisible, impenetrable barrier at the edge of town. She put a battery-powered gadget in each of her dolls. [*The Tommyknockers*]

22 July 1990

Al, Garvey, Ronnie, and Virge kidnapped Patty Kroger and killed the man she was with. They could handle eight women, so they killed an old one to make room for Patty.

June Brinkmeyer and Olivia Walker joined Nick Andros, Ralph Brentner, Tom Cullen, Dick Ellis, and Gina McCone about ninety miles south of Hemingford Home, NE.

>6:40 p.m.: Randall Flagg sent hundreds of weasels to get the chickens Mother Abagail had slaughtered for the Captain Trips survivors. They failed because of her faith in the Lord. [*The Stand: The Complete & Uncut Edition*]

The Stand: The Complete & Uncut Edition rose to number 4 on *The New York Times* Fiction Best Seller List, its eleventh week on the List.

22 July 2007

Richard Bachman's *Blaze* dropped to number 12 on *The New York Times* Fiction Best Seller List, its fourth week on the List.

22 July 2016, 12:00 p.m., PT

Simon & Schuster gave away 150 copies of the 1942 Fourth Edition of *Charlie The Choo-Choo* at Comic-Con International: San Diego, booth #1128. Author Beryl Evans inscribed each copy. Stephen King's and artist Ned Dameron's signatures were laid in.

22 July 2018, Sunday

Claude Bolton started a ten-day vacation; he visited his mother in Marysville, TX.

Ralph Anderson met with Jeannie Anderson, Howie Gold, and Alec Pelley; Lune Sablo Skyped in. Alec had seen the burned man, too. All agreed that the unknown, blurred finger-prints from the van came from the same person as the unknown, blurred prints from the belt buckle. They speculated that a man with burned hands wouldn't leave crisp prints. Alec said he knew someone they could send to Dayton for further investigation.

Gracie Maitland took a nap. A few hours later, she woke to a man sitting on her bed but thought she may still be dreaming. He said he'd go away if she relayed a message to Detective Anderson. That evening, she excused herself from watching a movie, went upstairs, and found Howie Gold's number on her mother's cell. She asked him to give a message to the detective. A man that may have been in a dream told her to tell Detective Anderson to stop or something bad would happen. This time, the man looked better; the Play-Doh face was gone, but he didn't look "done."

night: Alec Pelley called Finders Keepers hoping to leave a message for Bill Hodges. Holly

Gibney answered and told him Bill had died two years before. He told her about the case and that he needed someone to back-check Terry Maitland's April trip to Dayton, OH.

With Google, Holly found the Fairview Hotel was the closest lodging to The Tommy and Tuppence Pub and Café. Sarah Maitland had said the restaurant was near their hotel, so the Fairview was probably where the Maitlands had stayed. [*The Outsider*]

The Outsider dropped to number 4 on *The New York Times* Hardcover Fiction Best Seller List, its seventh week on the List.

July 23

23 July 1789

Robert Boone wrote Johns and Goodfellow about getting a copy of *De Vermis Mysteriis* (*The Mysteries of the Worm*) for his brother. Philip wanted to get it for James Boon. ["Jerusalem's Lot"]

23 July 1958

Bill Denbrough, Ben Hanscom, and Richie Tozier got two bearing molds from Kitchener Precision Tool & Die. At the Denbroughs', the Losers made two silver slugs from one of Ben's four silver dollars his father had given him. [*IT*]

23 July 1961, Sunday

George Amberson's second timeline: Mimi and Deke Simmons left for Mexico. They went more for alternative medical treatment for Mimi than for a honeymoon. With eight to twelve months to live, she wanted to die on a Mexican beach instead of in an American hospital. Also, the painkillers wouldn't be limited in Mexico. [*11/22/63*]

23 July 1963, Tuesday

Selena St. George was a counselor at Lake Winthrop for the summer. Dolores St. George called her and told her that her father was missing. [*Dolores Claiborne*]

23 July 1970

"Slade," Chapter 6, appeared in *The Maine Campus*.

23 July 1988, Saturday

Hillman Brown, almost catatonic, was still in the hospital. He had lost ten teeth. [*The Tommyknockers*]

23 July 1992

The Night Flier killed Buck Kendall at Lakeview Airport in Alderton, NY. ["The Night Flier"]

23 July 1995

Rose Madder stayed at number 2 on *The New York Times* Fiction Best Seller List, its fourth week on the List.

23 July 2018, Monday

9:50 a.m.: Holly Gibney left for Dayton, OH.

3:17 p.m.: She arrived at the Fairview Hotel. The Tommy and Tuppence Pub and Café was less than a block away. City Parking was a block beyond the Pub. She talked with Mary Hollister, the Pub's hostess and part owner.

At the hotel, she emailed Alec Pelley. Pub leaflets were distributed on April 19th so that was the day Merl Cassidy left the van. It was most likely stolen the same day, two days before the Maitlands arrived in Dayton. [*The Outsider*]

July 24

24 July 1963, Wednesday

Melissa Caron drove Selena St. George home from Lake Winthrop. Selena and Dolores St. George talked. Selena suspected her mother killed her father; Selena felt responsible. [*Dolores Claiborne*]

24 July 1976, Sunday

THE POWER AND GRACE OF HE WHO WALKS BEHIND THE ROWS was the sermon of what had been the Grace Baptist Church in Gatlin, NE. ["Children of the Corn"]

24 July 1983

Christine stayed at number 4 on *The New York Times* Fiction Best Seller List, its sixteenth week on the List.

24 July 1988, Sunday

Ruth McCausland wished to signal the outside world that something was wrong in Haven. Knowing she was going crazy from the Tommyknocker effects, she wanted to die sane. She rigged her dolls to the town hall clock so they would explode at 3:00 p.m. She fell through the clock tower trap door and broke a few ribs when bats flew into her.

3:05 p.m.: An M–16 firecracker Ruth had gotten from Hump Jernigan went off five minutes later than expected. The tower was blown off; she died in the explosion.

The Tommyknockers needed a picture of the tower to project in its place. Christina Lindley, 17, and Bobby Tremain created a new picture from an old one, changing the time from 9:45 to 3:05. After finishing, Christina had Bobby take her virginity.

5:15 p.m.: Maine State Police Troopers Peter Gabbons and Bent Rhodes arrived in Haven, ME, to investigate the explosion that killed Ruth McCausland. They got there before the Tommyknockers projected a picture of the clock tower in place of the missing tower. Haven officials told them the furnace exploded. The troopers thought they talked with Tug Ellender at their base; they actually talked with Tommyknocker Buck Peters. He could read their thoughts and told them what they expected to hear.

7:45 p.m.: The troopers left Haven. On their way back to Derry, ME, they stopped by Beach Jernigan's truck in the road. Jernigan disintegrated them with a Tommyknocker gadget. He placed a freshly killed and gutted dear by their car to make their disappearance look like a poacher's crime.

John Leandro of the Bangor *Daily News* talked with Haven Volunteer Fire Department Chief Dick Allison about the explosion. Allison told him the town hall furnace exploded. Angry after calls from the Associated Press and various law officers from nearby towns, Allison slammed his fist on his desk. He broke four fingers. [*The Tommyknockers*]

24 July 1990

Nick Andros, Ralph Brentner, June Brinkmeyer, Tom Cullen, Dick Ellis, Gina McCone, and Olivia Walker were the first Captain Trips survivors to arrive at Mother Abagail's in Hemingford Home, NE. They spent the night there. [*The Stand: The Complete & Uncut Edition*]

24 July 1992, 5:00 a.m.

Jenna Kendall found her husband's body, with two holes on opposite sides of his neck. Most of his blood was gone. ["The Night Flier"]

24 July 1994

On their way to California, the Garins—Bill, June, Mary Lou, and Seth—passed the China Pit mine in Desperation, NV. Seth, autistic, spoke clearly and coherently; he asked to go back to see the Ponderosa. Engineer Allen Symes showed the Garins the China Pit Mine and the entrance to the newly uncovered Rattlesnake Number One Mine. Tak influenced Seth to go down a quarter mile to a crack where Tak entered and possessed him. [*The Regulators*]

24 July 2000

The Plant Book One: *Zenith Rising*, Part 1 e-book (Philtrum Press, $1.00) published

24 July 2013

The Dark Tower: The Gunslinger—So Fell Lord Perth ONE-SHOT (Marvel Comics, $3.99) published

24 July 2016

End of Watch dropped to number 5 on *The New York Times* Hardcover Fiction Best Seller List, its fifth week on the List.

24 July 2018, Tuesday

morning: Mrs. Kelly welcomed Holly Gibney to the Heisman Memory Unit then got poopy when Holly asked about Peter Maitland. From their brief conversation, Holly learned reporters and police had been to see Mr. Maitland, and Mrs. Kelly didn't know Peter's son, Terry, was dead.

>11:00 a.m.: With a Starbucks latte and her laptop, Holly sat on a bench in Andrew Dean Park. She perused the archives of the Dayton *Daily News*. Heath Holmes, an orderly at the Heisman Memory Unit was arrested for the murder and molestation of Amber and Jolene Howard in April. (Terry Maitland was in nearby Dayton.) In early June, Heath Holmes killed himself.

2:30 p.m.: Holly went back to the Heisman Memory Unit and parked in the employee lot.

~3:00 p.m.: A nurse, Candy Wilson, walked to an old Honda Civic and lit a cigarette. Thinking the woman could use some extra money, Holly followed her home. She offered $100 to talk about Heath Holmes and his connection to Peter Maitland. Since her job was on the line, Candy agreed, but needed $250; she invited Holly in. Candy had seen Holmes at work one day during the week he was on vacation.

Holly called Alec Pelley and asked whether she could speak with Detective Anderson. Pelley said he'd have to check with Howard Gold and Marcy Maitland. Later, Ralph called. She told him a similar killer was an orderly who had bumped into Terry. Ralph told her the orderly had cut Terry, and another person (Claude Bolton) had been cut, too. He asked her to fly down for a meeting the next evening. [*The Outsider*]

July 25

25 July 1932, Monday

Eduard Delacroix had been convicted for the rape and murder of a young girl. The girl's apartment caught fire when he burned her body behind it. Two more children and three or four adults died. To await his execution, he arrived in Cold Mountain State Penitentiary's E Block. Percy Wetmore pulled him out of the wagon too fast, causing him to fall; his hands brushed Wetmore's pants. Thinking Delacroix was grabbing his crotch, Wetmore dragged him to his cell, beating him with a baton. Paul Edgecombe and Brutal Howell pulled off the out-of-control Wetmore. Percy's hate for Delacroix grew as Del's Date Of Execution got closer. [*The Green Mile*]

25 July 1958

The Losers went to 29 Neibolt Street to kill IT. In the bathroom, they found an uncovered toilet drain and the commode in many pieces. When IT as the Teenage Werewolf came out of the drain, Beverly Marsh shot at IT with a silver slug but missed. IT cut Ben Hanscom's stomach when IT picked him up and threw him into the bathtub. Beverly shot IT near the right eye. IT escaped into the drain when they bluffed that they had more slugs. Silver bullets kill werewolves, so a silver slug could hurt IT when IT was a werewolf. This was the first time IT had ever been hurt, the first time IT had almost died, the first time IT had experienced fear. The Losers were responsible; IT wanted to kill them. [*IT*]

25 July 1988

Hilly Brown, in a constant, deep sleep, was still in Derry Home Hospital, Room 371.

David Bright's article about the disappearance of Peter Gabbons and Benton Rhodes appeared on page 1 of the Bangor *Daily News*. Johnny Leandro's article about Ruth McCausland's death also appeared on the front page. [*The Tommyknockers*]

25 July 1990

Trash reached western Utah.

Saving herself for the Dark Man, Nadine Cross stopped Larry Underwood from making love to her. [*The Stand: The Complete & Uncut Edition*]

25 July 1994

The vacationing Garins expected to be in San Jose, CA, to visit with the Calabreses, old college friends. [*The Regulators*]

25 July 1996

The Green Mile, Part Five: Night Journey (Signet, $2.99) published with a first printing of 2,000,000 copies

25 July 1999

The Girl Who Loved Tom Gordon dropped to number 11 on *The New York Times* Fiction Best Seller List, its fourteenth week on the List.

25 July 2004

The Dark Tower VI: Song of Susannah dropped to number 8 on *The New York Times* Fiction Best Seller List, its fifth week on the List.

25 July 2014, Friday

Charlie Jacobs told Jamie Morton to be at Goat Mountain Resort on Sunday. [*Revival*]

25 July 2018, Wednesday

2:00 a.m.: Jack Hoskins woke with a vodka hangover, sunburn on the back of his neck, and needed a bowel movement. Someone stood behind the shower curtain as he read the *Flint City Call* on the toilet. The outsider called his name and told him his neck wasn't sunburned. The outsider had given him cancer but would take it back if Jack agreed to do something. Jack fainted.

4:06 AM: Jeannie Anderson woke to pee. A light was on downstairs; she hadn't noticed it before going to the bathroom. It was the light over the stove. A kitchen chair was missing. Someone told her not to move or scream else he'd kill her. A man sat on the missing chair in the living room. He said to tell Ralph to stop; otherwise, he'd kill Ralph, he'd kill them all. She knew it was the man who had killed Frankie Peterson. She fainted.

Later, she told Ralph about the man. With all doors and windows locked, the burglar alarm set, and no imprints of anyone sitting in a chair on the new carpet, he didn't believe her. Yet, he recognized her description of the man, down to MUST tattooed on his hand, as Claude Bolton.

7:00 p.m.: Jeannie Anderson, Ralph Anderson, Holly Gibney, Howie Gold, Marcy Maitland, Alec Pelley, Yune Sablo, and Bill Samuels met in Howie's conference room. They discussed how the Howard murders mirrored the Peterson case: brutal killing, overwhelming evidence, and perp in two places at once. Heath Holmes had cut Terry Maitland who then cut Claude Bolton. A man matching Bolton's description had visited Gracie Maitland and Jeannie Anderson, yet Bolton was in Texas.

Holly Gibney explained how there were three men in two places at one time. First, she showed a few scenes from *Mexican Wrestling Women Meet the Monster* where the Wrestling Women defeat *El Cuco*, a Mexican legend of a being that lived off the blood and fat of children. *El Cuco* took the form of Professor Espinoza and killed a child, for which the professor was executed. Near the end of the movie, *El Cuco* had a lumpy face and prongs for eyes. The legend was known as *El Hombre con Saco* in Spain and Pumpkinhead in Portugal. Holly said that, while legends aren't real, they are based on bits of truth.

The outsider, not Terry or Heath, was the killer. In the shape of a chosen scapegoat, the outsider kills and feeds on a child (or two), marks (cuts) the next scapegoat, and rests while transforming into the new scapegoat. The transformation could take several weeks. During the change, the outsider could appear lumpy or burned.

She showed pictures of abandoned structures bordering Peaceful Rest Cemetery—a car wash, a factory, a train station, and two boxcars. She expected more evidence inside one.

Next step: Ralph, Alec, Howie, and Holly would go to Marysville, TX, to interview Claude Bolton. Holly figured he was the outsider's next scapegoat.

Jack Hoskins sat half a block away. The outsider told him to drive to Texas then was gone. [*The Outsider*]

July 26

26 July 1976, Tuesday

Malachi Boardman slit Japheth's throat and threw his body from the cornfield for trying to leave Gatlin, NE. Burt Robeson hit the body while driving through Nebraska. He and his wife took it to Gatlin to report what they found. He Who Walks Behind the Rows worshipers attacked them and took Vicky Robeson. They sacrificed her to He Who Walks Behind the Rows. Burt Robeson found her body on a cross and was also taken as a sacrifice. ["Children of the Corn"]

26 July 1987

The Eyes of the Dragon dropped to number 16 on *The New York Times* Fiction Best Seller List, its twenty-sixth and last week on the List.

Misery dropped to number 2 on *The New York Times* Fiction Best Seller List, its eighth week on the List.

26 July 1988, Tuesday

Ev Hillman asked Maine State Police Trooper Butch Dugan to watch for a flare while attending Ruth McCausland's funeral. Ev told him he would be going to Haven, ME, and if he got into any trouble, he'd set off a flare. Feeling as if something was wrong with Ruth the last time he talked with her, Butch said he'd go with Hillman. Ev rented breathing equipment from Maine Med Supplies. [*The Tommyknockers*]

26 July 1990, 1:00 p.m.

Nick Andros led the group from Hemingford Home toward Boulder, CO. He left a sign at Mother Abagail's to tell later arrivers they went to Boulder and would monitor CB channel 14. [*The Stand: The Complete & Uncut Edition*]

26 July 1992

Gerald's Game stayed at number 1 on *The New York Times* Fiction Best Seller List, its second week on the List.

26 July 2014

Stephen King finished *Finders Keepers*.

26 July 2015

Finders Keepers dropped to number 7 *The New York Times* Hardcover Fiction Best Seller List, its sixth week on the List.

26 July 2018, Thursday

Howard Gold chartered a King Air from Regal Air. He, Alec Pelley, Holly Gibney, Ralph Anderson, and Yune Sablo flew to Texas. Claude Bolton and his mother, Lovie Ann, met them at Plainville Airfield, sixty miles from Marysville. Holly rode with the Boltons and filled them in with the high points. In a blue SUV Howie had rented, the others followed them to the Indian Motel and Café.

Jack Hoskins drove to the Marysville Hole, a cave system that had been a tourist attraction but was closed years before. He took a Winchester .300 bolt-action with a Leupold VX–1 riflescope and climbed up a path on a hill. Modern graffiti gave way to older Indian pictographs on the rocks. He perched in a spot with a view of the gift shop, parking lot, and the Hole's entrance. His job was to keep the meddlers away.

~3:00 p.m.: Yune Sablo took a call from the Montgomery County PD. The outsider, linked with Claude Bolton, knew what Claude knew. So they could talk without being eavesdropped on, Lovie sent Claude to Highway Heaven in Tippit, forty miles away, to get chicken dinners for everybody. Howie insisted on paying.

Yune told them bloody clothes—including a Heisman Memory Unit orderly's jacket—had been found in the abandoned factory next to the Peaceful Rest Cemetery in Regis.

Lovie talked about the Jamieson twins getting lost in the Marysville Hole. Roger Bolton, her brother-in-law, led a search party. A cave-in trapped them forever when someone fired a pistol to create sound for the boys to follow. Because of the outsider's attraction to burial grounds, the Marysville Hole was the place to look for him.

dusk: No one showed up. Jack Hoskins drove to his room at the Indian Motel and Café. [*The Outsider*]

July 27

27 July 1963, Saturday, >1:00 p.m.

As part of Garrett Thibodeau's search party, Sonny Benoit and Duke Marchant looked for Joe St. George's body. Sonny found it. [*Dolores Claiborne*]

27 July 1964

Rodney Conklin's article, "MILLIONAIRE DERWENT BACK IN COLORADO VIA BACK DOOR?" discussed the possible association between Horace Derwent and High Country Investments. [*The Shining*]

27 July 1988, Wednesday

Butch Dugan had planned to speak at Ruth McCausland's funeral. Instead, he went to help Ev Hillman find out what was going on in Haven, ME. His official reason for not attending was a stomach flu. In a Jeep Cherokee Hillman rented from Derry AMC, they entered Haven from Albion, the far side of Haven from Derry. Ev gave Butch an oxygen mask after Butch vomited twice and lost three teeth. Dick Allison and Bobbi Anderson attended Ruth McCausland's funeral. Bobbi and other Tommyknockers heard voices at the spaceship. They went to the dig site, where she hit Hillman on the back of the neck with a gun. Dugan shot her; the .45 bullet went through her right lung. Kyle Archinbourg and Adley Mckeen saved her life by taking her into the shed for intense Tommyknocker becoming. They took Dugan into the shed, programmed him, and let him go. They kept Hillman in the shed; part of his skull was removed to allow a cable to be connected to his brain, a power source. [*The Tommyknockers*]

27 July 1990

Stu Redman's group spent the night at Kunkle Fairgrounds, north of Kunkle, OH. [*The Stand: The Complete & Uncut Edition*]

27 July 2007

Dr. John Bonsaint had been counting things and making sure they were an even number. Under the guise of writing a research paper, he consulted Dr. J., his mentor-psychiatrist, about the transitive nature of OCD from patient to analyst. Dr. J. said it was possible but rare. Dr. Bonsaint wrote himself a prescription for Neurontin. ["N."]

27 July 2014, Sunday

Jamie Morton arrived at Goat Mountain Resort. For a couple of days, his duties would be to cook the meals, be available for safety during Charlie Jacobs's showers, and rub prescription Voltaren Gel on Charlie twice a day. [*Revival*]

Mr. Mercedes dropped to number 8 on *The New York Times* Hardcover Fiction Best Seller List, its sixth week on the List.

27 July 2018, Friday

4:00 a.m.: Jack Hoskins woke up aching from the previous day's hill climb. He drove back to the Marysville Hole. A rattler slept in his sniper's nest; he eased the Winchester's barrel under it and flung it twenty feet.

Ralph Anderson, Holly Gibney, Howie Gold, Alec Pelley, and Yune Sablo went to the Marysville Hole. The main entrance was secure; no one had gotten in. As the outsider had been close to burial grounds instead of in them, Alec suggested they check the abandoned gift shop. This gave Jack Hoskins a clear shot. He killed Howie Gold and Alec Pelley and hit Yune Sablo's left arm.

With Yune providing cover fire and Jack dealing with the rattlesnake that had returned and bit him, Holly and Ralph ran fifty yards to a boulder by the service road. They heard Hoskins coming down and watched from behind a sign with Chief Ahiga's portrait, which marked the path to the Ahiga entrance. Ralph stepped out when Jack staggered into view, thirty feet away. Ralph told Jack to drop the rifle he was using as a cane. Instead, Jack lifted it and pointed it at Holly. Ralph moved in front of her and killed Hoskins with three shots. He and Holly followed the Ahiga path.

The entrance had a door, ajar. Ralph went first. Holly's UV flashlight showed the outsider's trail. At the Chamber of Sound, a metal stairway spiraled in both directions, up toward the main entrance and down to the large chamber where the outsider waited.

Up close, they saw the outsider was still changing from Terry Maitland to Claude Bolton. While he mostly looked like Claude, he still had some Terry features.

The outsider warned Ralph that firing his weapon would kill them all. Holly's saying he was just a sexual sadist and impotent pedophile offended him. He explained he needed to eat like everyone else, and children were the tastiest. The ejaculations provided a wonderful DNA counter-measure.

Holly turned the UV flashlight on his face and hit his head with her Happy Slapper, a white athletic sock filled with ball bearings. He fell to his knees; his face flipped through the faces he had become before. She hit his cheekbone. Reddish-brown worms poured from its face. A third blow, on the top of its head, split its face down the middle. The worms were its life. Ralph and Holly climbed the stairs; the worms couldn't and died.

They developed a plausible story: Following Terry Maitland's solid alibi, they continued investigating and re-interviewing witnesses. As Claude Bolton was in Texas, they needed to go to Marysville. Jack Hoskins called and told them the guy they were looking for was hiding out in the Marysville Hole. When they arrived, Jack ambushed them, killing Howie Gold and Alec Pelley and wounding Yune Sablo before Ralph could take him out. [*The Outsider*]

July 28

28 July 1985

Richard Bachman's *Thinner* dropped to number 15 on *The New York Times* Fiction Best Seller List, its twenty-second week on the List.

Skeleton Crew stayed at number 1 on *The New York Times* Fiction Best Seller List, its sixth week on the List.

28 July 1988, Thursday

3:05 a.m.: As the Haven Tommyknockers had programmed him, Butch Dugan woke up, wrote a suicide note, and shot himself with his .357 magnum service revolver.

Anne Anderson's father put his Leighton Street house up for sale. He didn't want to sell, but Anne wanted it sold. [*The Tommyknockers*]

28 July 1990, ~4:10 p.m.

Mark Braddock died while Stu Redman performed an appendectomy from a book. Overnight, Mark's girlfriend, Perion McCarthy overdosed on Veronal. [*The Stand: The Complete & Uncut Edition*]

28 July 1996

The Green Mile, Part One: The Two Dead Girls stayed at number 13 on *The New York Times* Paperback Fiction Best Seller List, its sixteenth week on the List.

The Green Mile, Part Two: The Mouse on the Mile stayed at number 12 on *The New York Times* Paperback Fiction Best Seller List, its twelfth week on the List.

The Green Mile, Part Three: Coffey's Hands was still on *The New York Times* Paperback Fiction Best Seller List, its eighth week on the List.

The Green Mile, Part Four: The Bad Death of Eduard Delacroix stayed at number 1 on *The New York Times* Paperback Fiction Best Seller List, its fourth week on the List.

28 July 2010

American Vampire #5 (Vertigo Comics, $3.99), with Stephen King's "If Thy Right Hand Offend Thee..." published

28 July 2013

Joyland stayed at number 1 on *The New York Times* Paperback Trade Fiction Best Seller List, its sixth week on the List.

July 29

29 July 1957

Gatlin, NE, child Moses Richardson was born Henry Richardson. ["Children of the Corn"]

29 July 1963, Monday

Dr. John McAuliffe interrogated Dolores St. George about Joe St. George's death. The autopsy and investigation showed that Joe didn't die right away, he had yelled a lot and a rock had bashed his face. He suspected that Dolores was involved by either ignoring Joe's screams or bashing his face. He couldn't trip her up. Before answering each question, she counted to three, with a my-pretty-pony after each number. She hadn't heard Joe's screams because of the noise from the people and boats gathered for the eclipse. Constable Garrett Thibodeau offered that Joe could have bashed himself in the face while trying to climb out of the well. [*Dolores Claiborne*]

29 July 1979, Sunday

"MISSING TROOPER'S SISTER LEFT WITH MANY QUESTIONS; Edith Hyams Calls For Full Investigation" appeared on the front page of the *Pittsburgh Post-Gazette*. [*From a Buick 8*]

29 July 1988

Johnny Leandro's article about Butch Dugan's death was on the front page of the Bangor *Daily News*. [*The Tommyknockers*]

29 July 1990

Al, Garvey, Ronnie, and Virge spotted Fran Goldsmith's group. [*The Stand: The Complete & Uncut Edition*]

The Stand: The Complete & Uncut Edition stayed at number 4 on *The New York Times* Fiction Best Seller List, its twelfth week on the List.

~29 July 2003

Chief Dale Gilbertson held a Fisherman press conference at La Follette Park. Two hundred French Landing residents, who won a seating lottery, sat up front, with about four hundred newspeople behind them. Wanda Kinderling, the 199th lottery winner, emptied her six-shot bulldog .32 into Jack Sawyer and shouted, "See you in hell, Hollywood." She fired the gun at her own head, but she was out of bullets. Doc Amberson jumped off the platform and tackled her, breaking her neck, left shoulder, and four ribs. Speedy Parker flipped Jack to the Territories, where he lay unconscious for ten days. He would recover but could return to his world for only short visits. [*Black House*]

29 July 2007

Richard Bachman's *Blaze* dropped to number 14 on *The New York Times* Fiction Best Seller List, its fifth and last week on the List.

29 July 2009

The Dark Tower: Fall of Gilead #3 of 6 (Marvel Comics, $3.99) published

29 July 2018

The Outsider stayed at number 4 on *The New York Times* Hardcover Fiction Best Seller List, its eighth week on the List.

July 30

30 July 1963, Tuesday

The coroner's inquest for Joe St. George ruled death by misadventure. Although she wasn't prosecuted, everybody knew Dolores St. George killed him. They thought she did so because Joe hit her when he was drunk. Nobody knew about his fondling their daughter, Selena. For the next thirty years, Dolores was gossip material, and she kept hearing the rock hit Joe's face, his body hitting bottom, and his screams. [*Dolores Claiborne*]

30 July 1970

"Slade," Chapter 7, appeared in *The Maine Campus*.

30 July 1988

One of Haven, ME, resident and Tommyknocker Johnny Enders's eyes bled, an effect of being too close to the spaceship. [*The Tommyknockers*]

30 July 1990

Al, Garvey, Ronnie, and Virge stopped Glen Bateman, Fran Goldsmith, Harold Lauder, and Stu Redman to kill the men and kidnap Fran. After a gunfight, Al, Garvey, Ronnie, Virge, and three of the eight kidnapped women, including Rachel Carmody and Helen Roget, were dead. Shirley Hammett, Dayna Jurgens, Patty Kroger, Susan Stern, and another woman joined Glen's group. They spent the night in a Columbia, IN, farmhouse. [*The Stand: The Complete & Uncut Edition*]

30 July 1992

Stating an origin of Bayshore Airport, DE, the Night Flier used the name Dwight Renfield to land at Duffrey Airfield in Duffrey, MD. He stayed on the runway until the next night. ["The Night Flier"]

30 July 1994

The Garins, on vacation, stayed with college friends the Calabreses in San Jose, CA. MotoKops in the Tracker Arrow Power Wagon shot and killed Bill, Junie, John, and Mary Lou Garin while they played croquet in the front yard. Lieutenant Robert Alvarez was a police spokesperson in the Garin murders investigation. [*The Regulators*]

30 July 1995

Rose Madder dropped to number 5 on *The New York Times* Fiction Best Seller List, its fifth week on the List.

July 31

31 July 1963, Wednesday

Lucien Mercier's Mercier Funeral Home, Little Tall Island's only mortuary, handled Joe St. George's funeral. Joe was buried in The Oaks Cemetery. [*Dolores Claiborne*]

31 July 1983

Christine dropped to number 5 on *The New York Times* Fiction Best Seller List, its seventeenth week on the List.

31 July 1988, Sunday, 11:15 a.m.

Hank Buck sent Albert Pits Barfield to Altair-4 for cheating at poker; Barfield disintegrated. Davey Brown was still alive on Altair-4. [*The Tommyknockers*]

31 July 1990

Harold Lauder saw Fran Goldsmith and Stu Redman make love near Brighton. [*The Stand: The Complete & Uncut Edition*]

31 July 1992, late night

The Night Flier killed Ellen and Ray Sarch and drank their blood. With no one left to run it, Duffrey Airfield shut down. ["The Night Flier"]

31 July 1994

"MEMBERS OF TOLEDO FAMILY SLAIN IN SAN JOSE: Four Killed in Suspected Gang Drive-by; Six-Year-Old Survives," an article about the Garin shootings the day before, appeared in the Columbus *Dispatch*. [*The Regulators*]

31 July 2014, Thursday: The Revival of Mary Fay

Severe thunderstorms were forecast. Charlie Jacobs's research during the years since his wife and child were killed led to this day. Upon death, a person passed to the other side. He wanted to know what happened after death.

Lightning is a power that feeds secret electricity. Secret electricity is a tributary that feeds *potestas magnum universum*, an incomprehensible power. Charlie wanted to tap into that power to open a doorway to the other side.

Jenny Knowlton had taken Mary Fay to the green-and-white cottage at Skytop. Without life support, Mary Fay died. Charlie Jacobs put a tin metallic headband on her head, clasping her temples. After several lightning bolts struck Skytop's iron rod, Mary opened her eyes. Charlie asked where she had been, what was on the other side? She grabbed Charlie's hand; Jamie Morton took the other. The world appeared as an illusion. Jamie Morton saw large, ant-like creatures drive an endless line of naked people through a ruined city. If the people fell, the ants bit and prodded them until they got back in line. Most had many bite holes, bloodless because the people were dead. A huge black leg split the sky. A large claw of human faces—the Mother—reached for Jamie Morton. Jamie tore his hand free of Charlie's, breaking the connection. The world beyond the world was gone.

Charlie called out to Patsy Jacobs and Morrie Jacobs, his dead wife and son. He asked where they were. The Mother, through Mary, answered that they were serving the Great Ones in the Null. The leg, with a claw at the end, emerged from Mary's mouth. At the end of the claw, was Morrie's screaming face; Patsy's face joined it. Mary's body rose toward Jamie. From the top bureau drawer, Jamie pulled a gun. Four of his five shots hit the thing. The Mother was gone. Mary Fay's dead body, with four bullet holes, lay on the bed.

A cataclysmic stroke had killed Charlie. Jamie propped his body against the bureau, put the revolver in Charlie's hand, and fired the last shot into the wall above Mary Fay's body.

Jenny Knowlton had run out during the experiment. At home, Astrid Soderberg stabbed her in the throat then slashed her own wrists. [*Revival*]

31 July 2016

End of Watch dropped to number 6 on *The New York Times* Hardcover Fiction Best Seller List, its sixth week on the List.

July

July 1880

Bram Percy hired the Pinkerton Agency to apprehend Skinner Sweet. Special Agent James Book caught Skinner in a Sidewinder, Colorado, brothel after Hector Camillo turned him in. Book and Deputy Felix Camillo took Sweet on a train to be hanged in New Mexico. Percy rode along to celebrate Sweet's capture.

Ronnie Jeeks and the Blackmouth Twins, part of Sweet's gang, damaged the railroad tracks, causing the train to crash when it rounded a curve. Skinner and his gang opened fire. Skinner shot James Book; the bullet grazed his head. Percy, a European vampire, couldn't be killed. He bit Skinner, and then Skinner shot him in the left eye. Some of Percy's blood splashed on Skinner. Jeeks and the Twins rode off when they saw Percy kill Skinner.

Five days later, James Book woke up from a coma in Mrs. Pruitt's Boarding House. Felix Camillo told him Ella Langum, Book's fiancée, was dead. Skinner Sweet had sent her a bottle of poisoned wine, with a fraudulent note from James Book.

Skinner Sweet was buried in Sidewinder, Colorado's Boot Hill. From Percy's blood, he became a different vampire. A better vampire. The first American Vampire. Undead, he lay in Boot Hill for thirty-nine years. [*American Vampire*]

July 1911

The Overlook Hotel's season opened too late for a full summer crowd. ["Before the Play"]

July 1958, Sunday

Roland LeBay, Veronica LeBay, and Rita LeBay stopped to eat while motorvating in Christine. Roland's daughter, Rita, choked on a burger; Roland put her in Christine to die. Marcia LeBay, Marcia's husband, and her children went to the funeral at Libertyville Methodist Church. (Marcia was Rita's aunt.) Rita was buried in Libertyville Heights Cemetery. [*Christine*]

July 1959

George Shavers, an intern at Sisters of Mercy Hospital in New York City, was on-call when lightning hit a TWA Tri-Star at Idlewild. Sixty of sixty-five people on board were killed; three were severely injured. [*The Dark Tower II: The Drawing of the Three*]

July 1969

Checking in with a stolen South Carolina driver's license, The Funhouse Killer and Linda Gray spent the night at the Luna Inn. At Joyland the next day, they visited Annie Oakley's Shootin' Gallery, had lunch at Rock Lobster, and rode the Carolina Spin. Halfway into Horror House's ride, the Funhouse Killer slit Linda's throat and tossed her body out of the monorail car. The tunnel's double-S curve between Dungeon and the Chamber of Torture was the ride's darkest part. One hundred yards farther, he dropped his outer shirt; farther still, he discarded his gloves. Stuck in the tunnel, Linda Gray haunted Horror House. Crewmembers mentioned the ghost of a woman in a blue sleeveless blouse and a blue skirt standing next to the track. Publicized pictures were in black-and-white. Witnesses also said they saw her wearing a blue Alice band, information never released to the public. [*Joyland*]

July 1970

Charlie Dawes's left hand was paralyzed. [*Roadwork*]

July 1971

Frank Dodd became a Castle County deputy in Castle Rock. [*The Dead Zone*]

July 1974

Through Larry Crockett, Richard Straker bought the Marsten House and The Village Washtub in Jerusalem's Lot, ME. Straker and Kurt Barlow would live in the Marsten House on the Brooks Road. Straker turned the Washtub, at 27 Jointner Avenue, into Barlow and Straker—Fine Furnishings. [*'Salem's Lot*]

July 1975

"The Revenge of Lard Ass Hogan" (incorporated as a Gordie Lachance story in "The Body") appeared in the July issue of *The Maine Review*.

July 1976

Morris Bellamy got a job with Donahue Construction, a housing-development contractor in Boston. He became friends with ex-cons Freddy Dow and Curtis Rogers. Although they didn't work the same job sites often, they had lunch together daily. For the next two years, Bellamy made weekend trips to Talbot Corners, NH, John Rothstein's town. Freddy and Curtis joined him in the second year. [*Finders Keepers*]

"The Ledge" (collected in *Night Shift*) appeared in the July issue (Volume 7, Number 11) of *Penthouse*.

July 1977

After an evening of drinking, Mrs. Massey overdosed on sleeping pills and died in the bathtub of The Overlook Hotel's Room 217. [*The Shining*]

July 1979

"The Crate" appeared in the July issue (Vol. 7, No. 8) of *Gallery*.

July 1981

"The Slow Mutants" (collected in *The Dark Tower I: The Gunslinger*) appeared in the July issue (#362; Volume 61, Number 1) of *The Magazine of Fantasy & Science Fiction*.

July 1982

Creepshow (Plume, $6.95) published

July 1989

An Introductory Note to *Four Past Midnight*

July 1991

The Corson brothers loaned Ace Merrill $85,000 to finance a cocaine deal. Ducky Morin ripped him off by giving him only two pounds. The Corsons gave Ace three months to pay back the money, or they would kill him. [*Needful Things*]

July 2001

Drunken Bradley Roach hit and killed Trooper Curt Wilcox near the intersection of Pennsylvania State Road 32 and Humboldt Road. [*From a Buick 8*]

Dave Streeter was diagnosed with an aggressive and fast-moving form of cancer. ["Fair Extension"]

July 2002

Arky Arkanian, Phil Candleton, Eddie Jacubois, Shirley Pasternak, and Huddie Royer helped Sandy Dearborn tell Ned Wilcox about the Buick Roadmaster in Shed B. After everybody had left, Ned returned to destroy the car. Sandy and others had inklings, so they went back to save Ned from the Buick. [*From a Buick 8*]

July 2009

"Morality" (collected in *The Bazaar of Bad Dreams*) appeared in the July issue (Vol. 152, No. 1) of *Esquire*.

July 2012

Jodie, TX's Centennial Celebration featured Sadie Dunhill, the Citizen of the Century. George Amberson had DJ Donald Bellingham play the Glenn Miller Orchestra's "In the Mood" then danced with Sadie. For a short time, he relived the good times he had had with her in another life. [*11/22/63*]

July 2014

Charlie Jacobs hired Jenny Knowlton to look after Mary Fay. For this short-term job, he paid her enough to retire. [*Revival*]

July 2017

Mr. Ross Albright gave the hitchhiking Angel Fitzroy a ride on Route 2, east of Chinook, MT. She used her real name and did not need the knife she would have carried years earlier. [*Sleeping Beauties*]

July 2018

A month after Heath Holmes hanged himself in jail, his mother, Mrs. Mavis Holmes, hanged herself in her basement. She was buried in Peaceful Rest Cemetery. [*The Outsider*]

August
Happenings

August 1

1 August 1947

"USAF SAYS 'CANNOT EXPLAIN' ARNOLD SIGHTING; 850 Additional Sightings Since Original Report" appeared in the Chicago *Daily Tribune*. [*Dreamcatcher*]

1 August 1960

<u>George Amberson's second timeline</u>: George Amberson had left Florida after a hunch that Eduardo Gutierrez wouldn't take his winning a $2,000 5–1 bet kindly. In Gulfport, MS, The Red Top Inn was only for Negroes; they recommended The Southern Hospitality. [*11/22/63*]

~1 August 1979, >6:00 p.m.

The Buick Roadmaster in Troop D's Shed B performed its first lightquake, which lasted almost an hour. The temperature in the Shed was fifty-four degrees. [*From a Buick 8*]

1 August 1988

Bobbi Anderson's father died in Utica Soldier's Hospital after three strokes in three years. [*The Tommyknockers*]

1 August 1990

Stu Redman's group was near Elkhart, IN. Overnight, Harold Lauder unknowingly left a chocolate thumbprint in Fran Goldsmith's diary. [*The Stand: The Complete & Uncut Edition*]

1 August 1992, ~12:00 a.m.

The Night Flier flew out of Duffrey Airfield. ["The Night Flier"]

1 August 1999

The Girl Who Loved Tom Gordon rose to number 9 on *The New York Times* Fiction Best Seller List, its fifteenth week on the List.

1 August 2004

The Dark Tower VI: Song of Susannah dropped to number 11 on *The New York Times* Fiction Best Seller List, its sixth week on the List.

1 August 2007

The Dark Tower: Gunslinger Born #7 of 7 (Marvel Comics, $3.99) published

The Dark Tower: Gunslinger's Guidebook #1 (Marvel Comics, $3.99) published

1 August 2018, Wednesday, 11:15 a.m.

Holly Gibney's flight home [*The Outsider*]

August 2

2 August 1963

The Funhouse Killer murdered Claudine Sharp in a movie theater during the long and loud *Lawrence of Arabia*. After killing his second known victim, he left his bloody shirt and gloves behind. [*Joyland*]

~2 August 1979, 3:00 p.m.

The outside temperature was eighty-seven degrees; it was forty-seven in Shed B. [*From a Buick 8*]

2 August 1987

Misery dropped to number 3 on *The New York Times* Fiction Best Seller List, its ninth week on the List.

2 August 1988

Anne Anderson arranged her father's funeral. [*The Tommyknockers*]

2 August 1990

Harold Lauder started a journal.

Stu Redman's group camped near Joliet, IL. They arrived in the Free Zone within eight days. [*The Stand: The Complete & Uncut Edition*]

2 August 1992

Gerald's Game stayed at number 1 on *The New York Times* Fiction Best Seller List, its third week on the List.

2 August 2015

Finders Keepers dropped to number 13 *The New York Times* Hardcover Fiction Best Seller List, its seventh week on the List.

August 3

3 August 1962

<u>George Amberson's second timeline</u>: With his new omnidirectional microphone, George Amberson listened as Snakeskin Boots rented the house across the street to the Oswalds. [*11/22/63*]

3 August 1988

Unable to contact her sister after their father died, Anne Anderson tried to call Haven officials. She couldn't reach the town constable, but Newt Berringer, the town manager, said he would give her message to Bobbi Anderson. He didn't.

The Tommyknockers hit water in their spaceship dig. [*The Tommyknockers*]

3 August 1999

"Low Men In Yellow Coats" appeared in *Family Circle*.

3 August 2007

The key to Ackerman's Field sat on the wrong side of the drawer. Dr. John Bonsaint moved it to the other side and put his safe-deposit key in its old place; two keys—even. The Neurontin he had prescribed for himself wasn't helping. ["N."]

3 August ≥2008

"BROWN BAGGERS ANNOUNCE SPEAKING SCHEDULE FOR FALL" appeared in the Chicopee *Weekly Reminder*. ["Big Driver"]

3 August 2011

The Dark Tower: The Gunslinger—The Battle of Tull #3 of 5 (Marvel Comics, $3.99) published

3 August 2014

Mr. Mercedes dropped to number 10 on *The New York Times* Hardcover Fiction Best Seller List, its seventh week on the List.

August 4

4 August 1789

Robert Boone met James Boon. He thought Boon sinister. ["Jerusalem's Lot"]

4 August 1927

That summer, Joe Newall's sixteen cows died, some from anthrax. He wouldn't let Castle County health officer Clem Upshaw inspect them without a court order. While Upshaw got the order, Newall disposed of fifteen cows. He left one that might not have been his. Upshaw returned, inspected it, and found no anthrax. ["It Grows on You"]

4 August 1977

Frankie Stone pulled up as Gwendy Peterson took the garbage to the end of her driveway. She declined his offer of going for a ride. As Gwendy walked back up the drive, Frankie threw a beer can; it hit the back of her neck. He drove off, shouting obscenities. That night, she dreamed she reached into his car and crushed his left arm. [*Gwendy's Button Box*]

4 August 1983

Afterword to *Cycle of the Werewolf*

4 August 1985

Richard Bachman's *Thinner* rose to number 14 on *The New York Times* Fiction Best Seller List, its twenty-third week on the List.

Skeleton Crew stayed at number 1 on *The New York Times* Fiction Best Seller List, its seventh week on the List.

4 August 1988

After hitting water, Freeman Moss installed a Tommyknocker-built pump at the spaceship dig site. They used it the next day. [*The Tommyknockers*]

4 August 1990

Trash reached the edge of the desert near Las Vegas—bumpty-bumpty-bump! After spending the day in a car, he went toward Vegas that night. [*The Stand: The Complete & Uncut Edition*]

4 August 1996

The Green Mile, Part One: The Two Dead Girls stayed at number 13 on *The New York Times* Paperback Fiction Best Seller List, its seventeenth week on the List.

The Green Mile, Part Two: The Mouse on the Mile stayed at number 12 on *The New York Times* Paperback Fiction Best Seller List, its thirteenth week on the List.

The Green Mile, Part Three: Coffey's Hands was number 9 on *The New York Times* Paperback Fiction Best Seller List, its ninth week on the List.

The Green Mile, Part Four: The Bad Death of Eduard Delacroix stayed at number 1 on *The New York Times* Paperback Fiction Best Seller List, its fifth week on the List.

4 August 2005

Stephen King finished *Lisey's Story* in Center Lovell, ME.

4 August 2010

The Stand: Hardcases #3 of 5 (Marvel Comics, $3.99) published

4 August 2013

Joyland stayed at number 1 on *The New York Times* Paperback Trade Fiction Best Seller List, its seventh week on the List.

August 5

5 August 1963

<u>George Amberson's second timeline</u>: Identifying himself as John Lennon, George Amberson called George de Mohrenschildt. He implied he was CIA and could help with de Mohrenschildt's Haiti oil leases, but he was concerned about his relationship with Lee Harvey Oswald. He had de Mohrenschildt meet him at a parking lot on Mercedes Street that night to show proof he wasn't part of the Walker assassination attempt.

8:40 p.m.: In the parking lot, de Mohrenschildt showed Lennon a clipping from the April 12th Dallas *Morning News*. The AROUND TOWN column reported that the de Mohrenschildts celebrated Jeanne de Mohrenschildt's birthday at the Carousel Club on Wednesday night (April 10th). A picture showed the de Mohrenschildts partying. (Jack Ruby had also attended.) George was satisfied that Oswald acted alone in the Walker assassination attempt. [*11/22/63*]

5 August 1964

The bodies of James Cheney, Andrew Goodman, and Michael Schwerner were found in Longdale, MS. [*The Dark Tower VI: Song of Susannah*]

5 August 1974

Carpenter Herb Smith broke his leg in an accident at a house he was building in Gray. [*The Dead Zone*]

5 August 1988

Neurosurgeon Peter Bailey was flying his Cessna Hawk XP from Teterboro, NJ, to Bangor, ME, to consult on the Hillman Brown case. When he wandered off his flight path and flew over the Tommyknocker spaceship in Haven, ME, he flew back to get a closer look. He got a headache and lost a tooth. He turned to resume his course. His instruments malfunctioned, and the engine stalled; his left eye ruptured, and his brain burst. The plane crashed and exploded on Ezra Dockery's land in Newport. [*The Tommyknockers*]

5 August 1990

In Los Angeles, Eric Strellerton gave strong suggestions on how the Randall Flagg operation should be run. Flagg looked at him, turning him crazy. He was dumped in the Mojave Desert. [*The Stand: The Complete & Uncut Edition*]

The Stand: The Complete & Uncut Edition stayed at number 4 on *The New York Times* Fiction Best Seller List, its thirteenth week on the List.

5 August 2018

The Outsider stayed at number 4 on *The New York Times* Hardcover Fiction Best Seller List, its ninth week on the List.

August 6

6 August 1960, ~3:30 p.m.

Bobby Garfield ambushed Harry Doolin on Harry's way home from work. Bobby used Harry's baseball bat to beat him for beating Carol Gerber a month and a half earlier. He had been staking out Commonwealth Park, waiting for Doolin to walk home alone. Later, when Harry and his mother accompanied Officer Raymer to talk with Liz Garfield, Liz said Bobby was home cleaning with her during the attack. She seemed pleased when she learned Harry was the boy who had beaten Carol. ["Low Men in Yellow Coats"]

6 August 1970

"Slade," Chapter 8, appeared in *The Maine Campus*.

6 August 1991

The Dark Tower III: The Waste Lands (Donald M. Grant, $38) published with a first printing of 30,000 to 40,000 copies

6 August 1988

Hester Brookline and Tommy Jacklin went on a battery run for Haven, ME. Tommy saw a clown with balloons in a Derry sewer. Upon returning, Hester passed out from exposure to non-Tommyknocker air. Three days later, she regained consciousness but was blind from being away too long. She died after word of the Haven Tommyknockers got out. [*The Tommyknockers*]

6 August 1995

Rose Madder dropped to number 6 on *The New York Times* Fiction Best Seller List, its sixth week on the List.

6 August 2014

Introduction to *The Bazaar of Bad Dreams*

August 7

7 August 1945

General Douglas MacArthur gave General Hecksler a platinum-plated Zippo lighter, engraved, "TO TONY FROM DOUGLAS/AUG. 7th 1945." [*The Plant* Book One: *Zenith Rising*]

7 August 1983

Christine dropped to number 7 on *The New York Times* Fiction Best Seller List, its eighteenth week on the List.

7 August 1988

With her right arm in a sling, Bobbi Anderson came out of the shed. Her hairline had receded to the middle of her head. She and Jim Gardener made love near the ship. Gard's steel plate didn't prevent him from becoming, it just delayed it; he lost his first tooth. [*The Tommyknockers*]

7 August 1998, evening

Stephen King took Fred Hauser to Alcoholics Anonymous in Fryeburg. On the way back, he agreed to sponsor Hauser. [*The Dark Tower VI: Song of Susannah*]

7 August 2016

End of Watch dropped to number 9 on *The New York Times* Hardcover Fiction Best Seller List, its seventh week on the List.

August 8

8 August 1970

Richard Pine used a lifeboat inspection log to write a diary. The boat's last log entry was August 8th. ["Survivor Type"]

8 August 1980, Friday

The Shop had had the McGees under surveillance, including bugging their phones, since 1978. They panicked when Charlie McGee stayed with a friend; they thought the McGees were on to them and had hidden her. Norville Bates headed the McGee operation to abduct Charlie and her father. They wanted Charlie; they would need Andy for a while, then he could be killed.

<12:00 p.m.: Baldy and another Shop agent removed four fingernails from Vicky McGee's right hand before she told them where Charlie was. (She was staying with Terri Dugan, on Blassmore Place in the Lakeland section of Harrison, OH, for a couple of days.) They stuffed Vicky's mouth with a rag, broke her neck, and put her body in a cabinet.

>2:00 p.m.: After a hunch that something was wrong at home and finding Vicky dead, Andy McGee followed the turnpike to a rest area, where he found the Shop with Charlie. Andy pushed one agent into thinking he was blind then pushed Baldy into believing his gun was hot. Baldy's hand blistered; he dropped the gun. Andy pushed him to sleep. He was in a coma for six months and fell asleep for four hours whenever anyone mentioned sleep. Andy took Charlie back. They spent the night in Hammersmith, twenty miles away. [*Firestarter*]

8 August 1982

Different Seasons entered *The New York Times* Fiction Best Seller List at number 7. It was on the List for thirty-two weeks.

8 August 1990

Trash was sent to Boulder Dam to help restore the power. [*The Stand: The Complete & Uncut Edition*]

8 August 1992

Inside View reporter Rick Dees flew to Washington National Airport then drove sixty miles to Duffrey, MD, to investigate the Sarch murders. Later, he saw a pattern to The Night Flier murders. At a Days Inn, he discovered The Night Flier would strike next in Wilmington, NC. ["The Night Flier"]

8 August 1999

The Girl Who Loved Tom Gordon dropped to number 10 on *The New York Times* Fiction Best Seller List, its sixteenth week on the List.

8 August 2004

The Dark Tower VI: Song of Susannah stayed at number 11 on *The New York Times* Fiction Best Seller List, its seventh week on the List.

August 9

9 August 1963

Lee Harvey Oswald was arrested while handing out "Fair-Play for Cuba" flyers. Dutz Murret paid his bail. [*11/22/63*]

9 August 1969

George Amberson's second timeline: Vice President Curtis LeMay commanded the mission to drop atomic bombs on Hanoi. [*11/22/63*]

9 August 1978

Ed Ferman, editor in chief at *Fantasy and Science Fiction*, bought the first chapter of Stephen King's *The Dark Tower*. He called it "The Gunslinger." [*The Dark Tower VI: Song of Susannah*]

9 August 1987

Misery stayed at number 3 on *The New York Times* Fiction Best Seller List, its tenth week on the List.

9 August 1988

Anne Anderson left for Haven, ME. On Delta flight 230, she arrived in Bangor, ME. She had flown from LaGuardia Airport to Logan Airport to Bangor International Airport. She rented an Oldsmobile Cutlass and checked in to the Cityscape Hotel. [*The Tommyknockers*]

9 August 1990

Randall Flagg arrived at the M-G-M Grand Hotel in Las Vegas, NV. He had Hector Drogan crucified for freebasing cocaine. Later, Drogan died, his body badly burned. [*The Stand: The Complete & Uncut Edition*]

9 August 1992

Gerald's Game stayed at number 1 on *The New York Times* Fiction Best Seller List, its fourth week on the List.

9 August 2015

Finders Keepers stayed at number 13 *The New York Times* Hardcover Fiction Best Seller List, its eighth week on the List.

August 10

10 August 1958

Mr. Robert Gray from Derry, ME, sent Henry Bowers balloons and a new, six-inch switch-blade. IT's voice, speaking from the moon, told Bowers to kill his father and the Losers. He stabbed his father in the throat. Later that day, he, Victor Criss, and Belch Huggins caught Beverly Marsh on her way to the Barrens. She kicked Bowers in the balls and ran away. From the Barrens, they chased the Losers into the sewer system. Bowers saw IT remove Criss's head. While IT, as Frankenstein's monster, was busy killing Huggins, Bowers ran. He became insane from what he had seen in the sewers. By the end of the year, he was convicted for the murders of his father and several Derry children.

The Losers entered a disused part of the drain system. IT as the Eye attacked them. Eddie Kaspbrak sprayed IT with his aspirator; IT left. They entered a large cavern, fifty feet high, with glowing walls. IT as a large bird attacked them. Stan Uris called out bird names, saying he didn't believe in the IT-bird; IT left. They entered a larger cavern with a pile of children's bones next to a three-foot high door at the end. They went through the door and saw IT as a spider on a web with pieces of silk-wrapped bodies. Bill Denbrough faced IT. IT subjected him with illusions; he ignored them. He saw beyond IT to the Turtle, which said it wouldn't interfere. Bill sensed a Final Other beyond the Turtle. The Ritual of Chüd began. IT sent Bill's consciousness hurtling through the void. Bill believed in all he had ever believed in. His will was stronger; he was returned to his body. IT, punctured and wounded in many places, ran deeper into the bowels of Derry. When IT ran, Bill let go of IT, as he had promised to do if IT brought him back. Not knowing whether IT was dead, they started home. They got lost in the tunnels. To stay friends forever and to help them find their way out, Beverly had the boys make love to her. Eddie was first, followed by Stan, Mike Hanlon, Richie Tozier, Ben Hanscom (she had an orgasm), and Bill (she had another orgasm). Outside the drainage system, Stan cut their palms with a broken Coke bottle. They held hands and swore to come back if IT was alive and became active again. This was the last time all seven were together. Although they didn't kill IT, the Losers hurt IT badly. Derry suffered heavy storms and floods when IT was hurt. [*IT*]

10 August 1962

Lee Harvey and Marina Oswald moved into 2703 Mercedes Street in Fort Worth, TX. Robert Oswald brought their belongings in a trailer. [*11/22/63*]

10 August 1978, Thursday, ~4:00 p.m.

After years of neglect, Christine was for sale in poor condition. She had a broken wind-shield, smashed rear deck, dangling rear bumper, ripped upholstery, bald tires, a large rusted dent, rusted exhaust, nonfunctioning horn, an oil puddle under her engine, and 97,432.6 miles on her odometer. On his way home from work, Arnie Cunningham saw her and had to have her. Roland LeBay wanted a 10% deposit on his $250 asking price to hold her for a day. Arnie borrowed $9 from Dennis Guilder. That night, his mother (Regina Cunningham) let him buy the car but only because he threatened to take vocational training in-stead of college high school courses. [*Christine*]

10 August 1988

Anne Anderson entered Haven, ME. Metal bridgework in her mouth helped her resist becoming a Tommyknocker, but she got a headache and vomited. Early that evening, after losing track of time, she arrived at Bobbi Anderson's. Bobbi took her to the shed, where the Tommyknockers removed part of her skull and connected a cable to her brain to use her as a power source.

Hearing Bobbi sneeze and seeing dog hairs on her dress after she returned from the shed, Jim Gardener thought Peter was in the shed. Gard lost his second tooth that day and two more that night. [*The Tommyknockers*]

10 August 2007

Dr. John Bonsaint felt the eighth stone at Ackerman's Field weakening. ["N."]

10 August 2011

The Stand: Night Has Come #1 of 6 (Marvel Comics, $3.99) published

10 August 2014

Mr. Mercedes stayed at number 10 on *The New York Times* Hardcover Fiction Best Seller List, its eighth week on the List.

10 August 2018

Flint County District Attorney Bill Samuels held a press conference at the courthouse. After further investigation into the Frankie Peterson case, the Flint City District Attorney's office considered the late Terry Maitland innocent. Irrefutable evidence showed Terry was in Cap City during the crime. None of the evidence against him had held up to further scrutiny: witnesses were no longer sure it was Terry they had seen, and, because the DNA samples were mixtures from the killer and the victim, they led to inaccurate results. The DA's office believed Terry's fingerprints had been planted in the dirty white van and at the murder scene. They thought Jack Hoskins was involved with the killer.

Although he mentioned that the collected DNA samples had also been compromised in unrelated testing, he didn't report that the outsider's DNA samples left as forensic counter-measures to implicate Heath Holmes and Terry Maitland had degraded and developed unknown white spots. [*The Outsider*]

August 11

11 August 1978, Friday

Arnie Cunningham paid the balance for Christine. She had a flat tire on the way to Darnell's Garage. Arnie parked her in front of Ralph's house while Dennis Guilder went to a Texaco station to get a new Firestone black wall tire on his rim for $28.50 plus tax and a $2.00 tip. Ralph didn't want Christine there and almost started a fight. [*Christine*]

11 August 1985

Richard Bachman's *Thinner* stayed at number 14 on *The New York Times* Fiction Best Seller List, its twenty-fourth week on the List.

Skeleton Crew stayed at number 1 on *The New York Times* Fiction Best Seller List, its eighth week on the List.

11 August 1990

A group of nineteen, including Laurie Constable, Nadine Cross, Tony Donahue, Sandy DuChiens, Harry Dunbarton, Richard Farris, Jack Jackson, Joe, Rennett, Smith, Lucy Swann, Andrea Terminello, Larry Underwood, Dick Vollman, and Mark Zellman, arrived in the Free Zone. Ralph Brentner took them to see Mother Abagail. (Sally Vollman had gotten sick at Hemingford Home; she died two days later.)

The Ad Hoc Committee was established with Nick Andros, Glen Bateman, Ralph Brentner, Dick Ellis, Fran Goldsmith, Stu Redman, and Sue Stern its first members. [*The Stand: The Complete & Uncut Edition*]

11 August 1996

The Green Mile, Part One: The Two Dead Girls rose to number 12 on *The New York Times* Paperback Fiction Best Seller List, its eighteenth week on the List.

The Green Mile, Part Two: The Mouse on the Mile dropped to number 13 on *The New York Times* Paperback Fiction Best Seller List, its fourteenth week on the List.

The Green Mile, Part Three: Coffey's Hands dropped to number 11 on *The New York Times* Paperback Fiction Best Seller List, its tenth week on the List.

The Green Mile, Part Four: The Bad Death of Eduard Delacroix dropped to number 2 on *The New York Times* Paperback Fiction Best Seller List, its sixth week on the List.

11 August 2007

Dr. John Bonsaint took his camera to Ackerman's Field to bring back the eighth stone. He saw a darkness—a darkness with an eye. ["N."]

11 August 2013

Joyland dropped to number 2 on *The New York Times* Paperback Trade Fiction Best Seller List, its eighth week on the List.

August 12

12 August 1939, 1:45 p.m.

Hubie Marsten shot his wife, Birdie, then hanged himself in a Marsten House bedroom. Birdie's sister, Minella Corey, felt a bolt of pain and fainted in Cape Cod, three hundred miles away. [*'Salem's Lot*]

12 August 1977

Johnny Smith was staying in Ft. Lauderdale, FL. [*The Dead Zone*]

12 August 1978, Saturday

Arnie Cunningham began restoring Christine in Darnell's Garage; stall 20 cost a too-much $20 a week. He earned the use of tools and a lift by running errands for Will Darnell. Arnie soon discovered Christine could repair herself. Her odometer ran backward two to five miles for every mile traveled. She got newer and removed damage as her odometer moved before the incidents that caused the damage—as if she were moving back in time, negating aging, damage, and wear and tear. To regenerate, she had to be moving, either under her own power or by being pushed. No matter what station she was tuned to, she played broadcasts from the 1950s and 1960s, and WDIL-AM, the oldies station. [*Christine*]

12 August 1988

Slowly becoming a Tommyknocker, Jim Gardener unconsciously read Bobbi Anderson's thoughts. He found Anne Anderson's rented Cutlass buried in a gravel pit at the end of Nista Road, about two miles from Bobbi's place. [*The Tommyknockers*]

12 August 1990

Laurie Constable, RN, began working with Dick Ellis, the Free Zone's doctor. By the end of the month, Laurie and Dick considered having a baby. [*The Stand: The Complete & Uncut Edition*]

The Stand: The Complete & Uncut Edition dropped to number 6 on *The New York Times* Fiction Best Seller List, its fourteenth week on the List.

12 August 2007

Dr. John Bonsaint wasn't sure he saw anything the day before. ["N."]

12 August 2018

The Outsider stayed at number 4 on *The New York Times* Hardcover Fiction Best Seller List, its tenth week on the List.

August 13

13 August 1962, Monday, 5:30 p.m.

When Lee Harvey Oswald got home after work, he saw his mother had been there, so he hit his wife in the face. [*11/22/63*]

13 August 1978, Sunday

Arnie Cunningham and Dennis Guilder saw a Chuck Norris movie at the State Twin. [*Christine*]

13 August 1990

Fran Goldsmith found Harold Lauder's chocolate thumbprint on her diary's August 1st entry.

Rona Hewett, a Free Zone resident, had a flu but not Captain Trips.

7:00 p.m.: In a private, closed Ad Hoc Committee meeting, veterinarian Dick Ellis withdrew from the Committee because he was the closest thing to a doctor in the Free Zone; Larry Underwood took his place. They decided to send three spies to Las Vegas to see what Randall Flagg was doing. Nick Andros nominated Tom Cullen, Larry nominated Judge Farris, and Susan Stern nominated Dayna Jurgens.

late evening: Regina Wentworth had twins on her way to the Free Zone. [*The Stand: The Complete & Uncut Edition*]

~13 August 1992

At the Wilmington, NC, airport, The Night Flier killed at least nine people, including a man, a woman, a thirteen-year-old girl, and another girl whom he beheaded.

Rick Dees almost crashed in a storm at the Wilmington airport when Farmer John gave him and a 727 clearance to land on the same runway at the same time.

7:45 p.m.: He landed on runway 34. He found The Night Flier's latest victims. In the restroom, he saw that The Night Flier was a vampire. In a mirror reflection, he saw nothing but red urine streaming down a urinal. The Night Flier took his film and warned him to stop following him.

The police arrived and arrested Dees. ["The Night Flier"]

13 August 1995

Rose Madder dropped to number 7 on *The New York Times* Fiction Best Seller List, its seventh week on the List.

August 14

14 August

As part of a vacation that included two weeks in England and a week in Barcelona, Spain, the Freemans—Lonnie, Doris, Norma, and Danny—arrived in London. They stayed at the Hotel Inter-Continental. ["Crouch End"]

14 August 1923

Gary Paulson drove by the Newalls' house. Cora Newall had just gotten her newspaper when she saw Gary. She lifted her dress, showing him something he found attractive, and thrust her hips at him three times. He thought of that moment whenever he was intimate with another woman. ["It Grows on You"]

14 August 1933

Clayton Blaisdell Jr. was born. One Saturday morning, his father threw him down the stairs. After recovering in the hospital, he was sent to Hetton House, a county home in Cumberland, ME, where he picked up the nickname Blaze. The bullies left him alone after he beat up the biggest one. In and out of foster homes, he kept returning to Hetton House until he was sixteen. He served two years in prison for assaulting the headmaster, whom he blamed for his best friend's death. After prison, he drifted around, lived a life of petty crime, and teamed with George Rackley. His last caper—kidnapping Joseph Gerard IV—didn't go well. [*Blaze*]

14 August 1967

beginning of a nuclear attack [unpublished *The Aftermath*]

14 August 1976

The police finished investigating the old dude's murder. Richard Drogan had been living with the old dude and was freaked out by the old dude's cataract. Each night for a week, Drogan watched the old dude sleep to look at the eye, which was closed. On the eighth night, he made a noise, waking the old dude. Drogan remained silent for an hour and heard the old dude's ticker getting louder . . . louder . . . louder—so loud, he feared the neighbors would hear. He smothered the old dude until the ticker stopped. The police arrived to check out a neighbor's report of a scream. Drogan was cool and explained the scream away. Vietnam vets, he and the police officer swapped Vietnam stories. He heard the old dude's ticker again, getting louder . . . louder . . . louder—so loud he was sure the police could hear it. He blurted out that the sound they were all hearing was the old dude's ticker under the floorboard, with the rest of the cut-up body pieces. ["The Old Dude's Ticker"]

14 August 1983

Christine stayed at number 7 on *The New York Times* Fiction Best Seller List, its nineteenth week on the List.

14 August 1988

Bobbi Anderson and Jim Gardener dug through to the ship's hatch. That night, Gard went into the shed while the Tommyknockers checked out the uncovered hatch. He saw Anne Anderson, Ev Hillman, and Peter with cabling coming from where parts of their skulls had been removed. [*The Tommyknockers*]

14 August 1990

dawn: Mother Abagail was proud that everyone who came to the Free Zone wanted to stop and see her first. To repent for committing the sin of pride, she left the Free Zone. Ralph Brentner, Harold Lauder, and Stu Redman searched in vain for her. Harold planned to kill Ralph and Stu when they met in Chautauqua Park at dusk. Nick Andros and Glen Bateman thwarted these plans by arriving with Ralph.

Fran Goldsmith entered Harold's house through an unlocked cellar window. She noticed a loose hearthstone, but didn't move it. [*The Stand: The Complete & Uncut Edition*]

14 August 2016

End of Watch dropped to number 10 on *The New York Times* Hardcover Fiction Best Seller List, its eighth week on the List.

August 15

15 August 1982

Different Seasons rose to number 1 on *The New York Times* Fiction Best Seller List, its second week on the List.

15 August 1988

Johnny Leandro, of the Bangor *Daily News*, investigated Haven, ME. Hazel McCready controlled a Coke machine, a Tommyknocker border guard. It killed Leandro on Route 9.

With breathing equipment to protect them from the concentrated poisonous air inside the spaceship, Bobbi Anderson and Jim Gardener went in. They found a pile of four Tommyknocker bodies; one had a knife. All were badly cut from the knife and from their claws (each had a single claw on a single foot). They had crashed because they were fighting. In another section of the ship, Bobbi and Gard found the power source: hundreds of Tommyknockers in slings and with cables in their heads.

Back in the house, Bobbi forced Gard to take 140 mg of Valium, enough to kill him. He shot at her; the gun misfired. As she shot a Tommyknocker phaser at him, he pushed the kitchen table on her. A Tommyknocker-modified radio fell into spilled beer and exploded. The kitchen and Bobbi caught fire. He shot her to end her misery. Her telepathic screams alerted the other Tommyknockers. He drank saltwater and vomited several times to get rid of the Valium then went to the shed. Anne Anderson and Ev Hillman used their mind power to help him shoot green fire with a Tommyknocker weapon. Freeman Moss, the first Tommyknocker to arrive, died. Bobbi's and Freeman's trucks exploded, and Bobbi's house caught fire. Anne died from the strain. Dick Allison arrived and strangled Newt Berringer. With a Tommyknocker device in the shed, Gard brought Davey Brown back from Altair-4. To end Ev's and Peter's miseries, Gard burned the shed. Gard started the spaceship; Allison died when the ship vibrated. Many Tommyknockers died when he drained their power on takeoff.

Henry Amberson, a Newport, ME, forest ranger, investigated the fire in Big Injun Woods, set by Jim Gardener's Tommyknocker fight. He died when his pacemaker exploded.

The FBI and The Shop investigated Haven. During the next two weeks, The Shop took the twenty-six surviving Tommyknockers to their Virginia compound. By the end of October, all had died. [*The Tommyknockers*]

15 August 1990

As a wolf, Randall Flagg visited Mother Abagail in her dreams. [*The Stand: The Complete & Uncut Edition*]

15 August 1997

The Dark Tower IV: Wizard & Glass (Donald M. Grant, $45) published with a first printing of 40,000 copies

15 August 1998

Legends: Short Novels by the Masters of Modern Fantasy, edited by Robert Silverberg (Tor Books, $27.95), with "The Dark Tower: The Little Sisters of Eluria" (collected in *Everything's Eventual*), published

15 August 1999

The Girl Who Loved Tom Gordon stayed at number 10 on *The New York Times* Fiction Best Seller List, its seventeenth week on the List.

15 August 2004

The Dark Tower VI: Song of Susannah rose to number 10 on *The New York Times* Fiction Best Seller List, its eighth week on the List.

15 August 2012

The Dark Tower: The Gunslinger—Man in Black #3 of 5 (Marvel Comics, $3.99) published

August 16

16 August 1980

"'ALIEN ABDUCTEES' REMAIN CONVINCED; Psychologists Question Drawings of So-Called Gray Men" appeared in *The New York Times*. [*Dreamcatcher*]

16 August 1981

Cujo entered *The New York Times* Fiction Best Seller List at number 5. It was on the List for thirty-four weeks.

16 August 1987

Misery stayed at number 3 on *The New York Times* Fiction Best Seller List, its eleventh week on the List.

16 August 1988

Word about the Haven, ME, Tommyknockers had gotten out of Haven. Tommyknocker Poley Andrews killed himself by drinking Drano; Queenie Golden committed suicide by jumping in a well. [*The Tommyknockers*]

16 August 1990, early afternoon

Kojak, who had been left in New Hampshire, was beaten and missing an eye when he found Glen Bateman in the Free Zone. Dick Ellis treated him. Kojak had fought four wolves at Mother Abagail's place in Hemingford Home, NE. [*The Stand: The Complete & Uncut Edition*]

16 August 1992

Gerald's Game stayed at number 1 on *The New York Times* Fiction Best Seller List, its fifth week on the List.

16 August 2010

Marjorie Duvall, Beadie's last victim, donated type A-positive blood. ["A Good Marriage"]

16 August 2015

Finders Keepers dropped to number 15 *The New York Times* Hardcover Fiction Best Seller List, its ninth week on the List.

August 17

~17 August 1939

Postman Larry McLeod went to see why the Marstens' mail had piled up for five days. He found the Marstens dead in their house. [*'Salem's Lot*]

17 August 1966, Saturday afternoon: The Stone Incident

Attracted to loud radio music, Carrie White, almost 3, wandered next door. Stella Horan was sunbathing on her stomach. When she woke up and rolled over, the top of her new white bikini fell, exposing the tops of her breasts. Carrie saw them and said she wanted some but knew she never would. Her mother had taught her only bad girls grew dirtypillows. Her mother had them because she had done a bad thing with Carrie's father—a bad thing that resulted in Carrie.

When Margaret White saw her daughter talking with a bikini-clad woman, she shrieked for Carrie to come home. To impress upon Carrie the urgency, she clawed her own face. After much yelling from inside the White house, a storm dropped large balls of ice over the Whites' house and yard.

More screaming caused several neighbors to come out of their houses. They could hear sounds of things breaking in the house. They didn't know about Carrie's telekinesis, and wondered how someone could have thrown a 300-pound mahogany table halfway through a window. The Stone Incident ended with a storm of granite stones that punctured the Whites' roof and cratered their yard. [*Carrie*]

17 August 1990

In a private, closed meeting, the Ad Hoc Committee planned to have each member find someone to nominate one member of the temporary Ad Hoc Committee for the permanent Free Zone Committee at the next night's meeting so they could stay in power. [*The Stand: The Complete & Uncut Edition*]

17 August 2014

Mr. Mercedes dropped to number 12 on *The New York Times* Hardcover Fiction Best Seller List, its ninth week on the List.

August 18

18 August 1907

Ellen Rimbauer went to Anna Herr Clise's Children's Orthopedic Hospital fund-raising luncheon; John had given her the required $20 donation. Afterward, Ellen invited Tina Coleman for Earl Grey tea, cucumber sandwiches, and huckleberry scones. She asked what Tina knew about John Rimbauer's nighttime activities. Tina said it was unfounded gossip. [*The Diary of Ellen Rimbauer: My Life at Rose Red*]

18 August 1984

Stephen King and his agent, Kirby McCauley, met with Elaine Kostner of NAL in New York. She tried in vain to persuade him to publish *The Gunslinger* as a trade paperback.

Stephen King had an idea about a clown monster. [*The Dark Tower VI: Song of Susannah*]

18 August 1985

Richard Bachman's *Thinner* dropped to number 15 on *The New York Times* Fiction Best Seller List, its twenty-fifth and last week on the List.

Skeleton Crew stayed at number 1 on *The New York Times* Fiction Best Seller List, its ninth week on the List.

18 August 1990

In a public meeting, the Free Zone Committee was established to replace the temporary Ad Hoc Committee. At Harold Lauder's suggestion, the people voted the Ad Hoc Committee as the Free Zone Committee. Mother Abagail had veto power. In other business, the Burial Committee, headed by Chad Norris, was set up, with the responsibility of burying the Free Zone's Captain Trips victims. The Power Committee was created to restore electricity to the Free Zone, and the Search Committee, led by Harold Lauder, was established to find Mother Abagail. [*The Stand: The Complete & Uncut Edition*]

18 August 1994

Audrey Wyler wrote to her college friend, Janice Conroy. She had taken in her nephew Seth Garin after his family was killed while vacationing in California. [*The Regulators*]

18 August 1996

The Green Mile, Part Three: Coffey's Hands dropped to number 14 on *The New York Times* Paperback Fiction Best Seller List, its eleventh week on the List.

The Green Mile, Part Four: The Bad Death of Eduard Delacroix dropped to number 5 on *The New York Times* Paperback Fiction Best Seller List, its seventh week on the List.

The Green Mile, Part Five: Night Journey entered *The New York Times* Paperback Fiction Best Seller List at number 1. It was on the List for ten weeks.

18 August 2010

The Dark Tower: The Gunslinger—The Journey Begins #4 of 5 (Marvel Comics, $3.99) published

18 August 2013

Michael Roch

Joyland stayed at number 2 on *The New York Times* Paperback Trade Fiction Best Seller List, its ninth week on the List.

August 19

19 August

Doris and Lonnie Freeman took a cab to Crouch End to visit John Squales. They left the cab to call John for directions. When they returned, the cab was gone, yet they hadn't paid their fare. After running from something behind a hedge on Hillfield Avenue in Crouch End, they reached the corner of Crouch Lane and Norris Road. A sign showed Slaughter Towen a mile away. (A towen was a Druid site of ritual human sacrifice.) Something took Lonnie in an underpass on Norris Road. A scary, human cat asked Doris for a cigarette. She ran and found her way out of Crouch End Towen. Evvie accompanied her to the Crouch End police station on Tottenham Lane, where she reported her husband's disappearance. The police had never heard of Crouch Lane, Norris Road, or Slaughter Towen. ["Crouch End"]

19 August 1959

As Odetta Holmes waited for the A-train in Greenwich Village's Christopher Street station, Jack Mort pushed her in front of the subway train. She lost her legs at the knees. An old black woman jumped in and put tourniquets on her thighs. Paramedics Julio Estevez, the Bobbsey Twins, and ride-along intern George Shavers, treated her and took her to Sisters of Mercy Hospital on Twenty-Third Street.

Detta Walker, a second personality within Odetta, was the opposite of Odetta; while Odetta was nice, Detta was nasty. Odetta had been the dominant personality, but Detta's control gradually increased. Odetta had headaches before becoming Detta. When she returned to herself, she didn't realize she had been gone. Neither personality knew of the other. Detta had always been a part of Odetta, influencing her, but they didn't live as two separate people until the subway accident. [*The Dark Tower II: The Drawing of the Three*]

19 August 1964

In Ur 7,191,974, Ernest Miller Hemingway died. (Our Ernest Hemingway died on 2 July 1961.) ["Ur"]

19 August 1966

The Westover, ME, *Enterprise* reported the Stone Incident. [*Carrie*]

19 August 1972

Patricia Blum and Stan Uris married. [*IT*]

19 August 1975

morning: Johnny Smith touched Eileen Magown, his physical therapist, and saw her house burning. He sent her home. She had left the stove on; a dishtowel then the curtains had caught fire.

early evening: At a press conference, Lewiston *Sun* feature editor Roger Dussault wanted Johnny Smith to tell his future. When Johnny mentioned Roger's sister Anne's drug addiction and resulting death after a heart attack, Dussault called Johnny a freak, punched him, ran, and fainted. Later, he wrote an article that said Johnny was a fake. Vera Smith had a stroke while watching the conference, which aired on TV at 11:00 p.m. [*The Dead Zone*]

19 August 1976

At Greg Stillson's campaign rally at the Trimbull, NH, town park, Johnny Smith shook Stillson's hand. He passed out after seeing President Stillson start World War III. He woke up in a cell; his forehead was bruised, most likely from being kicked. Trimbull Police Chief Bass and FBI agent Edgar Lancte talked with him then released him. [*The Dead Zone*]

19 August 1982, The Blackout

> 3:30 p.m.: The Shop's power went out in a storm. Since April, Rainbird had been masquerading as John the friendly orderly to gain Charlie McGee's trust. He won her over when he pretended to be afraid of the dark because of his Vietnam experience. In about three weeks, he persuaded Charlie to take part in the Shop's tests, but she had to get something in return each time. Also, he had scared her into needing to control her power.

Andy McGee's Thorazine was late. As it wore off, he had a hunch Charlie was in danger. This was the first hunch since before their capture. He thought the Thorazine may have been hindering his abilities (except early in his testing, where he wasn't drugged—he was probably just tapped out). In his sleep, he pushed himself off his Thorazine addiction. He pretended to continue taking the pills. [*Firestarter*]

Stephen King started *The Tommyknockers*.

19 August 1990

early a.m.: So she would not be for the Dark Man, Nadine Cross asked Larry Underwood to make love to her. He declined.

In a private meeting, the Free Zone Committee decided when to send the three spies to Las Vegas. Judge Farris was to leave on August 21st, Dayna Jurgens on the 27th, and Tom Cullen on the 28th. The dates changed later. [*The Stand: The Complete & Uncut Edition*]

The Stand: The Complete & Uncut Edition stayed at number 6 on *The New York Times* Fiction Best Seller List, its fifteenth week on the List.

19 August 1993, Thursday afternoon

Ed Deepneau beat up his wife, Helen, after he saw her name on a petition to have the pro-choice Susan Day speak in Derry. She spent the night in the hospital, recovering from two lost teeth, a broken cheekbone, cuts, bruises, torn-out hair, and a possible concussion. Detective Johnny Leydecker and Officer Chris Nell, Aloysius Nell's grandson, arrested Ed for second-degree assault in violation of Maine's Domestic Violence law.

After four months of insomnia, Ralph Roberts experienced hyper-reality, where he could see auras around people. He could read information about people and see their changing emotions in the auras. The aura around a ringing telephone allowed him to know who was calling. [*Insomnia*]

19 August 1997

Stephen King received author's copies of *Wizard and Glass*. [*The Dark Tower VI: Song of Susannah*]

19 August 2007

Sure his OCD wasn't normal, Dr. John Bonsaint was going to call Dr. J., but Dr. J.'s phone number, 1–207–555–1863, had eleven digits—bad. Valium had been working better than Neurontin. ["N."]

19 August 2009

The Stand: American Nightmares #5 of 5 (Marvel Comics, $3.99) published

19 August 2018

The Outsider rose to number 3 on *The New York Times* Hardcover Fiction Best Seller List, its eleventh week on the List.

August 20

20 August, ~3:00 a.m.

While looking for Police Constable Ted Vetter, Crouch End PC Robert Farnham entered the Crouch End Towen and never returned. ["Crouch End"]

20 August 1975

8:05 a.m.: Vera Smith died in Cumberland General Hospital, Room 35.

Chief Wiggins arrested Ridgeway, NH, town council member George Harvey's nephew for wearing a T-shirt with profanity. Mayor Greg Stillson talked some sense into him, painfully.

Johnny Smith moved in with his dad, Herb Smith, at RFD #1, Pownal, ME.

David Bright's article, "REAWAKENED COMA PATIENT DEMONSTRATES PSYCHIC ABILITY AT DRAMATIC NEWS CONFERENCE," appeared in the Bangor *Daily News*. [*The Dead Zone*]

20 August 1976

Ngo Phat, the Chatsworths' groundskeeper, told Johnny Smith that Greg Stillson reminded him of a tiger that had gone bad after getting the taste for human meat. Stillson should be killed—politically. [*The Dead Zone*]

20 August 1993

Insomniac Ralph Roberts's wake-up time was 3:30 a.m., with about four hours' sleep. [*Insomnia*]

20 August 1994, Saturday afternoon

Stockbroker Howie Cottrell played Derry Municipal Golf Club. As Howie looked for his ball in the rough off the 14th hole, a rare snake that escaped from a house nearby bit his left calf. Dr. Jennings, part of a foursome Howie played through earlier, pronounced him dead. He woke up in a body bag on a gurney heading to Autopsy Room Four. He could see, hear, smell, feel, and sense movement, but he couldn't talk or move. Dr. Arlen's assistant, Peter, did a whole-body, visual examination and took his temperature—94.2 degrees. He didn't see the snakebite because Howie had many insect bites from wearing shorts and lying in the rough. Peter was ready to start the pericardial cut. Dr. Arlen saw a scar Peter had missed and stopped him. She lifted Howie's penis and got close to view the scar, close enough that Howie could feel her breath. Rusty, an orderly, stopped the autopsy because a snake from Howie's golf bag bit another orderly. When Dr. Arlen looked back, Howie's penis was erect. ["Autopsy Room Four"]

20 August 1995

Rose Madder stayed at number 7 on *The New York Times* Fiction Best Seller List, its eighth week on the List.

August 21

21 August 1977, Friday night

Frankie Stone, probably drunk, hit a tree on Hanson Road. He was banged up, with his shattered left arm his most severe injury. [*Gwendy's Button Box*]

21 August 1983

Christine dropped to number 8 on *The New York Times* Fiction Best Seller List, its twentieth week on the List.

21 August 1990

The Burial Committee began the corpse cleanup. Within a couple of weeks, they had buried 25,000. Before the Free Zone, most Boulder, CO, residents left town because they believed Captain Trips came from the US Meteorological Air Testing Center on Broadway.

Larry Underwood asked Judge Farris to be a spy and go to Las Vegas.

Randall Flagg sent Nadine Cross to Harold Lauder. She was waiting for him and introduced herself when he got home. They made love without intercourse; she moved in. [*The Stand: The Complete & Uncut Edition*]

21 August 1994, Sunday

"PARALYZED MAN ESCAPES DEADLY AUTOPSY," an article about Howie Cottrell's almost having an autopsy while alive, headlined the local Derry newspaper. ["Autopsy Room Four"]

21 August 2000

The Plant Book One: *Zenith Rising*, Part 2 e-book (Philtrunm Press, $1.00) published

21 August 2003

Author's Note to *The Dark Tower VII: The Dark Tower*

21 August 2012

A Face in the Crowd (Scribner, $1.99, e-book; $9.99, audio), by Stephen King and Stewart O'Nan, published

Road Rage comic (hardcover, IDW Publishing, $24.99), with Stephen King and Owen King's "Throttle," published

21 August 2016

End of Watch dropped to number 16 on *The New York Times* Hardcover Fiction Best Seller List, its ninth and last week on the List.

August 22

22 August 1961

DeeDee Mowbray, from Waycross, GA, disappeared. [*Joyland*]

22 August 1974, Thursday

Mr. Richard Farris had been reading *Gravity's Rainbow* on a Castle View bench. On Thursday, he talked with Gwendy Peterson and gave her a beautiful, mahogany button box. It had eight hard-to-push, colored buttons on top, a small lever on each side, and a slot in the middle. Six buttons represented the continents except for Antarctica. The red button was for whatever she wished, and the black one was for everything. She knew pushing the buttons would cause destruction. The lever near the red button dispensed an animal-shaped chocolate treat that would curb her overeating and sweet tooth. She pulled it and ate the tiny chocolate rabbit. At Mr. Farris's invitation, she pulled the other lever. The box dispensed a mint condition 1891 Morgan silver dollar (value: $600). When she got home, she hid the box under the exposed roots of the oak out back. For dinner, she had single helpings of everything but skipped the chocolate cake her father had picked up at the Castle Rock Bake Shop. [*Gwendy's Button Box*]

22 August 1977, Saturday

At breakfast, Gwendy Peterson's father told her Frankie Stone made the newspaper for hitting a tree the night before. When he said Frankie's arm had the most severe injury, she knew it was his left one. That night, she realized it was exactly three years since she got her button box. [*Gwendy's Button Box*]

22 August 1982

Different Seasons dropped to number 2 on *The New York Times* Fiction Best Seller List, its third week on the List.

22 August 1990

8:15 a.m.: In a Land Rover, Judge Farris left for Las Vegas without knowing whether there were other spies. He took Route 7 east through Brighton to I-25 north to Cheyenne, where he picked up I-80 west. He planned to follow I-80 to Salt Lake City and Reno before turning north to Las Vegas.

early afternoon: Nick Andros, Ralph Brentner, and Stu Redman hypnotized Tom Cullen with Stan Nogotny's word—elephant—to explain they wanted him to go to Las Vegas on a spy mission. They programmed him to say he was sent away from the Free Zone because he was feebleminded and to come back at the full moon.

Sue Stern asked Dayna Jurgens to be a spy. [*The Stand: The Complete & Uncut Edition*]

22 August 1994, Monday

Walter Kerr didn't show up at work. A couple of weeks later, the woman next-door reported a foul stink from his house. Police found more than sixty snakes, half of them dead. Many were dangerous. Some were rare, with one that zoologists thought had been extinct for almost fifty years. They found a snake for every cage except one. The missing snake may have been the one that sent Howie Cottrell to Autopsy Room Four. Derry Municipal Golf

Course was a half mile of vacant lots and scrub woods away. ["Autopsy Room Four"]

22 August 1999

The Girl Who Loved Tom Gordon dropped to number 15 on *The New York Times* Fiction Best Seller List, its eighteenth and last week on the List.

22 August 2004

The Dark Tower VI: Song of Susannah dropped to number 14 on *The New York Times* Fiction Best Seller List, its ninth week on the List.

August 23

23 August 1974, Friday

Gwendy Peterson was hungry after her Suicide Stairs run. A small chocolate turtle from her button box satisfied her. For lunch, she had a bologna-and-cheese sandwich, salad with French dressing, and a glass of milk; she looked at the leftover chocolate cake but didn't want any. [*Gwendy's Button Box*]

23 August 1981

Cujo rose to number 1 on *The New York Times* Fiction Best Seller List, its second week on the List.

23 August 1987

Misery stayed at number 3 on *The New York Times* Fiction Best Seller List, its twelfth week on the List.

23 August 1992

Gerald's Game stayed at number 1 on *The New York Times* Fiction Best Seller List, its sixth week on the List.

23 August 1994, Tuesday

afternoon and evening viewings for Johanna Noonan at Dakin's Funeral Home in Motton, ME [*Bag of Bones*]

August 24

24 August 1848

Robert Howell, a character in Bobbi Anderson's *The Buffalo Soldiers*, camped near a Sand Hill Country stream in the Nebraska panhandle. [*The Tommyknockers*]

24 August 1947

Andy Dufresne followed his wife to Glenn Quentin's and confirmed the rumors she was having an affair with her golf instructor. ["Rita Hayworth and Shawshank Redemption"]

24 August 1954

Rocky Mountain Express, Inc., shipped four hundred cases (one gross/case) of Delsey toilet tissue from Sidey's Warehouse to The Overlook Hotel. [*The Shining*]

24 August 1974, Saturday

Gwendy Peterson and her parents went to visit Aunt Dottie and Uncle Jim (her father's brother) in Yarmouth, ME. They watched *Thunderbolt and Lightfoot* and *Gone in 60 Seconds* at Pride's Corner Drive-In. [*Gwendy's Button Box*]

24 August 1980

Firestarter entered *The New York Times* Fiction Best Seller List at number 6. It was on the List for thirty-five weeks.

24 August 1994, Wednesday morning

Johanna Noonan, in a blue dress, was buried in Fairlawn Cemetery. [*Bag of Bones*]

24 August 2012

Stephen King finished *Joyland*.

24 August 2014

Mr. Mercedes dropped to number 15 on *The New York Times* Hardcover Fiction Best Seller List, its tenth and last week on the List.

August 25

25 August 1962, Saturday evening

<u>George Amberson's second timeline</u>: George followed the Oswalds. When it looked as if they'd be awhile at Peter Gregory's, he went to install the bug in the lamp he had already placed in 2703 Mercedes Street. He entered through the unlocked back door. He put the bug in the base of the lamp and ran the wire though the hole he had drilled in the wall when he placed the lamp. Outside, he hooked up the tape recorder, hiding it in a rusty Crisco can under a pile of bricks and boards. [*11/22/63*]

25 August 1974, Sunday

The Petersons went back home to Castle Rock, ME. Mrs. Peterson had a Ladies Aid meeting. [*Gwendy's Button Box*]

25 August 1977

"The King Family and the Wicked Witch" appeared in *Flint*.

25 August 1985

Skeleton Crew stayed at number 1 on *The New York Times* Fiction Best Seller List, its tenth week on the List.

25 August 1990

Al Bundell arrived in the Free Zone with a group of more than forty, including George Richardson and Regina Wentworth.

The Census Committee, headed by Sandy DuChiens, and the Department of Law and Order, with Stu Redman the Free Zone Marshall, were established at a public Free Zone Committee meeting held in Munzinger Auditorium. For a Free Zone judicial system, the Law Committee was set up with Al Bundell as the head and Judge Farris and three others to serve him. Glen Bateman became a member of the Representative Government Committee. The Free Zone had 814 residents. [*The Stand: The Complete & Uncut Edition*]

25 August 1996

After a week off, *The Green Mile, Part One: The Two Dead Girls* re-entered *The New York Times* Paperback Fiction Best Seller List at number 14, its nineteenth week on the List.

The Green Mile, Part Three: Coffey's Hands dropped to number 15 on *The New York Times* Paperback Fiction Best Seller List, its twelfth week on the List.

The Green Mile, Part Four: The Bad Death of Eduard Delacroix dropped to number 8 on *The New York Times* Paperback Fiction Best Seller List, its eighth week on the List.

The Green Mile, Part Five: Night Journey stayed at number 1 on *The New York Times* Paperback Fiction Best Seller List, its second week on the List.

25 August 2013

Joyland dropped to number 5 on *The New York Times* Paperback Trade Fiction Best Seller List, its tenth week on the List.

August 26

26 August 1926

Dave Davis was a Florida bootlegger. His Table Whiskey arrived in Florida via Duma Key. Friend John Eastlake stored the whiskey in his barn. Davis gave him a gift of champagne. [*Duma Key*]

~26 August 1961

<u>George Amberson's second timeline</u>: Mimi Simmons died. She was to be cremated. [*11/22/63*]

26 August 1974, Monday

After running the Suicide Stairs, Gwendy Peterson ate a little chocolate cat. Her button box produced another 1891 Morgan silver dollar when she pulled what she called the Money Lever. [*Gwendy's Button Box*]

26 August 1978, Saturday

At Darnell's Garage, Buddy Repperton broke one of Christine's headlights. Arnie Cunningham hit his hand and spilled Coke on him. Repperton gave him bruises and a black eye. When the fight changed to Arnie's favor and Arnie bloodied Repperton's nose, Will Darnell stopped it and kicked Arnie out of the Garage.

afternoon: Roland LeBay died suddenly. [*Christine*]

26 August 1986

Bred Any Good Rooks Lately?: Original Puns, Shaggy Dogs, Spoonerisms, Feghoots & Malapropriate Stories, gathered by James Charlton (Doubleday, $4.95), with "For the Birds," published

26 August 1990

Sue Stern accompanied Dayna Jurgens as far as Colorado Springs. On Sue's way back to the Free Zone, she found a puppy near Monument, CO. She took it with her. [*The Stand: The Complete & Uncut Edition*]

The Stand: The Complete & Uncut Edition rose to number 5 on *The New York Times* Fiction Best Seller List, its sixteenth week on the List.

26 August 2009

The Dark Tower: Fall of Gilead #4 of 6 (Marvel Comics, $3.99) published

26 August 2018

The Outsider dropped to number 4 on *The New York Times* Hardcover Fiction Best Seller List, its twelfth week on the List.

August 27

27 August 1961, Sunday morning

<u>George Amberson's second timeline</u>: Coach Borman and Ellen Dockerty told George that Mimi Simmons had died. George agreed to organize a memorial assembly during the upcoming school year. [*11/22/63*]

27 August 1976

Charlie Decker was convicted for the murders of Jean Underwood and John Vance. Judge Samuel K. N. Deleavney sentenced Charlie to Augusta State Hospital because five state psychiatrists had determined he wasn't responsible for his actions. [*Rage*]

27 August 1982

Different Seasons (Viking, $16.95) published with a first printing of 200,000 copies

27 August 1990

Judge Farris camped in northwest Wyoming. [*The Stand: The Complete & Uncut Edition*]

27 August 1994, Saturday

Dr. Arlen planned to shampoo her dog. ["Autopsy Room Four"]

27 August 1995

Rose Madder dropped to number 8 on *The New York Times* Fiction Best Seller List, its ninth week on the List.

August 28

28 August 1962

<u>George Amberson's second timeline</u>: John Clayton sent ex-wife Sadie Dunhill a manila envelope with horrifying pictures of Japanese atomic-bomb blast victims, suggesting the United States was heading toward a nuclear war. [*11/22/63*]

28 August 1973

The Blue Ribbon Laundry needed more space, and it was going to be demolished for the Route 784 extension. It had a ninety-day option on a Douglas Street building in Waterford; if they didn't buy it during that time, the Thom McAn shoe company would. Barton Dawes was in charge of securing the building. [*Roadwork*]

28 August 1978, Monday

"LIBERTYVILLE VETERAN DIES AT 71," headlined Roland LeBay's obituary.

After a movie with girlfriend Roseanne, Dennis Guilder dreamed of a decaying Roland LeBay driving Christine as a Death Car. As she raced toward him, she transformed from an old car into a new one. [*Christine*]

28 August 1983

Christine rose to number 7 on *The New York Times* Fiction Best Seller List, its twenty-first week on the List.

28 August 1990

Sue Stern returned to the Free Zone after seeing Dayna Jurgens off at Colorado Springs.

Free Zone residents Jack and Candy Jones had poison ivy in embarrassing places.

dusk: Tom Cullen left for Las Vegas with no knowledge of other spies. He followed Route 70. Judge Farris entered Idaho through Targhee Pass. [*The Stand: The Complete & Uncut Edition*]

28 August 2012

the September issue of *Harper's Magazine*, with "Batman and Robin Have an Altercation" (collected in *The Bazaar of Bad Dreams*), published

28 August 2014, Thursday night

Sadie MacDonald, a nurse in Brady Hartsfield's ward at the Traumatic Brain Injury Clinic, killed herself. [*Finders Keepers*][*End of Watch*]

August 29

29 August 1945

New owner Horace Derwent celebrated The Overlook Hotel's grand reopening with a masked ball. [*The Shining*]

29 August 1963, Thursday

George Amberson's second timeline: George Amberson took Sadie Dunhill to the Dallas Auditorium to watch the Case-Tiger fight on closed-circuit TV. Tommy Case knocked out Dick Tiger in the fifth round. This was the last sports-result entry in the notebook Al Templeton had given to Jake Epping (Amberson). [*11/22/63*]

29 August 1978, Tuesday

Will Darnell kicked Buddy Repperton out of the Garage; Arnie Cunningham could stay. Darnell offered him his tool fees, lift fees, and garage space for half price if he worked twenty hours a week. Part of his job was to bring wrecked cars from the Philly Plains races to Darnell's junkyard.

2:00 p.m.: Roland LeBay received an American Legion burial at Libertyville Heights Cemetery. Arnie, Dennis Guilder, and George LeBay, Roland's brother, attended. Later that night, Dennis visited George at the Rainbow Motel to learn more about Roland. [*Christine*]

29 August 1980

Dark Forces: New Stories of Suspense and Supernatural Horror, edited by Kirby McCauley (Viking, $16.95), with "The Mist" (collected in *Skeleton Crew*), published.

29 August 1982

Different Seasons rose to number 1 on *The New York Times* Fiction Best Seller List, its fourth week on the List.

29 August 1990

The Census Committee estimated the Free Zone population at more than a thousand. [*The Stand: The Complete & Uncut Edition*]

29 August 1996

The Green Mile, Part Six: Coffey on the Mile (Signet, $3.99) published with a first printing of 2,000,000 copies

29 August 2004

The Dark Tower VI: Song of Susannah rose to number 12 on *The New York Times* Fiction Best Seller List, its tenth and last week on the List.

29 August 2014, Friday

Pete Saubers had good news he wanted to deliver in person. Bill Hodges followed the path from the Birch Street Rec and met Pete at the stream in the undeveloped land where Pete had found the trunk with the Rothstein money and notebooks. *The New Yorker* was doing a photo shoot to go with an article about Pete's finding the trunk. Pete would write the article. He planned to use the $15,000 from *The New Yorker* to send Tina to Chapel Ridge.

Bill Hodges visited Brady Hartsfield. He tried to elicit a response by saying Brady had a small penis and had sex with his mother. Nothing. After Hodges left, a Zappit game console turned on, cycled through animated fish, Angry Birds, Barbie Fashion Walk, and Galactic Warming then turned off. Water in the bathroom went on then off. Brady looked at the picture of himself and his mom; it fell over. [*Finders Keepers*]

August 30

30 August 1960, Tuesday

Ray Brower went to pick blueberries. A GS&WM train hit him near Back Harlow Road in South Harlow, ME. The train knocked him out of his shoes and killed him. ["The Body"]

30 August 1963, Friday

George Amberson's second timeline: George Amberson had already told the landlord that August was the last month he'd be renting the Neely Street apartment. He went back to get the rest of his belongings. As he went up the steps, a speeding panel truck stopped in front of the building. George went into his apartment and locked the door. Four guys, sent by Eduardo Gutierrez, busted it open. Two large, winning bets were more than a coincidence, and they wanted to know how he knew. All they got was the satisfaction of beating him up. They broke his nose, cheekbone, left knee, and left arm, dislocated one to three fingers on his left hand, and knocked out some teeth. After they left, he made his way outside but couldn't walk or drive. Neighbor Alberta Hitchinson, the woman with the Elsa Lanchester hair, found him and called an ambulance. Dr. Malcom Perry treated him at Parkland Memorial Hospital. After seven weeks, he was transferred to Eden Fallows, a rehabilitation facility in north Dallas. [*11/22/63*]

30 August 1979

The Dead Zone (Viking, $11.95) published with a first printing of 50,000 to 80,000 copies

30 August 1981

Cujo stayed at number 1 on *The New York Times* Fiction Best Seller List, its third week on the List.

30 August 1987

Misery stayed at number 3 on *The New York Times* Fiction Best Seller List, its thirteenth week on the List.

30 August 1990

Rutland, VT's Brian Ball had won third prize for his walkie-talkie-based device that rang a bell on voice command up to twelve miles away. Harold Lauder used this concept, which was featured in *65 National Science Fair Prize Winners*, to build a detonation device for a bomb made from eight sticks of dynamite.

Judge Farris reached Butte City, ID. [*The Stand: The Complete & Uncut Edition*]

30 August 1992

Gerald's Game stayed at number 1 on *The New York Times* Fiction Best Seller List, its seventh week on the List.

30 August 2015

Stephen King finished *End of Watch*.

August 31

31 August 1961

The body of Delight Mowbray, the Funhouse Killer's first known victim, was found next to a trail on the edge of the Okefenokee Swamp. The Funhouse Killer had cut her throat and driven away in a truck. [*Joyland*]

31 August 1978, Thursday

Michael Cunningham asked Dennis Guilder to see how Arnie Cunningham was doing with restoring Christine. [*Christine*]

31 August 1980

Firestarter rose to number 2 on *The New York Times* Fiction Best Seller List, its second week on the List.

31 August 1990

Judge Farris left Butte City, ID.

evening: Fran Goldsmith and Larry Underwood talked about the loose stone in Harold Lauder's house. They wanted to find out what was under it. [*The Stand: The Complete & Uncut Edition*]

31 August 1992

Charles Sutlin abandoned his dog, Prince, to avoid paying a $70 dog tax. Prince survived by scavenging Kashwakamak Lake trash cans. A couple of months later, Prince found a hearty meal—the dead Gerald Burlingame. [*Gerald's Game*]

31 August 2012

Jamie Morton's grandniece, Cara Lynne, was born. [*Revival*]

31 August 2013, Saturday

Terry Morton threw a party to commemorate his wedding anniversary, and his granddaughter's (Cara Lynne) first birthday. The party started in the afternoon at home. Cara Lynne loved Jamie Morton, and couldn't get enough of him. In the evening, the party moved to the Eureka Grange No. 7. The Castle Rock All-Stars was scheduled to play. Short a rhythm guitarist, Norm Irving invited Jamie Morton to fill in. With three ex-members of Chrome Roses, the All-Stars played as Chrome Roses, an impromptu reunion in more than thirty years. [*Revival*]

31 August 2016

The Dark Tower: The Drawing of the Three—Bitter Medicine #5 of 5 (Marvel Comics, $3.99) published

August

August 1900

Bradley Colson preached in Ilium, ME. He said the town was a haven and shouldn't be named after an Italian. Seven months later, Ilium voted to change its name to Haven. [*The Tommyknockers*]

August 1901

On a nice Sunday afternoon, Harry Auster, George Armbruster, Fred Dean, Jared Devore, Draper Finney, Ben Merrill, and Oren Peebles raped Sara Tidwell then killed her and her son. For almost a hundred years, Sara haunted the Dark Score Lake area, causing child descendants of these men to be killed. [*Bag of Bones*]

August 1922

Owner James Parris died of a heart attack between two topiary lions at The Overlook Hotel. Bob T. Watson's son, Dick, found his body the next morning. ["Before the Play"]

A Norway rat had grabbed and bitten into one of Achelois's teats. The cow freed the rat, but it took the teat with it. Wilfred James put Rawleigh Antiseptic Salve on her. She stopped producing milk. ["1922"]

August 1929

As Lottie Kilgallon Pillsbury slept at The Overlook Hotel, a hand grabbed her wrist. She had nightmares for the rest of her life. ["Before the Play"]

August 1938

Saturday afternoon: Moira Alderson slashed her wrists in the bathtub.

George Alderson took the boys (Rhett, Jack, and Pete) to her house so each could pick an item to remember her by. Rhett chose her blue ceramic cookie jar. A week or two later, Jack and Rhett ate cookies from the jar. They noticed it was always full of fresh cookies. ["Cookie Jar"]

August 1939

Roger Breakstone was born. [*Cujo*]

August 1951

The Oklahoma Rancher's and Cattlemen's Association hired rainmaker Greg Stillson. After a drought, it rained for three days, yet they paid Stillson just $17. [*The Dead Zone*]

August 1955

Four hundred people answered an enticing ad in the Sacramento *Bee*. After two rounds of testing, a hundred, including Ted Brautigan, remained. A couple of months later, Ted was a Breaker at Devar-Toi. [*The Dark Tower VII: The Dark Tower*]

August 1956

Jamie Morton was born in Harlow, ME. [*Revival*]

August 1960

The Garfields moved from Harwich, CT, to Danvers, MA. ["Low Men in Yellow Coats"]

August 1964

The children of Gatlin, NE, killed everyone over the Age of Favor (nineteen) and started worshiping He Who Walks Behind the Rows. ["Children of the Corn"]

August 1967

Andy McCandless had always been more successful than his younger brother Jack. For example, Andy did better in school, got his driver's license with fewer tries, and he and Jenna Farrell were Homecoming King and Queen. The rivalry darkened when Jack won the Minuteman rifle club's annual Hawkeye Shooting Competition and Jenna's affections. After the competition, all three went to Club 41 then to the McCandlesses' lake cabin. A few drinks later, Andy put an apple on his head and suggested Jack enter a real shooting competition. At first, Jack wouldn't, but Andy egged him on. In a quick motion, Jack put the rifle to his shoulder and fired. He missed the apple but hit Andy in the forehead. Jack wrote a suicide note, explaining that Andy's death was an accident and that he and Jenna couldn't live with what had happened. In each other's arms at the cliff at the end of Lookout Road, they had second thoughts. Joe McCandless, the baby of the family, had eavesdropped that evening and ran to the cliff to save his brother. Startled by the screaming Joe, Jack lost his footing and fell over the cliff, pulling Jenna with him. Joe kept quiet; for forty years, everybody thought the lovers had committed suicide. ["Ghost Brothers of Darkland County" *libretto*]

August 1972

Barton Dawes went to the Route 784 extension groundbreaking. He discussed his disapproval of the project with newscaster Dave Albert. [*Roadwork*]

August 1973

Barton Dawes wrote a letter to the newspaper objecting to the Route 784 extension. [*Roadwork*]

Ophelia Todd was fond of finding shortcuts between Castle Rock and Bangor, ME, which was seventy-nine miles as a crow flies. Roads that traversed the distance in as little as 31.6 miles weren't on any map and took her past strange trees and animals. In August, she went on a shortcut and never returned. ["Mrs. Todd's Shortcut"]

Over a Wednesday-night dinner on the beach, Dev Jones told Erin Cook and Tom Kennedy about Linda Gray's haunting of Horror House at Joyland. The next day, they took the Horror House ride. Tom saw Linda Gray holding out her hands. He remembered this to within a month of his death.

Later that August, Dev Jones collected his favor from Mr. Easterbrook. He wanted to skip a year of school and stay on with Joyland after the summer. Mr. Easterbrook agreed, so long as Dev told his father. [*Joyland*]

August 1974/1980

Professor Dexter Stanley told Henry Northrup about a creature that had been found in a crate and had killed a Horlicks University janitor and graduate student. Northrup used the creature to kill his wife, who had made married life miserable. ["The Crate" / "The Crate" from *Creepshow*]

August 1977

"The Man Who Loved Flowers" (collected in *Night Shift*) appeared in the August issue (Vol. 5, No. 9) of *Gallery*.

August 1978

Buddy Repperton bought a blue 1976—77 Camaro from Will Darnell's friend. It had been rolled on Route 46 near Squantic Hills State Park. He started smuggling runs for Darnell. [*Christine*]

August 1979

The Stillson Committee held a hearing to find out why Johnny Smith tried to assassinate Greg Stillson. Chief Counsel Norman D. Verizer and Deputy Counsel Albert Renfrew interviewed Stuart Clawson, Herman Joellyn, Keith Strang, and Dr. Weizak. Senator William Cohen of Maine chaired the Committee. [*The Dead Zone*]

August 1980

Ewen High School student Norma Watson was one of the few survivors of Carrie's Prom Night. She told her story in "We Survived the Black Prom," a "Drama in Real Life" feature in the August *Reader's Digest*. [*Carrie*]

Harry Streeter had planned to take Gwendy Peterson on his family's ten-day vacation on the coast. [*Gwendy's Button Box*]

August 1982

Ayana kissed Doc Gentry on the cheek and cured his pancreatic cancer. ["Ayana"]

"Before the Play," a prologue to *The Shining*, appeared in Volume 5, Number 1–2 (issue 17–18) of *Whispers*.

August 1983

The Creed family moved to Ludlow, ME. Louis Creed, a Chicago doctor, had a new job running University Medical Services at the University of Maine at Orono. [*Pet Sematary*]

August 1984, Saturday, full moon

The Beast killed Constable Neary while the Constable drank in his pickup truck in west Tarker's Mills. [*Cycle of the Werewolf*]

August 1988

Troop D's dog, Mister Dillon, alerted Troop D about a seven-foot humanoid creature that had come out of the Buick Roadmaster's trunk. Four members of Troop D killed it. It was poison to Mister Dillon, who had to be put down. They buried him in a field near the barracks. [*From a Buick 8*]

Popular writer Scott Landon was honorary groundbreaker for the University of Tennessee Nashville's Shipman Library. After the ceremony, Gerd Allen Cole shot him. As Cole aimed for a fatal second shot, Lisey Landon clubbed him with the ceremonial spade. [*Lisey's Story*]

August 1989

American Pride Flight 29 from Los Angeles, CA, to Boston, MA, flew through a time-rip into the recent past. All passengers who were awake were vaporized; those who slept lived. At Bangor International Airport, they discovered that the Langoliers ate the past. They refueled, took off, and headed back toward the time-rip, just ahead of the Langoliers. Nick Hopewell gave his life by staying awake to fly the plane back through the rip to the present. ["The Langoliers"]

August 1994

Johanna Noonan died of a stroke. Kia Noonan drowned in her womb. [*Bag of Bones*]

August 1997

Bob Anderson had taken a trip to Mickelson's Coins in Waterville, ME. Beadie killed Stacey Moore, who lived in Waterville. This seventh murder started Beadie's new cycle. ["A Good Marriage"]

the October/November issue (#556; Volume 93, Number 4 & 5) of *The Magazine of Fantasy & Science Fiction*, with "Everything's Eventual" (collected in *Everything's Eventual*), published

August 1998

Rosalie joined Natalie Deepneau walking down Harris Avenue. Atropos slapped Rosalie, causing her to run in the road. Pete Sullivan swerved to avoid hitting her and headed right at Natalie. Ralph Roberts, who had been taken to Long-Time levels to fulfill his promise, returned to Short-Time levels in front of Sullivan's car and pushed Natalie to safety. The 20 MPH car broke his leg on impact. When he hit the ground, he broke his skull and back, his ribs punctured his lungs, his liver smashed, and his intestines burst. He lived for a short time, without pain. [*Insomnia*]

August 2001

Monday evening: Under a yellow umbrella on the Harris Avenue Extension, Mr. George Elvid had set up a card table to sell extensions. He offered a life extension to Dave Streeter for 15% of his income over the next fifteen years. It was just a fair extension, not immortality.

Wednesday afternoon: An MRI showed that Dave's tumors had shrunk and his lungs were clear. The technician thought the MRI computer must have malfunctioned.

Friday evening: Dave returned to the Harris Avenue Extension with one of Tom Goodhugh's Atenolols, which Mr. George Elvid then swallowed. Dave would get fifteen to twenty-five years of good health and send his 15% to The Non-Sectarian Children's Fund's Cayman Island bank. ["Fair Extension"]

August 2004

Robert Fornoy conducted a sociology/geology experiment in Waco, TX. He found Waco much less violent than other towns of its size. Believing something was in the water, he spent the next three years in La Plata forty miles from Waco. Violence increased proportionally from La Plata. He found a sub-microscopic protein in the water, a protein found only in human brains. His purer, concentrated form of the water had a calming effect. The next eruption of Gulandio, a volcano near Borneo, could distribute the water all over the world, calming everyone and ending war. ["The End of the Whole Mess"]

August 2006

Amateur photographer N. went to Motton, ME, for a weekend landscape photography outing along the Androscoggin River. Ackerman's Field was a field of uncut hay with seven stones, from three to five feet high. He noticed when he looked through the camera, there were eight stones. Before leaving, he felt he had to touch all the stones to preserve the order of the world. As he reached his car, he looked back and saw a black-and-green thing turning among the stones. It watched him with sick, pink eyes. He realized the Field was a thin spot between worlds and the creature was not from this one. When he got home, he locked the doors, double-checked them, and counted them—six. He couldn't sleep that night. He counted ninety-three books in his bedroom bookcase, a bad number: 93/3 = 31 = 13 backward. A book from the hall bookcase brought the total to ninety-four, but 9+4 = 13, so he added six more. Fifty-six books remained in the hall, a good number: 56/2 = 28—good enough for him to sleep. ["N."]

August 2007

Joe McCandless had seen his brothers' sibling rivalry lead to their deaths. When his sons' rivalry involved a broken arm, Joe intervened. He called a family meeting at the cabin to stop his sons from following in their uncles' footsteps. He explained what had happened forty years earlier—the public story and the part of his own involvement, which he had kept private until then. The next morning, the boys—Frank McCandless and Drake McCandless—tried to be brothers instead of enemies. Fearing that Frank wouldn't take her to New York with him after his writing success, Anna Wicklow got nasty, saying ugly things about Drake and his parents. Drake started choking her; Monique McCandless broke it up. Anna pushed Monique on her way out. Monique fell into the grandfather clock (which had been broken when Andy McCandless was shot forty years before). Drake couldn't revive his mother and resumed choking Anna. Frank, smaller than Drake, couldn't stop him, so he shot him. The bullet killed Drake and Anna. When Joe McCandless entered the room, Frank blamed him, shot him, and then turned the gun on himself. ["Ghost Brothers of Darkland County" *libretto*]

August 2009

Tom Goodhugh's son, Carl, died choking on a piece of apple. ["Fair Extension"]

Cathy Morse killed herself. "WOMAN IN DEATH JUMP FROM CYRUS AVERY MEMORIAL BRIDGE" appeared in the Tulsa *World*. [*Revival*]

Stephen King's poem "Mostly Old Men" appeared in the Summer 2009 issue (#40; Volume 10, Number 4) of *Tin House*.

August 2010

While the family was away for the day, Pete Saubers went to the embankment for the notebooks. He reburied the empty trunk. At home, he stashed the notebooks under blankets in the far corner of the seldom-used attic. [*Finders Keepers*]

August 2013

Freddi Linklatter had dropped off a picture of Brady Hartsfield and his mother that summer. Brady sent Z-Boy to show her a Zappit and ask how to modify it to make people linger on the Fishin' Hole demo. She said to make an eye-trap by turning the demo into a game. First, install a rootkit that could accept future programming.

Later, *Prize Surprise* on TV gave Brady the idea for his Zappit eye-trap. A contestant had to tap five red dots, moving with other colored dots on a computer screen, to win a trip to Aruba. The tapped dots turned into numbers. If the sum was enough, she'd win. Brady would offer prizes when people tapped enough fish that changed to numbers. Brady chose the Fishin' Hole's pink fish because they were the fastest and pink was soothing. [*End of Watch*]

August 2014

Jamie Morton stopped by his brother Terry's house. Cara Lynne was terrified of him. She wouldn't stop screaming until he went outside. [*Revival*]

Howard Gamache thought Paul Massimo's last firework was the rare Rooster of Destiny. He didn't know how Massimo had gotten it into the country. Alden McCausland offered $1,000 for something that could top that. For a $50 referral fee, Howard vouched for Alden with Johnny Shining Path Parker. ["Drunken Fireworks"]

August 2017

Howard Timlin, Peter Robinson, and Gandalf were sick with radiation poisoning. Timlin shot himself. Robinson put Gandalf down with a shot of Demerol then rode his 2014 Harley-Davidson Fat Bob down Dead Man's Curve at top speed. ["Summer Thunder"]

September
Happenings

September 1

1 September 1789

Philip Boone was baptized in James Boon's church in Jerusalem's Lot. ["Jerusalem's Lot"]

1 September 1939

A Stranger's assassinating of the King in the Territories kicked off a three-week war, which killed about a hundred people. The war ended when Laura DeLoessian became Queen. Events in The Territories and our world are linked. This war caused World War II here. [*The Talisman*]

1 September 1960, Thursday

Charlie Hogan, Marie Dougherty, Billy Tessio, and Beverly Thomas stole a Dodge. They went joyriding then parking near Back Harlow Road in Harlow, ME. Hogan and Tessio found Ray Brower's body while urinating. ["The Body"]

1 September 1985

Skeleton Crew dropped to number 2 on *The New York Times* Fiction Best Seller List, its eleventh week on the List.

1 September 1990

Power was turned on in the Free Zone for a short time. Everything had been left on during the Captain Trips epidemic, so there was an overload.

1:00 p.m.: Fran Goldsmith and Larry Underwood broke into Harold Lauder's house and stole his journal. It showed Harold's plans to kill Stu Redman, learn all he could about the Free Zone, and report to Randall Flagg.

Nadine Cross planted Harold's bomb-in-a-shoe-box in Nick Andros's closet. Nick and Ralph Brentner would host a Free Zone Committee meeting the next night. Nadine lost her virginity when Randall Flagg made love to her. Her black hair, which had streaks of white, became completely white. Nadine and Harold left the Free Zone after discovering that Fran and Larry had stolen Harold's journal (Flagg told her). They headed for Las Vegas, Flagg's base, spending the night at Sunrise Amphitheater. [*The Stand: The Complete & Uncut Edition*]

1 September 1996

The Green Mile, Part One: The Two Dead Girls stayed at number 14 on *The New York Times* Paperback Fiction Best Seller List, its twentieth week on the List.

The Green Mile, Part Three: Coffey's Hands dropped to number 16 on *The New York Times* Paperback Fiction Best Seller List, its thirteenth week on the List.

The Green Mile, Part Four: The Bad Death of Eduard Delacroix dropped to number 9 on *The New York Times* Paperback Fiction Best Seller List, its ninth week on the List.

The Green Mile, Part Five: Night Journey stayed at number 1 on *The New York Times* Paperback Fiction Best Seller List, its third week on the List.

1 September 2011

Mile 81 e-book (Scribner, $2.99) published (collected in *The Bazaar of Bad Dreams*)

1 September 2013

Joyland rose to number 4 on *The New York Times* Paperback Trade Fiction Best Seller List, its eleventh week on the List.

September 2

2 September 1939, 6 o'clock

A German truck knocked Dr. Weizak's mother through a clock-shop window. She suffered amnesia and a broken hip. She took the name Johanna and later married Helmut Borentz, from Switzerland. [*The Dead Zone*]

2 September 1960, Friday

While looking for pennies under his porch, Vern Tessio overheard his brother Billy and Charlie Hogan talk about seeing Ray Brower's body. Vern told Chris Chambers, Teddy Duchamp, and Gordie Lachance. To become famous by finding and reporting the body, they began their twenty-to-thirty-mile trek. They followed the GS&WM railroad tracks; a train almost hit them as they crossed Castle River. At the Castle Rock Dump, Gordie lost a coin-flip to get food at the Florida Market. When he returned, the others were gone, and Dump-keeper Milo Pressman sicced Chopper on him. Gordie climbed the fence without being bit. When they camped for the night in the woods in Harlow, ME, Gordie told his story "The Revenge of Lard Ass Hogan." ["The Body"]

2 September 1973, Sunday

Dev Jones wore the fur twelve times. [*Joyland*]

2 September 1990

The Power Committee set up the Turning-Off Crew to turn off everything in the Free Zone before power was turned on again.

7:45 p.m.: Unwell, Mother Abagail returned to the Free Zone. Leo Rockway (Joe) found her and led her home, where she collapsed.

~8:25 p.m.: Harold Lauder remotely detonated his bomb at a semiprivate Free Zone Committee meeting. Nick Andros, Chad Norris, Dale Pedersen, Sue Stern, Patsy Stone, Andrea Terminello, and Dean Wykoff died. Glen Bateman, Ralph Brentner, Lewis Deschamps, Fran Goldsmith, Brad Kitchener, Stu Redman, and Teddy Weizak were among the twenty wounded. Most got out in time because of Mother Abagail's return. Harold and Nadine Cross headed west. [*The Stand: The Complete & Uncut Edition*]

The Stand: The Complete & Uncut Edition stayed at number 5 on *The New York Times* Fiction Best Seller List, its seventeenth week on the List.

2 September 1995

A van almost hit Stephen King as he walked on Route 7. [*The Dark Tower VI: Song of Susannah*]

2 September 2002, Monday, Labor Day

Jonesy and Carla Jones had Henry Devlin over for a cookout at their summer cottage on Pepper Pond in North Ware, MA. [*Dreamcatcher*]

Fred and Judy Marshall took Tyler Marshall to Maui Wowie, a Hawaiian-style VFW picnic at La Follette Park. [*Black House*]

2 September 2015

The Dark Tower: The Drawing of the Three—Lady of Shadows #1 of 5 (Marvel Comics, $3.99) published

2 September 2018

The Outsider stayed at number 4 on *The New York Times* Hardcover Fiction Best Seller List, its thirteenth week on the List.

September 3

3 September 1960, Saturday

Taking a shortcut through a culvert of water on their way to find Ray Brower's body, Chris Chambers, Teddy Duchamp, Gordie Lachance, and Vern Tessio got a good scare when leeches covered them. Near the Royal River, Vern found the body.

To become famous in Castle Rock, Fuzzy Bracowicz, Eyeball Chambers, Vince Desjardins, Charlie Hogan, Ace Merrill, Jack Midgett, and Billy Tessio went to discover Ray Brower's body while fishing the Royal River. They found Chris, Teddy, Gordie, and Vern near the body. Ace told them to go away, that they would report the body. Gordie and his friends refused to leave. Chris fired his father's .45. Ace and the others left but threatened to get them later. ["The Body"]

3 September 1973, Monday, Labor Day

Joyland's last day of the season: Dev Jones dropped off Erin Cook at the Wilmington train station. She took a cab to the bed and breakfast, where she and Tom Kennedy spent that night. [*Joyland*]

3 September 1979, Monday, Labor Day

Troop D held their annual Labor Day picnic at the old Academy soccer field near Redfern Stream. [*From a Buick 8*]

3 September 1990

Teddy Weizak died from wounds received in Harold Lauder's Free Zone Committee meeting explosion the day before. [*The Stand: The Complete & Uncut Edition*]

3 September 1995

Rose Madder dropped to number 11 on *The New York Times* Fiction Best Seller List, its tenth week on the List.

3 September 2014

The Dark Tower: The Drawing of the Three—The Prisoner #1 of 5 (Marvel Comics, $3.99) published

September 4

4 September 1914, evening

Douglas Posey and John Rimbauer argued about business in Europe. Posey didn't want to profit from the war; John did. Posey threatened to sell his shares in the partnership; Rimbauer offered to buy them. Later, Rimbauer bought him out but kept him on as an employee.

Madame Stravinski presided over a séance in the Ladies Library at Rose Red. She relayed a message from Rose Red to Ellen: Ellen could live, without fear, forever if she kept building onto the house. [*The Diary of Ellen Rimbauer: My Life at Rose Red*]

4 September 1945

Gatlin, NE, child Amos Deigan was born Richard Deigan. ["Children of the Corn"]

4 September 1955

Life magazine related an incident about Andrea Kolintz, as told by her brother. She had telekinetically thrown things around after a spanking for crawling onto the roof. [*Carrie*]

4 September 1960

After walking all night, Chris Chambers, Teddy Duchamp, Gordie Lachance, and Vern Tessio arrived back in Castle Rock. They told their parents they camped in Vern's backyard then moved to Brickyard Hill. They didn't report finding Ray Brower's body. Ace Merrill did so in an anonymous call. ["The Body"]

4 September 1964

Amos Deigan was sacrificed to He Who Walks Behind the Rows on his nineteenth birthday. Earlier in the year, Gatlin, NE, children killed everyone over nineteen, the Age of Favor, and started worshiping He Who Walks Behind the Rows. ["Children of the Corn"]

4 September 1973, Tuesday

Joyland was closed, but there was a lot to do. Dev Jones ate warm croissants while walking along the beach to work. [*Joyland*]

4 September 1977

Chuck Chatsworth left to go to Stovington Preparatory Academy (where *The Shining*'s Jack Torrance had taught). Johnny Smith had recommended a year of prep school before going to college. [*The Dead Zone*]

4 September 1983

Christine rose to number 6 on *The New York Times* Fiction Best Seller List, its twenty-second week on the List.

4 September 1984

Marty Coslaw returned home to Tarker's Mills, ME, after spending much of the summer with his Aunt Ida and Uncle Jim in Stowe, VT. [*Cycle of the Werewolf*]

4 September 1990

Another Free Zone resident died from Harold Lauder's September 2nd bomb.

Randall Flagg, as a crow with red-rimmed eyes, saw Judge Farris at the Ranchland Motel in New Meadows, ID.

8:00 p.m.: In a public Free Zone Committee meeting at Munzinger Auditorium, Brad Kitchner reported that power was expected the next day. [*The Stand: The Complete & Uncut Edition*]

4 September 1998

Merton Askew was born. He went missing in 2010. [*Doctor Sleep*]

4 September 2000, Monday, Labor Day

Trooper Paul Loving fell off a tire swing and sprained his knee at Troop D's annual Labor Day picnic. [*From a Buick 8*]

4 September 2018

Flight or Fright: 17 Turbulent Tales, edited by Stephen King and Bev Vincent (Cemetery Dance, $27.95 trade hardcover; $85, 1000-copy limited Slipcased Hardcover Artist edition, signed by Bev Vincent and artist Cortney Skinner; $1500, 52-copy Traycased Hardcover Lettered edition, signed by the artist and each editor), with "The Turbulence Expert," published

September 5

5 September 1975

After twenty-four years, Ben Mears returned to Jerusalem's Lot, ME, to write a novel about the Marsten House. His third-floor room at Eva's Rooms had a view of the house. [*'Salem's Lot*]

5 September 1982

Andy McGee had been unsuccessful in the Shop's tests. Dr. Patrick Hockstetter and Dr. Pynchot decided to send him to the Shop's Maui compound. [*Firestarter*]

Different Seasons stayed at number 1 on *The New York Times* Fiction Best Seller List, its fifth week on the List.

5 September 1990, Power Day

Judge Farris crossed the Snake River into Homestead, OR.

noon: Power was turned on in the Free Zone with one casualty. Rich Moffat, drunk in an auto body shop on Pearl Street, died when the shop exploded.

Judge Farris reached the Salmon River Mountains. [*The Stand: The Complete & Uncut Edition*]

September 6

6 September 1964

Gatlin, NE, child Job Gilman was born Clayton Gilman. ["Children of the Corn"]

6 September 1977

Richard Bachman's *Rage* (Signet, $1.50) published with a first printing of 75,000 copies

6 September 1981

Cujo stayed at number 1 on *The New York Times* Fiction Best Seller List, its fourth week on the List.

6 September 1987

Misery stayed at number 3 on *The New York Times* Fiction Best Seller List, its fourteenth week on the List.

6 September 1990

sunrise: Before dying, Mother Abagail spoke about a mission from God, where several Free Zone people shall go forth and stand against Randall Flagg.

~12:00 noon: Glen Bateman, Ralph Brentner, Kojak, Stu Redman, and Larry Underwood left to take the stand. They spent the night in Golden, CO. Hugh Petrella succeeded Stu as Free Zone Marshall. [*The Stand: The Complete & Uncut Edition*]

6 September 1992

Gerald's Game stayed at number 1 on *The New York Times* Fiction Best Seller List, its eighth week on the List.

6 September 1993, Monday, Labor Day

Insomniac Ralph Roberts's wake-up time was 2:45 a.m., with about three and a quarter hours' sleep. [*Insomnia*]

6 September 2015

After two weeks off, *Finders Keepers* re-entered *The New York Times* Hardcover Fiction Best Seller List at number 15. This was its tenth and last week on the List.

September 7

7 September 1900

During the summer, Bradley Colson had gone to Ilium, which later became Haven, ME. On Derry Road, he set up a tent from which to preach. His congregation grew. He went to bed with many women in town, including Faith Clarendon. On September 7th, he held the Harvest Home Revival of 1900, where he persuaded his congregation to donate cash as an offering to God. Before leaving town that night, he made love to six women, three of which were virgins. [*The Tommyknockers*]

7 September 1958, Sunday

Bill Titus, of Titus Chevron in Lisbon Falls, ME, took Arlene Hadley's 1954 Ford Sunliner convertible in on a trade. [*11/22/63*]

7 September 1960

Chris Chambers, Teddy Duchamp, and Gordie Lachance started junior high school. ["The Body"]

7 September 1979

"The Legacy of TK: Scorched Earth and Scorched Hearts," an article about the aftermath of Prom Night, appeared in the Lewiston *Daily Sun*. The death toll had reached 440, with eighteen still missing. [*Carrie*]

7 September 1980

Firestarter stayed at number 2 on *The New York Times* Fiction Best Seller List, its third week on the List.

7 September 1990, ~3:30 p.m.

Dave Roberts and Bobby Terry killed Judge Farris outside Copperfield, OR, after seeing him drive by on Oregon Highway 86. Terry accidentally shot and killed Roberts. For shooting the Judge in the face, Randall Flagg bit Terry to death. Flagg had wanted to send the head to the Free Zone. [*The Stand: The Complete & Uncut Edition*]

7 September 1999

999: New Stories of Horror and Suspense, edited by Al Sarrantonio (Avon Books, $27.50), with "The Road Virus Heads North" (collected in *Everything's Eventual*), published

7 September 2011

The Dark Tower: The Gunslinger—The Battle of Tull #4 of 5 (Marvel Comics, $3.99) published

September 8

8 September 1947

Considering suicide after confirming his wife's affair, Andy Dufresne bought a six-shot .38 Police Special at Wise Pawnshop in Lewiston, ME. ["Rita Hayworth and Shawshank Redemption"]

8 September 1958

Chuck Chatsworth was born in Durham, NH. [*The Dead Zone*]

8 September 1961, Friday

<u>George Amberson's second timeline</u>: George Amberson and Sadie Dunhill went to a Denholm Lions football game. The cheerleaders led the crowd in the Jim Cheer (for star quarterback Jim LaDue): the crowd called out, "Jim," and the cheerleaders followed, "La." Together, they chanted, "Jimla, Jimla, Jimla." [*11/22/63*]

8 September 1981

Cujo (Viking, $13.95) published with a first printing of 150,000 to 200,000 copies

8 September 1985

Skeleton Crew dropped to number 3 on *The New York Times* Fiction Best Seller List, its twelfth week on the List.

8 September 1990

Dayna Jurgens saw Tom Cullen in Las Vegas.

Power was off in the Free Zone for a short while after an overload on Arapahoe.

Four-year-old Dinny McCarthy was the youngest of about twenty children in Las Vegas. The oldest was fifteen. [*The Stand: The Complete & Uncut Edition*]

8 September 1996

The Green Mile, Part Four: The Bad Death of Eduard Delacroix dropped to number 11 on *The New York Times* Paperback Fiction Best Seller List, its tenth week on the List.

The Green Mile, Part Five: Night Journey stayed at number 1 on *The New York Times* Paperback Fiction Best Seller List, its fourth week on the List.

8 September 2001

The True Knot arrived in Hoboken, NJ. Crow Daddy had secured a private lot for ten days. [*Doctor Sleep*]

8 September 2013

Joyland dropped to number 6 on *The New York Times* Paperback Trade Fiction Best Seller List, its twelfth week on the List.

September 9

9 September 1905

After beer and eggs at The Sleepy Silver Dollar in Derry, ME, Claude Heroux used his ax on other patrons who might have taken part in the May 1905 killings. He cut off Floyd Calderwood's right hand, beheaded El Katook, and killed Eddie King and Tinker McCutcheon. Stugley Grenier shot him in the thigh then ran outside. The others in the bar acted as if nothing had happened. Later, a mob lynched Heroux from an elm near the Canal. This marked the start of another IT cycle; Pennywise was in The Bloody Bucket, a nearby bar. [*IT*]

9 September 1908

Ellen Rimbauer had a miscarriage in Paris. She blamed John Rimbauer for pushing her into two weeks of constant socializing. The doctor prescribed seven to ten days' bed rest. She feared John, out alone, would resume his womanizing. [*The Diary of Ellen Rimbauer: My Life at Rose Red*]

9 September 1909, early a.m.

Adam Rimbauer was born. Sukeena was Ellen Rimbauer's midwife. [*The Diary of Ellen Rimbauer: My Life at Rose Red*]

9 September 1915

John Rimbauer took Adam Rimbauer to the Cheshire Academy in Portland, OR, to start the first grade. [*The Diary of Ellen Rimbauer: My Life at Rose Red*]

9 September 1947

Deciding not to commit suicide after confirming his wife's affair, Andy Dufresne threw his gun from the Pond Road Bridge into the Royal River. ["Rita Hayworth and Shawshank Redemption"]

9 September 1958, Tuesday, 11:58 a.m.

Lee Harvey Oswald and his Marine unit were in the South China Sea.

There were a few places—bubbles—where one could travel in time. Each had a guardian posted near its stationary end. The guardian warned others not to use the bubble. When people went back in time, they created strings of existence. Strings gummed up the machine; too many, and the machine—reality—stopped. The guardians tried to keep track of the strings, but doing so took a toll on their sanity. People who traveled back in time had no trouble getting around them.

One such bubble extended from the back of Al Templeton's diner to 9 September 1958, Tuesday, 11:58 a.m., in Lisbon Falls, ME. Whenever he went through the portal, it was always two minutes later when he returned. He went to the 1958 Red & White market for fifty-four cents/pound ground chuck often. He'd buy ten to fourteen pounds from Mr. Warren. Because things reset each time someone went through the portal, he'd always buy the same meat.

George Amberson's first timeline: Jake Epping arrived in Lisbon Falls, ME, as George T. Amberson. On his way into town, he passed a white-over-red Plymouth Fury in the Worumbo Mills and Weaving parking lot. In town, he bought some clothes of the period and opened a checking account with a $1,000 deposit. A $2.50 taxi ride took him to the Tamarack Motor Court.

George Amberson's second timeline: Jake Epping arrived in Lisbon Falls, ME, as George T. Amberson. He went to the Tamarack Motor Court.

George Amberson's third timeline: Jake Epping arrived in Lisbon Falls, ME, as George T. Amberson. He checked in to the Tamarack Motor Court, Unit 7. At the market up the road, he bought two dozen legal pads and ten black-ink refills for the fountain pen from Bobbi Jill Allnut and Mike Coslaw. He planned to write about his trips to the past. [*11/22/63*]

9 September 1978

Burt Hatlen called Stephen King about the possibility of King doing a year as a writer in residence at the University of Main. [*The Dark Tower VI: Song of Susannah*]

Saturday: The Libertyville High School Terriers' first football game of the season was an away game against the Luneburg Tigers. They lost 54–48, their first loss against Luneburg in more than twenty years. [*Christine*]

"The Gunslinger" (collected in *The Dark Tower I: The Gunslinger*) appeared in the October issue (#329; Volume 55, Number 4) of *Fantasy and Science Fiction*. [*The Dark Tower VI: Song of Susannah*]

9 September 1979

The Dead Zone entered *The New York Times* Fiction Best Seller List at number 8. It was on the List for thirty-two weeks.

9 September 1981

Stephen King started *IT* in Bangor, ME.

9 September 1982

10:00 a.m.: To delay his going to the Shop's Maui compound, Andy McGee pushed Dr. Pynchot into recommending another three-month series of tests. [*Firestarter*]

Annie Wilkes's trial for the murder of Girl Christopher began in Denver, CO. During the trial, Letters to the Editor called her the Dragon Lady; the name stuck throughout the trial. The only evidence was a hand mark and ring mark like Annie's. [*Misery*]

9 September 1990

Dayna Jurgens was discovered as a spy. To escape Randall Flagg's torture, she killed herself with a piece of glass from a window she had tried to jump through. She died before she could tell him who the third Free Zone spy was. [*The Stand: The Complete & Uncut Edition*]

The Stand: The Complete & Uncut Edition stayed at number 5 on *The New York Times* Fiction Best Seller List, its eighteenth week on the List.

9 September 2012

A Face in the Crowd entered *The New York Times* E-Book Fiction Best Seller List at number 17, its only week on the List.

9 September 2018

The Outsider dropped to number 5 on *The New York Times* Hardcover Fiction Best Seller List, its fourteenth week on the List.

September 10

10 September 1947

Andy Dufresne, upset at his wife's affair, decided to confront her and her lover. He had three whiskeys in three minutes at the Falmouth Hills Country Club bar. As he left, he told the bartender he was going to Glenn Quentin's place and his actions would be in the morning newspaper. After about three hours of drinking beer and smoking in his car outside Quentin's bungalow, he decided his wife could have the guy and left. Elwood Blatch killed Linda Dufresne and Glenn Quentin while burgling Quentin's bungalow. Andy was convicted for the murders. ["Rita Hayworth and Shawshank Redemption"]

10 September 1958, Wednesday

George Amberson's first timeline: For $315 cash, George Amberson bought a cherry-red 1954 Ford Sunliner convertible from Bill Titus's used-car lot in Lisbon Falls, ME. He drove to Derry, ME, passing Bowers produce stand. In his third-floor room at Derry Town House, he found ninety-six Dunnings in the phone book.

George Amberson's second timeline: George Amberson bought the 1954 Ford Sunliner for $300. He was still wearing a shirt he had bought in his first timeline; he bought it again. [*11/22/63*]

10 September 1983, Saturday

Jud Crandall took the Creeds—Louis, Rachel, Ellie, and Gage—to see the Pet Sematary. Death started to become real to Ellie. [*Pet Sematary*]

10 September 1990

Julie Lawry recognized Tom Cullen in Las Vegas. He left before she told anybody. [*The Stand: The Complete & Uncut Edition*]

Stephen King started *Insomnia*.

10 September 1993, Friday morning

Insomniac Ralph Roberts's wake-up time was 2:30 a.m., with about three hours' sleep.

The Friends of Life demonstrated in front of WomanCare to protest Susan Day's coming to speak. After being questioned at Derry Police Headquarters, most were released. Ed Deepneau and five others were arrested and charged with malicious mischief, a misdemeanor. Ed was released on his own recognizance. Anne Rivers, a *News at Noon* reporter on Channel 4, interviewed him outside the police station. [*Insomnia*]

10 September 1995

Rose Madder rose to number 10 on *The New York Times* Fiction Best Seller List, its eleventh week on the List.

10 September 2008

The Dark Tower: Treachery #1 of 6 (Marvel Comics, $3.99) published

The Stand: Captain Trips #1 of 5 (Marvel Comics, $3.99) published

10 September 2019

The Institute (Scribner, $30) published

September 11

11 September 1947

Glenn Quentin's maid found him and Linda Dufresne dead in bed. Each been shot four times. In "FOUR FOR HIM AND FOUR FOR HER," a Portland *Sun* article called suspect Andy Dufresne The Even-Steven Killer. ["Rita Hayworth and Shawshank Redemption"]

11 September 1958, Thursday

George Amberson's first timeline: Mrs. Starrett at the Derry library told George Amberson the 1950 census records had been moved to City Hall in 1954. Miss Marcia Guay at City Hall said the 1957 flood destroyed most of the records.

Late that afternoon, George walked out Kansas Street. The sound of the Glenn Miller Orchestra drew him to the Barrens. Beverly Marsh and Richie Tozier were learning to swing dance to a 78-RPM record. They saw him watching and talked with him. He learned they went to school with Tugga Dunning, the Dunnings lived on Kossuth Street, and Dunning worked at the Center Street Market. After leaving the kids, he walked to Kossuth Street and found that the Dunnings lived at #379.

George Amberson's second timeline: afternoon: George Amberson drove to Derry, ME. He checked in to Derry Town House and had dinner at the hotel's restaurant. [*11/22/63*]

11 September 1959

Lee Harvey Oswald was discharged from the Marines. [*11/22/63*]

11 September 1961, Monday, first day of school

George Amberson's second timeline: At Denholm County Consolidated High School, George Amberson organized an assembly in memory of Mimi Simmons. [*11/22/63*]

11 September 1983

Christine dropped to number 8 on *The New York Times* Fiction Best Seller List, its twenty-third week on the List.

11 September 2001, Tuesday

In a lobby beneath The Dixie Pig in New York City, tickets were sold for the terrorist event on this date. [*The Dark Tower VII: The Dark Tower*]

Abra Stone cried for hours. Her mother dreamed of Abra crying in an airplane bathroom. In what looked like blood, "11" was written on Abra's chest. Her father dreamed of Abra crying in a burning mall. "175" was on her chest.

8:46 a.m.: American Airlines Flight 11 hit the World Trade Center's North Tower.

9:03 a.m.: United Airlines Flight 175 hit the South Tower. [*Doctor Sleep*]

Most employees of the home office of Light and Bell, Insurers, on the 110th floor of the World Trade Center, died in the terrorist attack. Only Warren Anderson and Scott Staley survived because they were away from the office. Almost a year later, things the deceased left behind at the office appeared in Staley's apartment. ["The Things They Left Behind"]

From Sinatra Park, the True Knot watched the aftermath and inhaled the steam from those who died. [*Doctor Sleep*]

September 12

12 September 1915, Sunday

Ellen Rimbauer and Sukeena took April Rimbauer to Madame Lu, hoping the Great Lady could help April, who stopped speaking seven months earlier. Madame Lu explained that Douglas Posey had gone to the other side, where he communicated—without using his mouth—with her from. April was OK after this. [*The Diary of Ellen Rimbauer: My Life at Rose Red*]

12 September 1958, Friday

<u>George Amberson's first timeline</u>: George Amberson picked up some apples, oranges, and a few other things at the Center Street Market. He saw that Frank Dunning was the head butcher. That evening, he sat on a bench by the Canal and watched the Market.

6:45 p.m.: Market employees left the store. Dunning caught the bus near the Market, George down the street. Dunning got off at the corner of Witcham Street and Charity Avenue; he went into EDNA PRICE ROOMS on Charity Avenue. George got off two stops farther.

<u>George Amberson's second timeline</u>: George Amberson rented the same Harris Avenue apartment he had rented in his first timeline. [*11/22/63*]

12 September 1968

Dr. Wanless recommended testing Lot Six on college students. Lot Six is a name for DLT, dilysergic triune acid, a synthetic pituitary extract. This little-understood substance caused telekinesis, thought transference, and mental domination by altering the chromosome structure and the pituitary gland composition. Its unclassified description was a mild hallucinogenic and hypnotic. [*Firestarter*]

12 September 1980

"Carrie: the Black Dawn of TK," by Jack Gaver, appeared in the September 12th issue of *Esquire* magazine. It covered Estelle Horan's account of the Stone Incident (17 August 1966). [*Carrie*]

12 September 1981

Morgan Sloat had two men from The Territories kill Tommy Woodbine. In a black van with "Wild Child" written on the side, they ran him down. He died on La Cienega Boulevard in Los Angeles, CA. [*The Talisman*]

12 September 1982

Dr. Pynchot requested another series of Andy McGee tests. [*Firestarter*]

Different Seasons dropped to number 2 on *The New York Times* Fiction Best Seller List, its sixth week on the List.

12 September 1983, Monday

Tremont Withers, driving too fast on the University of Maine at Orono campus, hit Victor Pascow, who was jogging with his fiancée and a friend. Pascow was taken to the UMO Student Medical Center, where Louis Creed treated his severe head injuries. Pascow gave Creed a vague warning about the Pet Sematary then died. They became linked because Louis was close when Victor's soul discorporated. This was Judy DeLessio's and Carla Shavers's first day on the job as University Medical Services candy stripers. Carla returned to keep her job; Judy didn't. The police arrested Withers for vehicular manslaughter, driving while intoxicated, and negligent driving. [*Pet Sematary*]

12 September 1990

After Randall Flagg's men made fun of him, Trash set incendiary fuses on the fuel trucks and helicopters at Indian Springs. He ran into the desert. A fuel truck exploded. Freddy Campanari died after being badly hurt in a fire; Carl Hough was mildly burned.

Nadine Cross's Vespa motor scooter died. She walked the rest of the day. About a week earlier, she had left Harold Lauder to die after he broke his leg in a motorcycle accident caused by Randall Flagg. Harold had shot at her, but Flagg telepathically caused him to miss.

~9:00 p.m.: Randall Flagg met Nadine Cross. Wanting her to bear his son, he raped and impregnated her.

Tom Cullen left Las Vegas and headed back for the Free Zone. He traveled at night and slept during the day. [*The Stand: The Complete & Uncut Edition*]

September 13

13 September 1958, Saturday

<u>George Amberson's second timeline</u>: George bought a Colt .38 Police Special revolver for $10 at Machen's Sporting Goods. [*11/22/63*]

13 September 1981

Cujo stayed at number 1 on *The New York Times* Fiction Best Seller List, its fifth week on the List.

13 September 1982

Dr. Patrick Hockstetter allowed Dr. Pynchot six to eight more weeks of Andy McGee testing. [*Firestarter*]

13 September 1983, Tuesday

The dead Victor Pascow took Louis Creed to the Pet Sematary and warned him never to go over the deadfall, which turned into a pile of writhing bones. Later that morning, Louis thought it was a dream until he saw dirt and pine needles on his feet and bed. That afternoon, he dismissed it as sleepwalking. [*Pet Sematary*]

13 September 1987

Misery stayed at number 3 on *The New York Times* Fiction Best Seller List, its fifteenth week on the List.

13 September 1990

Nick Andros visited Tom Cullen in a dream and told him to be careful because Randall Flagg's men were going after him. [*The Stand: The Complete & Uncut Edition*]

13 September 1992

Gerald's Game stayed at number 1 on *The New York Times* Fiction Best Seller List, its ninth week on the List.

September 14

14 September 1965

"NEW HAMPSHIRE UFO SIGHTINGS MOUNT; Most Sightings in Exeter Area; Some Residents Express Fear of Alien Invasion" appeared in the Portland, ME, *Press-Herald*. [*Dreamcatcher*]

14 September 1980

Firestarter stayed at number 2 on *The New York Times* Fiction Best Seller List, its fourth week on the List.

14 September 1983, Wednesday

Rachel Creed wanted to keep Ellie Creed's cat, Winston Churchill, from wandering in the truck-busy road. She dropped him off at Dr. Quentin L. Jolander's office to be neutered. [*Pet Sematary*]

14 September 1986

IT entered *The New York Times* Fiction Best Seller List at number 1. *IT* was on the List for thirty-five weeks.

14 September 1990

After Nadine Cross reminded Randall Flagg how his operation was failing, he threw her through the M-G-M Grand Hotel's penthouse window. She and his unborn son died. [*The Stand: The Complete & Uncut Edition*]

14 September 1999

Hearts in Atlantis (Scribner, $28) published with a first printing of 1,750,000 copies

14 September 2010

He Is Legend: An Anthology Celebrating Richard Matheson (Tor Books, $21.99), with "Throttle," by Joe Hill and Stephen King, published

14 September 2011

Foreword to *The Dark Tower 4.5: The Wind Through the Keyhole*

The Stand: Night Has Come #2 of 6 (Marvel Comics, $3.99) published

14 September 2013

Stephen King finished *Mr. Mercedes*.

September 15

15 September 1962, Saturday

George Bouhe introduced Lee Harvey Oswald to George de Mohrenschildt. They talked about Russia, socialism, Cuba, General Edwin Walker, and America's (not Kennedy's) desire to stop Cuba's socialist ways. Oswald said he had started a Hands Off Cuba protest group. [*11/22/63*]

15 September 1975

Shawshank State Prison inmate Red received a postcard from escapee Andy Dufresne. It was sent from McNary, TX. Red, who was close to Andy in prison, started writing the story of Andy Dufresne. ["Rita Hayworth and Shawshank Redemption"]

Kevin Delevan was born in Castle Rock, ME. ["The Sun Dog"]

15 September 1985

Skeleton Crew stayed at number 3 on *The New York Times* Fiction Best Seller List, its thirteenth week on the List.

15 September 1986

IT (Viking, $22.95) published with a first printing of 800,000 to 1,000,000 copies

15 September 1990

Glen Bateman, Ralph Brentner, Kojak, Stu Redman, and Larry Underwood found The Kid's body near the Eisenhower Tunnel. He seemed to have been attacked by wolves, so they called him The Wolfman. [*The Stand: The Complete & Uncut Edition*]

For his birthday, Kevin Delevan got a pair of mittens his sister knitted, $10 from his grandmother, a string tie and clasp from Aunt Hilda, and a Polaroid Sun 660 camera from his parents. No matter what he took a picture of, the resulting photograph was always the same outdoor scene of a dog. The Sun dog was shown from behind, near a picket fence. Each picture differed slightly from the one before. Kevin had bad feelings about them. ["The Sun Dog"]

15 September 1991

For his birthday, Kevin Delevan got a $1,700 WordStar 70 laptop PC and a word processing software package. He typed into the computer. It responded with a message that the Sun dog was after him again. ["The Sun Dog"]

15 September 1994

Insomnia (Viking, $27.95) published with a first printing of 1,300,000 to 1,500,000 copies

15 September 1996

After a week off, *The Green Mile, Part One: The Two Dead Girls* re-entered *The New York Times* Paperback Fiction Best Seller List for the third time. Its twenty-first week on the List, it was at number 12.

After four weeks off, *The Green Mile, Part Two: The Mouse on the Mile* re-entered *The New York Times* Paperback Fiction Best Seller List at number 14, its fifteenth week on the List.

After a week off, *The Green Mile, Part Three: Coffey's Hands* re-entered *The New York Times* Paperback Fiction Best Seller List at number 15, its fourteenth week on the List.

The Green Mile, Part Four: The Bad Death of Eduard Delacroix rose to number 10 on *The New York Times* Paperback Fiction Best Seller List, its eleventh week on the List.

The Green Mile, Part Five: Night Journey dropped to number 4 on *The New York Times* Paperback Fiction Best Seller List, its fifth week on the List.

The Green Mile, Part Six: Coffey on the Mile entered *The New York Times* Paperback Fiction Best Seller List at number 1. It was on the List for nine weeks.

15 September 2001

Stephen King and Peter Straub's *Black House* (Random House, $28.95) published with a first printing of 2,000,000 copies

15 September 2013

Joyland dropped to number 13 on *The New York Times* Paperback Trade Fiction Best Seller List, its thirteenth week on the List.

September 16

16 September 1789

Robert Boone gave Philip Boone a copy of *De Vermis Mysteriis*. Philip, who worshiped with James Boon, gave it to James. The book contained the secret of The Worm; only five copies existed in the United States. Boone got it through Johns and Goodfellow, a Boston company that acquired obscure books. ["Jerusalem's Lot"]

16 September 1958, Tuesday

<u>George Amberson's first timeline</u>: For $65 a month, George Amberson rented a partially furnished apartment on Harris Avenue. Since he paid three months in advance, Mrs. Joplin, the landlady, didn't mind that he had no references. [*11/22/63*]

16 September 1975, Tuesday

Kurt Barlow arrived at the Portland Harbor.

Ben Mears met Susan Norton in the park. They went to a movie that night.

Doc, Win Purinton's black, half cocker spaniel had white patches around the eyes. Richard Straker killed Doc because a dog with white eyes kept vampires away. [*'Salem's Lot*]

16 September 1978, Saturday

The Ridge Rock Bears beat the Libertyville High football Terriers 40–6. Norman Aleppo broke his arm, and Fred Dann suffered a concussion. Dennis Guilder scored the Terriers' six points in this home game. [*Christine*]

16 September 1979

The Dead Zone rose to number 5 on *The New York Times* Fiction Best Seller List, its second week on the List.

16 September 1983, Friday

The Creeds picked up Winston Churchill from Dr. Jolander's office. [*Pet Sematary*]

16 September 1990

Glen Bateman, Ralph Brentner, Kojak, Stu Redman, and Larry Underwood found Harold Lauder's body.

Ace High, Jenny Engstrom, Whitney Horgan, and Ronnie Sykes planned to leave Randall Flagg and Las Vegas. [*The Stand: The Complete & Uncut Edition*]

The Stand: The Complete & Uncut Edition dropped to number 6 on *The New York Times* Fiction Best Seller List, its nineteenth week on the List.

Four Past Midnight entered *The New York Times* Fiction Best Seller List at number 1. It was on the List for twenty-two weeks.

16 September 1992

Notes to *Nightmares & Dreamscapes*

16 September 2007

When Dr. John Bonsaint brought back the eighth stone at Ackerman's Field, he saw a three-lobed eye. He considered suicide to lock the eighth stone in place. ["N."]

16 September 2018

The Outsider rose to number 4 on *The New York Times* Hardcover Fiction Best Seller List, its fifteenth week on the List.

September 17

17 September 1958, Wednesday

<u>George Amberson's first timeline</u>: George moved into the Harris Avenue apartment he rented the day before. [*11/22/63*]

17 September 1973, Monday

Eddie Parks had Dev Jones wax the Horror House ride's cars. When he finished, he walked along the tracks to the double-S curve where the Funhouse Killer had murdered Linda Gray. He didn't see her, but he felt something; the air was colder, and he heard a long, slow, unhuman sigh. Then nothing.

On his way back home along the beach, he saw Annie Ross struggling to fly a kite for Mike, her son. At Mike's insistence, she agreed to let Dev try. He held the kite into the wind, which caught it. The kite felt alive to Mike, who held the string. Mike asked his mother whether Dev could stay for dinner. Seeing she'd rather not, Dev politely declined. She asked him to stop by for a smoothie on his way to work the next morning. [*Joyland*]

17 September 1975, Wednesday

10:00 a.m.: With a lucky break, new kid Mark Petrie beat Stanley Street Elementary School bully Richie Boddin in a fight.

6:00–7:15 p.m.: Ben Mears had dinner with the Nortons.

7:30 p.m.: Danny Glick and Ralphie Glick went to see Mark Petrie. On the way, Richard Straker kidnapped Ralphie and bled Danny.

~10:30 p.m.: Danny returned home, remembering nothing.

11:59 p.m.: In Harmony Hill Cemetery, Richard Straker sacrificed Ralphie to the Dark Father for Kurt Barlow's admittance into Jerusalem's Lot, ME. [*'Salem's Lot*]

17 September 1981, Thursday

Jack Sawyer had to travel west to get the Talisman to save his mother and another woman. Speedy Parker gave him a road atlas, a bottle of magic juice to help him flip between the two worlds, and a guitar pick. Because the Territories was smaller than the US, Speedy recommended traveling there as much as possible. The guitar pick (a tooth with gold in The Territories) was for the Captain of the Outer Guards. He would let Jack see Laura DeLoessian, the other woman Jack was going to try to save. In the Territories, Captain Farren, loyal to the Queen of the Territories, helped Jack get into the summer palace to see the Queen. They said Jack was his son, Lewis Farren. Afterward, Captain Farren gave Jack a special Territories coin, which became a 1921 silver dollar in our world, and showed him the Outpost Road, heading west. In our world, Jack used Lewis Farren as a traveling name. [*The Talisman*]

17 September 1990

Mr. Baker, Kevin Delevan's teacher, referred Kevin to Pop Merrill to check his camera. ["The Sun Dog"]

4:00 a.m.: Trash found an atomic bomb with A161410USAF stamped on it at Nellis Air Force Range.

Tom Cullen spent the day in Gunlock, UT. Glen Bateman, Ralph Brentner, Kojak, Stu Redman, and Larry Underwood camped near Grand Junction, CO. They had traveled 362.4

miles since leaving the Free Zone. [*The Stand: The Complete & Uncut Edition*]

17 September 1995

Rose Madder dropped to number 14 on *The New York Times* Fiction Best Seller List, its twelfth week on the List.

17 September 2013, Tuesday

Abra Stone saw Bradley Trevor in the HAVE YOU SEEN ME? column on the back page of *The Anniston Shopper*. With her left hand, she touched his picture. She followed him from the moment he left the cornfield and got in Barry the Chink's RV. A line of RVs went to an old, rundown factory. She had already seen what happened when they took him around back.

late afternoon: Abra Stone found herself in Rose the Hat's head in Sam's Supermarket. Rose felt her presence and jumped into the conduit, into the girl that was in her head. Rose was knocked down in the supermarket when the girl screamed to force her out of her head. Rose recognized her as the looker when she tortured Bradley Trevor. The girl was much more powerful than Rose thought back then. Instead of killing her to harvest her steam all at once, Rose wanted to capture the girl and milk her steam for years. She was also irked that the girl pushed her out of her head so easily. The girl needed to be taught a lesson. While she was in Abra's head, Rose heard the thought that the kids called it Lickety-Spliff. Through a window, she saw mountains.

When Abra Stone forced Rose out of her head, she caused what seemed to be a small earthquake, local to Richland Court in Anniston, NH. It cracked Dane Borland's driveway. Cassie and Matt Renfrew threw an Earthquake Barbecue. Almost everyone on Richland Court attended. [*Doctor Sleep*]

17 September 2014

The Dark Tower: The Drawing of the Three—The Prisoner #2 of 5 (Marvel Comics, $3.99) published

September 18

18 September 1958, Thursday, 12:00 p.m.

<u>George Amberson's first timeline</u>: George went to Machen's Sporting Goods and bought a Colt .38 Police Special for $9.99. [*11/22/63*]

18 September 1973, Tuesday, ~7:00 a.m.

On the boardwalk, Annie Ross served smoothies with fresh strawberries and homemade yogurt. Dev Jones brought blueberry muffins and croissants from Betty's Bakery. Mike Ross told him about his medical condition. Mike also told him, "it's not white," but didn't know what that meant. [*Joyland*]

18 September 1983

Christine stayed at number 8 on *The New York Times* Fiction Best Seller List, its twenty-fourth week on the List.

18 September 1989

A McKee, KY, high school senior took eleven students hostage for about nine hours. Although two shots had been fired, no one was hurt. He surrendered an hour and a half after releasing the last two hostages. Police found a copy of *Rage* in his bedroom. Stephen King felt that a disturbed individual was responsible, not his fiction.

18 September 1990

4:00 p.m.: Kevin Delevan took his camera and the twenty-eight pictures he had snapped to Pop Merrill. Pop couldn't find anything wrong. He asked Kevin to take thirty more pictures at specific times and bring all fifty-eight back in a few days. He gave Kevin $12 toward film. Just before he left, Kevin saw the photographer's shadow in the pictures. He told Pop. ["The Sun Dog"]

Glen Bateman, Ralph Brentner, Kojak, Stu Redman, and Larry Underwood spent the night in Loma, CO, near the Colorado-Utah border. [*The Stand: The Complete & Uncut Edition*]

18 September 2010

"NONAGENARIAN WOUK TO PUBLISH NEW BOOK," by Motoko Rich, appeared in *The New York Times*. The article reported that ninety-four-year-old Herman Wouk was to publish a book-length essay the next year.

After winning $2,700 in the Pick-3 lottery, Brenda took old friend Jasmine and their combined seven children on a road trip up I-95 to their hometown of Mars Hill, ME, to see their folks. After she loosened up with Allen's Coffee Brandy, Brenda wondered aloud how fast the new red Chevy Express rental van from Hertz could go. When Jasmine suggested she find out, she accelerated to almost 100 MPH before veering into the breakdown lane, crossing the entrance ramp to the Mile 109 rest area near Fairfield, ME, and crashing into a tree. All nine people on board were killed.

On their way to a poetry festival at the University of Maine at Orono, semiretired poets Pauline Enslin and Phil Henreid stopped at the rest area for a picnic lunch. After eating, Phil read Pauline's poem, then she read his. Phil saw the accident as Pauline read his poem. ["Herman Wouk Is Still Alive"]

18 September 2011

Mile 81 entered *The New York Times* E-Book Fiction Best Seller List at number 10. It was on the List for twelve weeks.

September 19

19 September 1945

Gatlin, NE, child Isaac Renfrew was born William Renfrew. ["Children of the Corn"]

19 September 1958, Friday evening

George Amberson's first timeline: Frank Dunning went to The Lamplighter on Witcham Street and sat at Tony Tracker's table. George Amberson followed and sat at the bar. Chaz Frati talked with him. George didn't know Chaz's friendliness was at Bill Turcotte's request, to find out what George was up to concerning Frank Dunning. [*11/22/63*]

19 September 1964, dusk

Isaac Renfrew was sacrificed to He Who Walks Behind the Rows. ["Children of the Corn"]

19 September 1965

"ENORMOUS OBJECT SIGHTED NEAR EXETER WAS OPTICAL ILLUSION; Air Force Investigators Refute State Police Sighting; Officer Cleland Adamant: 'I Know What I Saw'" appeared in the Manchester, NH, *Union-Leader*. [*Dreamcatcher*]

19 September 1982

Different Seasons dropped to number 3 on *The New York Times* Fiction Best Seller List, its seventh week on the List.

19 September 1986

Stephen King finished *The Drawing of the Three*. He got drunk and stoned to celebrate. [*The Dark Tower VI: Song of Susannah*]

19 September 1990

Glen Bateman, Ralph Brentner, Kojak, Stu Redman, and Larry Underwood spent the night in Harley Dome, UT. Randall Flagg sent his Eye to check on them; they felt Something. [*The Stand: The Complete & Uncut Edition*]

19 September 1993

Umney's Last Case e-book (The Online Bookstore, $5.00) published (collected in *Nightmares & Dreamscapes*)

19 September 1996

Allen Symes, Geological Mining Engineer for the Deep Earth Mining Corporation at the China Pit copper mine in Desperation, NV, died of a heart attack. [*The Regulators*]

19 September 2010

"9 DIE IN HORRIFIC I-95 CRASH; Spontaneous Mourning at Scene," by Ray Dugan, appeared in The Portland *Press Herald*. A one-vehicle accident on I-95, near Mile 109 in Fairfield, ME, left two adults and seven children dead. Within six hours, the Mile 109 picnic area had nine crosses. An "ANGELS GATHER HERE" sign marked where the two youngest children were found. ["Herman Wouk Is Still Alive"]

19 September 2012

The Dark Tower: The Gunslinger—Man in Black #4 of 5 (Marvel Comics, $3.99) published

19 September 2013, Thursday

Andrew Gould's article, "'POCKET EARTHQUAKE' REPORTED IN ANNISTON," appeared in the *Union-Leader*. Andrew Sittenfeld, spokesman for the Geological Survey Center in Wrentham, MA, said there was no earthquake activity in the region on Tuesday afternoon. What the residents felt was probably a sewer-system event or a military plane breaking the sound barrier. [*Doctor Sleep*]

September 20

20 September 1917

Andy Dufresne was born. ["Rita Hayworth and Shawshank Redemption"]

20 September 1981

Cujo stayed at number 1 on *The New York Times* Fiction Best Seller List, its sixth week on the List.

20 September 1982

In the Shop's first Charlie McGee test, she burned wood chips. Later, in the second test, she burned more wood chips. [*Firestarter*]

20 September 1987

Misery dropped to number 5 on *The New York Times* Fiction Best Seller List, its sixteenth week on the List.

20 September 1992

Gerald's Game dropped to number 3 on *The New York Times* Fiction Best Seller List, its tenth week on the List.

20 September 1993

Mike Hanlon offered Helen Deepneau a job at the Derry Public Library. She'd be the Children's Library assistant in the afternoons and evenings. [*Insomnia*]

September 21

21 September 1859, 1:10 p.m.

Two hundred feet down the Rattlesnake Number One shaft, the Diablo Mining Company broke into a chamber containing thousands of *can tahs*—statues of coyotes, rats, spiders, and wolves. All had absorbed evil from Tak's *ini* at the center of the chamber. Those miners who touched the *can tahs*, and those closest to them, became crazed and violent, attacking one another. Ch'an Lushan and Shih Lushan looked into the chamber but didn't touch anything. They headed out; a foreman with a gun told them to get back to work. Ch'an held him while Shih disarmed and shot him. Sixty feet from the mine's entrance, the brothers, working for God, dug at the shaft's roof to bring it down. Yuan Ti, possessed by Tak, ran out of the shaft. Shih shot him several times. The roof came down after Shih removed a crossbar support. Other cave-ins trapped Tak in its *ini*. Like the other miners, the Luchans went crazy, but it took longer. They lived in the desert, eating small animals for which they had an extraordinary, new knack of summoning. Almost two weeks later, crazed, the Lushans went to the Lady Day Saloon. Shih waved the foreman's empty gun; the miner patrons attacked the Lushans. Ch'an was shot six times then hanged two days later. Shih was stabbed to death, but the popular story was that Henry Brophy cut his throat by throwing a playing card at him. [*Desperation*]

21 September 1947

Stephen King was born. [*The Dark Tower VI: Song of Susannah*]

21 September 1963, 1:30–6:00 p.m.

Carrie White, to her mother's surprise and screams heard by several nearby neighbors, was born at home—47 Carlin Street, Chamberlain, ME 02249. Margaret White hadn't known she was pregnant; she thought she had cancer.

Ralph White, Carrie's father, died seven months before her birth. She was raised in a single-parent, fundamentalist Baptist household. A four-foot, bloodily detailed crucifix and righteous-wrath pictures throughout the house caused many nightmares. Punishment included being locked in a closet to pray for several hours up to an entire day. Perhaps because of this upbringing, Carrie was subjected to constant pranks, practical jokes, and cruelties throughout her school career.

Carrie, offspring of two parents, each having a recessive TK gene, had a dominant TK gene. Said to occur in people under extreme psychic stress, telekinesis is the ability to move objects with the mind, without physical means. During the year after her birth, she dangled her bottle in midair over her crib. Thinking Carrie was possessed by the same Devil's Power as Carrie's great-grandmother, Sadie Cochran, Margaret tried to kill her. Somehow, Carrie's father, Ralph, saved her from beyond the grave. [*Carrie*]

21 September 1978

The Rocky Mountain *News* mentioned Laura D. Rothberg's death at Denver Receiving Hospital. Nobody knew Annie Wilkes killed her. [*Misery*]

21 September 1980

Firestarter stayed at number 2 on *The New York Times* Fiction Best Seller List, its fifth week on the List.

21 September 1986

IT stayed at number 1 on *The New York Times* Fiction Best Seller List, *IT*'s second week on the List.

21 September 1989, ~10:00 a.m.

While Stephen King wrote at his word processor, Bangor House of Flowers delivered a dozen roses from Dave and Sandy Mansfield for his forty-second birthday. He became interested in a rose and wanted to return to writing *The Dark Tower*. He thought of a name for a bookstore: The Manhattan Restaurant of the Mind. [*The Dark Tower VI: Song of Susannah*]

21 September 1990

Glen Bateman, Ralph Brentner, Kojak, Stu Redman, and Larry Underwood passed through Sego, UT. [*The Stand: The Complete & Uncut Edition*]

21 September 1993

Ralph Roberts's hyper-reality experience deepened. From people's auras, he could read information, such as their names and what's been going on with their families. Unconsciously, he sucked aural energy from people; he looked and felt better. Aural energy reversed the effects of aging—hair colored and thickened, skin tightened, wrinkles smoothed, teeth became fuller, etc. [*Insomnia*]

21 September 1997

The Dark Tower IV: Wizard and Glass (Donald M. Grant edition) entered *The New York Times* Fiction Best Seller List at number 12, its only week on the List.

21 September 2004

The Dark Tower VII: The Dark Tower (Donald M. Grant, $35) published with a first printing of 700,000 copies

21 September 2013

Abra Stone met with Dan Torrance outside the Anniston Public Library. She learned that her gifts were called a shining. She filled him in on what had happened to Bradley Trevor. Barry the Chink had worn Trevor's baseball glove, and they buried it with his body. She said she could find Barry the Chink if she could touch the glove.

Jimmy Numbers researched Lickety-Splits that had views of mountains. He and Rose the Hat narrowed Abra Stone's probable location to Fryeburg, ME, Madison, NH, or Anniston, NH. [*Doctor Sleep*]

September 22

22 September 1960, Thursday

<u>George Amberson's second timeline</u>: George Amberson found an apartment on Blackwell Street in North Dallas. He didn't like the racist attitude of Mr. Ray Mack Johnson, the owner-landlord. [*11/22/63*]

22 September 1973, Saturday afternoon

Because it rained that weekend, Dev Jones stayed in to read *The Lord of the Rings: The Return of the King*. Mrs. Shoplaw asked whether he'd like to play Scrabble with her and Tina Ackerley. He didn't like Scrabble but said he'd be happy to. Miss Ackerley won. [*Joyland*]

22 September 1975, Monday

~4:00 a.m.: With a preliminary diagnosis of delayed emotional shock, Danny Glick was admitted into Central Maine General. A later diagnosis was pernicious anemia.

6:58 p.m.: Hank Peters and Royal Snow took a Hepplewhite sideboard crate (with Kurt Barlow's coffin) from the Portland Docks' Customs House Wharf to the Marsten House. Hank saw Ralphie Glick's clothes in the basement. [*'Salem's Lot*]

22 September 1985

Skeleton Crew dropped to number 4 on *The New York Times* Fiction Best Seller List, its fourteenth week on the List.

22 September 1990

Glen Bateman, Ralph Brentner, Kojak, Stu Redman, and Larry Underwood spent the night near Green River, UT. [*The Stand: The Complete & Uncut Edition*]

22 September 1992

The Grant edition of *The Waste Lands* had sold out.

Stephen King had an idea about a woman who buys a picture and falls into it—into Mid-World. [*The Dark Tower VI: Song of Susannah*]

22 September 1996

The Green Mile, Part One: The Two Dead Girls stayed at number 12 on *The New York Times* Paperback Fiction Best Seller List, its twenty-second week on the List.

The Green Mile, Part Two: The Mouse on the Mile dropped to number 15 on *The New York Times* Paperback Fiction Best Seller List, its sixteenth week on the List.

The Green Mile, Part Three: Coffey's Hands rose to number 14 on *The New York Times* Paperback Fiction Best Seller List, its fifteenth and last week on the List.

The Green Mile, Part Four: The Bad Death of Eduard Delacroix dropped to number 13 on *The New York Times* Paperback Fiction Best Seller List, its twelfth week on the List.

The Green Mile, Part Five: Night Journey stayed at number 4 on *The New York Times* Paperback Fiction Best Seller List, its sixth week on the List.

The Green Mile, Part Six: Coffey on the Mile stayed at number 1 on *The New York Times* Paperback Fiction Best Seller List, its second week on the List.

22 September 1998

Bag of Bones (Scribner, $28) published with a first printing of 1,260,000 to 1,750,000 copies

22 September 2010

The Dark Tower: The Gunslinger—The Journey Begins #5 of 5 (Marvel Comics, $3.99) published

22 September 2013, Sunday

Walnut identified a drug the True Knot could use to keep the girl they were after [Abra Stone] knocked out but not cause an overdose. Jimmy Numbers found the September 19th article about the small earthquake on Richland Court in Anniston, NH. Rose the Hat was 80% sure it was her girl. [*Doctor Sleep*]

Joyland stayed at number 13 on *The New York Times* Paperback Trade Fiction Best Seller List, its fourteenth week on the List.

September 23

23 September 1909

While Ellen Rimbauer and Sukeena strolled Rose Red's halls with Adam Rimbauer, they saw Laura Hirtson's spirit, with her blouse open and her skirt missing. Ellen and Sukeena investigated Laura's disappearance and found her skirt behind a horse blanket in the hay wagon's stall in the Carriage House. They saw images of Laura being raped in the wagon. Although they saw only Laura, not her attacker, Ellen was sure it was Daniel. They saw John Rimbauer return home and talk with Daniel. Laura appeared again and pointed to the two men. [*The Diary of Ellen Rimbauer: My Life at Rose Red*]

23 September 1922, Saturday afternoon

Sallie Cotterie discovered her daughter, Shannon, was pregnant when she saw her drying after a shower. Harlan Cotterie arranged with Sister Camilla to have Shannon sent to St. Eusebia Catholic Home for Girls in Omaha, NE. She could return home after the baby was born and put up for adoption. ["1922"]

23 September 1960, Friday

George Amberson's second timeline: George Amberson left Dallas for a five-room house, with central air conditioning and a garage, in Jodie, TX. At Al's Diner that evening, he introduced himself to Deke Simmons and Mimi Corcoran, who invited him to join them. By the end of their conversation, Mimi had hired him as a substitute teacher, with a full-time position when Phil Bateman retired. [*11/22/63*]

23 September 1978, Saturday

The Libertyville High School Terriers' third football game of the season was at home against the Philadelphia City Dragons. The Terriers lost. [*Christine*]

23 September 1979

The Dead Zone rose to number 3 on *The New York Times* Fiction Best Seller List, its third week on the List.

23 September 1981, Wednesday

After washing dishes for Minette Binberry at the Golden Spoon in Auburn, Jack Sawyer hit the road. He reached Oatley, in western New York. [*The Talisman*]

23 September 1984

Stephen King started *Misery* in Lovell, ME.

23 September 1990, Monday

Kevin Delevan had taken thirty more pictures and gave all fifty-eight to Pop Merrill. Pop told him to come back with the camera on Friday. Pop said he'd ask Kevin's father to come, too. ["The Sun Dog"]

~12:00 noon: Crossing a washed-out section of I-70 in Utah, Stu Redman fell and broke his right leg in several places. All agreed that Glen Bateman, Ralph Brentner, and Larry Underwood should continue without him. They splinted his leg, and Glen left a bottle of morphine-based pills, three to four of which would be enough to kill him. Kojak stayed with Stu; the others went west another sixteen miles and camped for the night. Kojak caught a rabbit for Stu. [*The Stand: The Complete & Uncut Edition*]

The Stand: The Complete & Uncut Edition dropped to number 8 on *The New York Times* Fiction Best Seller List, its twentieth week on the List.

Four Past Midnight stayed at number 1 on *The New York Times* Fiction Best Seller List, its second week on the List.

23 September 1993

A conflict between the Friends of Life and a pro-choice group near WomanCare and Derry Home Hospital resulted in fifteen arrests on each side, including Ed Deepneau's. [*Insomnia*]

23 September 1997

Screamplays, edited by Richard Chizmar (Del Rey, $14.50), with "General," published

23 September 2012, afternoon

With his family by his side, Goldman Sachs investment banker William Andrews died of colon cancer. When the white light faded, he found himself in a hallway. He knocked at the door at the end. Mr. Isaac Harris invited him in—for the fifteenth time. They discussed events in each other's lives. Again, Isaac told Bill to choose a door. The door to Isaac's left led to Bill reliving his life, exactly as he had before. The door to Isaac's right led to the end of Bill's existence. Bill regretted four things in his life: cutting off the tip of his brother's pinky finger in an accident while playing flashlight tag, stealing a watch at the Mall of New Jersey, letting two friends have sex with Annmarie Winkler immediately after he did, and not having a colonoscopy. Although he knew there were no second chances, and he'd been through it fifteen times, he hoped he'd remember something this time, so he could fix a regret. He chose the door to Isaac's left. ["Afterlife"]

23 September 2013, Monday

1:30 a.m. MDT: After meditating for several hours, Rose found the girl she was looking for [Abra Stone] and entered her mind while she slept. Rose saw a person's mind as a set of file drawers. Abra was ready for her. When Rose opened a drawer, a loud piercing alarm went off and the drawer slammed shut on her hand, causing great pain. Abra jumped into her mind; Rose pushed her out. While Abra was in Rose, she learned what the True Knot were and that they lived on steam—the stuff that came out of kids with the shining when they died.

7:45 p.m.: Grampa Flick cycled out (died). The True Knot didn't catch rube diseases, yet Grampa Flick had caught the measles from Bradley Trevor. [*Doctor Sleep*]

23 September 2018

The Outsider dropped to number 7 on *The New York Times* Hardcover Fiction Best Seller List, its sixteenth week on the List.

September 24

24 September 1909

After hearing Sukeena's Rose Red theory, Ellen Rimbauer wanted to consult Madame Lu. The theory was that Rose Red was alive, possessed by the spirits of Indians whose graves were disturbed in Rose Red's construction. Because of its Indian heritage, men were warriors; Rose Red didn't need warriors, so any men it dealt with were killed. Women, not being warriors, lived longer and knew the history of the tribe. Rose Red took women for two purposes. First, was to learn from them. Second, it took them if they had had relations with John Rimbauer. The Rimbauers were off-limits because they continued the construction, making Rose Red bigger and stronger. [*The Diary of Ellen Rimbauer: My Life at Rose Red*]

24 September 1962

George Amberson's second timeline: George Amberson moved into Apartment 1, the bottom of a two-apartment building at 214 West Neely Street in Dallas, TX. The Oswalds rented the upstairs apartment later. [*11/22/63*]

24 September 1975, Wednesday

1:00 a.m.: A nurse found Danny Glick found dead of pernicious anemia. His red blood cell count was 45%; normal for his age was 85% to 98%. The hospital room window was open.

>3:00 p.m.: Constable Parkins Gillespie talked with newcomers Ben Mears and Richard Straker about Ralphie Glick's disappearance. Straker said Mr. Barlow was on a buying trip in New York and wouldn't be in town for a couple of weeks. [*'Salem's Lot*]

24 September 1976, Friday

Herb Smith asked Johnny Smith to be his best man. They celebrated with champagne. [*The Dead Zone*]

24 September 1981, Thursday

Jack Sawyer traveled under the name of Jack Sawtelle. Smokey Updike, owner of the Oatley Tap, paid Jack $4.90 ($9.00 minus $4.10 for food) for his first day's work (4:00 p.m. to 1:00 a.m.). Jack earned $1.00 an hour, with a noon-to-1:00 a.m. shift. [*The Talisman*]

24 September 1990

Glen Bateman, Ralph Brentner, and Larry Underwood traveled thirty miles and spent the night near San Rafael Knob. [*The Stand: The Complete & Uncut Edition*]

Four Past Midnight (Viking, $22.95) published with a first printing of 1,200,000 to 1,500,000 copies.

24 September 1995

Rose Madder stayed at number 14 on *The New York Times* Fiction Best Seller List, its thirteenth week on the List. Fifteen weeks later, *Rose Madder* appeared on the List again.

24 September 1996

Richard Bachman's *The Regulators* (Dutton, $24.95) was published with a first printing of 1,250,000 copies. Douglas Winter had confirmed the manuscript was a genuine Richard

Bachman book.

Desperation (Viking, $27.95) published with a first printing of 1,750,000 copies

24 September 2002

From a Buick 8 (Scribner, $28) published with a first printing of 1,750,000 copies

24 September 2013, Tuesday

morning: Dan Torrance and John Dalton went to Iowa to get Bradley Trevor's baseball glove.

>10:00 p.m. MDT: Crow Daddy led Barry the Chink, Jimmy Numbers, Snakebite Andi, and Walnut on a mission to capture the girl they were after [Abra Stone]. Rose the Hat wanted to milk steam from her for years. [*Doctor Sleep*]

Doctor Sleep (Scribner, $30) published with a first printing of 1,100,000 copies

September 25

25 September 1922, Monday

Harlan Cotterie was upset that Wilfred's son, Henry James, had gotten Shannon Cotterie pregnant. For $300, Harlan had sent Shannon away to have the baby. He knew Wilfred couldn't afford to split that fee but demanded Wilfred pay the $75 tutor fee to keep Shannon's studies current. ["1922"]

25 September 1975, Thursday

After dinner at the Nortons', Ben Mears and Susan Norton made love on the grass near the War Memorial in the park.

Ben met Matt Burke at Dell's tavern. ['Salem's Lot]

25 September 1983

Christine dropped to number 9 on *The New York Times* Fiction Best Seller List, its twenty-fifth week on the List.

25 September 1990

Glen Bateman, Ralph Brentner, and Larry Underwood spent the night 260 miles from Las Vegas. [*The Stand: The Complete & Uncut Edition*]

25 September 2000

The Plant Book One: *Zenith Rising*, Part 3 e-book (Philtrum Press, $1.00) published

25 September 2011

Mile 81 rose to number 4 on *The New York Times* E-Book Fiction Best Seller List, its second week on the List.

25 September 2013, Wednesday, >12:00 a.m. EDT

Dan Torrance woke up Abra Stone. She directed him to Bradley Trevor's grave. [*Doctor Sleep*]

September 26

26 September 1922, Tuesday

Wilfred James searched the house for money Arlette James may have hidden. He found $40 in the inner band of a red hat in a hat box in the bedroom closet. This left him $35 short for Shannon Cotterie's tutor fee. ["1922"]

26 September 1978, Tuesday

Leigh Cabot met Arnie Cunningham when she asked him for an English class assignment.

In the school's smoking area during lunch, Buddy Repperton smashed Arnie's lunch and pulled out an eight-inch switchblade. Arnie knocked the knife from Repperton's hand when Dennis Guilder protested that the fight wasn't fair. Repperton reached for the knife, and Arnie stomped on his hand. Don Vandenberg threw Arnie on the ground. Dennis kicked Vandenberg; Moochie Welch grabbed Dennis. Mr. Casey ended the fight. Repperton was expelled from school. [*Christine*]

26 September 1981, Saturday

Elroy, a werewolf-like creature from The Territories, stopped Jack Sawtelle (one of Jack Sawyer's traveling names) from leaving the Oatley Tap. Jack ran; Elroy ran after him. Jack escaped by flipping to the Territories. On the Western Road, he heard Morgan of Orris approach. As he flipped back to the United States, near Angola, NY, the village suffered its first earthquake. Several Speiser Construction men were killed when the Rainbird Towers condominium building collapsed. Joseph Gargan reported the collapse in the Angola *Herald*. [*The Talisman*]

26 September 1982

Different Seasons dropped to number 4 on *The New York Times* Fiction Best Seller List, its eighth week on the List.

26 September 1989

My Pretty Pony (Alfred A. Knopf, $27) published with a first printing of 15,000 copies (collected in *Nightmares & Dreamscapes*)

26 September 2013, Thursday

Jimmy Numbers showed Crow Daddy pictures of three girls from Anniston Middle School—Julianne Cross, Emma Deane, and Abra Stone. Two lived on Richland Court, one around the corner. One of these kids was the girl Rose the Hat wanted.

Barry the Chink had the measles.

Dan Torrance and John Dalton took Bradley Trevor's baseball glove to Abra Stone. She learned that several True Knot were on their way to get her. The rest of the True Knot was at the Bluebird or Bluebell Campground in Sidewinder, CO. [*Doctor Sleep*]

26 September 2017

Sleeping Beauties (Scribner, $32.50), by Stephen King and Owen King, published

September 27

27 September 1909

Tina Coleman took Ellen Rimbauer to Madame Lu's. The Great Lady couldn't help Ellen; she would need to be inside Rose Red to contact the missing women, but she couldn't leave Seattle's China district. She offered to write to Madame Stravinski, the only person she'd recommend. Madame Stravinski was in Europe, so Ellen may have had to wait years for her to be in Seattle again. [*The Diary of Ellen Rimbauer: My Life at Rose Red*]

27 September 1958, Saturday

George Amberson's first timeline: Frank Dunning went to a flea market in Brewer. George Amberson followed in a rented Hertz Chevrolet. [*11/22/63*]

27 September 1980, Saturday

On the first day of tournament play, the Pee Wee League Tigers, Georgie Bruckner's baseball team in Castle Rock, ME, were eliminated. ["Gramma"]

27 September 1981

Cujo dropped to number 2 on *The New York Times* Fiction Best Seller List, its seventh week on the List.

27 September 1983

Stephen King's *Pet Sematary* (Doubleday, $15.95) was published with a first printing of 250,000 to 340,000 copies. The list of works in the front showed *The Dark Tower*. [*The Dark Tower VI: Song of Susannah*]

27 September 1987

Misery stayed at number 5 on *The New York Times* Fiction Best Seller List, its seventeenth week on the List.

27 September 1990, Friday

~4:00 p.m.: John Delevan and Kevin Delevan arrived at Pop Merrill's. In his apartment upstairs, Pop played a videotape he had made from Kevin's pictures. The Sun dog walked, sniffed, turned around, and growled. Something was under its neck; only Kevin knew what it was. They went out back and Kevin smashed the camera with a sledgehammer. John and Kevin didn't know Pop had switched cameras. Inside, they looked at the pictures with a microscope. The Sun dog was wearing a string tie with a woodpecker clasp—the tie Aunt Hilda had given Kevin for his birthday—suggesting it was Kevin he wanted to kill once he got out of the two-dimensional picture world. They burned the pictures then went home; the tie was missing. ["The Sun Dog"]

Glen Bateman, Ralph Brentner, and Larry Underwood spent the night at Fremont Junction. [*The Stand: The Complete & Uncut Edition*]

27 September 1992

Gerald's Game stayed at number 3 on *The New York Times* Fiction Best Seller List, its eleventh week on the List.

27 September 2013, Friday

Abra Stone was in two places at once. She was in her physical body in Anniston, NH, and, through her shining, she was in Dan Torrance. David Stone and Torrance were in The Helen Rivington train on their way to Cloud Gap. The idea was to fool the sick Barry the Chink into thinking she was on a picnic with her father.

Before Barry the Chink cycled out (died), he detected the girl they wanted [Abra Stone]. She was going on a picnic with her father at Cloud Gap, near Frazier, NH. For a moment, he saw her in two places—on the picnic and in a bathroom in a house in Anniston. Aware of the possibility she was gaming them, he told Crow Daddy he was mostly sure she was in Frazier. Crow Daddy stayed in Anniston, while the others went to Frazier.

Jimmy Numbers, Snakebite Andi, and Walnut arrived at Cloud Gap. John Dalton, Dave Stone, and Dan Torrance ambushed and killed them. Dan compelled Snakebite Andi into telling him where Crow Daddy was before she died.

Abra had gone to Emma Deane's after school. Feigning her period, she excused herself and went home.

Under an oak at the end of Richland Court, Crow Daddy pretended to read *The Anniston Shopper*. Down the street, two girls he recognized as Emma Deane and Abra Stone came out of a house. Emma went back in. Abra crossed the street and gave a thumbs-up to a man sitting in a pickup truck. Thus, Abra Stone was the girl they wanted, and the man was her protection. He caught Billy Freeman off-guard and injected him; he injected Abra in her house. He took them in Billy's truck and headed west.

Crow Daddy stopped for gas. When Abra needed to use the restroom, he injected a bit more of the drug in the back of her hand.

Back on the road, Dan Torrance in Abra's body overpowered Crow Daddy and shot him with the gun in Crow Daddy's hand. Rose felt the death when Crow Daddy cycled out. No longer did she want to capture Abra Stone to milk her. She wanted to kill her.

>10:30 p.m.: Abra Stone's grandmother, Chetta Reynolds, had cancer and was in a coma in Room 9 of Massachusetts General Hospital's Intensive Care. Dan Torrance visited her and woke her enough for them to communicate via Dan's shining. Before he helped her cross over, she told him enough to confirm Dan's hypothesis that he and Lucy Stone (Abra's mother) had the same father. To save Abra, she allowed him to inhale her last essence as she died. Dan created a lockbox for it, but it leaked and made him sick. Too much could kill him. During the next couple of days, he could only keep down thin soup. [*Doctor Sleep*]

September 28

28 September 1958, Sunday

Frank Dunning took his kids to the Aladdin Theater for a Disney double feature. [*11/22/63*]

28 September 1960

George Amberson's second timeline: George Amberson had about $14,000 and thought he'd add to that with a bet. At Faith Financial on Greenville Avenue in Dallas, he placed a $600, 2–1 bet that the Pittsburgh Pirates would beat the Yankees in seven games. [*11/22/63*]

28 September 1975, Sunday

Father Callahan presided over Danny Glick's funeral, both the private family church service at St. Andrew's and the public service at Harmony Hill Cemetery. Mike Ryerson and Royal Snow had dug his grave.

6:50 p.m.: Sure that Danny's eyes had popped open, Ryerson broke the coffin's lock and raised the lid; Danny bit him. Mike fell asleep and awoke the next morning; the grave had been tidied, but he didn't remember doing it.

~9:30 p.m.: Kurt Barlow bit Dud Rogers. [*'Salem's Lot*]

28 September 1980

Firestarter reached number 1 on *The New York Times* Fiction Best Seller List, its sixth week on the List.

28 September 1986

IT stayed at number 1 on *The New York Times* Fiction Best Seller List, *IT*'s third week on the List.

28 September 1988

The Dark Tower: The Gunslinger (Plume, $10.95) published

28 September 1990, Saturday

Pop Merrill tried to sell Kevin Delevan's camera to Cedric McCarty. They took a picture of each other. When Cedric saw the resulting Sun dog pictures, he thought it was a trick and didn't want the camera. ["The Sun Dog"]

12:00 p.m.: Eight of Randall Flagg's men, including Paul Burlson and Barry Dorgan, picked Glen Bateman, Ralph Brentner, and Larry Underwood up on Route 70 and took them to Las Vegas County Jail. [*The Stand: The Complete & Uncut Edition*]

28 September 2013, Saturday

Billy Freeman and Dan Torrance headed west to confront Rose the Hat.

Abra Stone called Rose and taunted her, calling her a coward, repeatedly. Abra challenged Rose to meet her, alone, on Roof O' the World on Monday, with the rest of the True Knot out of the way in the Overlook Lodge. Rose accepted. [*Doctor Sleep*]

September 29

29 September 1980

Firestarter (Viking, $13.95) published with a first printing of 100,000 copies

29 September 1982, Wednesday

Charlie McGee produced 20,000 degrees of heat in a four-second flash in the Shop's third test of her abilities.

That night, Dr. Pynchot wore his wife's clothes and put his arm in his garbage disposal. He died. [*Firestarter*]

29 September 1985

Skeleton Crew rose to number 3 on *The New York Times* Fiction Best Seller List, its fifteenth week on the List.

29 September 1990, 10:00 a.m.

Glen Bateman died in jail when Randall Flagg ordered Lloyd Henreid to shoot him for laughing at Flagg. [*The Stand: The Complete & Uncut Edition*]

29 September 1996

The Green Mile, Part One: The Two Dead Girls dropped to number 14 on *The New York Times* Paperback Fiction Best Seller List, its twenty-third week on the List.

The Green Mile, Part Four: The Bad Death of Eduard Delacroix stayed at number 13 on *The New York Times* Paperback Fiction Best Seller List, its thirteenth week on the List.

The Green Mile, Part Five: Night Journey dropped to number 6 on *The New York Times* Paperback Fiction Best Seller List, its seventh week on the List.

The Green Mile, Part Six: Coffey on the Mile stayed at number 1 on *The New York Times* Paperback Fiction Best Seller List, its third week on the List.

29 September 2011

A Book of Horrors, edited by Stephen Jones (Jo Fletcher Books, £16.99), with "The Little Green God of Agony" (collected in *The Bazaar of Bad Dreams*), published

29 September 2013

Abra Stone called Rose the Hat to let her know her Uncle Billy would drive her to the True Knot's campground. [*Doctor Sleep*]

Joyland dropped to number 14 on *The New York Times* Paperback Trade Fiction Best Seller List, its fifteenth week on the List.

September 30

30 September

The Overlook Hotel's annual season ended. [*The Shining*]

30 September 1958

George Amberson's third timeline: After three weeks of writing, George Amberson had filled twenty-three legal pads. [*11/22/63*]

30 September 1965

"FOOD POISONING EPIDEMIC IN PLAISTON STILL UNEXPLAINED; Over 300 Affected, Most Recovering; FDA Officer Says May Have Been Contaminated Wells" appeared in the Manchester, NH, *Union-Leader*. [*Dreamcatcher*]

30 September 1975, Tuesday

Barlow and Straker—Fine Furnishings, a front for Kurt Barlow's presence in The Lot, opened.

Author Ben Mears talked to Matt Burke's Period 4 creative writing class. Ben had dinner with Matt that evening. [*'Salem's Lot*]

30 September 1977, Closing Day

Jack Torrance and his family moved into The Overlook Hotel. Jack was the winter caretaker. He planned to write "The Little School," a play.

Mrs. Brant demanded to pay her Overlook Hotel bill with American Express, a card the hotel no longer accepted. [*The Shining*]

30 September 1978, Saturday

On his first date with Leigh Cabot, Arnie Cunningham took her to the Hidden Hills-Libertyville High School football game in Hidden Hills. This was the first time Arnie had driven Christine since he had taken her to Darnell's Garage. She wasn't quite street-legal, but Will Darnell lent her an inspection sticker and a dealer license plate. The Terriers won 27–18. Dennis Guilder scored three times for the Terriers, including a ninety-yard run, his longest ever. [*Christine*]

30 September 1979

The Dead Zone rose to number 2 on *The New York Times* Fiction Best Seller List, its fourth week on the List.

30 September 1982, Thursday

Andy McGee pushed Captain Hollister for information about Charlie McGee and to take Andy to Dr. Pynchot's funeral. [*Firestarter*]

30 September 1990, morning

Randall Flagg killed Whitney Horgan for making a statement against him.

Almost dead of radiation poisoning—one eye, hair, teeth, and nails gone—The Trashcan

Man arrived in Las Vegas with the A-bomb for Randall Flagg. God detonated it, killing Stan Bailey, Ralph Brentner, Paul Burlson, Barry Dorgan, Jenny Engstrom, Ratty Erwins, Lloyd Henreid, Trash, Larry Underwood, and hundreds more. Just before the bomb went off, Flagg disappeared. Brentner Rock in the Free Zone was named as a memorial to Ralph. [*The Stand: The Complete & Uncut Edition*]

The Stand: The Complete & Uncut Edition dropped to number 9 on *The New York Times* Fiction Best Seller List, its twenty-first week on the List.

Four Past Midnight stayed at number 1 on *The New York Times* Fiction Best Seller List, its third week on the List.

30 September 2001

Black House entered *The New York Times* Fiction Best Seller List at number 1. It was on the List for fifteen weeks.

30 September 2009

The Dark Tower: Fall of Gilead #5 of 6 (Marvel Comics, $3.99) published

30 September 2013

Billy Freeman dropped Dan Torrance at a picnic area a mile past the road to the Bluebell Campground. With a mannequin that looked like a young girl, Billy drove to the parking lot. While the True Knot watched Billy, Danny Torrance and a far-seeing Abra Stone made their way to the Overlook Lodge. On the way, Dan released Horace Derwent, who was happy to be back home. Inside the Lodge, Dan let the cancerous essence of Chetta Reynolds out of the lockbox. The True Knot inhaled it as if it were steam and cycled out.

Silent Sarey couldn't become invisible, but she could become dim. Rose the Hat had her hide in a shed near Roof O' the World. If Rose needed help, she'd call on Sarey to come out and kill Abra Stone. Horace Derwent found Silent Sarey. He kissed her then strangled her.

Combining their shinings, Dan Torrance and Abra Stone overpowered Rose the Hat and pushed her off Roof O' the World. Rose landed headfirst, shattered her neck, and cycled out. [*Doctor Sleep*]

30 September 2018

The Outsider dropped to number 10 on *The New York Times* Hardcover Fiction Best Seller List, its seventeenth week on the List.

September

September 1910

Bob T. Watson hired Keystone Paving Works of Golden to pave the last twenty (of sixty) miles of road from Estes Park to The Overlook Hotel. ["Before the Play"]

September 1912

Paul Edgecombe married Janice. [*The Green Mile*]

September 1914

Rutherford, Bob T. Watson's accountant, advised bankruptcy. The Overlook Hotel's debts, not counting two mortgages, totaled $200,000, including outstanding salaries and contractor bills. ["Before the Play"]

September 1951: Fire of '51

A boy started a fire in the woods. A wind from the west spread it across the Marshes into Jerusalem's Lot. Ralph Miller led the Jerusalem's Lot Sawmill crew in building a firebreak that turned the fire south, where it was brought under control. Nobody knew a boy had started the fire that burned half the town; a stray cigarette was suspected. Two years later, the boy graduated valedictorian and landed a hundred-thousand-dollar Wall Street job. [*'Salem's Lot*]

September 1957

Roland LeBay received a new 1958 Plymouth Fury sport coupe from Norman Cobb's Plymouth dealership. It came with a 382 CID engine, dual exhaust, cruise control, Air Conditioning, Automatic Transmission, four doors, AM radio, tailfins, 120 MPH speedometer, red upholstery, whitewall tires, and six miles on the odometer. He had paid $2,100 and traded in a clunker for the $3,000 car. Chrysler didn't have the colors he wanted, so he had her custom-painted Autumn Red and ivory. He named her Christine. [*Christine*]

September 1970

Sarah Bracknell and Johnny Smith became Cleaves Mills High School teachers after graduating from UMO. They met at a freshman dance and started dating. [*The Dead Zone*]

September 1972

"Battleground" (collected in *Night Shift*) appeared in the September issue (Vol. 22, No. 11) of *Cavalier*.

September 1975

Hangtown, Roberta Anderson's second book and first Western, was published. [*The Tommyknockers*]

September 1976

Charlene MacKenzie accepted Herb Smith's marriage proposal. [*The Dead Zone*]

"I Know What You Need" (collected in *Night Shift*) appeared in the September issue of *Cosmopolitan*.

September 1977

Johnny Smith worked on the Phoenix Public Works Department road crew with Herman Joellyn and Larry McNaughton. Keith Strang was the boss. [*The Dead Zone*]

Stephen King started *Cujo*.

September 1978

Leigh Cabot and her family moved from Weston, MA, to Libertyville, PA. [*Christine*]

<u>Monday</u>: In colored ski masks, Morris Bellamy (yellow), Freddy Dow (blue), and Curtis Rogers (red) went to John Rothstein's house in Talbot Corners, NH. At gunpoint, they got the combination to Rothstein's safe. Already upset at Rothstein for selling out and making Jimmy Gold an everyday suburbanite in the trilogy's final book, Bellamy shot Rothstein in the head. They left with four duffels bags and a leather valise filled with cash and Moleskine notebooks of unpublished writing.

They drove across New Hampshire into Vermont then picked up Route 92 in upstate New York. Bellamy didn't want either ex-con to get caught on something else and offer up Morris for leniency. He killed Freddy Dow and Curtis Rogers in a rest area.

At an Ohio antiques barn, he bought a trunk for $20 to stash the Rothstein material.

He went to his childhood home, which his mother still owned but didn't live in, and ate an old Hungry Man Meatloaf dinner from the freezer.

<u>Tuesday</u>: Morris Bellamy found Andy Halliday on a coffee break outside The Happy Cup on Ellis Avenue. Rothstein's murder changed everything. It would be many years before they could sell the unpublished work. In case the police found a trail leading to Bellamy, Andy suggested he hide the loot.

Bellamy buried the trunk under a tree overhanging a stream in the undeveloped land behind his house. He planned to retrieve it a few weeks later. That night, he got drunk on Jack Daniels at Shooter's Tavern.

<u>Wednesday</u>, early a.m.: Outside the tavern, Morris Bellamy dragged Miss Cora Ann Hooper to an alley. She triggered her Police Alert and scratched him; he broke her nose and raped her. Officer Philip Ellenton pulled him off her. That afternoon, in front of Judge Bukowski, he was arraigned on three counts—resisting arrest, aggravated assault, and aggravated rape. [*Finders Keepers*]

Gwendy Peterson got her driver's license! [*Gwendy's Button Box*]

Shadows, edited by Charles L. Grant (Doubleday), with "Nona" (collected in *Skeleton Crew*), published

September 1984

full moon: The Beast disemboweled and killed eleven of Elmer Zinneman's pigs. [*Cycle of the Werewolf*]

Mike Hanlon's feeling that IT was active again became stronger when he read that Chris Unwin saw a clown under the bridge over which Adrian Mellon was thrown in July. [*IT*]

September 1985

Norman Daniels beat Rose Daniels again. To avoid future suspicions, he became creative in his beatings, so that she didn't have to go to the hospital. [*Rose Madder*]

September 1986

The Long Ride Back, Roberta Anderson's tenth Western, was published. [*The Tommyknockers*]

September 1987

The New Adventures of Sherlock Holmes: Original Stories by Eminent Mystery Writers, edited by Martin Harry Greenberg and Carol-Lynn Rossel Waugh (Carroll & Graf, $18.95), with "The Doctor's Case" (collected in *Nightmares & Dreamscapes*), published

September 1988

scheduled publication date for *Massacre Canyon*, Roberta Anderson's eleventh Western [*The Tommyknockers*]

September 1990

Daniel Landry had signs of Kaposi's sarcoma. ["Umney's Last Case"]

September 1991

Undercover federal agents almost caught Ace Merrill in a firearms scam. In the bathroom, a stranger in the next stall tipped Ace off. He sneaked out. [*Needful Things*]

September 1992

Jamie Morton played with Kelly Van Dorn's crossover country band at the Tulsa State Fair. Van Dorn fired him for missing a gig and a sound check. Looking for heroin, Jamie went to Bell's Amusement Park, next to the Fair. He found a couple of guys that looked right for scoring some dope. Around the corner, a crows and strange electric crackles attracted his attention.

As Dan Jacobs, Charlie Jacobs sold Lightning Portraits at the amusement park. His performance started with demonstrations of his Lightning Maker, which drew a crowd. He selected a pretty girl, Miss Cathy Morse, to volunteer. He sat her, blindfolded, in a chair. On the stage behind them was a twenty-foot portrait of a beautiful woman wearing a ballroom gown, diamond earrings, and bloodred lipstick. He got under the cloth cover of an old-style camera. After a flash of blue light, Cathy Morse's face, without the blindfold, replaced the beautiful woman's face on the large portrait. Through motion picture projection, the girl in the large portrait turned away from the audience, looked back at them, and winked. After a free portrait for the volunteer, he sold portraits to whoever else wanted one.

Jamie Morton fainted. He had the flu. Charlie nursed him back to health. With what looked like a pair of headphones plugged into what resembled a Marshall amplifier, Charlie Jacobs used electricity to cure Jamie's heroin addiction. Something happened. Jamie got stuck saying the two words "something" and "happened." He snapped out of it when Charlie slapped him. Charlie took Jamie on as his assistant. [*Revival*]

September 2005

"The Furnace" appeared in the September issue of *Know Your World Extra*.

September 2006

N. took his second trip to Ackerman's Field. He had hoped if he went in the middle of the day, and saw there was nothing at Ackerman's Field, he'd be OK and stop his OCD behavior. A chain, with an ABSOLUTELY NO TRESSPASSING sign (twenty-three letters—a terrible number, worse than thirteen), stretched across the dirt road. Five pines and an oak, all cut with a chainsaw, blocked the road. He parked at Serenity Ridge Cemetery and walked back up the dirt road. There was a faded area where the eighth stone belonged in the middle of the seven stones. The sky above it looked grayish, while the rest of the sky was blue. The faded area turned black, with two yellow eyes looking at him. A breeze came from the black spot. A voice spoke unrecognizable words, interspersed with his name. With a digital camera, he took six to eight pictures; through the viewfinder, he saw eight stones. The pictures didn't take. Instead, the camera fried. ["N."]

September 2007

While haggling over fresh tomatoes at the open-air market in Tamazunchale, Mexico, Jerome Wireman had a fatal heart attack. [*Duma Key*]

As Andy Dickerson drove home from work, a drunk driver veered into his lane; Andy died in the crash. Broke, Gracie Goodhugh Dickerson moved back with her father, Tom Goodhugh, and her brother, Carl. ["Fair Extension"]

September 2008

Bree Donlin and Jamie Morton began sleeping together. It wasn't a serious relationship. At twice her age, Jamie was the old wreck she learned on. [*Revival*]

September 2011

Reverend George Winston, recovering from a stroke, had sinned, but he had never committed a major sin. He offered Nora Callahan, his assisted-living nurse, $200,000 to injure a small child enough to draw blood. She accepted. ["Morality"]

Brady Hartsfield woke up from his coma but didn't let on. At first, he remembered only his name. Later, his memories returned as images on seven computer screens he saw in his head. He found he could move objects without touching them. [*End of Watch*]

September 2012

Ralph M. Kiner Memorial Hospital received twelve Zappit Commander game consoles. They wound up on a back shelf in the library. [*End of Watch*]

September 2013

Pete Saubers sent $340, the last of the money, with a note saying he was sorry there was no more. He dropped it in a mailbox near Discount Electronix at Birch Hill Mall. [*Finders Keepers*]

September 2016

End of Watch: Bill Hodges died of pancreatic cancer. He left the Finders Keepers investigative agency to Holly Gibney. Not able to run it by herself, she hired Pete Huntley to do the legwork in the field, while she researched on the computer. [*End of Watch*]

Elaine Geary gave $800 to the church, money Frank Geary thought they couldn't afford. Her response that it was hers, not theirs, angered him. He punched a hole in the kitchen wall. Elaine worried Frank might one day hit her or Nana, so she offered him a choice of separation or divorce. He chose separation. [*Sleeping Beauties*]

October
Happenings

October 1

1 October 1922, Sunday

Wilfred James was short $35 to pay Shannon Cotterie's $75 tutor expenses. He told Henry James to take the Model T to school the next day because he needed the truck to go into town for a loan. With interest, he expected to pay back $38 by Christmas. Wilf would pay half and get the other half from Henry's chore money. ["1922"]

1 October 1958

George Amberson's third timeline: George Amberson wondered whether John Clayton had known about his relationship with Sadie Dunhill. Perhaps, if he stayed away from her, Clayton wouldn't go after her. [*11/22/63*]

1 October 1973, Monday

When Dev Jones got to work, he saw Eddie Parks finish a cigarette then fall forward in a somersault. Eddie had had a heart attack. Dev cracked four of Eddie's ribs and broke a fifth while saving his life with CPR. Lane Hardy called an ambulance. Dev was sure Eddie was too old to have been the Funhouse Killer, but he took off Eddie's gloves to be sure. No tattoo, just psoriasis.

4:00 p.m.: Dev visited Eddie Parks at Heaven's Bay Community Hospital, ICU Room 315. He dropped off Eddie's gloves and a picture of Eddie and his wife he had found in Eddie's shack at Joyland. On his way out, Dev saw Annie Ross in the lobby. While they were talking, Mike Ross returned from his appointment and asked Annie to take him to Joyland with Dev. Reluctantly, she agreed.

Mike Ross called Dev Jones after dinner, excited about going to Joyland. He told Dev they were going for the girl (Linda Gray), who had been there a long time and wanted to leave. [*Joyland*]

1 October 1975, Wednesday night

Mike Ryerson dreamed someone was at his window. He was bitten again. [*'Salem's Lot*]

1 October 1993

Susan Day, a pro-choice advocate, was coming to Derry, ME, to give a speech. Detective Sergeant Johnny Leydecker's colleagues threw him a party for being chosen to head her protection. He'd lead a team of four to augment Day's security detail. [*Insomnia*]

1 October 2003, Wednesday

3:03 p.m. EST: The Pulse, presumably a terrorist attack, began. It zapped anybody talking on a cell phone, wiping the user's brain clean, leaving only the base, killer instinct. A few committed suicide. Most became crazy and violent, attacking normal people and one another. As their brains rebooted, they grouped in flocks, going out during the day to eat, returning to large open areas to roost at night. Each flock became a single, collective intelligence, with little individuality among its members. All the flocks were connected telepathically, and they could communicate with normal people through telepathy.

Clay Riddell had a meeting in which he sold his first graphic novel, *Dark Wanderer*, and its sequel, to Dark Horse comics. People around him became crazy on his walk back to the Atlantic Avenue Inn. Cars smashed into one another; others drove off the road and crashed into buildings, fountains, etc. People screamed gibberish and ran everywhere; some jumped off buildings. There were explosions, looting; much of Boston burned. Tom McCourt, the only other sane person around, talked with him.

~3:18 p.m.: They went to Clay's hotel, about five blocks away. The doors were locked, but they persuaded Mr. Ricardi, the desk clerk, to let them in. Alice Maxwell, being chased by a phone-crazy, pounded on the doors. They let her in.

>4:45 p.m.: Clay, Tom, and Alice left Boston, crossing the Mystic River Bridge. They walked the two miles to Tom's house, where they spent the night. [*Cell*]

1 October 2014

The Dark Tower: The Drawing of the Three—The Prisoner #3 of 5 (Marvel Comics, $3.99) published

~1 October 2014

Alden McCausland met with Johnny Shining Path Parker to discuss fireworks. Johnny said the Close Encounters of the Fourth Kind should top all other fireworks. ["Drunken Fireworks"]

October 2

2 October 1850

Charles Boone arrived at Chapelwaite after inheriting it from Stephen Boone, his cousin. Chapelwaite, a twenty-three-room mansion on the coast of Maine, sat on four acres about two miles northwest of Jerusalem's Lot. ["Jerusalem's Lot"]

2 October 1922, Monday

Wilfred James got a $35 loan from Home Bank & Trust. He declined Mr. Stoppenhauser's suggestion of a $750 mortgage.

Henry James didn't go to school. Instead, he went into town, found his father's truck outside the bank, and took it. He left the Model T in its place, with a note saying he was going to Omaha to get Shannon Cotterie. The truck ran out of gas east of Lyme Biska. He drove it off the road into a field of high grass. He removed the grass under the truck so it wouldn't catch fire. ["1922"]

2 October 1962

George Amberson's second timeline: The people moved out of the upstairs apartment at 214 West Neely Street. George Amberson easily got past the door's spring lock and installed his other bugged lamp. [*11/22/63*]

2 October 1971

James Robert Boone, the last of the Boone family line descended from James Boon, lived at Chapelwaite. He heard what sounded like rats in the walls. ["Jerusalem's Lot"]

2 October 1973, Tuesday

Dev Jones worried he had made a promise he couldn't keep, that Fred Dean wouldn't let him take Annie Ross and Mike Ross to Joyland. Lane Hardy said he'd tell the *Banner* about Dev's saving Eddie Parks. With that free publicity, Dean would allow the visit. [*Joyland*]

2 October 1975, Thursday night

Matt Burke saw Mike Ryerson at Dell's and, concerned about Mike's health, asked him to spend the night. [*'Salem's Lot*]

2 October 1982, Saturday

Clapper worked with Brad Hyuck in the fourth of the Shop's Charlie McGee tests. With no trouble, she created 30,000 degrees of spot heat and burned a cinder block wall. She refused further testing until she saw her father.

At Dr. Pynchot's funeral, Andy McGee pushed Captain Hollister into helping the McGees escape from the Shop. Andy gave him a note for Charlie. It told the truth about John and described the escape plan. The push ricocheted; snakes and golfing bounced around in Hollister's head. [*Firestarter*]

2 October 1983

Christine rose to number 8 on *The New York Times* Fiction Best Seller List, its twenty-sixth week on the List.

2 October 1990, early a.m.

Tom Cullen found Stu Redman and Kojak. [*The Stand: The Complete & Uncut Edition*]

2 October 1993, Saturday

Insomniac Ralph Roberts's wake-up time was 1:58 a.m., after about two and a half hours' sleep. [*Insomnia*]

2 October 2003, Thursday evening

Clay Riddell, Tom McCourt, and Alice Maxwell noticed the phone-crazies' flocking behavior and left Tom's house after the phone-crazies had gone to roost. First stop: the Nickersons, Tom's gun-nut neighbors across the street, for guns. They headed north. Clay worried about his son and estranged wife, back home in Kent Pond, ME. [*Cell*]

2 October 2011

Mile 81 dropped to number 9 on *The New York Times* E-Book Fiction Best Seller List, its third week on the List.

October 3

3 October 1922, Tuesday

With a crowbar, Henry James threatened the eighty-year-old woman working at the grocery-ethyl station in Lyme Biska, NE. She handed him $23.

During the next week and a half, Henry bought a nickel-plated .32 caliber pistol for $5 at a pawn shop on Dodge Street in Omaha, NE. Wearing a flat cap and a red bandanna over his mouth and nose, he robbed the First Agricultural Bank, Omaha branch. He thanked teller Rhoda Penmark when she gave him the money. On his way out, he fired the gun in the air as a warning to the portly security guard. He got away with $150-200, most in one- and five-dollar bills. ["1922"]

3 October 1963

Lee Harvey Oswald moved back to Dallas, TX. As O. H. Lee, he rented an apartment on Beckley Street, where he lived during the week. He spent the weekends with his family at Ruth Paine's. He kept his rifle wrapped in a blanket in Ruth Paine's garage. [*11/22/63*]

3 October 1975, Friday

~12:00 a.m.: Matt Burke heard Danny Glick bite Mike Ryerson. The punctures in Mike's neck disappeared when he died.

~4:00 a.m.: Matt Burke called Ben Mears to help with Mike and to explain his vampire theory.

Because roses had adverse effects on vampires, Richard Straker bought all the roses from the closest florist in Cumberland.

afternoon: Mike Ryerson bit Carl Foreman, the undertaker.

~4:15 p.m.: Floyd Tibbits attacked Ben Mears for dating Susan Norton. With bruises and a hairline fracture in his head, Ben was admitted into a third-floor Cumberland Receiving Hospital room. Jimmy Cody became his doctor. Constable Parkins Gillespie put Tibbits in the drunk tank.

6:30 p.m.: Susan Norton visited Ben Mears.

~8:30 p.m.: The Undead Mike Ryerson visited Matt Burke. Matt had a heart attack and was admitted into Cumberland Receiving Hospital, Room 402. [*'Salem's Lot*]

3 October 1982, Sunday, 4:45 p.m.

Captain Hollister delivered Andy McGee's note to Charlie McGee. [*Firestarter*]

Different Seasons stayed at number 4 on *The New York Times* Fiction Best Seller List, its ninth week on the List.

3 October 1990, morning

Tom Cullen, Kojak, and Stu Redman left Stu's accident site. Tom pulled Stu on a travois for three hours until they found A. C.'s car and push-started it. They stayed at the Utah Hotel in Green River until Stu recovered. [*The Stand: The Complete & Uncut Edition*]

3 October 1992, ~2:00 a.m.

Jamie Morton had an aftereffect of Charlie Jacobs's electrical treatment. Wearing only one sock, he woke up in the rooming house's backyard. A rubber tube was wrapped around his forearm. He was pricking his forearm with a fork. Stuck repeating, "something happened," he bit his tongue to pull himself out of it. Back in his room, his foot was bleeding. He had stepped on broken glass. [*Revival*]

3 October 1993, Sunday, ~2:00 p.m.

Ralph Roberts was alone in a library reading room. Charlie Pickering, with a bright aura, went in, called him a Godless baby-killing Centurion, and twice pushed a knife into his left side—not stabbing but enough to draw blood. Ralph thought he had put his Bodyguard spray in a kitchen cabinet, yet it was there in his right jacket pocket. He fell to the floor. When Pickering bent over with the knife, Ralph sprayed his face. When Ralph returned home, he found a note from which he deduced Dorrance Marstellar had been in his apartment and put the Bodyguard in his pocket. [*Insomnia*]

3 October 1999

Hearts in Atlantis entered *The New York Times* Fiction Best Seller List at number 4. It was on the List for sixteen weeks.

3 October 2000

On Writing (Scribner, $24.50) published with a first printing of 500,000 copies

3 October 2003, Friday

day: Clay Riddell, Tom McCourt, and Alice Maxwell stayed in a barn in North Reading, MA. They watched phone-crazies flock southwest along Route 62, toward Wilmington, MA. Several carried boom boxes.

>9:00 p.m.: They continued north and met other people. Several told them the State Police had closed the New Hampshire border. They reached North Andover, MA. [*Cell*]

October 4

4 October 1958, Saturday

Frank Dunning took the kids to the University of Maine in Orono for a Black Bears football game. They had dinner at the Ninety-Fiver after the game. [*11/22/63*]

4 October 1973, Thursday

"JOYLAND EMPLOYEE SAVES SECOND LIFE," headlined the *Banner*, the Heaven's Bay weekly newspaper. [*Joyland*]

4 October 1975, Saturday

Floyd Tibbits was found dead of acute anemia. He was taken to the county morgue in Portland.

6:45 p.m.: Matt Burke told Father Callahan about the vampire problem.

~8:15 p.m.: Reggie Sawyer caught Corey Bryant with his wife, Bonnie. He put an unloaded shotgun in Bryant's mouth, pulled the trigger, and told him to take that night's bus out of town. Kurt Barlow bit Corey outside.

9:45 p.m.: Cumberland County Morgue attendants Buddy Bascomb and Bob Greenberg found Randy McDougall's and Floyd Tibbits's slabs empty.

Danny Glick scratched at Mark Petrie's window. With a cross, Mark sent him away.

Ruthie Crockett had three orgasms as Dud Rogers bit her. [*'Salem's Lot*]

4 October 1981

Cujo stayed at number 2 on *The New York Times* Fiction Best Seller List, its eighth week on the List.

4 October 1985

The Bachman Books: Four Early Novels by Stephen King (NAL Books, $19.95), a collection of four little-known Richard Bachman novels (*Rage*, *The Long Walk*, *Roadwork*, and *The Running Man*), published with a first printing of 15,000 to 25,000 copies

4 October 1987

Misery dropped to number 7 on *The New York Times* Fiction Best Seller List, its eighteenth week on the List.

4 October 1990, early a.m.

In a dream, Nick Andros told Tom Cullen that Stu Redman had pneumonia. He showed Tom antibiotics and vitamins then told Tom how to save Stu. Nick also said he (Nick) had died. [*The Stand: The Complete & Uncut Edition*]

4 October 1991

Needful Things (Viking, $24.95) published with a first printing of 1,497,000 to 1,500,000 copies

4 October 1992

Gerald's Game dropped to number 4 on *The New York Times* Fiction Best Seller List, its twelfth week on the List.

4 October 1993, Monday, early a.m.

Mrs. May Locher, old and sick, lived at 86 Harris Avenue, across from Ralph Roberts in Derry, ME. Clotho and Lachesis walked through her locked doors to cut her lifelines. Ralph, awake with insomnia, saw them outside her door. One carried what at first looked like a knife but was a pair of scissors. Anonymously, he called 911 and reported two strangers outside her house. Several police officers arrived, kicked open her door, and found her dead in bed. [*Insomnia*]

4 October 2003, Saturday

day: Clay Riddell, Tom McCourt, and Alice Maxwell spent the day at the Sweet Valley Inn, at Highway 28 and 110, near Methuen, MA.

8:45 p.m.: Before leaving, Clay picked up maps of Massachusetts and New Hampshire. They took 110 west for eight to nine miles then picked up Dostie Stream Road. They found no State Police at the New Hampshire border, four miles down the road. New Hampshire Route 38 took them to 128. [*Cell*]

4 October 2005

The Colorado Kid (Hard Case Crime, $5.99) published with a first printing of 1,000,000 copies

October 5

5 October 1958, Sunday

<u>George Amberson's second timeline</u>: Frank Dunning went to Longview Cemetery to place flowers on his parents' graves. George Amberson shot him three times and put his body in the Tracker mausoleum.

<u>George Amberson's third timeline</u>: George Amberson went to the Lisbon Drive-In, its last night of the season. After *Macabre*, he went to the snack bar for coffee. He bought a postcard, too, and went back to his room. [*11/22/63*]

5 October 1973, Friday

Fred Dean allowed Dev Jones to give Annie Ross and Mike Ross a tour of Joyland, but Lane Hardy had to go with them.

evening: Dev Jones picked up Erin Cook and Tom Kennedy at the Wilmington train station. They, Miss Tina Ackerley, and Mrs. Shoplaw had a picnic dinner on the beach. [*Joyland*]

5 October 1975, Sunday

morning: Marjorie Glick died. Danny Glick had bitten her three or four of the previous nights. Dr. Reardon took her to Green's Mortuary.

9:10 a.m.: Ben Mears, Matt Burke, and Susan Norton met in Matt's hospital room. Later, Ben and Susan told Jimmy Cody everything they knew and suspected about The Lot's vampire problem. Jimmy agreed to have Danny Glick exhumed to test the theory.

12:30 p.m.: Mark Petrie went to kill Kurt Barlow. He waited in the woods for Richard Straker to go away.

1:30 p.m.: When they learned Marjorie Glick had died, they went to Maury Green's Mortuary in Cumberland to watch Mrs. Glick's body at sunset.

2:00 p.m.: Susan Norton went to kill Barlow.

late afternoon: Mark Petrie found Susan in the woods near the Marsten House. Together, they broke in through a window. An end table had a book written in Latin and containing a picture of a child sacrifice. Richard Straker caught them and hog-tied Mark. With patience and concentration, Mark freed himself.

~7:00 p.m.: He killed Straker with a metal cot leg. At the cellar door, he called for Susan to run. Barlow asked him to come down; Mark ran home.

7:02 p.m., sunset: At Green's Mortuary, the Undead Marjorie Glick bit Jimmy Cody. He pulled her off before she could finish her bite then forced her away with a cross.

Kurt Barlow bit Susan Norton. To avoid being caught at the Marsten House, Barlow left a note threatening Mark Petrie's parents and moved to Eva's Rooms. Susan bit her mother, Ann Norton. [*'Salem's Lot*]

5 October 1980

Buddy Bruckner broke his leg at home plate in a championship baseball game. Ruth Bruckner, his mother, went to CMG Hospital in Lewiston, ME. His brother, Georgie, stayed home with Gramma. After about an hour, Georgie heard Gramma make a strange gurgling noise. He looked in on her; she was dead. When he pulled the sheet over her head, she grabbed his wrist. He pulled free and ran out. Gramma called him back. He ran out again when he saw her sitting in a chair. She followed, grabbed him, and transferred herself from her dead body into his living one. Later that night, Gramma uttered some Latin and Druidic grunts through Georgie. Aunt Flo died of a brain hemorrhage in Minnesota. Over the phone, Aunt Flo had told Georgie to use Hastur's name to keep Gramma away from him. ["Gramma"]

Firestarter stayed at number 1 on *The New York Times* Fiction Best Seller List, its seventh week on the List.

5 October 1986

IT stayed at number 1 on *The New York Times* Fiction Best Seller List, *IT*'s fourth week on the List.

5 October 1990

Pop Merrill tried to sell Kevin Delevan's camera to the Pus Sisters for $10,000. He took a picture of them. Most of the Sun dog's teeth were visible. The Pus Sisters suggested he destroy the camera. On his way out, Pop took a picture of their chauffeur. The dog had finished turning and was approaching the photographer. ["The Sun Dog"]

5 October 1993, Tuesday, >7:20 a.m.

Atropos, an agent of the Random, cut Rosalie's balloon-string lifelines, which shortened her lifespan. He took her bandanna. Later, fulfilling circumstances, Joe Wyzer ran over Rosalie, killing her. Atropos took Joe's pocket comb.

Lois Chasse and Ralph Roberts met with Clotho and Lachesis at Derry Home Hospital. Ed Deepneau had not been designated as either Random or Purpose, but Atropos had cut his lifeline anyway. For several months, Clotho and Lachesis had been bringing Lois and Ralph into their reality; insomnia was a side effect. Today, Clotho and Lachesis explained that they were needed to fix the repercussions of cutting Ed's cord. Ed will kill all 2,000 people attending Susan Day's speech at the Derry Civic Center. Their job was to prevent Ed from doing this. At Long-Time levels, they had talked for a couple of hours. When Lois and Ralph returned to Short-Time levels, it was Friday morning. They each looked fifteen to twenty years younger than they had that Monday. [*Insomnia*]

5 October 2003, Sunday

early a.m.: On Route 102, east of Manchester, NH, and about two miles outside Gaiten, Clay Riddell, Tom McCourt, and Alice Maxwell heard faint music. Two old men walked with them awhile. The old guys told them to leave their shoes outside when they found a place to stay. The phone-crazies wouldn't take them, and normal people would go somewhere else.

In Gaiten, NH, Route 102 was Main Street, then Academy Avenue, which had nicer houses but all with shoes out front. An old man with a cane and a young boy with a lantern stood at the entrance to Gaiten Academy, offering shelter. Because of a flock's trail of food and litter into the Academy, everybody declined. It was getting close to daylight, so Clay, Tom, and Alice went with them. The music they had been hearing came from the Academy's Tonney Field. Headmaster Charles Ardai and Jordan (the old man and young boy) took them to a spot around two hundred yards from the field. About a thousand phone-crazies, lying close together, covered the field. After hamburgers off a gas grill that afternoon, Clay and the others slept in Cheatham Lodge, the Headmaster's residence.

night: They tried to burn the flock with gasoline from the Academy's motor pool but ran into one complication after another. They'd have to find another way. [*Cell*]

5 October 2011

The Dark Tower: The Gunslinger—The Battle of Tull #5 of 5 (Marvel Comics, $3.99) published

October 6

6 October 1850

Charles Boone heard what sounded like rats behind the walls at Chapelwaite. ["Jerusalem's Lot"]

6 October 1889

Hubie Marsten was born. A wealthy organized crime figure and contract killer, he retired to Jerusalem's Lot, ME, in 1928. ['Salem's Lot]

6 October 1922, Friday

Wilfred James's truck had been found east of Lyme Biska, NE. Sheriff Jones had Lars Olsen drive it to Wilfred's farm. ["1922"]

~6 October 1957

Jersey Joe DiPunno, manager of American League baseball team the New Jersey Titans, had a heart attack. He was watching the World Series at Milwaukee's County Stadium. Although he lived five more years, 1957 was his last year as manager. [*Blockade Billy*]

6 October 1958, Monday

George Amberson's third timeline: Saving President Kennedy had affected many lives and caused an unwieldy number of strings. Worried about the changes he'd cause by everything he did, George Amberson decided to go back to the future. [*11/22/63*]

6 October 1973, Saturday afternoon

Miss Tina Ackerley, Tom Kennedy, and Mrs. Shoplaw played Scrabble.

On folded chairs in front of Madame Fortuna's shy at Joyland, Erin Cook told Dev Jones the results of her Funhouse Killer investigation. She had determined two crucial things. First, the tattoos on the killer's hand were fake tattoos used as conversation starters. Second, the killer was a carny who had worked with *Manly Wellman's Show of 1000 Wonders* then with Southern Star Amusements. Something in the photos of the killer nagged Dev, but he couldn't quite place it. [*Joyland*]

6 October 1975, Monday

~12:05 a.m.: Kurt Barlow and Susan Norton bit Homer McCaslin after he found Susan's car off the Brooks Road. Later, McCaslin bit deputy Nolly Gardener after Nolly found his car.

early a.m.: Danny Glick bit Jack Griffen. Jack bit his brother, Hal.

Larry Crockett thought he had the flu or something and stayed home from the office. Sunlight bothered him.

8:45 a.m.: Mark Petrie told Ben Mears that Susan Norton was Undead. They met with Matt Burke and Jimmy Cody. With Matt in the hospital, the others would go after Barlow.

11:00 a.m.–1:00 p.m.: Father Callahan heard their confessions then joined them. They went to Cumberland for vampire-fighting tools—Jimmy's office for two stakes and a hammer, a supermarket for garlic, and a florist for roses. The florist was sold out.

>12:00 p.m.: Kurt Barlow visited Ann Norton. He had a job for her.

>2:15 p.m.: They broke into the Marsten House and found Straker's body upstairs. Downstairs, they found Barlow's note and Susan Norton. Ben drove a stake through her Undead heart. Mark Petrie and Father Callahan went to warn Mark's parents.

~7:00 p.m.: Kurt Barlow killed Henry Petrie and June Petrie. Barlow forced Father Callahan to drink his blood after the Father lost his faith and was no longer a threat.

Ann Norton took Bill Norton's .38 to Cumberland County Hospital to kill Matt Burke. An orderly knocked her out with a punch to the jaw after a visitor grabbed her from behind.

<10:15 p.m.: Unclean, Father Callahan couldn't go in the church. The door handle burned his hand.

11:10 p.m.: Father Callahan took a one-way bus to New York City.

11:50 p.m.: Danny Glick and other Undead children bit school bus driver Charlie Rhodes. ['Salem's Lot]

6 October 1976

Ben Mears and Mark Petrie returned to Jerusalem's Lot, ME, and set fire to the town to rid it of its Undead. They set it at the same place the Fire of '51 had been started. ['Salem's Lot]

6 October 1982, Wednesday

12:45 p.m.: Don Jules took Charlie McGee to the stables for a horse ride. She warmed his gun and threatened to burn him to make him leave. He left to issue a Condition Bright Yellow alert then returned. Charlie killed him when he tried to shoot her. Her force threw him forty feet.

~1:00 p.m.: Captain Hollister took Andy McGee to the Shop's stables to get Charlie. From the loft, Rainbird threatened to kill Andy to get Charlie to climb up. Andy pushed Rainbird to jump. He pushed harder than he ever had before; the left side of his body went numb. Rainbird jumped, broke his leg, and shot Andy. When Rainbird shot at Charlie, she burned the bullet. Her fire trail burned Rainbird and Hollister. Andy died after telling Charlie to destroy the Shop's compound. She burned those agents who tried to kill her, destroyed the compound, climbed the gate, and left. [Firestarter]

6 October 1985

Skeleton Crew stayed at number 3 on The New York Times Fiction Best Seller List, its sixteenth week on the List.

6 October 1996

The Green Mile, Part One: The Two Dead Girls stayed at number 14 on The New York Times Paperback Fiction Best Seller List, its twenty-fourth week on the List.

The Green Mile, Part Four: The Bad Death of Eduard Delacroix rose to number 12 on The New York Times Paperback Fiction Best Seller List, its fourteenth week on the List.

The Green Mile, Part Five: Night Journey dropped to number 8 on The New York Times Paperback Fiction Best Seller List, its eighth week on the List.

The Green Mile, Part Six: Coffey on the Mile stayed at number 1 on The New York Times Paperback Fiction Best Seller List, its fourth week on the List.

6 October 2003, Monday

1:00 p.m.: Clay Riddell and Tom McCourt went to the Academy Citgo across Route 102 and drove two propane tanker trucks to the middle of Tonney Field. While Clay and Tom were in the Citgo getting the keys to the trucks, two crazies in the street fought over a box of Twinkies. They emitted energy that moved ashes in an ashtray, jingled hanging keys, fluttered papers, and knocked a gas pump nozzle out of place.

10:00 p.m.: The phone-crazies roosted on Tonney Field, under and around the propane tankers. With a Colt .45 revolver, loaded with dum dums, Clay shot into the left truck. Although the explosion destroyed most of the phone-crazies, Clay felt they should leave as soon as possible. An hour later, they were packed and ready to go. The Head was too old to travel on foot and would stay. Jordan wouldn't go without him, Alice wouldn't go without Jordan, Tom wouldn't go without Alice, and Clay wouldn't go without Tom and Alice. They didn't go. [*Cell*]

6 October 2013

Joyland dropped to number 16 on *The New York Times* Paperback Trade Fiction Best Seller List, its sixteenth week on the List.

October 7

7 October 1922

The Overlook Hotel closed for its last season under James Parris. ["Before the Play"]

7 October 1929

The Bradley Gang bought ammunition at Machen's Sporting Goods in Derry, ME. Lal Machen recognized them, sold them some ammo, and said he could have the rest in two days. Machen told everybody they were coming back in two days. [*IT*]

7 October 1958, Tuesday

George Amberson's second timeline: "BUSINESS MAN FOUND MURDERED IN LOCAL CEMETERY; Dunning Was Prominent in Many Charity Drives" appeared in the Derry *Daily News*.

George Amberson's third timeline: On the postcard, George Amberson wrote a message to Mr. Deacon Simmons. He asked Deke to look out for his new librarian; she'd need a good angel in April 1963. He reconsidered. If Sadie Dunhill were meant to die, preventing her death wouldn't be good for the future; he tore up the postcard. He walked back to Lisbon Falls and returned to 2011. [*11/22/63*]

7 October 1973, Sunday

Dev Jones took Erin Cook and Tom Kennedy to the Wilmington train station. Tom's Coastal Express to New Jersey left two hours after Erin's train to Annandale-on-Hudson in upstate New York, so he and Dev went to the rib joint across the street for an early dinner. [*Joyland*]

7 October 1975, Tuesday

<3:00 a.m.: Heading to the second floor on the Cumberland Receiving Hospital elevator, Ann Norton died.

Weasel Craig bit Eva Miller.

4:15 a.m.: The Undead Corey Bryant returned to the Sawyers'. Reggie Sawyer shot him with both barrels of a shotgun. Bryant tossed him aside and bit Bonnie Sawyer.

3:07 p.m.: Matt Burke died of a heart attack in his hospital room.

Mark Petrie and Jimmy Cody marked locations of vampires in 'Salem's Lot. Mark had seen blue chalk on Barlow; Jimmy remembered Eva Miller had an old pool table in her basement.

Jimmy when he fell into the basement at Eva's Rooms. The stairs had been replaced with kitchen knives in a door.

~4:10 p.m.: Mark told Ben Mears that Jimmy Cody was dead.

6:23 p.m.: Ben sprinkled holy water on an ax and broke into the padlocked root cellar at Eva's Rooms.

6:55 p.m.: Ben drove a stake through Kurt Barlow's heart. The body turned to dust, leaving only his teeth. Ben and Mark left town.

Carl Foreman and Homer McCaslin bit Delbert Markey, Larry and Mrs. Crockett bit Royal Snow, Milt Crossen's Undead customers bit Crossen, Glynis Mayberry bit Mabel Werts, and George Middler bit some high school boys. ['*Salem's Lot*]

7 October 1978, Saturday

The Libertyville High School Terriers lost their fifth football game of the season. [*Christine*]

7 October 1979

The Dead Zone stayed at number 2 on *The New York Times* Fiction Best Seller List, its fifth week on the List.

7 October 1982, Thursday

The Shop explained Charlie McGee's destruction of their Longmont, VA, compound as a terrorist attack. Double agent John Rainbird had planted bombs for a terrorist organization. [*Firestarter*]

7 October 1986

Stephen King finished *Misery* in Bangor, ME.

7 October 1989

Stephen King started *The Wastelands*, the next *Dark Tower* book. Again, it felt as if he weren't writing it, that it was flowing through him and he was just recording it. [*The Dark Tower VI: Song of Susannah*]

7 October 1990

Stu Redman's fever lifted. [*The Stand: The Complete & Uncut Edition*]

The Stand: The Complete & Uncut Edition dropped to number 12 on *The New York Times* Fiction Best Seller List, its twenty-second week on the List.

Four Past Midnight stayed at number 1 on *The New York Times* Fiction Best Seller List, its fourth week on the List.

7 October 1992

With a hammer, Cathy Morse broke a display case in J. David Jewelry in Broken Arrow, OK. She took out a pair of diamond earrings, saying they were hers and went with her dress. On the broken glass, she cut herself enough to get stitches. [*Revival*]

7 October 2001

Black House stayed at number 1 *The New York Times* Fiction Best Seller List, its second week on the List.

7 October 2003, Tuesday, midafternoon

The phone-crazies had piled melted boom boxes from Tonney Field at the front door of Cheatham Lodge and pulled back. Twenty-one crazies formed a 'V,' with Raggedy Man, their spokesman, at the point. For ten minutes, Clay Riddell and his group heard the agonizing screams of normal people being executed in the street in retaliation for the previous night's flock destruction. Raggedy Man offered free access to Academy Avenue. Upstairs, they found the flock had made Charles Ardai kill himself. Clay Riddell, Tom McCourt, Alice Maxwell, and Jordan buried him in the garden behind the Lodge. Jordan, exhausted, needed rest. [*Cell*]

7 October 2007

At Ackerman's Field, Dr. John Bonsaint saw a crow swerve to avoid flying over the stones. ["N."]

7 October 2015

The Dark Tower: The Drawing of the Three—Lady of Shadows #2 of 5 (Marvel Comics, $3.99) published

7 October 2018

The Outsider dropped to number 11 on *The New York Times* Hardcover Fiction Best Seller List, its eighteenth week on the List.

October 8

8 October 1850

Housekeeper Mrs. Cloris told Charles Boone that Chapelwaite was bad and it wasn't ghosts lurking behind the walls. ["Jerusalem's Lot"]

8 October 1966, Saturday

Hugh Brennan, Ronnie Malenfant, Ashley Rice, and Pete Riley played Hearts in the Chamberlain Hall dormitory's third-floor lounge. A Hearts epidemic began that resulted in nineteen of thirty-two third-floor residents transferring to another dorm, leaving school, or flunking out. Of the original four, only Pete returned for the spring semester. ["Hearts in Atlantis"]

8 October 1973, Monday, 12:00 p.m.

Fred Dean sent Dev Jones home early, promising a full day's pay. Fred and Lane Hardy prepared Joyland to be mostly operational, instead of just a tour, for Annie Ross and Mike Ross the next day.

Fred Dean told Lane Hardy that Erin Cook and Dev Jones had spent much of Saturday afternoon poring over a folder. Paranoid, Lane was sure Dev had figured out he was the Funhouse Killer. [*Joyland*]

8 October 1975, Wednesday morning

Ben Mears returned to Jerusalem's Lot. He buried Mr. and Mrs. Petrie and Jimmy Cody in a wooded clearing behind the Petries' house. [*'Salem's Lot*]

8 October 1991, Tuesday afternoon

Needful Things had a brief preview opening. Leland Gaunt sold a Topps 1956 Sandy Koufax baseball card to Brian Rusk, his first customer. The price was eighty-five cents plus a deed involving Wilma Jerzyk. The card was worth about a hundred times the cash price. [*Needful Things*]

8 October 1993, Friday

Lois Chasse and Ralph Roberts figured out Ed Deepneau would kill all 2,000 people at Susan Day's speech by flying an explosive-laden plane into the Derry Civic Center. Tragedies affecting more than 2,000 people happen frequently. Confused about why this one was different, Ralph summoned Clotho and Lachesis. They explained that people in such disasters are designated Random, and it wouldn't disturb the balance for them to die. Everybody at the Civic Center, except Patrick Danville, was designated Random. Patrick's untimely death would cause the Tower of all existence to fall. Because Ed was undesignated as either Random or Purpose, only he could harm Patrick. If successful in his flight, he would unwittingly kill Patrick. Earlier that day, Ralph had taken Ed Deepneau's wedding ring from Atropos's storeroom and had forced Atropos to leave Lois Chasse and Ralph alone; Atropos backed off but said he'd kill Natalie Deepneau. Ralph would help Clotho and Lachesis only if they saved Natalie. They agreed, but Ralph had to promise to die in her place when the time came.

Lois let Ralph siphon most of her aural energy so he could stop Ed. Ralph went into a MEN's

Portosan and, with Ed's ring, could see Derry from the plane. With Lois's energy, he put himself on the plane. The Crimson King intervened. Ralph caused higher levels to open, blowing the Crimson King into the deadlights. Twelve hundred feet from the Civic Center, Ralph returned to Short-Time levels to disconnect the detonation wires from the explosives and incapacitate Ed. He steered the plane away from the Center. Lois sucked energy from a wino and went into the Portosan to pull Ralph back just before the plane crashed in the parking lot. A piece of flying glass beheaded Susan Day. Ralph and Lois went to Lois's house and slept for twenty-two hours.

Ralph fulfilled his promise almost five years later. Patrick died eighteen years later while preserving the Random/Purpose balance by saving two men, one of whom must not have died then. [*Insomnia*]

8 October 2003, Wednesday

8:00 a.m.: Clay Riddell was keeping watch behind Cheatham Lodge. Raggedy Man approached and stood on Charles Ardai's grave. When they talked, Raggedy Man spoke through Clay. He said to head north that night and gave Clay an image of the words, "KASH-WAK=NO-FO." Later, Clay told the others about the meeting, leaving out the part of Raggedy Man controlling his voice. On the map, Jordan showed them Kashwak, ME, north of Fryeburg. An unincorporated area designated TR-90, it had no cell phone service.

8:00 p.m.: Clay Riddell, Tom McCourt, Alice Maxwell, and Jordan left Gaiten Academy. For half a mile along Route 102, they saw the carnage, the torn-apart bodies of the normal people the phone-crazies had killed after the Gaiten flock was blown up. The phone-crazies had no trouble finding them—they went to houses with shoes out front. [*Cell*]

8 October 2008

The Dark Tower: Treachery #2 of 6 (Marvel Comics, $3.99) published

The Stand: Captain Trips #2 of 5 (Marvel Comics, $3.99) published

~8 October 2014

Waitress Angie McCain found short-order cook Dale Barbara behind Sweetbriar Rose, put her arms around him, and kissed him. He kissed her back but pushed her away when she thrust her hips against him. Hurt and angry, she told Frankie DeLesseps that Barbie raped her. [*Under the Dome*]

October 9

9 October 1850, evening

Calvin McCann, a Chapelwaite servant, showed Charles Boone a Jerusalem's Lot map, which linked The Worm to the church. ["Jerusalem's Lot"]

9 October 1929, 2:25 p.m.

The Bradley Gang stopped where Canal, Kansas, and Main Streets intersected in Derry, ME. Feeling as if something were wrong, Al Bradley got out of his car to tell the others to go back. Lal Machen shot Al Bradley in the shoulder. Fifty to seventy-five Derry residents shot and killed the Bradley Gang. Another IT cycle had started, with Pennywise taking part in the shootout. [*IT*]

9 October 1961, Monday

George Amberson's second timeline: George Amberson paid a $100 deposit on $140 worth of surveillance equipment at Silent Mike's Satellite Electronics on Lower Main Street in Dallas. At 2703 Mercedes Street in Fort Worth, TX (the house where Lee and Marina Oswald would live), he gave Ivy Templeton $5 to call him when she and her family moved out. He gave her an extra dollar to cover the 75-cent long-distance call. [*11/22/63*]

9 October 1965

"GERALD FORD CALLS FOR UFO INVESTIGATION; Republican House Leader Says 'Michigan Lights' May Be Extraterrestrial in Origin" appeared in the Michigan *Journal*. [*Dreamcatcher*]

9 October 1973, Tuesday

Fred Dean, Lane Hardy, and Dev Jones gave Mike Ross and Annie Ross a day of fun at Joyland they would never forget.

Mike Ross showed Linda Gray the way out of Horror House. Only Mike saw her. She thanked him and said for Dev to be careful because it wasn't white.

That evening, after Mike was sound asleep, Annie invited Dev upstairs. He lost his virginity to her.

On his way from the ICU to the Cardiac Recovery Floor, Eddie Parks had a fatal heart attack in the elevator. [*Joyland*]

9 October 1983

Christine dropped to number 11 on *The New York Times* Fiction Best Seller List, its twenty-seventh week on the List.

9 October 1989

Stephen King felt *The Waste Lands* was a better title, from the T. S. Eliot poem "The Waste Land." [*The Dark Tower VI: Song of Susannah*]

9 October 1991, Wednesday

10:00 a.m.: Grand Opening of Leland Gaunt's Needful Things in Castle Rock, ME

10:02 a.m.: Polly Chalmers gave a welcome-to-town, devil's food cake to Leland Gaunt. Nettie Cobb had baked it.

Leland Gaunt sold a Lalique vase to Cyndi Rose Martin for $31.

late afternoon: Nettie Cobb and Rosalie Drake went to Needful Things. Leland Gaunt gave Nettie an appointment to look at some carnival glass the next day.

10:10 p.m.: Leland Gaunt sold a foxtail to Hugh Priest for $1.50 plus a deed involving Nettie Cobb. [*Needful Things*]

9 October 1993, Saturday, 7:00 p.m.

Lois Chasse and Ralph Roberts woke after sleeping for twenty-two hours. They couldn't change levels of existence anymore. People's auras faded after a couple more nights of sleep, and they could no longer see them in a week. Memories of what had happened also faded. [*Insomnia*]

9 October 2003, Thursday

Clay Riddell, Tom McCourt, Alice Maxwell, and Jordan passed a flock roosting in West Side Cemetery, next to Rochester Mall in Rochester, NH. In collaboration with the flock, normies with rifles were posted around the cemetery.

Route 19 would take them into Maine. Its many clear stretches, some up to a quarter mile, invited people, mostly drunk, to speed. Jordan called them sprinters. Gunner sped by in a black Cadillac Escalade and shouted a derogatory comment at Alice. Up around a bend, Gunner crashed. They found the Cadillac flipped on its side, with Gunner and passenger Harold banged up but walking around. The other passengers had run off. Gunner and Harold recognized the group from their dreams (courtesy of the phone-people flocks) and refused first aid. Fearing Gunner might react like a cornered dog, Clay hit him across the face with a pistol butt. [*Cell*]

9 October 2007

Dr. John Bonsaint felt better about Ackerman's Field. ["N."]

9 October 2011

Mile 81 dropped to number 14 on *The New York Times* E-Book Fiction Best Seller List, its fourth week on the List.

October 10

10 October 1850, ~11:00 a.m.

Charles Boone and Calvin McCann visited the Boar's Head Inn, a couple of houses, and the church in Jerusalem's Lot. All were deserted but hadn't been vandalized or looted. They found *De Vermis Mysteriis* (*The Mysteries of the Worm*); the church shuddered when Boone touched the book. ["Jerusalem's Lot"]

10 October 1914

Construction started on a new, two-floor, 12,000-square-foot wing on Rose Red. The wing included four rooms for Sukeena, three visitor suites, school facilities, a Bird Room, a Map Room, and a Projection Room. A model of Rose Red, with which April Rimbauer was playing, showed the new wing. Earlier that day, the model lacked the wing. [*The Diary of Ellen Rimbauer: My Life at Rose Red*]

10 October 1958, Friday

George Amberson's second timeline: George Amberson had placed a $500 bet with Chaz Frati, at 6–1 odds, that the Yankees would win the World Series after being down three games to one. At Frati's pawn shop, Chaz cheerfully paid his winnings, having $3,500 ready in an envelope.

"HUNT FOR MYSTERY KILLER GOES ON AS FRANK DUNNING IS LAID TO REST" appeared in the Derry *Daily News*. [*11/22/63*]

10 October 1973, Wednesday, early a.m.

A banging shutter woke Dev Jones. He went outside to secure it but couldn't go back to sleep. In the parlor, he went over Erin Cook's photos. The man's hat was always at an angle, but it kept changing sides, right and left, just as Lane Hardy's hat changed sides. Also, the killer in the photos had blond hair. Dev remembered he had seen Lane without his hat once and thought he saw strands of white hair. It wasn't white; it was blond. Lane had dyed his hair black.

From the payphone outside the drugstore in the little shopping center on Beach Drive, Lane Hardy called Dev Jones. He threatened to kill Annie Ross and Mike Ross if Dev didn't meet him at Joyland.

They got on the Carolina Spin. Lane had Dev start the Spin with a modified Genie garage-door opener and toss the remote over the side. Lane wanted to know how Dev was on to him. Dev said he hadn't known for as long as Lane suspected, he had just figured it out, and then told him how he knew.

The ghost of Eddie Parks told Mike Ross that Dev Jones was going to get killed at Joyland. Mike woke his mother. Annie Ross grabbed a rifle and went to help. She found Devin and Hardy on the Carolina Spin. Hardy had a gun on Devin. She shouted for Devin to duck then shot Hardy in the head. She didn't want Mike involved, so they decided to tell the police Dev had called to warn her before he left for Joyland. Fearing sirens would spook Hardy, she went to help without calling the police.

In the papers, Hardy became known as the Carny Killer. "BEAUTY AND THE BEAST," an article in an *Inside View* extra edition, showed side-by-side photos. One was of seventeen-year-old Annie Ross at a Camp Perry shooting match, the other of twenty-one-year-old

Lane Hardy when he was arrested for indecent exposure in San Diego. [*Joyland*]

10 October 1980

New Terrors 2, edited by Ramsey Campbell (Pan Books), with "Big Wheels: A Tale of the Laundry Game" (collected in *Skeleton Crew*), published

10 October 1982

Different Seasons dropped to number 5 on *The New York Times* Fiction Best Seller List, its tenth week on the List.

10 October 1985

Ed Paladin quit smoking. ["The Reploids"]

10 October 1991, Thursday

~10:30 a.m.: At Needful Things, Nettie Cobb bought a $300 carnival-glass lamp shade for $10.40 and a deed involving Dan Keeton. Leland Gaunt gave her a key to Keeton's house.

afternoon: Myra Evans knew her best friend, Cora Rusk, wanted the Elvis Presley picture at Needful Things, but she went to buy it anyway. As she held the picture, she experienced the best orgasm of her life—with Elvis on stage. Leland Gaunt sold it to her for $140 and a deed involving Henry Beaufort.

Brian Rusk smeared mud on Wilma Jerzyck's laundry hanging in the backyard. Later, Wilma thought Nettie Cobb had done it.

~9:00 p.m.: Leland Gaunt sold a Bazun fishing rod and reel to Norris Ridgewick. The deal included a prank on Hugh Priest. [*Needful Things*]

10 October 1992, last day of the Tulsa State Fair

Charlie Jacobs answered a knock at his RV's door. Mr. Morse punched him in the mouth, blaming him for his daughter's getting arrested. Jamie Morton hit Mr. Morse with a pot. The man was still upset but no longer in a fighting mood. Jamie talked with him outside and bought him a Coke at a nearby refreshment stand. [*Revival*]

10 October 1999

Hearts in Atlantis stayed at number 4 on *The New York Times* Fiction Best Seller List, its second week on the List.

10 October 2003, Friday

Clay Riddell, Tom McCourt, Alice Maxwell, and Jordan heard another sprinter but didn't think anything of it. As Harold drove a Chevrolet sedan, Gunner threw a cinder block and hit Alice in the head. Clay and Tom carried her up the slope by the side of the road and stayed with her under some apple trees. Throughout the night, she seemed delirious. [*Cell*]

10 October 2004

The Dark Tower VII: The Dark Tower entered *The New York Times* Fiction Best Seller List at number 1. It was on the List for eight weeks.

10 October 2007

The eighth stone was still in Ackerman's Field, so Dr. John Bonsaint didn't have to do anything. It was approaching the winter solstice, after which he could relax until spring. The summer solstice was the most dangerous time. The force breaking through the thin spot between worlds was strongest. It was weakest at the winter solstice. ["N."]

October 11

11 October 1981

Cujo stayed at number 2 on *The New York Times* Fiction Best Seller List, its ninth week on the List.

11 October 1987

Misery dropped to number 8 on *The New York Times* Fiction Best Seller List, its nineteenth week on the List.

11 October 1990

John Delevan took the day off when Kevin Delevan told him Pop Merrill had switched cameras. The camera he had taken to Pop's had no film, but the one he smashed had three pictures left. They went to see Merrill—no answer. They bought another camera at LaVerdiere's Super Drug Store and returned to Merrill's shop, where they saw Pop working on the camera. Part of the camera exploded as another picture was taken. Pop was killed. The Sun dog started to jump out of a picture. Kevin took a picture of it, sending it back. The new camera was destroyed. ["The Sun Dog"]

Stu Redman had a relapse. [The Stand: The Complete & Uncut Edition]

11 October 1991, Friday

Wilma Jerzyck had been driving by and parking in front of Nettie Cobb's house. After returning four times to make sure things were locked, Nettie called Polly Chalmers to have the day off. She said she was sick to her stomach, but, actually, she wanted to guard her lamp shade and house against Wilma Jerzyck.

Leland Gaunt sold a cloisonné vase to June Gavineaux for $97 and a deed involving Father Brigham, a teddy bear to the Gendrons, a pewter teapot to Slopey Dodd for seventy-one cents and a prank on Lester Pratt, another Lalique vase to Cindi Rose Martin for a deed involving Norris Ridgewick, seventy-two nude photos of a seventeen-year-old actress-model to Ricky Bissonette for $36 and a prank on Reverend Rose, a piece of "petrified wood from the holy land" to Sally Ratcliffe for $17 and a deed involving Frank Jewett, and a pipe that had belonged to Herman Göring to Ev Frankel for $12 and a prank on Sally Ratcliffe.

Leland Gaunt sold a pair of Elvis Presley's sunglasses to Cora Rusk for $19.50. Part of the price was to tell him who would be good to watch Alan Pangborn; she suggested Eddie Warburton. He sold Warburton a Saint Christopher's medal; part of the price was to watch Pangborn. [*Needful Things*]

11 October 1992

morning: Charlie Jacobs left a note under Jamie Morton's door. The letter told him to see Hugh Yates for a job. An Amtrak *Mountain Express* ticket from Tulsa, OK, to Denver, CO, was enclosed. Jamie took the train to Denver then a bus to Nederland. As a favor to Charlie Jacobs, Hugh Yates hired Jamie to work at the Wolfjaw Ranch recording studio. [*Revival*]

Gerald's Game dropped to number 5 on *The New York Times* Fiction Best Seller List, its thirteenth week on the List.

11 October 1998

Bag of Bones entered *The New York Times* Fiction Best Seller List at number 1. It held the number 1 spot for four of its twenty weeks on the List. It entered the List three times, with seventeen weeks its longest run.

11 October 2003, Saturday, dawn

Alice Maxwell died. Using shovels from the shed of a nearby farmhouse, Clay Riddell, Tom McCourt, and Jordan buried her under an apple tree. [*Cell*]

October 12

12 October 1914

Omicron Oil shares had doubled in six months. Douglas Posey had made some bad investments since he sold his shares to John Rimbauer and asked Rimbauer for help. Rimbauer turned him away. [*The Diary of Ellen Rimbauer: My Life at Rose Red*]

12 October 1980

Firestarter stayed at number 1 on *The New York Times* Fiction Best Seller List, its eighth week on the List.

12 October 1986

IT stayed at number 1 on *The New York Times* Fiction Best Seller List, *IT*'s fifth week on the List.

12 October 1991, Saturday

Bazooka Joan won the night's first horse race at Lewiston Raceway. Filly Delfia won the second, Tammy's Wonder the third, I'm Amazed the fourth, By George the fifth, Pucky Boy the sixth, Casco Thunder the seventh, Delightful Son the eighth, Tiko-Tiko the ninth, and Malabar the tenth.

~7:15 a.m.: Leland Gaunt sold *Winning Ticket*, a horse race game, to Dan Keeton for a $2 bill. He told Keeton the game predicted race results in the 1930s. They would negotiate further if the game still worked. That night, Keeton won $18,000 at Lewiston Raceway.

~10:30 a.m.: Eddie Warburton called to tell Leland Gaunt that Alan Pangborn was on his way to say, "Hi." Gaunt replaced the OPEN sign with one saying he was in Portland for business. [*Needful Things*]

12 October 1993

Helen Deepneau started her new job at the Derry Public Library. Mike Hanlon had offered her the position of Children's Library assistant in the afternoons and evenings. [*Insomnia*]

12 October 1998

George Staub's girlfriend was sick, so he went to Thrill Village in Laconia, NH, alone and rode the Bullet four times. He stopped for beer on his way home and crashed his Mustang, knocking out his teeth and decapitating himself. He was buried in a small graveyard on Ridge Road outside Gates Falls, ME. His inscription read, "Well Begun, Too Soon Done." [*Riding the Bullet*]

12 October 2003, Sunday

12:00 a.m.: Clay Riddell, Tom McCourt, and Jordan reached the intersection of Main and Livery Lane in Kent Pond, ME. Clay's old house on Livery Lane was empty, but there was a note from his son on the back door. It said Johnny Riddell and friends went to the Town Hall.

The bulletin board inside the deserted Town Hall had about two hundred notes, many of them proclaiming Kashwak a safe place to go. A note from Johnny said he was going. On their way to Kashwak, Clay, Tom, and Jordan met Daniel Hartwick, Denise Link, and Ray

Huizenga, another group the phoners and everybody else shunned.

~3:00 a.m.: They thought it was suicide to go to Kashwak, but Clay had to get his son. He went north on Route 11, to pick up Route 160, on which he planned to travel eighty miles to TR-90, the unincorporated township at Kashwak. Tom and Jordan accompanied Dan and the others heading west on Route 11.

Clay spent the day in a small cottage next to the Springvale, ME, Logging Museum. After a breakfast of oatmeal, with powdered milk, raisins, sugar, and a foil packet of concentrated bacon and eggs, he slept in the back room.

Tom and the others thought they spent a wonderful day at the Twilight Motel in Vaughan Woods. The huge breakfast, dancing, and sleeping were a virtual reality the phoners created. They had already walked the night. The phoners pushed them to walk during the day, too, to exhaust them so they'd be less resistant at night, when the phoners slept and lost control of them. They were redirected toward Kashwak and spent that night at a motel on Maine Route 47. [*Cell*]

12 October ≥2008, Friday

Tessa Jean, the author of the Willow Grove Knitting Society mystery novels, had a speaking engagement for Books & Brown Baggers at the Chicopee Public Library.

12:00 p.m.: She gave a forty-five-minute speech to about four hundred people in the library auditorium. In the Question & Answer session, people asked the standard questions: where did she get her ideas, were her characters based on real people, how does one get an agent, and so on. The event ended with a few autographs. Ramona Norville paid her and gave her a shortcut that eliminated much of I-84's out-of-the-way part. Sixteen miles along the scenic Stagg Road would take her to US 47, leaving her about twelve miles on I-84.

Four miles from US 47, she rounded a curve on Stagg Road and ran over nail-studded debris. She pulled over at a deserted, broken-down store, with a faded ESSO sign over an island that no longer had gas pumps. A rusty spike held a piece of wood in her left, front tire.

A Zombie Bakers van rounded the curve and swerved around the debris without seeing her. She cleaned the debris off the road.

An old F-150 pickup truck stopped short; Lester Strehlke looked at the debris in the ditch. When Tess called out to him, he parked next to her Expedition and offered to change her tire. In the back of his truck, she noticed nail-studded debris like that she had just cleared. He punched her with his right hand, the hand with a red-stoned ring, and knocked her out.

She woke up under him, inside the deserted store. Her panties hung from a pocket of his bib overalls; her pants were under an old counter. He knocked her out again and raped her some more, lots more. When she woke up again, he knocked her out by choking her. The third time she woke up, he was carrying her outside. Her Expedition was gone. She stayed limp, hoping he'd think she was dead. He pushed her into a drainage pipe in a ditch across Stagg Road from the store then drove away.

She stayed in the culvert's pit, in the water and rotting leaves, so he wouldn't see her if he came back. She thought about crawling across the street in the pipe but found the corpses of two women. One was a skeleton, the other, a fresher body. Tess's forehead, cheeks, lips, and throat were bruised and swollen. She had two black eyes. It felt as if her nose was broken. Naked below the waist, she went back to the store, where she found her slacks and flat shoes. Her cell phone was there but smashed. Her diamond drop earrings were missing.

Hiding off to the side of Stagg Road every time she heard a vehicle, she walked four miles to The Stagger Inn. The Zombie Bakers played "Mustang Sally" in the roadhouse. She needed privacy, so she walked a half mile to the intersection of Stagg Road and US 47. The Gas & Dash had restrooms and two pay phones. She used her AT&T calling card to call Royal Limousine to take her home, paying them with the credit card they had on file.

11:00–11:30 p.m.: She took some Vicodin then showered. ["Big Driver"]

12 October 2011

The Stand: Night Has Come #3 of 6 (Marvel Comics, $3.99) published

~12 October 2014

At Dipper's Roadhouse, Frank DeLesseps poured a glass of beer on the back of Dale Barbara's shirt. Frank walked away then returned with a pitcher of Bud Light, which he splashed in Barbie's face. Barbie accepted Frank's invitation to take it outside. Junior Rennie, Melvin Searles, and Carter Thibodeau ambushed him. Chief Perkins stopped the fight. He saw that Barbie was innocent and smoothed everything over. He suggested Barbie leave town, however, because Big Jim Rennie was sure to make trouble for him. [*Under the Dome*]

12 October 2016

The Dark Tower: The Drawing of the Three—The Sailor #1 of 5 (Marvel Comics, $3.99) published

October 13

13 October 1958, Monday

George Amberson's second timeline: Before leaving Derry, ME, George Amberson left a note with Pete at the Sleepy Silver Dollar. The note told Bill Turcotte to see a doctor about his heart. [*11/22/63*]

13 October 1985

Skeleton Crew dropped to number 5 on *The New York Times* Fiction Best Seller List, its seventeenth week on the List.

13 October 1990

Stu Redman was coherent and talking. He recovered from his pneumonia during the next five days. [*The Stand: The Complete & Uncut Edition*]

13 October 1991, Sunday

Leland Gaunt visited Brian Rusk in a dream to have him throw rocks into Wilma Jerzyck's house. Later, Brian threw about a dozen, breaking several windows, a Sony TV, a microwave oven, and more. Each rock had a note implying Nettie Cobb was the culprit.

~9:45 a.m.: Hugh Priest killed Nettie Cobb's dog, Raider, and left a note that appeared to be from Wilma Jerzyck.

>10:15 a.m.: Leland Gaunt gave Nettie a book of traffic tickets to play a prank on Dan Keeton. She taped them throughout his house. When she returned home, she found Raider dead and the note. With a meat cleaver, she headed toward Wilma Jerzyck's. Wilma had just found her house vandalized; she headed for Nettie's with a carving knife.

~1:30 p.m.: An old woman called the Sheriff's Office to report two women killing each other with knives. Deputy Andy Clutterbuck sent Seat Thomas to check it out, called Sheriff Pangborn and the state police, and met the Sheriff at the scene. They found Nettie Cobb and Wilma Jerzyck dead.

~1:45 p.m.: At Needful Things, Leland Gaunt gave Polly Chalmers an Egyptian amulet that eased pain. She could pay for it later if it worked. [*Needful Things*]

13 October 1993

Nightmares and Dreamscapes (Viking, $27.50) published with a first printing of 1,500,000 copies

13 October 1996

The Green Mile, Part One: The Two Dead Girls rose to number 12 on *The New York Times* Paperback Fiction Best Seller List, its twenty-fifth and last week on the List.

After two weeks off, *The Green Mile, Part Two: The Mouse on the Mile* re-entered *The New York Times* Paperback Fiction Best Seller List a third time. Its seventeenth and last week on the List, it was number 14.

The Green Mile, Part Four: The Bad Death of Eduard Delacroix rose to number 11 on *The New York Times* Paperback Fiction Best Seller List, its fifteenth and last week on the List.

The Green Mile, Part Five: Night Journey stayed at number 8 on *The New York Times* Paperback

Fiction Best Seller List, its ninth week on the List.

The Green Mile, Part Six: Coffey on the Mile dropped to number 3 on *The New York Times* Paperback Fiction Best Seller List, its fifth week on the List.

Desperation entered *The New York Times* Fiction Best Seller List at number 1. It was on the List for fifteen weeks.

Richard Bachman's *The Regulators* entered *The New York Times* Fiction Best Seller List at number 2. It was on the List for fourteen weeks.

13 October 2002

From a Buick 8 entered *The New York Times* Fiction Best Seller List at number 1. It was on the List for eleven weeks.

13 October 2003, Monday

Daniel Hartwell, Ray Huizenga, Jordan, Denise Link, and Tom McCourt found a pickup truck with keys. They followed Route 47 to Route 11, south of Route 160, and then switched to a school bus Ray saw behind the Newfield Trading Post. With Ray driving, they continued up Route 160. At the Gurleyville Quarry, he rigged the back of the bus with explosives, to be detonated by cell phone.

Clay Riddell spent much of the day in the only motel in Gurleyville, ME, an unincorporated township on Route 160. He left before dark, knowing it was safe because he was going to Kashwak, where the phoners wanted him to go. He crested a hill on Route 160 and saw a yellow school bus with Tom and the others. Ray Huizenga walked off to relieve himself and called for Clay to check for poison ivy or poison oak. He gave Clay a cell phone and a piece of paper with a ten-digit number and told Clay he'd know when to use it. He didn't tell Clay his plan because the flock could read minds. So the flock wouldn't read *his* mind, Ray took Clay's .45 and killed himself.

The phoners urged them on to Kashwak, where there was no cell phone service. They stopped at the Parachute Drop ride outside the Kashwakamak Hall. Surrounded by about 5,000 phoners, they walked to the hall and were locked in. Clay figured out Ray's plan and told the others. Because of the fair each year, the New England Amusement Corporation carnies had put up an illegal cell phone tower in the Parachute Drop ride. The phoners didn't know, but Ray and Clay did.

The Hall's windows were too small for an adult, so they broke one with a crowbar and helped Jordan out. He drove the school bus, not to the edge of the flock as Clay suggested, but over the flock, parking in the middle. When Jordan was safely away, Clay dialed the number. An explosion destroyed most of the flock; the few stragglers weren't a threat. The blast damaged the Hall enough for Clay and the others to get out.

Clay left the group. People who went to Kashwak were given cell phones at the edge of service and were zapped with The Pulse. The Pulse had mutated; these new phoners didn't exhibit the same behavior as the original phoners. They were more likely to wander around than flock. Clay walked south, hoping his son was one of the new phoners who had wandered away from the flock. [*Cell*]

13 October ≥2008, Saturday

6:00 a.m.: Tessa Jean woke up. Thinking of the two dead women while showering, she was sure he'd do it again. She decided to go to Stoke Village Mall and anonymously report the dead women, the guy, and his pickup to the State Police.

~7:45 a.m.: She fell asleep.

9:45 a.m.: The phone woke her. Betsy Neal from The Stagger Inn left a message that they had her car. After 5:00 p.m., it would be towed at Tess's expense. They didn't have her car keys but had other property she'd need to pick up at the office. Tess took a cab.

The Stagger Inn was closed but unlocked. She went in. Betsy Neal found her and returned her TomTom GPS. Since her car wasn't locked, they had removed the GPS for safekeeping. Tess assured Betsy her injuries hadn't happened at the bar but afterward, at the Gas & Dash, with her boyfriend. A nice man had helped her. She wondered whether Betsy knew the big man, who wore a brown hat with bleach spots and drove an old blue pickup truck. Betsy said it sounded like Big Driver, a man with a Polish name, who ran a trucking company with his brother.

It was odd that Ramona Norville hadn't given the usual speaking-engagement, morning-after phone call. With Google, she found "Librarian Ramona Norville Announces 'Willow Grove Friday'," a Chicopee *Weekly Reminder* article, with a picture of Ramona Norville. She was a large woman who resembled the man who raped Tess; she could have been the man's mother. A search of trucking companies led her to Red Hawk Trucking's website. There was a picture of Big Driver behind the wheel of a truck; he looked like Ramona. The Books & Brown Baggers website mentioned that Ramona Norville hosted the June 10th meeting at her home in Brewster. A search of Brewster Township's tax records showed her address. ["Big Driver"]

13 October 2013

Joyland rose to number 7 on *The New York Times* Paperback Trade Fiction Best Seller List, its seventeenth week on the List.

Doctor Sleep entered *The New York Times* Hardcover Fiction Best Seller List at number 1. It was on the List for twenty-one weeks.

October 14

14 October 1945

Gatlin, NE, child Zepeniah Kirk was born George Kirk. ["Children of the Corn"]

14 October 1960

George Amberson's second timeline: George Amberson collected his $1,200 winnings at Faith Financial. [*11/22/63*]

14 October 1961, Saturday night

Bobbi Jill Allnut and Mattie Shaw's cartoon mural of Miss Sadie Hawkins was displayed at the Denholm County Consolidated High School Sadie Hawkins Dance. Donald Bellingham DJ'd as Donny B. [*11/22/63*]

14 October 1964, dusk

Zepeniah Kirk was sacrificed to He Who Walks Behind the Rows. ["Children of the Corn"]

14 October 1978, Saturday

The Libertyville High School Terriers lost their sixth football game of the season. [*Christine*]

14 October 1979

The Dead Zone rose to number 1 on *The New York Times* Fiction Best Seller List, its sixth week on the List. Stephen King's first #1 Best Seller, it stayed at number 1 for two weeks.

14 October 1990

The Stand: The Complete & Uncut Edition rose to number 10 on *The New York Times* Fiction Best Seller List, its twenty-third week on the List.

Four Past Midnight stayed at number 1 on *The New York Times* Fiction Best Seller List, its fifth week on the List.

14 October 1991, Monday

dawn: Ricky Bissonette left an offensive, threatening note for Reverend Rose. It was signed THE CONCERNED CATHOLIC MEN OF CASTLE ROCK.

~7:45 a.m.: At Needful Things, Leland Gaunt gave Ev Frankel an envelope with "Lovey" on it. He put it in Lester Pratt's car.

10:15 a.m.: With a phony book by Reginald Merrill, *Lost and Buried Treasures of New England*, Leland Gaunt enticed Ace Merrill into his shop. He coerced Merrill into working for him by giving him cocaine from the Plains of Leng and showing him a map that marked where Pop Merrill buried his fortune. He sold Ace the book with the map for $1.50 and agreeing to work for Gaunt. With a 10% employee discount, the cost was $1.35. The book alternated between *Treasure Island* and the Reginald Merrill book. He sent Ace to 85 Whipple Street, in a deserted, decaying section of Boston, to get his car and weapons. A crate contained automatic handguns that David Friedman, a firearms expert, had never seen. The bullets had been treated with an unknown, deadly poison.

~1:15 p.m.: While Sally Ratcliffe's car had been in the shop, her fiancé, Lester Pratt, let her use his. She found an envelope addressed to Lovey in the car. A picture showed Lester and Judy Libby kissing in The Mellow Tiger; a letter suggested they had slept together. Sally returned his car with a message to go to hell spray painted in pink on the windshield. She spent the night with her friend Irene Lutjens.

overnight: Melissa Clutterbuck pulled many of Lenore Potter's flowers and threw them into the street. The prank was part of the price when she bought a set of Limoges china from Leland Gaunt. [*Needful Things*]

14 October 2000, Wednesday

Mrs. McCurdy told Al Parker his mother had a stroke but was OK. While hitchhiking, he sat on a stone wall outside a small country graveyard on Ridge Road, near Gates Falls, ME. He went in and was startled by the inscription on George Staub's gravestone: "FUN IS FUN AND DONE IS DONE," a phrase his mother always said. Walking back to the road, he tripped and almost hit his head on a gravestone. Looking at the gravestone again, he saw the inscription was "Well Begun, Too Soon Done." A car passed, stopped, and picked him up. The driver, with stitches around his neck and on his abdomen, was George Staub. Speeding along at 80 MPH, George knew Al was too afraid to ride the Bullet when his mother took him to Thrill Village when he was a kid. Twelve miles outside Lewiston, George asked who rides the Bullet with him and who stays—either Al or his mother. Al had to decide before they reached Lewiston or George would take them both. Seven miles outside Lewiston, Al said to take his mother because she had lived most of her life (she was forty-eight) and he was just beginning his (he was twenty-one). George pinned a Riding the Bullet button on him and pushed him out. He never hit the ground—he was already down in the Ridge Road graveyard. The back of his head was bloody. A farmer in a pickup gave him a ride to Central Maine Medical Center. The hospital allowed him to visit his mother for a few minutes even though visiting hours were over. He hitchhiked home. His mother lived another nine years. He had lost Staub's Riding the Bullet button. He found it under his mother's bed after she died. [*Riding the Bullet*]

14 October 2001

Black House dropped to number 2 *The New York Times* Fiction Best Seller List, its third week on the List.

14 October 2003, Tuesday

Clay Riddell spent the night in a trailer near Gurleyville, ME. [*Cell*]

14 October ≥2008, Sunday

>4:00 p.m.: Dressed in dark clothing, Tessa Jean visited Ramona Norville. The look of shock on Ramona's face told Tess she was in on the rape. Tess pulled her gun and went in. Ramona got the gun from her, told her she had sent Tess to her son, and shot at her—nothing. Tess had learned never to leave a round in the chamber. She stabbed Ramona in the stomach with a butcher knife then shot her. Upstairs, she found Ramona's Apple Mac computer on but sleeping. A couple of keystrokes woke it; she found Alvin Strehlke's and Lester Strehlke's addresses in Ramona's desktop address book. On her way out, Tess retrieved her diamond drop earrings she had seen in a glass candy dish on the TV.

~9:10 p.m.: She passed Red Hawk Trucking on her way to Al Strehlke's house. Big Driver's pickup was at a gas pump outside Richie's Township Road Truck Stop. Big Driver was in the store. She drove on to wait for him at his house.

9:35 p.m.: Al Strehlke pulled up and parked in his driveway. Tess opened the passenger door and fired twice, hitting him in the throat and above the right eyebrow. For the last couple of days, she thought Big Driver was the man who had raped her. This man was older and even bigger than her attacker. She had killed the wrong man. Lester Strehlke, his younger brother, was the one; Lester wore his big brother's hat and ring when he went hunting. She left her Expedition and drove Al's pickup to Lester's house. She wore Big Driver's hat and put his ring in her pocket.

almost midnight: She parked in Lester's driveway, toward the back of the house. The sound of his brother's pickup truck didn't alarm him. He was surprised, however, when Tess walked in on him while he was watching TV. She shot him in the temple. In a travel-tote on the closet shelf in his bedroom, she found a bunch of women's panties. She replaced hers with a four-foot piece of yellow boat line. She put the hat and ring on Lester then returned to Al's to see whether she could find any evidence that he took part in Lester's crimes.

Between Al's mattress and box spring, were three purses, including her expensive, cream-colored, Kate Spade clutch. On the closet's top shelf was a stuffed duck, with a missing eye, patches of missing fur from being petted often, and a dark maroon splash on its beak. This suggested a child victim. ["Big Driver"]

14 October 2018

The Outsider dropped to number 12 on *The New York Times* Hardcover Fiction Best Seller List, its nineteenth week on the List.

October 15

15 October 1984

"Urban Energy Conservation and the Young Turks," an article in *Time* magazine, commented on Ben Hanscom's architectural competence. [*IT*]

15 October 1991, Tuesday

8:00 a.m.: Leland Gaunt sold black pearls to Lucille Dunham for $38 and a prank on Reverend Rose.

2:46 p.m.: Polly Chalmers's amulet was easing her arthritis pain. At Needful Things, Leland Gaunt charged $46 plus a prank on Ace Merrill. She went to the old Camber place, dug up a Crisco can from behind the barn, put an envelope in place of photographs of a woman getting it on with a collie, and burned the photos. She heard growling from the barn and saw two red things that might have been Cujo's eyes.

Leland Gaunt had gotten John LaPointe's wallet in an earlier prank. He gave it to Slopey Dodd to put in Lester Pratt's car.

Norris Ridgewick slashed the tires on Hugh Priest's car, smashed the headlights and taillights, and left a note that showed it was from Henry Beaufort. Myra Evans put a note that seemed to be from Priest on Beaufort's windshield, slashed all his tires, and scratched the paint on his car.

3:40 p.m.: Henry Beaufort, owner-bartender of The Mellow Tiger in Castle Rock, went to the bar to get his shotgun and go after Hugh Priest. Billy Tupper suggested they have a drink first, after which Beaufort calmed down. Outside, Hugh Priest shot Tupper in the neck, came in, and shot Beaufort in the right cheek. Henry and Priest shot each other; Priest died. Beaufort died on the way to the hospital, not from gunshot wounds but from an unknown, deadly poison on the bullets, a toxin that ruptured his brain and heart. Leland Gaunt had given Priest an automatic handgun.

Lester Pratt found John LaPointe's wallet in his car. In had a picture of John and Sally Ratcliffe, Lester's fiancée. Slopey Dodd saw the picture and said it was the same guy who took Sally out Friday night, and, before getting in the car, Sally and John did some serious kissing. Pratt found LaPointe outside the Municipal Building and beat him. Sheila Brigham called Sheriff Pangborn and hit Pratt on the head with a gun butt, killing him. She was treated for shock at the hospital. LaPointe was sent to the hospital in Norway, ME, where he was treated for internal injuries, a broken nose, and a broken jaw. Feeling responsible for Pratt's death, Sally Ratcliffe hanged herself.

Ace Merrill dug up a can at the Camber place and found a note that said Alan Pangborn found $200,000 in it.

after dark: In a dispute over car repairs, Eddie Warburton shot and killed Ricky Bissonette at Sonny's Sunoco. He thought Ricky was Sonny Jackett. Sonny shot and killed Warburton.

evening: Lenore Potter shot and killed Melissa Clutterbuck while Melissa was pulling Potter's flowers. She thought Melissa was Stephanie Bonsaint, whom she thought had pulled her flowers the night before.

7:00 p.m.: The Baptist Anti-Gambling Christian Soldiers of Castle Rock, led by Reverend Rose, had been having meetings to discuss a strategy to fight the Catholics' Casino Nite. After Leland Gaunt's pranks set them against the Catholics, the meetings were to discuss ways of fighting and protecting themselves from Father John Brigham and the Catholics.

More than seventy people attended their fourth meeting, during which Don Hemphill burst in and said the Catholics stink-bombed his market. A stink bomb, which Sonny Jackett had planted in the Baptist Church earlier that day, went off. Escaping through a window because the doors were jammed, they went after the Catholics. Meanwhile, at the Knights of Columbus Hall, a stink bomb that June Gavineaux had planted went off. Father Brigham's Catholics broke through a window because the doors wouldn't open and met the Daughters of Isabella in the parking lot. (A stink bomb, which Myrtle Keeton had planted, had gone off in the Daughters of Isabella Hall while they were discussing Casino Night. They, too, broke out a window because Babs Miller had jammed the doors.) The Baptists and the Catholics clashed at the bottom of Castle Hill. Trooper Morris, Henry Payton, Baptists Lucille Dunham, Norman Harper, Nan Roberts, and Bill Sayers, and Catholics Albert Gendron, Jake Pulaski, and Betsy Vigue were injured. Len Milliken died.

Cora Rusk entered Myra Evans's bedroom with a gun. Myra was expecting her. After a shootout, Myra had gunshot wounds in the thigh and knee, and Cora was dead.

Ace Merrill and Dan Keeton put dynamite bombs under the Castle Stream Bridge and in several Main Street business establishments. All bombs went off, killing nineteen people.

Polly Chalmers figured out Leland Gaunt was behind Castle Rock's trouble. She found Alan Pangborn leaving Needful Things. As Polly explained what Gaunt was doing, Ace Merrill approached, held her at gunpoint, and demanded Pangborn give him his $200,000. While Alan used magic to force Gaunt out of town, Ace aimed to shoot Polly. Norris Ridgewick shot and killed him. [*Needful Things*]

15 October 2003, Wednesday

Clay Riddell saw Johnny Riddell sitting on a curb outside the Gurleyville Café. [*Cell*]

15 October ≥2008, Monday

7:30 a.m.: Tessa Jean woke up after less than three hours' sleep. Betsy Neal was a loose end, so Tess researched her on the computer. She found twelve Neals in the phone listings. E. Neal could've been Elizabeth (Betsy) Neal. Tess called it; a machine answered, with Betsy's voice speaking the greeting. As Tess explained that she had been raped and tried to make it right, Betsy picked up.

>1:00 p.m.: Over lunch in the Colewich town common, Tess told Betsy the rest. Betsy supported her, saying she'd need a backup story because there *will* be a police investigation that could lead to Tess through the limo driver or the cab driver. Betsy asked Tess to keep her out of it. ["Big Driver"]

15 October 2010

The Secretary of Dreams, Volume Two (Cemetery Dance, $75 5,000-copy gift edition; $300 750-copy limited edition; $1,500 52-copy lettered edition) published

15 October 2012, Monday

Little Green God of Agony, a serial eComic, page 1 of 24, online at www.stephenking.com

15 October 2017

Sleeping Beauties entered *The New York Times* Hardcover Fiction Best Seller List at number 1. It was on the List for fourteen weeks.

October 16

16 October 1961, Monday, 7:00 p.m.

<u>George Amberson's second timeline</u>: George Amberson picked up the surveillance equipment he had put a deposit on at Silent Mike's Satellite Electronics. [*11/22/63*]

16 October 1973, Tuesday

Dev Jones drove Annie Ross and Mike Ross to Wilmington International Airport. A Buddy Ross Ministries, Inc. private jet flew them to Chicago. [*Joyland*]

16 October 1975

Richard Dees offered Johnny Smith a contract for an *Inside View* psychic column. Johnny threatened to get a shotgun to force Dees off his porch. [*The Dead Zone*]

16 October 1978, Monday

Dennis Guilder dreamed of Arnie Cunningham driving Christine, with a decaying Roland LeBay in the passenger seat. [*Christine*]

16 October 1983

Christine dropped to number 12 on *The New York Times* Fiction Best Seller List, its twenty-eighth week on the List.

16 October 2011

Mile 81 dropped to number 18 on *The New York Times* E-Book Fiction Best Seller List, its fifth week on the List.

October 17

17 October 1850

Calvin McCann ordered a five-pound tin of Rat's Bane for thirty cents from a Summer 1850 catalog. He had it shipped to Chapelwaite. ["Jerusalem's Lot"]

17 October 1920

An entire Wing of Rose Red burned. Ellen Rimbauer may have set the fire in retaliation for John Rimbauer's delaying the construction of the Tower that Ellen had ordered more than two years before. Construction began a couple of weeks later. [*The Diary of Ellen Rimbauer: My Life at Rose Red*]

17 October 1963

Lee Harvey Oswald started working at the Texas School Book Depository. Buell Frazier had gotten him the job. [*11/22/63*]

17 October 1973, Wednesday

Mike Ross started seeing a round of specialists in Chicago. [*Joyland*]

17 October 1975

'Salem's Lot (Doubleday, $8.95, reduced to $7.95) published with a first printing of 8,000 to 20,000 copies

17 October 1977

In a letter to Johnny Smith, Chuck Chatsworth wrote he had scored three touchdowns, hyperventilated, and passed out in the Stovington Tigers' sole win in four games. He also wrote that most people in Greg Stillson's congressional district thought Stillson was doing a better job than President Carter. [*The Dead Zone*]

17 October 1982

Different Seasons dropped to number 6 on *The New York Times* Fiction Best Seller List, its eleventh week on the List.

17 October 1993

Nightmares & Dreamscapes entered *The New York Times* Fiction Best Seller List at number 3. It was on the List for eighteen weeks.

17 October 1999

Hearts in Atlantis stayed at number 4 on *The New York Times* Fiction Best Seller List, its third week on the List.

17 October 2004

The Dark Tower VII: The Dark Tower stayed at number 1 on *The New York Times* Fiction Best Seller List, its second week on the List.

17 October 2005

Stephen King finished *Cell* in Center Lovell, ME.

17 October 2012, Wednesday

The Dark Tower: The Gunslinger—Man in Black #5 of 5 (Marvel Comics, $3.99) published

Little Green God of Agony, a serial eComic, page 2 of 24, online at www.stephenking.com

October 18

18 October 1939

Lee Harvey Oswald was born in New Orleans, LA. [*11/22/63*]

18 October 1971, Monday

Sarah Bracknell accepted Walter Hazlett's marriage proposal. [*The Dead Zone*]

18 October 1981

Cujo stayed at number 2 on *The New York Times* Fiction Best Seller List, its tenth week on the List.

18 October 1987

Misery dropped to number 9 on *The New York Times* Fiction Best Seller List, its twentieth week on the List.

18 October 1992

Gerald's Game dropped to number 6 on *The New York Times* Fiction Best Seller List, its fourteenth week on the List.

18 October 1998

Bag of Bones stayed at number 1 on *The New York Times* Fiction Best Seller List, its second week on the List.

18 October 2016

mass market paperback version of *The Bazaar of Bad Dreams* (Pocket Books, $9.99), with "Cookie Jar," a short story not included in the first (hardcover) edition, published

October 19

19 October 1850

The noises inside Chapelwaite were worse. Calvin McCann thought they were coming from the cellar. He and Charles Boone suspected more than rats. ["Jerusalem's Lot"]

19 October 1947

"SO-CALLED SPACE WHEAT A HOAX, ANGRY FARMER DECLARES; Andrew Hoxon Denies 'Saucer Connection;' Red-Tinged Wheat 'Nothing But Prank,' He Insists" appeared in the Roswell, NM, *Daily Record.* [*Dreamcatcher*]

19 October 1980

Firestarter dropped to number 2 on *The New York Times* Fiction Best Seller List, its ninth week on the List.

19 October 1986

IT stayed at number 1 on *The New York Times* Fiction Best Seller List, *IT*'s sixth week on the List.

19 October 1987

Stephen King didn't like the way he was living his life, with all the drinking, drugging, and smoking. [*The Dark Tower VI: Song of Susannah*]

19 October 1988

Public announcement of a working Jaunt was given. Developed from Victor Carune's particle transmission research, the Jaunt grew to an inexpensive means of transporting goods and people over long distances throughout the solar system. ["The Jaunt"]

19 October 1995

Audrey Wyler received a response from Allen Symes, geological mining engineer for the China Pit copper mine in Desperation, NV. She had written to ask whether anything unusual happened when the Garins visited the mine. His reply said nothing happened; she knew he lied. [*The Regulators*]

Stephen King finished *Wizard and Glass*. [*The Dark Tower VI: Song of Susannah*]

19 October 2012, Friday

Little Green God of Agony, a serial eComic, page 3 of 24, online at www.stephenking.com

October 20

20 October 1850

Charles Boone and Calvin McCann saw the Undead Marcella Boone and Randolph Boone in Chapelwaite's cellar. Charles passed out for thirty-six hours. ["Jerusalem's Lot"]

20 October 1965, Wednesday

George Barton drove his Ford F-150 pickup, with his potato digger, toward his south field. An epileptic seizure caused him to veer onto the wrong side of Route 9. Patsy Jacobs and Morrie Jacobs died in a head-on collision after they emerged from around a curve. Barton was OK but never drove again. [*Revival*]

20 October 1977

Jack Torrance found a wasp's nest while shingling The Overlook Hotel's roof. He killed and chased away its inhabitants with a wasp bomb then gave the empty nest to Danny Torrance. In nightmares that night, Danny had premonitions of his father chasing him with a roque mallet. Three wasps stung his hands eleven times. Jack put a glass bowl over the nest. Later, there were fifty to a hundred wasps inside the bowl. [*The Shining*]

20 October 1985

Skeleton Crew dropped to number 6 on *The New York Times* Fiction Best Seller List, its eighteenth week on the List.

20 October 1990

Stu Redman went outside. [*The Stand: The Complete & Uncut Edition*]

20 October 1991

Needful Things entered *The New York Times* Fiction Best Seller List at number 2. It was on the List for twenty weeks.

20 October 1996

The Green Mile, Part Five: Night Journey dropped to number 14 on *The New York Times* Paperback Fiction Best Seller List, its tenth and last week on the List.

The Green Mile, Part Six: Coffey on the Mile dropped to number 6 on *The New York Times* Paperback Fiction Best Seller List, its sixth week on the List.

Desperation stayed at number 1 on *The New York Times* Fiction Best Seller List, its second week on the List.

Richard Bachman's *The Regulators* stayed at number 2 on *The New York Times* Fiction Best Seller List, its second week on the List.

20 October 2000

Jean Parker was discharged from Central Maine Medical Center after being treated for a stroke. [*Riding the Bullet*]

20 October 2002

From a Buick 8 dropped to number 2 on *The New York Times* Fiction Best Seller List, its second week on the List.

20 October 2010

The Stand: Hardcases #4 of 5 (Marvel Comics, $3.99) published

20 October 2013

Joyland dropped to number 20 on *The New York Times* Paperback Trade Fiction Best Seller List, its eighteenth week on the List.

Doctor Sleep stayed at number 1 on *The New York Times* Hardcover Fiction Best Seller List, its second week on the List.

October 21

21 October 1978, Saturday

At Ridge Rock, the Bears beat the Libertyville Terriers 46–3. Seven minutes into the third quarter, three Bears hit Dennis Guilder after he caught a pass. He fractured his skull, injured his lower back, and broke his right forearm, his right leg, and his left leg twice. He passed out. Dr. Arroway treated him at Libertyville Community Hospital, where he stayed in Room 240. Teammate Brian McNally, who was to replace him after he graduated, assumed his position. [*Christine*]

21 October 1979

The Dead Zone stayed at number 1 on *The New York Times* Fiction Best Seller List, its seventh week on the List.

21 October 1990

The Stand: The Complete & Uncut Edition dropped to number 12 on *The New York Times* Fiction Best Seller List, its twenty-fourth week on the List.

Four Past Midnight dropped to number 2 on *The New York Times* Fiction Best Seller List, its sixth week on the List.

21 October 2001

Black House stayed at number 2 *The New York Times* Fiction Best Seller List, its fourth week on the List.

21 October 2003, Tuesday

Clay Riddell and Johnny Riddell had been staying in the caretaker's cottage at the Springvale Logging Museum. Johnny wasn't getting any better, so Clay dialed 911 on his cell phone and put the phone to Johnny's ear. He hoped for a reboot of the original Johnny programming. [*Cell*]

21 October 2009

The Talisman: The Road of Trials #0 of 6, a prequel to *The Talisman* (Del Rey Comics, Free) published

The Stand: Soul Survivors #1 of 5 (Marvel Comics, $3.99) published

21 October 2014, Saturday: Dome Day

Leatherheads, children from another world, created a force field Dome around Chester's Mill, ME, that caused a few accidents:

—2,000 feet up, following Route 119 out of town on an instructional flight, Claudie Sanders flew into the Dome. The plane exploded, killing her and Chuck Thompson, her instructor. During the investigation, Chief Perkins got too close to the Dome; his pacemaker exploded, killing him.

—Billy and Wanda Debec argued on their way to the flea market in Oxford Hills. Billy turned around and headed back home. At 60+ MPH on Route 117, they hit the Dome. His airbag didn't deploy; the steering column killed him. The car's engine broke Wanda's left leg and right arm, her head hit the dashboard, and the windshield sliced off part of her scalp.

—Heading south on Route 117, into Chester's Mill, Elsa Andrews and Nora Robichaud found the Debec accident scene. Wanda Debec was dragging herself along the highway's white line. They put her in the backseat of Nora's car to take her to Cathy Russell Hospital. Elsa got in the back with her. Nora drove around the Debecs' Chevy and crashed into the Dome. Elsa hit the driver's seat and was OK.

—Listening to James Blunt's "You're Beautiful" on his iPod, Bob Roux drove his Deere tractor, at 15 MPH, home for lunch. He ran into the outside of the Dome and was thrown forward onto the Dome, breaking his neck and splitting his skull.

—Myra Evans was reaching for a Blue Hubbard squash in her vegetable garden when the Dome came down. With the garden crossing the line between Chester's Mill and Motton, the Dome severed her right hand. She went inside but died of blood loss.

—Vera Appleton and her children, Aidan and Alice, were staying in a cabin at Chester's Pond. Vera went to Yoder's to get Whoopie Pies and other supplies when the Dome came down, trapping her out and her kids in.

Junior Rennie, with a tumor-induced migraine, went to see Angie McCain. It angered him when she answered with a smile and called him Junior. He slapped her. He went in and beat her so bad that she had a seizure. To stay out of Shawshank State Prison, he strangled her.

On Chief Perkins's home computer, Brenda Perkins found a file documenting the Chief's investigation of Big Jim Rennie's unlawful activities.

>9:15 p.m.: Junior Rennie went back to the McCains'. He cleaned up the crime scene and put Angie's body in the pantry. Dodee Sanders knocked at the front door then went in. Junior strangled her and put her body in the pantry.

10:40 p.m.: The military found that the Dome was a force field. Colonel Cox asked Dale Barbara to find and shut down the generator, which had to be inside the Dome. [*Under the Dome*]

21 October 2018

The Outsider dropped to number 14 on *The New York Times* Hardcover Fiction Best Seller List, its twentieth and last week on the List.

October 22

22 October 1962, Monday, 8:30 p.m.

<u>George Amberson's second timeline</u>: After President Kennedy announced the Cuban Missile Crisis, Johnny Clayton's Japanese atomic bomb blast pictures concerned Sadie Dunhill. Because of Johnny's statistical analysis and his past, correct predictions, she feared nuclear war. She took a few pills of the sedative Nembutal. When they didn't kick in, she drank a little Scotch. The combination made her sick; she vomited in the bathroom and passed out on her bed.

On his evening walk, George Amberson stopped at the Ivy Room for a beer. When he saw how frightened everyone at the bar was after President Kennedy spoke, he phoned Sadie—no answer. He went to Jodie, TX. [*11/22/63*]

22 October 2000

On Writing entered *The New York Times* Non-Fiction Best Seller List at number 2. It was on the List for sixteen weeks.

22 October 2012, Monday

Little Green God of Agony, a serial eComic, page 4 of 24, online at www.stephenking.com

22 October 2014, Sunday: Day 2

Dale Barbara had been a Captain in the Army. Colonel Cox told him the President had declared martial law in Chester's Mill. Reinstated and promoted to Colonel, Barbie was the officer in charge in Chester's Mill and the town's link to the outside.

A protest demonstration and a group prayer were held at Alden Dinsmore's farm, the site of Chuck Thompson's plane crash. Romeo Burpee, of Burpee's Department Store, paid Dinsmore $600 for the rights to set up a tent to sell hot dogs and lemonade. Dinsmore charged $5 a car to park. The events ended when Rory Dinsmore tried to save the town. He fired his father's .30-.30 rifle into the Dome, hoping to pierce it. Instead, the bullet ricocheted back in two pieces; the smaller put out his left eye and lodged in his brain. He died in surgery.

>10:00 p.m.: Thuds at Sammy Bushey's front door woke her. Frankie DeLesseps, Georgia Roux, Melvin Searles, and Carter Thibodeau forced themselves in. The men raped her, while Georgia cheered them on. [*Under the Dome*]

22 October 2017

Sleeping Beauties dropped to number 2 on *The New York Times* Hardcover Fiction Best Seller List, its second week on the List.

October 23

23 October 1962, Tuesday, ~12:30 a.m.

<u>George Amberson's second timeline</u>: George Amberson pulled into Sadie Dunhill's driveway. When she didn't answer the front doorbell or his knocks at the back door, he let himself in with her spare key under the back step. He saw she had taken some pills with Scotch. Too many pills remained for her to have tried to kill herself, but she was passed out on her bed. He got her half-awake, and a cold shower woke her fully. He told her not to worry about the Cuban Missile Crisis; it would be over in a few days. He explained how it would happen: through an intermediary from the United States media—ABC News correspondent John Scali—the Russians would agree to dismantle their missiles in Cuba if the United States removed theirs from Turkey and agreed not to invade Cuba. She didn't know how he could know this but trusted him. [*11/22/63*]

23 October 1965, Saturday:

Reverend David Thomas gave the eulogy at the funeral for Morrie Jacobs and Patsy Jacobs. For friend Charlie Jacobs, Pastor Stephen Givens led the graveside service at Willow Grove Cemetery. He read from First Corinthians. [*Revival*]

23 October 1978, Monday afternoon

Fifty hours after his football accident, Dennis Guilder regained consciousness. Prognosis: he would walk, limping for at least two years but never play football again. Coach Puffer gave him a bottle of rose hips to help his bones heal faster. [*Christine*]

23 October 1983

Christine dropped to number 13 on *The New York Times* Fiction Best Seller List, its twenty-ninth week on the List.

23 October 1994

Insomnia entered *The New York Times* Fiction Best Seller List at number 1. It was on the List for sixteen weeks.

23 October 2000

The Plant Book One: *Zenith Rising*, Part 4 e-book (Philtrum Press, $2.00) published

23 October 2005

The Colorado Kid entered *The New York Times* Paperback Fiction Best Seller List at number 5. It was on the List for three weeks.

23 October 2011

Mile 81 rose to number 17 on *The New York Times* E-Book Fiction Best Seller List, its sixth week on the List.

23 October 2014, Monday: Day 3

morning: Alone without food (except an onion with sugar) since Saturday morning, Aidan Appleton and Alice Appleton left the cabin. Special Deputies Frankie DeLesseps and Junior

Rennie found them and dropped them off with Thurston Marshall and Carolyn Sturges at Sweetbriar Rose.

1:00 p.m.: The military fired two Cruise missiles into the Dome; each failed to penetrate it. Joe McClatchey set up his PowerBook Pro computer to webcast the event. Norrie Calvert and Benny Drake showed the capture on the big screen at Dipper's Roadhouse. Intense heat from the missiles started brush fires inside the Dome. Brenda Perkins led a firefighting team to put them out.

>1:00 p.m.: Sammy Bushey woke to a crash and Little Walter Bushey crying. He cut his forehead when his crib collapsed. She stopped his bleeding the best she could. Her car's front tires had been punctured, so she packed Little Walter in his Papoose and walked. From the rape, she had bled in bed for the past twelve hours. She passed out. Reverend Piper Libby found them and took them to the hospital.

Colonel Barbara sneaked into the Town Hall's fallout shelter and took the Geiger counter. He gave it to Rusty Everett, who gave it to Julia Shumway. She gave it to Joe McClatchey.

9:00 p.m.: The military tried to burn through the Dome with acid. It failed.

Junior Rennie went to Dale Barbara's apartment to get something identifiable as Barbie's. He took Barbie's dog tags. [*Under the Dome*]

October 24

24 October 1932, 9:45 p.m.

Eduard Delacroix played with Mr. Jingles, his pet mouse. He'd throw a colored spool, and Mr. Jingles would roll it back. One throw put the spool out onto the Green Mile. When Mr. Jingles ran after it, Percy Wetmore stomped on him and broke his back. John Coffey asked for Mr. Jingles while there was still time and helped him. The mouse lived another sixty-four years. [*The Green Mile*]

24 October 1939

Sally Druse was admitted to Gottreich Hospital with Bordetella pertussis—whooping cough. Her friend Maddy Kruger was admitted for whooping cough about the same time. Both girls became Dr. Ebenezer Gottreich's research subjects. [*The Journals of Eleanor Druse*]

24 October 1980

Betsy Moriarty's article, "MYSTERY OF THE DEAD FISH," appeared in *The Bridgton News*. It reported the finding of many dead fish in Casco, ME's Crystal Lake. Hal Shelburn had put a toy monkey in a bag with three rocks and dropped it in the deepest part of the lake. Each time the monkey had clapped its cymbals, someone close to the Shelburn family died. ["The Monkey"]

24 October 1981

Buddy Parkins picked up Jack Sawyer, traveling as Lewis Farren, on Route 40 and gave him a ride from Cambridge, OH, to Zanesville, OH. Jack called his mother from the Buckeye Mall. Morgan Sloat cut into the conversation and told him to go home. [*The Talisman*]

24 October 1982

Different Seasons stayed at number 6 on *The New York Times* Fiction Best Seller List, its twelfth week on the List.

24 October 1988

Stephen King started *Needful Things*.

24 October 1989

Preface to *The Stand: The Complete & Uncut Edition*

24 October 1993

Nightmares & Dreamscapes rose to number 2 on *The New York Times* Fiction Best Seller List, its second week on the List.

24 October 1999

Hearts in Atlantis dropped to number 5 on *The New York Times* Fiction Best Seller List, its fourth week on the List.

24 October 2004

The Dark Tower VII: The Dark Tower stayed at number 1 on *The New York Times* Fiction Best

Seller List, its third week on the List.

24 October 2006

Lisey's Story (Scribner, $28) published with a first printing of 1,250,000 copies

24 October 2012, Wednesday

Little Green God of Agony, a serial eComic, page 5 of 24, online at www.stephenking.com

24 October 2014, Tuesday: Day 4

~12:00 a.m.: Reverend Lester Coggins talked with Big Jim Rennie in Rennie's study. The Reverend explained that God put the Dome over Chester's Mill as punishment for their crystal meth business and that he and Rennie had to confess their sins publicly. With a gold-plated souvenir baseball, Rennie bludgeoned Coggins to death. Junior Rennie took care of the body.

A crowd formed outside Food City when people found it closed until further notice. The crowd became a mob when Randy Killian, Ricky Killian, and Sam Verdreaux threw rocks at specific people, arranged by Big Jim Rennie to incite a riot. The crowd broke through the doors and forced their way in, trashing the store and looting. They ignored police but responded to Rose Twitchell, who talked to them as neighbors. Most got their sanity back, but many still took their looted items.

Julia Shumway, owner-editor of the local newspaper, The Chester's Mill *Democrat*, wasn't at the paper's office. So Brenda Perkins dropped off Chief Perkins's file about Big Jim Rennie at Andrea Grinnell's instead. Andrea was going cold turkey to break her OxyContin habit, so she didn't pay attention to the envelope. Brenda confronted Big Jim Rennie. He broke her neck. Junior Rennie put her in the McCains' pantry.

Special Deputy Junior Rennie put Dale Barbara's dog tags in Angie McCain's hand then called in his finding the bodies of Angie, Dodee Sanders, Lester Coggins, and Brenda Perkins.

Norrie Calvert, Benny Drake, and Joe McClatchey checked the Town Common with the Geiger counter. They started there because it was the center of town. They noted only noise. Norrie suggested they try Black Ridge, the highest part of town, after lunch.

>2:30 p.m.: Chief Randolph, Freddy Denton, Linda Everett, Jackie Wettington, Frank DeLesseps, Junior Rennie, and Carter Thibodeau, all with weapons drawn, arrested Dale Barbara for the murders of Angela McCain, Dorothy Sanders, Lester Coggins, and Brenda Perkins. After Barbie was photographed, fingerprinted, and locked in a cell, Mel Searles punched him a couple of times. Barbie called out to Linda Everett to have Rusty Everett examine the bodies; Chief Randolph Maced him.

Norrie Calvert, Benny Drake, and Joe McClatchey rode their bikes to Black Ridge. The Geiger counter registered +50 at Black Ridge Road then +75 when they crossed the road. On the other side of a patch of woods, they saw what looked like a radio beacon in the apple orchard. The beacon, which flashed a purple light every fifteen seconds, was the Dome's generator.

Sammy Bushey left the hospital. Alden Dinsmore found her walking along Route 119. He gave her a ride to the Evanses' house, where she took Jack Evans's .45 automatic from his desk, a spare clip, and the keys to their Malibu. She drove back to the hospital, said goodbye to Little Walter Bushey, and went to Georgia Roux's room. She killed Frankie DeLesseps, who had been sleeping in a chair, and Georgia. She turned the gun and shot herself in the temple.

~9:30 p.m.: Junior Rennie and Carter Thibodeau threw four Molotov cocktails at the offices of Julia Shumway's *Democrat*. The office and her apartment above burned. They made it sound as if Dale Barbara were behind it by calling over a bullhorn to release Dale Barbara from jail or else.

10:45 p.m.: Rusty Everett examined the bodies at Bowie Funeral Home. He saw impressions of baseball stitches on Lester Coggins. He knew Big Jim Rennie had a gold-plated baseball and was sure Rennie had killed Coggins.

night: Andy Sanders told Phil Bushey that Sammy Bushey was dead. Phil turned him on to some crystal meth.

Julia Shumway and Horace, her Welsh Corgi, spent the night at Andrea Grinnell's. [*Under the Dome*]

October 25

25 October 1850

Calvin McCann gave sleeping powder to Charles Boone to keep him away from Jerusalem's Lot. ["Jerusalem's Lot"]

25 October 1932, Eduard Delacroix's Date of Execution

Earlier in the month, Wild Bill Wharton had grabbed Percy Wetmore, scaring him enough to pee in his pants. Eduard Delacroix laughed; Percy remembered. Wetmore, presiding at Delacroix's execution, failed to soak the sponge that went between a convict's head and Old Sparky's metal cap. Instead of being electrocuted to death quickly, Del burned to death slowly. They put him out with a fire extinguisher. [*The Green Mile*]

25 October 1981

Emory Light picked up Jack Sawyer, traveling as Lewis Farren, near Dayton, OH. He offered Jack $50 for sex. At a rest stop in Lewisburg, OH, Jack went into a bathroom and didn't come out. Light left. Seeing Morgan Sloat's car in the rest area, Jack flipped to The Territories, where he met Wolf. Sloat ungracefully migrated to the Territories as Morgan of Orris and killed several of Wolf's cow-sheep. Jack grabbed Wolf and used the last of his magic juice to flip back to our world. To travel faster, Wolf carried him horsey-back. Wolf had known Phil Sawyer and knew Jack was his son because of their similar smells. [*The Talisman*]

Cujo stayed at number 2 on *The New York Times* Fiction Best Seller List, its eleventh week on the List.

25 October 1987

Misery dropped to number 10 on *The New York Times* Fiction Best Seller List, its twenty-first week on the List.

25 October 1992

Gerald's Game dropped to number 8 on *The New York Times* Fiction Best Seller List, its fifteenth week on the List.

25 October 1998

Bag of Bones stayed at number 1 on *The New York Times* Fiction Best Seller List, its third week on the List.

25 October 2014, Wednesday: Day 5

morning: Romeo Burpee, Benny Drake, Norrie Calvert, Rusty Everett, and Joe McClatchey drove to Black Ridge. Rusty, in a makeshift radiation suit, found the Dome's generator. The others stayed behind, where the Geiger counter registered +400. The radiation reached +1000 before dropping off to 0. The generator wasn't the source of the radiation. Instead, there was a radiation belt surrounding the area to keep people away. The generator was about the size of an Apple TV box. Rusty couldn't move it, but when he grasped it, he could see alien children watching.

late afternoon: Big Jim Rennie wanted to remove all traces of his crystal meth business. He sent Fern Bowie, Stewart Bowie, and Roger Killian to return the propane he had stolen and kept at the storage barn behind the WCIK studio. Phil Bushey and Andy Sanders, each armed, sent them back to town.

While examining Big Jim Rennie at the hospital, Rusty Everett told Rennie he knew he killed Lester Coggins and said he'd give Rennie a good heart drug for stepping down as Second Selectman. Freddy Denton and Carter Thibodeau came out of the bathroom. Carter hit Rusty in the mouth after discussing criminal wrongdoing. Rennie pressed his foot on Rusty's left hand, breaking the fifth metacarpal and dislocating three fingers. They withheld medical treatment and arrested him for extortion, criminal withholding, attempted murder, and resisting arrest (by sitting in a chair after having been pushed into it). Later, they added criminal complicity in the murders of Lester Coggins and Brenda Perkins.

evening: Rummaging behind Andrea Grinnell's couch for popcorn, Horace found a manila envelope, labeled for Julia Shumway. He took it to Andrea. She remembered Brenda Perkins had dropped it off then had gotten killed, so she looked inside and learned about Big Jim Rennie's unlawful activities. [*Under the Dome*]

October 26

26 October 1789

Preacher's Corners townspeople Frawley the Blacksmith, Goody Randall, and others saw signs of evil from nearby Jerusalem's Lot. ["Jerusalem's Lot"]

26 October 1954, Tuesday night

Annie Wilkes and her family left their apartment because the kitchen had a water leak. There was a fatal fire in the building the next day. [*Misery*]

26 October 1979, Friday

In a front-loaded honeymoon, Lisey (rhymes with CeeCee) Debusher and Scott Landon went to The Antlers, a bed-and-breakfast in Rome, NH, to celebrate the paperback sale of Scott's *Empty Devils*. They had unexpected snow. [*Lisey's Story*]

26 October 1980

Firestarter stayed at number 2 on *The New York Times* Fiction Best Seller List, its tenth week on the List.

26 October 1981

While traveling in our world with Jack Sawyer, Wolf from The Territories climbed a tree for an apple. Wasps stung him. [*The Talisman*]

26 October 1986

IT stayed at number 1 on *The New York Times* Fiction Best Seller List, *IT*'s seventh week on the List.

26 October 2012, Friday

Little Green God of Agony, a serial eComic, page 6 of 24, online at www.stephenking.com

26 October 2014, Thursday: Day 6

While setting up for Visitors Day outside the Dome, Private Clint Ames talked with Ollie Dinsmore, who was inside the Dome.

Carolyn Sturges took Aidan Appleton and Alice Appleton to Big Jim Rennie's town meeting. While confronting Rennie, Andrea Grinnell had drug withdrawal shakes and dropped her bag. Aidan saw her gun and called out. Mel Searles shot at Carolyn when she bent to get Aidan. When she stood, Freddy Denton shot her between the eyes. Linda Everett took the kids home with her. Carter Thibodeau had waited for a clear shot and killed Andrea.

~7:00 p.m.: Romeo Burpee, Ernie Calvert, and Jackie Wettington went to break Dale Barbara and Rusty Everett out of jail. Junior Rennie had killed the three cops at PD and was downstairs, aiming to kill Barbie. Jackie Wettington shot him. They sprung Barbie and Rusty then they all went to the abandoned McCoy Orchard on top of Black Ridge, where the Dome's generator was. [*Under the Dome*]

October 27

27 October 1850, 5:00 a.m.

Charles Boone and Calvin McCann went to the Jerusalem's Lot church, where The Worm killed McCann. Charles burned *De Vermis Mysteriis*, forcing The Worm to leave the church (but not Jerusalem's Lot). The Undead James Boon still unlived under the church. Charles ran when he saw him. Later, people thought Charles had brain fever and killed McCann. ["Jerusalem's Lot"]

27 October 1932, early a.m.

Paul Edgecombe, Brutal Howell, and Harry Terwilliger drugged Wild Bill Wharton, put a straitjacket on Percy Wetmore, and locked him in the restraint room. They took John Coffey to help the warden's wife, Melinda Moores. Coffey inhaled her sickness, healing her inoperable brain tumor. Upon returning to Cold Mountain State Penitentiary, Coffey grabbed Wetmore and exhaled the sickness into him, causing him to shoot Wild Bill Wharton six times. Wharton had raped and killed the Detterick twins, a crime for which Coffey was to be executed. Percy, catatonic for the rest of his life, was sent to the Briar Ridge mental facility, where he had an administration job application. [*The Green Mile*]

27 October 1954, early Wednesday morning

Adrian Krenmitz and most of his family died in a fire in their apartment building. He saved eighteen-month-old Laurene but died when he tried to save the others. Three-year-old Alison, six-year-old Frederick, eight-year-old Paul, and their neighbor Irving Thalman died. Adrian's wife, Jessica, survived. Eleven-year-old Annie Wilkes had set the fire, but Fire Chief Michael O'Whunn thought a careless wino had started it with a cigarette. [*Misery*]

27 October 1960

For a few months, Thad Beaumont suffered headaches that got worse; Dr. Seward thought they were migraines. While waiting outside his house for the school bus, he suffered convulsions. Mr. Reed, the school bus driver, arrived and prevented him from choking on his tongue. In an X-ray at Bergenfield County Hospital, Dr. Hugh Pritchard found something that suggested a brain tumor. [*The Dark Half*]

27 October 1965

Steve King's "Codename: Mousetrap" appeared in Vol. 3 No. 1 of the Lisbon High School newsletter *The Drum*, "Lisbon's Best Selling Newspaper."

27 October 1979, Saturday

The owner of The Antlers outfitted Lisey Debusher and Scott Landon with snowshoes and parkas to walk the trail behind the inn. They stopped under a willow tree (under the yum-yum tree) to eat their picnic lunch. Scott told Lisey he shouldn't have children because of a blood-bool lunacy that ran through his family. He illustrated with a four-part story, giving her details about the first two parts—the first about his father cutting his brother deep to coerce three-year-old Scott to jump off the hall bench, and the second about the best bool hunt (a treasure hunt) that his brother Paul had set up. Exiting the willow's overhanging branches, Scott took her to Boo'ya Moon for a moment. That night he gave her details about Paul's death, the third part of the story. He told her he had killed his father soon after, but she didn't learn the details for almost twenty-seven years. He took her to Boo'ya Moon again. It was almost dark there, so they couldn't stay long, but it was long enough for her to realize she was there (unlike that afternoon). [*Lisey's Story*]

27 October 1981

Wolf and Jack Sawyer, with a 102-degree fever and a cough, reached Muncie, IN. They tried to watch *Wizards* and *The Lord of the Rings* at the Town Line Sixplex's Cinema 6. When the movie started, Wolf became scared and howled; they were thrown out. They spent the night in an empty house in Cammack, IN. [*The Talisman*]

27 October 1985

Skeleton Crew dropped to number 10 on *The New York Times* Fiction Best Seller List, its nineteenth week on the List.

27 October 1991

Needful Things stayed at number 2 on *The New York Times* Fiction Best Seller List, its second week on the List.

27 October 1995

Allen Symes wrote about the Garins' 24 July 1994 visit to the Rattlesnake Number One Mine. He sealed the typed manuscript in an envelope marked, "concerns strange incident in china pit and read after my death, pls." [*The Regulators*]

27 October 1996

Afterword to *The Dark Tower IV: Wizard and Glass*, in Lovell, ME

The Green Mile, Part Six: Coffey on the Mile stayed at number 6 on *The New York Times* Paperback Fiction Best Seller List, its seventh week on the List.

Desperation dropped to number 2 on *The New York Times* Fiction Best Seller List, its third week on the List.

Richard Bachman's *The Regulators* dropped to number 4 on *The New York Times* Fiction Best Seller List, its third week on the List.

27 October 2002

From a Buick 8 dropped to number 3 on *The New York Times* Fiction Best Seller List, its third week on the List.

27 October 2011

Granta, Issue 117, Fall/Winter 2011 (£10.55), with "The Dune" (collected in *The Bazaar of Bad Dreams*), published

27 October 2013

Doctor Sleep dropped to number 2 on *The New York Times* Hardcover Fiction Best Seller List, its third week on the List.

27 October 2014, Friday: Day 7, Visitors Day

The government organized a Visitors Day, where people inside the Dome could meet with loved ones from outside the Dome. Twelve hundred loved ones met at two rally points, the Castle Rock Fairgrounds and the Oxford Plains Speedway. School buses took them to the Motton, ME, side of the Dome. Eight hundred Chester's Mill residents attended.

12:02 p.m.: Two teams went to deal with Phil Bushey and Andy Sanders at the WCIK studio. Freddy Denton's team approached from an access road in the back to surprise them. Bushey, expecting the raid, opened fire from behind a Meals On Wheels truck. He killed Marty Arsenault, Lauren Conree, Freddy Denton, George Frederick, and Stubby Norman. He fired again, killing Denton. Mel Searles and Aubrey Towle ran into the woods and regrouped. Towle went back and wounded Bushey. Chief Randolph's team—Fern Bowie and Stewart Bowie—assuming the gunfire came from Freddy Denton's team, headed to the studio. Andy Sanders killed them from behind then went around back to help Bushey. Together, they pushed the white button on Bushey's garage door opener. Mel Searles killed both just before eighty pounds of plastic explosive and 10,000 gallons of propane in the storage barn/meth lab exploded. The shock wave hit the whole town like an earthquake. A fire cloud expanded southeast until it hit the Dome, destroying 70% of the town and killing all except 397 of its 2,000 residents. When the fire burned itself out, it had consumed most of the oxygen within the Dome, leaving noxious gases.

Ollie Dinsmore took the oxygen tanks and mask that had been left when Grampy Tom was staying with them. He buried himself under potatoes in the barn's cellar.

Dale Barbara had arranged with Colonel Cox to have a series of Air Max industrial generator-powered fans set up outside the Dome. After the explosion, Barbie and others drove to the Dome at the TR-90 border and had Lieutenant Colonel Stringfellow turn on the fans, driving some air through the partially permeable Dome. [*Under the Dome*]

October 28

28 October 1954

With "FIVE DIE IN APARTMENT HOUSE FIRE," the *Bakersfield Journal* reported how the Krenmitzes died the day before. [*Misery*]

28 October 1960

Dr. Lester Albertson assisted Dr. Hugh Pritchard in exploratory brain surgery on Thad Beaumont; Thad had a small scar on his forehead for the rest of his life. Before the operation, Thad heard sparrows. Such sensory precursors are common with brain tumor victims. In his case, he heard sparrows because actual sparrows flocked. During surgery, Dr. Pritchard found pieces of a twin, whom Thad absorbed before birth. The twin's remaining parts had begun to grow again, causing Thad's tumor-like symptoms. Dr. Pritchard told Thad's parents he removed a small benign tumor. After the operation, a flock of sparrows flew into the Intensive Care wall. Three hundred dead sparrows were found on the ground. (Dr. Loring was the anesthesiologist. Hilary, an Operating Room nurse, ran out when she saw an eye in Thad's brain. Dr. Pritchard had her fired.) [*The Dark Half*]

28 October 1979

The Dead Zone dropped to number 4 on *The New York Times* Fiction Best Seller List, its eighth week on the List.

28 October 1981

Jack Sawyer and Wolf spent the night in the ruins of a burned house. Wolf made Jack medicine from water and plants. When Jack drank it, he almost flipped into The Territories. He began to think he could flip without the magic juice. (He didn't know it, but the magic juice was Purple Jesus wine.) [*The Talisman*]

28 October 1984

The Talisman entered *The New York Times* Fiction Best Seller List at number 1. It was on the List for twenty-one weeks.

28 October 1990

The Stand: The Complete & Uncut Edition dropped to number 14 on *The New York Times* Fiction Best Seller List, its twenty-fifth week on the List.

Four Past Midnight dropped to number 3 on *The New York Times* Fiction Best Seller List, its seventh week on the List.

28 October 2001

Black House dropped to number 4 *The New York Times* Fiction Best Seller List, its fifth week on the List.

28 October 2014, Saturday: Day 8

sunrise: While on Visitors Day cleanup detail, Private Clint Ames heard knocking from inside the Dome. Ollie Dinsmore needed air. Private Ames had the few Air Max fans outside the Dome turned on to get some air into the Dome. He had Ollie clear the char on the inside of the Dome to improve the airflow.

morning: Ernie Calvert died of a heart attack.

<12:00 p.m.: Aidan Appleton died from the poor air quality. [*Under the Dome*]

October 29

29 October 1970, Thursday

On their last date, Sarah Bracknell and Johnny Smith went to the Esty Fair. His car was in Tibbets' Garage in Hampden, so Sarah drove. Johnny won almost $600—more than three weeks' salary—at Sol Drummore's Wheel of Fortune. Sarah got sick and threw up, so he drove her home in her car, arriving after midnight. [*The Dead Zone*]

~29 October 1975

The Castle Rock Strangler raped and killed Etta Ringgold, his fifth victim. [*The Dead Zone*]

29 October 1979

Ed Ferman, editor in chief at *Fantasy and Science Fiction*, decided to publish the second chapter of Stephen King's *The Dark Tower*. He called it "The Way Station."

A Cianbro truck almost hit Owen King in the road near his Orrington home. Behind the house was a pet cemetery, with a sign, "PET SEMATARY." Stephen King thought of doing a story about it. [*The Dark Tower VI: Song of Susannah*]

29 October 2000

On Writing dropped to number 3 on *The New York Times* Non-Fiction Best Seller List, its second week on the List.

29 October 2012, Monday

Little Green God of Agony, a serial eComic, page 7 of 24, online at www.stephenking.com

29 October 2014, Sunday morning: Day 9

Julia Shumway persuaded a young female leatherhead to release them. She took over the leatherhead's mind and showed her that the Chester's Mill people were real, living beings.

The Dome rose. Ollie Dinsmore passed out while Private Ames carried him to a helicopter to take him to Central Maine General. [*Under the Dome*]

29 October 2017

Sleeping Beauties stayed at number 2 on *The New York Times* Hardcover Fiction Best Seller List, its third week on the List.

October 30

30 October 1970, Friday, 12:00–2:00 a.m.

Johnny Smith took a Bangor & Orono Yellow Cab home from Sarah Bracknell's. On Carson's Hill at Carson's Bog, Brad Freneau was drag racing his Dodge Charger with a Ford Mustang. Heading east in the wrong lane of Route 6, Freneau hit Johnny's cab head-on. Freneau and the cab driver were killed. Mary Thibault, Freneau's girlfriend, died later that morning at Eastern Maine Medical Center. The Cleaves Mills Rescue Squad took Johnny to the Medical Center, too, where Dr. Strawns treated his severe head injuries. After a long operation, he wasn't expected to live. At first, he stayed in Intensive Care room 619. He was in a coma for fifty-five months. [*The Dead Zone*]

30 October 1983

Christine rose to number 12 on *The New York Times* Fiction Best Seller List, its thirtieth week on the List.

30 October 1994

Insomnia stayed at number 1 on *The New York Times* Fiction Best Seller List, its second week on the List.

30 October 2005

The Colorado Kid stayed at number 5 on *The New York Times* Paperback Fiction Best Seller List, its second week on the List.

30 October 2006

The Secretary of Dreams, Volume One (Cemetery Dance, $75 5,000-copy gift edition; $300 750-copy limited edition; $1,500 52-copy lettered edition) published

30 October 2011

Mile 81 dropped to number 18 on *The New York Times* E-Book Fiction Best Seller List, its seventh week on the List.

30 October 2018

Elevation (Scribner, $19.95) published

October 31

31 October 1789

James Boon, Philip Boone, and all Jerusalem's Lot residents disappeared after Boon summoned The Worm. ["Jerusalem's Lot"]

31 October 1938

Jack Alderson felt he was too old, so Rhett Alderson went trick-or-treating by himself. ["Cookie Jar"]

31 October 1955, 5:00 p.m.

Ted Brautigan, Dick, Dave Ittaway, Tanya Leeds, and Jace McGovern met Frank Armitage and two other humes outside the Mark Hopkins Hotel in San Francisco. In a woody station wagon, Frank took them to an empty freight depot in Santa Mira, CA, where they went through a door marked, "Thunderclap Station." Phil drove them to Devar-Toi. They became Breakers. [*The Dark Tower VII: The Dark Tower*]

31 October 1958, Friday, Halloween

original timeline:

5:20 p.m.: Frank Dunning killed his wife, Doris, and two of his sons, Tugga and Troy, with a hammer. He severely injured his daughter, Ellen, and son Harry. A neighbor hit him on the back of the head with an ash shovel. Dunning died of acute stomach poisoning at Shawshank State Prison. Ellen died in a coma. Harry's leg, broken in four places, caused him to limp for life.

George Amberson's first timeline:

5:20 p.m.: George Amberson parked near the Witcham Street Baptist Church. He walked to 202 Wyemore Lane, a vacant house on the street behind Kossuth Street.

5:45 p.m.: George hid between the garage and a hedge behind 202 Wyemore Lane. Bill Turcotte sneaked up behind him and held a bayonet to his left temple, drawing blood. Turcotte knew Amberson was after Frank Dunning but said George couldn't have him because he was going to get him for killing his little sister. George disarmed Bill.

When it was time to go, Turcotte, having heart trouble, didn't try to stop him. George made his way to the Dunnings' back door. In the main room, Dunning had already hit Mrs. Dunning with a twenty-pound sledgehammer. George shot Frank in the shoulder; a second shot missed; the third hit Dunning's right cheek. Frank hit Arthur (Tugga) Dunning in the head and killed him. Frank swung at George. He ducked, but the hammer skidded across his head, leaving a six-inch gash. George dropped the gun; Frank went after him. Bill Turcotte had come through the front door and stabbed Frank in the back with his bayonet. George went out the back door, walked to his car, and left Derry.

George Amberson's third timeline:

Frank Dunning killed half his family and severely injured the others. [*11/22/63*]

31 October 1959, Halloween, night

In homemade Batman and Robin costumes, Dougie Sanderson and his father went trick-or-treating. Dougie's father was drunk, but Dougie had fun anyway. At Norma Forester's door, Norma said, "trick or treat," to Dougie and, "trick or drink," to his father. ["Batman and

Michael Roch

Robin Have an Altercation"]

31 October 1965, Sunday:

The First Methodist Church of Harlow deacons arranged for a guest preacher while Reverend Charlie Jacobs mourned the death of his wife and son. [*Revival*]

31 October 1971

Stephan King's poem "Woman with Child" appeared in *Contraband* #1.

31 October 1974, night

After nine hours of labor, Sarah Hazlett gave birth to Dennis Edward Hazlett at Eastern Maine Medical Center. He was named after his grandfather, Dennis Hazlett. In the same hospital, Johnny Smith lay in a coma. [*The Dead Zone*]

31 October 1981

Zenith House would close on October 31st if, on 30 June 1981, they hadn't had three books sure to hit *The New York Times* Bestseller List by the end of the year. [*The Plant* Book One: *Zenith Rising*]

Jack Sawyer bought a $10 padlock from a Daleville, IN, True Value Hardware store. He thought he would have to lock Wolf in the woodshed they had been using until Wolf's werewolf transformation wore off. Jack was Wolf's herd. To protect him, Wolf locked *him* in the shed. [*The Talisman*]

31 October 1982

Different Seasons rose to number 5 on *The New York Times* Fiction Best Seller List, its thirteenth week on the List.

31 October 1983, 7:00-7:30 p.m.

Norma Crandall had a small heart attack in her kitchen. Louis Creed, who had been visiting, treated her and sent her to the hospital for a few days' observation. A Bangor MedCu ambulance took her to Eastern Maine Medical Center. There was little heart damage and no scarring. [*Pet Sematary*]

31 October 1984

Herman Coslaw took his son, Marty, trick-or-treating. Marty saw Reverend Lowe with an eye patch and knew he was The Beast. [*Cycle of the Werewolf*]

31 October 1988

Alice Kimball, the last living Haven, ME, Tommyknocker, died at The Shop's facility in Virginia. [*The Tommyknockers*]

31 October 1990

Tom Cullen, Kojak, and Stu Redman left Green River, UT. [*The Stand: The Complete & Uncut Edition*]

31 October 1991, Thursday

Casino Night was scheduled to be held at the Knights of Columbus Hall. [*Needful Things*]

31 October 1993

Nightmares & Dreamscapes stayed at number 2 on *The New York Times* Fiction Best Seller List, its third week on the List.

31 October 1994

"The Man in the Black Suit" (collected in *Everything's Eventual*) appeared in the October 31st issue of *The New Yorker*.

31 October 1995

Aunt Audrey took Seth Garin trick-or-treating. Seth didn't want to be a cowboy or a Mo-toKop, so he dressed as a pirate. [*The Regulators*]

31 October 1997

Trisha McFarland and Pepsi Robichaud wanted to go trick-or-treating dressed as the Spice Girls. Quilla McFarland wouldn't let her daughter dress that way. [*The Girl Who Loved Tom Gordon*]

31 October 1999

Hearts in Atlantis dropped to number 8 on *The New York Times* Fiction Best Seller List, its fifth week on the List.

31 October 2004

The Dark Tower VII: The Dark Tower dropped to number 2 on *The New York Times* Fiction Best Seller List, its fourth week on the List.

31 October ≥2017, Halloween, 6:30 p.m.

180 pounds: He asked a boy and girl, the last tricker-or-treaters, how they fared at the house up the street. Their mother had told them to skip that house because the ladies weren't nice. [*Elevation*]

October

October

<u>Tuesday</u>: Deke, La Verne, Rachel, and Randy went to Cascade Lake. They stripped to their underwear and swam the 45 to 50-degree water to a raft. A blob on the lake trapped them. It hypnotized and killed Rachel. After it grew from five feet in diameter to eight feet, it slowly pulled Deke through a crack in the boards; he died before it got his thigh. It grew to 15 feet. La Verne and Randy made love. Her hair fell into the water; the blob killed her. Randy spent the night sitting on the raft. He slept while he sat.

<u>Wednesday</u>: The blob got Randy with its hypnotic effect. ["The Raft"]

October 1900

Sara Tidwell performed with the Red-Top Boys at the Fryeburg Fair. [*Bag of Bones*]

October 1922

Victoria Stevenson helped Shannon Cotterie and Henry James exchange notes. The kids arranged for Shannon to sneak away from St. Eusebia Catholic Home for Girls.

Henry had already helped his father kill his mother, so robbing banks to survive didn't bother him. He and Shannon became known as The Sweetheart Bandits. ["1922"]

October 1926

Dave Davis (bootlegger and friend of John Eastlake), Dave's bodyguard, and a bathing beauty set sail for Europe. The bathing beauty and bodyguard made it to Paris. Davis was lost at sea. [*Duma Key*]

October 1951

Ben Mears had been living with his Aunt Cindy in Jerusalem's Lot, ME, for about four years. Aunt Cindy sent him back to his mother, who had recovered from a nervous breakdown. [*'Salem's Lot*]

October 1957

Bill Denbrough made a paper boat for his little brother, Georgie. It floated in the rain-filled gutters of Witcham Street to a storm drain, where Pennywise caught it and offered it to him. When Georgie reached for it, Pennywise tore off his left arm. The resulting shock or blood loss killed him. [*IT*]

October 1960

Vera Donovan knew her husband was cheating on her. She and Ted Kenopensky caused a car accident in which he died. Kenopensky worked for Vera in Baltimore then Little Tall Island, satisfying her sexual needs. [*Dolores Claiborne*]

October 1961

Vera Donovan's children, Donald and Helga, had been drinking, upset at their mother's involvement in their father's death the year before. Driving Donald's Corvette at more than 100 MPH, Helga missed a turn and splashed into a quarry. Both died. On Little Tall Island, Vera Donovan talked about them as if they never died, creating careers and lives for them.

[*Dolores Claiborne*]

October 1962

Reverend Charlie Jacobs moved to Harlow, ME. The Ladies Auxiliary had fixed up the church's parsonage for him. Jamie Morton was playing with his toy army in the front yard when Reverend Jacobs went to thank Mrs. Morton. The Reverend introduced himself, joined the army play for a while, and then went inside to talk with Mrs. Morton. [*Revival*]

October 1970

Barton Dawes's son, Charlie, died after a three-week coma. [*Roadwork*]

"Graveyard Shift" (collected in *Night Shift*) appeared in the October issue (Vol. 20, No. 12) of *Cavalier*.

October 1972

Vera Smith returned home after living with The American Society of the Last Times on a St. Johnsbury, VT, farm. They had been waiting for a flying saucer to take them to heaven, which they believed was in the Orion constellation. [*The Dead Zone*]

Stephen King started *'Salem's Lot*.

October 1973

"Gray Matter" (collected in *Night Shift*) appeared in the October issue (Vol. 23, No. 12) of *Cavalier*.

October 1974

Gwendy Peterson got a Robby Benson poster and a small TV for her thirteenth birthday. [*Gwendy's Button Box*]

October 1975

Three-year-old Danny Torrance ransacked his father's study and poured beer on a manuscript. His father, Jack Torrance, grabbed him by the arm and broke it. [*The Shining*]

Ridgeway, NH, Mayor Greg Stillson blackmailed investment partner Chuck Gendron with pictures of Gendron having sex with a waitress from Bobby Strang's truck stop. He wanted Gendron to round up $50,000 in campaign contributions for his run for Congress. [*The Dead Zone*]

Donald Callahan found Home at the corner of First Avenue and Forty-Seventh Street in Manhattan, two blocks from Tom and Jerry's Artistic Deli (the site of the vacant lot). He volunteered for a couple of days then Rowan Magruder gave him a paid job. He and Lupe Delgado became friends. [*The Dark Tower V: Wolves of the Calla*]

October 1977

For her sixteenth birthday, Gwendy Peterson got an Eagles poster and an eight-track/cassette stereo.

A coin shop valued one of Gwendy's silver dollars at $750. [*Gwendy's Button Box*]

October 1978

After school, Richie Grenadeau beat up Duddits behind the abandoned Tracker Brothers depot. Grenadeau was about to make Duddits eat a dog turd when Beaver, Henry Devlin, Jonesy, and Pete Moore arrived and stopped him. Beaver and the others had gone to the depot hoping to see an old picture of Tina Jean Schlossinger with her skirt up. After taking Duddits home, they went back to look at the picture. It wasn't the pantiless high school girl; it was an older woman, revealing panties. [*Dreamcatcher*]

Gwendy Peterson got a bright orange, slightly used Ford Fiesta from Castle Rock Ford for her seventeenth birthday. The radio worked sometimes. [*Gwendy's Button Box*]

October 1979

While visiting Johnny Smith's grave, Sarah Hazlett felt someone touch her shoulder. She turned, expecting to see Johnny. No one was there. [*The Dead Zone*]

October 1981

Norville Bates, Orville Jamieson, and John Mayo tracked Andy McGee and Charlie McGee in Manhattan and Albany, NY. At the Albany County Airport, Eddie Delgado lied to Sally Bradford that he had a vasectomy and couldn't be the father of her child. Charlie sensed her emotions and set Delgado's shoes on fire. He put his feet out in a Ladies Restroom toilet. Jim Paulson drove the McGees from the airport to the Slumberland Motel in Hastings Glen, NY.

Bruce Cook, Orville Jamieson, and eight other Shop agents looked for the McGees in Hastings Glen. Irving Manders gave the McGees a ride to his farm.

The Incident at the Manders Farm: Al Steinowitz succeeded Norville Bates as head of the McGee operation. Bates was part of Steinowitz's team at the Manders farm, where Charlie McGee let loose her pyrokinetic powers on the Shop agents who came to take her and kill her father. Bruce Cook fell on a bean stake, which pierced his neck and killed him. Al Steinowitz, several other Shop agents, and three chickens were killed; a few Shop agents suffered burns but lived. The Manderses' farmhouse and the Shop's cars burned. Orville Jamieson hurt his ankle and lost The Windsucker, his .357 Magnum, while running away. Later, while scrutinizing the farm, the Shop found the gun. The McGees, in Manders's old Willys Jeep, headed to Granther McGee's cottage. A week after they arrived, the Shop knew they were there; they watched the McGees for five months. [*Firestarter*]

Paul Devane told Dave Bowie of *The Weekly Islander* that the tax stamp on John Doe's cigarettes might show where they came from. Bowie talked with Sergeant Murray of the Attorney General's Office Evidence Storage and Filing Department. Murray called back later to say the cigarettes were from Colorado and called John Doe The Colorado Kid. After pictures of The Colorado Kid ran in seventy-eight Colorado newspapers, Arla Cogan identified the man as James Cogan. [*The Colorado Kid*]

"The Lawnmower Man" comic appeared in the October issue (Volume 1, Number 29) of *Bizarre Adventures*.

Shadows 4, edited by Charles L. Grant (Doubleday), with "The Man Who Would Not Shake Hands" (collected in *Skeleton Crew*), published

October 1982

Dolores Claiborne became Vera Donovan's live-in paid companion after Ted Kenopensky died. A linen closet separated their bedrooms. [*Dolores Claiborne*]

October 1983

Annie Wilkes gave Andrew Pomeroy a ride. He was going to Sidewinder, CO, to sketch the ruins of The Overlook Hotel. She took him home for a few days, found he was no artist, and killed him with an ax. She bathed the body to remove evidence then dumped it. [*Misery*]

"Uncle Otto's Truck" (collected in *Skeleton Crew*) appeared in the October issue of *Yankee Magazine*.

October 1984, full moon

The Beast killed four deer near the turnpike. [*Cycle of the Werewolf*]

October 1986

"The End of the Whole Mess" (collected in *Nightmares & Dreamscapes*) appeared in the October issue (Volume 9, Number 1) of *Omni*.

October 1989

John Shooter accused Morton Rainey of publishing Shooter's "Secret Window, Secret Garden" as Rainey's own "Sowing Season." The similarities were beyond coincidence. He wanted Rainey to write a story for Shooter to publish. Shooter killed Greg Carstairs and Tom Greenleaf, two Tashmore Lake caretakers, with Rainey's tools. Amy Rainey went to their Tashmore Lake home to discuss insurance payments on their destroyed Derry, ME, home. John Shooter, a second personality in Morton Rainey, attacked her. She ran out the back door. Arson investigator Fred Evans shot and killed Morton Rainey as he ran after her. The John Shooter entity lived. ["Secret Window, Secret Garden"]

Stephen King started *Dolores Claiborne*.

October 1991

The Daughters of Isabella organized Casino Night to raise money to fix the Our Lady of Serene Waters Church roof. There was no real gambling; people donated at the door, gambled with play money, and then took part in a prize auction at the end of the night. [*Needful Things*]

October 1992

Gerald and Jessie Burlingame did their bondage thing at their summer home; they usually did that at their main home. He handcuffed her—wearing only see-through panties—to the bedposts. She didn't like it and asked him to uncuff her. He ignored her and made love to her, roughly. She kicked him off; he had a heart attack, fell off the bed, and died. Autumn in a summer-vacation area, there was no one to hear her screams. Prince, an abandoned stray dog, ate from Gerald's body. During the night, Prince's barking woke her. In the corner, she saw Death. He opened his case filled with jewelry and human bones and teeth. She passed out; when she awoke, he was gone. The next day, she had a jar of Nivea face cream that she planned to use to grease her wrists so she could slide out of the cuffs. Prince returned and startled her, causing her to drop the jar. Late that afternoon, she broke a glass and pushed a pointed piece of glass into her right wrist and cut the skin most of the way around her wrist. The skin peeled off the back of her hand when she pulled her hand through the cuff. She could then reach the keys on the bureau to unlock her left hand. [*Gerald's Game*]

Screaming about dust bunnies, Vera Donovan fled her bedroom. Her wheelchair over-turned in the doorway. Dolores Claiborne saw her try to walk and tumble down the front stairs. Vera said she wanted to die there, not in a hospital. Dolores went for a rolling pin. When she returned, Vera was dead.

Dolores was a suspect in Vera's death. To the police, she explained why she had killed her husband nineteen years earlier, told about her relationship with Vera, and about Vera's fatal accident. [*Dolores Claiborne*]

Tom Kennedy died at 2:00 p.m. Erin, whom he had married in 1974, was with him. [*Joyland*]

October 1993

First Words: Earliest Writing from Favorite Contemporary Authors, edited by Paul Mandelbaum (Algonquin Books of Chapel Hill, $24.95), with "Jhonathan and the Witchs," published

October 1994

Antaeus #75/76, Fall 1994, The Final Issue (Ecco Press, $17), with "Blind Willie" (greatly revised and collected in *Hearts in Atlantis*), published

October 2003

Carl Goodhugh's roommate at Emerson College found him on the kitchen floor and administered CPR. Carl had had a heart attack from a thin atrial wall, an undetected congenital heart defect. With severe brain damage from oxygen deprivation, he moved back home. His father, Tom Goodhugh, hired a companion to take care of him. ["Fair Extension"]

October 2006

Talking on her cell phone and smoking while driving her Hummer too fast, Mrs. Fevereau hit and mortally wounded Gandalf, eleven-year-old Monica Goldstein's Jack Russell terrier. Edgar Freemantle put him out of his misery. [*Duma Key*]

October 2008

Costing $4 million, more than 60,000 gallons of The Calmative (Robert Fornoy's calming water) was produced and shipped to Borneo. Gulandio erupted and distributed the water around the world. Over the next three years, everybody was calm, but Fornoy's concentrated form of the water made people senile. The world became calm, senile, and then dead. ["The End of the Whole Mess"]

Bree Donlin learned that Robert Rivard was a patient at Gad's Ridge, a mental hospital. Semicatatonic, he would often be found standing in the corner of his room. Six years later, he hanged himself. [*Revival*]

October 2009

Jamie Morton and Bree Donlin had researched people Charlie Jacobs had cured. Several had negative aftereffects. Jamie visited Charlie at the Latches in upstate New York to persuade him to stop his healings. Charlie estimated that three to 5% of his healings showed aftereffects. He told Jamie not to worry, his secret electricity research had progressed, and he no longer healed people. [*Revival*]

October 2010

While looking for batteries for the TV remote, Darcy Anderson found Marjorie Duvall's identification hidden in the garage. Duvall was Beadie's eleventh victim. Researching Beadie on the computer, she cross-referenced her husband's business trips with recent victims. She realized her husband, Robert Emory Anderson, was a serial killer. Bob returned home in the middle of the night. From talking on the phone and checking her computer, he could tell she knew. He promised to stop if it meant not losing her. ["A Good Marriage"]

October 2011

Nora and Chad Callahan went to Forest Park. At the playground, Nora punched a four-year-old boy in the face. She bloodied his nose and lips, and she may have knocked out a tooth. Chad videotaped the attack. At their apartment, they watched the video five times. At first, they wanted to make sure the boy got up. In the later viewings, they focused on the punch. The next day, Nora collected her money. ["Morality"]

October 2013

After symptoms of myoclonus, ataxia, and seizures, a spinal tap identified the Creutzfeldt-Jakob (C-J) prion in Mary Fay. When she was five, her family was in a head-on collision while touring Ireland. Her parents were killed. Mary survived, but blood transfusions with tainted blood infected her with mad cow's disease. It had remained dormant until the previous summer. [*Revival*]

October 2014

Brady Hartsfield started entering Dr. Babineau's mind and taking control of his body. Brady took a couple of months to create Dr. Z, a second personality within Dr. Babineau. Taking control of Dr. Babineau gave him access to the doctor's finances. [*End of Watch*]

October ≥2017

240-pound Scott Carey noticed he had been losing around a pound a day but he didn't shrink. At any weighing, the scale showed the same with clothes, without clothes, and whether he held anything. A complete checkup with Dr. Adams revealed nothing. (He didn't tell the doctor about his weight loss.) As the weight came off, he felt better and his appetite increased. At 212 pounds, he told retired Doctor Bob Ellis.

Neighbors Missy Donaldson and Deirdre McComb took their two boxers running; they wouldn't clean up when their dogs pooped in Scott's yard. After seeing Doctor Bob, he talked with Deirdre about it. She denied it and accused him of discriminating against the women for their same-sex marriage. That afternoon, he caught the dogs pooping in his yard again. From his screened-in porch he took pictures with his tablet. He showed the photos to Deirdre that evening. She was dismissive but promised to take the dogs to the park to run.

A few days later, Missy Donaldson apologized and explained that Deirdre's cold behavior was because the town wasn't patronizing their restaurant out of prejudice.

204 pounds: During lunch at Patsy's Diner the next day, Scott chastised Trevor Yount for making a crude comment about the Mexican restaurant's owners. Patsy Denton told Scott to leave when Yount threatened to punch him for butting in.

On his walk home, he stopped at the Book Nook. Owner Mike Badalamente told him Holy

Frijole was failing because the predominantly Republican town was prejudiced against the restaurant's married lesbian owners.

Friday evening: Scott and Doctor Bob dined at Holy Frijole. Hostess McComb was friendly toward Doctor Bob but cold toward Scott. As the restaurant was vegetarian, Scott had a salami sandwich at home. His weight loss had picked up; he weighed 199 pounds. [*Elevation*]

late October ≥2017

Garage band Big Top played as Pennywise and the Clowns at the Castle Rock high school's Halloween dance. [*Elevation*]

October 2025

To earn money for a doctor for his daughter, Ben Richards appeared on *The Running Man*, a game show where contestants got a twelve-hour head start then were hunted. Contestants who eluded the Hunters for thirty days won a billion New Dollars; those who were caught within thirty days, however, were killed. The game was rigged in favor of Network Games. Eight days, seven hours after leaving the Network Games Building, Richards broke *The Running Man* record by two hours. With Amelia Williams as a hostage, he forced the Network to give him a plane. He killed most of the Network personnel on board. Mortally wounded in a shootout with Evan McCone, the Chief Hunter, he gave Amelia Williams the only parachute and flew the plane into the 67th floor of the Games Building, destroying most of the building and killing himself and Dan Killian, *The Running Man*'s executive producer. [*The Running Man*]

November
Happenings

November 1

1 November 1957

Roland LeBay registered Christine. [*Christine*]

1 November 1958, Saturday, >12:00 a.m.

George Amberson's first timeline: "MURDEROUS RAMPAGE ENDS IN 2 DEATHS," appeared on the bottom of page 1 (and continued on page 12) of the *Derry News*. It reported Bill Turcotte's cover story: After an argument, Frank Dunning broke Doris Dunning's arm with a hammer then killed Arthur Dunning, who had tried to intervene. Hearing screams and shouts, passerby Turcotte ran into the house. He confronted Dunning and grabbed a hunting knife from Dunning's belt. Their struggle resulted in Dunning's being stabbed to death.

George Amberson left his car outside the Kennebec Fruit Company in Lisbon Falls and walked behind the Mill's drying shed. He couldn't find the steps back to June 2011. Just as he gave up looking, he heard Al Templeton calling to him. He followed Al's voice. [*11/22/63*]

1 November 1978, Wednesday

Christine was street-legal. Registration fees included $8.50 excise tax, $2.00 municipal road tax, and $15.00 for Pennsylvania license plate HY–6241–J. She still had much rust, but she had new rocker panels, hood, back deck, front-end kit, headlights, and exhaust pipes. With about 79,500 miles on her odometer, Christine's restored value was between $2,000 and $5,000. Arnie Cunningham's mother, Regina, refused to let him keep her at home. At his father's (Michael's) request, Arnie kept her in the $5.00-a-month airport parking lot, twenty miles away. Later, lot attendant Sander Galton told Buddy Repperton that Arnie had Christine there. [*Christine*]

1 November 1981

Cujo dropped to number 3 on *The New York Times* Fiction Best Seller List, its twelfth week on the List.

1 November 1987

Misery dropped to number 11 on *The New York Times* Fiction Best Seller List, its twenty-second week on the List.

1 November 1989

The Dark Half (Viking, $21.95) published with a first printing of 1,500,000 copies, the largest hardcover print run to date

1 November 1991

The Corson brothers' $85,000 from Ace Merrill was due. Instead of killing him, they wanted him to take them to Ducky Morin so they could kill Morin, who had ripped off Merrill of the $85,000. [*Needful Things*]

1 November 1992

Gerald's Game dropped to number 12 on *The New York Times* Fiction Best Seller List, its sixteenth week on the List.

1 November 1994

Stephen King started *Desperation*

1 November 1998

Bag of Bones stayed at number 1 on *The New York Times* Fiction Best Seller List, its fourth week on the List.

1 November 2005

'Salem's Lot, Illustrated Edition (Doubleday, $35) published

1 November ≥2017, 9:00 a.m.

Scott Carey walked to the Castle Rock Rec and paid the $5 local adult entry fee for the Turkey Trot 12K (7-1/2 mile) run. [*Elevation*]

November 2

2 November 1869, All Souls' Day

The Gates Falls Textile Mill, owned by Ebenezer Gottreich, Dr. Ebenezer Gottreich's uncle, burned. Most adults escaped. Many child laborers, who worked in the underground levels, perished. In 1870, Gottreich Hospital was built on the Mill site. [*The Journals of Eleanor Druse*]

2 November 1928, All Souls' Day

Eleanor Sarah Druse (maiden name unknown) was born in Gottreich Hospital in Lewiston, ME. [*The Journals of Eleanor Druse*]

2 November 1939, All Souls' Day

Sally Druse was taken to the Pain Room, Dr. Gottreich's laboratory in the basement of Gottreich Hospital, where he conducted pain-alleviation research. He worried her when he talked about her being bad and having bad thoughts. To make those thoughts go away, he started a transorbital lobotomy. He got the ice pick-like tool through the eye socket bone above her left eye but couldn't finish the procedure—Sally pushed him away. There was a focal earthquake at the hospital; gas jets in the back of the lab started a fire. The ghost of Mary led Sally to safety. Dr. Gottreich and Paul Morlock, another research subject, died in the fire. Gottreich Hospital, built on the site of the burned-down Gates Falls Textile Mill, burned. Kingdom Hospital was built in its place. [*The Journals of Eleanor Druse*]

2 November 1966, Tuesday afternoon

Carol Gerber was with five carloads of University of Maine at Orono students who went to Derry to protest the Vietnam War outside the recruitment office. She marched awhile then stood aside. The demonstration was peaceful until construction workers arrived with opposing viewpoints. The police took the marching students to the police station then released them. ["Hearts in Atlantis"]

2 November 1975

Etta Ringgold's body was found in a culvert. [*The Dead Zone*]

2 November 1976, Tuesday

With 46% of the votes, Greg Stillson beat Harrison Fisher (31%) and David Bowes (23%) for New Hampshire's Third District US House of Representatives seat. [*The Dead Zone*]

2 November 1980

Firestarter stayed at number 2 on *The New York Times* Fiction Best Seller List, its eleventh week on the List.

2 November 1986

IT stayed at number 1 on *The New York Times* Fiction Best Seller List, *IT*'s eighth week on the List.

2 November 1990

Tom Cullen, Kojak, and Stu Redman reached Grand Junction, CO, where they were snowed in. They planned to stay at the Grand Junction Holiday Inn until spring. [*The Stand: The Complete & Uncut Edition*]

2 November 2003

Sally Druse finished her yearlong journal about the goings-on at Kingdom Hospital. She sent it to Stephen King, asking whether he could have it typed for submission to a paranormal investigation organization. Still worried about Mary, who was stuck between life and death at the hospital, she asked whether he could find someone to help the girl if something happened to Sally. [*The Journals of Eleanor Druse*]

2 November 2017

Stephen King's Introduction to *Flight or Fright: 17 Turbulent Tales*

November 3

3 November 1966, Wednesday

A Derry *News* article reported the previous day's demonstration. Although no names were given, Carol Gerber could be seen in the accompanying picture. ["Hearts in Atlantis"]

3 November 1969

Warden Norton ran an Inside-Out program, where Shawshank State Prison inmates did physical construction labor outside the prison grounds. A ten-point buck walked up to a construction site in Sabbatus. While guard Henry Pugh shot it, three Insider-Outers walked away. Two were caught in Lisbon; the third was never found. ["Rita Hayworth and Shawshank Redemption"]

3 November 1976

Catatonic since May, Ted Jones had not improved. Dr. Andersen requested four to six weeks of Will Greenberger's hallucination therapy before shock therapy. [*Rage*]

3 November 1985

Skeleton Crew rose to number 9 on *The New York Times* Fiction Best Seller List, its twentieth week on the List.

3 November 1987

Stephen King started *The Dark Half*.

3 November 1991

Needful Things stayed at number 2 on *The New York Times* Fiction Best Seller List, its third week on the List.

3 November 1996

The Green Mile, Part Six: Coffey on the Mile dropped to number 14 on *The New York Times* Paperback Fiction Best Seller List, its eighth week on the List.

Desperation stayed at number 2 on *The New York Times* Fiction Best Seller List, its fourth week on the List.

Richard Bachman's *The Regulators* stayed at number 4 on *The New York Times* Fiction Best Seller List, its fourth week on the List.

3 November 2002

From a Buick 8 dropped to number 5 on *The New York Times* Fiction Best Seller List, its fourth week on the List.

3 November 2013

Doctor Sleep rose to number 1 on *The New York Times* Hardcover Fiction Best Seller List, its fourth week on the List.

3 November 2015

Michael Roch

The Bazaar of Bad Dreams (Scribner, $30) published

November 4

4 November 1850

Believing he was the last of the Boone family line and The Worm needed a Boon/Boone in Jerusalem's Lot, Charles Boone committed suicide. ["Jerusalem's Lot"]

4 November 1978, Saturday

Leigh Cabot and Arnie Cunningham were petting at the Embankment. Feeling uncomfortable in Christine, she stopped. She felt Christine was watching them and Arnie was somebody else when he was with Christine.

That night, Arnie realized something was going on. Much more of Christine than he had fixed or replaced was new. [*Christine*]

4 November 1979

The Dead Zone stayed at number 4 on *The New York Times* Fiction Best Seller List, its ninth week on the List.

4 November 1981

The full moon was over; Wolf's werewolf period had passed. Jack Sawyer slid the key under the shed door, and Wolf let him out. Bill Thompson gave them a ride from Daleville, IN, to Cayuga, IN. Officer Williams arrested Jack Parker and Philip Wolf as runaways on French Lick Road. Corrupt Judge Ernest Fairchild sent them to the Sunlight Gardener Scripture Home for Wayward Boys. He and Officer Williams each earned a $20 referral fee from the Sunlight Home. Other inmates harassed and beat them often. [*The Talisman*]

4 November 1982

After escaping from the Shop in October, Charlie McGee cut her arm and back on a barbed-wire fence while trying to get away from a mad pig. Her cuts became infected. [*Firestarter*]

4 November 1984

The Talisman stayed at number 1 on *The New York Times* Fiction Best Seller List, its second week on the List.

4 November 1990

The Stand: The Complete & Uncut Edition stayed at number 14 on *The New York Times* Fiction Best Seller List, its twenty-sixth week on the List.

Four Past Midnight stayed at number 3 on *The New York Times* Fiction Best Seller List, its eighth week on the List.

4 November 2001

Black House dropped to number 6 *The New York Times* Fiction Best Seller List, its sixth week on the List.

4 November 2003

The Dark Tower V: Wolves of the Calla (Donald M. Grant, $35) published with a first printing of 660,000 copies

November 5

5 November 1978, Sunday, ~4:00 a.m.

The dead Roland LeBay drove Christine to Leigh Cabot's house. Leigh awoke from a dream and saw a driverless Christine in front of her house. [*Christine*]

5 November 1982

Charlie McGee arrived at the Manderses' farm and collapsed. Irving Manders called Dr. Hofferitz, who treated her infections, 101-degree temperature, malnutrition, and dehydration. As Roberta McCauley, she stayed with the Manderses. [*Firestarter*]

5 November 1989

The Dark Half entered *The New York Times* Fiction Best Seller List at number 1. It was on the List for nineteen weeks.

5 November 1992

A coroner's inquest into Vera Donovan's death (and Dolores Claiborne's statement) absolved Dolores of any wrongdoing. [*Dolores Claiborne*]

5 November 2000

On Writing stayed at number 3 on *The New York Times* Non-Fiction Best Seller List, its third week on the List.

5 November 2014

The Dark Tower: The Drawing of the Three—The Prisoner #4 of 5 (Marvel Comics, $3.99) published

5 November 2017

Sleeping Beauties dropped to number 4 on *The New York Times* Hardcover Fiction Best Seller List, its fourth week on the List.

November 6

6 November 1983

Christine stayed at number 12 on *The New York Times* Fiction Best Seller List, its thirty-first week on the List.

Pet Sematary entered *The New York Times* Fiction Best Seller List at number 4. It was on the List for thirty-two weeks.

6 November 1992

"ISLAND WOMAN CLEARED," an Ellsworth, ME, *American* front-page article, reported that Dolores Claiborne didn't murder Vera Donovan. [*Dolores Claiborne*]

6 November 1994

Insomnia stayed at number 1 on *The New York Times* Fiction Best Seller List, its third week on the List.

6 November 2005

The Colorado Kid dropped to number 6 on *The New York Times* Paperback Fiction Best Seller List, its third and last week on the List.

6 November 2011

Deirdre McComb placed fourth in the New York Marathon's Women's Division. [*Elevation*]

Mile 81 rose to number 15 on *The New York Times* E-Book Fiction Best Seller List, its eighth week on the List.

November 7

7 November 1958

<u>George Amberson's first timeline</u>: "LOCAL POLICE SEEK MYSTERY MAN," appeared on page 2 of the Lisbon *Weekly Enterprise*. They had found George's bloodstained car and worried about his well-being. [*11/22/63*]

7 November 1965, Sunday:

The First Methodist Church of Harlow deacons arranged for a second guest preacher. Reverend Charlie Jacobs was mourning the death of his wife and son. [*Revival*]

7 November 1975

Johnny Smith's mail included a small manila envelope with page three of the previous week's *Inside View*. "MAINE 'PSYCHIC' ADMITS HOAX," appeared at the bottom. Richard Dees had written the non-by-lined article to discredit Johnny for refusing his contract offer in mid-October. The article said Johnny admitted being a fake for a ride on the gravy train to get enough money to pay his medical bills and retire for a couple of years. This suited Johnny because he didn't want any publicity. [*The Dead Zone*]

7 November 1982

Different Seasons dropped to number 6 on *The New York Times* Fiction Best Seller List, its fourteenth week on the List.

7 November 1993

Nightmares & Dreamscapes dropped to number 3 on *The New York Times* Fiction Best Seller List, its fourth week on the List.

7 November 1999

Hearts in Atlantis dropped to number 9 on *The New York Times* Fiction Best Seller List, its sixth week on the List.

7 November 2004

The Dark Tower VII: The Dark Tower dropped to number 6 on *The New York Times* Fiction Best Seller List, its fifth week on the List.

7 November 2012, Wednesday

Little Green God of Agony, a serial eComic, page 8 of 24, online at www.stephenking.com (delayed because of Hurricane Sandy)

Little Green God of Agony, a serial eComic, page 9 of 24, online at www.stephenking.com (delayed because of Hurricane Sandy)

Little Green God of Agony, a serial eComic, page 10 of 24, online at www.stephenking.com (delayed because of Hurricane Sandy)

Little Green God of Agony, a serial eComic, page 11 of 24, online at www.stephenking.com

November 8

8 November 1981

Cujo stayed at number 3 on *The New York Times* Fiction Best Seller List, its thirteenth week on the List.

8 November 1982

Dr. Hofferitz examined Roberta McCauley (Charlie McGee) and found her much better. The following weekend, he declared her well. [*Firestarter*]

8 November 1984

Stephen King and Peter Straub's *The Talisman* (Viking, $18.95) published with a first printing of 492,000 to 600,000 copies

8 November 1987

Misery dropped to number 12 on *The New York Times* Fiction Best Seller List, its twenty-third week on the List.

8 November 1988, Tuesday

Gerald and Jessie Burlingame went to a party at the restaurant on the roof of the Hotel Sonesta to celebrate the election of George H. W. Bush as President. Jessie wore her best black dress. Before leaving for the party, she couldn't find her special pair of gold earrings earrings. Gerald saw she was wearing them. [*Gerald's Game*]

8 November 1992

Gerald's Game dropped to number 13 on *The New York Times* Fiction Best Seller List, its seventeenth week on the List.

8 November 1998

Bag of Bones dropped to number 3 on *The New York Times* Fiction Best Seller List, its fifth week on the List.

8 November 2011

11/22/63 (Scribner, $35) published

November 9

9 November 1975, Sunday

"THE DO-NOTHING COPS IN OUR SISTER STATE" appeared in a Manchester, NH, *Union-Leader* supplement after The Castle Rock Strangler was still at large after five victims in Maine during the past five years. [*The Dead Zone*]

9 November 1980

Firestarter dropped to number 3 on *The New York Times* Fiction Best Seller List, its twelfth week on the List.

9 November 1986

IT stayed at number 1 on *The New York Times* Fiction Best Seller List, *IT*'s ninth week on the List.

9 November 2009

"Premium Harmony" (collected in *The Bazaar of Bad Dreams*) appeared in the November 9th issue of *The New Yorker*.

~9 November 2009

Wesley Smith ordered an Amazon Kindle. ["Ur"]

9 November 2010

Full Dark, No Stars (Scribner, $27.99) published with a first printing of 1,200,000 copies

9 November 2012, Friday

Little Green God of Agony, a serial eComic, page 12 of 24, online at www.stephenking.com

9 November 2016

The Dark Tower: The Drawing of the Three—The Sailor #2 of 5 (Marvel Comics, $3.99) published

November 10

10 November 1912

Daniel, the Carriage House master at Rose Red, seemed to have been trampled to death in the hay wagon's stall. There were no horses in that stall, so Dirk moved the body to Black Thunder's stall before the police arrived. Daniel had had sexual relations with the Rose Red staff, without consent from some. [*The Diary of Ellen Rimbauer: My Life at Rose Red*]

10 November 1947, Tuesday

Haven, ME, resident Delbert McCready got lost hunting in Big Injun Woods. He lost track of time and slept the entire day, losing a tooth while he slept. [*The Tommyknockers*]

10 November 1985

Skeleton Crew dropped to number 10 on *The New York Times* Fiction Best Seller List, its twenty-first week on the List.

10 November 1987

The Tommyknockers (Putnam, $19.95) published with a first printing of 1,200,000 copies

10 November 1991

Needful Things stayed at number 2 on *The New York Times* Fiction Best Seller List, its fourth week on the List.

10 November 1993

Stephen King finished *Insomnia*.

10 November 1996

The Green Mile, Part Six: Coffey on the Mile dropped to number 16 on *The New York Times* Paperback Fiction Best Seller List, its ninth and last week on the List.

Desperation dropped to number 3 on *The New York Times* Fiction Best Seller List, its fifth week on the List.

Richard Bachman's *The Regulators* dropped to number 6 on *The New York Times* Fiction Best Seller List, its fifth week on the List.

10 November 2001, Saturday

In their annual Kineo, ME, hunting trip, Rick McCarthy, Steve Otis, Nat Roper, and Becky Shue split into pairs—Becky and Nat, Steve and Rick. Within days, they were considered missing. [*Dreamcatcher*]

10 November 2002

From a Buick 8 dropped to number 7 on *The New York Times* Fiction Best Seller List, its fifth week on the List.

10 November 2006

Several months earlier, builder-contractor Edgar Freemantle almost died. A twelve-story

Link-Belt ran into his pickup truck on a bank-building job site on Sutton Avenue in Minnesota. Over the next several months, his anger led to divorce and depression. Dr. Xander Kamen suggested he move far away and take up something that made him happy. On November 10th, he moved to Duma Key, on the Gulf of Mexico in Florida. He had hired Jack Cantori to help with whatever he needed. They became friends. [*Duma Key*]

10 November 2009

Under the Dome (Scribner, $35) published with a first printing of 925,000 to 950,000 copies

~10 November 2009

Wesley Smith received his Amazon Kindle in one day, but he hadn't requested express delivery. He didn't know they only came in white, so he didn't think it odd that his was pink. He wondered why it didn't come with an instruction booklet. ["Ur"]

10 November 2013

Doctor Sleep dropped to number 3 on *The New York Times* Hardcover Fiction Best Seller List, its fifth week on the List.

November 11

11 November 1912

For his quick thinking the day before, Ellen Rimbauer gave Dirk an extra month's wages and promoted him from stable hand to stable master. [*The Diary of Ellen Rimbauer: My Life at Rose Red*]

11 November 1979

The Dead Zone dropped to number 6 on *The New York Times* Fiction Best Seller List, its tenth week on the List.

11 November 1984

The Talisman stayed at number 1 on *The New York Times* Fiction Best Seller List, its third week on the List.

11 November 1990

The Stand: The Complete & Uncut Edition dropped to number 15 on *The New York Times* Fiction Best Seller List, its twenty-seventh week on the List.

Four Past Midnight stayed at number 3 on *The New York Times* Fiction Best Seller List, its ninth week on the List.

11 November 2001

Beaver Clarendon, Henry Devlin, Jonesy, and Pete Moore arrived at Hole in the Wall, Beaver's place in Maine's Jefferson Tract, for their annual hunting trip. [*Dreamcatcher*]

Black House dropped to number 7 *The New York Times* Fiction Best Seller List, its seventh week on the List.

11 November 2006

Edgar Freemantle walked on the beach, thirty-eight steps out and back, without his crutch. [*Duma Key*]

11 November 2007

Helen Shaverstone's and Robert Shaverstone's bodies were found. A couple of days earlier, Bob Anderson was in Saugus, MA, for two estate sales, then Boston for a coin auction. Beadie killed the Shaverstones, from Tassel Village, MA. ["A Good Marriage"]

11 November 2008

Just After Sunset (Scribner, $28) published with a first printing of 900,000 copies

11 November 2014

Revival (Scribner, $30) published

November 12

12 November 1907

Ellen and John Rimbauer married, with Priscilla Schnubly as Ellen's maid of honor. They spent the night in the Grand's Presidential Suite. Ellen bought the bed sheets as a souvenir of her wedding night. [*The Diary of Ellen Rimbauer: My Life at Rose Red*]

12 November 1932

Curtis Anderson, the warden's chief assistant, signed John Coffey's Date Of Execution (DOE) papers. [*The Green Mile*]

12 November 1945

Gatlin, NE, child Mary Wells was born Roberta Wells. ["Children of the Corn"]

12 November 1947, Thursday

A search party began looking for Delbert McCready, who went hunting in Haven's Big Injun Woods two days earlier. About a week later, they found him when he followed Preston Stream out of the woods. In 1952, still the town laughingstock, he moved to East Eddington, ME, where he started a small engine-repair facility. [*The Tommyknockers*]

12 November 1963, Tuesday

The Dallas *Morning News* printed an editorial about President Kennedy's upcoming Dallas trip. [*11/22/63*]

12 November 1964, dusk

Mary Wells was sacrificed to He Who Walks Behind the Rows. ["Children of the Corn"]

12 November 1970, >3:07 p.m.

The Castle Rock Strangler strangled then raped Alma Frechette, his first victim, on the Castle Rock Park bandstand. They had dated a couple of times. [*The Dead Zone*]

12 November 1972

Frank Dodd raped and strangled Ann Simons in Colorado. He and Tom Harrison were taking a Rural Law Enforcement Class at the University of Colorado at Pueblo. [*The Dead Zone*]

12 November 1989

The Dark Half stayed at number 1 on *The New York Times* Fiction Best Seller List, its second week on the List.

12 November 2000

On Writing stayed at number 3 on *The New York Times* Non-Fiction Best Seller List, its fourth week on the List.

12 November 2006

Edgar Freemantle had established a morning routine: painkillers with orange juice, a walk along the beach, yogurt for breakfast, then catching up on current events on cable TV. This morning, he walked forty-five steps out. He created a Numbers Game where he would walk one step, restart the count, then walk two steps, restart, three steps, restart, etc. Thus, nine Numbers Game steps were forty-five steps. Walking nine steps back to the house was less mentally debilitating than walking forty-five steps back. [*Duma Key*]

Lisey's Story entered *The New York Times* Fiction Best Seller List at number 1. It was on the List for ten weeks.

12 November 2008

The Dark Tower: Treachery #3 of 6 (Marvel Comics, $3.99) published

The Stand: Captain Trips #3 of 5 (Marvel Comics, $3.99) published

12 November 2012, Monday

Little Green God of Agony, a serial eComic, page 13 of 24, online at www.stephenking.com

12 November 2017

Sleeping Beauties stayed at number 4 on *The New York Times* Hardcover Fiction Best Seller List, its fifth week on the List.

November 13

13 November 1907

The SS *Ocean Star* departed from Pier 47. Heading for the Pacific Atolls, its first stops were Victoria and the Tahitian Islands. Ellen and John Rimbauer expected to travel for at least a year on a combination honeymoon and Omicron business trip. The grand house's construction was to be complete upon their return. During the voyage, John allowed Ellen to accompany him for meals but otherwise kept her in their presidential stateroom, while he, himself, was free to go to other areas of the ship. [*The Diary of Ellen Rimbauer: My Life at Rose Red*]

13 November 1970

Alma Frechette's body was found on the Castle Rock Park bandstand. [*The Dead Zone*]

13 November 1983

Christine dropped to number 14 on *The New York Times* Fiction Best Seller List, its thirty-second and last week on the List.

Pet Sematary rose to number 1 on *The New York Times* Fiction Best Seller List, its second week on the List.

13 November 1984

At his trial in Derry District Court, Steve Dubay received a first-degree manslaughter conviction and a fifteen-year Shawshank State Prison sentence for the death of Adrian Mellon. John Garton received a first-degree manslaughter conviction and a fifteen-to-twenty-year Thomaston State Prison sentence. [*IT*]

13 November 1994

Insomnia dropped to number 2 on *The New York Times* Fiction Best Seller List, its fourth week on the List.

13 November 2006

Edgar Freemantle walked ten Numbers Game steps (fifty-five actual steps), about ninety yards. [*Duma Key*]

13 November 2011

Mile 81 dropped to number 21 on *The New York Times* E-Book Fiction Best Seller List, its ninth week on the List.

November 14

14 November 1965, Sunday:

The First Methodist Church of Harlow deacons arranged for a third guest preacher. Reverend Charlie Jacobs was mourning the death of his wife and son. [*Revival*]

14 November 1968

In Caslin, NE, Nick Andros was born with neither eardrums nor vocal cords. His mother taught him to read lips and write his name. [*The Stand: The Complete & Uncut Edition*]

14 November 1978

Duddits, with the combined psychic power of Beaver, Henry Devlin, Jonesy, and Pete Moore, caused Richie Grenadeau to have a fatal car accident on Route 7, the old Derry-Newport Road. Mud filled the eyes of Grenadeau's decapitated head; the three others in the car were killed. Beaver and his friends thought they were sharing Duddits's dream but suspected they took part in the killing. [*Dreamcatcher*]

14 November 1982

Different Seasons dropped to number 8 on *The New York Times* Fiction Best Seller List, its fifteenth week on the List.

14 November 1993

Nightmares & Dreamscapes stayed at number 3 on *The New York Times* Fiction Best Seller List, its fifth week on the List.

14 November 1999

Hearts in Atlantis rose to number 8 on *The New York Times* Fiction Best Seller List, its seventh week on the List.

14 November 2001, Wednesday

"MYSTERIOUS SKYLIGHTS, MISSING HUNTERS SPARK PANIC IN JEFFERSON TRACT" appeared in the Derry, ME, *Daily News*.

Richard McCarthy wandered past Jonesy, hunting in a tree-stand. They went inside Hole in the Wall to get out of the twenty-degree cold.

Under Abraham Kurtz's command, Blue Base was set up at Gosselin's Country Market to handle the extermination, containment, and cleansing after a grayboys' spaceship, designated Blue Boy, crashed in Maine's Jefferson Tract. The barn, stable, and corral were set up as Blue Holding, an area to keep any civilians—mostly hunters—found in the area. Blue Group, consisting of a Kiowa OH–58 chopper and four Chinook gunship helicopters, flew to the Blue Boy site. While playing The Rolling Stones' "Sympathy for the Devil," they killed most of the sixty remaining grayboys outside the ship. Four surviving grayboys set off an explosion, bringing down two gunships. Kurtz and Owen Underhill were on the helicopters that made it.

Decayed grayboys left a reddish-gold fungus called byrus. Weasel-like creatures—byrum—grew inside humans who became infected with byrus by direct contact. A byrum chewed its way out of Richard McCarthy and splashed into the toilet at Hole in the Wall. Beaver sat on the toilet lid while Jonesy went for a roll of friction tape. Beaver, who had a habit of chewing toothpicks, leaned too far over to pick up his spilled toothpicks. The byrum escaped the toilet and killed him. When Jonesy returned, the head of Mr. Gray, the last surviving grayboy, exploded, expelling ether-smelling particles. Jonesy inhaled them, inviting Mr. Gray into his body. Jonesy/Mr. Gray left on a Sno-Cat.

Henry Devlin and Pete Moore, returning from a supply run, flipped Henry's Scout to avoid hitting a woman sitting in the road. After finding shelter, Henry walked back to Hole in the Wall. He found McCarthy's byrum, with many hatching eggs, in the bed. He shot it and burned the eggs.

Jonesy/Mr. Gray picked up Pete Moore for his directional ability. When he finished with Pete, Mr. Gray killed him. On the turnpike between Presque Isle and Millinocket, Mr. Gray stopped Andy Janas, killed him, and took his truck. Later, he killed another for a 4WD Dodge Ram. With a rotting grayboy from Janas's truck, Mr. Gray infected Lad, the driver's border collie, with byrus. They continued south.

Henry cross-country skied toward Gosselin's Market; on the way, he found Pete gone. Soldiers near the Market picked him up and put him in the holding area. With a byrus-induced telepathy he had caught at Hole in the Wall, Henry could read some of Owen Underhill's thoughts. He used those thoughts to persuade Underhill to help him escape early the next morning to catch Jonesy/Mr. Gray. [*Dreamcatcher*]

14 November 2004

The Dark Tower VII: The Dark Tower dropped to number 10 on *The New York Times* Fiction Best Seller List, its sixth week on the List.

14 November 2012, Wednesday

Little Green God of Agony, a serial eComic, page 14 of 24, online at www.stephenking.com

November 15

15 November 1958, Saturday

<u>Original timeline</u>: ~2:00 p.m.: While hunting in the Bowie Hill woods of Durham, ME, Andy Cullum shot at a deer but hit Carolyn Poulin. She was paralyzed and wheelchair-bound for life.

<u>Al Templeton-altered timeline</u>: On his way to hunt in the Bowie Hill woods, Andy Cullum stopped to help Bill Laidlaw (an Al Templeton alias) move a felled tree from the road. When Bill showed symptoms of a heart attack, Andy took him to Central Maine General in Lewiston. After Bill was diagnosed with indigestion, Andy returned him to his car. Andy didn't go hunting that day.

<u>George Amberson's second timeline</u>: Previously, George had offered Andy Cullum $200 to teach him how to play cribbage. Instead of going hunting, Andy played cribbage.

<u>George Amberson's third timeline</u>: Andy Cullum accidentally shot Carolyn Poulin. [*11/22/63*]

15 November 1981

Cujo stayed at number 3 on *The New York Times* Fiction Best Seller List, its fourteenth week on the List.

15 November 1987

Misery rose to number 11 on *The New York Times* Fiction Best Seller List, its twenty-fourth week on the List.

15 November 1992

Gerald's Game dropped to number 14 on *The New York Times* Fiction Best Seller List, its eighteenth week on the List.

15 November 1998

Bag of Bones stayed at number 3 on *The New York Times* Fiction Best Seller List, its sixth week on the List.

15 November 2001, Thursday

Early in the morning, Henry Devlin telepathically told the people in Blue Holding that soldiers were going to kill them. He persuaded them to form a mob and force their way into the woods to save themselves. As the mob broke through the front of the holding area, Owen Underhill helped Henry get out the back. Abraham Kurtz shot at Underhill, driving away in a Sno-Cat.

Kurtz and Freddy Johnson brought Gene Cambry and Archie Perlmutter, who were infected with the telepathy-inducing byrus, along as telepathic trackers to catch Underhill. With Perlmutter the primary tracker, Kurtz shot and killed Cambry.

Kate Gallagher led a search-and-destroy mission to hunt and kill all the barn people and Blue Group troops that had gotten away. At one point, she estimated that more than a hundred civilians had been killed in Clean Sweep One, the code name for the valley where most of the runaways were found. Jocelyn McAvoy reported more than forty killed in Quadrant Four. Dawg Brodsky armed five civilian men and two civilian women with automatic weapons and led them on a surprise attack to kill Gallagher and McAvoy.

After swapping their Sno-Cat for a Humvee, Henry and Underhill picked up Duddits to help find Mr. Gray and Jonesy. They tracked them to Quabbin Reservoir's Shaft 12, where Mr. Gray was trying to contaminate the water supply with Lad, a byrus-infected border collie. In Duddits's dreamcatcher—a psychic plane of existence held together by Duddits and where each strand was a different place and time—Henry and Jonesy found Mr. Gray in a Massachusetts General Hospital bed and killed him, freeing him from Jonesy at Shaft 12. Jonesy grabbed the byrum as it emerged from Lad; he threw it and shouted for Owen Underhill to shoot it. Owen froze; Duddits telekinetically lifted Owen's gun. Underhill took over and killed the byrum.

Near Shaft 12, Kurtz and Freddy Johnson heard gunshots and lay low to see who returned. They ambushed Owen Underhill. Knowing Kurtz was going to kill him, Johnson killed Kurtz first. From inside his Humvee, Henry saw Johnson pass him, get in the other Humvee, and get killed by Perlmutter's byrum. With an Army carbine from the back of his Humvee, Henry shot the gas tank of Freddy's Humvee. He slipped in the snow just before the force of the explosion went over him. When he was sure the byrum was dead, Henry found Jonesy and dragged him on a travois back to the Humvee. [*Dreamcatcher*]

November 16

16 November 1921

Ellen Rimbauer had gone to the Tower often to talk with April, who usually appeared during a full moon. John Rimbauer forbade further visits. Ellen threatened to bring back some prominent guests and show them the secret passages John had used to view their wives. He relented. [*The Diary of Ellen Rimbauer: My Life at Rose Red*]

16 November 1960

George Amberson's second timeline: George Amberson sat on a bench at the corner of Ballinger and West Seventh in Fort Worth, TX. He watched Marguerite Oswald chase Robert Oswald one and a half blocks down West Seventh. [*11/22/63*]

16 November 1963, Saturday

The Dallas *Morning News* reported that President Kennedy would be in a motorcade on Main Street on the 22nd. The *Times Herald* published the motorcade route, from Love Field to the Trade Mart.

Kennedy was scheduled to speak to the Dallas Citizen Council. [*11/22/63*]

16 November 1980

Firestarter stayed at number 3 on *The New York Times* Fiction Best Seller List, its thirteenth week on the List.

16 November 1986

IT stayed at number 1 on *The New York Times* Fiction Best Seller List, *IT*'s tenth week on the List.

16 November 1991

John T. Spier wrote a letter to Stephen King expressing his extreme displeasure at the cliffhanger ending to *The Waste Lands*. [*The Dark Tower VI: Song of Susannah*]

Stephen King finished *Gerald's Game*.

16 November 1993, Tuesday, 11:00 a.m.

Johanna Noonan accepted delivery of two plastic owls at her Dark Score Lake summer home. After learning the secrets of Sara Tidwell and the Dark Score Lake area, she wanted the owls to, according to Indian folklore, keep evil spirits away from the house. For almost a hundred years, Sara Tidwell's ghost had a power over the town, where she caused specific residents to kill their children. These residents were descendants of the seven men who had killed her son. Johanna's husband, Mike, was in the same family as one of the men but not a direct descendant. Pregnant and fearing for her daughter's life, she got the owls. [*Bag of Bones*]

16 November 2007

Ackerman's Field had eight stones. ["N."]

16 November 2009, Monday

Wesley Smith found UR FUNCTIONS under an EXPERIMENTAL MENU item on his Kindle. Under Ur Books, he typed, "Ernest Hemingway." The Kindle found 17,894 entries across 10,438,721 Urs. He selected Ur 7,191,974. Of the many works displayed he didin't recognize three or four. He bought *Cortland's Dogs*, an unfamiliar title, for $7.50. He continued until dawn. ["Ur"]

16 November 2011

The Stand: Night Has Come #4 of 6 (Marvel Comics, $3.99) published

16 November 2012, Friday

Little Green God of Agony, a serial eComic, page 15 of 24, online at www.stephenking.com

November 17

17 November 1907

On board the SS *Ocean Star* heading for Tahiti, Mr. Jamerson sat at the captain's table, to Ellen Rimbauer's right, for dinner. That evening, Ellen smelled Miss Pauling's perfume on John Rimbauer when he returned to their stateroom. Miss Pauling was the *Ocean Star*'s entertainer. [*The Diary of Ellen Rimbauer: My Life at Rose Red*]

17 November 1958, Monday

George Amberson's second timeline: George Amberson had been renting a cabin on Sebago Lake near Durham, ME. He dropped off the keys and headed south. He spent that night at the Parker House in Boston, MA. [*11/22/63*]

17 November 1971, ~10:00 a.m.

The Castle Rock Strangler raped and strangled Pauline Toothaker, his second victim, in her Carbine Street apartment. [*The Dead Zone*]

17 November 1985

Skeleton Crew dropped to number 11 on *The New York Times* Fiction Best Seller List, its twenty-second week on the List.

The Bachman Books entered *The New York Times* Fiction Best Seller List at number 10. It was on the List for two weeks.

17 November 1991

Needful Things stayed at number 2 on *The New York Times* Fiction Best Seller List, its fifth week on the List.

17 November 1992

Dolores Claiborne (Viking, $23.50) published with a first printing of 1,500,000 copies

17 November 1994

Stephen King finished *Rose Madder*.

17 November 1996

Desperation stayed at number 3 on *The New York Times* Fiction Best Seller List, its sixth week on the List.

Richard Bachman's *The Regulators* dropped to number 9 on *The New York Times* Fiction Best Seller List, its sixth week on the List.

17 November 2002

From a Buick 8 dropped to number 14 on *The New York Times* Fiction Best Seller List, its sixth week on the List.

17 November 2010

The Stand: Hardcases #5 of 5 (Marvel Comics, $3.99) published

17 November 2013

Doctor Sleep dropped to number 5 on *The New York Times* Hardcover Fiction Best Seller List, its sixth week on the List.

November 18

18 November 1932

John Coffey was taken to D Block for a shower so the E Block guards could rehearse his execution. While talking with Paul Edgecombe when he returned, Coffey transferred something to him. Paul lived with little sickness to at least 104. [*The Green Mile*]

18 November 1958, Tuesday

George Amberson's second timeline: George Amberson went south on US 1 and checked in to Hotel Harrington in Washington, DC. [*11/22/63*]

18 November 1963, Monday

George Amberson's second timeline: George Amberson remembered he had tossed his pistol under the steps at his West Neely Street apartment.

President Kennedy spent nine hours making five speeches in Florida. [*11/22/63*]

18 November 1973

Vinnie Mason worked for Steve Ordner at The Blue Ribbon Laundry. Ordner had the Masons over for dinner to find out how far long Barton Dawes was in getting the building for the Laundry's relocation. [*Roadwork*]

18 November 1979

The Dead Zone rose to number 5 on *The New York Times* Fiction Best Seller List, its eleventh week on the List.

18 November 1984

Stephen King had an idea where a Beam held one or more Earths. [*The Dark Tower VI: Song of Susannah*]

The Talisman stayed at number 1 on *The New York Times* Fiction Best Seller List, its fourth week on the List.

18 November 1990

Four Past Midnight dropped to number 4 on *The New York Times* Fiction Best Seller List, its tenth week on the List.

18 November 2001

Black House dropped to number 10 *The New York Times* Fiction Best Seller List, its eighth week on the List.

18 November 2009

The Talisman: The Road of Trials #1 of 6 (Del Rey Comics, $3.99) published

The Stand: Soul Survivors #2 of 5 (Marvel Comics, $3.99) published

18 November 2015

The Dark Tower: The Drawing of the Three—Lady of Shadows #3 of 5 (Marvel Comics, $3.99)

Michael Roch

published

18 November 2018

Elevation entered *The New York Times* Hardcover Fiction Best Seller List at number 1. It was on the List for ten weeks.

November 19

19 November 1884

Stella Flanders was born Stella Godlin on Goat Island, ME. She never left the island until she died. ["Do the Dead Sing?" / "The Reach"]

19 November 1907

Ellen and John Rimbauer argued about the clothes she wore. He didn't like that parts of her breasts were exposed when she laughed. She pointed out that he wouldn't let her wear her shawl. [*The Diary of Ellen Rimbauer: My Life at Rose Red*]

19 November 1932

Old Sparky got leg-clamp extensions so the clamps would fit John Coffey. [*The Green Mile*]

19 November 1962

In Ur 4,121,989, this was the final date of archived *New York Times* articles. The *Times* reported that the Cuban Missile Crisis ended badly. Radiation killed more than six million in Manhattan. Russia was obliterated. Europe and Asia had incalculable losses. China took part in launching forty ICBMs. ["Ur"]

19 November 1963, Tuesday

George Amberson's second timeline: George Amberson got his gun from under the steps outside his West Neely Street apartment. Later, sitting on a park bench across from the Texas School Book Depository, he planned to kill Lee Harvey Oswald on the 22nd.

President Kennedy made a campaign stop in Miami, FL. [*11/22/63*]

19 November 1975

An article on page 27 of the Portland *Press-Herald* reported that Charles V. Pritchett had moved out of Jerusalem's Lot after hearing funny noises. They had bought the Griffen Farm at a bargain only a month before. [*'Salem's Lot*]

19 November 1978

"CALTECH SCIENTISTS REPORT SIGHTING HUGE DISC-SHAPED OBJECT IN MOJAVE; Tickman: 'Was Surrounded by Small Bright Lights;' Morales: 'Saw Red Growth Like Angel Hair,'" appeared in the *Los Angeles Times*. [*Dreamcatcher*]

19 November 1979

Most Goat Island, ME, residents, including Mary and Richard Dodge, Alden Flanders, Sarah Havelock, and Hattie Stoddard, went to Stella Flanders's ninety-fifth birthday party. Hattie and Vera Spruce baked the cake. This was Stella's last birthday; she died the following March. ["Do the Dead Sing?" / "The Reach"]

Lisey Debusher married Scott Landon in a civil ceremony at the University of Maine's Newman Chapel. Lisey's four sisters attended. The reception was at The Rock, a raunchy, rowdy, low-down-and-dirty, rock-and-roll bar in Cleaves Mills. [*Lisey's Story*]

19 November 1984

The Sidewinder *Gazette* reported that Grider Wildlife Preserve hikers found Andrew Pomeroy's remains in Colorado. His body was twenty-seven miles from where Annie Wilkes had dumped it thirteen months earlier. [*Misery*]

Richard Bachman's *Thinner* (NAL, $12.95) published with a first printing of 20,000 to 50,000 copies. The book felt like a Stephen King book. Speculation that Richard Bachman was a pseudonym snowballed.

19 November 1989

The Dark Half stayed at number 1 on *The New York Times* Fiction Best Seller List, its third week on the List.

19 November 2000

On Writing dropped to number 4 on *The New York Times* Non-Fiction Best Seller List, its fifth week on the List.

19 November 2006

Lisey's Story dropped to number 3 on *The New York Times* Fiction Best Seller List, its second week on the List.

19 November 2009, Thursday

Wesley Smith showed his Ur Kindle to office-mate Don Allman and student Robbie Henderson. They looked through Ur Books. That evening, they browsed Ur News Archive, an archive of *The New York Times* across many Urs. ["Ur"]

19 November 2012, Monday

Little Green God of Agony, a serial eComic, page 16 of 24, online at www.stephenking.com

19 November 2017

Sleeping Beauties dropped to number 7 on *The New York Times* Hardcover Fiction Best Seller List, its sixth week on the List.

November 20

20 November 1932

John Coffey was executed on Cold Mountain State Penitentiary's Old Sparky. "I'm sorry for what I am," were his last words. [*The Green Mile*]

20 November 1963, Wednesday

George Amberson's second timeline: 9:00 a.m.: George Amberson left the Eden Fallows rehabilitation facility in Dallas to go to Fort Worth. He paid Merritt $50, almost a month's rent, for a weekend at 2703 Mercedes Street.

9:15 a.m.: Sadie Dunhill arrived at Eden Fallows. A note from George said he loved her too much to include her in his mission. [*11/22/63*]

20 November 1973

Barton Dawes bought a .44 Magnum handgun, a .460 Weatherbee rifle, and ammunition at Harvey's Gun Shop. He said he was buying a Christmas present for his cousin, Nick Adams. He paid with American Express. [*Roadwork*]

20 November 1983

Pet Sematary stayed at number 1 on *The New York Times* Fiction Best Seller List, its third week on the List.

20 November 1992

The Boston *Globe* reported an anonymous windfall for The New England Home for Little Wanderers in the front-page article, "*A Happy Thanksgiving in Somerville*—ANONYMOUS BENEFACTOR GIVES 30M TO ORPHANAGE." Alan Greenbush handled Dolores Claiborne's anonymous donation of her inheritance from Vera Donovan. [*Dolores Claiborne*]

20 November 1994

Insomnia stayed at number 2 on *The New York Times* Fiction Best Seller List, its fifth week on the List.

20 November 2000

The Plant Book One: *Zenith Rising*, Part 5 e-book (Philtrum Press, $2.00) published

20 November 2006

Edgar Freemantle walked seventeen Numbers Game steps (153 actual steps).

Edgar asked Jack Cantori to get a plain, straight-backed chair, an artist's easel, and a Cybex treadmill for the large, empty, second-floor room. [*Duma Key*]

20 November 2009, Friday, 12:00 p.m.

The Lady Meerkats left Moore College for the Bluegrass Pre-Season Invitational Tournament at Rupp Arena in Lexington, KY, eighty miles away. The Meerkats were the only Division Three team in the tournament; the other seven teams were Division Two.

Wesley Smith had a late breakfast at Susan and Nan's, where he found that his Kindle's UR

LOCAL function showed Moore *Echo* articles from the future. When he saw the Lady Meer-kats' bus go by, he typed in Monday's date to see whether they were going to win. Instead of good news, he saw the article, "COACH, 7 STUDENTS KILLED IN HORRIFIC BUS CRASH; 9 OTHERS CRITICAL." He ran to Robbie Henderson's apartment above the café. Articles from the following Tuesday and Wednesday showed that a drunken Candy Rymer would cause the accident. They decided to stop her. ["Ur"]

20 November 2011

Mile 81 dropped to number 25 on *The New York Times* E-Book Fiction Best Seller List, its tenth week on the List.

November 21

21 November 1958, Friday

<u>George Amberson's second timeline</u>: George was on Florida's west coast. For the next year and a half, he rented a conch shack on the beach in Sunset Point, about sixty miles south of Tampa. He lived off his gambling winnings, but his cover story was that his rich uncle supported him while he wrote a novel. He placed bets with Eduardo Gutierrez, who had been part of Carlos Marcello's New Orleans Mob organization. [*11/22/63*]

21 November 1963, Thursday

<u>George Amberson's second timeline</u>: Sadie Dunhill remembered George Amberson had said something about living on Cadillac Street, but that wasn't quite right. She called Deke Simmons. He checked his maps and found a Mercedes Street in Fort Worth.

President and Mrs. Jackie Kennedy arrived in San Antonio, TX. They met with Lyndon and Lady Bird Johnson and Governor and Nellie Connally. In Houston, they all went to a dinner event hosted by the League of Latin American Citizens. [*11/22/63*]

21 November 1965, Sunday, The Terrible Sermon

Reverend Charlie Jacobs gave his first sermon after the deaths of his wife and son. It started well enough. After reading from First Corinthians, he said he had suffered a great loss and didn't sense the presence of God. He told about his recent research and conclusions that led to his loss of faith: At the library in Castle Rock, he read *New York Times* articles on microfilm. He found many examples of tragedies killing and injuring innocent people. Nothing in his Christianity studies from Methodist Youth Fellowship to divinity school answered the question, "Why?" that followed any tragedy. The most successful religions, whether they were branches of Christianity or other religions, were built on the deaths of those who didn't follow their way. Religion was based on coercion. Heaven was the carrot to entice us to follow; hell was the stick to keep us following their preaching. Religion was like an insurance scam where one paid into for life, then, when one needed it, found it wasn't there. He ended by saying there were too many conflicting beliefs among the various churches for God to be the God of any of them. [*Revival*]

21 November 1982

Different Seasons dropped to number 9 on *The New York Times* Fiction Best Seller List, its sixteenth week on the List.

21 November 1993

Nightmares & Dreamscapes stayed at number 3 on *The New York Times* Fiction Best Seller List, its sixth week on the List.

21 November 1999

Hearts in Atlantis dropped to number 9 on *The New York Times* Fiction Best Seller List, its eighth week on the List.

21 November 2004

The Dark Tower VII: The Dark Tower stayed at number 10 on *The New York Times* Fiction Best

Seller List, its seventh week on the List.

21 November 2009

The Lady Meerkats played the Truman State, IN, Bulldogs in their first game of the Blue-grass Preseason Invitational Tournament. ["Ur"]

21 November 2012, Wednesday

Little Green God of Agony, a serial eComic, page 17 of 24, online at www.stephenking.com

November 22

22 November 1963, Friday

Lee Harvey Oswald carpooled to work with Buell Frazier.

~10:30 a.m.: After President Kennedy gave a speech to the Fort Worth Chamber of Commerce at the Texas Hotel, his motorcade headed to Carswell Air Force Base.

~11:30 a.m.: Air Force One landed at Love Field.

11:50 a.m.: Lee Harvey Oswald set up his sniper's nest behind some cartons in the southeast corner of the Texas School Book Depository's sixth floor.

Original timeline:

12:29 p.m.: President Kennedy's motorcade arrived in Dealey Plaza.

12:30 p.m.: Lee Harvey Oswald's third shot killed President Kennedy.

Police questioned people they found in the Depository. They let Oswald go after Roy Truly said he was an employee.

1:00 p.m.: Dr. Malcolm Perry couldn't save the President at Parkland Memorial Hospital. Kennedy was pronounced dead.

Oswald shot and killed Dallas police officer J. D. Tippit with a Smith & Wesson Victory .38 revolver.

George Amberson's second timeline:

Sadie Dunhill drove along Mercedes Street until she found George Amberson's car.

8:15 a.m.: She woke him. He had had a mostly sleepless night.

8:40 a.m.: They drove to the bus stop at Winscott Road, waited a few minutes for the Number Three to Main Street in Dallas, and followed it. Their right front wheel broke off on Vickery Boulevard. They walked half a block to the next bus stop.

9:30–10:00 a.m.: They got on a Number Three bus. It turned onto Harry Hines Boulevard.

10:18 a.m.: A Dallas Public Works dump truck ran the red light at Inwood Avenue and hit the bus. They got off and walked four blocks in twenty minutes. Sadie waved a $10 bill and offered $50 to anyone who would drive them to Main Street in Dallas. A cowboy in a Studebaker stopped, saw the money, and grabbed her purse. She didn't let go; instead, she reached in, pulled out a butcher knife, and cut his arm. George pulled his .38 and told the man to run toward Love Field, three miles away. They took the cowboy's car.

11:20 a.m.: The Studebaker's engine blew at North Pearl Street, about three miles from the Texas School Book Depository at Houston and Elm. They saw a midnight blue Ford Sunliner convertible parked at the intersection of North Pearl and San Jacinto. He broke in, checked the glove box, and found a key in a Sucrets box.

12:05 p.m.: Knowing Main Street would be blocked, they took side streets. The last two blocks of Havermill served as a parking lot. George paid the attendant $5, and Sadie tossed him the keys. They walked to the Depository.

12:20 p.m.: Inside the locked Depository, a man in a poor boy cap waved for them to move along.

12:21 p.m.: George remembered the man's name—Bonnie Ray Williams—from Al Templeton's notes. Williams let them in when George called him by name and said they knew Oswald.

12:28 p.m.: On the fifth floor, three boxes of books blocked the stairs up. George pushed his way between them. He reached the northwest corner of the sixth floor; Oswald crouched in the southeast corner.

12:29 p.m.: President Kennedy's motorcade arrived in Dealey Plaza. George Amberson ran toward the southeast corner, called out to Oswald, and shot in Oswald's direction. He missed, but his shot caused Oswald to jerk; Oswald's shot went high, missing the President. George fired again, as Oswald prepared to shoot him. George stumbled and fell; Oswald's shot hit Sadie in the chest. From outside, police fired at the window and killed Oswald. George went to Sadie and held her. He told her the President was safe when she asked about him. She said, "How we danced!" before dying in his arms.

Two police officers took George to the Dallas Police station. Captain Will Fritz and FBI Agent James Hosty interrogated him. They wanted to be sure he prevented Lee Harvey Oswald from killing the President and that he wasn't part of the assassination attempt. They seemed satisfied with his answers. They took him to the Adolphus Hotel, to the same room he had when he arrived in Dallas three years earlier.

President Kennedy continued to Austin, TX, to give a scheduled dinner speech.

9:00 p.m.: Agent Hosty arrived. Amberson had no history before Derry, ME. He knew things he shouldn't have known, things that could embarrass the FBI and damage the public's opinion of them. He was no private citizen. Hosty told him they wanted him to go back to wherever and whomever he came from. Hosty would make public the story that George was so grief-stricken over losing his fiancée that he went away. The FBI took him to the bus station and gave him a choice of three tickets—Tampa, Little Rock, or Albuquerque. He chose Little Rock.

<u>George Amberson's third timeline</u>: Lee Harvey Oswald assassinated President John F. Kennedy. [*11/22/63*]

One of the many doors in the rotunda under the Fedic Dogan was labeled, "DALLAS (NOVEMBER 1963)/FEDIC." JFK's assassination was quite the tourist attraction. [*The Dark Tower VII: The Dark Tower*]

22 November 1978, Wednesday

Leigh Cabot visited Dennis Guilder in the hospital and told him about Buddy Repperton's vandalizing Christine. [*Christine*]

22 November 1981

Cujo stayed at number 3 on *The New York Times* Fiction Best Seller List, its fifteenth week on the List.

22 November 1987

Misery dropped to number 12 on *The New York Times* Fiction Best Seller List, its twenty-fifth week on the List.

22 November 1992

Gerald's Game dropped to number 15 on *The New York Times* Fiction Best Seller List, its nineteenth week on the List.

22 November 1998

Bag of Bones dropped to number 7 on *The New York Times* Fiction Best Seller List, its seventh week on the List.

22 November 1999

Blood and Smoke audio (Simon & Schuster Audio, $27.50), with "1408," "In the Deathroom," and "Lunch at the Gotham Café," (all collected in *Everything's Eventual*), was published. "Lunch at the Gotham Café" was published before (November 1995).

22 November 2007

Stephen King started *Under the Dome*.

22 November 2009, Sunday

The Lady Meerkats won the Bluegrass Preseason Invitational Tournament.

afternoon: After getting drunk at The Pot o' Gold in Central City, KY, Candy Rymer went to The Broken Windmill in Eddyville, twenty miles north of Cadiz.

~5:00 p.m.: Candy Rymer was on her way to Banty's Bar in Hopson, KY.

7:00 p.m.: Candy Rymer left Banty's Bar after the bartender tried to take her keys.

Original timeline:

Candy Rymer pulled over and took a nap on the road.

almost 9:00 p.m.: Two miles west of Cadiz, KY, Candy Rymer, speeding westbound on Highway 80, struck the Lady Meerkats' school bus, traveling on Route 139, the Princeton Road. Herbert Allison, the bus driver, tried to swerve; the bus overturned and exploded in a ditch. Coach Ellen Silverman and seven students died; nine others, including Josie Quinn, were critically injured. Rymer was barely hurt.

Timeline after Robbie Henderson and Wesley Smith intervened:

5:00–7:00 p.m.: While Candy Rymer was in Banty's Bar, Wesley slashed her front tires, and then Robbie slashed her spare and rear tires.

7:00 p.m.: When Candy Rymer came out of Banty's Bar, Wesley shook her, slapped her twice, told her she's going to kill people, and slapped her again. Wes and Robbie went to the intersection of Route 139 and Highway 80 and waited for the bus.

almost 9:00 p.m.: The bus and about a dozen cars went through the intersection. Wes and Robbie followed the parade back to Moore, KY.

When Wesley Smith got home, the Paradox Police (two low men in yellow coats) were in his apartment. They explained that his changing the timeline could have serious, unknown repercussions. He told them why he did it. Warning him not to do it again, they took his Kindle and let him go. ["Ur"]

22 November 2013

The Kileen *Weekly Gazette*'s "Jodie Doin's" column reported Texas millionaire Trevor Anderson's surprise birthday party for his wife, Sadie. In the fifty years since Sadie Dunhill married Trevor Anderson, they had five children, eleven grandchildren, and six great-grandchildren. All attended the party at JFK Memorial Park. ["Final Dispatch," alternate final chapter to *11/22/63*]

22 November 2015

The Bazaar of Bad Dreams entered *The New York Times* Hardcover Fiction Best Seller List at number 1. It was on the List for eleven weeks.

22 November 2016

Charlie the Choo-Choo, by Beryl Evans, with illustrations based on artwork by Ned Dameron (Simon & Schuster Books for Young Readers, $14.99) published with a first printing of 30,000 copies

November 23

23 November 1963, Saturday

In more than seventy Urs, *The New York Times* reported that Lee Harvey Oswald had tried to assassinate John F Kennedy. In some Urs, he succeeded; in others, he missed or wounded the President. [Kindle "Ur"]

Original timeline: "JFK SLAIN IN DALLAS, LBJ TAKES OATH; FIRST LADY EMERGES UNHARMED; SHOOTER CHARGED AS KILLER," by Max H. Littell, appeared on page one of the *Daily News* EXTRA.

George Amberson's second timeline: "JFK ESCAPES ASSASSINATION, FIRST LADY ALSO OK!" headlined the evening edition of the *Daily News* EXTRA. "AMERICANS BREATHE A SIGH OF RELIEF," by Philip Scudder, appeared on page one. "PANIC STRIKES DURING DRIVE THROUGH DALLAS," was on page 3.

From Little Rock, AK, George Amberson took the bus to Pittsburgh, PA. It stopped in Indianapolis, IN; he had breakfast in the bus depot's diner.

George Amberson's third timeline: The *Daily News* EXTRA reported JFK's assassination. [*11/22/63*]

23 November 1973, 8:00 p.m.

Steve Ordner, Barton Dawes's boss at The Blue Ribbon Laundry, invited Dawes to dinner for an update on the purchase of the Waterford building for the Laundry's relocation. Dawes lied and said he expected to close the deal the following Friday. [*Roadwork*]

23 November 1978, Thanksgiving

Arnie Cunningham took turkey sandwiches, beer, and apple pie to Dennis Guilder, in the hospital. Dennis had Arnie sign his cast again (the first time was shortly after breaking his leg). The signatures differed as if signed by two people. [*Christine*]

23 November 1980

Firestarter stayed at number 3 on *The New York Times* Fiction Best Seller List, its fourteenth week on the List.

23 November 1983

Horace Derwent visited Danny Torrance in a stairwell at Alafia Elementary School. Danny walked away. That night, he asked Dick Hallorann how many lockboxes he could have in his mind. As many as he needed. [*Doctor Sleep*]

23 November 1986

IT dropped to number 2 on *The New York Times* Fiction Best Seller List, *IT*'s eleventh week on the List.

23 November 2003

The Dark Tower V: Wolves of the Calla (as *The Dark Tower*: Volumes 1–5 because, since *The Green Mile*, a series of books could have only one spot on the List) entered *The New York Times* Fiction Best Seller List at number 2. It was on the List for nine weeks.

23 November 2006

Edgar Freemantle's second floor was furnished with the three items he had requested. He used the second floor to draw and paint, and, on rainy days, to exercise. [*Duma Key*]

23 November 2009, Monday

Josie Quinn and another Moore College student died from Sunday night's crash. ["Ur"]

23 November 2012, Friday

Little Green God of Agony, a serial eComic, page 18 of 24, online at www.stephenking.com

23 November 2017, Thanksgiving

Lila Norcross had pushed Clint Norcross away. He drove to Coughlin to see Shannon Parks. Parked outside her house, he saw she was spending the holiday with other women; he left and stopped at O'Byrne's.

Frank Geary decided to absorb the inevitable abuse from his ex-in-laws to have Thanksgiving with his daughter. On the way, he found Clint Norcross at O'Byrne's. They had a drink together, neither showing any ill will toward the other. [*Sleeping Beauties*]

November 24

24 November 1965, Wednesday

To show her gratitude for restoring Con Morton's voice, Mrs. Morton took a turkey with sweet potatoes to Charlie Jacobs. She suggested he might find his faith if he left Harlow and started over in a new place. [*Revival*]

24 November 1978

"STATE POLICE, USAF INVESTIGATORS FIND NO 'ANGEL HAIR' AT MOJAVE SITE; Tickman and Morales Take, Pass, Lie Tests; Possibility of Hoax Discounted" appeared in the *Los Angeles Times*. [*Dreamcatcher*]

24 November 1983, Thanksgiving, 5:30 p.m.

Jud Crandall found Ellie Creed's cat, Winston Churchill, dead on his lawn. Church's neck was broken, probably from being hit in the road. Jud took Louis Creed to the Micmac burial ground, three miles beyond the Pet Sematary. Jud knew Church would come back different. Ellie would learn that sometimes dead is better; she'd still love Church but wouldn't be upset when he died again. Louis buried Church in a 2' W x 3' L x 30" D grave with a stone cairn. [*Pet Sematary*]

24 November 1985

Skeleton Crew dropped to number 13 on *The New York Times* Fiction Best Seller List, its twenty-third week on the List.

The Bachman Books dropped to number 16 on *The New York Times* Fiction Best Seller List, its second and last week on the List.

24 November 1991

Needful Things dropped to number 3 on *The New York Times* Fiction Best Seller List, its sixth week on the List.

24 November 1996

Desperation dropped to number 6 on *The New York Times* Fiction Best Seller List, its seventh week on the List.

Richard Bachman's *The Regulators* dropped to number 12 on *The New York Times* Fiction Best Seller List, its seventh week on the List.

24 November 2009, Tuesday

The death of a Lady Meerkats cheerleader, badly burned in Sunday night's crash, brought the death toll to eleven. ["Ur"]

24 November 2013

Doctor Sleep dropped to number 7 on *The New York Times* Hardcover Fiction Best Seller List, its seventh week on the List.

November 25

25 November 1922

A farmer, on his way to Lyme Biska, NE, found three coy dogs fighting over the mostly skeletal remains of a woman with auburn hair. The woman was missing two back teeth. ["1922"]

25 November 1973

The Mustangs-Chargers football game was televised. The Chargers intercepted three of Hank Rucker's passes, beating the Musties 37–6. [*Roadwork*]

25 November 1979

The Dead Zone rose to number 4 on *The New York Times* Fiction Best Seller List, its twelfth week on the List.

25 November 1983, Friday, ~1:00 p.m.

After being killed in the road and buried in the Micmac burial ground beyond the Pet Sematary, Winston Churchill came back alive but different, wrong. He wasn't mean, but he killed small animals and seldom purred. He smelled bad, and his green eyes had become yellow-green. [*Pet Sematary*]

25 November 1984

The Talisman stayed at number 1 on *The New York Times* Fiction Best Seller List, its fifth week on the List.

25 November 1990

Four Past Midnight rose to number 3 on *The New York Times* Fiction Best Seller List, its eleventh week on the List.

25 November 2009, Wednesday

"CANDACE RYMER CHARGED WITH MULTIPLE COUNTS OF VEHICULAR HOMICIDE," appeared on the lower half of page 1 of the Moore *Echo*. ["Ur"]

The Dark Tower: Fall of Gilead #6 of 6 (Marvel Comics, $3.99) published

25 November 2018

Elevation dropped to number 6 on *The New York Times* Hardcover Fiction Best Seller List, its second week on the List.

November 26

26 November 1914, Thanksgiving Day

John Rimbauer provided Thanksgiving dinner in the Carriage House for about fifty Rose Red servants. [*The Diary of Ellen Rimbauer: My Life at Rose Red*]

26 November 1922, night

Wilfred James woke up. Arlette James, dead, opened the door from the back porch. A group of rats brought her into the kitchen. She told Wilfred about Henry James's activities, both those that had happened and those that hadn't yet. ["1922"]

26 November 1963, Tuesday, ~12:00 p.m.

George Amberson's second timeline: George Amberson's Greyhound bus pulled into Auburn, ME's Minot Avenue station. After almost eighty hours of bus rides, he took a cab to Tamarack Motor Court, on Route 196. He got the same room he had before. [*11/22/63*]

26 November 1973

The ninety-day option on the Waterford building for The Blue Ribbon Laundry's relocation expired. Real estate agent Patrick J. Monohan had made a good offer, but Barton Dawes rejected it. [*Roadwork*]

26 November 1989

The Dark Half dropped to number 2 on *The New York Times* Fiction Best Seller List, its fourth week on the List.

26 November 2000

On Writing dropped to number 6 on *The New York Times* Non-Fiction Best Seller List, its sixth week on the List.

26 November 2006

Lisey's Story dropped to number 5 on *The New York Times* Fiction Best Seller List, its third week on the List.

26 November 2012, Monday

Little Green God of Agony, a serial eComic, page 19 of 24, online at www.stephenking.com

<26 November 2015, Thanksgiving

Dinah Scott responded to a tweet about badconcert.com. People who had gone to the ruined 'Round Here concert qualified for a free Zappit as a consolation. She sent a picture of herself at the concert. A week later, she received her green Zappit. A letter said she could win a Wave 50cc moped-scooter by watching the Fishin' Hole demo screen. When the pink fish turned to numbers, she would be entered by tapping them. Numbers for the moped: 7459. Prizes were to be claimed on zeetheend.com. [*End of Watch*]

26 November 2017

Sleeping Beauties dropped to number 11 on *The New York Times* Hardcover Fiction Best Seller

List, its seventh week on the List.

November 27

27 November 1922

Sheriff Jones told Wilfred James that Arlette James was dead. He didn't take Wilfred's question, "I killed her, didn't I?" as a confession. The Sheriff took him to the hospital to have his infected hand treated. ["1922"]

27 November 1963, Wednesday

George Amberson's second timeline: George Amberson took a taxi to The Kennebec Fruit, on the corner of Main Street and the Old Lisbon Road in Lisbon Falls. At the time portal, guardian Zack Lang explained that George had created an enormous number of strings. George had to go back to the future, see what he had done, and then come back to 1958 to reset everything. Otherwise, all humanity could be destroyed.

George went from the Land of Ago to the Land of Ahead. Saving President Kennedy affected so many lives and created so many strings that the world was messed up. [*11/22/63*]

27 November 1973

Barton Dawes visited Sal Magliore, who told him to return the next day after Magliore had him checked out. With less than two months to move before his house was to be demolished for the Route 784 extension, Dawes told his wife that Olsen was looking for a new home for them. Olsen was a bogus name. [*Roadwork*]

27 November 1980, evening: The Famous Thanksgiving Jag of 1980

Drunk, Jim Gardener shot and almost killed his wife, Nora. She agreed to drop it if he gave her an uncontested divorce. The State of Maine allowed the arrangement but had him seek counseling. [*The Tommyknockers*]

27 November 1983

Pet Sematary stayed at number 1 on *The New York Times* Fiction Best Seller List, its fourth week on the List.

27 November 1991

Stephen King put John T. Spier's 11/16/1991 letter in his journal. [*The Dark Tower VI: Song of Susannah*]

27 November 1994

Insomnia stayed at number 2 on *The New York Times* Fiction Best Seller List, its sixth week on the List.

27 November 2011

11/22/63 entered *The New York Times* Fiction Best Seller List at number 1. It was on the List for twenty-one weeks.

Mile 81 rose to number 22 on *The New York Times* E-Book Fiction Best Seller List, its eleventh week on the List.

November 28

28 November 1965, Sunday

Reverend Davis Thomas was the guest preacher at the First Methodist Church of Harlow. Reverend Charlie Jacobs had been fired for giving The Terrible Sermon the week before. [*Revival*]

28 November 1973

Because he let the Waterford option expire, Barton Dawes cleared his desk at The Blue Ribbon Laundry and gave his resignation to Steve Ordner. He returned to Magliore's Used Cars for explosives to blow up the Route 784 extension when it was built. Sal Magliore wouldn't help. [*Roadwork*]

28 November 1978

The Stand (Doubleday, $12.95) published with a first printing of 70,000 copies

28 November 1982

Different Seasons stayed at number 9 on *The New York Times* Fiction Best Seller List, its seventeenth week on the List.

28 November 1993

Nightmares & Dreamscapes stayed at number 3 on *The New York Times* Fiction Best Seller List, its seventh week on the List.

28 November 1999

Hearts in Atlantis dropped to number 12 on *The New York Times* Fiction Best Seller List, its ninth week on the List.

28 November 2004

The Dark Tower VII: The Dark Tower dropped to number 13 on *The New York Times* Fiction Best Seller List, its eighth and last week on the List.

28 November 2010

Full Dark, No Stars entered *The New York Times* Fiction Best Seller List at number 2. It was on the List for eight weeks.

28 November 2012, Wednesday

Little Green God of Agony, a serial eComic, page 20 of 24, online at www.stephenking.com

November 29

29 November 1977

Danny Torrance played in The Overlook Hotel's playground. The topiary animals came to life and chased him. As he jumped on the hotel's porch, a topiary lion pounced and clawed his legs. When his parents opened the door, the animals were back in their original positions. [*The Shining*]

29 November 1981

Cujo dropped to number 5 on *The New York Times* Fiction Best Seller List, its sixteenth week on the List.

29 November 1987

Misery dropped to number 14 on *The New York Times* Fiction Best Seller List, its twenty-sixth week on the List.

The Tommyknockers entered *The New York Times* Fiction Best Seller List at number 1. It was on the List for twenty-three weeks.

29 November 1989

During The Tonight Show's taping, Reploid Ed Paladin walked on stage when Johnny Carson was announced. He mimed a juggling act before being arrested. When the police tried to call Albert K. Dellums, his lawyer, they reached a stock brokerage at the business phone number and housekeeper Howlanda Moore at the home number. The lawyer's firm was not in the yellow pages. ["The Reploids"]

29 November 1990

Tom Cullen, Kojak, and Stu Redman decided to leave Grand Junction, CO, the next day and try to make it to Boulder, CO, the Free Zone. [*The Stand: The Complete & Uncut Edition*]

29 November 1992

Gerald's Game rose to number 13 on *The New York Times* Fiction Best Seller List, its twentieth week on the List.

29 November 1998

Bag of Bones rose to number 5 on *The New York Times* Fiction Best Seller List, its eighth week on the List.

29 November 2009

Under the Dome entered *The New York Times* Fiction Best Seller List at number 1. It was on the List for nine weeks.

29 November 2015

The Bazaar of Bad Dreams dropped to number 2 on *The New York Times* Hardcover Fiction Best Seller List, its second week on the List.

November 30

30 November

Gun hunting season ended in the Lake Charles area. [*End of Watch*]

30 November 1929, Joe Newall's funeral

Joe had hanged himself in the new section of his house; the house grew some more. Cleve Torbutt found his body; Noble Upshaw cut it down. Hay & Peabody took care of his funeral. He was buried next to his wife and daughter in Gates Falls, ME. ["It Grows on You"]

30 November 1963

As part of the rumor that Johnnie Dillinger hadn't died in Chicago in July 1934, a sixty-year-old Dillinger was said to have succumbed to a heart attack. ["The Death of Jack Hamilton"]

30 November 1965, Tuesday

Jamie Morton said goodbye to Charlie Jacobs. Charlie didn't know where he would end up but wanted to make Portsmouth that night. [*Revival*]

30 November 1975, Sunday

"THE HUNT FOR THE CASTLE ROCK STRANGLER GOES ON . . . AND ON" appeared in a Maine newspaper supplement. [*The Dead Zone*]

30 November 1977

The Overlook Hotel's elevator moved with nobody on it. Danny Torrance and Wendy Torrance heard party noises; Wendy found confetti in the elevator. [*The Shining*]

30 November 1978, Thursday

Nicky Bellingham, Richie Trelawney, and Moochie Welch saw Jackson Browne perform at the Pittsburgh Civic Center. Welch lost the others while mooching money outside; he netted $30. After the concert, he hitchhiked back to Libertyville. [*Christine*]

30 November 1980

Firestarter stayed at number 3 on *The New York Times* Fiction Best Seller List, its fifteenth week on the List.

30 November 1986

IT stayed at number 2 on *The New York Times* Fiction Best Seller List, *IT*'s twelfth week on the List.

30 November 1990

Tom Cullen, Kojak, and Stu Redman left for the Free Zone. In a large Colorado Highway Department snowmobile, they went sixteen miles. [*The Stand: The Complete & Uncut Edition*]

30 November 2003

The Dark Tower V: Wolves of the Calla (as *The Dark Tower*: Volumes 1–5) dropped to number 2 on *The New York Times* Fiction Best Seller List, its second week on the List.

30 November 2008

Just After Sunset entered *The New York Times* Fiction Best Seller List at number 2. It was on the List for eight weeks.

30 November 2012, Friday

Little Green God of Agony, a serial eComic, page 21 of 24, online at www.stephenking.com

30 November 2014

Revival entered *The New York Times* Hardcover Fiction Best Seller List at number 1. It was on the List for ten weeks.

November ≥2017

Thursday, Thanksgiving:

Myra and Bob Ellis hosted Thanksgiving dinner. Two of their five children, a few grandchildren, and Scott Carey attended. After dinner, Scott weighed 141 pounds.

Friday after Thanksgiving: Castle Rock's Forty-Fifth Annual Turkey Trot 12K:

Deirdre McComb had made it clear she didn't want to have anything to do with Scott Carey and hadn't appreciated his efforts to intervene in her struggle with prejudice. He offered her a wager: If she won the race, she could let her dogs poop in his yard and he'd clean it up; if he won the race, she and Missy had to have dinner (vegetarian) at his house and at least try to be neighborly; they'd keep the status quo if neither won.

9:10 a.m.: Mayor Dusty Coughlin announced and started the race. Scott Carey ran past the 3K and 6K markers with ease. He increased his speed at the 8K and 9K markers. Aches and labored breathing started on Hunter's Hill. Beyond the 10K marker at the top of the Hill, he felt an elevation and ran easily again.

Nearing 11K, it rained. Deirdre had pulled into the lead, with three runners between them. One of those runners stopped. At the 11K marker, Scott picked up his speed as the rain pounded. He could see only Deirdre's red shirt as he passed the other two runners. Surprised to see Scott over her shoulder, Deirdre picked up her pace; he picked up his more.

Less than seventy yards from the finish line, Deirdre tripped when she turned to look again. When Scott stopped to help her, she asked how he had cheated. A newspaper photographer snapped a photo as he picked her up; Scott felt her weight, but she didn't. He put her on her feet, told her to run, and followed her across the finish line at Tin Bridge.

evening: Recognizing she would have lost without Scott's help, Deirdre honored their wager and suggested Monday for their dinner. She apologized for saying he had cheated and looked forward to his explaining the weightless feeling she had when he held her.

An online *Press-Herald* article, LOCAL RESTAURANT OWNER WINS CASTLE ROCK TURKEY TROT, mentioned the restaurant and quoted a favorable review from August. The photo of Scott helping her up was captioned, SHE GOT BY WITH A LITTLE HELP FROM A FRIEND. A second photo showed Missy Donaldson and Deirdre hugging; the camera angle made it look as though Scott was in the hug. Following publication of the article and photos, the townspeople made Holy Frijole a hit, almost giving the restaurant more business than it could handle.

Scott weighed 137 pounds.

Monday after Thanksgiving:

Missy Donaldson and Deirdre McComb and Myra and Bob Ellis had vegetarian lasagna Florentine with garlic toast points for dinner at Scott Carey's. After dessert, Scott told them about his weight loss. Missy didn't believe it until he took her hand and she went weightless.

They became friends and got together at Holy Frijole every week. Deirdre reserved a table for the Dr. Ellis Party. [*Elevation*]

November

November 1889

Ten-year-old Rebecca Cline got a silver dollar for her birthday. She took it to the apothecary on Main Street in a town in the Black Hills of Dakota to buy candy. After a couple of drinks at the Chuck-a-Luck, Jim Trusdale strangled her and took her dollar. He didn't realize he had lost his Plainsman hat until after he returned home.

Mr. Cline, concerned when his daughter didn't come home, led a search party. They found her in Barker's Alley. Trusdale's hat was under her party dress. Sheriff Barclay deputized six townsmen to bring him in. A thorough search of Trusdale's shack and body cavities failed to find the dollar. During Trusdale's testimony at the trial, the Sheriff began to believe in Trusdale's innocence. If Trusdale had taken the girl's dollar, he would have gone back to the Chuck-a-Luck for more whiskey.

The jury deliberated for an hour and a half to find Trusdale guilty of murder in the first. He was hanged three days later. Undertaker Abel Hines summoned the Sheriff. When a man is hanged, his sphincter often loosens. In Trusdale's excrement was Rebecca Cline's silver dollar. Hines supposed Trusdale had swallowed it, and, whenever it had passed, he had cleaned and reswallowed it. ["A Death"]

November 1899

Lord Hull's sons and wife conspired to kill him for disinheriting them and being a lousy man. Inspector Lestrade consulted with Sherlock Holmes and Dr. Watson about the murder, a seemingly perfect locked-room crime. Because of his cat-allergy symptoms, Holmes couldn't see the subtle clues. Dr. Watson could and solved the case. Because Lord Hull was a nasty man, Lestrade, Holmes, and Watson altered the crime scene to show the crime as murder during an attempted burglary. The family wasn't implicated. ["The Doctor's Case"]

November 1922

Two men stopped while Henry James changed a blown tire. One drew a bandit hammer claw shotgun and robbed him. Henry and Shannon Cotterie, the Sweetheart Bandits, robbed a nearby farmer of his rattletrap Reo car and cash. They abandoned the car near the McCook train depot then stole a Hupmobile in McCook. A day or two later, Henry robbed the Frontier Bank of Arapahoe, CO, for less than $100. The next day, The Sweetheart Bandits robbed the First Bank of Cheyenne Wells for $400. Later in the month, they robbed a bank in Grand Junction, CO, and another in Ogden, UT. A man at the Ogden bank tried to stop them outside. Henry shot him in the chest. The man's death two days later qualified them for Utah's death penalty.

Wilfred James wanted to be busy with home improvement projects over the winter so he wouldn't have time to think about Arlette James or Henry James. He took out a $750 mortgage, getting $200 in cash. As he reached for a hat box to hide the money, a two-foot, six-pound Norway rat bit the webbing between his left thumb and forefinger. He stomped on the rat and killed it, but his hand became infected. He was sure it was the same rat that had attacked Achelois in August. ["1922"]

November 1930

The Maine Legion of White Decency burned Company E's The Black Spot nightclub. Dick Hallorann helped Trevor Dawson and Will Hanlon get out of the club. Sixty to eighty people died. IT was at this event, which marked the end of IT's 1929–1930 cycle. [*IT*]

November 1933

Sadie Dunhill was born. ["Final Dispatch," alternate final chapter to *11/22/63*]

November 1951

Oklahoma City townspeople had stopped buying from The Oklahoma Rancher's and Cattlemen's Association after Greg Stillson had run a *Herald* ad saying he saved many thousands of dollars yet received only $17. The Association sent two men to rough up Stillson. He beat them up and rammed their brass knuckles where the sun doesn't shine. [*The Dead Zone*]

November 1960

Ruthie Creed, Louis Creed's cousin, was driving her father's car when a kid started a Public Works Department payloader and couldn't stop it. It struck and totaled the car, killing Ruthie. Mortician Donny Donahue buried her. [*Pet Sematary*]

November 1969

Charlie Dawes, Barton and Mary's son, began having headaches and double vision. [*Roadwork*]

November 1972

Castle County Sheriff Carl M. Kelso didn't catch The Castle Rock Strangler. The voters replaced him with George Bannerman, a Castle Rock law officer. [*The Dead Zone*]

November 1974

The Castle Rock Strangler raped and strangled Carol Dunbarger, his fourth victim, near Strimmer's Brook between Castle Rock and Otisfield, ME. [*The Dead Zone*]

November 1975

Philip Sawyer, Morgan Sloat, and Tommy Woodbine hunted in Blessington, UT, as they did every year. Sunlight Gardener substituted for Randy Glover, who was on a cruise. Gardener/Osmond shot and killed Phil. Sloat called and told Phil's family he died in a hunting accident. Phil's Twinner was killed about the same time. [*The Talisman*]

November 1977

Congressman Louis Quinn was thrown out of office when Greg Stillson disclosed his involvement in a parking-lot kickback scheme. [*The Dead Zone*]

Mrs. Massey, dead for four months, got out of the bathtub of The Overlook Hotel's Room 217 and half-strangled Danny Torrance. [*The Shining*]

Gwendy Peterson wanted to try the red button on her button box. During fifth-period study hall, she went to Mr. Anderson's empty classroom to look at the pull-down maps. South America had much of the world's unpopulated areas, so she picked three countries. In the library, she narrowed it down to one, an unpopulated country with mostly jungle. After school, she thought of that country and pushed the red button. With a fever, Gwendy slept most of the next day. The evening news was all about the Jim Jones-led mass suicide in

Jonestown, Guyana. [*Gwendy's Button Box*]

November 1978

Johnny Smith experienced double vision. Dr. Weizak suggested he see Dr. Vann.

Representing New Hampshire's Third District, Greg Stillson was re-elected into the US House of Representatives. [*The Dead Zone*]

Buddy Repperton, Richie Trelawney, Don Vandenberg, and Moochie Welch demolished Christine. They smashed her windows, pried off half her front bumper, punched holes in her body, smashed her dashboard, ripped her seats, cut off her distributor cap, smashed her taillights, defecated on her dashboard, slashed her tires, broke off her antenna, put sugar in her gas tank and Texas Driver wine in her carburetor, and damaged her radiator. Arnie Cunningham helped her repair herself.

Arnie began running cigarettes and liquor into New York and fireworks into Burlington for Will Darnell. Once, he ran a brown package of drugs to Wheeling and exchanged it for a brown package of money. [*Christine*]

November 1979

For Gwendy Peterson and Harry Streeter that summer, it was almost love at first sight. In November, Gwendy approached her mother about birth control. Understanding, Mrs. Peterson made the doctor's appointment. [*Gwendy's Button Box*]

November 1980

"The Monkey" (collected in *Skeleton Crew*) appeared in the November issue (Vol. 8, No. 11) of *Gallery*.

November 1981

"The Gunslinger and the Dark Man" (collected in *The Dark Tower I: The Gunslinger*) appeared in the November issue (#366; Volume 61, Number 5) of *The Magazine of Fantasy & Science Fiction*.

"Do the Dead Sing?" (collected as "The Reach" in *Skeleton Crew*) appeared in the November issue of *Yankee Magazine*.

November 1982

"The Raft" (collected in *Skeleton Crew*) appeared in the November issue (Vol. 10, No. 11) of *Gallery*.

November 1984, full moon

For four nights, Elmer Zinneman and his brother, Pete, led a team of men and dogs to search for The Beast in Tarker's Mills. The Beast killed Milt Sturmfuller at The Driftwood motel in Portland, ME. [*Cycle of the Werewolf*]

November 1985

Norman Daniels raped Rose Daniels anally with a tennis racket. [*Rose Madder*]

November 1995

Dark Love: Twenty-Two All-Original Tales of Lust and Obsession, edited by Nancy A. Collins, Edward E. Kramer, and Martin H. Greenberg (ROC, $22.95), with "Lunch at the Gotham Café" (collected in *Everything's Eventual*), published

November 1997

The Dark Tower IV: Wizard & Glass (Plume, $17.95) published

November 2003

Borderlands 5, edited by Thomas F. Monteleone and Elizabeth Monteleone (Borderlands Press, $35), with "Stationary Bike" (collected in *Just After Sunset*), published

November 2007

"Ayana" (collected in *Just After Sunset*) appeared in the Fall 2007 issue (No. 182) of *The Paris Review*.

November 2008

The EPS shut down Tom Goodhugh's garbage business over groundwater contamination and unlawful dumping of medical waste. They planned to sue and considered criminal proceedings. ["Fair Extension"]

November 2009

After the City Center Massacre, Brady Hartsfield struck up conversations with Mrs. Trelawney on Under Debbie's Blue Umbrella, an anonymous social media site. He said he had used her car to kill those people in the massacre. He had been taking the same medication as Mrs. Trelawney. When he stopped taking it, he knew what he had done was wrong. Mrs. Trelawney stopped her meds.

Late at night in November, Brady played the SPOOKS audio file he had installed on her computer. Baby Patricia Cray cried, and the baby's mother accused Mrs. Trelawney of letting him murder her baby. Mrs. Trelawney thought they were ghosts of the victims. She killed herself. [*Mr. Mercedes*]

"The Bone Church" (collected in *The Bazaar of Bad Dreams*) appeared in the November issue (Volume 56, Number 11) of *Playboy*.

November 2010

Detective Bill Hodges retired with forty years of service. [*Mr. Mercedes*]

November 2011

For two years, Andrew Newsome, the sixth-richest man in the world, was in constant pain. He sought help from specialists around the world; none could help. His private investigation led him to consult Reverend Rideout. The Reverend exorcised a demon god from Newsome, but the exertion cost Rideout his life. ["The Little Green God of Agony"]

3:15 p.m.: Outside Brady Hartsfield's hospital window was a parking garage. Flashes of sunlight reflected off cars as they went up the ramp. After tending to Brady, Nurse Sadie MacDonald watched the cars. The light flashes caused mini-seizures, which allowed Brady in her head. He watched with her, seeing what she saw. He could also see her thoughts. Without knowing he was even there, she pushed him out.

A few days later, Brady opened his eyes in front of Nurse Norma Wilmer. He told her his head hurt and asked for his mother. [*Mr. Mercedes*][*Finders Keepers*] [*End of Watch*]

November 2012

Library Al Brooks found the Zappits in Kiner Memorial Hospital's library and took one. [*End of Watch*]

November 2015

When Dave Calhoun was sixteen, he saw a woman get out of her boyfriend's Humble Oil truck. Her skirt rode up so he could see her panties. Many years later, sitting on a bench outside the Lakeview Assisted Living Center, he saw a representation of her. He called her Miss Yummy. She smiled, waved, and pulled her skirt up above her knees.

The following week, his son Peter took him to dinner. Miss Yummy sat at the next table. She pulled her skirt up higher, showing him a thigh. As she was for him, only Dave could see her. He told Peter he was tired and ready to go back to the Center. ["Mister Yummy"]

City Center Massacre victim Gerald Stansbury died of a heart attack. Heart disease ran in his family. [*End of Watch*]

December
Happenings

December 1

1 December

Quitters, Inc. considered Dick Morrison an ex-smoker. At 5' 11" and 174 pounds, they set his maximum weight at 182 pounds. He was to be weighed monthly. Quitters, Inc. would cut off a loved one's little finger if a client exceeded the maximum weight.

One to two months earlier, Quitters, Inc. caught Morrison smoking in a Midland Tunnel traffic jam. He had to watch as they gave his wife a series of electric shocks. This one offense was enough for him to quit smoking. ["Quitters, Inc."]

1 December 1960, Thursday

<8:00 a.m.: Stokely Jones spray-painted antiwar graffiti in five-foot high letters on Chamberlain Hall's north wall. Snow had changed to rain, so the paint never set. The message became illegible.

>4:30 p.m.: On his way to the dining hall, Stokely Jones fell in the icy, slushy water and couldn't get up. The Hearts group from Chamberlain Three had been cheering him on until he fell. They carried him and his crutches to the infirmary. At Skip Kirk's suggestion, the group went back and drew peace signs on many of their belongings.

9:00 p.m.: Dearborn (Chamberlain Three's floor-proctor), the Dean of Men, and the Disciplinary Officer held a meeting to confirm Stokely Jones was the graffiti artist. They suggested it had to have been Jones because he had a peace sign on his coat and the graffiti contained peace signs. Tony DeLucca, Lennie Doria, Nate Hoppenstand, Skip Kirk, Ronnie Malenfant, Billy Marchant, Nick Prouty, Pete Riley, and Brad Witherspoon said they had been using peace signs, too. They offered to go to their dorm rooms to show them. Hugh Brennan showed peace signs on his socks. The meeting ended without identifying the artist. ["Hearts in Atlantis"]

1 December 1971

Stephan King's poem "The Hardcase Speaks" appeared in *Contraband* #2.

1 December 1973

Barton Dawes never got over the death of his son in October 1970. Relations with his wife became strained after Dawes lost his job and didn't get a new house to replace the one to be demolished for the Route 784 extension. She left him and went to her parents. [*Roadwork*]

1 December 1977

Tony showed Danny Torrance redrum in a mirror—murder—and told him it would happen the next day. Danny sent a telepathic distress call from The Overlook Hotel in Colorado to Dick Hallorann in St. Petersburg, FL. Dick left for Colorado. [*The Shining*]

1 December 1978, Friday, 1:25 a.m.

After the Jackson Browne concert, Moochie Welch walked along JFK Drive toward Vandenberg's Happy Gas to ask Buddy Repperton for a ride home. Christine and the dead Roland LeBay ran down Welch, their first victim, breaking his back and knocking him out of his boots. They ran over him repeatedly; his remains had to be scraped up with a shovel. Christine suffered a bloodied hood, broken headlight, broken muffler, dented bumper, and a dented grill. She repaired herself while returning to Darnell's Garage. Later, the FBI laboratory in Washington, DC, determined paint from Welch's body was Autumn Red—one of Christine's colors. Pennsylvania State Police Detective Rudy Junkins talked with Leigh Cabot, Arnie Cunningham, and Michael Cunningham about Moochie Welch's death. [*Christine*]

1 December 1980

the December issue (volume 76, #6) of *Ellery Queen's Mystery Magazine*, with "The Wedding Gig" (collected in *Skeleton Crew*), published

1 December 1985

Heroes for Hope: Starring the X-Men, Volume 1 #1 (Marvel Comics, $1.50), published

Skeleton Crew stayed at number 13 on *The New York Times* Fiction Best Seller List, its twenty-fourth week on the List.

1 December 1986

Afterword to *The Dark Tower II: The Drawing of the Three*

1 December 1991

Needful Things stayed at number 3 on *The New York Times* Fiction Best Seller List, its seventh week on the List.

1 December 1996

Desperation dropped to number 8 on *The New York Times* Fiction Best Seller List, its eighth week on the List.

Richard Bachman's *The Regulators* dropped to number 13 on *The New York Times* Fiction Best Seller List, its eighth week on the List.

1 December 1997

A West Paducah, KY, high school freshman shot eight students, killing three at a school prayer meeting. A copy of *Rage* was found in his locker. After this last of several apparently *Rage*-related incidents of increasing violence (4/26/1988, 9/18/1989, 1/18/1988, 2/2/1996, 12/1/1997), Stephen King let *Rage* fall out of print.

1 December 2013

Doctor Sleep rose to number 6 on *The New York Times* Hardcover Fiction Best Seller List, its eighth week on the List.

December 2

2 December 1922

"'SWEETHEART BANDITS' ELUDE ELKO POLICE, ESCAPE AGAIN" appeared in the papers after Henry James and Shannon Cotterie were seen heading toward Elko, NV, but weren't caught by the police waiting for them. They had gone to a diner in Deeth, NV, for eggs and coffee. The counterman recognized them and tried to make a citizen's arrest. The man fired his gun when Henry got up to ask them to just let them pay and leave; it misfired. Henry paid $2 for their meal, and they headed out. The man shot Shannon in the back. Henry helped Shannon to the car. The man fired again; the gun blew up and took out his left eye. Henry drove toward Elko, thirty miles away. Two miles from Elko, they may have hit a pothole. The car skidded into a ditch and stalled. Henry carried Shannon to an empty shack with a stove. He shot himself after Shannon died in his lap. Their bodies were discovered later that month.

Wilfred James's hand had been amputated because of gangrene. At the hospital, Sheriff Jones told Wilfred about the woman a farmer had found a week earlier. He asked Wilfred about Arlette James's back teeth; Wilfred lied and said she had lost them to a gum infection. Arlette was considered dead, having been robbed on the road. ["1922"]

2 December 1977

Danny Torrance's shine would strengthen The Overlook Hotel. If Danny were to be killed inside, he and his shine would become part of the hotel. After the Torrances arrived in late September, the hotel caused Jack Torrance to become crazier and crazier, with the goal of having him kill Danny. By this day, Jack had disabled all remaining means of contact with the outside world—the radio and snowmobile.

A recovering alcoholic not having had a drink since February 1976, Jack drank in The Colorado Lounge. Delbert Grady, who killed himself in The Overlook Hotel the winter of 1970–1971, served him, though there wasn't any alcohol on the premises. Wendy Torrance found him drunk in the Lounge. He tried to strangle her. Danny distracted him long enough for her to knock him out. They locked him in the kitchen pantry.

Later, Delbert Grady opened the pantry. Jack hit Wendy several times with a roque mallet, breaking her back and three ribs; she stabbed him in the lower back. He followed her to their rooms. When he broke a hole in the bathroom door, she cut his hand with a razor. He left when he heard a snowmobile; he waited. It was Dick Hallorann. Jack knocked him out with the roque mallet, breaking his left cheek and several teeth.

Wendy woke Dick Hallorann. Danny, remembering the boiler, told them they had to leave at once. [*The Shining*]

2 December 1978, Saturday

After a 150-mile run to Jamesburg for Will Darnell, Arnie Cunningham took Leigh Cabot out. They had ice cream at Baskin-Robbins then went Christmas shopping at Monroeville Mall. On their way home, they picked up hitchhiker Barry Gottfried at the intersection of Route 17 and JFK Drive. They stopped at McDonald's for takeout. When they dropped Gottfried off at the corner of JFK Drive and Center, Leigh choked on her burger as Christine played songs from dead singers. Gottfried saved Leigh's life with the Heimlich Maneuver. Arnie had forgotten the Maneuver. When he was in Christine, he was in the 1950s, before the technique was invented. He thought Gottfried was hurting Leigh, so he hit Gottfried in the mouth. Outside her house, she told Arnie she didn't want to drive in Christine again. She explained how she felt in Christine, how Christine changed him, how Christine tried to kill her that night. They broke up. [*Christine*]

2 December 1979

The Dead Zone dropped to number 5 on *The New York Times* Fiction Best Seller List, its thirteenth week on the List.

2 December 1984

The Talisman stayed at number 1 on *The New York Times* Fiction Best Seller List, its sixth week on the List.

2 December 1990

Four Past Midnight stayed at number 3 on *The New York Times* Fiction Best Seller List, its twelfth week on the List.

2 December 2001

After a week off, *Black House* re-entered *The New York Times* Fiction Best Seller List at number 15, its ninth week on the List.

2 December 2018

Elevation dropped to number 8 on *The New York Times* Hardcover Fiction Best Seller List, its third week on the List.

December 3

3 December 1973

Consumer expert Mrs. Virginia Knauer gave a television public-service announcement on saving electricity. [*Roadwork*]

3 December 1977

12:00 a.m.: Distracted by trying to kill his family after going crazy, Jack Torrance had forgotten to turn back the pressure on The Overlook Hotel's boiler; the pressure crept. Just as Dick Hallorann, Danny Torrance, and Wendy Torrance got out the door, the boiler exploded, killing Jack and destroying—but not killing—the hotel; it burned in less than four hours. Dick, Danny, and Wendy took Dick's snowmobile to Sidewinder, CO. Wendy was treated for minor exposure and shock at Estes Park Community Hospital. [*The Shining*] ["After the Play"]

"OVERLOOK HOTEL BURNS; Famed Colorado Resort Hotel Goes Up in Flames; 'Arson Possible.' Says County Police Chief Clinton," by Robert T. McCord, appeared in *The Estes Park Echo*.

"FAMED COLORADO LANDMARK DESTROYED; Overlook Hotel Burns; Mystery Man at Scene," by Hal Collier, appeared in *The Denver Post*. ["After the Play"]

The Jicarilla County fire marshal ruled a defective boiler. An inoperative steam valve caused the pressure to build. John Torrance, the off-season caretaker, was killed in a heroic effort to dump the pressure. John Torrance's wife was injured in the explosion; his son was physically unhurt. Richard Hallorann, who had checked on the Torrances because of a powerful hunch, was injured. [*Doctor Sleep*]

3 December 1978, early a.m.

As Arnie Cunningham motorvated in Christine, the dead Roland LeBay told him they must make the shitters pay for hurting Christine. [*Christine*]

3 December 1989

The Dark Half stayed at number 2 on *The New York Times* Fiction Best Seller List, its fifth week on the List.

3 December 2000

On Writing stayed at number 6 on *The New York Times* Non-Fiction Best Seller List, its seventh week on the List.

3 December 2006

Lisey's Story dropped to number 7 on *The New York Times* Fiction Best Seller List, its fourth week on the List.

3 December 2009

The Talisman: The Road of Trials #2 of 6 (Del Rey Comics, $3.99) published

The Dark Tower: Battle of Jericho Hill #1 of 5 (Marvel Comics, $3.99) published

3 December 2012, Monday

Little Green God of Agony, a serial eComic, page 22 of 24, online at www.stephenking.com

3 December 2017

Sleeping Beauties dropped to number 12 on *The New York Times* Hardcover Fiction Best Seller List, its eighth week on the List.

December 4

4 December 1973

A drunken Barton Dawes begged Mary Dawes to come back. With both crying, Mary hung up. She didn't go back. [*Roadwork*]

4 December 1977

"COUNTY POLICE SILENT ON RESORT HOTEL ARSON POSSIBILITY; Mystery Remains in Fire Which Claimed One Life" appeared in a Special to *The New York Times*. ["After the Play"]

4 December 1983

Pet Sematary stayed at number 1 on *The New York Times* Fiction Best Seller List, its fifth week on the List.

4 December 1994

Insomnia dropped to number 3 on *The New York Times* Fiction Best Seller List, its seventh week on the List.

4 December 2011

11/22/63 dropped to number 2 on *The New York Times* Fiction Best Seller List, its second week on the List.

Mile 81 dropped to number 23 on *The New York Times* E-Book Fiction Best Seller List, its twelfth and last week on the List.

December 5

5 December

After arranging travel to the Far East, Gerard Nately inflated landlady Mrs. Leighton with a blue air compressor until she exploded. He buried the pieces under her shed. She had laughed and ridiculed him when she read "The Hog," his story about her. ["The Blue Air Compressor"]

5 December 1973

This was the Arlins' scheduled move date. An extension to Route 784 was going to go through their street. [*Roadwork*]

5 December 1976

Charlie Decker's gunshot wounds had almost healed. He received a letter from friend Joe McKennedy. Although censored, it told how their high school classmates were doing. [*Rage*]

~5 December 1981

morning: Jack Sawyer flipped Wolf and himself out of the Sunlight Home into the Pits, a Territories hell-prison with gargoyle-like guards. When they saw a cart run over and kill Ferd Janklow, they flipped back. Sonny Singer and Andy Warwick caught them. They injected Wolf and closed him in a coffin-sized box. After Jack broke Singer's nose, they injected Jack and put him in a straightjacket.

evening: Wolf's change happened early. He broke out of the box to save Jack Sawyer. He decapitated George Irwinson at the kitchen door, killed Heck Bast and Pedersen in the confession room, and killed Casey when he found Jack downstairs. Sonny Singer fired twice at Jack. Wolf jumped in front of Jack and caught the bullets. Sonny shot him two more times. Wolf tore off Singer's arm, changed back to his normal form, and faded away. Jack sneaked out. [*The Talisman*]

5 December 1982

Different Seasons dropped to number 10 on *The New York Times* Fiction Best Seller List, its eighteenth week on the List.

5 December 1993

Nightmares & Dreamscapes stayed at number 3 on *The New York Times* Fiction Best Seller List, its eighth week on the List.

5 December 1995

Stephen King finished *Desperation*.

5 December 1999

Hearts in Atlantis rose to number 10 on *The New York Times* Fiction Best Seller List, its tenth week on the List.

5 December 2010

Full Dark, No Stars dropped to number 5 on *The New York Times* Fiction Best Seller List, its second week on the List.

5 December 2012, Wednesday

Little Green God of Agony, a serial eComic, page 23 of 24, online at www.stephenking.com

December 6

6 December

Marian Sunderland died from a glioblastoma in March. Six months later, Lloyd Sunderland's sister, Beth Young, brought him a Border Collie-Mude puppy. He didn't want it but Beth went shopping for supplies and persuaded him to try her. Soon, the dog, which he named Laurie, became the center of his daily routine.

Six Mile Path was an old wreck of a boardwalk that ran for a mile alongside a canal that ran beneath the drawbridge to Caymen Key. Every day, Laurie and Lloyd walked it to lunch at the Caymen Key Fish House's dog-friendly Puppy Patio. On December 6th, Laurie found an alligator atop the body of Lloyd's next-door neighbor, Don Pitcher, on the boardwalk. Lloyd unhooked Laurie's leash and sent her home. The alligator went for Lloyd. Don's mahogany cane broke when Lloyd hit the alligator. The boardwalk broke beneath the alligator when Lloyd stabbed first into the soft side of its head then its eye. He let go of the cane as the gator fell into the canal. ["Laurie"]

~6 December 1907

The SS *Ocean Star* crossed the Equator; the ship's passengers celebrated. Ellen Rimbauer was so stricken by a black waitress that she wanted to kiss her and touch her all over. [*The Diary of Ellen Rimbauer: My Life at Rose Red*]

6 December 1973

Tired of the drug lifestyle, Olivia Brenner left college to get a job in Las Vegas. Barton Dawes picked up the hitchhiking Brenner at exit 15 of Route 784. He took her home for a meal and a good night's sleep. She got the bed upstairs, while he slept on the couch. At first, he declined her invitation to join her but went up later. [*Roadwork*]

6 December 1981

Cujo rose to number 4 on *The New York Times* Fiction Best Seller List, its seventeenth week on the List.

6 December 1984

Marty Coslaw told Uncle Al about Reverend Lowe as The Beast. He asked Uncle Al for two silver bullets, a gun, and his presence on New Year's Eve, the next full moon. [*Cycle of the Werewolf*]

6 December 1987

The Tommyknockers stayed at number 1 on *The New York Times* Fiction Best Seller List, its second week on the List.

6 December 1990

Tom Cullen, Kojak, and Stu Redman reached Rifle, CO, where they were snowed in. [*The Stand: The Complete & Uncut Edition*]

6 December 1992

Gerald's Game dropped to number 14 on *The New York Times* Fiction Best Seller List, its twenty-first week on the List.

Dolores Claiborne entered *The New York Times* Fiction Best Seller List at number 1. It was on the List for fourteen weeks.

6 December 1998

Bag of Bones rose to number 4 on *The New York Times* Fiction Best Seller List, its ninth week on the List.

6 December 2009

Under the Dome dropped to number 2 on *The New York Times* Fiction Best Seller List, its second week on the List.

6 December 2015

The Bazaar of Bad Dreams dropped to number 4 on *The New York Times* Hardcover Fiction Best Seller List, its third week on the List.

6 December 2016

In Sunlight or in Shadow: Stories Inspired by the Paintings of Edward Hopper, edited by Lawrence Block (Pegasus Elliot Mackenzie Publishers Ltd., $25.95), with "The Music Room," published

December 7

7 December 1941

Lenny Stillmach, a good friend of Sally Druse, manned a gun on the USS *Tucker*, one hundred yards from the USS *Arizona*. [*The Journals of Eleanor Druse*]

7 December 1973

Barton Dawes drove Olivia Brenner to Landry, where the turnpike resumed, and gave her $200 to help her get to Las Vegas. She gave him a mescaline pill. [*Roadwork*]

7 December 1978

A small capillary ruptured in Johnny Smith's right eye. Later, Dr. Vann found a tumor in Johnny's parietal lobe, the area he bruised when he fell on the ice in 1953 and injured again in the 1970 car crash—his dead zone. Johnny declined surgery, without which he had eight to twenty months to live. [*The Dead Zone*]

7 December 1980

Firestarter dropped to number 4 on *The New York Times* Fiction Best Seller List, its sixteenth week on the List.

7 December 1986

IT stayed at number 2 on *The New York Times* Fiction Best Seller List, *IT*'s thirteenth week on the List.

7 December 2003

The Dark Tower V: Wolves of the Calla (as *The Dark Tower*: Volumes 1–5) dropped to number 4 on *The New York Times* Fiction Best Seller List, its third week on the List.

7 December 2008

Just After Sunset dropped to number 6 on *The New York Times* Fiction Best Seller List, its second week on the List.

7 December 2012, Friday

Little Green God of Agony, a serial eComic, page 24 of 24, online at www.stephenking.com

7 December 2014

Revival dropped to number 2 *The New York Times* Hardcover Fiction Best Seller List, its second week on the List.

December 8

8 December

Gibson, a Florida Fish and Wildlife game warden told Lloyd Sunderland they had found the alligator. She had been protecting her nest. ["Laurie"]

8 December 1981

Miles P. Kiger, from Ogden, IL, gave Jack Sawyer a ride, a coat, and $10 for lunch. He dropped Jack off at the Empire Diner. After lunch, a trucker gave Jack a ride to Decatur, IL. [*The Talisman*]

8 December 1985

Skeleton Crew rose to number 12 on *The New York Times* Fiction Best Seller List, its twenty-fifth week on the List.

8 December 1991

Needful Things stayed at number 3 on *The New York Times* Fiction Best Seller List, its eighth week on the List.

8 December 1996

Desperation stayed at number 8 on *The New York Times* Fiction Best Seller List, its ninth week on the List.

Richard Bachman's *The Regulators* dropped to number 14 on *The New York Times* Fiction Best Seller List, its ninth week on the List.

8 December 2010

The Dark Tower: The Gunslinger—The Little Sisters of Eluria #1 of 5 (Marvel Comics, $3.99) published

8 December 2013

Doctor Sleep dropped to number 7 on *The New York Times* Hardcover Fiction Best Seller List, its ninth week on the List.

December 9

9 December

Bow hunting season ended in the Lake Charles area. [*End of Watch*]

9 December 1908

Ellen Rimbauer, John Rimbauer, and Sukeena arrived in Seattle, WA. Ellen's mother and governess met them at the train station. [*The Diary of Ellen Rimbauer: My Life at Rose Red*]

9 December 1919

Sukeena brought an icicle to Ellen Rimbauer to share some phallic fun. [*The Diary of Ellen Rimbauer: My Life at Rose Red*]

9 December 1973

On a public service announcement, Barton Dawes heard a gallon of gas equaled twelve sticks of dynamite. [*Roadwork*]

9 December 1979

The Dead Zone dropped to number 7 on *The New York Times* Fiction Best Seller List, its fourteenth week on the List.

9 December 1981

Jack Sawyer found Richard Sloat in Entry 5, Nelson House, Thayer School in Springfield, IN. That afternoon, everybody on the Thayer campus disappeared. Humanlike creatures—the Twinners of students Buckley, Etheridge, Garson, Littlefield, and Norrington—wanted Jack. Running toward Thayer's Depot, Jack flipped Richard and himself to the Outpost Depot in The Territories. [*The Talisman*]

9 December 1984

The Talisman stayed at number 1 on *The New York Times* Fiction Best Seller List, its seventh week on the List.

9 December 1990

After three weeks off, *The Stand: The Complete & Uncut Edition* re-entered *The New York Times* Fiction Best Seller List at number 15, its twenty-eighth week on the List.

Four Past Midnight rose to number 2 on *The New York Times* Fiction Best Seller List, its thirteenth week on the List.

9 December 2001

Black House rose to number 14 on *The New York Times* Fiction Best Seller List, its tenth week on the List.

9 December 2006

Edgar Freemantle and Dr. Xander Kamen exchanged emails. Dr. Kamen felt Edgar was improving. [*Duma Key*]

9 December 2018

Elevation dropped to number 10 on *The New York Times* Hardcover Fiction Best Seller List, its fourth week on the List.

December 10

10 December 1919

John Rimbauer had a honey-covered icicle served at dinner. [*The Diary of Ellen Rimbauer: My Life at Rose Red*]

10 December 1966

At George Waterhouse's request, David Adley returned to the club at 249 B East 35th Street in New York City for his second visit. ["The Breathing Method"]

10 December 1973, 1:00 p.m.

Barton Dawes and Mary Dawes had Andyburgers at Handy Andy's. Nothing was resolved; she wanted him to see a psychiatrist. [*Roadwork*]

10 December 1977

"A BLAZING—AND MYSTERIOUS—FINALE FOR A NOTORIOUS RESORT HOTEL" appeared in *Newsweek*'s "Crime" column.

"THE MYSTERIOUS FLAME-OUT OF A COLORADO GRAND HOTEL" appeared in *Time*'s "The Nation" column. ["After the Play"]

10 December 1981

Jack Sawyer and Richard Sloat met Anders, who thought Jack was Jason DeLoessian. They took his train and headed west. Morgan of Orris reached the Outpost Depot in the Territories the same time his Twinner, Morgan Sloat, arrived at Thayer School. Anders was supposed to drive the train loaded with weapons to the west coast of The Territories to meet Morgan of Orris. Morgan was going to use the weapons to stop Jack from reaching the Black Hotel. [*The Talisman*]

10 December 1984

Uncle Al called Marty Coslaw and told him he'd be there on New Year's Eve. [*Cycle of the Werewolf*]

10 December 1989

The Dark Half stayed at number 2 on *The New York Times* Fiction Best Seller List, its sixth week on the List.

10 December 1990

Tom Cullen, Kojak, and Stu Redman left Rifle, CO. [*The Stand: The Complete & Uncut Edition*]

10 December 1992

Jolene Aubuchon completed a 2,000-piece Mt. St. Helen jigsaw puzzle. [*Dolores Claiborne*]

10 December 2000

On Writing dropped to number 8 on *The New York Times* Non-Fiction Best Seller List, its eighth week on the List.

10 December 2006

Lisey's Story rose to number 6 on *The New York Times* Fiction Best Seller List, its fifth week on the List.

10 December 2017

Sleeping Beauties stayed at number 12 on *The New York Times* Hardcover Fiction Best Seller List, its ninth week on the List.

10 December ≥2017

Castle Rock's Christmas ceremony featured a helicopter bringing Mayor Coughlin dressed as Santa and Deirdre McComb lighting the Christmas tree.

Scott Carey weighed 114 pounds. [*Elevation*]

December 11

~11 December 1961, Monday, 7:00 p.m.

<u>George Amberson's second timeline</u>: Ivy Templeton called George Amberson and said she was moving out of her rented house. He offered two months back rent ($100) plus another $100 if she agreed to meet him at the Montgomery Ward warehouse parking lot at the end of her street and give him a duplicate key to the house she was vacating. That evening, he gave her his coat and the $200. [*11/22/63*]

11 December 1981

As Jack Sawyer and Richard Sloat rode west on Morgan of Orris's train, humanlike creatures attacked with bows and arrows. They stopped when Jack and Richard shot two of them. [*The Talisman*]

11 December 1983

Pet Sematary stayed at number 1 on *The New York Times* Fiction Best Seller List, its sixth week on the List.

11 December 1994

Insomnia stayed at number 3 on *The New York Times* Fiction Best Seller List, its eighth week on the List.

11 December 2001

Introduction to *Everything's Eventual*, in Bangor, ME

11 December 2006

Jack Cantori took Edgar Freemantle to get a Salvador Dalí art book, $119 after his Barnes & Noble discount. [*Duma Key*]

~11 December 2010

Bob Anderson came home with a 1955 double-date wheat penny. He took Darcy Anderson to Portland's Pearl of the Shore to celebrate with champagne and dinner. He drank most of the two bottles of Moët et Chandon, so she drove home. They hadn't had sex since she discovered he was a serial killer. She went upstairs, leaving him the promise of sex if he brought her a Perrier with lime. When he reached the top step, she pushed him. He tumbled, breaking his nose, several teeth, neck, back, and arm. After pretending to call 911, Darcy suffocated him with a dishrag in a plastic bag. She called 911 to report that her husband had fallen while drunk. ["A Good Marriage"]

11 December 2011

11/22/63 stayed at number 2 on *The New York Times* Fiction Best Seller List, its third week on the List.

December 12

12 December 1973

When Barton Dawes resigned from the Blue Ribbon Laundry, Vinnie Mason got his job. After the laundry closed, the Laundry's parent company had Vinnie manage the Westfall Cinema. When he told Dawes about it, Dawes said they put him in a dead-end job. Vinnie punched him in the eye. [*Roadwork*]

12 December 1977

"HALLORANN RELEASED FROM CUSTODY; Police Satisfied Cook Had No Part in Blaze; Refuses to Talk to Reporters," by Robert T. McCord, appeared in *The Estes Park Echo*. ["After the Play"]

12 December 1978, Tuesday

In a 54–48 home-game basketball loss to the Buccaneers, Terrier Lenny Barongg scored thirty-four points for a Libertyville High School record.

Christine had been restored twice, yet nobody had ever seen Arnie Cunningham do any real work on her. The haphazard way Arnie had restored her—new windshield wipers, antenna, rear seat cover, and half the grill—led Will Darnell to think Christine repaired herself.

~10:15 p.m.: Buddy Repperton, Bobby Stanton, and Richie Trelawney went to the closed Squantic Hills State Park to drink. Christine and the dead Roland LeBay followed in a high-speed chase. Repperton's car crashed into the park gatehouse, rolled, and exploded. Stanton and Trelawney, Christine and LeBay's second and third victims, died in the crash. Repperton was thrown clear. Injured with a sliced-off ear, two broken legs, broken ribs, a smashed left foot, and a punctured lung, he climbed a snowbank where Christine couldn't get him. The decaying LeBay told him he was done. Repperton, the fourth victim, died from exposure and his injuries. Christine repaired herself while returning to Darnell's Garage. [*Christine*]

12 December 1982

Different Seasons rose to number 8 on *The New York Times* Fiction Best Seller List, its nineteenth week on the List.

12 December 1993

Nightmares & Dreamscapes stayed at number 3 on *The New York Times* Fiction Best Seller List, its ninth week on the List.

12 December 1999

Hearts in Atlantis stayed at number 10 on *The New York Times* Fiction Best Seller List, its eleventh week on the List.

12 December 2001

Norma Goodhugh's MRI at Derry Home Hospital showed the cancer in her left breast had spread to her lymph nodes. Meanwhile, Dr. Henderson declared Dave Streeter cancer-free. ["Fair Extension"]

12 December 2002, Thursday

Dr. Egas dilated Theresa Bradley's pulmonary valve, a routine procedure. Unknowingly, he punctured her heart with a balloon catheter. [*The Journals of Eleanor Druse*]

12 December 2010

Full Dark, No Stars rose to number 3 on *The New York Times* Fiction Best Seller List, its third week on the List.

December 13

13 December 1977

"CARETAKER'S WIFE ABSOLVES OVERLOOK CHEF; Only Crime was Saving Our Lives, Winnifred Torrance Says" appeared in *The Rocky Mountain News*. ["After the Play"]

13 December 1978, Wednesday, early a.m.

Will Darnell saw Christine, driverless, return to stall 20 in Darnell's Garage. He got inside her, she started up; he got out, she shut off. Her odometer showed 52,107.8 miles. [*Christine*]

13 December 1981

Cujo rose to number 3 on *The New York Times* Fiction Best Seller List, its eighteenth week on the List.

13 December 1982

The jury in Annie Wilkes's trial for the murder of Girl Christopher deliberated about three months after the trial began. [*Misery*]

13 December 1987

After two weeks off, *Misery* re-entered *The New York Times* Fiction Best Seller List at number 15, its twenty-seventh week on the List.

The Tommyknockers stayed at number 1 on *The New York Times* Fiction Best Seller List, its third week on the List.

13 December 1990

Tom Cullen, Kojak, and Stu Redman approached Shoshone, CO. [*The Stand: The Complete & Uncut Edition*]

13 December 1992

Gerald's Game stayed at number 14 on *The New York Times* Fiction Best Seller List, its twenty-second week on the List.

Dolores Claiborne stayed at number 1 on *The New York Times* Fiction Best Seller List, its second week on the List.

13 December 1998

Bag of Bones dropped to number 5 on *The New York Times* Fiction Best Seller List, its tenth week on the List.

13 December 2002, Friday, full moon, early a.m.:

Theresa Bradley died on the operating table during emergency surgery, caused by an error in a routine medical procedure earlier that day. Her death stirred up Mary, a little girl's ghost attached to Kingdom Hospital. Sarah Bradley, Theresa's mother, cut Dr. Egas, the responsible surgeon, with a scalpel. He needed forty stitches.

Sally Druse went to visit childhood friend Madeline Kruger. When she got to her room,

Madeline was dead. Sally fell and hit her head. [*The Journals of Eleanor Druse*]

13 December 2006

The Dark Tower: The Gunslinger Born Sketchbook #1 (Marvel Comics, Free) published

13 December 2009

Under the Dome dropped to number 4 on *The New York Times* Fiction Best Seller List, its third week on the List.

~13 December 2010

Bob Anderson was buried in Peach Cemetery in Yarmouth. His wife and children attended. His accounting firm, Benson, Bacon & Anderson, closed for the day, with all accountants going to his funeral. ["A Good Marriage"]

13 December 2015

The Bazaar of Bad Dreams dropped to number 5 on *The New York Times* Hardcover Fiction Best Seller List, its fourth week on the List.

December 14

14 December 1946

Andy McGee was born. [*Firestarter*]

14 December 1978, Thursday

A picture of Buddy Repperton's burned Camaro accompanied "THREE KILLED IN CAR CRASH AT SQUANTIC HILLS STATE PARK" on the Libertyville *Keystone*'s front page. [*Christine*]

14 December 1980

Firestarter rose to number 3 on *The New York Times* Fiction Best Seller List, its seventeenth week on the List.

14 December 1981

Elroy was part of Morgan of Orris's army, chosen to defend the Black Hotel against Jack Sawyer. Jack and Richard Sloat surprised the army camp by arriving in Morgan's train early and killed most of the soldiers. Jack shot and killed Elroy. Shooting Osmond's son (Reuel Gardener's Twinner) had no effect. Jack pushed the special Territories coin from Captain Farren in his head; this killed him. Reuel died in an epileptic seizure when his Twinner died. Morgan of Orris/Morgan Sloat arrived, splitting the air between the two worlds. Jack flipped into Camp Readiness, an abandoned World War II survivalist camp in our world. They followed train tracks south to Point Venuti, north of San Francisco. Sunlight Gardener and several of Sloat's men were outside the Black Hotel. On the beach, Speedy Parker, whom Sloat had made critically ill, helped Jack get to the Black Hotel from the water. Jack defeated five Guardian Knights in the Black Hotel to get the Talisman. Outside, Sunlight Gardener tried to shoot Jack. Light rays from the sun reflected, amplified, from the Talisman to the gun. The Weatherbee hunting rifle exploded, taking Gardener's left hand, the right side of his face, and his right eye. Gardener attacked with a knife. Jack grabbed Gardener's wrist and touched the Talisman to him. He melted away. Jack dropped the Talisman, an offer for Morgan to break it. Morgan of Orris turned his lightning rod on it; the lightning was reflected, amplified, back to him. He and Morgan Sloat burned to death. Jack healed Speedy with the Talisman. Jack, Richard, and Speedy flipped to the Territories. Speedy went on his way; Jack and Richard slept. [*The Talisman*]

14 December 1986

IT stayed at number 2 on *The New York Times* Fiction Best Seller List, *IT*'s fourteenth week on the List.

14 December 1992

"Nosey Nettie" reported Jolene Aubuchon's completing a 2,000-piece Mt. St. Helen jigsaw puzzle and Mrs. Lottie McCandless's winning $240 in a Beano game in *Notes from Little Tall*, her column in Little Tall Island, ME's *The Weekly Tide*. The article also reported Selena St. George's plans to visit Dolores Claiborne for Christmas, her first time back on the Island in more than twenty years. [*Dolores Claiborne*]

14 December 2003

The Dark Tower V: Wolves of the Calla (as *The Dark Tower*: Volumes 1–5) dropped to number 5 on *The New York Times* Fiction Best Seller List, its fourth week on the List.

14 December 2008

Just After Sunset rose to number 4 on *The New York Times* Fiction Best Seller List, its third week on the List.

14 December 2011

The Dark Tower: The Gunslinger—The Way Station #1 of 5 (Marvel Comics, $3.99) published
The Stand: Night Has Come #5 of 6 (Marvel Comics, $3.99) published

14 December 2014

Revival dropped to number 4 *The New York Times* Hardcover Fiction Best Seller List, its third week on the List.

14 December 2016

The Dark Tower: The Drawing of the Three—The Sailor #3 of 5 (Marvel Comics, $3.99) published

December 15

15 December 1907, morning

On a South Pacific Island, Ellen Rimbauer got excited watching a fifteen-year-old chamber-maid change the bed sheets. The maid noticed that Ellen's neck bothered her and massaged out the kink for fifteen minutes. The maid wanted her to undress to continue the massage. Ellen declined but liked the idea of another woman touching her. [*The Diary of Ellen Rimbauer: My Life at Rose Red*]

15 December 1978, Friday

Libertyville High School's last day of classes before the Christmas break [*Christine*]

15 December 1981

In The Territories, Jack Sawyer and Richard Sloat flipped to our world and followed a road to a Mobil station in Storyville, CA. They met Wolf's brother, Wolf, in a Cadillac El Dorado. He drove them to Arcadia Beach, NH. [*The Talisman*]

15 December 1985

Skeleton Crew dropped to number 13 on *The New York Times* Fiction Best Seller List, its twenty-sixth week on the List.

15 December 1991

Needful Things stayed at number 3 on *The New York Times* Fiction Best Seller List, its ninth week on the List.

15 December 1996

Desperation rose to number 5 on *The New York Times* Fiction Best Seller List, its tenth week on the List.

Richard Bachman's *The Regulators* rose to number 13 on *The New York Times* Fiction Best Seller List, its tenth week on the List.

15 December 2002

Stephen King wrote the Author's Afterword to, and finished writing, *The Dark Tower V: Wolves of the Calla*, in Bangor, ME.

After three weeks off, *From a Buick 8* re-entered *The New York Times* Fiction Best Seller List at number 13, its seventh week on the List.

15 December 2013

After seven weeks off, *Joyland* re-entered *The New York Times* Paperback Trade Fiction Best Seller List at number 18, its nineteenth week on the List.

Doctor Sleep rose to number 6 on *The New York Times* Hardcover Fiction Best Seller List, its tenth week on the List.

December 16

16 December 1971, ~2:00 p.m.

The Castle Rock Strangler raped and strangled Cheryl Moody, his third victim. [*The Dead Zone*]

16 December 1978, Saturday

Arnie Cunningham ran two hundred cartons of cigarettes to Henry Buck in Albany, NY, for Will Darnell. The New York State Police, with a warrant, pulled him over and searched his car. They found the cigarettes, arrested him, and took him to Albany. They offered to let him go if he told what he knew about Darnell's operation. He declined because he feared Darnell would hurt Christine. Buck was arrested for receiving smuggled goods. He explained Darnell's fireworks-and-cigarettes smuggling operation: Buck supplied Darnell with used cars; Darnell ran cigarettes to Buck. Three policemen gave Darnell's accountant, Bill Upshaw, court orders to turn over all business and personal tax records on Darnell.

Pennsylvania, New York, the Federal Drug Control Task Force, the IRS, and the Bureau of Alcohol, Tobacco, and Firearms worked together. Rudy Junkins led a raid on Darnell's Garage; they arrested Will Darnell and took him to Harrisburg. Rick Mercer led the arrests and impounds. [*Christine*]

16 December 1979

The Dead Zone rose to number 5 on *The New York Times* Fiction Best Seller List, its fifteenth week on the List.

16 December 1981, night

Jack Sawyer, Richard Sloat, and Wolf's brother, Wolf, stopped in Julesburg, CO. [*The Talisman*]

16 December 1982

The prosecution in Annie Wilkes's trial for the murder of Girl Christopher had circumstantial evidence and no proof. The jury found her not guilty. [*Misery*]

16 December 1984

The Talisman stayed at number 1 on *The New York Times* Fiction Best Seller List, its eighth week on the List.

16 December 1990

The Stand: The Complete & Uncut Edition rose to number 14 on *The New York Times* Fiction Best Seller List, its twenty-ninth week on the List.

Four Past Midnight stayed at number 2 on *The New York Times* Fiction Best Seller List, its fourteenth week on the List.

16 December 2001

Black House dropped to number 15 on *The New York Times* Fiction Best Seller List, its eleventh week on the List.

16 December 2002, Monday

Sally Druse woke up in Boston General Medical Center's ICU. Radiologists had found a dot in the left frontal lobe. They wanted to keep an eye on this lesion, from her almost-lobotomy on 2 November 1939, which may have been related to her recent fall. [*The Journals of Eleanor Druse*]

16 December 2015

The Dark Tower: The Drawing of the Three—Lady of Shadows #4 of 5 (Marvel Comics, $3.99) published

16 December 2018

Elevation dropped to number 11 on *The New York Times* Hardcover Fiction Best Seller List, its fifth week on the List.

December 17

17 December 1919

Ellen Rimbauer ground a rare African herb from Sukeena into John Rimbauer's creamed spinach. He had diarrhea for three days. [*The Diary of Ellen Rimbauer: My Life at Rose Red*]

17 December 1975

morning: Johnny Smith refused Sheriff Bannerman's request to help find the Castle Rock Strangler.

10:10 a.m.: The Castle Rock Strangler raped and strangled Mary Kate Hendrasen, his sixth victim, in the Castle Rock town common. She was nine.

evening: After hearing about Mary Kate Hendrasen's murder, Johnny reconsidered and met with the Sheriff at Jon's Restaurant in Bridgton. At Alma Frechette's and Mary Kate's murder scenes in the town common, Johnny knew who the Castle Rock Strangler was. Bannerman had trouble accepting it was Frank Dodd, one of his deputies. They argued; Bannerman punched Johnny then considered it. [*The Dead Zone*]

17 December 1977

"THE PSYCHIC CONNECTION," in *Newsweek*'s "Periscope" column, reported the DA's office suspected psychic activity related to Richard Hallorann's presence at The Overlook Hotel when it burned. ["After the Play"]

17 December 1978, Sunday

Arnie Cunningham was extradited to Pennsylvania, charged, and released on $1,000 bail. A preliminary hearing was scheduled for January. The previous day's arrests were front-page news in Libertyville, but Arnie wasn't named. [*Christine*]

17 December 1981

Jack Sawyer, Richard Sloat, and Wolf's brother, Wolf, passed through Nebraska into Iowa. [*The Talisman*]

17 December 1983

As on any other workday, William Shearman woke up. As Bill Shearman, he commuted to Western States Land Analysts, one of two offices he rented in a New York City office building. He climbed from his fifth-floor office into his sixth-floor office, where he changed into Willie Shearman, a technician for Midtown Heating and Cooling. Leaving on an apparent service call, Willie went to a public restroom at the Whitmore Hotel to transform into Blind Willie, a homeless, blind Vietnam veteran. By 10:45 a.m., he had $400 to $500, leading to a $3,000 day working in front of St. Patrick's Cathedral. As the day wore on, his vision diminished then returned in the late afternoon when Blind Willie reversed the process. In a Sheraton Gotham restroom, Blind Willie transformed back into repairman Willie Shearman, who went back to his sixth-floor office and changed back to Bill Shearman. He dropped to the fifth-floor office and commuted home to be William Shearman. ["Blind Willie"]

17 December 1989

The Dark Half stayed at number 2 on *The New York Times* Fiction Best Seller List, its seventh week on the List.

17 December 2000

On Writing dropped to number 9 on *The New York Times* Non-Fiction Best Seller List, its ninth week on the List.

17 December 2002, Tuesday evening

The order was given to move Sally Druse from Boston General Medical Center's ICU to the neurology ward. [*The Journals of Eleanor Druse*]

17 December 2006

Lisey's Story dropped to number 10 on *The New York Times* Fiction Best Seller List, its sixth week on the List.

17 December 2013

Turn Down the Lights, edited by Richard Chizmar (Cemetery Dance, $35), with "Summer Thunder" (collected in *The Bazaar of Bad Dreams*), published

17 December 2017

Sleeping Beauties stayed at number 12 on *The New York Times* Hardcover Fiction Best Seller List, its tenth week on the List.

December 18

18 December 1973

The Blue Ribbon Laundry was demolished for the Route 784 extension. Barton Dawes watched. [*Roadwork*]

18 December 1975

After finding that Ann Simons had been raped and strangled in Colorado while Frank Dodd was there in 1972, Sheriff Bannerman and Johnny Smith went to talk with Frank. They found him dead; he had slit his throat with a Wilkinson Sword razor blade. [*The Dead Zone*]

18 December 1981

Jack Sawyer, Richard Sloat, and Wolf's brother, Wolf, passed the Sunlight Home. [*The Talisman*]

~18 December 1981

A snow plow driver found the body of Beadie's sixth victim in Barre, VT. Preceding a sixteen-year break, this ended Beadie's first cycle. ["A Good Marriage"]

18 December 1983

Pet Sematary stayed at number 1 on *The New York Times* Fiction Best Seller List, its seventh week on the List.

18 December 1994

Insomnia dropped to number 5 on *The New York Times* Fiction Best Seller List, its ninth week on the List.

18 December 2000

The Plant Book One: *Zenith Rising*, Part 6 e-book (Philtrum Press, Free) published

18 December 2002, Wednesday morning

Nurse Claudia took Sally Druse from Boston General Medical Center's ICU to Room 959, Bed 2, in the neurology ward. Nancy Conlan, in a persistent vegetative state because of a Dr. Stegman surgical error, had Bed 1. [*The Journals of Eleanor Druse*]

18 December 2010

Stephen King finished *11/22/63* in Lovell, ME.

18 December 2011

11/22/63 stayed at number 2 on *The New York Times* Fiction Best Seller List, its fourth week on the List.

December 19

19 December 1973, early a.m.

Barton Dawes blew up a crane at the Route 784 extension site with gasoline. He threw Molotov cocktails at other construction equipment and in the Lane Construction Co. contractor's office-trailer. Damage: about $100,000. [*Roadwork*]

19 December 1975

"MAINE PSYCHIC DIRECTS SHERIFF TO KILLER DEPUTY'S HOME AFTER VISITING SCENE OF THE CRIME" appeared in *The New York Times*. [*The Dead Zone*]

19 December 1977

"SIDEWINDER DA DENIES NEWSWEEK STORY; Says Overlook Hotel Case is Closed" appeared in *The Denver Post*. ["After the Play"]

19 December 1982

Different Seasons stayed at number 8 on *The New York Times* Fiction Best Seller List, its twentieth week on the List.

19 December 1983, Monday, 4:20 p.m.

Donald Frank Callahan (nineteen letters), Ward Huckman, and Al McCowan, representing The Lighthouse Shelter for the homeless in Detroit, MI, kept their appointment with The Sombra Corporation. They were to meet with Richard P. Sayre to talk about The Lighthouse Shelter's candidacy for one of twenty $1 million charitable contributions Sombra would make before the end of the year. A man escorted them to a conference room on the thirty-third floor and wished them God luck. In the room were three low men, all smoking, nine Type Three Vampires, and Sayre. Another low man and a low woman entered and stunned Huckman and McCowan. By this time, Callahan had killed hundreds of vampires in a dozen Americas. To stop him, they needed to kill him in all worlds. The nine vampires all had AIDS and were about to attack and infect him. He ran, crashed through the window, and fell thirty-three floors toward Michigan Avenue. Callahan died in his world but, without AIDS, could live in another. He heard chimes, saw a light, and went to it. He found himself in a way station in a desert. Behind him was a door, standing by itself, labeled UNFOUND in hieroglyphics. A man in a black robe, Walter, beckoned him to follow and showed him two dots moving on the horizon—Jake Chambers and Roland Deschain. Walter thought Jake and Roland would die soon. If not, Black Thirteen, in a box he held, would kill them after they met Callahan later. The door appeared; with Black Thirteen, Callahan fell through it, into a cave. He passed out and woke up three days later with the Manni. Henchick and Jemmin had found him in the Doorway Cave in Calla Bryn Sturgis. [*The Dark Tower V: Wolves of the Calla*]

19 December 1993

Nightmares & Dreamscapes stayed at number 3 on *The New York Times* Fiction Best Seller List, its tenth week on the List.

19 December 1999

Hearts in Atlantis stayed at number 10 on *The New York Times* Fiction Best Seller List, its twelfth week on the List.

19 December 2002, Thursday

Michael Baxley did Sally Druse's MRI. [*The Journals of Eleanor Druse*]

19 December 2010

Full Dark, No Stars dropped to number 4 on *The New York Times* Fiction Best Seller List, its fourth week on the List.

December 20

20 December 1919

John Rimbauer visited Ellen Rimbauer, tied her face-down to the bed, and sodomized her. [*The Diary of Ellen Rimbauer: My Life at Rose Red*]

20 December 1973

Barton Dawes told his wife he saw a psychiatrist—Nicholas Adams or Nicholas Aarons. The bogus names didn't fool her.

John T. Gordon, of the City Council, wrote Barton Dawes to remind him he had to vacate his home at 1241 Crestallen Street West before January 20th. [*Roadwork*]

20 December 1977

Wendy Torrance was discharged from Estes Park Community Hospital. She and Danny planned to stay in Sidewinder with the Durkins for further recuperation. Longer term, they would live with her mother in New Hampshire. ["After the Play"]

20 December 1981

Jack Sawyer, Richard Sloat, and Wolf's brother, Wolf, reached New England. [*The Talisman*]

Cujo stayed at number 3 on *The New York Times* Fiction Best Seller List, its nineteenth week on the List.

20 December 1987

Misery dropped to number 16 on *The New York Times* Fiction Best Seller List, its twenty-eighth week on the List.

The Tommyknockers stayed at number 1 on *The New York Times* Fiction Best Seller List, its fourth week on the List.

20 December 1992

Gerald's Game rose to number 11 on *The New York Times* Fiction Best Seller List, its twenty-third week on the List.

Dolores Claiborne stayed at number 1 on *The New York Times* Fiction Best Seller List, its third week on the List.

20 December 1998

Bag of Bones rose to number 2 on *The New York Times* Fiction Best Seller List, its eleventh week on the List.

20 December 2002, Friday

After studying Sally Druse's MRI results, Dr. Stegman and others told Sally she had a seizure disorder with frequent, complex, partial seizures—seizures Sally knew were mystical experiences. Later, Nurse Claudia warned her about Dr. Stegman's patient overload. She should never let him operate on her. [*The Journals of Eleanor Druse*]

20 December 2009

Under the Dome stayed at number 4 on *The New York Times* Fiction Best Seller List, its fourth week on the List.

20 December 2015

The Bazaar of Bad Dreams rose to number 4 on *The New York Times* Hardcover Fiction Best Seller List, its fifth week on the List.

December 21

21 December 1961

A few weeks after suffering a bad cut on her face from a car accident, Bobbi Jill Allnut tried to overdose on her mother's sleeping pills. She spent two nights in Parkland Memorial Hospital. [*11/22/63*]

21 December 1968

Jack Sawyer was born in Los Angeles, CA. [*The Talisman*]

21 December 1977

"MRS. TORRANCE DISCHARGED; Says She and Her Son Plan to Fly Back to New Hampshire in Near Future" appeared in *The Estes Park Echo*. ["After the Play"]

21 December 1980

Firestarter stayed at number 3 on *The New York Times* Fiction Best Seller List, its eighteenth week on the List.

21 December 1981, 5:15 p.m.

Laura DeLoessian and Lily Sawyer were dying. Jack Sawyer, Richard Sloat, and Wolf's brother, Wolf, arrived at the Alhambra Inn and Gardens. Jack gave the Talisman to his mother, who weighed only seventy-eight pounds because of pneumonia. It healed her and Laura DeLoessian, Lily's Twinner, and then disappeared. [*The Talisman*]

21 December 1986

IT rose to number 1 on *The New York Times* Fiction Best Seller List, *IT*'s fifteenth week on the List.

21 December 2002, Saturday morning

Dr. Metzger put Sally Druse on 100 milligrams of Scyllazine twice a day for seizures. He suggested Charybdisol to counter the side effects. The Scyllazine affected her meditations. She called the out-of-it feeling her soma fog. [*The Journals of Eleanor Druse*]

21 December 2003

The Dark Tower V: Wolves of the Calla (as *The Dark Tower*: Volumes 1–5) stayed at number 5 on *The New York Times* Fiction Best Seller List, its fifth week on the List.

21 December 2008

Just After Sunset dropped to number 6 on *The New York Times* Fiction Best Seller List, its fourth week on the List.

21 December 2014

Revival stayed at number 4 *The New York Times* Hardcover Fiction Best Seller List, its fourth week on the List.

December 22

22 December 1922

Reverend Thursby gave the eulogy to a packed house at Shannon Cotterie's funeral service at Hemingford Glory of God Methodist Church. ["1922"]

22 December 1966, Thursday

At the club at 249 B East 35th Street, Peter Andrews told the club's Christmas tale. ["The Breathing Method"]

22 December 1985

Skeleton Crew rose to number 10 on *The New York Times* Fiction Best Seller List, its twenty-seventh week on the List.

22 December 1990

Near Avon, CO, Tom Cullen, Kojak, and Stu Redman's snowmobile ran off the road and down an embankment. They jumped off and spent the night in Avon. [*The Stand: The Complete & Uncut Edition*]

22 December 1991

Needful Things stayed at number 3 on *The New York Times* Fiction Best Seller List, its tenth week on the List.

22 December 1996

Desperation dropped to number 6 on *The New York Times* Fiction Best Seller List, its eleventh week on the List.

Richard Bachman's *The Regulators* dropped to number 15 on *The New York Times* Fiction Best Seller List, its eleventh week on the List.

22 December 1998

Author's Note to *Hearts in Atlantis*

22 December 2002

From a Buick 8 rose to number 12 on *The New York Times* Fiction Best Seller List, its eighth week on the List.

22 December 2013

Joyland rose to number 12 on *The New York Times* Paperback Trade Fiction Best Seller List, its twentieth week on the List.

Doctor Sleep rose to number 4 on *The New York Times* Hardcover Fiction Best Seller List, its eleventh week on the List.

December 23

23 December 1976, Thursday

At the club at 249 B East 35th Street in New York City, Emlyn McCarron told the club's Christmas tale. He related Sandra Stansfield's staying alive until her baby was born, despite having been decapitated in a car accident. ["The Breathing Method"]

23 December 1979

The Dead Zone stayed at number 5 on *The New York Times* Fiction Best Seller List, its sixteenth week on the List.

23 December 1984

The Talisman stayed at number 1 on *The New York Times* Fiction Best Seller List, its ninth week on the List.

23 December 1990

The Stand: The Complete & Uncut Edition stayed at number 14 on *The New York Times* Fiction Best Seller List, its thirtieth week on the List.

Four Past Midnight stayed at number 2 on *The New York Times* Fiction Best Seller List, its fifteenth week on the List.

23 December 2001

Black House rose to number 13 on *The New York Times* Fiction Best Seller List, its twelfth week on the List.

23 December 2006, morning

Edgar Freemantle exchanged emails with his daughter Ilse. She told him she would visit for a few days during the Christmas break and she had special news. [*Duma Key*]

23 December 2009

The Dark Tower: Battle of Jericho Hill #2 of 5 (Marvel Comics, $3.99) published

The Stand: Soul Survivors #3 of 5 (Marvel Comics, $3.99) published

Afterword to *Full Dark, No Stars* in Bangor, ME

23 December 2018

Elevation dropped to number 13 on *The New York Times* Hardcover Fiction Best Seller List, its sixth week on the List.

December 24

24 December

After checking on patient Mrs. Carl Simmons, Dr. Thorpe got a rush call to report to the hospital president's office. A boy pinned under a car needed someone to remove his appendix. Dr. Thorpe volunteered and saved him. ["Rush Call"]

24 December 1922

Reverend Thursby presided over Henry James's funeral service at Hemingford Glory of God Methodist Church. Wilfred James was the only mourner. ["1922"]

24 December 1935

Sandra Stansfield called a cab and Dr. Emlyn McCarron when her contractions were every twenty-five minutes. The cab collided with an empty ambulance leaving the hospital. She was decapitated and thrown from the cab. Dr. McCarron arrived. Her body continued to breathe as governed by The Breathing Method while he delivered her baby son. When he finished, her head mouthed, "Thank you, Dr. McCarron," and the vocal cords in her body, twenty feet away, said the words. She died. ["The Breathing Method"]

24 December 1975

"THE NEW HURKOS," an article about Johnny Smith, appeared on page 41 of *Newsweek*. [*The Dead Zone*]

24 December 1978, Sunday

11:00 a.m.: Dennis Guilder was discharged from Libertyville Community Hospital.

10:00 p.m.: Don Vandenberg worked at Vandenberg's Happy Gas. In a blizzard with eight inches of snow on the ground, he went to help a customer—Christine and the dead Roland LeBay. They killed him, their fifth victim. Next, they rammed their way into Will Darnell's house. Darnell ran upstairs, had a heart attack, and fell down the stairs. LeBay and Christine finished him, their sixth victim. Christine repaired herself while returning to Darnell's Garage.

Arnie Cunningham and his parents were in Ligonier visiting Aunt Vicky and Uncle Steve. [*Christine*]

24 December 1989

The Dark Half rose to number 1 on *The New York Times* Fiction Best Seller List, its eighth week on the List.

24 December 1990

Tom Cullen, Kojak, and Stu Redman spent the night near Silverthorne, CO. [*The Stand: The Complete & Uncut Edition*]

24 December 2000

On Writing dropped to number 11 on *The New York Times* Non-Fiction Best Seller List, its tenth week on the List.

24 December 2001

"The Death of Jack Hamilton" (collected in *Everything's Eventual*) appeared in the December 24th issue of *The New Yorker*.

24 December 2006

Edgar Freemantle drew a young man, with dark blond hair, holding a Bible, and wearing work boots, jeans, and a Minnesota Twins T-shirt, Number 48. He knew this was Ilse Freemantle's special news, her fiancé. Edgar named the picture *Zales*, after the jewelry store where the young man bought Ilse's engagement ring, and wrote, "Hummingbirds," on it. He felt there would be trouble between Ilse and her fiancé. [*Duma Key*]

Lisey's Story stayed at number 10 on *The New York Times* Fiction Best Seller List, its seventh week on the List.

24 December 2008

The Dark Tower: Treachery #4 of 6 (Marvel Comics, $3.99) published

24 December 2014

The Dark Tower: The Drawing of the Three—The Prisoner #5 of 5 (Marvel Comics, $3.99) published

24 December 2017

Sleeping Beauties dropped to number 13 on *The New York Times* Hardcover Fiction Best Seller List, its eleventh week on the List.

December 25

25 December 1973

Olivia Brenner called Barton Dawes from Las Vegas. He sent her $500 after the call. Later, Sal Magliore congratulated him for his demolition work the week before and told him the Route 784 extension construction wasn't hindered. [*Roadwork*]

25 December 1977

Todd Bowden's father gave him a Winchester .30–.30. He thought about going to a freeway near his house and sniping. Later the next year, he sniped for five hours before police killed him. ["Apt Pupil"]

25 December 1983

Pet Sematary dropped to number 2 on *The New York Times* Fiction Best Seller List, its eighth week on the List.

25 December 1990

Tom Cullen, Kojak, and Stu Redman spent the night near Colorado's Loveland Pass. [*The Stand: The Complete & Uncut Edition*]

25 December 1994

Lois Roberts gave Ralph Roberts a beagle puppy for Christmas. He named it Rosalie after a homeless dog he had befriended the year before. [*Insomnia*]

Insomnia stayed at number 5 on *The New York Times* Fiction Best Seller List, its tenth week on the List.

25 December 2007

Dr. John Bonsaint had Christmas dinner with his sister, Sheila Bonsaint LeClair, and her family. ["N."]

25 December 2011

11/22/63 rose to number 1 on *The New York Times* Fiction Best Seller List, its fifth week on the List.

December 26

26 December 1957

IT had killed Betty Ripsom, a thirteen-year-old Derry girl. Her mutilated body was found on Outer Jackson Street. Three weeks before her death, her mother heard voices in the kitchen drain. [*IT*]

26 December 1972, Tuesday

In an old Ford with "Snake Eyes" written on the side, Vinnie Corey, David Garcia, and Bob Lawson killed Billy Stearns in a hit-and-run while Billy crossed Rampart Street. This made room for Lawson in Jim Norman's class. ["Sometimes They Come Back"]

26 December 1973

Dr. Strawns, the doctor who treated Johnny at Eastern Maine Medical Center after his car accident, died from burns when his house was on fire. Doctors Brown and Weizak took Johnny's case. [*The Dead Zone*]

26 December 1978

"FOUL PLAY SUSPECTED IN BIZARRE DEATH OF SUSPECTED CRIME FIGURE," headlined the Libertyville *Keystone* the day after Will Darnell's murder.

2:02 p.m.: Leigh Cabot arrived at Dennis Guilder's to talk about Christine. They kissed and later fell in love. [*Christine*]

2:30 p.m.: Bud Prescott sold Johnny Smith a .243 Remington 700 rifle at the Phoenix Sporting Goods Store on Fourth Street. [*The Dead Zone*]

26 December 1982

Different Seasons dropped to number 9 on *The New York Times* Fiction Best Seller List, its twenty-first week on the List.

26 December 1993

Nightmares & Dreamscapes stayed at number 3 on *The New York Times* Fiction Best Seller List, its eleventh week on the List.

26 December 1999

Hearts in Atlantis rose to number 9 on *The New York Times* Fiction Best Seller List, its thirteenth week on the List.

26 December 2006

Ilse Freemantle arrived in Florida. She told Edgar Freemantle her special news and showed him a picture of her fiancé. It was exactly what Edgar had drawn the other day as if he had copied the picture. After dinner, he showed her his drawings. She suggested he show them to a professional. [*Duma Key*]

26 December 2010

Full Dark, No Stars dropped to number 7 on *The New York Times* Fiction Best Seller List, its fifth week on the List.

December 27

27 December 1902

Abagail Trotts sang and played guitar in a talent show at the Hemingford Home Grange Hall after Gretchen Tilyons performed a racy French dance. Abagail was the Hall's first black performer. [*The Stand: The Complete & Uncut Edition*]

27 December 1922

Wilfred James had lost most of his livestock while he was in the hospital. After the front of the barn collapsed in a blizzard, he brought Achelois, his last cow, into the house. ["1922"]

27 December 1978

10:30 a.m.: Dean Clay sold a briefcase to Johnny Smith at Phoenix Office Supply, Inc.

late afternoon: Bonnie Alvarez sold a January 3rd Amtrak ticket to Johnny Smith. [*The Dead Zone*]

Leigh Cabot got copies of Roland LeBay's 11/1/57 car registration and Arnie Cunningham's 11/1/78 registration. She and Dennis Guilder compared the signatures to Arnie's two signatures on Dennis's leg cast: Arnie's second signature matched LeBay's 1957 signature. [*Christine*]

27 December 1981

Cujo dropped to number 4 on *The New York Times* Fiction Best Seller List, its twentieth week on the List.

27 December 1987

The Tommyknockers stayed at number 1 on *The New York Times* Fiction Best Seller List, its fifth week on the List.

27 December 1992

Gerald's Game rose to number 9 on *The New York Times* Fiction Best Seller List, its twenty-fourth week on the List.

Dolores Claiborne stayed at number 1 on *The New York Times* Fiction Best Seller List, its fourth week on the List.

27 December 1998

Bag of Bones stayed at number 2 on *The New York Times* Fiction Best Seller List, its twelfth week on the List.

~27 December 2002

Sally Druse was discharged from Boston General Medical Center. At home, she learned that nurse Laurel Werling was in Kingdom Hospital. Sally went to visit her. She saw an old man, dressed as an exterminator and carrying rat poison labeled with warnings about the toxic dangers of Warfarin. When she got in to see Laurel Werling, the nurse was dead of an apparent Warfarin overdose. After Sally reported the man with rat poison, hospital staff called him a ghost and nicknamed him Dr. Rattigan. Later, she determined that the old man was the same Dr. Gottreich who had died in the 2 November 1939 fire. [*The Journals of Eleanor*

Druse]

27 December 2006
Walking along the beach before breakfast, Edgar Freemantle and Ilse Freemantle planned to drive to the southern end of Duma Key Road the next day. [*Duma Key*]

27 December 2009
Under the Dome stayed at number 4 on *The New York Times* Fiction Best Seller List, its fifth week on the List.

27 December 2013
Stephen King finished *Revival.*

27 December 2015
The Bazaar of Bad Dreams stayed at number 4 on *The New York Times* Hardcover Fiction Best Seller List, its sixth week on the List.

December 28

28 December 1922

Wilfred James offered Arlette James's hundred acres of farmland to Harlan Cotterie for pennies on the dollar. Believing the land cursed, Harlan declined. ["1922"]

28 December 1980

Firestarter dropped to number 4 on *The New York Times* Fiction Best Seller List, its nineteenth week on the List.

28 December 1981

Captain Hollister's wife, Georgia, died of cancer. [*Firestarter*]

28 December 1985

Stephen King finished *IT* in Bangor, ME.

28 December 1986

IT stayed at number 1 on *The New York Times* Fiction Best Seller List, *IT*'s sixteenth week on the List.

28 December 2003

The Dark Tower V: Wolves of the Calla (as *The Dark Tower*: Volumes 1–5) stayed at number 5 on *The New York Times* Fiction Best Seller List, its sixth week on the List.

28 December 2006

After tuna sandwiches for lunch, Edgar Freemantle and Ilse Freemantle headed down Duma Key Road; Ilse drove. Not long after they passed *El Palacio*, Elizabeth Eastlake's hacienda, the road narrowed, and its condition worsened. Twelve-foot-high vegetation placed the road in shadows. Roots in the road made them slow to 5 MPH. He didn't feel right; his vision clouded with red. She felt worse—she vomited out the car. Edgar drove, backing up to *El Palacio*, where he could turn around. [*Duma Key*]

28 December 2008

Just After Sunset stayed at number 6 on *The New York Times* Fiction Best Seller List, its fifth week on the List.

28 December 2014

Revival rose to number 3 *The New York Times* Hardcover Fiction Best Seller List, its fifth week on the List.

December 29

29 December 1959

"Jumper," Part 1, appeared in *Dave's Rag*. Parts 2 and 3 were published in 1960.

29 December 1978, Friday

Dennis Guilder called Richard McCandless, an American Legion buddy of Roland LeBay's, for George LeBay's address. McCandless promised to get it for him then told Dennis more about Roland. [*Christine*]

29 December 1985

Skeleton Crew rose to number 8 on *The New York Times* Fiction Best Seller List, its twenty-eighth week on the List.

29 December 1991

Needful Things rose to number 2 on *The New York Times* Fiction Best Seller List, its eleventh week on the List.

29 December 1996

Desperation stayed at number 6 on *The New York Times* Fiction Best Seller List, its twelfth week on the List.

Richard Bachman's *The Regulators* rose to number 14 on *The New York Times* Fiction Best Seller List, its twelfth week on the List.

29 December 2002

From a Buick 8 rose to number 10 on *The New York Times* Fiction Best Seller List, its ninth week on the List.

29 December 2013

Joyland stayed at number 12 on *The New York Times* Paperback Trade Fiction Best Seller List, its twenty-first week on the List.

Doctor Sleep dropped to number 5 on *The New York Times* Hardcover Fiction Best Seller List, its twelfth week on the List.

December 30

30 December 1979

The Dead Zone dropped to number 9 on *The New York Times* Fiction Best Seller List, its seventeenth week on the List.

30 December 1984

The Talisman stayed at number 1 on *The New York Times* Fiction Best Seller List, its tenth week on the List.

30 December 1990

The Stand: The Complete & Uncut Edition rose to number 11 on *The New York Times* Fiction Best Seller List, its thirty-first week on the List.

Four Past Midnight stayed at number 2 on *The New York Times* Fiction Best Seller List, its sixteenth week on the List.

30 December 2001

Black House rose to number 10 on *The New York Times* Fiction Best Seller List, its thirteenth week on the List.

30 December 2004

Stephen King started *Cell* in Center Lovell, ME.

30 December 2018

Elevation rose to number 10 on *The New York Times* Hardcover Fiction Best Seller List, its seventh week on the List.

December 31

31 December 1922

Wilfred James went to Mr. Stoppenhauser to sell the hundred acres to the bank and settle his mortgage. Stoppenhauser said the bank was not a real estate agency. Wilfred knew they had bought the Rideout place when it went up for auction in the summer and had bought the Triple M. Wilf thought Stoppenhauser had made a deal with Andrew Lester, the Farrington Company's lawyer. By not buying the hundred acres, Stoppenhauser would have to foreclose Wilfred's mortgage and take his farm. Farrington would get the land.

Rats in the house spooked Achelois. She ran outside, jumped off the porch, and broke her front legs. Wilfred James put her down when he came home and found her lying in the front yard. ["1922"]

31 December 1962

Six months after Bobbi Jill Allnut's facial reconstruction surgery, her scar was a faint, pink line. She and Mike Coslaw celebrated New Year's Eve at a dance at Jodie, TX's Bountiful Grange. [*11/22/63*]

31 December 1970

Chrome Roses played New Year's Eve at the Eureka Grange No. 7. During a break, rhythm guitarist Jamie Morton kissed Astrid Soderberg under the fire escape. After the break, the band led with "Wild Thing," at Astrid's request. She blew Jamie a kiss. [*Revival*]

31 December 1973

Barton Dawes took the mescaline pill Olivia Brenner had given him then went to Wally Hamner's New Year's Eve party. [*Roadwork*]

31 December 1975

Johnny Smith was to teach at Cleaves Mills High School in January, substituting for Anne Beatty, who would be on maternity leave. He received a letter from assistant principal Dave Pelsen, telling him of the school board's 5–2 decision to reject his contract. [*The Dead Zone*]

31 December 1978, Sunday, New Year's Eve

Dennis Guilder's father dropped him off at Arnie Cunningham's. Dennis and Arnie had always spent New Year's Eve together. [*Christine*]

31 December 1980

Billy and Heidi Halleck hosted a New Year's Eve party. Cary Rossington fondled Heidi's breast at midnight. [*Thinner*]

31 December 1981

deadline for Zenith House's three books to hit The New York Times Bestseller List [*The Plant* Book One: *Zenith Rising*]

31 December 1983

Jud and Norma Crandall spent New Year's Eve at the Creeds'. [*Pet Sematary*]

31 December 1984, full moon

Uncle Al and Marty Coslaw stayed up after the rest of the family went to bed. Later, The Beast crashed through the picture window and went after Marty. Marty shot at it with two silver bullets. The second shot hit its right eye. Around midnight, it died and transformed back into Reverend Lowe, dead. [*Cycle of the Werewolf*]

31 December 1989

The Dark Half dropped to number 2 on *The New York Times* Fiction Best Seller List, its ninth week on the List.

31 December 2000

On Writing stayed at number 11 on *The New York Times* Non-Fiction Best Seller List, its eleventh week on the List.

31 December 2001, New Year's Eve

Dr. Clinton Norcross went to a seminar in Georgetown. Staying the night because of car trouble, he saw his old friend Shannon Parks working at a bar. She wanted to hook up, but he said he couldn't. [*Sleeping Beauties*]

31 December 2006

Edgar Freemantle and Jack Cantori took Ilse Freemantle to the airport. During her stay, Edgar drew *The End of the Game*, which he gave to her when she asked whether she could have it. At Arts & Artifacts on the way back, Edgar bought almost $1,000 of art supplies—for painting instead of drawing. [*Duma Key*]

Lisey's Story rose to number 9 on *The New York Times* Fiction Best Seller List, its eighth week on the List.

31 December 2009

Dipper's Roadhouse had a record crowd when the Vatican Sex Kittens performed. [*Under the Dome*]

31 December 2017

Sleeping Beauties rose to number 10 on *The New York Times* Hardcover Fiction Best Seller List, its twelfth week on the List.

December

December 1951

The Oklahoma Rancher's and Cattlemen's Association paid Greg Stillson $700. [*The Dead Zone*]

December 1962

Carrie White was conceived. [*Carrie*]

December 1972

"The Mangler" (collected in *Night Shift*) appeared in the December issue (Vol. 23, No. 2) of *Cavalier*.

December 1974

Jamie Morton answered an ad on the University of Maine's bulletin board. Jay Pederson hired him to play rhythm guitar for the Heaters. [*Revival*]

December 1975

At the Gaiety movie theater, Donald Callahan saw his first Type Three vampire. [*The Dark Tower V: Wolves of the Calla*]

December 1978

After stabbing Albany bus driver Herman T. Schneur, General Hecksler was committed to Oak Cove Asylum in Cutlersville, NY. [*The Plant* Book One: *Zenith Rising*]

"Man with a Belly" appeared in the December issue (Vol. 29, No. 2) of *Cavalier*.

December 1979

Gwendy Peterson got two Bs on her report card, and she had gained six pounds. She knew her weight gain and her subpar athletic and academic performance were because she had stopped using her button box. She was happy, so she figured she neither needed nor wanted the box. [*Gwendy's Button Box*]

December 1982

Paul Sheldon's *Misery's Quest* published [*Misery*]

Stephen King finished *Pet Sematary*.

December 1984

An IT victim, Steven Johnson's mutilated body was found in Memorial Park. One of his legs was gone from the knee down. [*IT*]

December 1988

Stephen King finished *The Stand: The Complete & Uncut Edition*.

December 1990

"The Moving Finger" (collected in *Nightmares & Dreamscapes*) appeared in the December issue (#475; Volume 79, Number 6) of *The Magazine of Fantasy & Science Fiction*.

December 2002

Dave Streeter sent $15,000 (15% of that year's income) to the Non-Sectarian Children's Fund. ["Fair Extension"]

December 2003

"Rest Stop" (collected in *Just After Sunset*) appeared in the December issue (Vol. 140, No. 6) of *Esquire*.

December 2006

Someone sent N. an envelope marked PERSONAL to his work address. It contained a key, with a tag labeled, "A. F." No note, but the message was clear: the sender had tried to keep him out of Ackerman's Field; N. wouldn't stay away, so the Field became his responsibility.

That weekend he went back. The key was to the chain across the dirt road. The fallen trees were out of the way. This time, it felt different. He saw eight stones, as if they occurred naturally, not in a circle. N. understood he had unlocked the place by looking at it, by trying to take a picture of it. He was OK. For a while. ["N."]

"Willa" (collected in *Just After Sunset*) appeared in the December issue (Volume 53, Number 12) of *Playboy*.

December 2007

"Mute" (collected in *Just After Sunset*) appeared in the December issue (Volume 54, Number 12) of *Playboy*.

December 2008

Evangelist C. Danny Jacobs held the last show of his Healing Revival Tour in San Diego, CA. [*Revival*]

December 2012

Library Al liked the Zappit's Fishin' Hole demo. He showed it to Brady Hartsfield in Kiner Memorial's Lakes Region Traumatic Brain Injury Center. Brady didn't purposely go into Al —it just happened as Al watched the demo. With control of Al's body, Brady walked around the hospital. In a lobby restroom stall, he looked at the Zappit. The Fishin' Hole demo had a hypnotic effect. He kept the Zappit, the first one he ever saw, and called it Zappit Zero. Over the next few months, he created Z-Boy, a second personality within Library Al. He had Z-Boy take the Zappits from the hospital. [*End of Watch*]

December 2015

Janice Ellerton and Martine Stover lived at 1601 Hilltop Court in Ridgedale. Before Christmas, at Ridgeline Foods, at the bottom of the hill, Dr. Z gave Janice a pink Zappit Commander. It was free, with the request she fills out a questionnaire. Brady Hartsfield began working on her. Shortly after, it looked as if something were bothering her; she seemed depressed. [*End of Watch*]

December 2016

Michael Roch

Hugh Yates invited Georgia Donlin to his office in the big house for a surprise. He strangled her with a lamp cord then put her body in his Lincoln Continental. He killed himself with the car's exhaust. [*Revival*]